Metarules of Pāṇinian Grammar

CRITICAL STUDIES IN PĀṆINIAN SYSTEM

The series is intended to stem the dwindling concern towards, and to rekindle interest in Sanskrit grammar, which is an essential tool to unravel the richness of values enshrined in Sanskrit language. This would include studies which would provide insight into the technical aspects such as descriptive language of Pāṇini's Aṣṭādhyāyī (metalanguage), the metarules, the principle of suspension, the principle of *anuvṛtti*, its bearing on the elliptical nature of the aphorisms of Pāṇini's Aṣṭādhyāyī and the like. We hope that studies in this series would help interpret correctly the principles sought to be explained by Pāṇini in his grammar.

1

Metarules of Pāṇinian Grammar

The *Vyāḍīyaparibhāṣāvṛtti*

Critically Edited with Translation and Commentary

DOMINIK WUJASTYK

VOLUME I

(2 Vols. Bound in One)

MOTILAL BANARSIDASS PUBLISHERS
PRIVATE LIMITED • DELHI

First Indian Edition : ***Delhi, 2017***
Earlier Published by **Egbert Forsten**, *Groningen, The Netherlands*

Designed and Typeset by the Author

ISBN : 978-81-208-3982-3

MOTILAL BANARSIDASS
41 U.A. Bungalow Road, Jawahar Nagar, Delhi 110 007
8 Mahalaxmi Chamber, 22 Bhulabhai Desai Road, Mumbai 400 026
203 Royapettah High Road, Mylapore, Chennai 600 004
236, 9th Main III Block, Jayanagar, Bengaluru 560 011
8 Camac Street, Kolkata 700 017
Ashok Rajpath, Patna 800 004
Chowk, Varanasi 221 001

MLBD Cataloging-in-Publication Data
Metarules of Pāṇinian Grammar
The Vyāḍi's Paribhāṣāvṛtti
Critically Edited with Translation and Commentary by
Dominik Wujastyk
ISBN : 978-81-208-3982-3
Includes the Text of the *Paribhāṣāvṛtti*,
Alphabetical and Page index of *Paribhāṣās*,
Their cross-references, texts cited in the
Vyāḍīyaparibhāṣāvṛtti, and *sūtras* of the *Aṣṭādhyāyī*.
I. Pāṇinian Grammar II. Wujastyk, Dominik

Printed in India
by RP Jain at NAB Printing Unit,
A-44, Naraina Industrial Area, Phase I, New Delhi–110028
and published by JP Jain for Motilal Banarsidass Publishers (P) Ltd,
41 U.A. Bungalow Road, Jawahar Nagar, Delhi-110007

To my parents, with endless love

Prefatory Note

The importance of Pāṇini's Aṣṭādhyāyī is borne out by the vastness of works and commentaries woven around it but an access to the richness of Pāṇinian system requires adequate familiarity with the language and techniques Pāṇini made use of in composing the Aṣṭādhyāyī, which, along with the vārttikas of Kātyāyana attracted the genius of Patañjali to write his magnum opus, the Mahābhāṣya. It is fondly remarked about the Mahābhāṣya of Patañjali that to comprehend its intricacies is nothing short of governing an empire (mahābhāṣyaṁ vā paṭhanīyaṁ mahārājyaṁ vā pālanīyam). It is in the Mahābhāṣya that we come across analytical discussion of paribhāṣās for the first time. It first identifies a possible fault or redundancy in a sūtra. Then it explains how this redundant situation intimates some general principle which renders the sūtra efficient and operationally meaningful and helps tide over other such derivational problems. It may safely be said in this context that Dr. Dominik Wujastyk's two-volume work *Metarules of Pāṇinian grammar: Vyāḍi's Paribhāṣāvṛtti* is a fitting introduction to the present series as it enters into useful elaborate details having a bearing on the complexities of derivational method of Pāṇini's Aṣṭādhyāyī.

In preparing a critical edition, Wujastyk has made a proper use of the available manuscripts. On the basis of these manuscripts he has given as many variant readings as possible, which enhances the value of the present work. He also discusses the authorship of the work fairly well. However, he could have been more elaborate to decide the issue of authorship unequivocally. Similarly, he could have given more grounds to buttress his position that the Paribhāṣāvṛtti was not written by the ancient grammarian Vyāḍi mentioned by Kātyāyana in vārttika 45 on Pā. 1.2.64. Wujastyk however opines that Vyāḍi's Paribhāṣāvṛtti was written after Patañjali as there is overwhelming evidence that the author of Vyāḍi's Paribhāṣāvṛtti has used the Mahābhāṣya. He rather locates the commentator in the period preceding Bhartṛhari and Candra.

Wujastyk has taken due care in translating the Sanskrit text, for he remains consistent in translating the technical terms and phrases throughout the work. The translation is accompanied by very useful explanation and enriching comments, which do constitute an invaluable aid in understanding the characteristics of the metarules. It is also clearly noticed that in the process of preparing his work Wujastyk has made judicious use of the relevant works available to him.

It is hoped that the present work, despite some negligible typographical errors, would go a long way in serving the purpose for which the present series has been undertaken.

KANSHI RAM

Contents

VOLUME I

Foreword ix

Acknowledgements xi

Introduction to the text xiii

The discovery of the *Paribhāṣāvṛtti* xiii
The editio princeps xv
The present edition xvi
Manuscripts xvii
Stemma Codicum xix
Provenance xx
The critical apparatus xxi
Sigla xxiii

Text of the *Paribhāṣāvṛtti* 1

Appendix: interpolated text 87

Indexes 89

Alphabetical index of *paribhāṣās* 89
Page index to *paribhāṣās* 93
Paribhāṣās cross-referenced in the text 93
Texts cited in the *Vyāḍīyaparibhāṣāvṛtti* 94
Sūtras of the *Aṣṭādhyāyī* 94
Other texts 96

Foreword

In these volumes I have attempted to give a clear account of the work of an early Sanskrit grammarian of the school of Pāṇini. A major chapter of the history of linguistics concerns the achievements of the Indian grammarians in their analysis of Sanskrit. Since Bloomfield, this achievement has been repeatedly praised by Western linguists who have learned enough Sanskrit to plunge into the formidable literature. But the density and technicality of Sanskrit grammatical literature have discouraged many from getting an analytical understanding of what the Indian grammarians were doing. Furthermore, few commentarial texts have been adequately presented in modern languages.[1]

I hope this book will have some appeal to two groups of readers. Sanskritists will find here another work from the huge literature, presented in a critical text. The translation and interpretation will give guidance and ease of initial understanding, as well as providing a springboard for higher criticism. Linguists and historians of linguistics will be introduced to some of the complex issues and arguments that arose from putting Pāṇini's famous grammar to work in practice.

Paribhāṣās, 'principles' or 'rules of interpretation' constitute one of the few topics in Sanskrit grammatical literature which is sufficiently circumscribed in extent, yet sufficiently general in content, to give the student a broad grasp of the main lines of Pāṇini's generative system. For this reason I believe that this literature is a useful point of entry into the field for anyone who has gained some familiarity with the basics of Pāṇini's system.

The *Vyāḍīyaparibhāṣāvṛtti* has been a controversial work for some time. The name Vyāḍi is known from the *Mahābhāṣya* to refer to an ancient philosopher of language who lived between Pāṇini (4th century BC or earlier) and Kātyāyana (3rd century BC?). Arguments have been proposed both for identifying the ancient philosopher with our *Paribhāṣā* commentator, and for distinguishing them. I believe I have settled this question decisively in favour of the latter position.

Volume I of this work contains the critical edition of the *Paribhāṣāvṛtti*. Volume II contains the translation, parallel passages, analysis and discussion. The translation and its explanation are broken down into individual arguments, so the reader will find here a compendium of distinct examples of grammatical

[1]Outstanding exceptions exist, of course, such as the translations of Patañjali's *Mahābhāṣya* by S. D. Joshi and J. A. F. Roodbergen, the translations of the first pāda of the *Kāśikāvṛtti* by Yutaka Ojihara and Louis Renou, and others.

debate. In my commentary, the Vyāḍi commentator's arguments are sifted, evaluated and compared with those of other grammarians, so as to pinpoint his intellectual position in the history of Indian grammar.

The Sanskrit grammatical literature on *prakriyā*, 'derivation' (as opposed to philosophy), consists, in a fundamental way, not of connected exposition but of discrete gobbets of discussion. In this it is rather like, for example, the *subhāṣita* literature, which consists of separate poems, each expressing a single, poignant theme. In the grammatical literature, these discrete discussions have a textual life of their own, being separately quoted by subsequent authors – not always in the same contexts – to solve recurrent problems. My treatment of the arguments used by the Vyāḍi commentator, and my attempt to trace their provenance and development, highlights this feature of the literature, and I hope it will contribute to the future study of *vyākaraṇa* texts.

The purpose of this study is twofold. The first aim is to present as good a text of the *Paribhāṣāvṛtti* as can be established on the basis of the available manuscripts. I trust that no Indologist today would dispute the central importance of critically edited texts. The English translation of such a text is, perhaps, an oddity. For even to understand the English, a thorough knowledge of *vyākaraṇa* is necessary, and such a knowledge is unlikely to exist without the ability to read *vyākaraṇa* texts. Nevertheless, the translation will be of use to students, and it does at least demonstrate to all what I believe the text means. The exercise of translation is also useful in forcing an editor to account explicitly and publicly for every syllable of the text.

The second aim of the study is to identify the Vyāḍi commentator's sources and affiliations, and to locate him intellectually and temporally. Since he explicitly quotes almost no one other than Pāṇini, and is explicitly quoted by no later authors, this is an arduous task, requiring minute examination of his arguments.

To avoid misunderstanding, I should like to clarify what this study is not. It is not a general examination of the *paribhāṣā* literature. Nor is it intended to be a completely general study of this *paribhāṣā* text. This was not the primary aim of the study. Once the main affiliations of the commentary became clear, I judged it unnecessary to continue to dissect each argument in full detail. Furthermore, most of the arguments not discussed in detail in these volumes may be further explored in other texts.[2] Although the Vyāḍi text is of interest historically for several of its ideas, as well as for being perhaps the first separate commentary on *paribhāṣās*, I do not believe it to be the best text upon which to base a general study of *paribhāṣās*. It is too idiosyncratic (a criticism I would also level at the *Paribhāṣenduśekhara*, for different reasons). Such a general study would, in my view, be better based on Puruṣottamadeva's *Laghuparibhāṣāvṛtti*, or Sīradeva's *Bṛhatparibhāṣāvṛtti*, both outstandingly clear, comprehensive and balanced works, each supported by a rich manuscript tradition. The present work seeks merely to explore some of the Vyāḍi commentator's ideas and primarily to discover his place relative to the rest of the Sanskrit grammatical tradition.

---

[2]E.g., F. Kielhorn, *The Paribhāṣenduśekhara of Nāgojībhaṭṭa* (Poona: Bhandarkar Oriental Research Institute, 1960).

Acknowledgements

I wish to thank the authorities of the libraries in Berlin, Jammū and Poona who were all most helpful in providing microfilms and facilities for photographing the manuscripts.[1] In particular I thank Professor Dandekar of the Bhandarkar Institute for writing letters that gained me permission to enter the Raghunātha Temple Library in Jammu. I also wish to thank Dr. Karan Singh MP for the permission itself.

Jenny Kenyon, Marika Antoniw, Vivian Wren and Wiesław Micał all have my thanks for typing various parts of the book. It was a monstrous job and they executed it with admirable accuracy.

These volumes were typeset on a personal computer using the program TeX, so generously placed in the public domain by Professor D. E. Knuth (Stanford).[2] The TeX macro program for formatting critical editions was written by John Lavagnino (Brandeis) and myself.[3] The beautiful Devanāgarī font was created in METAFONT by Frans Velthuis (Groningen): it fully deserves to revolutionize the typesetting of Sanskrit and Hindī.

For initial guidance in research and for much sane advice I warmly thank Professor R. F. Gombrich. Professor B. K. Matilal steered me through most of the translating and commenting: his patience, interest and expertise in *vyākaraṇa* were invaluable. It is very sad for me that his recent death has robbed me of the opportunity of presenting these volumes to him in gratitude.

While in India, I often took my grammatical queries to Professor S. D. Joshi at Poona University. It was he who first suggested that I should study Vyāḍi's curious text. He has a wonderful capacity of making other people's textual problems his own, and of offering original and insightful solutions.

I reserve special gratitude for Professor S. Bhaṭe with whom, in 1979, I studied the first part of the *Vyāḍīyaparibhāṣāvṛtti*. Without her patient guidance I would be struggling with the text even now. Professor Bhaṭe was also kind enough to read a draft of this edition, and offered many helpful corrections and comments.

[1]Grants from the Boden Fund also made it possible for me to visit India to study and photograph manuscripts in 1978, 1979 and 1980.

[2]Donald E. Knuth, *The TeXbook* (Reading, Mass., etc.: Addison Wesley, 1986).

[3]See John Lavagnino and Dominik Wujastyk, "An Overview of EDMAC: A plain TeX format for critical editions" in *TUGboat: the Communications of the TeX Users Group* **11** (1990), pp. 623–643. A book by the same authors describing the program in detail is in press.

My greatest thanks go to Professor Bhaṭe's teacher, and mine, Paṇḍit V. B. Bhāgavata. This marvellous man began studying grammar at least twenty years before I was born. I started reading *vyākaraṇa* texts with him in 1978 and I have returned to him whenever I could. With him I first read the latter portions of the *Vyāḍīyaparibhāṣāvṛtti*. It has been a privilege and a joy to study with so fine an exemplar of the *śāstrika* tradition.[4]

Professor G. Cardona was kind enough to read an early draft of this book, and to make several helpful comments and corrections. He encouraged me to seek publication at a time when I was feeling very discouraged; his goodwill counted for a great deal. Professor Gary Tubb improved several readings in the text, and helped with acute comments on the text's arguments. Professor J. Bronkhorst has been a staunch colleague throughout, and helped greatly with stimulating discussions, suggestions and corrections. Professor Hans Bakker and the editors and publisher of the Groningen Oriental Series have my heartfelt thanks for their encouragement and enormous patience in prising this book out of my hands.

Any remaining errors are, of course, my own responsibility.

Finally, without the love and moral support of my family and friends, this book would never have been finished.

[4]Some notes on Pt. Bhāgavata's own traditional education were published as 'Notes on Traditional Sanskrit Teaching' in *South Asia Research*, no. 1 (May 1981), pp. 30–36.

Introduction to the text

The discovery of the *Paribhāṣāvṛtti**

In July 1875, the great Indologist Georg Bühler set out from Bombay on a search for manuscripts in Kashmir and elsewhere which was to prove extremely rewarding in several fields of Sanskrit literature. It was during this tour that the *Paribhāṣāvṛtti* first came to light. Bühler probably found the text in late 1875 or early 1876. His first move was to consult Kielhorn. He also sent a manuscript of the work to Weber in Berlin. It is not clear from Bühler's 1887 account of his trip in what order he did these actions, nor whether he had extra copies of the manuscripts made. At any rate the manuscript for Weber (B) arrived in Berlin on the 19th January 1878, and concerning the two manuscripts he sent to Kielhorn (P_1 and P_2) Bühler made the following remarks:

> ... the *Vyāḍīyaparibhāshāvṛtti* ... bears the most ancient name. The Kashmirian Pandits are unanimous in declaring it to be a production of the author of the *Saṃgraha*. But Dr. Kielhorn, to whom I submitted the book immediately after its discovery, tells me that he cannot discover in it any proof of great antiquity, and that it contains only the well know *Paribhāshās*. He thinks it not unlikely that the title has been given to it because some Pandit believed the *Paribhāshās* to belong to Vyāḍi. I must leave the question to the decision of those Sanskritists who make the *Vyākaraṇaśāstra* their speciality.[1]

Weber was the first to publish notice of the work, with the appearance in 1886 of the second volume of his catalogue of the Royal Library of Berlin, which contained an article on the manuscript Bühler had sent him. He made no comment, apart from noting in his introduction that this work among others,

*An earlier version of this introduction, and that of volume 2, appeared in *Oxford University Papers on India*, vol. 1, part 1, ed. N. J. Allen, R. F. Gombrich, et. al. (Oxford, OUP, 1986).

[1]Georg Bühler, *Detailed report of a tour in search of Sanskrit MSS, made in Kashmir, Rajputana and Central India.* (Bombay, London: Bombay branch of the Royal Asiatic Society, 1877), p. 69.

was 'besonders werthvoll'.[2] Bühler's report, containing Kielhorn's comment was published a year later.

It was nearly twenty years after Bühler's first discovery that in 1894 Stein published his catalogue of the Raghunātha temple library in Jammu, where he had found a fourth manuscript (J). In his introduction he mentioned:

> ... The rare commentary on the Paribhāshās, attributed to Vyāḍi and first discovered by Professor Bühler in Kashmir. The Jammu manuscript, though written by a modern Kashmirian hand, is fairly correct and bears no signs of having been transcribed from a śāradā original.[3]

Although Stein is right that the manuscript does not show outward signs of being a transcription from the Śāradā script, the critical examination of variant readings and emendations tells another story (see p. xx below).

After this early interest in the work, it ceased to attract much attention, possibly because of Kielhorn's slightly disparaging remarks. It was not discussed again until Abhyankar began to focus scholarly interest on the *paribhāṣā* literature, first with a short article in 1955,[4] and later with a major edition of seventeen different *paribhāṣā* texts, including the *Vyāḍīyaparibhāṣāvṛtti*, published in 1967.[5] In these publications, and elsewhere,[6] Abhyankar renewed the claims originally made by the Kashmiri *paṇḍitas* for identifying the author of the *Paribhāṣāvṛtti* with the ancient Vyāḍi mentioned by *Kātyāyana* in *vārttika* 45 on P.1.2.64.

Abhyankar went extraordinarily far in his claims for the antiquity of our Vyāḍi. He suggested that Pāṇini might be Vyāḍi's maternal uncle,[7] and argued that Patañjali (*fl.* 140 BC) was heavily influenced by the *Paribhāṣāvṛtti*.[8] Once again this claim for the early date of our text aroused an opposing reaction, this time for Wezler.[9] After briefly summarizing the facts relating to the ancient Vyāḍi, Wezler ended with three possible assumptions about the *Paribhāṣāvṛtti*: either it is by a different Vyāḍi, or it was originally anonymous and

---

[2]Albrecht Weber, *Die Handschriften-Verzeichnisse der Königlichen Bibliothek zu Berlin, Fünfter Band, Verzeichnisse der Sanskrit- und Prākṛit-Handschriften, Zweiter Band, Erste Abtheilung* (Berlin: Königliche Bibliothek, 1886), p. x.

[3]Marc Aurel Stein, *Catalogue of the Sanskrit Manuscripts in the Raghunatha Temple Library of His Highness the Maharaja of Jammu and Kasmir* (Bombay: Nirnaya Sagara Press, 1894), p. xxi.

[4]Kashinath Vasudev Abhyankar, "A Short Note on Paribhāṣā works in Sanskrit grammar," *Annals of the Bhandarkar Oriental Research Institute* 36 (1955), pp. 157–62.

[5]idem, *Paribhāṣāsaṃgraha (a Collection of Original Works on Vyākaraṇa Paribhāṣās), Edited Critically with an Introduction and Index of Paribhāṣās*. (Poona: Bhandarkar Oriental Research Institute, 1967).

[6]E.g., idem, *A Dictionary of Sanskrit Grammar* (Baroda: Oriental Institute, 1961), p. 351 (p. 378 of 1986 ed.).

[7]*Paribhāṣāsaṃgraha*, p. 12

[8]ibid., p. 13 f.

[9]Albrecht Wezler, *Paribhāṣā IV, V und XV. Untersuchungen zur Geschichte der einheimischen indischen grammatischen Scholastik* (Bad Homburg v.d.H., Berlin, Zürich: Gehlen, 1969), pp. 19–23.

was subsequently attributed to the ancient Vyāḍi, or finally, it is a deliberate forgery.[10] But to resolve this question, Wezler says,

> ... müste eine genaue Prüfung dieses Textes nach inhaltlichen und stilistichen Besonderheiten ergeben.

This view was echoed by Cardona, who agreed that,

> ... general considerations are not sufficient to permit reaching conclusions; one has to study each *paribhāṣā* individually in the context of the commentatorial arguments associated with it.[11]

It is just this approach which has been adopted in the present study.

The editio princeps

The *Paribhāṣāvṛtti* was printed in 1967 as the first of the texts in the *Paribhāṣāsaṅgraha* edited by K. V. Abhyankar. It appears there under the title *Paribhāṣāsūcanaṃ*. This word is taken from the opening phrase of the text: '*atha paribhāṣāsūcanaṃ vyākhyāsyāmaḥ*'. But the author is not naming the work here; rather he is making a declaration of intent. The manuscript colophons are unanimous in calling the text the *Vyāḍīyaparibhāṣāvṛtti*.[12]

Abhyankar's edition was based on the two manuscripts in the Bhandarkar Oriental Research Institute, P_1 and P_2, which Abhyankar called B and A respectively. Abhyankar does not seem to have been aware of the manuscripts in Berlin and Jammu, but as luck would have it the Poona manuscripts represent the two versions of the transmitted text, so he had the advantage of access to most variant readings.

The publication of the text, and indeed of the *Paribhāṣāsaṅgraha* as a whole, was a major event for *vyakāraṇa* studies; it highlighted the importance, extent and continuity of the *paribhāṣā* literature, and made several texts available for the first time. Not least in importance is Abhyankar's own commentary on the Jainendra *paribhāṣās*, an achievement showing its author's great mastery of *vyākaraṇa*.

The virtues of the *Paribhāṣāsaṅgraha* are too obvious to need elaboration. But the editor did not use all the available manuscripts for the various texts, even though they are not particularly numerous. Nor did he follow the strictest codes of editorial technique in preparing the texts. In several places Abhyankar preferred to produce a text that made good sense to him, rather than a text which was derivable from the manuscripts. This preference, though wholly understandable, contravenes basic principles of textual criticism. A conjectural

---

[10]ibid., p. 23.

[11]George Cardona, *Pāṇini, a Survey of Research* (The Hague: Mouton, 1976; reprinted: Delhi: Motilal Banarsidass, 1980), p. 168.

[12]This title could be translated as 'A commentary on the *paribhāṣās* according to Vyāḍi', and is ambiguous regarding whether it is the commentary or the *paribhāṣās* which belong to Vyāḍi. The most natural reading is the latter, and this is discussed further in the introduction to volume II.

reading must be justified by more than the fact that it makes good sense. It must be accounted for, and weighed according to its place in the *stemma codicum*.

Suffice it to say that Abhyankar has blazed the trail for *paribhāṣā* studies. Other scholars must trim the kerbs, correct the signposts and make straight the way. A perusal of the critical apparatus of the edition offered here will show in more detail where changes to Abhyankar's edition have been necessary.

The present edition

Two guides were at my side throughout the process of editing: M. L. West and A. E. Housman. The first has, through his book *Textual Criticism and Editorial Technique*, taught me just how to proceed.[13] Housman's astringent introductions, particularly those to the *Astronomicon*, are so full of chastening wit and wisdom that their repeated study must be one of the finest ways of keeping one's standards high.[14] To any list of such books should be added S. M. Katre's *Introduction to Indian Textual Criticism*,[15] the only book I know devoted specifically to textual criticism in the Indian context.

In constituting the text it has, of course, been my intention throughout to correct the copyists, not the author. The difficulty of doing this has been felt particularly in those passages in which the author appears to be presenting a wrong argument. This type of problem is almost as old as the practice of textual criticism itself and, as Kenney says, 'it surely cannot be accounted a rational proceeding to print the indefensible merely because it is attested by all the extant MSS?'.[16] In the text here presented, it would have been possible to correct several apparent errors of reasoning and the non-traditional application of certain *sūtras*, and to a large extent this is what Abhyankar did in his edition. However, my practice has been much more conservative; if I have erred, it is in the direction of the text as transmitted by the MSS we have. I am well aware of the famous dictum of Haupt, quoted with approval by Housman, West, and others: 'If the sense requires it, I am prepared to write *Constantinopolitanus* where the manuscripts have the monosyllabic interjection *o*'.[17] But in spite of the risk of appearing too editorially timid, I have tried to correct the text only where the errors are explicable by reference to well understood mechanisms of scribal error. Bearing in mind the fact that estimates of the number of of learned conjectures that are actually correct, based on cases where it has been possible to check against subsequently discovered MSS or papyri, vary from 5 per cent to a mere 0.1 per cent,[18] any editor must surely hesitate before

[13] M. L. West, *Textual Criticism and Editorial Technique* (Stuttgart: Teubner, 1973).

[14] Alfred Edward Housman (ed.), *M. Manilii, Astronomicon, recensuit et enarravit A. E. Housman*, 5 vols (London: Grant Richards, 1903–30).

[15] Bombay: Karnatak Publishing House, 1941; reprinted Poona: Deccan College, 1954.

[16] E. J. Kenney, *The Classical Text: Aspects of Editing in the Age of the Printed Book* (Berkeley etc.: Univ. of California Press, 1974), p. 62.

[17] West, *op. cit.*, p. 58.

[18] Kenney, p. 148, f.n. 1.

proposing his own. In general I have preferred the author of the *Paribhāṣāvṛtti* to appear sometimes deficient, rather than to emend all difficulties away.

Ultimately, it is absurd for us to expect all Sanskrit authors, even *vaiyākaraṇas*, to be uniformly perfect in their knowledge. It is refreshing to discover a few erroneous arguments in a field usually so overwhelmingly learned, and this fact – I believe – tells us more about our author than would a text in which all arguments had been emended to conform with the standards of other authors. In producing a text, the fundamental aim is to discover what the author wrote, warts and all. For reasons that become abundantly clear from a reading of the *Paribhāṣāvṛtti*, I believe that the author of the work was not only idiosyncratic as a grammarian, but that he also made mistakes of reasoning and interpretation that go beyond what can reasonably be attributed to the faulty transmission of his text. If I had been confident that the Vyāḍi commentator was an infallible scholar of *vyākaraṇa*, I would have had no hesitation in adopting all Abhyankar's emendations, and indeed in proposing more. But my understanding of the author's style and skills in his subject force me to restrain the desire to improve and correct the text against the evidence of the manuscripts.

One fact more than any other has made it possible to improve upon Abhyankar's text while at the same time avoiding illicit conjectural readings. This is the discovery that the available manuscripts of the *Paribhāṣāvṛtti* are descended from an archetype written in the Śāradā alphabet. Numerous corrections are possible and justifiable in this knowledge. This single realization about the transmission of the text itself warrants the preparation of a fresh edition, leaving aside the discovery of additional manuscripts, and the changed editorial methodology.

Manuscripts

The following manuscripts have been used:

P_1

Bhandarkar Oriental Research Institute, Poona, India 411004.

Described by Belvalkar.[19] Catalogue number: 296. Library accession number: 319 of 1875–76. Earlier described by Bühler as number 319.[20]

Physical description: paper, 25 folios, foliated 7r–31r, size $14 \times 5\frac{3}{4}$ in., 12 lines per page, *ca.* 50 *akṣaras* per line. (Folios 1–6v contain the *Bhāṣānuśāsanam* of Sumati Śreyaskara.)

Incipit [fol. 7r]: ॐ अथ परिभाषासूचनं व्याख्यास्यामः । ओमथेत्ययमधिकारार्थः ॥

---

[19]Sh. K. Belvalkar, *Descriptive Catalogue of the Government Collections of Manuscripts in the Government Mss. Library...*, volume 2, *Grammar, Part 1: Vedic and Pāṇinīya* (Poona: Bhandarkar Oriental Research Institute, 1938), p. 231.

[20]Georg Bühler, *Detailed report*, pp. 69, xxi.

Explicit [fol. 31v]: ... प्रातिपदिकान्तनुंविभक्तिषु चेति णत्वं सिद्धं भवती'ति' सिद्धमिति श्रीव्यातीयपरिभाषावृत्तिः समाप्ता॥

The manuscript is not dated.

The calligraphy is good Kashmiri style Devanāgarī. The scribe uses *daṇḍas* to separate some sentences, and the *paribhāṣās* are numbered. There are a number of yellowed-out corrections throughout the text.

P_2

Bhandarkar Oriental Research Institute, Poona, India, 411004.

Described by Belvalkar.[21] Catalogue number: 295. Library accession number: 320 of 1875–76. Earlier described by Bühler as number 320.[22]

Physical description: paper, 28 folios, foliated 1–28, size $13\frac{3}{4} \times 6$ in., 10 lines per page, *ca.* 50 *akṣaras* per line. Two unnumbered folios precede this text, containing the *Vyāḍīyaparibhāṣāpāṭha*.

Incipit [fol. 1r]: ॐ नमो मुनित्रयाय अथ परिभाषासूचनं व्याख्यास्यामः अथेत्ययमधिकारार्थः

Explicit [fol. 28v]: .... प्रातिपदिकान्तनुम्विभक्तिषु चेति णत्वं सिद्धं भवति इति व्याडीयपरिभाषावृत्तिस्समाप्ता॥ शुभाय भवतात्॥

The manuscript is not dated.

The calligraphy is as P_1. The scribe uses no *daṇḍas*, as a rule, and the *paribhāṣās* are not numbered. There are yellowed-out corrections throughout the text, and insertions in a different hand are fairly common.

J

Sri Ranbir Sanskrit Research Institute, courtyard of the Raghunatha temple, Jammu, Jammu and Kashmir State, India.

Described by Stein.[23] Catalogue number: 954. Accession number: *gha* 150. Also described by Patkar.[24] Catalogue number: *vyākaraṇa* 59. Accession number: 150 *gha*.

Physical description: paper, folios, foliated 1–41r, *ca.* $11 \times 6\frac{1}{2}$ in., 11 lines per page, 33 *akṣaras* per line. (Fols. 41r–42v contains the *Paribhāṣāsutrāṇi*.)

Incipit [fol. 1r]: ॐ श्रीगणेशाय नमः ॐ अथ परिभाषासूचनं व्याख्यास्यामः अथेत्ययमधिकारार्थः

Explicit [fol. 41r]: ... प्रातिपदिकांतनुंविभक्तिषु चेति णत्वं सिद्धं भवती सिद्धं इति श्रीव्याडीयपरिभाषावृत्तिः समाप्तः

[21] Belvalkar, *Descriptive Catalogue*, p. 230.

[22] Georg Bühler, *Detailed report*, pp. 69, xxi.

[23] Marc Aurel Stein, *Catalogue of the Sanskrit Manuscripts in the Raghunatha Temple Library*, pp. 47, 262.

[24] M. M. Patkar, *Descriptive catalogue of manuscripts in the Shri Ranbir Sanskrit Research Institute, Jammu (Kashmir)*. (Jammu, 1970), p. 188.

The manuscript is not dated.

The calligraphy is a bold, clear Kashmiri style Devanāgarī. The scribe uses no *daṇḍas*, but does number the *paribhāṣās*. Few corrections and those that do occur seem to be by the hand of the original scribe.

B

Staatsbibliothek, Preußischer Kulturbesitz, Orientalische Abteilung, 1 Berlin 30, Reichpietschufer 72/76, Germany.

Described by Weber.[25] Catalogue number: 1637.

Accession number: 10508. Library number: MS. or. fol. 873.

Physical description: paper (now bound in codex form), *ca.* 39 × 10.5 cm., 21 folios, foliated 1–21, 14 lines per page, 48 *akṣaras* per line.

Incipit [fol. 1r]: ॐ श्रीगुरुवे नमः नमो मुनित्रयाय अथ परिभाषासूचनं व्याख्यास्यामः अथेत्ययमधिकारार्थः

Explicit [fol. 21v]: ... प्रातिपदिकांतनुंवि 'भ'क्तिषु चेति णत्वं सिद्धं भवति। इति श्रीव्याडीयपरिभाषावृत्तिस्समाप्ता शुभाय भवताच्छ्रोतॄणाम् ओन्तत्सत्। संवत्। शुभम्। [then, in *Śāradā*:] भद्रम्। कल्याणम्

The manuscript is not dated, in spite of the scribe's 'संवत्'.

The calligraphy is a clear, regular, close Kashmiri style Devanāgarī. The scribe uses no *daṇḍas* and does not number the *paribhāṣās*. Few corrections.

Finally, it is just possible that a manuscript of the *Vyāḍīyaparibhāṣāvṛtti* may exist amongst the Woolner and other collections of manuscripts at the Punjab University Library in Lahore.[26] But all my efforts at communicating with the librarians at the Punjab University over the years have met with silence.

Stemma Codicum

There are some readings of secondary origin, i.e., errors, shared by all four MSS (e.g., 1:8, 1:9, 3:4, 3:11, 3:16, 16:8, 23:9, 53:3, 68:9, 84:8, *et passim*), therefore all descend from a copy in which these readings were present. We call this archetype $\mathcal{X}$.

There are many readings of secondary origin common to P_2 and B which are not shared by P_1 and J (e.g., 1:49, 5:6, 5:14, 16:7, 19:1, 22:20, 23:8, *et passim*), therefore P_2 and B descend from their own hyparchetype, *b*, which cannot be the exemplar of P_1 and J. There are also readings of secondary origin common to P_1 and J which are not in *b* (e.g., 1:27, 2:23, 7:37, 9:8, 14:7, 18:8, 19:7, 22:35, *et passim*). Therefore P_1 and J have their own hyparchetype *a*, which cannot be the exemplar of *b*.

[25] Albrecht Weber, *Verzeichnisse der Sanskrit- und Prākṛt-Handschriften*, p. 204.

[26] See *Catalogue of the Sanskrit Manuscripts in the Panjab Universty Library* (Lahore: Univ. of the Panjab, 1932, 1941), volume II, p. 83, which lists an incomplete manuscript, consisting of only one leaf, of a *Paribhāṣāvṛtti* by Vyāḍi (acc. no. 1192).

Finally, all four manuscripts have readings of secondary origin unique to themselves, so none of them is descended from any other (e.g., P_2 – 7:29, 45:4, all of 46; B – 7:18, 30:7, 74:8–9; J – 13:24, 13:27, 20:9; P_1 – 18:2, 38:1, 51:9).

The resulting stemma is:

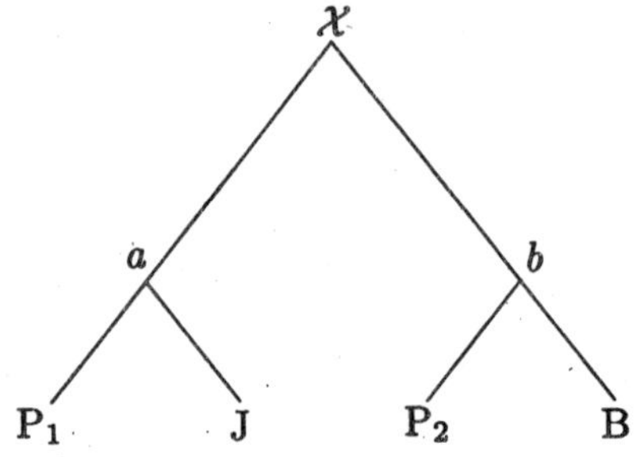

This picture is undoubtedly a simplification of the actual history of transmission. In the first place, there are very frequent variants between *a* and *b* which do not alter the sense but consist of a different word-order or choice of simple verb. This suggests that the tradition is in fact open, and that $\mathcal{X}$ represents more than one version of the text (e.g., 1:25, 1:43, 23:11, 31:4, *et passim*).

Secondly, the Poona MSS, P_1 and P_2, contain many corrections. P_2, in particular, is a contaminated MS containing many corrections not derived from the other MSS or hyparchetypes. Either the scribe of P_2 (or the corrector, if different) had access to some fifth MS, or was himself very learned (e.g., 11:6, 13:5). Abhyankar's text normally uses these innovations: perhaps they are his. Where it was possible to read the text of the manuscript under the correction, the older readings have been recorded in the apparatus as *ante correctionem* ('a.c.').

Provenance

All the manuscripts have many errors explainable by reference to letters which are similar in the Śāradā alphabet. There are literally hundreds of mistakes of this type, and if confirmation were needed, the post-colophon statement in MS B is actually in Śāradā. Errors in this category include the confusion of the following letter pairs: घ/च, ट/ड, द/च, ड/त, र्तै/त्रे, म्य/स्य, ऋ/रू, भ्य/व्य and so on.[27] Since each of the four manuscripts contain frequent errors of this type which do not occur at the same point in the others, it would seem that *a* and *b* were both in this script.

Another feature of the MSS, particularly P_2, which suggests a Kashmiri origin is the frequent tendency to replace *visarga* by *ś*, *ṣ or s*, when one of

[27]Vishnu S. Sukthankar, *The Ādiparvan, being the First Book of the Mahābhārata, the Great Epic of India* (Poona: Bhandarkar Oriental Research Institute, 1933), *Prolegomena* p. xi gives further examples of this type of error, as does Katre, *Indian Textual Criticism*, p. 57.

these sibilants follows (e.g., 1:4, 3:8, 3:14, 6:4, 7:18 etc.). This is an option recognized by Pāṇini (P.8.3.36; 8.4.40, 41), but it is not common in Devanāgarī MSS, while it is a characteristic feature of Śāradā MSS. (Whitney notes that this practice is also found in South Indian MSS.[28])

Errors explainable by reference to transliteration from Śāradā to Devanāgarī have been marked in the apparatus with wavy underlining; even a cursory examination of the apparatus will reveal how pervasively the text was corrupted at the time of transliteration.

There can be no doubt that the *Paribhāṣāvṛtti* has been preserved, until the present generation of MSS, in the Śāradā script, and therefore in Kashmir.

The critical apparatus

It would have been possible to exclude variants of *sandhi* altogether, considering them unimportant, as many editions do. However, as the study of Sanskrit manuscripts progresses it will be increasingly important to have access to information about scribal practices regarding *sandhi* as well as other classes of variant. Comparative study of such evidence may yield information about transmission, and regional and personal changes in fidelity to exemplars. It is interesting, for example, that scribes from Kashmir frequently use unfamiliar forms of *sandhi* that almost never appear in printed Devanāgarī texts and yet are sanctioned by Pāṇini. The suppression or silent normalization of such regional variations is undesirable from many points of view. Another reason for the apparatus being more minute than usual is the grammatical nature of the text, with its many single- and double-letter technical terms, which requires special documentation. Finally, in the absence of any manuscripts in the Śāradā script, it was necessary to give the full evidence of all the variants, including those of *sandhi*, which are traceable to errors in transliteration from Śāradā.

There is one exception to the above. It is common for scribes to use *anusvāra* for the class nasal even at the end of a sentence. In this text, for example, it is very frequent with the words *jñāpakaṃ* and *prayojanaṃ*. This has been passed over in the apparatus.

Those of Abhyankar's conjectures which I have accepted appear with his name, *honoris causa*.

Each entry begins with a specification of the place in the text which is in question, i.e. line number and lemma where necessary. Where sources are not mentioned, the reader may infer that they agree with the edited text.

When readings of P_1 and J agree they are referred to as α. Similarly P_2 and B are β. Thus, α and β readings can normally be taken as those of hyparchetypes *a* and *b*. However, α and β may not always be quite the same as the postulated hyparchetypes *a* and *b*, because if, say, P_1 introduces a mistake of its own then there is no α, but J still gives the reading of *a*.

[28] William Dwight Whitney, *Sanskrit Grammar, including both the Classical Language and the Older Dialects, of Veda and Brāhmaṇa* (Cambridge, Mass.: Harvard University Press, 1889; 14th issue of 2nd edition, 1975), p. 172.

Care has been taken to ensure that as far as possible variants and conjectures given in one entry all fit precisely the same portion of the text. In further details of usage I have followed West.[29]

Throughout the apparatus I have made every effort to explain the variants by reference to the known mechanisms of scribal error.

[29] West, *Textual Criticism*, pp. 86–94.

Sigla

Manuscripts

P_1	Poona 1
P_2	Poona 2
J	Jammu
B	Berlin
α	P_1 and J
β	P_2 and B

Abbreviations

a. c.	ante correctionem (before correction).
bis	repeated twice
codd.	codices (manuscripts).
f.n.	footnote.
ibid.	ibidem (the same).
in ras.	in rasura (over an erasure).
Kāś.	Kāśikā (Sāstri 1965).
Mbh.	Mahābhāṣya (Kielhorn 1880).
MS(S)	manuscript(s).
m. sec.	manus secunda (by a second hand).
om.	omittit (it omits).
P.	Pāṇini.
p. c.	post correctionem (after correction).
saut	saut du même au même (skipping from an item to the same item in another place).
sic	thus.
उण्°	उणादिसूत्र (पञ्चपदी)
का°	कात्यायन
प°	पाणिनि
पत°	पतञ्जलि
श्लो°वार्त्°	श्लोकवार्तिक
परि°	परिभाषा
वार्त्°	वार्तिक

Symbols used in the text

()	ordinary parentheses.
⟨⟩	angle brackets enclose letters, words or passages added to the transmitted text by conjecture.
⟨∗ ∗ ∗⟩	indicates the editor's belief that something has been omitted in the course of transmission.
⟨−n−⟩	indicates a lacuna of n akṣaras in the transmitted text.
† †	obeli mark words the editor judges to be corrupt. If only one word is suspect only one obelus is used, before the word.
{ }	braces enclose editorial deletions.

Additional symbols used in the apparatus

‖	separates MS evidence on different portions of the same line in the text.
:	separates different MS evidence on the same text portion.
:	between numbers indicates page and line. Thus 2:3 means page two, line three.
` ´	enclose insertions by a scribe, after completion of the original line. Most commonly insertions by a m.sec, often in a margin.
[ ]	square brackets around a whole entry enclose variant *sandhi* alone.
[[ ]]	Double brackets enclose letters or words that a scribe has deleted in the MS.
अ̰	wavy underlining marks variants explainable with reference to the Śāradā alphabet.
...	ellipses abbreviates a passage the beginning and end of which precede and follow it.
*	an asterisk indicates an illegible character.
च^{2}	a superscript number indicates which occurrence of the word in a line is meant.

ॐ

〈 व्याडीयपरिभाषावृत्तिः〉

अथ परिभाषासूचनं व्याख्यास्यामः। अथेत्ययमधिकारार्थः। परिभाषासूचनं शास्त्रमधिकृतं वेदितव्यम्। यदित ऊर्ध्वमनुक्रमिष्यामः इयमस्मिन्सूत्रे सिद्धा। इयमस्मिन्सिद्धेति किं कारणम्। अत्र हि ज्ञातपरिभाषः स्वयं शास्त्रं प्रतिपादयितुं समर्थो भवति। स तावत्सुखं ज्ञातपरिभाषो भवति। अतो व्याख्यानं द्रष्टव्यम्।

तत्रादित एव तावदियं परिभाषा भवति।

अर्थवद्ग्रहणे नानर्थकस्येति ॥ १[a] ॥

क्व पुनरियं परिभाषा ज्ञाप्यते। व्रश्चभ्रस्जादिसूत्रे (८।२।३६)।

कथं कृत्वा। अत्र हि राजभ्राजशब्दौ पठ्येते। अत्र हि राजशब्दग्रहणं शक्यमकर्तुम्। भ्राजशब्दः स एक एवेति। पश्यति त्वाचार्यः अर्थवतो राजशब्दस्येदं ग्रहणं स्यादिति। अतो राजशब्दः पठ्यते ऽस्याः परिभाषायाः प्रसिद्ध्यर्थमर्थवतो ग्रहणे नानर्थकस्येति।

नैतदस्ति ज्ञापकम्। अस्ति ह्यन्यदेतस्य वचने प्रयोजनम्। किमिति। इमौ द्वौ भ्राजशब्दौ। अत्रैकः फणादिषु पठ्यते ऽन्यो वर्चादिषु।

2 〈〉 Wujastyk, from colophon. 3 नमो मुनित्रयाय अथ P_2 : श्री गुरुवे 〈*sic*〉 नमः नमो मुनित्रंयाय अथ B : श्री गणेशाय नमः ॐ अथ J ‖ ॐ अथेत्य् P_1 (अथेति यम् a.c.) 5 [सिद्धेयम् α] 6 [॰भाषसु स्वयं P_2] ‖ प्रतिपादियतु J ‖ समर्थे P_2 a.c. ‖ सुखं P_2 : स्वयं B (very similar in Śāradā) : om. α 7 `अतो … द्रष्टव्यम्´ $P_1$ (in margin) ‖ द्रष्टव्यम् J 8 `तत्रादित … भवति´ P_1 (in margin) 2 व्रश्चभ्रजाति J : व्रश्चभ्रसदि P_1 a.c. 3 अत्रे J ‖ ॰शबदो P_1 (॰शब्दौ a.c.) ‖ पीठाते J ‖ राजशब्दग्रहणं codd. : भ्राज॰ Abhyankar 4 शक्यम् … राजशब्दस्येदं ग्रहणं om. α (saut) ‖ [शाब्दस् स P_2] ‖ ॰शब्द`:´ स `क´ एवेति B ‖ आचा`र्यः´ P_2 5 अर्थवते P_1 a.c. ‖ ॰शब्दस्ये स ग्रहणं P_1 a.c. (possible confusion of द and स in Śāradā) ‖ राजशब्दः β P_1 : राजशब्दः J : भ्राजशब्दः Abhyankar ‖ [पठ्यते अस्याः β] 6 अर्थवत योहणे P_1 a.c. (metathesis of ओ and अ and confusion of ग्र and य) 8 पध्यते P_1 a.c. ‖ [अन्यो β] : ऽत्यो J ‖ वर्चादिषु Abhyankar : र्धर्चादिषु codd. (scribe's attempt to improve a reading. वर्चादिषु is a small subgroup of the धातुपाठ (I. 175 ff.), whereas अर्धर्चादि is a well known गण)

फणादिपठितस्य ग्रहणं यथा स्यात्। वर्चादिपठितस्य ग्रहणं मा भूदिति। तस्य च विभ्राजिति भवति।

इदं तर्हि ज्ञापकम्। दयायासश्चेति (३।१।३७) आसिग्रहणात् कासेः सिद्धे यत्कासिग्रहणं करोति एतदस्य ज्ञापकम्। अतिप्रसङ्गनिवृत्त्यर्थं तत्स्यात्। एवं सति नासृप्रकाराणामपि प्राप्नोति। कासृग्रहणान्न दोषो भवति। इदं तर्हि अयग्रहणात्सिद्धे दयग्रहणं प्रत्युक्तम्। तदपि अयरयपयमयचयतयनयप्रकाराणां निवृत्त्यर्थम्।

इदं तर्हि ज्ञापकं स्वं रूपं शब्दस्याशब्दसंज्ञेति (१।१।६८)। अत्र रूपग्रहणं करोति।

कथं कृत्वा ज्ञापकम्। अस्मिन्सूत्रे रूपग्रहणं न कर्तव्यम्। स्वं शब्दस्येत्येव सिद्धम्। न हि शब्दस्य स्वमस्त्यन्यदतो रूपात्। पश्यति त्वाचार्यः अस्त्यन्यच्छब्दस्य स्वम्। किं पुनस्तत्। अन्यदर्थः। तेनेह रूपं न गृह्यते। अन्यत्र चार्थवान्गृह्यते नानर्थकः। किं कृतं भवति। अर्थवद्ग्रहणे नानर्थकस्येति परिभाषा कर्तव्या भवति।

किमेतस्या ज्ञापने प्रयोजनम्। काशे कुशे हरिशे बभ्रुश इति प्रगृह्यसंज्ञा न भवति इति।

सैषा परिभाषातिप्रसक्ता यत्र नेष्यते तत्र प्रतिषिध्यते।

9 फणाधि॰ P_1 a.c. ‖ ॰पटितस्य J ‖ अर्धर्चादि॰ codd. (॰आधि॰ P_1 a.c.) ‖ भूत् β (i.e. om. इति) **10** च : चर् J **11** दययासश् P_1 a.c. ‖ असि॰ P_1 a.c. ‖ कासे P_1 **12** एतदस्य : एतस्य P_1 ‖ ॰अर्थ J **13** नासृ॰ α : वासृ॰ B : कासृ॰ P_2 (वासृ॰ a.c.) ‖ ॰प्रकारणाम् J ‖ प्राप्नो`ति´ $P_2$ **15** ॰चय॰ $\alpha$ : ॰दूय॰ $\beta$ ‖ ॰तय॰ : ॰त॰ J : ॰डय॰ (?) $P_1$ a.c. **16** स्वरूपं J ‖ शाब्दस्या॰ J ‖ [॰संज्ञेत्यत्र B] **18** कृत्वा : कृत J ‖ `न´ P_1 P_2 **19** सिद्धं α ‖ न हि … रूपात् sic codd. Abhyankar's text is erroneous **20** आचर्यः P_2 a.c. ‖ अन्यत्स्वं शब्दस्य β ‖ अन्यशब्दस्य J : यदन्यच्छब्दस्य Abhyankar, again unfounded ‖ पुनस्तन् J ‖ तेनहे J (mere slip) **21** न : नु J ‖ न रूपं गृह्यते β ‖ ग्रह्यते B : दृ⟨?⟩ह्यते J ‖ नर्थकः B, P_2 a.c. **22** परिभाष ⟨*sic*⟩ क`र्त´ `व्या´ P_2 **23** हरिशे om. β ‖ बभूश J (an easy confusion in Śāradā) ‖ प्रागृह्य॰ P_1 a.c. **25** न यत्रेष्यते α

न वर्णग्रहणेषु ॥ १[b] ॥

कथं ज्ञायते। यदयमिट्वहिमहिङित्यत्रैकं टितं करोति। अस्य किल टित्करणं विशेषणार्थम्। तच्च शक्यमकर्तुम्। एरदिति वक्ष्यामः। न च वहिमह्योरपि इकारस्यात्प्राप्नोति अर्थवत इकारस्य ग्रहणात्। यश्च वहिमह्योरिकारो ऽसावनर्थकः। अनर्थकत्वादस्य न भविष्यति। अर्थवद्ग्रहणे नानर्थकस्येति सिद्धे सति यट्टकारं करोति विशेषणार्थं तज्ज्ञापयति वर्णग्रहणमिदमिति न चैषा परिभाषा वर्णग्रहणेषु भवति। न च सामान्यग्रहणमेतत्स्यात् आर्धधातुकेटश्च विभक्तेश्चेति। अस्य चाकारो यथा स्यात्। लविषीय पविषीय। न चात्रेष्यते। यद्यपि नेष्यते तथापि प्राप्नोति। न प्राप्नोति। कथम्। ङित् इति इड् विशिष्यते। ङितो य इडिति। यश्चार्धधातुके ऽसौ ङितश्चान्येषां च भवति। तेन तस्य न भविष्यति। एवमपि पुटिषीयेत्यत्र प्राप्नोति। अयं हि गाङ्कुटादिभ्यो ऽञ्णिन्ङिदिति (१।२।१) ङित् क्रियते। एवं तर्हि लस्येति (३।४।७७) एतदपि वर्तते तेन विशेषणं क्रियते। कथम्। लस्य ङितो य इडिति। तस्याकारो भवति स चेण्ङितो यदि भवतीति। तस्माज्ज्ञापनार्थमिदं टित्करणं न सामान्यग्रहणार्थम्।

27 कथं ज्ञायते om. α ‖ यदयं ⟨-4-⟩ वहिं॰ B : यदय`मिट् वहि॰ P_2 : यदयंह्रट॰ J (i.e. om. वहि) ‖ ॰महिट्रु P_2 a.c. ‖ [इति अत्र P_1 β] ‖ टितं : ङितं codd. (a very easy confusion in Śāradā) : टितं P_2 a.c. ‖ टित्॰ : ङुइत्॰ codd. **28** एरद् : एरज् P_1 β (द and ज are not alike in Śāradā, but द and च are. So if an original द were transliterated as च and the sandhi then regularized, the MS readings would be accounted for) : परज् J **29** वहिसह्योर् B, P_2 a.c. ‖ वहिमह्यरोपि J (metathesis) ‖ इकार॰ : द्रकार॰ J ‖ ॰आत्प्राप्नोति Abhyankar : ॰आच्प्राप्नोति J β : ॰आ [[-1-]] … आप्नोति P_1 (substitution of अच् for अत् is not obviously explicable) **30** यच्च J B ‖ वहिसह्योर् B : वह्यमोह्यर् J (saut and metathesis) : वह्रामोस्व P_1 a.c. (?) ‖ [इकारः असाव् β] **31** यट्टकारं Abhyankar : यड्रुकारं J, P_2 a.c. : ड्रुकारं P_1 : यटकारं P_2 : यदूकारं B (not obviously explicable) ‖ विशेषनार्थं P_1 **32** `तत्´ज्ञापयति B ‖ इति om. β **33** अर्ध॰ J B **35** इड् विशिष्यते : इत्त्विशिष्यते J : [इट् विशिष्यते P_1] ‖ य इडिति : य डिति J **36** [धातुके असौ β] ‖ ङितो ऽन्येषां α (i.e. om. च) **37** ॰कुटादि॰ : ॰अटादि॰ P_1 a.c. ‖ ॰भ्योंविह्रिदिति J : भ्योञ्[unclear]ङिदिति P_1 ‖ ङित् : तित् P_2 a.c. **38** [लस्येत्येतद् α] **39** ङितो : तिङो β (highly misleading metathesis) ‖ य डिति B ‖ तस्य कारो P_1 a.c. **40** टित्करणं Abhyankar : ङित्करणं codd. (see note to line 27)

यद्येतज्ज्ञाप्यते स्मिपूङ्रञ्ज्वशां सनीत्यत्र (७। २। ७४) च ऋवर्णग्रहणम्। तत्र ऋवर्णमात्रस्य प्राप्नोति। अर्तेश्चेष्यते। नैतदेवम्। अर्तेरिवेदं ग्रहणं न ऋवर्णस्य।

कथं ज्ञायते। यदयं किरश्च पञ्चभ्य इत्य् (७।२।७५) आह। अत्र हि यदि ऋवर्णस्य ग्रहणं स्यात्किरश्च पञ्चभ्य इत्येतन्न वक्तव्यं स्यात्। किरादयो हि ऋवर्णान्तास्तत्र पूर्वेणैव सिद्धम्। नैतदेवमर्थम्। तत्र तावत्प्रच्छेरवश्यं ग्रहणं कर्तव्यम्। एकाच इति प्रतिषेधार्थम्। किरादीनामप्यार्धधातुकस्येट् प्राप्तः। सनि ग्रहगुहोश्चेति (७। २। १२) उगन्तानां प्रतिषिद्धः। स्मिपूङ्रञ्ज्वशां सनीत्य् (७।२।७४) अनेनैव वर्णग्रहणेन पुनः प्रापितः। वॄतो वेति (७। २। ३८) वर्तमान इट् सनि वेति (७। २। ४१) विभाषितः। ततः इदं सूत्रं नित्यार्थं भवति। यद्येवमेतत्सूत्रं न कर्तव्यं किरश्च पञ्चभ्य इति (७। २। ७५)। कथम्। कॄगॄप्रच्छामिति वक्तव्यम्। तत्र हि ऋकारग्रहणादृकारान्तानां ग्रहणं ज्ञापयति। †न च किरादयः सर्वे ऋकारान्ताः। ननु च पञ्चग्रहणं करोति† । तज्ज्ञापयत्याचार्यः पूर्वसूत्रे ऋकारग्रहणे ऽर्थवद्ग्रहणमिति। वर्णग्रहणे च सति दृधृङोरिट् सिद्ध एव। ततो न चेदमकृतं भवति न वर्णग्रहणेष्विति। न च केचन दोषाः सन्ति॥१॥

42 स्मिङ्पूङ्ञ्जशां B : स्मिपूङ्रंजुशां J (correct but for Śāradāism) : स्मिपूङ्र`ञ्ज्व´शां P1 ‖ मनीत्य् J : [सनि इत्य् B] ‖ च om. P1 43 ऋवार्ण° P2 a.c. ‖ प्राप्नोति β : भवति α ‖ अत्रेश्चष्यते J ‖ तेनै`त´देवं P1 44 अर्तेर् : अत्रेर् J ‖ एवेवं P2 a.c. 45 किरिश् P1 a.c. 46 पञ्चव्य J ‖ इत्यतेन्न J (metathesis) 47 हि`ऋ´वर्णांता° B ‖ °आन्ता तत्र β 48 अवश्यग्रहणं P1 ‖ °कस्येट् : °कस्येड् B P1 : °कम्येजा J 49 उगिंतानां β 50 स्मिङ्पूङ्रञ्जशां β : स्मिपूङ्रंजुशां J ‖ °पूङ्° : °पूट्° P1 a.c. ‖ अनेन वर्ण° α (i.e. om. एव) ‖ पुन`:´ β 51 वॄतो : बूतेर् codd. ‖ इट् : इड् P1 a.c. : इड् J 52 ततः : तत्र J ‖ सूत्रं om. α 53 कॄगॄपृच्छाम् β : क्षॄगॄप्रच्छाम् J : ⟨-2-⟩ प्रच्छाम् P1 a.c. 54 ऋकार° P1 : रूकार° B, P2 a.c. (ॠ and रू are similar in Śāradā.) ‖ च om. β ‖ किरादया J : [किरादयस् P2] 55 तज्ज्ञाप इत्य् J : त`त´ज्ञापयत्य् B ‖ आचार्या P2 a.c. ‖ पूर्वं सूत्रे J 56 इति वर्ण° : इवर्ण° β ‖ सति : मति J ‖ इट् : इ J 57 ततो : तोते P1 a.c. ‖ चेदम् : चेदोम् J ‖ के`च´न P2 : केन B ‖ [दोषास् P2] ‖ १ om. β

लक्षणप्रतिपदोक्तयोः प्रतिपदोक्तस्यैव ग्रहणम् ॥ २ ॥

तस्य ज्ञापकं कर्तरि भुवः खिष्णुच्खुकञाविति (३। २। ५७) खिष्णुज्ग्रहणम्।

कथं कृत्वा ज्ञापकम्। अत्रोच्यते। अयं खिष्णुच् किमर्थमिकारादिः क्रियते न च क्स्नुरेवोच्यते। तत्रायमप्यर्थः चित्करणं न कर्तव्यं भवति। एकाचश्चित्करणानर्थक्यम् प्रत्ययस्वरेण कृतत्वादिति। का रूपसिद्धिः। आढ्यंभविष्णुरिति। इड्गुणावादेशमूर्धन्येषु कृतेषु सिद्धं भवति। सत्यमेवैतत्। स्वरे तु दोषो भवति। आढ्यंभविष्णुरित्यत्र कृत्योकेष्णुच्चार्वादयश्चेति (६। २। १६०) इष्णुज्ग्रहणेन ग्रहणं न प्राप्नोति। किं कारणम्। नायमिष्णुच्। किं तर्हि। क्स्नुः। ननु चायमिण्मूर्धन्ययोः कृतयोरिष्णुर्भवति। सत्यं भवति किं त्वत्र गुणो न प्राप्नोति कित्त्वात्। नायं ककारः। कस्तर्हि। खकारश्चर्त्वभूतो निर्दिश्यते। एवमयमिष्णुर्भवति। तत्र च सूत्रे इष्णुज्गृह्यते। तत्रापि सूत्रे इष्णुचार्वादयश्चेति वक्ष्यामि। †अथवेदं तावदयं प्रष्टव्यः। अथास्मिन् खिष्णुचि क्रियमाणे कस्य ग्रहणं स्यात्। ताच्छीलिकस्यालंकृञादिपठितस्य। अयमपीष्णुरेव यथाव्याख्यानम्†। तस्मान्नार्थ इडादिग्रहणेन। एवं सिद्धे सति

1 पतिपदोक्तस्यैव P1 ‖ °पदोक्तस्य β (i.e. om. एव) 2 खिष्णु ⟨-1-⟩ कञाव् P1 a.c. ‖ °खुकज्ञाव् J : °खुकाञाव् P1 a.c. : °खुकेञावं् P2 a.c. 3 खिष्णुज्ग्रहणम् : विष्णुत्ग्रहणं J : खिष्णु`ज्´ग्रहणम् P2 : खिष्णु [[-1-]] ग्रहणं B ‖ °ग्र`ह´णम् P1 5 क्स्नुर् Abhyankar : स्नुर् codd. (see argument 2.4 (line 11 ff. above)) ‖ [एव उच्यते P1 B] 6 चित्कारणा° P1 7 आढ्यं° : धुढ्यं° P2 a.c. ‖ इड्° : यद् P2 8 `आढ्यं° … दोषो भवति´ P1 (original saut) 9 कृतकेष्णुचादयश् J : कृत्यकेष्णुचादयश् P1 P2 B (°के`ष्णु´चा° P2) ‖ इष्णुज्° : इष्णुज° J : [इष्णुच् P1] 10 किं : कि J ‖ `क्स्नु:´ : P1 ‖ चायम् : चायसु् J, P1 a.c. ‖ इण्° : इङ्° J : इ`ण्´° P1 ‖ मूर्धन्योयोः P2 a.c. 11 कृतयोर् om. P1 ‖ सत्यं भवति om. J ‖ [किन्त्वत्र P2] ‖ कित्वा P1 12 चर्त्व° : चत्व° J ‖ °भूतौ P1 a.c. ‖ निर्द्`इ´श्यते [[त]] P1 ‖ एवमयमिष्णुर्भवति α : एवमप्ययमिष्णुर्भविष्यति β 13 च om. P2 ‖ सूत्रे : सूत्रे त्र P1 ‖ Abhyankar's reading यत्र is wrong ‖ इष्णुज्° J : इष्णुच्° P1 ‖ ग्रहयते B ‖ °चार्वादयश् : °चावादयश् β ‖ Abhyankar's reading इस्नु° is wrong ‖ वक्षामि P1 14 [अथवा इदं β] ‖ [प्रष्टव्यो ऽथा° α] ‖ खिष्णुचि : वष्णुचि P1 : क्स्नुचि Abhyankar, without MS evidence ‖ क्रियमा`न्´ए P2 15 °आलंकृञादि° : °आलंकृक्षादि° J ‖ [पठितस्यायम् codd.] ‖ [अपि इष्णुर् B] 16 तस्मानार्थ B ‖ सति : सति इ B

यदेतदादिग्रहणं करोति तज्ज्ञापयति लक्षणप्रतिपदोक्तयोः प्रतिपदोक्तस्य ग्रहणं भवति। अलंकृञादिषु (३।२।१३६) च प्रतिपदमिष्णुच् पठ्यते। अयं पुनरक्रियमाणे इदादित्वे लक्षणेन इष्णुच् क्रियते। तस्य प्रतिपदोक्तस्यैव ग्रहणं स्यात्। अस्य न स्यात्। तस्मादयमपि इष्णुजेव क्रियते।

नैतदस्ति ज्ञापकम्। असत्यां परिभाषायामवश्यमयमिकारादिः कर्तव्यः। मूर्धन्येन निर्देशं करिष्यामि। अस्य हीदागमे कृते पूर्वत्रासिद्धमिति लक्षणेन क्रियमाणं षत्वमसिद्धं भवति। तेनायमिस्नुर्भवति। स च इष्णुरुच्यते। ननु चालंकृञादिसूत्रे (३।२।१३६) इष्णुच् क्रियते। कुत एतत्। षत्वानित्यत्वज्ञापनार्थं मूर्धन्येन पठ्यते। तदपि ज्ञापितं स्यात्। एवं च सति लाक्षणिकं षत्वमसिद्धं भवति। तस्मादयमवश्यं खिष्णुच् कर्तव्यः सामान्यग्रहणार्थः न ज्ञापकार्थः।

इदं तर्हि ज्ञापकम्। व्रीह्यादिषु (६। २। ३८) महाप्रवृद्धेति तत्र प्रवृद्धग्रहणम्।

कथं कृत्वा ज्ञापकम्। अत्र प्रवृद्धग्रहणं नाख्यातव्यम्। कथं महाप्रवृद्ध इति। पूर्वपदप्रकृतिस्वरो भविष्यति कर्मधारये ऽनिष्ठेति (६।२।४६)। तत्र ह्यर्थे क्ते चेत्य् (६।२।४४, ४५) अतः प्रभृति क्त इत्यनुवर्तते। प्रवृद्धशब्दश्च क्तान्तः महच्छब्दश्चानिष्ठा। एवं सिद्धे सति यद्व्रीह्यादिषु प्रवृद्धशब्दं पठति तज्ज्ञापयत्याचार्यः यत्र पूर्वोत्तरपदानि प्रतिपदमुच्यन्ते

17 एतद् om. β **18** अलंकृज्ज्ञादिषु J ‖ प्रतिपदस् J **19** अक्रियमाने P_2 ‖ इदादित्वे Wujastyk : इचादित्वे codd. : Abhyankar's इजदि° is not helpful ‖ [लक्षणेनेष्णुच् P_1] (°ष्णुचि a.c.) ‖ इष्णुं J ‖ क्रि`इ´यते $P_1$ **20** प्रतिपदक्त° $P_1$ a.c. ‖ अयंम् J ‖ [अपीष्णुज् J] ‖ इष्णुचेव $\beta$ **21** इकारादि`:´ P_2 **22** अस्य पीडागमे J ‖ कृते om. Abhyankar **23** क्रियामणं P_1 a.c. ‖ षत्व सिद्धं J ‖ असिद्धिं P_1 a.c. ‖ तेना° … भवति om. α (saut) **24** इस्नुर् Wujastyk : इष्णुर् β : [चेष्णुर् J] ‖ अलंकृज्ञादि° J ‖ इष्णु`च्क्रि´यते $P_1$ **25** Abhyankar inserts तत् before कुत, against the MSS ‖ °नित्य`त्व´ज्ञापना° P_1 **26** लाक्षि`णि´कं P_2 : लाक्षिणाकं B ‖ स्विष्णुच J : स्विष्णुः β **27** षिष्णु[-?-]र्तव्यः P_1 a.c. ‖ सामान्यग्रहणार्थः bis P_1 ‖ न : नु J **28** महावृद्धेति α **30** नाख्यातव्यम् : न व्याख्यातव्यं P_2 : न ख्यातव्यं B ‖ कथ J **31** °स्वर P_1 a.c. ‖ भविष्यते P_2 a.c. ‖ निष्ठेति : तिष्ठति J **32** Abhyankar reads निष्ठा क्ते च against MSS ‖ क्ते : क्तो α ‖ चेत्य् Wujastyk : ने J : ने[[त्या]]त्य् P_1 : नेत्य् β ‖ अतः : तः J : अर्थः P_2 a.c. ‖ क्त : कु J ‖ अनुवर्तते [[त]] P_1 **33** महच्छब्दश् : महशब्दश् J ‖ चानिष्ठा एवं : च निष्ठैवो J : चानिष्ठैवं P_1 : च निष्ठा एवं B ‖ Abhyankar's readings are wrong **34** प्रवृ`द्ध´° $P_1$ ‖ °शब्द J ‖ पूर्वो`त्त´र° P_1

तत्रायं विधिर्भवति। क्त च पूर्वोत्तरपदानि प्रतिपदमुच्यन्ते। श्रेण्यादयः कृतादिभिरिति (२।१।४९)। अत्र ह्यनिष्ठान्तानि पूर्वपदानि क्तान्तानि चोत्तरपदानि। महाप्रवृद्ध इति पुनः सन्महत्परमोत्तमेत्य् (२।१।६१) अत्र पूर्वपदमेव प्रतिपदोक्तं भवति नोत्तरपदम्। अथ विशेषणविशेष्यसमासः उभयं नोक्तं भवति। एवं सति किं कृतं भवति। लक्षणप्रतिपदोक्तयोः प्रतिपदोक्तस्यैवेयं परिभाषा कर्तव्या भवति।

किमेतस्या ज्ञापने प्रयोजनम्। उस्यपदान्तादित्य् (६। १। ९६) अत्र का उस्रा कोस्रेति पररूपं न भवति। नैतदस्ति प्रयोजनम्। अत्रापदान्तादित्युच्यते अयं च पदान्तादुत्तरः। न चास्मिन्कश्चिदुस् प्रतिपदोक्तः पूर्वो ऽप्यादिश्यते। तस्मात्प्रयोजनाभावान्नास्त्येषा परिभाषा। ज्ञापकेषु परिहारा वक्तव्याः॥ २॥

गौणमुख्ययोर्मुख्ये संप्रत्ययः ॥ ३॥

गौणस्य च मुख्यस्य च ग्रहणे मुख्यस्य ग्रहणं भवति।

कथं ज्ञायते। यदयं द्यावापृथिवीशुनासीरेत्य् (४। २। ३२) अत्राग्नीषोमेत्यलाक्षणिकं षत्वं पठति। इहाग्नेः स्तुत्स्तोमसोमा इति (८। ३। ८२) षत्वं विधीयते ह्रस्वात्। तत्र कः प्रसङ्गः यद्दीर्घादग्निशब्दात्सोमशब्दस्य षत्वं स्यात्। ननु च वचनाद् भविष्यति। आहायमग्नेः परस्य षत्वं न चास्ति ह्रस्वो ऽग्निशब्दः। तत्र वचनाद्भविष्यति। अस्ति वचनस्यावकाशः। अग्निगुणो ऽग्निः सोमगुणः

36 क्तंतानि B a.c. 38 विशेषणविशेष° J : \`विशेषण´विशेष° P_1 40 [°ओक्तस्य इयं β] 41 ज्ञापनेन P_1 ‖ अस्य् : तुस्य् β 42 [कोस्रा इति β] 43 अत्रापदा° : अत्र पदा J β ‖ [चिद् : चित् α] ‖ उस् om. α 44 आदिश्यत J 45 ज्ञापकेषु : ज्ञापनेषु P_2 ‖ वक्तव्यः P_1 a.c. ‖ २ om. J β 1 मुख्ये : मुव्ये P_1 a.c. 2 गौण\`स्य´ P_2 ‖ च[1] om. P_2 ‖ मुख्यस्य च om. α B ‖ मुख्यस्य : मुख्यस्य च α B 4 शुनासीर् ये अत्रा° P_1 a.c. ‖ [अत्रा अग्° β] ‖ °अग्निषोमेत्य् sic codd. (i.e. all readings render the argument senseless) ‖ अलाक्षिणिकं β ‖ अलाक्षणिकं परि षत्वं J ‖ इह ग्निः J ‖ °स्तेम° : °स्तोसु° P_2 ‖ °सोमा : °सोम codd. 5 विधीयतै P_2 a.c. ‖ ह्रस्वात् : तूस्वात् J ‖ प्रसङ्ग P_1 6 दीर्घद् J ‖ च om. J 7 आहूयम् J ‖ ह्रस्वो : तूस्वो J 8 ऽग्नि\`:´ P_1 : ऽग्नि B ‖ [सोमगुणस् P_2]

सोमः अग्निश्च सोमश्चाग्निसोमावित्ययमवकाशः। ननु चात्रापीत्त्वेन भवितव्यं देवताद्वन्द्वे चेति (६।३।२६)। नैष देवताद्वन्द्वः। अस्मिन्नवकाशे सति यदग्नीषोमेति पठति तज्ज्ञापयत्याचार्यः मुख्योग्निशब्दो यस्तस्य तद्ग्रहणं भवतीति चात्र दीर्घः। एवं गौणमुख्ययोर्मुख्ये संप्रत्यय इति भवति।

किमेतस्याः परिभाषाया ज्ञापने प्रयोजनम्। अग्निसोमौ माणवकावित्यत्र षत्वं न भवति। †अथागौर्गौः समपद्यत गो ऽभवत्। ओदित्य् (१।१।१५) अनेन प्रगृह्यसंज्ञा न भवति। कथं पुनरस्य निपातः। च्विरव्ययमिति (उणादि° २।६६) गृह्यते तेन निपातत्वात् स्यादेव†। गौणमुख्ययोर्मुख्ये संप्रत्यय इति नैषा परिभाषा। कुतः। यो हि गौणाग्निः अग्निरिवायमग्निः सोम इवायं सोम इति। अन्यार्थोपदेशको वासौ भवति। एवं सति लाक्षणिक एवासौ भवति प्रायोगिको वा। यश्च मुख्यः प्रतिपदोक्तो ⟨ऽसौ औपदेशिको⟩ वा। तस्मादेषा लक्षणप्रतिपदोक्तयोः औपदेशिकप्रायोगिकयोर्वा अन्यतरया प्रत्युक्ता भवति।

यद्यप्यस्या ज्ञापकमुक्तं तदप्यज्ञापकमेव। असत्यां परिभाषायां सत्यवकाशे ह्रस्वात्षत्वमुच्यमानं दीर्घान्न प्राप्नोति। तदर्थमेतत्स्यात्। अथवा नेदमलाक्षणिकं षत्वं दीर्घो ह्यग्निशब्दः। एकदेशविकृतम् अनन्यवदिति ह्यग्निशब्द एव। तत्र तेनैव सूत्रेण ह्रस्वाद्दीर्घाच्च षत्वं प्राप्नोति। अथवा †सुषेण इति विभाषेट् इति (८।३।७९) विभाषा

9 चात्राप्येत्वेन J : चापीत्त्वेन β 10 °द्वन्द्वे : °त्वन्द्वे P_1 ‖ Abhyankar inserts ईदग्नेः ६। ३। २७ after च, against MSS ‖ °द्वन्द्वः J 11 अग्नी° : अग्नि° codd. (see notes to line 4) ‖ आचार्य J : आचार्याः P_2 a.c. ‖ मुख्यो° : मुख्ये° P_1 a.c. 12 एवं : एव J ‖ मुख्ये : मुखे P_1 a.c. ‖ भवती P_1 a.c. 13 अग्निसौमौ J 14 माणव° : साणव° B ‖ `न´ $P_1$ ‖ अथगौर्गाः J : अथा`गौ´र्गौः P_1 ‖ [गौसु P_2] ‖ समपद्यत : समपद्यत्य् J : समपद्य`ते´त्य $P_1$ a.c. : समपश्यत्य् $\beta$ ‖ गो ऽभवत् : अगो भ[-1-] J : अगो ऽभवत् $\beta$ 15 निपातः : `तिपातः J 16 च्विर् Wujastyk : अग्निर् codd. (it is just possible to confuse ग्न and च्व in Śāradā, but this does not fully explain the reading of the MSS) ‖ निपातत्वा`त्´ $P_1$ 17 परिभा`षा´ P_1 18 अग्नि J ‖ अन्या° : `अ´न्या° P_2 : ⟨-2-⟩ न्या° B 19 लाक्षिणिक B 20 ⟨⟩ Wujastyk (may have been omitted by homoeoteleuton) ‖ एषा : एश J : एष β ‖ लक्षण° : लाक्षणिक° B ‖ °पदोक्तयो J 21 [वान्यतरया J] 22 यद्यप्य् : यदप्य् P_2 ‖ अज्ञापकसु P_1 a.c. ‖ [एवासत्यां P_1] 23 सत्येवकाशे J ‖ ह्रस्वात् : तुस्वात् J 25 अनन्यवद् : अननन्यवद् P_2 ‖ इति ह्यग्नि : इति त्वग्नि P_1 (हग्नि a.c.) : इत्यग्नि β (i.e. om. हि) ‖ ह्रस्वाद् : तुस्वाद् J ‖ दीर्घश्च P_1 a.c. 26 विभाषेट इति om. α

प्रकृतानुवर्तते। सा तत्र व्यवस्थितविभाषा भवति। तेन ह्रस्वान्नैव भविष्यति। दीर्घाद्भविष्यत्येव। एवं च कृत्वा प्रयोजनमेतद्भविष्यति अग्निसोमौ माणवकाविति।

यदप्युक्तं गो ऽभवदिति तदप्यप्रयोजनम्। कस्मादेवात्र प्रगृह्यसंज्ञा न भवति। ओदित्(१।१।१५) अत्र तपरकरणं प्रत्याख्यायते सवर्णाभावात्। ओकारस्तत्कालतायामवधार्यं नास्तीति कृत्वा निपातसंज्ञायामवधारणं करिष्यते। निपात एव य ओकारस्तस्य प्रगृह्यसंज्ञा भवति। यो निपातश्चानिपातश्च तस्य संज्ञा मा भूदिति। यश्चायं च्व्यन्तः असौ च्वेरित्यत्र निपातः।

तस्माज्ज्ञापकाभावाच्च अन्यतरयोः प्रत्युक्तत्वान्नास्त्येषा परिभाषा॥ ३॥

औपदेशिकप्रायोगिकयोरौपदेशिकस्य ग्रहणम् ॥ ४॥

औपदेशिकस्य ग्रहणे प्रायोगिकस्य चौपदेशिकस्य ग्रहणं भवति न प्रायोगिकस्य च।

कथं ज्ञायते। यदयं श्वीदितो निष्ठायामिति (७।२।१४) श्विग्रहणं करोति। तत्र हि संप्रसारणे श्र्युकः कितीत्य् (७।२।११) एव सिद्धम्। पश्यति त्वाचार्यः औपदेशिकस्योको ग्रहणमिति। तस्माच्छ्विग्रहणं करोति।

किमेतस्या ज्ञापने प्रयोजनम्। तरप्तमपौ घ इति (१।१।२२) अत्रौपदेशिकस्य ग्रहणं न प्रायोगिकस्य। इह न भवति नदीतर इति।

नैतदस्ति परिभाषा। कुतः। उपदेशो नाम सूत्रपाठः खिलपाठः।

27 अनुवर्तेत P_1 ‖ सा : मा J ‖ व्यवस्थितविभाषा β : व्यवस्थिता α (व्ययस्थिता J) ‖ ह्रस्वान् : सृस्वान् J **28** [कृत्वा अप्र॰ P_1 P_2] **30** यदप्य् α : यद्यप्य् β **32** [ओकारः β] **33** एव य α : एवायम् β ‖ [ओकारः β] **34** निपातश्चा`निपातश्च´ $P_1$ (haplography) **35** च्व्यन्तः : च्यंतः J : ⟨-1-⟩ अन्तः $P_1$ a.c. ‖ च्वेर् : श्वेर् J : ⟨-1-⟩ $P_1$ a.c. ‖ [निपातस् $\alpha$] **36** ॰आभावाश् $P_2$ : ॰आभावश् B ‖ [चान्यतरयोः J $\beta$] ‖ प्रत्युत्क्तान् J ‖ ३ om. B **1** अपदेशिक॰ $P_1$ (औपदेशिक॰ a.c.!) ‖ पायोगिक`यो´र् P_2 **2** ग्रहणे om. B : `ग्रहणे´ $P_2$ **3** च om. B **4** निष्ठायम् B a.c. **5** संप्रसार`णे´ P_1 ‖ श्र्युकः unclear in B : [[-2-]] `श्र्यु´कः $P_2$ ‖ सिद्धं : सिर्द्ध J **6** [[॰देशिकस्य उको $\beta$]] ‖ ग्रहनम् $P_1$ a.c. ‖ तस्माच्छ्वि॰ J : तस्मा`च्छ्व॰´ P_1 : तस्माश्वि॰ B ‖ ॰ग्रहनम् P_1 a.c. **9** [अत्र आषदेश्॰ β] ‖ [प्रायोगिकस्येह α] ‖ नदीतीर J **10** उपदेशौ J : उपदेपो P_2 a.c. ‖ `खिलपाठः´ B

तत्र भव औपदेशिकः। औपदेशिको नाम प्रतिपदोक्तः। प्रायोगिकः प्रयोगमर्हतीति वा प्रयोगो भवतीति वा। तल्लक्षणप्रतिपदोक्तयोरिति अत्र संभवत्येषा परिभाषा। यदपि ज्ञापकमुक्तं तस्याप्यन्यत्प्रयोजनमस्ति। किम्। उकः कितीत्युच्यमाने श्वि त इति संप्रसारणं प्राप्नोति इट् च। तत्र परत्वादिटा भवितव्यम्। नित्यं संप्रसारणम्। कृते इटि प्राप्नोति। संप्रसारणे तु कृते इट् न प्राप्नोति। उकः कितीति प्रतिषिध्यते। एवं सत्येतज्ज्ञापकं भवति। यदा तु सर्वविधिभ्य इड्विधिर्बलवान् (परि० ५०) इत्यकृते संप्रसारणे इड्भवति तदोकः कितीति एष प्रतिषेधो ऽकिंचित्करः स्यात्। तत्राकृते संप्रसारणे इट्प्रतिषेधः कथं स्यादित्येवमर्थं श्विग्रहणं न ज्ञापनार्थम्। यद्यपि प्रयोजनमुक्तं नदीतर इति तदप्रयोजनं साहचर्यात्। †यस्तमपा सहचरितस्तरप् पठित आतिशायिकस्तेन कृत्प्रत्ययान्तस्य तरपो ग्रहणं न भविष्यति। एवं ज्ञापकाभावात्प्रयोजनाभावाच्चान्यस्य चासंभवान्नास्त्येवेयं परिभाषेति॥ ४॥

11 [भवः α] ‖ आपदे`शिकः औपदे´शिको नाम B ‖ नाम : नाप् $P_2$ ‖ प्रायौगिकः $P_1$ **12** प्रायोगा $P_2$ a.c. **14** [किति इत्य् B] ‖ उच्यमाने $P_1$ a.c. ‖ इट् च : इचा J : इ`ट् च´ P_1 : एट् च P_2 a.c. **15** पारत्वाद् P_1 ‖ इटा : इठा J ‖ भवतव्यं J, P_1 a.c. ‖ नित्यसम्प्रसारणं P_2 : नित्यसंप्रसारणे B (attraction to the following सप्तमी) ‖ कृते `इ´टि $P_2$: कृते टि $\alpha$ B (double *sandhi*?) **16** इ`ट् न´ प्राप्नोति [[:]] P_1 **17** ज्ञापकम् P_1 a.c. ‖ यदा : यथा P_1 ‖ इड्विधिर् : इड् निधिर् J : इडिधिर् P_1 a.c. **18** बलवानित्यकृते : बलीयान् इकृत्यत (superscript 2 1) B (superscript numbers indicate metathesis) ‖ [किति इति B] ‖ एष : ह्येष α : एष β **19** किञ्चि`त्क´रस्स्यात् $P_2$ ‖ तत्राकृते codd. : तत्र कृते Abhyankar ‖ [इट्० : इड्० $P_1$] ‖ ०प्रतिषेध`:´ B ‖ स्यादिति ह्येवमर्थकं α (none read as Abhyankar) **20** `ज्ञा´पनार्थं P_1 ‖ यदपि α ‖ नदीतीर J ‖ तदप्रयोजनं α : तस्यप्रयोजनं β (sense demands α reading; presumably this β reading gave rise to Abhyankar's spurious note, p. 5, note 6, by means of a saut) ‖ [साहचर्याद् P_1] **21** यस्तुमपा J : ए यस्तमपा B (suggests some omission) **22** तरपो : तरोप J ‖ ग्रहणो न B ‖ भविष्यति β : भवति α ‖ प्रयोजनाभावाश् J P_2 **23** परिभाषा α (i.e. om. इति). ‖ ४ om. β

कृत्रिमाकृत्रिमयोः कृत्रिमे संप्रत्ययः ॥ ५० ॥

कृत्रिमस्य ग्रहणे ऽकृत्रिमस्य च तत्र कृत्रिमे संप्रत्ययो भवति।

कथं ज्ञायते। यदयं महाराजाट्ठञिति (४। ३। ९७) निपातयति। अत्र हि समासान्तस्य टचः प्रतिषेधः न पूजनादिति (५। ४। ६९)। एतदाचार्यः पश्यति सुः पूजायामिति (१।४।९४) अतिरतिक्रमणे चेति (१।४।९५) स्वत्योरेव पूजितयोर्ग्रहणं भवति इह न भवति प्रतिषेधः।

नैतदस्ति ज्ञापकम्। न हि स्वती पूजायामेव विहितौ। एवं तर्हि न पूजनादिति (५। ४। ६९) ग्रहणे स्वत्योरेव ग्रहणम्। आश्रयिग्रहणादाश्रयग्रहणमपि भवति। तेन ज्ञापकम्।

किमेतस्या ज्ञापने प्रयोजनम्। महाराज इति समासान्तः सिद्धो भवति। कृत्रिमाकृत्रिमयोः कृत्रिमे संप्रत्यय इति। येषामेतत्सूत्रं (का० ५। ४। ६९। १) नास्ति तेषामेषा परिभाषा। किं ते ब्रुवते। काष्ठादिषु स्वती कल्याण इति कल्याणग्रहणं किमर्थम्। यावत्पूजनात्पूजितमित्य् (८।१।६७) अत्र पूजितशब्दे काष्ठादयो निर्दिश्यन्ते पूजने ये काष्ठादय इति। यदैव स्वती कल्याणार्थवाचिनौ तदैव पूजनम्। तस्मान्नार्थः कल्याणग्रहणेन। एवं प्रत्याख्यानस्य प्रयोजनं ब्रुवते। कथम्। स्वत्योः कल्याणवाचिनोः पूजनमिति संज्ञा स्यात्। किं कृतं भवति। न पूजनादित्य् (५।४।६९) अत्र वार्त्तिककारेणोक्तं स्वत्योर्ग्रहणं कर्तव्यं (का० ५।४। ६९।१) तन्न वक्तव्यं भवति। एवं सति ये पूजनशब्दास्तेभ्यो नैव प्रतिषेधः प्राप्नोति। तस्मान्नार्थः परिभाषया। न च प्रयोजनमस्ति भूयिष्ठम्।

एवं च

1 कृत्रिमा`कृत्रिमयोः´ $P_1$ (haplography) ‖ संप्रभृत्ययः J **2** Abhyankar's reading कृत्रिमग्रहणे अकृत्रिमस्य is not in MSS **3** कथ $P_1$ ‖ ज्ञापयते $P_2$ (conflation with ज्ञापकम्) ‖ ठञिति : टञ्जिति J : ठ`ञि´ति P_1 ‖ निपात इति J **4** हि om. α ‖ समामान्तस्य P_1 **5** सुः : सु J : स्वः B ‖ ०क्रमेणे J ‖ चेति : च P_2 (i.e. om. इति) **6** स्वत्येर् P_2 a.c. ‖ [पूजितयोः ग्र० B] ‖ भवति om. β **9** आश्रयि० : आश्रय० J, P_1 a.c. ‖ आश्रयग्रहणम् β : आश्रयम् α ‖ तेन om. B : ते`न´ $P_1$ **11** इति येषाम् : इति एषाम् $P_2$ a.c. : इत्येषाम् B **12** काष्टादिषु $P_2$ **13** [कल्याणे इति $P_1$] **14** काष्टादयो $P_2$ ‖ पूजने ये : पूजनीये $\beta$ ‖ काष्टादय $P_2$ **15** कल्या`णा´० P_1 ‖ ०वाचिनौ : ०वादिनौ α **17** ०वाचिनोः : ०वादिनोः α **18** अत्र om. β ‖ स्वत्योर् : स्वत्यो J : स्वत्यो`:´ P_2 : स्वत्योः B **19** तन्न : तन्त्व J (clarified as न्न in margin) ‖ ये : ये ते β ‖ नैव : नेव J **20** परिभाषयाः P_1 ‖ भूयिष्टं J β

कृत्रिमाकृत्रिमयोरुभयगतिर्भवति ॥ ५^{b}॥

साधकतमं करणमिति (१। ४। ४२) कृत्रिमस्य शब्दवैरकलहाभ्रकण्वमेघेभ्यः करणे (३। १। १७) ऽकृत्रिमस्य। आधारो ऽधिकरणमिति (१। ४। ४५) कृत्रिमस्य। विप्रतिषिद्धं चानधिकरणवाचीत्य् (२। ४। १३) ⟨***⟩ अत्रेच् कर्मव्यतिहार इत्य् (५। ४। १२७) अकृत्रिमस्य। संख्याकार्येषु चाकृत्रिमापि संख्या भवति॥

भवति च बहुव्रीहौ तद्गुणसंविज्ञानमिति ॥ ५^{c}॥

कथम्। यदयमाद्यादिषु च्व्यर्थेषु (३। २। ५६) इत्युक्ता अच्वाविति प्रतिषेधं करोति।

कथम्। च्विरर्थ एषामुपपदानां तानि च्व्यर्थानि। तेषु च्व्यर्थेषु। अन्यपदार्थत्वाद्बहुव्रीहिः। च्विरर्थो येषां तेषूपपदेषु भविष्यति नैव च्वौ प्राप्नोति। नार्थः प्रतिषेधेन। एतत्पश्यति अस्तीयं परिभाषा च्व्यर्थेषु च्वावपि प्रसज्यते। तस्मात्प्रतिषेधः।

किमेतस्या ज्ञापने प्रयोजनम्। सर्वादीनि सर्वनामानीत्य् (१। १। २७) अत्र सर्वनामसंज्ञा भूवादयो धातव इति (१। ३। १) च धातुसंज्ञा भवति।

22 \`कृत्रिमा´कृत्रिमयोर् $P_1$ **24** शब्दैवर॰ J, $P_1$ a.c. : शब्दवै\`र´॰ P_2 ‖ ॰कण्व॰ : ॰कनु॰ B ‖ ॰मेघभ्यः : ॰मेघङ् P_2 : ॰मेघं B ‖ Abhyankar inserts इत्य् after करणे, against MSS **25** [अकृत्रिमस्याधारो B] **26** [अत्र इच्॰ β] ‖ अत्रेच्छुर्म॰ P_1 : अत्रेघ्वुर्म॰ J ‖ Abhyankar's reading अत्र च is not found in any MSS ‖ इच् कर्तरि कर्मव्यतिहार इत्य् β (grammarian scribe confusing P.1.3.14 with 5.4.127) **27** इत्यकृत्रिम॰ : इति कृत्रिम॰ J (attraction to previous sentence) ‖ अकृतिमस्य P_1 a.c. **29** कथ J ‖ अयंम् J ‖ [॰अर्थेष्वित्य् J] ‖ [उत्त्वाच्वाव् P_1] : अत्त्वाम्वाव् J ‖ अश्वाव् P_2 a.c. ‖ अच्वाव् : अस्य च्वाव् B (grammarian scribe thinking of P.7.4.32) **30** करोति om. J **31** च्विर् : श्विर् J B, P_2 a.c. ‖ ॰अर्थ : ॰अथः β ‖ एषाम् : येषाम् P_2 p.c. ‖ उपदानां B (haplography) : उपपदांनां P_1 a.c. ‖ \`च्व्य´र्थानि $P_1$ ‖ तेष्वच्व्यर्थेषु J ‖ \`च्व्य´र्थेषु P_1 : [च्व्यर्थेष्व् B] **32** बहव्रहि : P_2 a.c. ‖ ॰ब्रीहि J ‖ च्विरोर्थे P_1 a.c. : श्वइरर्थो P_2 ‖ \`ते´षूप॰ $P_2$ ‖ भव्\`इ´ष्यति P_1 : भवति B ‖ \`च्व´औ P_1 : श्वौ P_2 **33** आस्तीयं J **34** च्वाव् : श्वाव् P_1 a.c., P_2 a.c. **35** सर्वतामानित्य् J ‖ Abhyankar's notes 7, 8 and 9, p. 6, are misleading and wrong. But see notes to line 37 **36** भवादयो J

बहुव्रीहौ तद्गुणसंविज्ञानात्। सर्वशब्दस्य सर्वनामसंज्ञा। सर्वनामसंज्ञायां च णत्वं प्राप्तं निपातनान्न भवति॥ ५॥

पुरस्तादपवादा अनन्तरान्विधीन्बाधन्ते ॥ ६॥

कथं ज्ञायते। यदयं से ऽसिचि कृतचृतच्छृदतृदनृत इति (७। २। ५७) नृतः से परतो वा इट्प्रतिषेधं शास्ति। नृतः श्यन्विकरणस्यापवादः। नैवास्य श्यन्विकरणः प्राप्नोति नार्थ इट्प्रतिषेधेन। एतत्पश्यत्याचार्यः पुरस्तादपवादो ऽनन्तरमेव शपं बाधते न श्यन्विकरणमिति पुरस्तादपवादा अनन्तरान्विधीन्बाधन्त इति।

किमेतस्या ज्ञापने प्रयोजनम्। विभाषा दिक्समास इत्य् (१।१।२८) अत्र बहुव्रीहिग्रहणं प्रत्याख्यायते। ततो ऽनन्तरवचनं न बहुव्रीहाविति (१।१।२९) प्रतिषेधो विभाष्यते। द्वन्द्वे चेत्य् (१।१।३१) असौ न विभाष्यते दक्षिणोत्तरपूर्वाणामिति॥ ६॥

37 बहव्रीहो P_1 ‖ तद्गुण॰ : तदण॰ P_1 a.c. ‖ ॰संज्ञानात् J ‖ \`सर्वनामसंज्ञा´ $P_2$ ‖ सर्वनाम\`संज्ञा सर्वनाम´संज्ञायां P_1 (i.e. scribal correction of original saut) **38** ण[[च]]॰ त्वं P_2 : नत्वम् J ‖ प्रासुं P_2 a.c. ‖ ५ om. β **2** से ऽसिचि : से सिच α P_2 : सि सेचि B, P_2 a.c. ‖ कृतनृत इति α (as न and च are easily confused in Śāradā, this is an abbreviation of the *sūtra*) : कृतशृत॰ P_2 **3** नृतः : शृतः P_2, B a.c. : चृतः B ‖ [परतः β] ‖ वेट्॰ J : वेड्॰ P_1 (corrected from an earlier वेङ्॰, which is a Śāradā misreading of वेट्॰) **4** [नृतश्श्यन्॰ B, P_2 a.c.] ‖ ॰विकरणस्या॰ : ॰विकरणस्य विकरणस्या॰ α (dittography), (॰विकर\`ण´स्या॰ $P_1$) ‖ श्यन्॰ om. $\beta$ ‖ ॰विकरण J : विकरण\`:´ P_2 : विकारणः B ‖ नर्थ J : [नार्थः β] **5** [अपवादः अनन्त॰ β] ‖ अनन्तम् P_2 ‖ एव om. α ‖ शापं J **6** अ\`न´तरान् ⟨*sic*⟩ B ‖ विधी\`न्´ B ‖ [बाधन्ते इति J β] **8** ऽनन्तारवचनं P_1 a.c. ‖ न om. P_2 **10** दक्षिणेत्तोर॰ P_1 a.c. ‖ ६ om. β

संनिपातलक्षणो विधिरनिमित्तं तद्विघातस्य ॥ ७॥

संनिपातेन लक्ष्यते यो विधिः सो ऽनिमित्तं तद्विघातस्य।

कथम्। यदयं अतो दीर्घो यञीति (७।३।१०१) ब्रवीति। एतत्किल न वक्तव्यं सूत्रमतो दीर्घो यञीति (७। ३। १०१) वृक्षाय प्लक्षाय अकृत्सार्वधातुकयोरिति (७।४।२५) भविष्यति। एवं सिद्धे यद्यञीति वक्ति तत्पश्यति नैवंजातीयकानां दीर्घो भविष्यति। कथंजातीयकश्चायम्। अकारान्तः संनिपातजातीयकः। नाकारविघातस्य निमित्तं भवति। अनेन वचनेन दीर्घत्वं भवति। किं कृतं भवति। संनिपातलक्षणो विधिरनिमित्तं तद्विघातस्येति।

किमेतस्या ज्ञापने प्रयोजनम्। शतानि सहस्राणीत्यत्र सर्वनामस्थानाश्रये नुमि कृते ष्णान्ता षड्दित्य् (१। १। २४) अनेन षट्संज्ञा प्राप्नोति। तत्र षड्भ्यो लुगिति (७। १। २२) जस्शसोर्लुक् प्राप्नोति। संनिपातलक्षणो विधिरनिमित्तं तद्विघातस्येति न दोषो भवति। अत्र हि सर्वनामस्थानजनितं नकारान्तत्वं न सर्वनामस्थानविघाताय भवति।

नैतदस्ति प्रयोजनम्। नैवात्र षट्संज्ञा प्राप्नोति। ष्णान्ता षडित्य् (१। १। २४) अत्र अन्तग्रहणं प्रत्याख्याय प्रयोजनमुपदिशति नित्यषकारनकारान्तायाः संख्याया इति। न चैषा नित्यनकारान्ता अतः षट्संज्ञैव नास्ति कुतः षट्संज्ञाश्रयो लुक्।

2 लक्षत P_1 ‖ यो om. β ‖ विधिः : विः J ‖ [स अनिमित्तं β] **3** अतो om. α ‖ यञीति J **4** \`न´ P_1 ‖ यज्ञीति J **5** अकृत्° : कृत्° J : आकृत्° P_1 ‖ यञीति J **6** °ईति वक्ति : ईत्याह α ‖ तत् : तन् J ‖ भविष्यति α : भवति β ‖ कथंजातोयकश् P_1 a.c. **7** [°जातीयको α] ‖ °विघाताय P_1, β (°विघातस्य reads better with निमित्तं and °तस्य is virtually identical to °ताय in Śāradā) : °विघातय J ‖ विघाताय [[कश्चायमक]] निमित्तं P_2 (scribe's eye slipped back to line 6) ‖ अने\`न´ $P_2$ **8** Abhyankar's reading वचनं is wrong ‖ कृतं भवति : कृतं कवति $P_1$ a.c. ‖ °लक्षणो $P_1$ a.c. **9** °विघातस्यैति $P_1$ a.c. **10** ज्ञापन J **11** सवनाम° $P_2$ ‖ अनेन om. $\alpha$ **12** लुक् : लक $\alpha$ **14** °जनि\`तं नकारान्त´ त्वं P_1 **16** नैवात्र : नवात्र α ‖ Abhyankar's न च is wrong ‖ प्राप्नोति [[ति]] P_2 **17** [अत्रांत J] ‖ °ग्रहमं P_1 a.c. **18** प्रयोजनम् ... संख्याया om. B (homoeoteleuton) ‖ नित्य° om. α ‖ [आन्तायासु P_2] ‖ संख्या\`या´ $P_2$ ‖ नित्यानकारा° J : नित्य\`न´कारा° P_2 ‖ अतः om. α : [ऽतः B] : [अतषु P_2] **19** कुतस् J : कु\`त´स् P_1 : [कुतष् P_2] ‖ षट्संज्ञाश्रयो β : तदाश्रयो α (°आश्रय P_1 a.c.) ‖ लुक् : लेक् P_1 a.c.

इदं तर्हि प्रयोजनम्। इयेष उवोष। अत्र हि उषेर्णलि गुणे कृते इजादेश्च गुरुमतो ऽनृच्छ इत्य् (३। १। ३६) आम्प्राप्तः। आमि सति आम इति (२। ४। ८१) च लेर्लुक् प्राप्नोति। संनिपातलक्षणो विधिरनिमित्तं तद्विघातस्येति दोषो न भवति। अत्र हि लिट्संनिपातनिमित्तं गुरुमत्त्वं न लिड्विघातस्य निमित्तं भवति।

एतदपि नास्ति प्रयोजनम्। अत्रापि इजादेश्च गुरुमतो ऽनृच्छ इति (३। १। ३६) चोच्यते मतुब्निर्देशो न वक्तव्यः। यथा गुरोश्च हल इति (३। ३। १०३)। तस्य प्रत्याख्यातस्य प्रयोजनमुपदिशति नित्यसंयोगे मतुबिति। न चायं नित्यं गुरुमान्। तेनात्र न भविष्यति।

इदं तर्हि प्रयोजनम्। शकटौ पद्धतौ॥ अत्र शकटि पद्धतीति स्थिते इदुद्भ्यामित्य् (७। ३। ११७) औकारे कृते अच्च घेरिति (७। ३। ११९) च शकटिपद्धतिशब्दादकारान्तादत इति टाप् प्राप्नोति। टापि च याडाप इति (७। ३। ११३) याट् स्यात्। तत्रानिष्टं रूपं भवति। संनिपातलक्षणो विधिरनिमित्तं तद्विघातस्येति न दोषो भवति। अत्र ह्यौकारसंनिपातजनितमदन्तत्वं तदिदानीमौकारविघातस्यानिमित्तं भवति।

20 इयेष om. α ‖ उवाष : उ ओष P_2 : उवषो P_1 a.c. ‖ उषेर् : इषेः P_2 : om. B ‖ णलि α : लिटि β (these readings are equivalent, णल् being the 1. sg. pf. suffix, लिट् the general pf. suffix) **21** इजादेर्गुरु° α (i.e. om. च) ‖ गुरुसतो B ‖ [आं प्राप्तः J B] ‖ आमि [[ति]] सति P_1 (अमि a.c.) **22** च लेर्लुक् : च्लेर्लु[[र्ण]]क् P_1 (चेर्लेर्णक् a.c.) ‖ अणिमित्तं P_1 a.c. **23** दोषे P_2 a.c. ‖ हि om. β ‖ \`लि´ट्° P_1 ‖ गुणमत्त्वं J : गुणसत्त्वं P_1 **24** लिड्° β : तद्° α ‖ °विघाताय P_2 (see notes to line 7 above) **25** अत्रापि इज्° : अत्रेज्° α (i.e. om. अपि) ‖ °आदेश्च : आदे J **26** मत्तब्° β ‖ मतुब्निर्देशो : म उ ⟨-1-⟩ ध्नि⟨-1-⟩ र्देशो P_1 **27** उपदिशिति P_1 a.c. ‖ नित्ययोगे α **28** मतुब् : मतुध् P_1 : मत्तब् P_2 : मत्तुर्ब् B ‖ न om. J ‖ भव्\`इ´ष्यति $P_1$ **29** पद्धतौ : पद्धोतौ $P_1$ a.c. ‖ शकति … अच्च घेरिति च om. $P_2$ (saut) ‖ [पद्धति इति B] ‖ Abhyankar's इ vowels not in MSS **30** अच्च : अश्च $\alpha$ B : यश्च $P_1$ a.c. ‖ घेर् : घोर् J, $P_1$ a.c. **31** शककटि° J (dittography) ‖ अकार्\`आ´न्ताद् P_1 **32** याडाप : यावाप P_2 a.c. ‖ तत्रनिष्टं J ‖ रूपं om. P_2 : \`रूपं´ B **34** [हि औकार° β] ‖ °विघातस्या° : °विघाताय° codd. (see also notes to line 7 above)

एतदपि नास्ति प्रयोजनम्। अत्रापि हि अच्च घेरिति (७।३।११९) समुच्चयकरणं प्रत्याख्याय प्रयोजनमुच्यते तदेवं यथा स्याद्यदन्यत्प्राप्नोति तन्मा भूदिति। किं च प्राप्नोति। टाबिति। तस्मात्प्रयोजनं मृग्यम्॥ ७॥

उच्चरितप्रध्वंसिनो ऽनुबन्धाः ॥ ८॥

उच्चरितमात्रा एवानुबन्धाः प्रध्वस्यन्ते।

कथं ज्ञायते। यदयं स्यसिच्सीयुट्तासिषु भावकर्मणोरुपदेश इति (६। ४। ६२) सिद्धे ऽज्ग्रहणेन हनो ग्रहणं करोति। अत्र हि हनग्रहावजन्तौ तत्राच इत्येव सिद्धम्। पश्यति त्वाचार्यः उच्चरितमात्रा एवानुबन्धाः प्रध्वस्यन्ते इति। अत्राकार उच्चरितमात्र एव लुप्यते। तत्राज्ग्रहणेन न सिध्यति। तस्माद्धनग्रहोर्ग्रहणम्॥ ८॥

36 एदपि J ‖ हि om. α ‖ अच्च : अच्छु : α B, P_2 a.c. ‖ घेर् : गेर् P_1 a.c. **37** समुच्चयकरणं : समुच्छयकरणं P_1 : अत्ताकरणं P_2 : अताकरणं B ‖ एवं : एव β ‖ यथा स्याद् om. α (saut) **38** मृग्यम् : कर्तव्यं α ‖ ७ om. β **1** उच्चारित° α : उच्छरित° B ‖ ऽनु`ब´न्धाः P_1 **2** उच्चारित° α : उच्छरित° B ‖ प्रध्वंस्यंते codd. (formation by analogy, in ignorance of P.6.4.24) : प्रध्वंमिन्ते P_1 a.c. **3** °सिच्° : °सिज्° P_2 : °सीज° B ‖ °सीयुट्° : °मीयट्° J : °मीयुट्° P_1 ‖ °कर्मणोरुप° : °कर्मणोडप° P_1 ‖ °देशा इति J **4** After सिद्धे J inserts a passage from a philosophical text on the definition of a वाक्य; see appendix ‖ सिद्धे`ज्ग्र´हणेन P_1 ‖ ऽजग्रहणेन J : ऽज्ग्रहणे β ‖ अत्र : इत्र P_1 a.c. (इ and त might be confused in Śāradā) : तत्र β ‖ हन° : हनु° J **5** इति ह्येव α ‖ उच्चारित° J : उच्चारीत° P_1 ⟨*sic*⟩ : उच्छरित° P_2 ‖ °मात्र B ‖ °बन्धः P_1 a.c. **6** प्रध्वंस्यंते codd. (see note above) ‖ इति om. α : इत्य् B ‖ उच्चारित° α : उच्छरित B, P_2 a.c. ‖ लुप्यंते P_2 a.c. ‖ °आज्° J ‖ तत्रा`ज्ग्र´हणेन P_1 ‖ न : सिद्धं α **7** धन° : धनु° J ‖ °ग्रहोर् : ग्रहो J ‖ ८ om. β

नानुबन्धकृतमनेकाल्त्वम् ॥ ९॥

अनुबन्धकृतमनेकाल्त्वं न भवति।

कथं ज्ञायते। यदयं अनेकाल्शित्सर्वस्येति (१। १। ५५) शिद्ग्रहणं करोति। तत्र हि सानुबन्ध आदेशो ऽनुबन्धेन सार्धमनेकालेव भवति। तत्रानेकालित्येव स सर्वादेशः सिद्धः। नार्थः शित्करणेन। पश्यति त्वाचार्यः यो ऽनुबन्धेन साकमनेकालादेशः स एकालेव। स च न सर्वादेशः। तस्माच्छिद्ग्रहणम्।

किमेतस्या ज्ञापने प्रयोजनम्। ऊदुपधाया गोह इति (६।४।८९)। †नास्त्ययमनेकाल्। सर्वादेशो न भवति ⟨***⟩ तु स्थानिनिर्देशेन सर्वाया ⟨*sic*⟩ ऊदुपधायाः सर्वादेशो न भवति †॥ ९॥

नानुबन्धकृतमसारूप्यम् ॥ १०॥

अनुबन्धैः सह प्रत्ययानामसारूप्यं न भवति।

कथं ज्ञायते। यदयं विभाषा कृवृषोरिति (३। १। १२०) विभाषया क्यपं शास्ति ण्यच्च यथा स्यादिति। अत्र हि क्यप् ण्यत् इति अनुबन्धैः सहासरूपौ। तत्र हि वासरूपो ऽस्त्रियामित्य् (३। १। ९४) एव सिद्धं भवति। नार्थो विभाषावचनेन। पश्यति त्वाचार्यः अनुबन्धैः सहासारूप्यं न भवति। लुप्तानुबन्धका ये ऽसरूपास्तेषां वा ऽसरूपन्यायेन समावेशो

1 ०कृतम् : कतम् J 3 अयंम् P_2 a.c. ‖ अनेका`ल्शि´त्सर्व० $P_1$  ‖ ०सर्वस्येति : सस्येति J  ‖ ०ग्रहनं $P_1$ a.c.  4 [सानुबन्धः : आ० $\beta$]  ‖ [आदेशः अन० $\beta$]  ‖ अनेकोल् $P_2$ a.c.  ‖ एव : ए J : ए`व´ P_2 5 स om. α ‖ नार्थ शित्० J : [नार्थश्शित्० P_2] 6 यो : ये P_1 a.c. 7 ०ग्रहणम् : ०ग्रहणे α 8 किम् … ज्ञापने om. α (i.e. the sense of the last sentence is reversed) ‖ इति om. α 9 नास्त्य् B : अस्त्य α P_2 (वग[?]स्त्य P_2 a.c.) ‖ भवति ⟨***⟩ तु om. α ‖ तु P_2: त B ‖ ०देशेन P_2 : ०देशः न α : ०देशन B, P_2 a.c. 10 ऊदुपधाया`:´ P_2 (र्यदुपधा० or र्थदुपधा० a.c.) ‖ ९ om. β 2 [[अनुबन्धैः … असारूप्यं]] अनुबन्धैः P_1 (i.e. erasure of dittography) 3 कृवृतोर् J ‖ विभाषा β 4 ण्यच्च P_1 : ण्यच्च P_1 a.c., J β ‖ स्याद् : स्माद् J 5 [०बन्धैस् सह P_2] ‖ सह सरूपौ β ‖ वसरूपो P_2 6 नार्थ वि० B ‖ ०वचेनन P_1 a.c. ‖ आचार्याः P_2 ‖ [०बन्धैस् सह० P_2] ‖ सहासारूप्यं : महामारूप्यं P_1 a.c. 7 ये रूपास् J[: ये असरूपास् β] ‖ ०न्यायेने P_1 a.c.

भवति। इह च ण्यत्क्यपोरनुबन्धलोपे कृते सारूप्यं भवति। ततो विभाषारभ्यते।

किमेतस्या ज्ञापने प्रयोजनम्। कर्मण्यण् (३।२।१) आतो ऽनुपसर्गे कः (३।२।३) अत्र वा ऽसरूपन्यायो न भवति नानुबन्धकृतमसारूप्यं भवतीति॥ १०॥

भूतपूर्वगतिरिह शास्त्रे संभवति ॥ ११॥

भूतपूर्वगत्येह शास्त्रे कार्याणि क्रियन्ते।

कथं ज्ञायते। यदयमोक उचः क इति (७।३।६४) ब्रवीति।

कथं कृत्वा ज्ञापकम्। †⟨-4-⟩ इत्येतस्मादिगुपधलक्षणः कः ⟨-2-⟩ वेत्संज्ञा। तत्र के इति न युज्यते वक्तुं ⟨-3-⟩ पूर्वो ऽयं क इति ज्ञात्वा उचः कादेशः ⟨-11-⟩† ।

किमेतस्या ज्ञापने प्रयोजनम्। पव्यमित्यत्रानुत्पन्ने प्रत्यये आर्धधातुकीये आर्धधातुकसामान्ये गुणे कृते यि प्रत्यये सामान्ये वान्तादेशे कृते (c.f. ६। १। ७९) हल इति (३। १। १२४) ण्यत् प्राप्नोति। अजन्तो ऽयं भूतपूर्व इति कृत्वा यद्भवति (c.f. ३। १। ९७)। यथा वायूनामिक्षूणाम्।

8 ण्य`त्क्य´प`ोर´ P_1 ‖ °क्ष्पोर् J : °कूपोर् P_2 a.c., B 10 एतस्या : अतेस्या J ‖ कर्मण्यं J : कमाण्यण् P_1 a.c. ‖ अतो ऽनुप° J, P_1 a.c. 11 °न्यायेन भवति α B (°न्याये[[ने]]न P_1) ‖ भवति om. α 12 १० om. β 1 इहा शास्त्रे B 2 [°गत्या इह β] ‖ क्रियते J 3 अयम् : अयसु P_1 a.c., P_2 a.c. 4 ⟨-4-⟩ : उच् Abhyankar (his footnote suggests that this reading appears in P_1; this is not so) : no lacuna in P_1 ‖ इत्य् α : त्त् β ‖ °उपधा° α (c.f. P.3.1.135) ‖ °लक्षणः क α : °लक्षण कः B ‖ ⟨-1-⟩ P_2 : ⟨-3-⟩ B 5 वेत् β : त् α ‖ के om. P_1 : क J ‖ ⟨-4-⟩ J : ⟨-2-⟩ P_1 : ⟨-1-⟩ P_2 ‖ ज्ञात्वा α : कृत्वा β 6 उचः : तुचः P_2 a.c. ‖ कादे α : कादेश B ‖ ⟨-3-⟩ J : ⟨-2-⟩ P_1 : `क्रियते´ P_2 m. sec. 7 पव्यसु B ‖ °उत्पन्नप्र° α ‖ प्रत्यये : प्राये α 8 °सामान्ये : °मामान्ये P_1 a.c. : °समान्ये B ‖ प्रत्यये [[प्र त्यये]] सा° P_1 9 लहे इति (i.e. scribe corrects metathesis) J ‖ इति om. β 10 कृत्वा om. α 11 इक्षुणाम् : इक्ष्वणां P_1 a.c.

ह्रस्वभूतपूर्वगत्या नामन्यतरस्यामित्य् (६ । १ । १७७) एष स्वरः सिद्धो भवति । भूतपूर्वगतिर्विज्ञायत इति ॥ ११ ॥

वसुप्रवृत्त्या इह शास्त्रे कार्यं भवति ॥ १२ ॥

कथं ज्ञायते । यदयं वस्वेकाजाद्घसाम् (७ । २ । ६७) इतीटमाह ।

कथं कृत्वा ज्ञापकम् । अत्रैकाज्ग्रहणं प्रत्याख्यायते । कथम् । न हि वसौ कश्चिदेकाजस्ति । अत्र हि द्विर्वचनेन भवितव्यम् । पश्यति त्वाचार्यः वसुप्रवृत्त्यैकाजयं भवति । कथम् । इटि कृते अत एकहल्मध्य इत्य् (६ । ४ । १२०) अभ्यासलोपो भवति । एकाजयं वत्स्यर्तीति इटं शास्ति ।

किमेतस्या ज्ञापने प्रयोजनम् । शदेः शित इत्य् (१ । ३ । ६०) आत्मनेपदं सिद्धं भवति । वत्स्यर्त्यत्र शिदिति ॥ १२ ॥

12 ह्रस्व° : तृस्व° J : ह्रम्व° P_1 a.c. ‖ °गत्या नाम् P_2 a.c., but then changed to गतीनाम् by scribe who took it for a genitive plural, not seeing the *sūtra* ‖ [स्वरस् P_2] . 13 सिद्धे P_2 a.c. ‖ भवति om. α ‖ [विज्ञायते β] ‖ इति om. B ‖ ११ om. β 1 वसु° : वस्व° P_2 a.c. ‖ इह शास्त्रे : इफलास्त्रे P_1 a.c. (mistaking the Śāradā ह for फ the scribe then saw the word as फल) ‖ शास्त्र J 2 एकाजद् J, P_1 a.c. ‖ [इति इटम् B] ‖ आह : आहे J 3 °आज्ग्रह° : °आजग्रह° J : °आ`ज्ग्र´ह° $P_1$ ‖ कथम् om. Abhyankar 4 काश्चिद् J 5 वसु : असु B ‖ [प्रवृत्त्या एकाज् $\beta$] ‖ After कथम् $P_1$ repeats भवति कथम् (dittography) ‖ [कृते त $\alpha$] ‖ हलाध्य J 6 एकंजयं J ‖ वत्स्यर्तीति Abhyankar : वत्स्यतीति codd. ‖ °तीत्य इटं J (a move towards *sandhi*) 7 शदेः : शदे J : शदे`:´ P_1 : शिदेशु β 8 वत्स्यर्त्य् Abhyankar : वत्स्यत्य् codd. ‖ अत्र शिद् : अशद् α ‖ १२ om. β

अनन्तरस्य विधिर्वा प्रतिषेधो वा ॥ १३ ॥

कथं ज्ञायते। यदयं णिश्व्योः प्रतिषेधं (c.f. ७। २। ५) शास्ति। ⟨-6-⟩।

कथं कृत्वा ज्ञापकम्। णिश्विप्रतिषेधो न वक्तव्यः। अत्र हि नेटीति (७। २। ४) प्रतिषेधे गुणे च कृते ऽयादेशे †चेष्टं सिध्येत्† । पश्यति त्वाचार्यः अनन्तराया हलन्तलक्षणाया वृद्धेः (c.f. ७। २। ३) प्रतिषेधः। न वृद्धिमात्रस्य। ततो णिश्व्योः प्रतिषेधं शास्तीति। कथम्। वृद्धेरपि णिश्व्योः सिचि प्रतिषेधः स्यादिति। एवं सति किं कृतं भवति। अनन्तरस्य विधिर्वा प्रतिषेधो वेत्येषा परिभाषा वक्तव्या भवति।

नैतदस्ति ज्ञापकम्। अन्यत्रापि ज्ञापितायामस्यां परिभाषायां णिश्व्योः प्रतिषेधो वक्तुं शक्यते। णिश्व्योः सिचि परतो गुणः प्राप्तः वृद्धिश्च। किमत्र वक्तव्यं। परत्वाद्गुणो नित्यत्वाद्वृद्धिः। कृते ऽपि गुणे प्राप्नोति अकृते ऽपीति नित्या वृद्धिः। न हि गुणे ऽपि कृते प्राप्नोति। इको गुणवृद्धी (१। १। ३) इत्युच्यते। एवं तर्हि अन्तरङ्गा वृद्धिः सिचीत्युच्यते। अन्तरङ्गतरो गुणः। कथम्। न हि वृद्धेः सिजेव निमित्तम्। किं तर्हि। परस्मैपदमपि। गुणस्य तु सिजेव भवति निमित्तम्। अन्तरङ्गत्वाद्गुणे कृते ऽयादेशे च हल⟨न्तलक्षणाया वृद्धेर् ह्म्यन्त⟩ इति (c.f. ७। २। ५) प्रतिषेधो भवति। नार्थो णिश्विग्रहणेन। एवं सिद्धे यदिह णिश्विग्रहणं करोति

1 प्रतिषेधे B a.c. **2** णिश्व्यः P_1 a.c. : णिच्व्योः B **3** ⟨ ⟩ om. α P_2 **4** °प्रतिषैधे P_1 a.c. ‖ अत्र Wujastyk (on stylistic grounds) : ⟨-2-⟩ J : त P_1 : `यतो´ $P_2$ m. sec. : ⟨-3-⟩ B ‖ नेटि ति $\alpha$, $P_2$ a.c., B **5** गुणे च कृते $\alpha$ : कृते गुणे $\beta$ ‖ [अयादेशे $\beta$] ‖ इष्टं सिध्येत् om. $\alpha$ : चे`ष्टं सिद्धेत्´ P_2 m. sec. : ⟨-3-⟩ B **6** प्रतिषेधः : कथं निषेधः P_2 **7** ततो निश्`व्योः´ $P_1$ : ततो णिच्व्योः B **8** णिश्`व्योः´ P_1 : [णिश्व्योस् P_2] : णिच्व्योः B ‖ मिचि P_1 ‖ [°षेधस् स्याद् P_2] **9** [वेति एषा α : वा इत्येषा β] **10** णि`श्व्योः´ $P_1$ : णिच्व्योः B **11** [प्रतिषेधश् $P_2$] ‖ वत्तुं $P_1$ ‖ शक्यते वक्तुं $\beta$ ‖ णि`श्´व्यो`:´ $P_1$ : `णि´श्व्योस् P_2 (च्व्योस् a.c.) : णिच्व्योः B **12** णित्य° J : नि`त्य°´ $P_2$ ‖ प्राप्नोति [[इ]] अकृते ऽपीति … कृते … इ[[ति]]को $P_2$ (saut) **13** इति om. $\alpha$ ‖ [वृद्धिर् $\alpha$] ‖ गुणो ऽपि J ‖ ऽपि om. B ‖ °वृद्धे J **14** °अङ्ग $P_1$ a.c., $P_2$ a.c., B **15** °अङ्ग`त´रो P_1 ‖ वृद्धेस् P_2 ‖ [किन्तर्हि P_1] **16** तु om. B ‖ सिजैव J : मिजेव P_1 ‖ [त्वात् α] **17** हल : फल J ‖ ⟨ ⟩ Wujastyk : ⟨-2-⟩ P_2 : ⟨-14-⟩ B : no lacuna α ‖ इति : `इ´ति P_2 : ति B **18** णिश्वग्रहणेन α : णिश्व्योर्ग्रहणेन P_2 (णिश्व्यो° a.c.) : णिच्व्योर्ग्रहणे B ‖ सिद्धे : B, P_2 a.c. ‖ इह om. β. Thus यण्णिश्वि°, but हुण्णिच्चि P_2 a.c. : हुणिश्वि° B

तत्पश्यत्याचार्यः न सिच्यन्तरङ्गमस्तीति। अतश्चैतदेवं यद् इको गुणवृद्धी (१।१।३) इत्यत्र वृद्धिग्रहणं करोति सिजर्थम्। सिचि वृद्धिरिग्लक्षणा यथा स्यादिति। तस्याश्च प्रतिषेधो यथा स्यात् क्ङिति चेति (१।१।५) तस्यां प्रतिषिद्धायां न्यनुवीत् इति उवङादेशः सिद्धो भवति। तस्मान्न ज्ञापकम्।

इदं तर्हि ज्ञापकम्। डाबुभाभ्यामित्यत्र (४। १। १३) उभाभ्यांग्रहणम्। ताभ्यामन्यत्रोणादय इति (३।४।७५) ताभ्यांग्रहणम्। यथाविध्यनुप्रयोगः पूर्वस्मिन्निति (३।४।४) पूर्वग्रहणम्। अनन्तरस्य प्राप्नोति विधिः पूर्वमात्रस्य न प्राप्नोति। इष्यते च। अत इदमुच्यते।

किमेतस्या ज्ञापने प्रयोजनम्। सुडनपुंसकस्येत्य् (१। १। ४३) अत्रानपुंसकग्रहणेनान्तरा या प्राप्तिः सा प्रतिषिध्यते। शि सर्वनामस्थानमिति (१। १। ४२) न प्रतिषिध्यते। तेन कुण्डानि तिष्ठन्तीत्यत्र सर्वनामस्थानसंज्ञा सिद्धा भवति। यद्येषा परिभाषास्ति सामन्त्रितमिति (२।३।४८) साग्रहणं किमर्थम्। नन्वनन्तरस्य विधिर्वा प्रतिषेधो वेति अनया संबोधनलक्षणाया एव प्रथमाया आमन्त्रितसंज्ञा भविष्यति न प्रातिपदिकलक्षणायाः। एवं तर्हि सिद्धे यत्साग्रहणं करोति

19 तत्पश्यत्याचार्यः α : तज्ज्ञापयति β ‖ सिच्य् : मिच्य् J ‖ अतश् : आतश् P_2 a.c. ‖ गुणवृद्धे J **20** Abhyankar's footnote alleging a reading °अर्थे in P_1 is from a misreading of an admittedly unclear form °अर्थ ‖ सिचि : सिवि J ‖ वृद्धिरितिग्लक्षणा J **21** प्रतिषेधे P_1 a.c. ‖ क्निति J : कृटिति P_2 a.c. **22** तस्यां च प्रति° P_2 ‖ इति om. β ‖ उवङ्° : उवजु° α, P_2 a.c. ‖ [°आदेशसु P_2] **24** इदं ... ज्ञापकम् om. J (saut from previous sentence end) ‖ डाब् : ह्राव् P_2 a.c. : द्वौ B ‖ इ`त्य´त्र $P_2$ **25** [अत्रोभा° $\alpha$] **26** यथा om. B ‖ °विध्यनु° J, $P_1$ a.c. **27** न om. J ‖ [चात B] **28** अनुपुंस° $P_1$ $\beta$ ‖ °कस्येत्य् : °केत्य् codd. **29** अत्रानुपुंसक° $P_1$ : अत्र`न´पुंसक P_2 ‖ [°ग्रहणेन अनन्तरा P_2] ‖ °आन्तन्तरा P_1 a.c. ‖ याः β ‖ [प्राप्तिसु P_2] : प्रा`प्तिः´ P_1 ‖ शि ... प्रतिषिध्यते repeated (dittography due to homoeoteleuton to प्रतिषिध्यते in previous sentence) **30** सर्व° : सव° P_2 ‖ °नामास्थानम् P_2 a.c. ‖ तेन : तेने P_1 a.c. **31** यद्येषा : यद्धेषा P_1 a.c. ‖ यदि ह्येषास्ति β ‖ परिभाषा om. β **32** सामांत्रितम् B ‖ इति om. J ‖ किमर्थम् : किमुक्तं J : कि`मु´क्तं $P_1$ ‖ ननुनंतरस्य J (नु and न्व easily confused in Śāradā) : अनन्तस्य $P_2$ ‖ [विधिः $\beta$] ‖ वा om. $\beta$ ‖ Abhyankar inserts a भवति after वा **33** संबोधन° : संबाध° $\alpha$ **34** भविष्यति : भवति $\alpha$ ‖ संज्ञा भवति `[[यद्येषा परिभाषा]]´ न P_1 (marginal correction by scribe whose eye slipped to an earlier line) ‖ प्रातिपतिक° P_2 ‖ लक्षणायः P_1 a.c.

तज्ज्ञापयति अनित्यैषा परिभाषेति।

किमेतस्या अनित्यत्वज्ञापने प्रयोजनम्। न गोश्वन्साववर्णेत्य् (६।१।१८२) अयं प्रतिषेध इति सावेकाजिति (६।१।१६८) काण्डस्य भवति नानन्तरस्य। विभाषा साकाङ्क्ष इत्य् (३।२।११४) अभिज्ञावचनमात्रस्य (३। २। ११२) भवति। नानन्तरस्य न यदीत्य् (३। २। ११३)। †एवमादयो योगास्तदस्मिन्नस्तीति देशे इत्य् (४।२।६७) एवमादिषु चतुर्ष्वेव भवन्ति नानन्तरस्येति† ॥१३॥

तद्भक्तस्तद्ग्रहणेन गृह्यते ॥१४॥

यो यस्य भक्तः स तद्ग्रहणेन भवति।

कथं ज्ञायते। यदयं न क्त्वा सेडिति (१। २। १८) कित्त्वप्रतिषेधं शास्ति।

कथं कृत्वा ज्ञापकम्। अत्र हि व्यवधानादेव किति प्रतिषेधो न भविष्यति। तस्मान् नार्थो ऽनेन प्रतिषेधेन। पश्यति त्वाचार्यः अयमिडागमः परं कितं भक्तः किद्ग्रहणेन गृह्यते इति। तस्माद्वचनम्।

अपरे आहुः न सेड्वचनं ज्ञापकम्। प्रतिषेधवचनमेव। कथम्। देवित्वा सेवित्वेति सार्वधातुकार्धधातुकयोः पुगन्तलघूपधस्य च (७। ३। ८४, ८५) उच्यते। न चायमिट् सार्वधातुकं नाप्यार्धधातुकम्। यस्त्वार्धधातुकमसाविटा व्यवहितः। तस्मादत्रासत्यपि

35 ज्ञापयति : ज्ञापइति P_1 a.c. ‖ [परिभाषा इति β] 36 अनित्यत्वं ज्ञापने B ‖ गोश्वत् J ‖ साववणेत्य् : साववर्णे इत्य् β : सावर्ण्य इति α (साव⟨?⟩ P_1 a.c. 37 भव`ति´. P_1 38 नानान्तरस्य ⟨*sic*⟩ P_1 (नानुन्तरस्य a.c.) ‖ [॰काङ्क्षे B] ‖ [इत्य् α : इति β] ‖ अभिज्ञार्वचन॰ J 39 [यदि इत्य् β] ‖ Abhyankar's अस्य ओरञ् इत्य् not in codd. 40 [योगास् β : योगाः α] ‖ तद् : नद् J 41 भवन्ति Abhyankar : भवति codd. ‖ इति om. β (thus नानन्तरस्य।) ‖ १३ om. β 2 [भक्तस् P_2] 3 यदयं : यदंय J : यदंयं P_1 a.c. ‖ कित्त्व॰ : कित्वे॰ P_2 (किन्त्व॰ a.c.) : किंत्व॰ B 4 शास्तीति B 5 ॰धानेदेव J ‖ प्रतिषेषो P_1 6 नार्थः α (नर्थः P_1 a.c.) : नार्थे P_2 a.c. ‖ ऽनेन om. α 7 परं कितं : पारं कितो α 8 सेड्॰ : मेट्॰ J 9 देवत्वा P_2 a.c. ‖ [सेवित्वा इति α] ‖ सर्व J ‖ ॰लघूपधस्य : लघूधस्य B 10 चायमिट् : चायसिङ् J ‖ `सा`र्वधातुकं P_1 11 नाप्य् : नप्य् P_2 a.c. ‖ यच्चा॰ P_1 (यस्त्वा॰ a.c. !) ‖ [असौ इटा β] ‖ अत्रासेत्यपि J

कित्त्वे न गुणः। नार्थः प्रतिषेधेन। पश्यति त्वाचार्यः आर्धधातुकभक्तो ऽयम् आर्धधातुकग्रहणेन गृह्यते तद्भक्तस्तद्ग्रहणेन गृह्यते इति। एवं सतीटि गुणः प्राप्नोतिं स कितीति प्रतिषिध्यते। तस्मात्कित्त्वप्रतिषेधो ज्ञापकार्थः।

किमेतस्या ज्ञापने प्रयोजनम्। सर्वेषामिति सुडागमः। सुब्भक्तः सुब्ग्रहणेन गृह्यते। तेन बहुवचने झल्येदित्य् (७। ३। १०३) एत्वं सिद्धं भवति॥ १४॥

तन्मध्यपतितस्तद्ग्रहणेन गृह्यते ॥ १५॥

यस्य मध्ये पतितस्तस्य ग्रहणेन गृह्यते। धातोर्मध्यपतितं धातुग्रहणेन गृह्यते। प्रातिपदिकमध्यपतितं प्रातिपदिकग्रहणेन गृह्यते।

कथं ज्ञायते। यदयं नेदमदसोरकोरिति (७।१।११) प्रतिषेधं शास्ति।

कथं कृत्वा ज्ञापकम्। क इदमदसोर्ग्रहणेन गृह्यते। तस्मात्प्रतिषेधो वक्तव्यः।

किमेतस्या ज्ञापने प्रयोजनम्। भिनत्ति छिनत्ति। श्नम् धातुमध्यपतितो धातुग्रहणेन गृह्यते। धातोर् (६। १। १६२) अन्त उदात्तो भवतीति सिद्धम्। भिनत्ति छिनत्ति मध्योदात्तं भवति॥ १५॥

12 कित्त्वे : किं त्वे J (presumably via किन्त्वे; see variants on कित्त्व below) ‖ नार्थः : Abhyankar's footnote 1 (p. 11), which would have been valid at line 6 above, is here spurious **13** अर्धधातुक॰ J ‖ ॰धातुकाग्रहणेन J ‖ ॰धातुकग्रहणे[[म्]]न P_2 ‖ गृह्यते स्तद्॰ J ‖ सतीडि J : [सति इटि β] **14** गुणाः P_1 a.c. ‖ सः β ‖ कित्त्व॰ : किन्त्व॰ P_2 a.c. : किं त्व B ‖ ज्ञापकर्थः P_1 a.c. **15** [॰आगमस्_ P_2] ‖ सुब्भक्तः : सुड्भक्तः J, P_1 in ras. : सुप्भक्तः B ‖ [॰भक्तस्_ P_2] **16** सुब्ग्रहणेन : सुड्ग्रहणेन J, P_1 in ras. : सु`प´ग्रहणेन B ‖ झल्य् : ऊल्य् J : झाल्य् P_1 a.c. ‖ [इल्य् : इति B] **17** १४ om. β **2** यस्य … ग्रहणेन β : यस्य च मध्यपतितस्तद्ग्रहणेन α ‖ धातोर् : धातु॰ P_2 (धातिर् a.c.) **3** प्रातिपद्यक॰ J ‖ Abhyankar omits these two sentences altogether, probably due to a saut from गृह्यते **4** नेदमघसोर् P_1 a.c. **5** इदम् : इ (in ras) दम् P_1 ‖ अदसोर् : अदसो J ‖ ग्रहणेन : गृहणोन J **6** ॰षेधो वक्तव्यः α : ॰षेधः कर्तव्यः β **7** भिन्नति J, P_2 a.c. : भिन्नत्ति B ‖ छिनत्ति : भिनत्ति J (*sic*) : छिनति P_1 : छिन्नत्ति β ‖ श्नम् धातु॰ : श्रस्वातु॰ J : श्नस्वातु॰ P_1 **8** उदोत्तो P_2 a.c. ‖ [भवति इति β] **9** भिन्नत्ति J B : भन्नत्ति P_2 a.c. ‖ छिन्नत्ति J, P_2 a.c., B ‖ (N.B. β reads छिनत्ति भिनत्ति) ‖ मध्योदात्तो α (॰ओदात्ते P_1 a.c.) : मध्योदा`त्तं´ P_2 ‖ १५ om. β

न निमित्तिकार्यं नैमित्तिकस्य ॥ १६ ॥

निमित्तिनो यत्कार्यमुच्यते तन्निमित्तस्य न भवति। इह रहाभ्यामुत्तरस्य यरो द्विर्वचनमुच्यते (c.f. ८। ४। ४६) रहौ निमित्तं भवतः। यस्य द्विर्वचनमुच्यते ऽसौ निमित्ती यर्। तेन यरो द्विर्वचनं रहयोर्निमित्तभूतयोर्न भवति।

कथं ज्ञायते। यदयं शिवादिषु क्षीरह्रदशब्दं पठति। अत्र ह्रद इति यो ऽसौ रेफस्तस्य द्विर्वचनं प्राप्तं तन्न भवति। आचार्याः सूत्रमात्रमेव पठन्ति ग्रामह्रदोत्तरपदाच्चेति (४। २। १४२) ह्रद इति निपातयन्ति निमित्तिकार्यं न निमित्तस्येति।

किमेतस्या ज्ञापने प्रयोजनम्। स्पर्धत इत्यत्र रेफस्य द्विर्वचनं न भवति॥ १६ ॥

अभ्यासविकारेष्वपवादा नोत्सर्गान्विधीन्बाधन्ते ॥ १७ ॥

अभ्यासविकारेष्वपवादा नोत्सर्गान्बाधन्ते।

कथं ज्ञायते। यदयं दीर्घो ऽकित इति (७। ४। ८३) प्रतिषेधं शास्ति।

कथं कृत्वा ज्ञापकम्। अत्र ह्यकित इति प्रतिषेधः क्रियते। जङ्गम्यत इति नुगागमे कृते दीर्घत्वं मा भूदिति। तच्चान्तरेणापि प्रतिषेधं सिध्यति।

1 निमित्ति° β : निमित्त° α **2** [भवतीह B] ‖ The context would suggest some phrases such as कथं ज्ञायते। यदयमचो रहाभ्यां द्वे (८। ४। ४६) इत्याह। to be added before इह **3** रहौ : रहो J **4** [उच्यते असौ β] ‖ यर् β : यत् α (the following letter is त; र्त and त्त are easily confused in Śāradā) **6** ह्रद इति : हृदय इति J : ह्रदय इति P_1 a.c. : ह्रय इति P_2 a.c. **7** रेफस् : रेढस् J ‖ भवति : भति P_1 ‖ आचार्याः α : आर्याः β (आर्यासु P_2) **8** ग्रामहृद° J ‖ °पदाश्चेति codd. (the author has added a च to the text of the सूत्र, which has then been misread as a श्) ‖ ह्रदे इति P_1 a.c. : ह्रदय इति B : हृद इति J **9** `नि´मित्ति P_1 ‖ °कार्यं : °कार्ये J **10** प्रयोजने J, P_1 a.c. (attraction) ‖ [स्पर्धते β] **11** १६ om. β
1 बाधन्ते : बाधेते J : बाधते B **5** [जङ्गम्यते α] : (जङ्गस्यते P_1 a.c.) **6** नुग्° : नुम्° α β ‖ दीर्घत्वं : दीर्घं J ‖ मा : सा P_1 a.c. ‖ तच्चा° : तश्चा J P_2, B a.c. ‖ स्`इ´ध्यति P_1 (स्° in ras.)

कथम्। अयं नुग् दीर्घत्वस्यापवादः। तत्रापवादत्वान्नुका दीर्घत्वं बाधिष्यते। नैवात्र दीर्घत्वं भवति। नार्थः प्रतिषेधेन। पश्यति त्वाचार्यः अयं नुगपवाद उत्सर्गं दीर्घत्वं न बाधिष्यते। तस्मात्प्रतिषेधो ऽकित इति। किति दीर्घत्वं मा भूदिति।

किमेतस्या ज्ञापने प्रयोजनम्। मीमांसत इत्यत्राभ्यासस्येत्वं च प्राप्नोति दीर्घत्वं च। अपवादत्वाद्दीर्घत्वमेव स्यात्। तेनाभ्यासविकारेष्वपवादा नोत्सर्गान्विधीन्बाधन्त इत्यनया परिभाषया इत्वे कृते दीर्घत्वं भवति॥ १७॥

असति संभवे बाधनं भवति ॥ १८॥

यत्र नास्ति संभवस्तत्र बाधनं भवति। वृक्षेभ्यः प्लक्षेभ्य इत्यत्र यञि दीर्घत्वं (c.f. ७।३।१०१) प्राप्नोति झल्येत्वं (c.f. ७।३।१०३)। तत्र नास्त्युभयोरेकस्मिन्संभवो दीर्घत्वमेत्वेन बाध्यते।

कथं पुनर्ज्ञायते संभवे ऽसति बाधनं भवति। यदयं दीर्घो ऽकित इति (७।४।८३) अकित इति प्रतिषेधं शास्ति।

कथं कृत्वा ज्ञापकम्। इह जङ्गम्यते इत्यत्रास्ति संभवः यदुभयं स्यात्। नुक् च दीर्घत्वं च। अभ्यासस्य नुगागमः अचो दीर्घत्वं च। पश्यति त्वाचार्यः संभवे सति बाधनं नास्ति। तस्मादकित इति प्रतिषेधादर्थादापन्नं संभवे सति बाधनं न भवति। असंभवे बाधनं भवतीति।

7 [नुग् : नुक् α B] ‖ दीर्घस्या॰ J 8 पश्य`ति´ $P_2$ 9 नु`ग´पवाद P_2 ‖ प्रतिषेधो ऽकित : प्रतिषेध किं तु J : प्रतिषेधं कितः P_1 ‖ ऽकित इति : ऽकित α 11 मीमांस इत्य् J : [मीमांसते इत्य् β] ‖ ॰आभ्याससत्वं P_1 a.c. 12 दी`र्घ´त्वं $P_1$ ‖ [चापवाद॰ $\alpha$] ‖ [विकारेषु अप्॰ $P_1$ B] 13 [बाधंते $\beta$] ‖ इत्वे : इत्वं J ‖ कृते : कृत्वे $P_2$ 14 १७ om. B ⟨*sic*⟩ 2 `यत्र … भवति´ P_1 (in margin, m. sec) ‖ यञि : यक्ष J : याञि P_2 a.c. 3 झल्येत्वं : ऊल्ल्येत्वं J : ञाल्येत्वं P_1 a.c. : `झ´लि एत्वं $P_2$ : [झलि एत्वं B] 4 संभवो : सम्मवो $P_1$ a.c. : मंभवो B ‖ एत्वेन : एतेन $P_2$ (एत्वेन a.c.) ‖ बा`ध्य´ते P_1 5 कित इ [[अकित इति]] अकित इति P_2 7 कृत्व J ‖ `इ´त्य $P_1$ ‖ उमयं $P_1$ a.c. 8 नुक् : नुश् $P_2$ ‖ च $P_1$ in ras. ‖ [चाभ्यास॰ B] ‖ अभ्यासस्य … दीर्घत्वं च om. $\alpha$ (saut) 9 प्रतिषेधार्थाद J 10 संभवे सति $\beta$ : सति संभवे $\alpha$ ‖ बाधनं न : बाधनं `न´ P_1 ‖ … न भवति असंभवे बाधनं न भवति असंभवे … J (saut: the scribe's eye skipped back from बाधनं) ‖ अ [[सति]] संभवे P_1 ‖ न भवतीति B (assimilation to previous sentence)

किमेतस्या ज्ञापने प्रयोजनम्। कार्यमित्यत्राचो यदिति (३।१।९७) यन्न भवति। न ह्यस्ति संभवो यद् †उक्तं ण्यद्यतौ स्यातामिति॥१८॥

सत्यपि संभवे बाधनं भवति ॥१९॥

कुतः। लोके दृष्टत्वात्। एवं हि दृश्यते लोके ब्राह्मणेभ्यो दधि दीयतां तक्रं कौण्डिन्यायेति सत्यपि संभवे दधिदानस्य तक्रदानं निवर्तकं भवति। अस्ति च संभवः यद्दधि कौण्डिन्याय दीयते तक्रं च। सत्यपि संभवे बाधनं भवति।

किमेतस्या ज्ञापने प्रयोजनम्। सर्वनाम्नो ऽकज्विधीयमानो ऽधिकृतं कं बाधते। अस्ति च संभवो यदुभयं पर्यायेण स्यात्॥१९॥

एकयोगनिर्दिष्टानामप्येकदेशानुवर्तनम् ॥२०॥

एकयोगनिर्दिष्टानामप्येकदेशः प्रवर्तते एकदेशश्च निवर्तते।

कथं ज्ञायते। यदयं तस्मादित्युत्तरस्येत्य् (१।१।६७) आह।

कथं कृत्वा ज्ञापकम्। अस्मिन्सूत्रे इतिकरणो न कर्तव्यः प्रकृतत्वात्। क्व प्रकृतत्वम्। तस्मिन्निति निर्दिष्टे पूर्वस्येति (१।१।६६)। अथवा तन्नानुवर्तते। निर्दिष्टग्रहणमपि कर्तव्यं भवति।

11 प्रयोजन्न B **12** [संभवः β] ‖ ण्यद्यतौ B : ण्ययोता J : ण्यद्योतौ P_1 a.c. : ण्यद्यतो P_2 ‖ स्याताम् : स्यात् P_2 ‖ इति om. β ‖ १८ om. β **1** बाधनं न भवति β **2** [कुतो P_1] ‖ दृश्यते लोके β : लोके दृश्यते α **3** कौडिन्यायेति P_2 **4** यद्दधि : य इ धि J : यद्ददि P_1 a.c. ‖ कोण्डिन्याय P_1 : कौडिन्याय P_2 ‖ दीयते : दे ई यते P_1 a.c. **6** कज्व्`इ´धीयमानो $P_1$ (°धीवमानो a.c.) ‖ °धिकृतं : यिकृतं $P_1$ a.c. **7** कं om. B ‖ [संभवः $P_1$] ‖ उभयं $\beta$ : उक्तं $\alpha$ ‖ पर्यायेन $P_1$ a.c. ‖ स्या`त्´ P_1 : स्यातां B ‖ १९ om. β : १८ J (but following rule is numbered 20) **2** °योग`नि´र्दिष्टा° P_2 **3** ज्ञायते : ज्ञापयत J (thinking of ज्ञापक) **4** अस्मिन् α : अत्र β (अत्र is the formula expression) ‖ इतिकरणं P_2 in ras. (°करणो a.c.) ‖ कर्तव्यं P_2 in ras. (°तव्यो a.c.) ‖ Abhyankar's reading of neuters is unwarranted and unnecessary, though more usual. **5** निर्दष्टे P_1 a.c. **6** अथवा : अथ β

एवं सिद्धे सति यदितिकरणं करोति तज्ज्ञापयत्याचार्यः इतिकरणो नानुवर्तते निर्दिष्टग्रहणमनुवर्तते इति। एवं सति किं कृतं भवति। एकयोगनिर्दिष्टानामप्येकदेशानुवर्तनमित्येतज्ज्ञापितं भवति।

किमेतस्या ज्ञापने प्रयोजनम्। कृते ग्रन्थे इत्य् (४। ३। ११६) अधिकृत्य संज्ञायामित्य् (४। ३। ११७) अत्र ग्रन्थ इति निवृत्तम्। तथा संख्याव्ययादेर्ङीप् (४। १। २६) दामहायनान्ताच्चेत्य् (४। १। २७) अत्र संख्यादेरित्यनुवर्तते अव्ययादेरिति निवृत्तम्॥ २०॥

इतरेतराश्रयाण्यपि कार्याणि शास्त्रेषु प्रकल्पन्ते ॥ २१॥

कथं ज्ञायते। यदयं वस्वेकाजाद्घसामित्याह (७। २। ६७)। एकाज्निमित्त इडागमः। इण्निमित्तमेकाच्त्वम्। तदेतदितरेतराश्रयं भवति। इतरेतराश्रयाणि कार्याणि प्रकल्पन्ते।

किमेतस्या ज्ञापने प्रयोजनम्। इग्यणः संप्रसारणं (१। १। ४५) भवति। अत्र संप्रसारणसंज्ञया यणः स्थाने इको भवन्ति। तेनैवेकः संप्रसारणसंज्ञा क्रियते। तदितरेतराश्रयं सिद्धं भवति॥ २१॥

7 ज्ञापयत्य् : ज्ञाप इ त्य् P_2 a.c. 8 निर्दिष्टा P_1 a.c. (thinking of the gen. pl. form) ‖ [इत्येवं B] 9 एकयोग ... ज्ञापितं भवति om. J (saut by homoeoteleuton) ‖ इत्येतज् : इति ह्येतज् P_1 ‖ ज्ञापितं [[भवपितं]] भवति P_2 (saut) 10 ग्रन्थो P_1 a.c. 11 निवृत्तम् : वृत्तम् P_1 12 °व्ययादीर् J ‖ ङीप् : ज्ञीप् P_1 a.c. ‖ दामहायना° : दासहाया° P_2 a.c. : दाम[[स]]हायना° B ‖ °आन्ताश्ु B P_1 : °आन्तश्ु (*sic*) J, P_2 a.c. ‖ [चेति अत्र β] 13 अव्ययादीर् J ‖ नुवृत्तं J ‖ २० om. β 1 इतरेतराण्यपि J : इतरेतरान्यपि P_1 ‖ प्र° om. α 2 वस्वेकांचसाम् J 3 एकाच्° : एकां° J ‖ इण्निमित्तम् : इङ्गिमित्तम् J : इङ्निमित्तम् β ‖ इण्निमित्त [[इडागमः इङ्गिमित्त]] मेकाच्त्वम् P_1 (saut.) ‖ एकाच्त्वम् : एकांचत्व J : एकांच्त्वं B ‖ एकाच्त्वं`त´देतद् $P_1$ (एकांच् तदेतद् a.c.) ‖ एतद् om. $\beta$ 5 [यणस्ु $P_2$] ‖ सस्प्रसारणं $P_2$ a.c. 6 भवति om. $\alpha$ ‖ °संज्ञाया $P_1$ $P_2$ ‖ यण्`स्था´ने (*sic*) P_2 ‖ [तेनैवेकस्ु β] 7 संप्रसारणे° P_2 a.c. ‖ तद् : नद् J ‖ २१ om. β

प्रातिपदिकग्रहणे लिङ्गविशिष्टस्यापि ग्रहणम् ॥ २२॥

प्रातिपदिकग्रहणे स्त्रीपुंनपुंसकलिङ्गविशिष्टस्यापि ग्रहणं भवति। कथं ज्ञायते। यदयं कुमारः श्रमणादिभिरित्याह (२।१।७०)। कथं कृत्वा ज्ञापकम्। अत्र कुमारशब्दस्य श्रमणादिभिः सह समासः क्रियते। अयं कुमारशब्दः पुंलिङ्गः। श्रमणादयश्च स्त्रीलिङ्गाः। समानाधिकरणाधिकारश्च वर्तते। तत्र सामानाधिकरण्यं न प्राप्नोति। पश्यति त्वाचार्यः कुमारग्रहणे लिङ्गविशिष्टस्यापि ग्रहणं भवति। तेन कुमारश्रमणेति कुमारशब्दस्य श्रमणादिभिः सह समास उपपन्नो भवति इति। प्रातिपदिकग्रहणे लिङ्गविशिष्टस्यापि ग्रहणं भवतीति।

किमेतस्या ज्ञापने प्रयोजनम्। युवा खलतिपलितवलिनजरतीभिरित्यत्र (२। १। ६७) समास उच्यते स च समासो युवतिशब्दस्यापि भवति। युवतिः पलितेति युवपलिता।

यदि तर्हि एषा ज्ञाप्यते ङ्याप्प्रातिपदिकादिति (४। १। १) ङ्याब्ग्रहणमनर्थकं भवति। अत्र हि प्रातिपदिकादित्येवं सति प्रातिपदिकग्रहणे लिङ्गविशिष्टस्यापि सिद्धं भवति। उत्तरार्थम्। वक्ष्यति तस्यापत्यमिति (४। १। ९२)। अत्र ग्रहणं तस्या न प्राप्नोति। तेन रक्तमिति (४। २। १) तया न प्राप्नोति। तत्र ङ्यापोरनुवृत्तिर्यथा

1 °`लि´ङ्ग° P_1 **3** [कुमारश् P_2] **4** [°भिस् सह P_2] **5** क्रियंते J **6** °धिकारश् : °बिकारश् P_1 ‖ वर्तते β : प्रर्वते α ‖ समानधिकरणाभावः प्राप्नोति α (समानावि° P_1 a.c. ‖ °कारणा° J) **8** कुमारश्रमनेति *sic* codd. (by splitting this compound Abhyankar renders the sentence absurd) ‖ श्रमाणादिभि`:´ (*sic*) $P_1$ ‖ [°भिस् सह $P_2$] **9** इति om. $\beta$ ‖ भवतीति $\beta$ : भवति $\alpha$ **11** खलितपतपल्नित° J ‖ खलितपलिन`वलिन´° P_1 ‖ °वलित° B ‖ इ[[त्य]]त्यत्र P_1 : इत्यत्यत्र J **12** युवति codd. : युवतिः Abhyankar ‖ पलितेति α : पलिता (i.e. om. इति) β ‖ युवपलिता om. α **13** एषा β : इयं α ‖ ङ्याप्° : ज्याप् α, P_2 a.c. : ज्या° B a.c. ‖ Thus : [[ज्या]]`ङ्या´प्प्राति° $P_2$ : ङ्या`प्´प्राति B **14** ङ्याब्° : ज्याट्° J : ज्याब्° P_1, P_2 a.c. ‖ हि प्रासि° P_1 a.c. **15** `सि´द्धं $P_1$ ‖ वकति (?) $P_1$ a.c. **16** तस्यापतिम् $P_1$ a.c. ‖ [इत्यत्र codd.] **17** तेन `र´क्तम् P_1 ‖ प्राप्नेति P_1 a.c. ‖ ङ्यापोर् : ज्यापोर् α, β a.c. ‖ अनुवृत्तिर् om. α

स्यात्। प्रातिपदिकात् ङ्याप्श्चेति । तेन यत्समर्थविभक्त्या गृह्यते तस्य ङ्याबुत्तरस्यापि प्रत्ययोत्पत्तिः सिद्धा भवति।

नैतदस्ति प्रयोजनमेकशेषनिर्देशात्समर्थविभक्तिषु। तस्य च तस्याश्च तस्य चेति नपुंसकमनपुंसकेनैकवच्चास्यान्यतरस्यामित्य् (१।२।६९) एकशेषो भवति। तेन सर्वतः प्रत्ययोत्पत्तिः सिद्धा भवति। नार्थो ङ्याब्ग्रहणेन।

इदं तर्हि प्रयोजनम्। †एतस्या एव प्रयोजनार्थं†। तत्र यद्वक्ष्यति प्रातिपदिकग्रहणे लिङ्गविशिष्टस्यापि ग्रहणमस्त्रीप्रत्यय इत्येतदुपपन्नं भवति। यदि तर्हि स्त्रीप्रत्ययो गृह्यमाणो लिङ्गविशिष्टं न गृह्णाति चटकाया ऐरगित्य् (४। १। १२८) अत्र चटकान्न प्राप्नोति। तथा एण्या ढञिति (४। ३। १५९) एणान्न प्राप्नोति। नैतौ स्त्रीनिर्देशौ। कथम्। चटकान्तात्ङसेर्यादेशः कृतः। अतो दीर्घो यञीति (७। ३। १०१) दीर्घत्वे कृते चटकाया इति सिद्धं भवति। यद्येवं चटकायैरगिति वृद्धिः किं न क्रियते। असंदेहार्थम्। चटकायैरगित्युच्यमाने संदिह्यते किमयमैरगेरग्वेति। नास्ति संदेहः। यद्ययमेरक् स्यात् ढ्रकमेव ब्रूयात्। तत्राप्यर्थः उत्तरत्र ग्रहणं न कर्तव्यं भवति। एवं तर्हि बहुलमिति वर्तते। क्व प्रकृतम्। †शेश्छन्दसि बहुलमिति (६। १। ७०)। तेन सर्व

18 ङ्याप्श् : ज्याप्श् α, β a.c. ‖ समर्थाविभक्त्या J ‖ तस्या α **19** ङ्याब्° : ज्यान्°J : ज्याव्° P_1, β a.c. ‖ उत्तर° : उर्त्तर° : P_1 ‖ उत्तरस्याज्यानुत्तरस्यापि J (i.e. saut back to the आ of तस्या (see note to line 18 on J (α) reading) ‖ [°त्यत्तिसु P_2] **20** न तदस्ति P_2 ‖ एकशेष : एकदेश β (a grammarian's mistake) ‖ तस्य च om. J **21** नमुंसकनुपुंसकेनैक° P_1 ‖ °वच्चान्यतर° (i.e. om. अस्य) codd. (but °वश्चा° P_2 a.c., B) ‖ [इत्य् : इति β] **22** [°त्पत्तिसु P_2] · **23** ङ्याब्ग्रहणेन : ज्याब्ग्रहणेन J : ज्या`प्ग्र´हनेन (*sic*) $P_1$ : `ङ्या´ब्ग्रहणेन P_2 **24** [°ग्रहणेनेदं B] ‖ प्रयोजनांर्थं P_1 **25** विशिष्ट`स्या´पि B ‖ प्रत्यय : प्रतिय $P_1$ a.c. ‖ उप`प´न्नं P_1 **26** ग्रह्यमाणो P_1 **27** एरक् (*sic*) β ‖ चटकन् : घटकान् J **28** एर्ण्या P_1 ‖ ढञ् : ढग् α : फञ् β ‖ इति एणान् : इत्यत्रैणान् B : इत्यत्रा एणान् P_2 **29** चटकांतां J ‖ चटकान्ता`ङ्ङ´से: $P_1$ ‖ ङसेर् : ङमे J ‖ यादेशः $\beta$ (°देश B) : या आदेशः $\alpha$ ‖ यङीति J **30** अग्`इ´ति P_2 **31** वृद्धि B ‖ [किन्न P_2] : क्किं न B ‖ चटकारग् J : चटकयैरग् B ‖ उच्युमाने P_1 **32** अयमैरगेरेग् J ‖ संदेहाः P_1 a.c. ‖ ढ्रकम् β : ढम् J : ढकम् P_1 (Abhyankar's फकम् is not attested) ‖ ब्रुयात् P_1 a.c. **33** `ब´हुलम् J **34** प्रकृते P_2 a.c. ‖ शेश् : शे J : शेचु P_1 F_2

एव संविहितो विधिर्बहुलं भवति। कारः प्रकार इत्येवमादीनि सिद्धानि भवन्ति। एण्या इति एणशब्दात् ङसेः स्थाने ड्या कृतः तत्र टिलोपे कृते सिद्धं भवति†। तस्मान्न चेदमकृतम्। अस्त्रीप्रत्यय इति च न दोषो ऽस्ति॥ २२॥

वर्णैकदेशा वर्णग्रहणेन गृह्यन्ते ॥ २३॥

वर्णानामेकदेशा वर्णग्रहणेन गृह्यन्ते।

कथं ज्ञायते। एच इग्घ्रस्वादेश इति (१।१।४८) योगमारभते।

कथं कृत्वा ज्ञापकम्। अयं योगो नारब्धव्यः। एच इग्घ्रस्वादेशेषु इकारोकारौ भविष्यतः। एङः सस्थानत्वादिकारोकारौ ऐच उत्तरभूयस्त्वाद्भविष्यतः। उत्तरं पूर्वमित्येकदेशशब्दावेतौ। एवं सति इकारोकारावेचः शब्दौ भवतः। यदि वर्णैकदेशा वर्णग्रहणेन गृह्यन्ते तत एषु प्रत्याहार उपपन्नो भवति। प्रयोजनमपि चास्य योगस्योच्यते। इमावैचौ समाहारवर्णौ मात्रावर्णस्य मात्रा इवर्णोवर्णयोस्तद्धस्वशासनेषु ऐचोरिवर्णोवर्णं मा कदाचिदवर्णं भूदित्येवमर्थं सूत्रारम्भः। यदि चैषा परिभाषास्ति तत एतत्प्रयोजनमुपपन्नं भवति।

35 विधि बंहुलं J ‖ कारः ... भवन्ति om. α ‖ कारः : काई P_2 a.c., B ‖ प्रकार : एकार P_2 a.c. : पकार B 36 एण्य B ‖ एण° : एन° α ‖ °शब्दात् ङसे : °शब्दांगमे J : °शब्दा`ङ्ङ´सेः $P_1$ ‖ ड्या : त्या $P_1$ a.c. : व्या $P_2$ 37 भवति om. $\beta$ 38 तस्मान् ... दोषो ऽस्ति om. $\alpha$ ‖ २२ om. $\beta$ 1 वर्णैक° : एकैक° $P_2$ a.c. 2 एक° : ऐक° J ‖ गृह्यते B 3 इति : ञति J 4 अयं योगमारम्भो नारब्धव्यः B ‖ इग्घ्र`स्वा´देशेषु P_1 5 इकारोकारो J ‖ एङः Wujastyk : एचः codd. : [एचस् P_2] ‖ सस्थानत्वाद् : स्वस्थानत्वाद् α, P_2 a.c., B: सस्थानत्वात् β ‖ इकारौकारौ P_2 6 उत्तर° : तत्तर P_1 a.c. ‖ भविष्यति P_1 ‖ उत्तरपूर्वम् P_1 ‖ एकेदेश° J 7 इकारोकारव् J : इंकारौकाराव् P_2 a.c. ‖ एचः : एवोः J : एचोः P_1, P_2 a.c. : अचोः B ‖ शब्दो J 8 एषु प्रत्याहार α : एष प्रत्याख्यान β ‖ उपपन्ने P_2 a.c. ‖ योगम्यो° J 9 ऐचौ Wujastyk : एचौ codd. (c.f. Mbh. I. 22:16) ‖ °हारवर्णो J ‖ मात्रावर्णस्य मात्रवर्णसौ J ‖ मात्रा om. J ‖ मात्रे`वर्णो°´ $P_1$ ‖ इवर्णो° : ञवर्णो° J (इ and ञ have been confused before; c.f. earlier note ‖ °वर्णयोस् : °वर्णेयोस् $P_1$ ‖ ध्रस्वाशनेषु $P_2$ a.c. 10 ऐचोर् Wujastyk : एचोर् $\alpha$ : `ए´चोः P_2 : एचोः B ‖ इवर्णेवर्णं P_2 ‖ मा : सा P_2 ‖ कदाचि`द´ J ‖ एवम् : अवम् $P_1$ ‖ आरम्भ`:´ P_2 11 °भाषास्ति β : °भाषा भवति α ‖ ए[[व]]तदुप° P_1 (i.e. om. प्रयोजनम्) : एवतद्दुप° P_1 a.c.

यच्चापि होतृप्रशास्तॄणामिति (६।४।११) कृतणत्वमुच्चारयति।

कथं कृत्वा ज्ञापकम्। इह रषाभ्यां (c.f. ८।४।१) णत्वमुच्यते। न चात्र रषौ पश्यामः। पश्यति त्वाचार्यः ऋवर्णे रेफो ऽस्ति यतो णत्वमुच्चारयति। यदि वर्णैकदेशा वर्णग्रहणेन गृह्यन्ते ⟨***⟩।

यच्चैकारौकारस्येदुतौ शास्ति।

कथं कृत्वा ज्ञापकम्। एचोः प्लुतिरुच्यमाना। कः प्रसङ्गो यदुत इदुतौ स्यातां यत्रेदुतावेव न स्तः। पश्यति त्वाचार्यः ऐचोरिदुतौ। यद्येतौ वर्णग्रहणेन गृह्यन्ते। यदि वर्णैकदेशा वर्णग्रहणेन गृह्यन्ते तत एतदुपपन्नं भवति।

किमेतस्या ज्ञापने प्रयोजनम्। आनृधुरित्यत्र ऋवर्णस्थं रेफं दृष्ट्वा द्विहल इति (c.f. ७।४।७१) नुट्सिद्धो भवति॥ २३॥

12 यशु चापि P_2 a.c., B ‖ चापि होतृ° : चाप्यहत्यो P_1 a.c. ‖ °प्रशास्तृ° J P_2 . ‖ इ[[?]]ति B ‖ उच्चारयति J 14 रषौ : रषो J : ऋका`रं´ P_2 (रोषा a.c.) (There is no reading रकारम् as alleged by Abhyankar, p. 14, f.n. 7) ‖ पश्यासः P_2 a.c. ‖ ऋवर्णे : ऋणवर्णे P_2 15 नत्वम् P_1 ‖ उच्चारयति P_1 16 यश्चैका° B ‖ चैकारोकार° β ‖ °कारम्येदुत्तौ J 17 ऐचोः Wujastyk : एचोः codd. ‖ उत ... स्यातां यत्रे om. J (saut) 18 [स्याताम् P_2] ‖ [यत्र इदुताव् B] : यत्र यदुताव् P_2 ‖ ऐचोर् Wujastyk : एचोर् α : `एचो´यदुतौ P_2 : एचोः B ‖ यद्येतौ om. J (homoeoteleuton) 19 गृह्यन्ते [[यदिवर्णैकदेशावर्ण]] तंत P_1 (saut back to गृह्येते) 20 उपपन्नं न भवति P_1 : उपपन्नं भवति J 21 आनृधुर् : अनृध्वर् (sic) J ‖ ऋवर्लस्थं P_1 a.c. : ऋवर्णस्वं P_2 a.c. : ऋवर्णस्तं B ‖ द्विहन P_2 a.c. 22 नुट् : नुाट् (sic) P_1 a.c. ‖ सिद्धिर् J ‖ २३ om. β

ताच्छीलिकेषु वासरूपविधिर्नास्ति ॥ २४ ॥

ताच्छीलिकेषु प्रत्ययेषु वासरूपविधिन्यायो न भवति।

कथं ज्ञायते। यदयं जुचङ्क्रम्येति (३।२।१५०) सूत्रे पदेर्युचं शास्ति। कथं कृत्वा ज्ञापकम्। अयं पदिरनुदात्तेत्। तस्यानुदात्तेतश्च हलादेरिति (३। २। १४९) युच् सिद्धः। नार्थः पुनः पदिग्रहणेन। एवं सिद्धे यत्पदिग्रहणं करोति तज्ज्ञापयत्याचार्यः ताच्छीलिकेषु वासरूपविधिर्न भवति।

किमेतस्या ज्ञापने प्रयोजनम्। भासते भास्वर इति वासरूपविधिना पुनरनुदात्तलक्षणो युज् न भवति। यद्येतज्ज्ञाप्यते सूददीपदीक्षश्चेति (३। २। १५३) दीपग्रहणमनर्थकम्। अस्माद्दीपो युज्विधीयते। नमिकम्पिस्म्यजसकमहिंसदीपो र इति (३।२।१६७)। स विशेषविहितः सामान्यविहितं युचं बाधिष्यते। एवं सिद्धे सति प्रतिषेधाधिकारे यद्दीपग्रहणं करोति तज्ज्ञापयत्याचार्यः युज्रयोः समावेश इति।

किमेतस्या ज्ञापने प्रयोजनम्। कम्रा कमनमिति च सिद्धं भवति॥ २४॥

1 वामरूप° J 3 °चङ्क्रम्येति : °चक्रम्य J (i.e. om. इति) : °च`ङ्´म्य $P_1$ (i.e. om. इति) : चट्रक्रम्येति $P_2$ (°क्रस्येति a.c.) ‖ सूत्रो $P_2$ a.c. ‖ पदेर् : पचेर् codd. (प`चे´र् P_1 : पदेर् P_2 a.c.) ‖ य्`उ`चं P_1 4 पदिर् : पचिर् codd. ‖ [तस्य अनु° P_2] ‖ °दात्तेतोश् P_2 a.c., B ‖ हलादेर् : फलादेर् J : हलादोर् P_1 a.c. : हनादेर् P_2 a.c. 5 युच् : फट् J : युट् P_1 P_2 ‖ सिद्धिः J ‖ पुन`: प´चि° P_2 (पुनःचि° a.c.) ‖ पदि° : पचि° codd. ‖ °गृहणेन J ‖ सिद्धे codd. : सति Abhyankar, contra codd. 6 यत्पदि° : यदिह α (i.e. om. पचि°) : यत्पचि° β ‖ आचार्यः om. β (thus ज्ञापयति) ‖ वामरूप° J 7 न भवति : नास्ति α β 8 कियेतस्या J ‖ भास्वते J ‖ वामरूप° J 9 अनुदातु° P_2 a.c. ‖ युज् न : ययण न J ‖ °दीपदेक्षश् P_1 a.c. 10 युज् : यण् J ‖ विधीयती P_1 a.c. 11 °कंमिःस्यज° J ‖ °सकमहिंस° : सुकसुहिंस α (°मुकमुहिंम° P_1 a.c.) : °संकसहिंस° P_2 ‖ विषेश° P_1 ‖ [°विहितस् β] 13 युजयोः J : [युज्रयोस् P_2] ‖ समवेश β 14 कस्रा α P_2 ‖ कसनम् β ‖ २४ om. β

प्रत्येकं वाक्यपरिसमाप्तिः ॥ २५ ॥

कथं ज्ञायते। लोकतः। तद्यथा देवदत्तयज्ञदत्तविष्णुमित्रा भोज्यन्तामिति। न चोच्यते प्रत्येकमिति। प्रत्येकं च भुजिः परिसमाप्यते। शास्त्रे चापीयमस्ति परिभाषा। कथं ज्ञायते । णल् उत्तमो वेत्याह (७।१।९१)।

कथं कृत्वा ज्ञापकम्। इह हि समुदितस्य त्रिकस्योत्तमसंज्ञा क्रियते। तत्रैकस्य णल उत्तम इति विशेषणं न प्राप्नोति। पश्यति त्वाचार्यः प्रत्येकं वाक्यपरिसमाप्तिर्भवति। तेन प्रत्येकं त्रिके उत्तमशब्दः क्रियते।

किमेतस्या ज्ञापने प्रयोजनम्। प्रत्येकं गुणवृद्धिसंज्ञे भवत इति न वक्तव्यं भवति॥ २५॥

समुदाये ऽपि वाक्यपरिसमाप्तिः ॥ २६ ॥

समुदाये ऽपि वाक्यं परिसमाप्यते। तद्यथा गर्गाः शतं दण्ड्यन्तामित्युक्ते अर्थिनश्च राजानो हिरण्येन भवन्ति न च प्रत्येकं दण्डयन्ति। शास्त्रे ऽपि चेयमस्ति परिभाषा। ज्ञापकं यदयं प्रथमयोः पूर्वसवर्ण इत्याह (६।१। १०२)।

कथं कृत्वा ज्ञापकम्। अयं प्रथमशब्दः सर्वत्रिकस्य समुदितस्य संज्ञा। तत इह प्रथमयोः त्रिकयोर्ग्रहणं भवति प्रथमद्वितीययोः। प्रथमयोरिति वचनात्। कथं पुनर्ज्ञायते त्रिकयोर्ग्रहणं न पुनरजाद्योः प्रथमयोरिति।

1 प्रत्यैकं P_1 a.c. **2** °विष्णुमित्र P_2 a.c. **3** \`प्रत्येकमिति´ P_1 m. sec. (om. through saut) **4** परिसमाप्येते B, P_2 a.c. : परिस[[˙]]माप्यते[[:]] P_1 ‖ [चापि इयम् β] ‖ उत्तमो : अत्तमो J ‖ उतुमो P_2 (उतुसो a.c.) **6** [त्रिकस्य उत्तम° β] **7** णल् B P_1 : णन P_2 a.c. ‖ इति : इव P_1 **8** त्रिको B **10** भवति om. α ‖ २५ om. β **2** गर्गः P_1 : गर्गाशु P_2 ‖ दाण्ड्यन्ताम् P_1 **3** राजानो भवन्ति हिरण्येन P_1 : राजानं भवंति हिरण्येन J **4** प्रथमयोः : प्रतिमयोः J ‖ पूर्वमुवर्ण J **6** °शब्द\`:´ $P_2$ : °शब्द B ‖ सार्व° B ‖ °त्र्\`इ´कस्य P_2 **7** इह : इत्याह B ‖ [प्रथमयोस् α B] : प्रथमयो\`:´ P_2 ‖ त्रिकयो J ‖ भवति α : करोति β **8** पुनर् : पुन J ‖ त्रिकयोर् : त्रिकयो J ‖ पुनर् : पुरर् (*sic ?*) P_1 a.c. ‖ अजाद्योः : प्रथमयोर् : अथद्योर् α (several small sauts)

आचार्यस्य प्रवृत्तिर्ज्ञापयति त्रिकयोस्तद्ग्रहणं यदयं तस्माच्छसो नः पुंसीति (६। १। १०३) तस्मादित्यनेन पूर्वसवर्णं निर्दिशति। तज्ज्ञापयति शसोऽपि तेन पूर्वसवर्ण इति। यदि च त्रिकयोस्तद्ग्रहणं तत एवमुपपन्नम्। तस्मात्प्रथमयोर्ग्रहणं ज्ञापकम्। समुदाये ऽपि वाक्यपरिसमाप्तिः। तेन ङे प्रथमयोरमित्य् (७।१।२८) एवमादि सिद्धं भवति॥ २६॥

भाव्यमानो ऽण् सवर्णान्न गृह्णाति ॥ २७°॥

कथं ज्ञायते। यदयमी हल्यघोरिति (६। ४। ११३) दीर्घमीकारं शास्ति।

कथं कृत्वा ज्ञापकम्। एतत्सूत्रमि हल्यघोरिति वक्तव्यम्। कथमिदानीमीकारो भविष्यति। अणुदित्सवर्णस्येति (१।१।६९) इवर्णो गृह्यते। तत्रास्य स्थाने सर्वस्मिन्निवर्णे प्रसक्ते स्थाने ऽन्तरतम इति (१।१।५०) दीर्घो भविष्यति दीर्घस्य। नार्थो दीर्घग्रहणेन। पश्यति त्वाचार्यः भाव्यमानो ऽणसवर्णान्न गृह्णाति ततो दीर्घोच्चारणं करोति।

किमेतस्या ज्ञापने प्रयोजनम्। इदम इश् इत्य् (५।३।३) अत्रेदमो ह्रस्वदीर्घप्लुताः पर्यायेणादेशा न भवन्ति। यद्येतज्ज्ञाप्यते दिव उदित्य् (६।१।१३१) अत्रोकारस्य तपरकरणं न कर्तव्यम्। कथम्। वकारस्य स्थाने

9 आचार्यप्रवृतिंर् β (J omits final र्) 10 इत्यनेन : इति नेन P_1 a.c. ‖ पूर्व° : पूर्ण° α ‖ ज्ञाप इति P_1 11 इति[[ति]] P_1 ‖ एवम् : एव B 12 प्रथमयोर् : प्रथमयो J ‖ ङे : ङेः β 13 अम् om. α ‖ २६ om. β 1 भाव्यमानो ऽण् : भाव्यमानः : P_1 (भाव्यसानः a.c.) ‖ सवर्णा`न्´गृह्णाति B 2 कथ $P_2$ ‖ ज्ञायते om. J ‖ ई : इं J : ओ $P_2$ a.c. 4 अगोर् $P_1$ 5 कथसु $P_1$ a.c. ‖ इदानीसु $P_2$ a.c. ‖ ईकारो : एकारो J 6 स्थाने … प्रसक्ते *sic* $\alpha$ (relegated to footnote by Abhyankar) ‖ स्थाने`तंर´स्मिन् P_2 : स्थाने[-4-]स्मिन् B (i.e. β had a lacuna for सर्व°, which was wrongly filled in by m. sec. on P_2) 8 भाव्यमानः α (i.e. om. अण्) ‖ °ओस्वारणं J B : °ओच्चारं P_2 (°ओस्वारं a.c.) 9 इदमः P_2 (इदसः a.c.) ‖ इत्यत्रेदमो : इत्येत्रदसो J : [इत्यत्र इदमो β] (इदसो P_2 a.c.) 10 °प्लुतः P_2 ‖ पर्यायेणा° : पर्यायेना° J : पर्यायोणा° P_1 : पर्याये[[न]]णा° P_2 ‖ उदित्य् : उद्यत्य् J 11 [अत्र उकारस्य β] ‖ तपर° : `त´पर° P_1 (उपर° a.c.)

ऽयमुकारो भाव्यते। तेन भाव्यमानो ऽण् सवर्णान्न ग्रहीष्यतीति ह्रस्व एव भविष्यति न दीर्घप्लुतौ। तस्मान्नार्थस्तत्परकरणेन। पश्यति त्वाचार्यः

उकार एवैको भाव्यमानो ऽपि सवर्णान्गृह्णाति ॥ २७^{b}॥

किमेतस्या ज्ञापने प्रयोजनम्। अदसो ऽसेर्दादु दो म इत्य् (८। २। ८०) अत्रोकारः सवर्णं गृह्णातीति। अमुष्मिन् अमूभ्याम् इत्यत्र ह्रस्वस्य ह्रस्वः दीर्घस्य दीर्घो भवति॥ २७॥

इह शास्त्रे व्यवस्थितविभाषा भवति ॥ २८॥

कथं ज्ञायते। यदयं वा क्यष इति (१। ३। ९०) ब्रवीति।

कथं कृत्वा ज्ञापकम्। एतत्किल सूत्रं नारब्धव्यम्। यदि नारभ्यते विभाषात्मनेपदं कथं भविष्यति। पटपटायति पटपटायते। नित्यवीप्सयोरिति (८। १। ४) द्विर्वचनं पटत् पटत्। अव्यक्तानुकरणाद् द्व्यजवरार्धादनितौ डाच् (५। ४। ५७) नित्यमाम्रेडिते डाचि (का० ६। १। ९९। १) पूर्वपररूपं तकारस्य पकारः पटपटा इति स्थिते क्यष् क्यङ् वा। कथम्। इह योगविभागं करिष्यामः। कर्तुः क्यङ् सलोपश्च (३। १। ११) भृशादिभ्यो भुव्यच्वेर्लोपश्च हलः (३। १।

12 ऽयसुकारे P_2 a.c. ‖ भाव्यमानः α (i.e. om. अण्) ‖ सवर्णा`न्´ग्रही° B ‖ ग्रहीष्यतीति : गृह्णातीति $\alpha$ ‖ एव : इव $P_1$ **14** सवर्णां गृह्णाति B **15** किमेतस्य … गृह्णातीति om. J (saut from गृह्णाति in l. 19 to l. 22) **16** [अत्र उकारसु $P_2$] **17** ह्रस्व`स्य ह्रस्वो´ भवति द्`ई´र्घस्य दीर्घः। P_2 : ibid. (as corrected) B ‖ २७ om. β **1** °विभाषा व भवति J **2** क्यष : कूष β a.c. **4** पटपटायते : पटपएयते J (ए and टा are easily confused in Śāradā) **5** नित्य° : निति° P_1 a.c. ‖ पटत् om. P_2 **6** °अनितौ : °अनितो J ‖ आम्रेडिते B ‖ आम्रेडिते डाचि : आम्रेडित इत्यादि α ‖ डाचि : ताचि(?) P_2 a.c. **8** क्यष् क्यङ् वा : क्यं क्यज्वा J : क्याष् क्यङ्वा P_1 a.c. : क्यज्वा P_2 : क्यङ् वा B (the ज् of क्यज् in these variants probably arises from a confusion of the Śāradā letters ज् and ङ्) ‖ करिष्यासः B ‖ कर्तुः : कतुं J : कर्त्[[तु]]र् P_2 ‖ क्यङ् : किट् J **9** मलोपश्च J ‖ अच्वेर् : अच्वे J : अश्वेर् β ‖ लोपश् : लोपिश् J

१२)। क्यङित्येव। तेन लोहितादिडाज्भ्य इत्य् (c.f. ३। १। १३) एव। तत्र यदा क्यङ् तदा ङित इत्य् (१। ३। १२) आत्मनेपदं भवति। यदा क्यष् तदा शेषादिति (१। ३। ७८) परस्मैपदं भवति। नार्थो वा क्यष इत्य् (१। ३। ९०) अनेन सूत्रेण। तदेतत्सूत्रं व्यवस्थितविभाषार्थमारभ्यते। कथम्। लोहितादिषु केषांचिदात्मनेपदमेव स्यात्केषां चिदुभयपदम्। योगविभागेन पुनः सर्वेषामुभयपदम्। तेन नीलादीनामात्मनेपदमेव भवति। लोहितशब्दस्योभयम्। तत्र यद्वक्ष्यति वार्त्तिककारः लोहिताडज्भ्यः क्यष्वचनं भृशादिष्वितराणि (का० ३। १। १३। १, २) तन्न वक्तव्यं भवति।

किमेतस्या ज्ञापने प्रयोजनम्।

देवत्रातो गलो ग्राह इतियोगे च सद्विधिः।
मिथस्ते न विभाष्यन्ते गवाक्षः संशितव्रतः॥ (श्लो० वार्त्० ३। ३। १५६। २, ७। ४। ४१। १)

देवत्रात इति नुदविदोन्दत्राघ्रा इत्य् (८। २। ५६) अत्रान्यतरस्यांग्रहणेन नाम्न्यनत्वमेव नाम्नोन्यत्रोभयम्। त्रातः त्राणः॥ तथा गलः। गॄ इत्येतस्यापि गुणे रपरत्वे च कृते ग्रो यङि अचि विभाषेति (८। २। २०, २१) लत्वे क्रियमाणे स्वाङ्ग एव गल इति भवति। स्वाङ्गादन्यत्र गरः॥ ग्राह इति विभाषा ग्रहः (३। १। १४३) णप्रत्ययो भवति। ग्राहश्चेज्जलचर एव भवति। जलचरादन्यत्राजेव भवति।

10 क्याङ् P_1 ‖ इत्येव : इतेव P_1 a.c. ‖ तेन : न P_2 ‖ °आदिडाज्भ्य : °आदित्वाज्ञा (*sic*) J ‖ °डाज्° : °डाङ्° P_2 **11** क्याङ् P_1 a.c. **14** व्यवस्थित° om. B **15** उभयपदम् : उभयम् α P_2 ‖ [पुनस् P_2] ‖ सर्वेषामेवोभय° P_2 ‖ उभयपदम् : उभयम् α P_2 **17** °डाज्भ्यः : °डाजभ्यः J : °डाज्व्यः P_1 a.c. : °डाज्भ्य`:´ P_2 (डाज्झः (?) a.c.) ‖ क्यष्वचनं : क्यपुचनं J : कृष्वपनम् (?) P_2 a.c. **19** किम् : विम् P_2 a.c. **20** गले β ‖ ग्रह β ‖ मद्विधिः J **21** [गवाक्षस् P_2] ‖ संशतव्रताः P_1 a.c. **23** नुदविदोन्यत्राघ्रा J : नुदविदोन्दात्राघ्रा P_1 : नुदविदोन्दात्राघ्रा P_2 (°विदोन्मा° a.c.) : नुदविदोन्मात्राघ्रा B **24** °आन्यतस्यां J ‖ नाम्न्यनत्वम् β : नाम्नि नत्वम् α (Abhyankar's reading in f.n. 5, p. 16, is spurious) ‖ त्राताः P_1 a.c. **25** गृ J ‖ च om. P_2 ‖ च कृते [[च कृते]] P_1 (erasure of dittography) ‖ ग्रो यङि : ग्र यङि α : गो षङि P_2 a.c. **26** क्रियमा`णे´ [[ने]] P_2 : क्रियमाने B **27** स्वाङ्ग ... भवति α : स्वाङ्गे गल एव भवति β ‖ स्वाङ्गदन्यत्र P_1 a.c. ‖ गरः : गाः J (particularly clear evidence of errors due to transliteration from Śāradā) **28** [चेत् जल° β] ‖ अन्यात्रजेव P_2 a.c. ‖ भवति : भवंति B

ग्रहः॥ इतियोगे च सद्विधिः। वर्षतीति धावतीति हन्तीति पलायत इति। अन्यत्र शतृशानचौ कदाचिद्भविष्यतः। नन्वोर्विभाषेति (३। २। १२१) वर्तमाने लटः शतृशानचावित्य् (३।२।१२४) अनेन व्यवस्थितविभाषया तु इतिशब्दे न भवतः॥ तथा च गवाक्ष इति अवङ्स्फोटायनस्य (६। १। १२३) वातायने नित्यं भवति। अन्यत्र विभाषा॥ संशितव्रत इति शाच्छोरन्यतरस्यामित्य् (७। ४। ४१) अनेनेत्वं क्रियमाणमत्र नित्यं भवति। अतो ऽन्यत्र विभाषा। संशितव्रतः संशातव्रतः॥ २८॥

स्वरविधौ व्यञ्जनमविद्यमानवत् ॥ २९॥

स्वरे क्रियमाणे यद्व्यवधायि व्यञ्जनं तदविद्यमानवद्भवति।

कथं ज्ञायते। यदयं यतो ऽनाव इत्य् (६। १। २१३) अनाव इति प्रतिषेधं शास्ति।

कथं कृत्वा ज्ञापकम्। नाव्यमित्यत्र यतो ऽनाव इति (६। १। २१३) प्रतिषेधः। यद्येवमर्थं नार्थोनेन। कथम्। अच उदात्तानुदात्तस्वरिता उच्यन्ते। स चात्रादौ न भवति। तस्मादत्राद्यभावादेवोदात्तत्वं न भविष्यति। नार्थः प्रतिषेधेन। एवं सिद्धे सति यत्प्रतिषेधं शास्ति तज्ज्ञापयति स्वरविधौ व्यञ्जनमविद्यमानवद्भवतीति।

29 ग्रह B ‖ धावतीति α : धावति β (i.e. om. इति) (धाव`ति´ P_2) ‖ [पलायते इति β] **30** भविष्यतः β : भवतः α ‖ नन्वोर् : ननो J : ननोर् P_1 β **31** इति वर्तमाने om. β (i.e. °भाषा) ‖ [लटशु β] ‖ [°शानचौ α] ‖ व्यवस्थित[[:]]विभाषया P_1 **32** तु : त J ‖ च om. α ‖ अवाङ् J ‖ स्फोटा° : मोटा° P_1 a.c. **33** वातायनो P_1 a.c. : वातायेन P_2 **34** शाच्छोर् : शाफो J : शाच्छो P_1 ‖ अन्यतरस्याम् : न्यतरस्योम् J : न्यतरंस्याम् P_1 **35** संशातव्रतः : संशात्तः β ‖ २८ om. β **1** सुरविधौ P_2 ‖ अविद्यमान्यत् J **2** क्रियमणे P_1 a.c. ‖ तदाविद्य° J **3** यदयं : यदयय् B ‖ यतो ऽनाव : योटे नाव P_1 a.c. : यंतो नाव B **4** प्रतिशेधं J **5** नाव्यम् : नान्यम् B ‖ यतो ऽनाव : योत नाव J (metathesis) **6** इति अनाव इति प्रतिषेधः β (dittography) ‖ °आनुदत्त° B a.c. **7** चात्रादौ : चन्नादो J ‖ तस्माद् : तस्याद् J ‖ अभावाद् : अभावोद् P_2 a.c. ‖ एवो`दा´त्तत्वं $P_2$ : एवोदात्तंत्व J **8** यत्प्रतिषेधं $P_1$ a.c. ‖ प्रतिषेधं [[?]] शास्ति $P_2$ ‖ शास्ति शास्ति J ‖ ज्ञापएति $P_1$ **9** व्यञ्जन`म्´अविद्यमान`वत्´भवतीति P_2

किमेतस्या ज्ञापनें प्रयोजनम्। गार्ग्यो वात्स्य इत्यत्राकारो नादिस्तस्याप्युदात्तत्वं सिद्धं भवति। तथा च पचति पठतीति उदात्तादनुदात्तस्य स्वरितः (८। ४। ६६) चकारठकारव्यवहितस्यापि स्वरितः सिद्धो भवति॥ २९॥

अङ्गवृत्ते †पुनर्वृत्तादविधिर्निष्ठितस्य ॥ ३०॥

अङ्गवृत्ते ऽङ्गकार्ये कृते †पुनर्वृत्तात्कार्यस्य विधिर्न भवति यो ऽन्यः त्प्राप्नोति।

कथं ज्ञायते। यदयं ज्ञाजनोर्जेत्याह (७। ३। ७९)। एतत्सूत्रं किल वक्तव्यं ज्ञाजनोर्ज इति। का रूपसिद्धिः। जानीते जायते। जभावे कृते पश्चादतो दीर्घो यञीति (७। ३। १०१) दीर्घत्वं भविष्यति। एवं सिद्धे सति यद्दीर्घमादेशं शास्ति तज्ज्ञापयति अङ्गनिमित्ते ऽजादेशे कृते पुनर्दीर्घत्वं न स्यादिति।

किमेतस्या ज्ञापने प्रयोजनम्। क्रियत इत्यत्र रिङादेशे कृते अकृत्सार्वधातुकयोर्दीर्घत्वं (c.f. ७। ४। २५) न भवति। अङ्गवृत्ते †पुनर्वृत्तादविधिर्निष्ठितस्येति॥ ३०॥

10 गौर्ग्य α ‖ वत्स्य P_2 a.c. **11** अत्राकारो नादिस् α : अत्राकारस्यानादिस् β ‖ भवति : भवती P_2 a.c. : भवतीति B ‖ च om. β **12** उदात्तादनुदात्तस्य स्वरितः Wujastyk : उदात्तानुदात्तस्वरितस्य codd. ‖ °व्यवर्हितस्या° J : °व्यवहतस्या° P_2 **13** [स्वरितसु P_2] ‖ २९ J : १९ P_1 : om. β **1** अङ्गवृत्तेः α B : अङ्गवृत्ते[[:]] P_2 (in spite of these readings, α अन्द् B read °वृत्ते in the final statement of the परिभाषा below ‖ अविधिर् : अवर्धिर् J : अव़धिर् P_1 β ‖ निष्टितस्य J β **2** अंगे वृत्तेंगकार्ये J : अंगवृत्ते कार्ये P_2 : अंगवृत्तेः कार्ये B ‖ न om. B **3** यो ऽन्यः α: यो ऽन्यत् β **4** सूत्रं om. α **5** ज्ञाजनोर्जा β (this, of course, confounds the argument) ‖ जानी`ते´ P_2 ‖ जाभावे P_2 (जभावे a.c.!) **6** पश्चाद् om. α : पश्चद् B ‖ Hence अतो : ऽतो α (ऽते P_1 a.c.) ‖ यजीति J **7** दीर्घमादेशं … पुनर् om. B (saut) ‖ पुनर् : पुन J **9** [क्रियते β] ‖ रिङ्° : रिज़ु° α : रिटू° P_2 a.c. **10** °धातुकयो दीर्घ° J ‖ भवति sic codd. : भविष्यति Abhyankar (groundless) ‖ °वृत्ते[[:]] P_2 **11** पुनर् : पुन P_1 P_2 ‖ अविधिर् : अवधिर् codd. (अवधि B) ‖ निष्टित° J B ‖ ३० om. β

सकृद्गतौ विप्रतिषेधे यद्बाधितं बाधितमेव तत् ॥ ३१॥

यत्र द्वौ विधी युगपत्प्राप्नुतः तत्र विप्रतिषेधे परमिति कृत्वा परस्मिन्कृते पुनःप्रसङ्गात्पूर्वो विधिः प्राप्नुवन्न भवति। किं कारणम्। यत्सकृद्बाधितं बाधितमेव तत्। न पुनर्भवति ।

कथं ज्ञायते। यदयं कर्तरि कर्मव्यतिहार इति (१।३।१४) कर्तृग्रहणं करोति।

कथं कृत्वा ज्ञापकम्। अत्र कर्मव्यतिहारे इति वक्तव्यम्। नार्थः कर्तृग्रहणेन। ननु च भावकर्मणोरपि कर्मव्यतिहारे इत्यात्मनेपदं प्रसज्येत। तत्र को दोषः। न खलु कश्चिदिहोत्तरत्र प्रतिषेधः स्यात्। यथा कर्तरि प्रतिषेधो भवति एवं भावकर्मणोरपि प्रतिषेधः प्रसज्येत। व्यतिगम्यन्ते ग्रामाः व्यतिहन्यन्ते दस्यवः। अस्तु। पुनःप्रसङ्गविज्ञानाद्भविष्यति (परि॰ ७६)। नार्थः कर्तृग्रहणेन। एवं सिद्धे सति यत्कर्तृग्रहणं करोति तज्ज्ञापयति सकृद्गतौ विप्रतिषेधे यद्बाधितं बाधितमेव तत्। सकृच्च व्यतिहारलक्षणेनात्मनेपदेन भावलक्षणमात्मनेपदं बाधितं न पुनः स्यात्।

किमेतस्या ज्ञापने प्रयोजनम्। शास् हि ⟨हन् हि⟩ इति तुह्योस्तातङ्ङाशिष्यन्यतरस्यामिति (७। १। ३५) तातङादेशश्च प्राप्तः। शाभावजभावौ च। परत्वात्तातङादेशे कृते पुनःप्रसङ्गाच्छाभावजभावौ न

1 सकृद्गौता J : सकृद्गो P_1 a.c. ‖ चाधितमेव J 2 युग`प´त् B ‖ प्राप्नतः B ‖ परमिति : पाम B 3 परस्मि`न्´ B ‖ `वि´धिः P_2 ‖ प्राप्न्[[आ]]उवन् J 4 सकृ[[त्]]द् P_2 ‖ बाधितमेव तत् β : तद्बाधितमेव α ‖ न पुनर्भवति : पुनर्न भवति J 5 [व्यतिहारें इति β] 7 ॰हारो P_1 a.c. ‖ इति om. β 8 कर्मव्यतिहारे α : व्यतिहारे β ‖ प्रसज्येते J : प्रयुज्येत β 9 दोष[[:]]: P_1 ‖ इहेत्तरत्र P_1 a.c. ‖ [प्रतिषेधस् P_2] 10 व्यतिगम्यते B 11 व्यतिहन्यते B ‖ ॰विज्ञानद् P_1 a.c. : विज्ञा[[?]]नाद् P_2 12 ॰ग्रहणेनैव (*sic*) B 13 ज्ञाप[[इ]]यति P_1 ‖ एव [[त]] तत् P_1 14 व्यतिहारंलक्ष॰ J ‖ भावल्लक्षण॰ J ‖ बाधितं om. P_2 ‖ [पुनस् P_2] 15 शासु J (for विराम?) 16 तुह्यौस् J : तुह्येस् P_2 a.c. ‖ तातङा॰ : तातङ्गा॰ J : तातङ P_1 a.c. : तातजा P_2 a.c., B ‖ तातङा॰ : तातङ्गा J : तातजा P_1 a.c., P_2 a.c., B 17 शभाव॰ codd. (see P.6.4.35, 36. Abhyankar's note, p. 18, no. 2, suggests that P_1 has शाभाव॰; this is not so) ‖ परत्वान् J ‖ तातङा॰ : नतजा॰ J : तातजा॰ P_1 a.c., P_2 a.c., B ‖ छभाव॰ codd. (छा॰ P_1 a.c.)

भवतः। सकृद्गतौ विप्रतिषेधे यद्बाधितं बाधितमेव तदिति न भवतः। शिष्टादित्यादि सिद्धं भवति॥ ३१॥

असिद्धं बहिरङ्गमन्तरङ्गे ॥ ३२॥

बहिरङ्गलक्षणमन्तरङ्गलक्षणे कर्तव्ये ऽसिद्धम् ।

कथं ज्ञायते। यदयं ओमाङोश्चेत्य् (६।१।९५) आह। अत्राङि परतः पररूपवचनमनर्थकम्। अद्य आ ऊढ इत्येवं स्थितस्य अकः सवर्णदीर्घत्वं (c.f. ६। १। १०१) प्राप्नोति पश्चाद्गुणः। पूर्वं तदेकादेशो भविष्यति। तस्मिन्गुणेन सिद्धम्। अद्योढः। एवं सिद्धे सति यदेतदाह तज्ज्ञापयति †धातूपसर्गयोरन्तरङ्गकार्यं भवति। बहिरङ्ग एकादेशः। तस्मिन्कृते ऽपि तस्यासिद्धत्वात्। पर आद्गुणः। स नित्यः। पश्चात्पुनर्वृद्धिः प्राप्नोति †। तस्मादारम्भ एवमर्थम्।

किमेतस्या ज्ञापने प्रयोजनम्। पट्व्या मृद्व्या इति परो यणादेशस्तस्यासिद्धत्वात्पूर्वो यणादेशो ऽन्तरङ्गो भवति॥ ३२॥

18 °षेधे ये यद् B ‖ बाधितं : बाधि J : om. P_1 ‖ बाधितमेव तद् : बाधितमेवत् J : बाधितंमेव तत् (*sic*) P_1 ‖ [तद् : तत् P_1 B] ‖ भवतः α : भवति β (scribe of βफ़ोर्गेत्तिन्ग् थे सुब्जेच्त् ओफ़् थे सेन्तेन्चे) **19** शिष्टद् J : शिष्याद् P_2 (शिष्टाद् a.c.) ‖ ३१ om. β **2** [बहिरङ्गलक्षणस् P_1] ‖ अन्तरं`गल´क्षणे $P_2$ ‖ कतंव्ये $P_2$ ‖ ऽसिद्धं भवति $P_2$ **3** ओमा`ङो´श्चेत्य् P_2 ‖ °आङोश्चेत्य् B ‖ अत्राणि P_1 **4** अं‍ा : अ P_1 a.c. ‖ ऊढ : रूढ P_2 a.c., B ‖ [इति एवं B] **5** प्रोप्नोति P_1 a.c. ‖ पश्चद् β a.c. ‖ गुण`:´ P_1 (गुप्ता (?) a.c.) **6** अद्योढा α B ‖ [अद्योढ एवं P_2] ‖ एतद् om. Abhyankar (P_1 has it, *pace* f.n. 6, p. 18) **7** धातूप° : not a separate rule in the MSS, nor in any other text, although Abhyankar prints it as one (but cf. discussion of paribhāṣā 33) ‖ सर्गयेरोन्त° P_1 a.c. ‖ °अङ्गकार्यं codd. : °अङ्गं कार्यं Abhyankar. ‖ बहिरंगा P_2 a.c. **8** तस्यसिद्ध° J ‖ आङ् गुणः P_1 ‖ पुनर् : पुन J **10** पटव्या J ‖ पट्व्य P_1 **11** याणादेशस् P_1 a.c. ‖ पूर्वो β : पूर्वं α ‖ ° ऽन्तरगो J (अनुस्वार dropped) ‖ ३२ om. β : ३१ राम P_2

समानाश्रयमसिद्धं व्याश्रयं सिद्धं भवति ॥ ३३॥

कथं ज्ञायते ऽस्त्येषा परिभाषा। यदयं हनः सिजिति (१।२।१४) सिचः कित्त्वे कृते सिचमाश्रित्यानुदात्तोपदेश इत्य् (६। ४। ३७) अनेनानुनासिकलोपः। सकारमाश्रित्य ह्रस्वादङ्गादिति (८। २। २७) सकारलोपः। एवमाहतेति सिद्धं भवति। असत्यपि सूत्रे सिचं च्लेः सिजिति (३।१।४४) कृत्वा हन् स् त इति स्थिते सार्वधातुकमपिदिति (१। २। ४) ङित्। तकारस्य ङित्त्वे सति तकारमाश्रित्यानिदितां हल उपधायाः क्ङितीति (६।४।२४) लोपः। ह्रस्वादङ्गादिति (८।२।२७) च सलोपः। तत आहतेति सिद्धं भवति। नार्थो हनः सिजिति (१।२।१४) सूत्रेण। मैवम्। अक्रियमाणे सूत्रे सकारलोपे कृते हकारे यो ऽकारस्तस्य सकारमाश्रित्यार्धधातुके ऽतो लोप इति (६।४।४८) लोपः प्रसज्येत। अथ सूत्रे क्रियमाणे एवमेव कस्मान्न भवति। असिद्धवदत्राभादिति (६। ४। २२) नकारस्यासिद्धत्वान्नकारेण व्यवधीयते। यावता अनिदितां हल इत्य् (६। ४। २४) अप्याभाच्छास्त्रम्। तस्मादुभयोरपि पक्षयोरसिद्धत्वान्नकारलोपस्याकारलोपो न भविष्यति। तस्मान्नार्थः

2 [ज्ञायते अस्त्य् β] ‖ परिभाषा om. J ‖ हनः : हतः J 3 कित्त्वे : क`इ´त्वे $P_1$ : क्कित्वे $P_2$ ‖ कृते : कृत्वे J ‖ आश्रित्या ⟨-२-⟩ नुदात्त° $P_1$ 4 अनेना`नुना´सिक° P_1 (saut) ‖ सकारम् Wujastyk : उकारस् J β : तकारम् P_1 ‖ आश्रित्य`आनुदात्तोपदेशेत्यनेनानुनासिकलोपः उकारमाश्रित्य´ ह्रस्वाद् $P_2$ (correction of a saut) ‖ ह्रस्वाद् J ‖ अङ्गाद् : अज्जाद् J 5 सकारो लोपः $P_1$ ‖ एवंम् J $P_2$ ‖ सूत्रे : सू J ‖ [च्लेस् $P_2$] 6 हन् स् त : ह त J : `ह´न् स त P_2 7 तकरस्य P_1 a.c. : तका`र´स्य B ‖ ङित्त्वे : दिते J ‖ तकारम् β : तम् α ‖ °आनिंदितां J 8 उपधाया J ‖ क्नितीति J ‖ ह्रुस्वाद् J ‖ इति : इते J 9 नार्थौं J ‖ [हनस् P_2] 10 मैवम् : सैवम् J : नैवम् β ‖ सूत्रे om. β ‖ यो कारस् α : यकारस् β ‖ Abhyankar's reading इकार (p. 18, note 11) in P_1 does not exist. 11 सकारम् β : शीकात्यम् J : शीछात्यम् P_1 (छ may be a misreading of Śāradā क; beyond this, the reading is mysterious) ‖ [आश्रित्य आर्ध° P_2] ‖ [ऽतो α : अतो β] ‖ लोप इति om. B (saut) ‖ प्रसज्येते J : प्रसज्यते β 12 क्रियमाने P_1 ‖ एवमेव[[मे]] J : एव`मेव´ $P_1$ : एव $P_2$ ‖ असिद्धवत्रा° J : असिद्धव`द´त्रा° P_1 (pointing to an α reading without द) 13 A reading 'नलोपस्यासिद्धत्वात्' would be preferable (see Discussion under 33.1) but is not supported in the MSS ‖ अनिपितां P_2 a.c. : अनितां B 14 [अपि आ° β] ‖ छास्त्तं J ‖ तस्मादुभ° : तस्मात्त् उभ° P_2 ‖ उभयोरपि α : उभयोः β (i.e. om. अपि) 15 नकारलोप° α : नकारस्य लोप° β ‖ °कारलोपे P_1 a.c. ‖ भविष्यति β : भवति α ‖ नार्थस् P_2 : नार्थ B

सूत्रेण। एवं सिद्धे सति यत्सूत्रमारभते तत्पश्यति समानाश्रयमसिद्धं व्याश्रयं सिद्धं भवति। आरभ्यमाणे हि सूत्रे सकारमाश्रित्य नकारलोपः अकारलोपो ऽपि सकारमेव। तदेतत्समानाश्रयं भवति। अनारभ्यमाणे सूत्रे तकारमाश्रित्य नकारलोपः ⟨अकारलोपः⟩ सकारमेव। तद्व्याश्रयं भवति। सूत्रमारभमाणस्तु पश्यति समानाश्रयमसिद्धं भवति।

किमेतस्या ज्ञापने प्रयोजनम्। पपुषः। द्वितीयाबहुवचने †पपिवसिति स्थिते वसोः संप्रसारणमिति (६। ४। १३१) शसमाश्रित्य संप्रसारणे परपूर्वत्वे चकृते (c.f. ६।१।१०८) †पप् उस् इति स्थिते उसमाश्रित्यातो लोप इति (६। ४। ६४) अजादे†र्ङिति आकारलोपे क्रियमाणे असिद्धवदत्राभादिति (६। ४। २२) संप्रसारणस्यासिद्धत्वादजेव नास्ति कुत आकारलोपः। अस्यां पुनः परिभाषायां सत्यां व्याश्रयत्वादेतत्सिद्धं भवति। अत्र शसमाश्रित्य वसोः संप्रसारणम्। उसमाश्रित्याकारलोपः। तदेतद्व्याश्रयं भवति। व्याश्रयं च सिद्धं भवतीति कृत्वाकारलोपे कृते पपुष इति सिद्धं भवति॥ ३३॥

16 [सूत्रेनैवं B] **17** नकारलो`पः´ $P_2$ **18** ऽपि om. J ‖ सकारम् $\beta$ : सकार $\alpha$ **19** तकारम् : उकारम् $P_2$ ‖ ⟨ ⟩ Wujastyk (cf. Abhyankar) (saut) **21** ब[[-1-]]`हु´वचने P_1 ‖ पपिवं इति J (presumably via पपिवम्) **22** वसो`:´ $P_1$ : [वसोस् $P_2$] ‖ °सारणम् : °मारणम् $P_1$ ‖ शमाश्रित्य B : शममाश्रित्य $P_2$ a.c. **23** उसमामाश्रि° B (dittography) ‖ [आश्रित्य आतो $\beta$] **24** अकारे J ‖ क्रियमाणे $\beta$ : कृते $\alpha$ **25** अत्राभा`दि´ति P_2 **26** [कुतः β] ‖ अकार° J ‖ अस्यां om. B **27** वसोः α : वसु β ‖ आश्रित्याकारलोपः : आश्रित्यालोपः α : [आश्रित्य आकारलोपः P_2] (a.c. अकार°) **28** [भवति इति α] ‖ [कृत्वा. आकार° P_2] ‖ कृते om. B **29** ३३ om. β

येन नाव्यवधानं तेन व्यवहिते ऽपि वचनप्रामाण्यात् ॥ ३४ ॥

येन वर्णेन वा संयोगेन वानन्तरेण †व्यवधानमुच्यमानस्य विधेः प्राप्तिरस्ति † तेन व्यवहिते ऽपि वचनप्रामाण्यादेव विधिर्भवति। तद्यथा शमामष्टानां दीर्घः श्यनीत्य् (७।३।७४) अनेन शाम्यतीत्यत्र दीर्घो न प्राप्नोतीति। किं कारणम्। यो ऽत्र दीर्घभावी सो ऽन्येन हला व्यवहितः। न च शमादीनामष्टानामपि कश्चिदजन्तो ऽस्ति यदर्थं वचनं स्यात्। उच्यते चेदं दीर्घत्वम्। तत्र वचनप्रामाण्यादनन्त्यस्यापि दीर्घो भवति।

कथम्। न ह्यन्तरेण व्यवधानमत्र दीर्घभावी अजस्ति। एवमियं परिभाषा ज्ञापिता विज्ञेया।

किमेतस्या ज्ञापने प्रयोजनम्। अधिजिगांसत इत्यत्राज्झनिगमां सनीति (६। ४। १६) गमेरन्त्यदीर्घत्वे सति मकारेणैव व्यवधायकेन धातोर्दीर्घत्वं भवति नाभ्यासस्य धातुव्यवाये॥ ३४॥

4 तेन [[अन्तरे]] व्यवहिते B 5 [दीर्घशु P$_2$] ‖ श्यनीत्[[इ]] यनेन P$_1$ (श्यनीति नेन a.c.) : [श्यनीति अनेन β] 6 प्राप्नोति P$_1$ (i.e. om. इति) ‖ यो ऽत्र : यत्रो J, P$_1$ a.c. 7 शसादीनाम् B ‖ अष्टानम् P$_2$ a.c. 8 चेदं : वेदं P$_1$ 9 दीर्घभावे J 11 अधिजिघांसते β ‖ [अत्र अज् P$_2$] ‖ °आजहनि° J : °आज्`ह´नि° P$_1$ ‖ °हनि° is read in the MSS, as against °हन° in the normal सूत्रपाठ texts. On this reading, cf. Mbh. III. 184:24–25 and Kāś. II. 735:2 with f.n. 1. 12 स[[न्]]नीति P$_2$ ‖ मकारेणै° Wujastyk : सकारेणै° $\alpha$ : पकारेणै° $\beta$ ‖ पकारेणै`व´ P$_2$ 13 धातोर् : धातो J B ‖ नभ्यास्° B a.c. ‖ ३४ om. β

निमित्ताभावे नैमित्तिकस्याप्यभावो भवति ॥ ३५ ॥

तद्यथा छत्त्रनिमित्ता छाया छत्त्रापाये न भवति। शास्त्रे ऽपि ज्ञापकं यदयं सुनोत्यादिषु स्तौतीति ब्रवीति।

कथं कृत्वा ज्ञापकम्। अत्र ष्टु इत्ययं शब्द उपदेशे पठितः। तस्य धात्वादेरिति (६। १। ६४) षकारस्य सकारः कृतः। षत्वनिमित्तं च ष्टुत्वम्। तस्याभावे ष्टुत्वस्याभावो भवति। ततः स्तौतीति भवति। एवं निमित्ताभाव इति सिद्धम्।

तस्या ज्ञापने प्रयोजनं पपुषः तस्थुष इत्यत्र वल्निमित्तक इट् वलभावे तस्याप्यभावः॥ ३५ ॥

संनियोगशिष्टानामेकतरापाये उभयोरप्यभावः ॥ ३६ ॥

कथं ज्ञायते। लोकतः। तद्यथा देवदत्तयज्ञदत्ताभ्यामिदं कर्तव्यम्। ⟨देवदत्तापाये⟩ यज्ञदत्तो ऽपि न करोति। शास्त्रे चापि ज्ञापकम्। यदयं बिल्वकादिभ्यश्छस्य लुगित्य् (६।४।१५३) आह।

कथं कृत्वा ज्ञापकम्। यदयमस्मिन्सूत्रे छग्रहणं करोति। अत्र हि बिल्वकादिभ्यो लुगित्युच्यमाने प्रत्ययस्य लुक्श्लुलुप इत्य् (१।१।६१) अनया परिभाषया बिल्वकादिभ्य उत्तरतस्तद्धिते परतो नैवान्यप्रत्ययो ऽस्ति विना छकारम्। तस्मादत्रान्तरेण च्छग्रहणं छस्यैव लुग्

1 नैमित्ताभावे J ‖ अप्यभावो : अपि भावो P_1 a.c. 2 यथाच्छत्र॰ J ‖ ॰निमित्ताच्छाया P_2 ‖ च्छा `या छत्रा´पाये $P_1$ 3 सुनोत्य् : सनोत्य् J B ‖ [स्तौति.इति B] 4 शब्दः B ‖ उपदेशो ऽपि B ‖ [पठितस् $P_2$] : पठित B 5 सकारः : मकारः J 6 तस्य भावे J ‖ भ`व´ति P_1 7 निमित्ताभाव : *sic* P_1 ; then altered to निमित्तभाव; then back again 8 तस्थूष P_1 B ‖ वल्निनिमित्तक J ‖ इट् व वलभावे J 9 अपि भावः J ‖ ३५ om. J β 1 अभावः β : अपायः α (c.f. the statement of the परिभाषा at the end of the second paragraph below) 2 [लोकतस् α] 3 ⟨ ⟩ Wujastyk (cf. Mbh. II. 216:1 etc) ‖ ऽपि om. β 4 ॰भ्य छम्स्य J : ॰भ्यचु छस्य P_1 B 5 छग्रहणं : फग्रहणं J 6 बिल्वकादिभ्यो : बिल्वकाल् P_2 : बिल्वका B ‖ प्रत्ययस्य : प्रत्यय J : प्रत्ययस्या P_1 ‖ लुक् : लुङ् P_1 ‖ लुप : लप J 7 [उत्तरतः β] ‖ [परतः β] 8 ऽस्ति विना छकारम् α : ऽस्त्यन्यत्र छकारात् β ‖ छकारम् : फकारम् J ‖ च्छग्रहणं : फग्रहणं J : छग्रहणं P_1 ‖ छस्यैव : फंम्यैव J

भवति। नार्थश्छग्रहणेन। तद्यथा बिल्वानामदूरभवं नगरमित्यस्मिन्विग्रहे नडादीनां कुक्चेत्य् (४।२।९१) अनेन बिल्वशब्दाच्छप्रत्ययो भवति कुक् चागमः। तत्र भव इति (४। ३। ५३) बिल्वकीया। तस्यां बिल्वकीयायां भव इत्यस्मिन्नर्थे ऽण्। तत्राकृतव्यूहाः पाणिनीयाः (परि॰ ५९)। बिल्वक् छ इति स्थिते अन्तरेण छवचनं छस्य लुकि कृते ऽणो ऽपि लुक् प्रसज्यते। अयमपि हि तदा बिल्वकशब्दादुत्तरो भवति। ननु च तद्धित इत्युच्यते न चाणस्तद्धितः परो ऽस्ति। नैष दोषः। यदा बैल्वकस्येदमित्यस्मिन्विग्रहे वृद्धलक्षणश्छः क्रियते तदाण्तद्धितपरो भवति। तस्मादण्निवृत्त्यर्थं छग्रहणं क्रियते। नैतदस्ति। अत्र ह्यणो लुकि क्रियमाणे असिद्धवदत्राभादिति (६।४।२२) छलुगसिद्धो भवति तेनाणो ऽलुग् भवति। तस्मान्नार्थश्छग्रहणेन। एवं सिद्धे यच्छग्रहणं करोति तत्पश्यति प्रत्ययस्य निवृत्तिः क्रियमाणा सागमकस्यापि भवति। तेन कथमिह छस्यैव स्यात्। कुतो मा भूदिति। अयं कुक् छसंनियोगशिष्ट इति। एवं सिद्धे किं कृतं भवति। संनियोगशिष्टानामन्यतरापाये द्वयोरप्यभाव इत्येषा परिभाषा कर्तव्या भवति।

अपर आह छकारोच्चारणं क्रियते छकारस्यैव लुग्यथा स्यात्ककारस्य मा भूदिति। तच्च न। प्रत्ययस्य लुगुच्यमाणः कः प्रसङ्गो यदप्रत्ययस्य। कुतः पूर्वभक्तस्य स्यादिति। पश्यति त्वाचार्यः अस्त्येषा परिभाषा यतश्छकारोच्चारणं करोति।

9 नार्थचु छ॰ α : नार्थः छ॰ β 10 नडादीना B 11 बिल्वकीयाः α (॰कीया`:´ $P_1$) 12 अस्मिन् `ऽ´र्थे `ऽ´ण् B 14 [ऽणो : अणो J $\beta$] 15 चाणस् : चानस् J : चाण $\beta$ (चा`ऽ´ण B) 16 बैल्ववक॰ J : बैलुक॰ B ‖ विगृहे J ‖ बृद्ध sic codd. ‖ लक्षणश् : लक्षणच् α P_2 : लक्षणाचु B ‖ तदाण् : तदाण J β 17 अण्निवृत्त्य्॰ : अनिवृत्त्य्॰ α β : अ`ण´निवृत्त्य् P_2 ‖ छग्रहणे J 18 तेनानो J ‖ ऽलुग् Wujastyk : लुग् Abhyankar 19 भव[[-1-]]ति P_1 ‖ नार्थश् : नार्थं J : नार्थचु β 20 ॰च्छग्रहणं … सागम॰ om. J (saut from छ to the क in सागमक॰ which is read as छ (c.f. P_1)) ‖ सागमकस्यापि : मागमछुस्यापि P_1 21 [इति : इत्य् B] ‖ सन्नियोगमिष्ट J 22 कृतं : कृते J 24 ॰कारोच्चारणं : ॰कारोश्चारणं P_1 B : ॰कारोच्चरणं P_2 ‖ ककारस्य : कारस्य J (haplography) 25 भू`दि´ति P_2 ‖ तच्च : तश्च P_2 a.c., B a.c. ‖ लुग् : लग् J 26 पश्यति om. P_2 27 यतश् : ययत J (dittography and छ for च्छ): यतचु P_1 P_2 ‖ ॰ओच्चारणं : ओश्चारणं J β

किमेतस्या ज्ञापने प्रयोजनम्। पञ्चेन्द्राण्यो देवता अस्येति (c.f. ४। २। २४) पञ्चेन्द्रः दशेन्द्र इति स्त्रीप्रत्ययस्य लुकि कृते ऽत्रानुको ऽपि निवृत्तिः सिद्धा भवति॥ ३६॥

येन नाप्राप्ते यो विधिरारभ्यते स तस्यैव बाधको भवति ॥ ३७॥

येन नाप्राप्ते इति द्विप्रतिषेधः प्रकृतं गमयति। नाप्राप्ते प्राप्त एव। येन लक्षणेन प्राप्ते सति अन्यो विधिरारभ्यते स तस्य बाधको भवति। येन तु क्वचित्प्राप्ते क्वचिदप्राप्ते न तस्य बाधकः।

कथं ज्ञायते ऽस्त्येषा परिभाषेति। यदयं सनीवन्तर्धेत्य् (७। २। ४९) अत्र स्वृशब्दं पठति विभाषार्थम्।

कथं कृत्वा ज्ञापकम्। अस्याप्यार्धधातुकेषु प्रत्ययेषु आर्धधातुकस्येत्य् (७।२।३५). अनेनेट् प्राप्तः। स एकाच उपदेशे ऽनुदात्तादिति (७।२। १०) प्रतिषिद्धः। तद्बाधनार्थं पुनः स्वरतिसूतीत्य् (७।२।४४) उच्यते। सन्यप्यार्धधातुकस्येट्प्राप्तः सनिग्रहगुहोश्च श्र्युकः कितीति (७।२।१२, ११) प्रतिषिद्धः। तस्याप्यनेन बाधनं स्यात्। सनीवन्तर्धादौ स्वृग्रहणे क्रियमाणे पश्यति त्वाचार्यः येन नाप्राप्ते तस्य बाधकं भवति।

29 पञ्चेन्द्रण्यो P_1 a.c. ‖ [देवतास्येति α] 30 लुकि : लकि P_1 ‖ कृते ऽत्रा° : कृते तत्रा° P_1 : [कृते अत्रा° β] 31 [निवृत्तिस् P_2] ‖ ३६ : ३९ J : om. β 1 नाप्रप्ते B a.c. ‖ यो : ये J, P_1 a.c. ‖ तस्यैव sic codd. Abhyankar omits एव 3 द्विप्रति° sic codd. In amending to द्विः प्रति° Abhyankar probably had in mind P.5.4.18. However this would go better with प्रतिषिद्धः than प्रतिषेधः. Abhyankar's choice suggests the construing of द्विः with गमयति ‖ गमयति : गम इति J ‖ [प्राप्ते एव P_2] 4 बाध[[ओ]]को P_1 (a.c. बाधोके): बधका P_2 a.c. 5 क्वचित् P_1 a.c. ‖ क्वचि प्राप्ते α 6 [ऽस्त्येषा α : अस्त्येषा β] ‖ परिभाषा α (i.e. om. इति) ‖ सनीवर्धेत्य् α : सनी om. β ; then वन्त्वर्धेति P_2 : वंतर्ध्`इ´तिं B 7 अत्र om. $\beta$ 8 अर्ध° $P_2$ a.c. ‖ अर्ध° B, $P_2$ a.c. 9 अनेनेजा प्राप्तः J : अनेने`ट्´ प्राप्तः P_1 ‖ एकाच [[-1-]] उप° P_1 10 त[[त्]] बाधना° P_2 ‖ [पुनस् P_2] ‖ सूति`त्यु´च्यते P_2 11 सन्यप्य् sic codd. Abhyankar's reading (and P_2 a.c.) सत्यप्य् is wrong. ‖ °कस्येट् : °कस्येजा J ‖ प्रप्तः P_1 a.c. ‖ श्र्यूकः J ‖ कितीति : कती B (i.e. om. इति) 12 सनीव[[र्]]त्यर्धादौ P_2 13 क्रियमाणे : ऽक्रियमाणे P_2

कथम्। न ह्यप्राप्ते क्वचिदपि स्वरतेरेकाज्लक्षणप्रतिषेधे ऽयं विभाषाविधिरारभ्यते अन्येष्वार्धधातुकीयेषु प्राप्ते च। एवमेकाज्लक्षणे सन्यप्राप्ते ग्रहगुहोश्चेति सनि प्राप्ते ऽन्यत्राप्राप्ते स्वरतिसूतित्य् (७। २। ४४) अनेन विभाषारभ्यते। स येन प्राप्ते ⟨ऽप्राप्ते⟩ न च तं बाधते तस्मात्स्वृग्रहणं क्रियते। पुनरेवं प्राप्ताप्राप्तयोरप्यारम्भः। आर्धधातुकस्येतीट् (c.f. ७। २। ३५) प्राप्तः। एकाच इति (c.f. ७। २। १०) प्रतिषिद्धः। अविभाषापक्षे ऽपि सनि ग्रहगुहोश्चेति (७। २। १२) उगन्तानामिति (७। २। ११) प्रतिषिद्धः। तद्बाधनार्थं पुनः स्वृग्रहणं क्रियते। सैषा स्वृग्रहणाज्ज्ञापिता भवति।

किमेतस्या ज्ञापने प्रयोजनम्। अदीधयुरिति पदकारस्य प्रत्याख्यानपक्षे उदाहरणमुपपन्नं भवति। कथम्। अयं जुसि गुणः (c.f. ७। ३। ८३) प्रतिषेधविषये आरभ्यमाणः येन प्राप्त एव प्रतिषेध आरभ्यते तं बाधते। येन प्राप्ते नाप्राप्ते च तं बाधते। क्ङितीत्य् (१। १। ४) एव प्रतिषिद्धः जुसि प्राप्तः। न हि कश्चिज्जुसस्ति यत्रायं प्रतिषेधो न स्यात्। दीधीवेवीटामिति (१। १। ६) पुनरनेन दीधीवेव्योरेवोत्तरस्मिञ्जुसि प्रतिषेधः प्राप्तः। अन्यस्य धातोर्जुस्यनेन प्राप्तः यो ऽसौ प्राप्ते चाप्राप्ते च। एवमयं जुसि गुणः येनास्य सर्वत्र प्रतिषेधः प्राप्तस्तं बाधते यः

14 ह्यप्राप्ते : हि प्राप्ते J ‖ स्वरतेर् α : स्वरिते β ‖ एकाजलक्षण॰ J **15** ॰षेधेयं [[-2-]] विभाषा P_1 ‖ विभाषां B ‖ विधिंर् B ‖ आर्धधातुकेयेषु P_1 a.c. ‖ प्राप्ते sic codd. Abhyankar's प्राप्तेषु is wrong. ‖ एकाज्॰ : एकाङ्॰ P_1 : एकां॰ J **16** सनि : सन्नि P_1 ‖ ऽन्यत्राप्राप्ते om. J (saut) **17** स येन sic codd. : स च येन Abhyankar ‖ ⟨ ⟩ Wujastyk (dropped by haplology) **19** अर्ध॰ P_1 : आर्धं॰ J ‖ ॰कस्येतीज़ा J : ॰कस्य P_2 (i.e. om. इतीट्): ॰कस्येट् B (i.e. om. इति) ‖ एकाच β : एकादेश α (mental association. See West 1973, p. 21) **20** प्रतिषिद्धा B ‖ सन्नि J **21** ॰अन्ताना[[˙]]म् P_2 **22** सैषा : मैषा J (on this *sandhi* cf. P.6.1:134) **23** किमेतस्या ज्ञापने प्रयोजनम् β : एतस्या ज्ञापने किं प्रयोजनं P_1 : एतंस्या पने किं प्रयोजनं J ‖ आदीधयुर् B **24** जुसि α : जुसिति β **25** आरभ्यमणः P_1 a.c. ‖ येन प्राप्त एव β : येन प्राप्तेरेव α **26** \`तं वाधते´ B ‖ येन न प्राप्ते B ‖ च β : न च α (partial saut?) ‖ तं न बाधते P_1 ‖ क्ङितीत्य J ‖ [॰ईति एव B] **27** जुस् : जस् J ‖ प्रतिषेधे P_1 a.c. **28** दीधी॰ : देधी॰ α (attraction to ॰वेवी॰): दिधी॰ Abhyankar (misprint) ‖ पुनरेनन J : पुनरेनेन P_1 (a.c. पुनरेणन) ‖ देधी॰ α ‖ ॰वेव्योर् : ॰वीव्योर् P_1 ‖ एवोत्तर॰ : अव्येत्तोर॰ J ‖ ॰अस्मिञ् : [॰अस्मिं J] : ॰अस्मिन् β **29** धातोर् : [धातोः β] (धातेः P_2 a.c.) ‖ यो ऽसौ : यः सो P_2 (येसो a.c.): यो सो B ‖ चाप्राप्ते : चप्राप्ते P_1 a.c. **30** प्राप्तस् β : [प्राप्तः α] ‖ यः : यत् B : य[[त्]]\`:´ P_2

क्वचित्प्राप्तः क्वचिदप्राप्तः न तं बाधते। क्ङितीत्य् (१।१।५) एवं बाधते दीधीवेवीटामिति (१।१।६) न बाधते। तस्मादन्यस्तस्यैव गुणो भवति न जुसि गुणः॥ ३७॥

लुग्विकरणालुग्विकरणयोरलुग्विकरणस्यैव ग्रहणम् ॥ ३८॥

लुग्विकरणस्यालुग्विकरणस्य च ग्रहणे ऽलुग्विकरणस्यैव ग्रहणं भवति।

कथं ज्ञायते। यदयं स्वरतिसूतीत्य् (७। २। ४४) अत्र सूतिसूयत्योर्ग्रहणं करोति। तन्निर्देशस्य प्रयोजनं सुवतिनिवृत्त्यर्थम्। नैतदस्ति। सूतिरिति ङानुबन्धस्यैव सूयतेरिष्यते। तेन सुवतेर्न भविष्यति। एवं सिद्धे सति यत्तन्निर्देशं करोति तज्ज्ञापयति भवतीयं परिभाषेति। षूङित्यस्य सूयतेरेवालुग्विकरणस्य {न} स्यात्। तस्मात्सूतिग्रहणं क्रियते। लुग्विकरणस्यापि यथा स्यात्।

किमेतस्या ज्ञापने प्रयोजनम्। गातिस्थाघुपेत्य् (२। ४। ७७) अत्र पाग्रहणे ऽलुग्विकरणस्यैव भवति। अपात्। लुग्विकरणस्य न स्यात्। अपासीत्। तत्रालुग्विकरणस्यैव स्यात्। †षूङित्युच्यमाने लुग्विकरणस्य न स्यात्। तस्मात्सूतिसूयतीति तिब्निर्देशः क्रियते ऽलुग्विकरणार्थम्। आचार्यप्रवृत्तिर्ज्ञापयति लुग्विकरणस्यैव ग्रहणमिति। यदयं गातिस्थाघुपेत्य् (२।४।७७) अत्र तिब्निर्देशं करोति तज्ज्ञापयति अस्त्येषा परिभाषेति †॥ ३८॥

31 क्ङितीत्य् J 32 देधी α 33 ३७ om. β 1 अलुग्विकरण[[-5-]]स्य ग्रहणम् P_1 (i.e. om. एव) 2 च om. α ‖ ऽलुग्° α : अलुग्° β : लुग् Abhyankar ‖ °स्यैवं J 4 °सूयत्योर् : °सूयत्यो J : सूयत्येर् B a.c. ‖ सुवति° : स्वति° J 5 सूतिरिति : सूतीति α : सूतिऱ्`इ´ति P_2 ‖ ङानुबन्ध° : ज़ानुबंध° J, P_1 a.c., P_2 a.c. 6 परिभाषेति β : परिभाषा α (i.e. om. इति) 7 षूङ् : पूङ् J ‖ एवालुक्ग्विकरण° J (scribe tampering with सन्धि) 9 °घुपेत्य् α : °घुपा इत्य् β 10 पाग्रहणे : प्राग्रहणे B ‖ ऽलुग्° α : अलुग् β 11 अपासीत् : पा अपासीत् B ‖ तत्रालुग्° β : तदत्रालुग्° α ‖ षूङ् : पूङ् P_2 12 तिब्निर्देशः : द्विन्निर्देशः J : द्विर्निदेशः P_1 : तिव्निदेशः (*sic*) P_2 13 ऽलुग् α : अलुग् β ‖ प्रवृत्तिर् : प्रवृत्ति J ‖ °विकर[[-1-]]स्यैव B ‖ °करणस्येव J 14 तिब्निर्देशं sic codd. : तिनिर्देशं Abhyankar (after correction; see p. 495) 15 ३८ om. β

उभयत आश्रये नान्तादिवद्भवति ॥ ३९ ॥

यत्रोभयं प्राप्नोति अन्तश्चादिश्च तत्रान्तादिवद्भावो न भवति। तद्यथा लोके उभयोस्तुल्यबलयोरेकः प्रेष्यो भवति स तयोः पर्यायेण कर्म करोति। यदा च तौ युगपदप्युपगच्छतः न च परस्परविरोधिनौ भवतः तदा क्रमेण करोति। यदा तु विरोधिनौ भवतः तदैकस्यापि न करोति कर्म। एवमिहापि यदि तावदन्तवदादिवन्न भवति।

किमेतस्या ज्ञापने प्रयोजनम्। परापूर्वस्यायतेः पलायत इति। तत्र यदा धातोरादिवन्न भवति तदोपसर्गस्यान्तवद्भवति। यदात्रोपसर्गस्यान्तवदेव ⟨न⟩ भवति तदा धातोरादिवत्। तत एकादेशे कृते उपसर्गस्यायतौ परत इत्येवं शक्यते वक्तुम्॥ ३९ ॥

1 नान्तादि॰ : नत्तादि॰ B (नान्ता and नत्ता are easily confused in Śāradā) 2 [यत्रोभयं P_1 P_2 : यत्र उभयं J B] ‖ चादिश् α : [च आदिश् P_2] ‖ आदिश् च om. B (saut from β reading च) 3 उभयस् J ‖ तुल्यबलयोर् α : तुल्यवर्णयोर् P_2 : त्वन्यबलयोर् B (वर्ण and वल are easily confused in Śāradā) 4 यदा च तौ α : यदा एतौ P_2 : यदैतौ B ‖ Abhyankar's reading of अपरस्पर (p. 22, f.n. 3) in P_2 is unfounded 5 विरोधिनः J ‖ भवतः α : om. β ‖ तदैकस्यापि न β : तदा नैकस्यापि α ‖ कर्म करोति P_1 6 यदि β : यदिह α ‖ तावदन्तवद् β : तावन्नान्तवन् α ‖ आदिवन्न β : नादिवद् α 7 ॰आयतेः : ॰आयते J 8 [पलायते इति β] ‖ तत्र यदा β : यदात्र α 9 यदात्रोप॰ α : यदत्रोप॰ P_2 : यदत्र उप॰ B ‖ ॰आन्तवद् : ॰आंतद् J : ॰आनवद् P_2 a.c. : ॰आंत`व´द् B ‖ एव : ए`व´ P_1 ‖ ⟨ ⟩ Wujastyk ‖ धातोर् : धौतर् J 10 परत [[:]] P_1 ‖ इत्येवं β : इत्येव α (इतेव P_1 a.c.) ‖ वक्तु[[-1-]]म् P_1 ‖ ३९ om. β

एकानुबन्धकृतमनित्यम् ॥ ४०॥

इह शास्त्रे एकानुबन्धकृतं ञित्त्वं णित्त्वं वा तदनित्यं भवति।

कथं ज्ञायते। यदयं मन्त्रे श्वेतवहोक्थशसिति (३। २। ७१) ण्विनित्याह। तत्र णित्करणं वृद्ध्यर्थम्। नित्करणं स्वरार्थं तत्त्वेतदेकानुबन्धेन शक्यते लब्धुम्। अत्र ञिरिति वक्तव्यम्। स्वरश्च वृद्धिश्च भविष्यति। एवं सिद्धे यदयं द्व्यनुबन्धं करोति तज्ज्ञापयति अस्तीयं परिभाषा एकानुबन्धकृतमनित्यमिति।

किमेतस्या ज्ञापने प्रयोजनम्। ज्योतिरधिकृत्य कृते ग्रन्थे ज्योतिषम्। सोमेन्द्रावस्य चरोर्देवता सोमेन्द्रश्चरुः। णकृतस्यानित्यत्वाद्वृद्धिर्न भवति॥ ४०॥

एकानुबन्धकग्रहणे न द्व्यनुबन्धकस्य ॥ ४१॥

एकानुबन्धकग्रहणे द्व्यनुबन्धकस्य ग्रहणं न भवति।

कथं ज्ञायते। यदयं वामदेव्याड्ड्यड्ड्यावित्य् (४।२।९) अत्र यस्येति लोपेन (c.f. ६। ४। १४८) सिद्धे यड्डित्करणमकारलोपार्थं करोति तज्ज्ञापयति एकानुबन्धकग्रहणे न द्व्यनुबन्धकस्य ग्रहणं भवति।

किमेतस्या ज्ञापने प्रयोजनम्। ययतोश्चातदर्थे इति (६। २। १५६) यत एव ग्रहणं भवति। अतस्तेन ⟨अ⟩वामदेव्यमिति॥ ४१॥

2 ञित्त्वं : जित्वं J : ञित्वं P_1 P_2 ‖ णित्त्वं : णित्वं α P_2 ‖ वा तद् codd. : तावद् Abhyankar (metathesis) ‖ आनित्यं J 3 [[य]]दयं P_1 4 °वहोक्त्थशमो ण्विन् (i.e. om. इति) J : °वहोक्त्यशसो ण्विन् (om. इति) P_1 : °वहो`क्थ´शस इति ण्विन् $P_2$ ‖ °शस इति B ‖ °अ`र्थं´ J 5 एकानुबन्धेन α : ओकानुबन्धेन P_2 a.c. : ओकारानुबन्धेन B ‖ अत्र : तत्र B ‖ ञिर् : जिर् J ‖ भविष्यति β : भवति α 6 द्व्यनुबन्धं : द्ध्यनुबन्धं P_2 ‖ आस्तीयं J 7 इति om. B 8 ज्योतिषां α 9 अस्य : असि J ‖ चरोर् : चोरेर् P_1 a.c. : चरोः B ‖ °आनित्यत्वाद् β : °आसिद्धत्वाद् α ‖ [°त्वाद् : °त्वात् β] 10 ४० om. β 1 एकानुबन्धक° α : एकानुबन्ध° β 3 वामदेवात्त्यड्त्याव् J : वामदेवा`ड्ड्य´ड्ड्याव् $P_2$ : वामदेवाद्ध्यड्ड्यौ B 4 सिद्धे यड् : सिद्ध येड् J (misplaced vowel) : सिद्धे यत् $P_1$ : सिद्ध योर्ड् $P_2$ : सिद्ध योड् B ‖ डित् : ड्`इ´त् P_2 6 ययतेश् B 7 यत α : एत β ‖ वामदेव्यम् codd. : ⟨ ⟩ Wujastyk. ‖ ४१ om. β

निरनुबन्धग्रहणे न सानुबन्धकस्य ॥ ४२॥

निरनुबन्धकग्रहणे सानुबन्धकस्य ग्रहणं न भवति।

कथं ज्ञायते। यदयं वामदेव्याड्ड्यड्ड्याविति (४। २। ९) यकारं ङितं करोति टिलोपार्थम्। अत्र हि यस्येति लोपेन (c.f. ६। ४। १४८) सिद्धम्। एवं तर्हि ज्ञापयति यकारस्याननुबन्धकस्य ग्रहणे न सानुबन्धकस्य तस्य ग्रहणं भवति।

किमेतस्या ज्ञापने प्रयोजनम्। ययतोश्चातदर्थे इति (६। २। १५६) यकारग्रहणे ⟨अ⟩वामदेव्यमित्यत्रैष स्वरो न भवति॥ ४२॥

यं विधिं प्रत्युपदेशो ऽनर्थकः स विधिर्बाध्यते ॥ ४३॥

यथा एकारविधिं प्रत्येकारोच्चारणमनर्थकम्। अकारविधिं प्रत्यकारोच्चारणमनर्थकम्। ओकारविधिं प्रत्योकारोच्चारणमनर्थकं भवति। एतेनैकारविधिः अकारविधिः ओकारविधिश्च पठ्यते। वक्ष्यते अतो भिस एसिति (c.f. ७।१।९)। इन्द्रवरुणसूत्रे (४।१।४९) अनुग्वक्तव्यः। ङसेश्चादेशः अद्वक्तव्यः (c.f. ७। १। १२)। आत ओ णल इति (c.f. ७।१।३४) वक्तव्यः। पश्चाद्वृद्धिसवर्णदीर्घत्वे सिद्धे वृक्षैः इन्द्राणी वृक्षात्पपावित्यत्र पररूपं प्राप्नोति। पररूपं प्रत्येते विधयो ऽनर्थका भवन्ति तेन पररूपं बाध्यते॥ ४३॥

2 निरनुबन्धग्रहणे P_2 ‖ सानुबन्धस्य J : सानुबन्ध`क´स्य $P_1$ ‖ ग्रहणं om. J 3 ज्ञायते यद् : ज्ञा यद् J (saut) ‖ वामदेवाड्त्यड्त्याव् J : वामदेवाड्ड्य[[आ]]अड्ड्याव् $P_2$ 4 ङितं : ङिते J ‖ टिलोपोर्थं J 5 `य´कारस्या° P_1 ‖ यकारस्या`न´नुबन्धक° $P_2$ 6 न … भवति $\alpha$ : सानुबन्धकस्येति एतस्य ग्रहणं न भवति $\beta$ 7 क्`द्ध´म् P_1 ‖ ययतेश् B ‖ [चातदर्थे इति β] 8 °ग्रहने P_1 a.c. ‖ ⟨ ⟩ Wujastyk ‖ अत्रैष : ऐत्रषु J : ऐत्रष P_1 ‖ स्वरे P_1 a.c. ‖ न : नो P_1 a.c. ‖ ४२ om. J β 1 β reads : यं विधिं प्रत्यनर्थकं भवति 2 तथा β ‖ °विधि B ‖ [प्रति β] ‖ °ओच्चारण° B P_1, P_2 a.c. 3 अका`रविधिं प्रत्य´रोच्चाण° $P_1$ (*sic.* saut from का to का) ‖ °ओच्चारण° B $P_1$, $P_2$ a.c. ‖ [प्रति B] ‖ प्रत्यकारो° J : `प्रत्यो´कारो° P_1 ‖ ओच्चारण° B P_1, P_2 a.c. ‖ भवति om. α 4 [एतेन एकार° β] ‖ अकारविधिः : अविधिः β ‖ पठ्यते J ‖ वक्ष्यति α (given as परस्मैपद in the धातुपाठ) 5 एस् : ऐस् P_1 (attraction to सूत्र) : एमु J ‖ आनुग्° P_2 (but अनुग्° a.c.; attraction to सूत्र) 6 ङसेश् : ङ्मेश् α ‖ ओ : औ β (attraction to सूत्र) ‖ [[?]]णल P_2 8 पापाव् P_2 : [पपौ α] ‖ [इति α P_2] 9 ४३ om. β

यस्य विधेर्निमित्तं नासौ बाध्यते ॥ ४४॥

तद्यथा लोके यमर्थं प्रति यद्वचनं निमित्तत्वेन कल्प्यते तस्यार्थस्य तद्वचनं प्रापकं भवति। यथा अभुक्तवति भुङ्क्ष्वेति। एवमिहापि यस्य विधेरकारैकारोच्चारणानि निमित्तं भवन्ति तानि तस्य विधेः प्रापकानि भवन्ति। अकारोच्चारणं सवर्णदीर्घत्वस्यैकारोच्चारणं च वृद्धिविधेः। कथं नाकृतेषु अकारैकारेषु एषां विधीनां प्राप्तिरस्ति वृक्षैरित्येवमादिषु। अत्र एकारः {उकारः} अकारो वानयोर्विध्योर्निमित्तमेव तेन तौ विधी भवतः। पररूपं च न भवति। अतो भिस ऐस् (७।१।९) आत औ णल इत्य् (७।१।३४) एवमादिषु वचनव्यतिरेकाद्विधिव्यतिरेको लभ्यते। अतिजरसैः अतिजरसात् ददरिद्राविति। यस्य विधेर्निमित्तं नासौ बाध्यते। अतो भिस ऐस् (७।१।९) टाङसिङसामिनात्स्याः (७।१।१२) आत औ णलः (७।१।३४)॥४४॥

कार्यकालं संज्ञापरिभाषम् ॥ ४५॥

को ऽस्यार्थः। कार्यं कालो यस्य तत्कार्यकालम्। कालो नाम पाठः। न्यास इत्यर्थान्तरम्। संज्ञाश्च परिभाषाश्च यत्रैव पठ्यन्ते स एव तासां कालः। यत्र यत्र कार्यं तत्र तत्र तासां कार्यः। तद्यथा सिचि वृद्धिः परस्मैपदेषु (७।२।१) उपस्थितमिदं भवति वृद्धिरादैजिति (१।१।१)। सैषा शास्त्राधिकृता सती अस्मात्सूत्रात्परा भवति । १।२) एषा

1 \`ना´सौ P_2 3 α transposes यथा to after भुङ्क्ष्वेति ‖ भुङ्क्ष्वेति : भुंत्क्ष्वेति J 4 [विधेः β] ‖ अकारैकार॰ : अकारोकार् P_1 a.c. ‖ ॰ओश्चारणानि β ‖ निमित्ते P_2 a.c. ‖ विधेः : विधी P_1 a.c. 5 अकारोश्चा॰ B, P_2 a.c. ‖ [॰दीर्घत्वस्य एकारो॰ β] ‖ ॰ओश्चारणं B, P_2 a.c. ‖ च β : तु α 6 [अकार एकारेषु β] ‖ विधीनां [[एषां विधीनां]] प्राप्तिर् P_2 7 [आदिष्वत्रैकारः B] ‖ अत्र … वा॰ β : अत्रैकारऐ⟨*sic*⟩ कारो ऽकारो वा J : अत्रैकारो [[-1-]] कारो वा P_1 ‖ [वा अनयोर् α β] (अनयो J B) ‖ विध्यो नि॰ B ‖ विधी : विधे J 8 ऐ[[-1-]]स् P_1 ‖ आत : अत P_2 11 ॰ङसाम् : ङसम् B a.c. 12 णलः : णतनः J : \`ण´[[-1-]]लः $P_2$ ‖ ४४ om. J $\beta$ 2 पाटः J 3 इ\`त्य´नर्थान्तरम् P_1 : इर्थान्तरम् P_2 ‖ अर्थान्तरम् : अनर्थोंतरं J 4 यत्र यत्र … तासां कार्यः om. P_2 ‖ तासां कार्यः : तासो कार्यः J ‖ वृद्धिः : वृद्धि P_2 : om. B

परा भवति। तथा राज्ञः क चेत्य् (४।२।१४०) अत्रालो ऽन्त्यस्येत्य् (१। १। ५२) एषा परा भवति। तथा अस्थिदधिसक्थ्यक्ष्णामनङुदात्त इति (७। १। ७५) अस्तेर्भूरिति (२। ४। ५२) ङिच्च (१। १। ५३) अनेकाल्शित्सर्वस्येति (१।१।५५) परा भवति। एवमेतत्कार्यकालं संज्ञापरिभाषं यत्र कार्यं तत्रोपस्थितं द्रष्टव्यम्।

कथं पुनर्ज्ञायते अस्त्येषा परिभाषेति। यदयं न मु न इत्य् (८।२। ३) आह।

कथं कृत्वा ज्ञापकम्। अत्र ह्यदःशब्दादुत्तरस्य टेत्येतस्य आङो नास्त्रियामिति (७। ३। १२०) क्रियमाणे नादेशे घिलक्षणो मुभावः सिद्धः। तत्र न मु न इत्य् (८। २। ३) अनेन मुभावस्य नाभावे क्रियमाणे पूर्वत्रासिद्धमिति (८। २। १) प्राप्ते सिद्धत्वमुच्यते। स तु नाभावः क्रियमाणो ऽप्यस्मिन्सूत्रे न प्राप्नोति। कथम्। यद्यप्ययं मुभावः नाभावसूत्रं प्रति सिद्धः घिसंज्ञां तु प्रत्यसिद्धः। तत्र मुभाव एव नास्ति। कुतो घिसंज्ञा। घिसंज्ञाभावाच्च कुतो नाभावः। तस्मान्न मु न इत्य् (८। २। ३) अत्र घिसंज्ञायां चेति वक्तव्यम्। न चोच्यते। तत्पश्यत्याचार्यः कार्यकालं संज्ञापरिभाषम्। यत्र कार्यं तत्रोपस्थितं द्रष्टव्यम्। अदसो ऽसेर्दादु दो म इत्य् (८।२।८०) उपस्थितमिदं भवति। शेषो घ्यसखीति (१। ४। ७) च मुत्वात्परा भवति। तस्मात्सिद्धायां सत्यां घिसंज्ञायां मुत्वं

7 राज्ञः : राज्ञा J ‖ क : कश् β : स P_1 a.c. ‖ [अत्र अलो P_2] 8 ऽन्त्ये`स्ये´षा $P_1$ (i.e. om. इति) ‖ एष ⟨-2-⟩ परा भवति J ‖ तथा om. J ‖ °सक्थ्य्° : °सक्त्य° J $\beta$ ‖ °सक्थ्`यक्ष्णा´म् P_1 ‖ अनङ् : अङ् J ‖ उ[[नु]]दात्त P_1 9 अस्तेर् : अस्ते J ‖ ङिच्च P_2 a.c., B 10 अनेकाल् : अकलि J : अ`ने´काल् $P_1$ ‖ शित् : शत् J 11 °परिभाषं : °पनिभाषं J ‖ तत्रेप° $P_2$ a.c. 12 [ने इत्य् $\alpha$] 14 ह्यदः° : हृदस्° J : [ह्यदस्° $P_1$] : [हि अदश् $P_2$] : [हिन्न`अदः B] ‖ टेत्य् α : [टा इत्य् β] 15 क्रियमाणे देशे P_2 (क्रियमानादेशे a.c.) ‖ घिलक्षणे β ‖ सुभावः B 16 मुभावो सिद्धः P_2 ‖ सिद्धा J ‖ मु : मू J ‖ ने इत्य् β] 17 क्रियम्[[आ]]आणे P_2 18 ना प्राप्नोति B ‖ न प्राप्नोति … नाभावसूत्रं om. J (saut from प्र to प्र) ‖ मुभावः : सुभावः B, P_2 a.c. 19 घिसंज्ञं J ‖ घिसंज्ञां तु : घिसंज्ञा तं B ‖ सुभाव P_2 20 घिसंज्ञा om. P_2 ‖ °भावाच्च P_2 a.c., B a.c. ‖ न इत्य् : नेत्य् B (secondary सन्धि) 21 अत्रा ⟨*sic*⟩ घिसंज्ञा संज्ञापरिभाषम् J (i.e. om. °यां चेति … कार्यकालं) ‖ वक्तव्यम् : वक्तम् P_2 23 असखीति : [असखि इति P_2] : असखि B (i.e. om. इति) 24 मत्वात् J ‖ परा : परि P_2 a.c. ‖ भवति। तस्मात् : भवति घिसंज्ञा तस्मात् J ‖ °संज्ञायामुत्वं β (i.e. om. अनुस्वार)

सिद्धं भवति। मुभावे त्वसिद्धे ततो ऽस्य मुभावस्य सिद्धत्वमनेन क्रियते। सैषा सूत्रारम्भाज्ज्ञापिता परिभाषा भवति।

किमेतस्या ज्ञापने प्रयोजनम्। अदसो ऽसेर्दा दु दो म इत्य् (८।२।८०) अत्र चोच्यते। ईत्वोत्वयोः प्रगृह्यसंज्ञोच्यते। एत ईद्बहुवचन इत्य् (८।२।८१) अस्मात्परा भविष्यति। कार्यकालं संज्ञापरिभाषमिति यदुक्तं तदुपपन्नं भवति॥ ४५॥

उक्तार्थानामप्रयोगः ॥ ४६ᵃ॥

सकृदुक्तस्यार्थस्य पुनः प्रयोगो न भवति। कुतः। लोके दृष्टत्वात्। तद्यथा लोके पुरुष इत्युक्ते †पुनस्तस्यैव द्वितीयश्च करणीयं कार्यमिति च† पुनः प्रयोगो न भवति। ⟨-220-⟩ यद्येवं न सामिवचन इत्य् (५।४।५) अयं प्रतिषेधो नोपपद्यते। कथम्। अत्र हि अनत्यन्तगतौ क्तादिति (५।४।४) कनि प्राप्ते ⟨***⟩ । †अवश्यं चैतदनुवर्त्यं लोप इत्येवमुक्तं तस्मान्नार्थश्चकारेण। पश्यति त्वाचार्यः अनन्त्यस्यापि वकारस्योदुच्यमानो ऽन्त्यसमानदेशस्यैव भवति। नानन्त्यमात्रस्य। यश्च ज्वरत्वरयोर्वकारः नासावन्त्यसमानदेशः। अकारेण व्यवहितस्य न भवति। स चकारेण बलात्क्रियते। तस्मादेष चकारो ज्ञापनार्थो भवति† ॥

25 मुभावे Wujastyk : नाभावे codd. ‖ मुभावस्य Wujastyk : नाभावस्य codd. ‖ सिद्धत्वम् : सिद्धम् J ‖ अनेन : उनेन P_2 a.c. 27 सेर् : मे J 28 ईत्वात्वयो J : ईत्वेत्वयोः P_2 a.c. ‖ [॰संज्ञा उच्यते β] ‖ ईद्॰ : यंद् J 29 भविष्यति : भवति J ‖ उक्तं om. J 30 ४५ om. β 1 परि॰ ४६, a and b, is omitted entirely by P_2 2 कुतो J 3 ईत्युक्ते J 4 न om. J ‖ ⟨ ⟩ om. α (after भवति B leaves about $4\frac{1}{2}$ lines, *c.*220 syllables, empty, resuming with यद्येवं etc.) 6 प्राप्ते : ′ B ‖ अवश्यं : [वश्यं B] ‖ उक्तं J : अर्थं B 8 वकारस्योद् : वकारस्योड् J : [यकारस्य ऊद् B] ‖ उच्यमानन्त्यो॰ J : [उच्यमानः अंत्य B] ‖ ॰समानदेश॰ : ॰समानेदश॰ J ‖ न चानन्त्य॰ Abhyankar : नान्त्य॰ B ‖ ज्वर॰ : ज्रुर॰ B ‖ ॰त्वरयोव॰ J 9 भवति J : प्राप्नोति B 10 एष : एषश् B ‖ ४६a om. codd.

अनन्त्यविकारे ऽन्त्यसदेशस्येति ॥ ४६[b]॥

किमेतस्या ज्ञापने प्रयोजनम्। अनस्तक्ष्ण इत्यल्लोपो (c.f. ६। ४। १३४) भवति। अनन्त्यस्याकारस्य लोप इत्युच्यमाने ऽन्त्यसमानदेशस्यैव भवति नान्त्यस्येति॥ ४६॥

संज्ञापूर्वको विधिरनित्यः ॥ ४७॥

इह यः संज्ञापूर्वको विधिरारभ्यते स किलानित्यो भवति।

कथं ज्ञायते। यदयमोर्गुण इत्य् (६। ४। १४६) आह। अत्र ह्योर्गुणे क्रियमाणे ओकारो भवति। तत्र लघ्वर्थमोरोदिति वक्तव्यम्। उवर्णस्य ओद्भवति। एवं सिद्धे सति यदयमाचार्यो गुणग्रहणं करोति तत्पश्यति संज्ञापूर्वको विधिरनित्यः। तत इहाप्यनित्यो गुणो यथा स्यात्। संज्ञापूर्वको विधिरनित्य इति।

किमेतस्या ज्ञापने प्रयोजनम्। स्वयम्भुवो ऽपत्यं स्वायम्भुव इति गुणो न भवति॥ ४७॥

11 °देशस्येति : °देशस्य Abhyankar (i.e. om. इति) 12 अनस् : अतस् J ‖ इत्य् : [इति B] 13 °लोपो भवति : °लोपो न भवति B ‖ लोप : लेप P_1 a.c. ‖ इत्यच्यमाने J ‖ °माने ऽन्त्य° : °मानः अंत्य° B 14 ४६ om. J β 1 °पूवको विधिर् J P_2 : °पूर्वकविधिर् B P_1 2 यः : यत् β ‖ °आनित्यो भवति : °आतित्यो भवति J : °आनित्ये भोवति P_1 3 ओर् : ओ J 4 ह्य् α : [हि β] ‖ ओर् : ओ J ‖ ओकारो : आकारे P_1 a.c. ‖ भवति : भोवति P_1 a.c. ‖ लघ्व° : घ्व° J ‖ °अर्थम् : °अर्थोम् P_1 a.c. ‖ ओरोद् : आरोद् J ‖ इति : इत J : इ B 5 आचार्यो om. α 6 तत्पश्यति : पश्यति तद् B : तपश्यति P_1 7 संज्ञा … इति om. α 8 [स्वयम्भुवः अपत्यं P_2] : स्वयंभुव अपत्यं B 9 ४७ om. β

नञिवयुक्तमन्यसदृशाधिकरणं तथा ह्यर्थः ॥ ४८॥

नञा युक्तमिवेन युक्तं यद्धि किंचिद्दृश्यते तदन्यस्मिंस्तत्सदृशे कार्यं ज्ञापयति। तद्यथा अब्राह्मणमानयेत्युक्ते ब्राह्मणसदृशस्तुल्योदरपाणिपादनयन एवानीयते नाश्वो गर्दभो वेत्येवं तावल्लोके। शास्त्रे ऽपि यदपि चायं सिपि धातो रुर्वेत्य् (८। २। ७४) अत्र धातुग्रहणं करोति।

कथं कृत्वा ज्ञापकम्। अत्र हि धातुग्रहणमनर्थकम्। सिपि परतो धातोरुच्यते। सिप्धातोरेव भवति न प्रातिपदिकात्। तत्र नार्थो धातुग्रहणेन। एवं सिद्धे सति यद्धातुग्रहणं करोति तज्ज्ञापयति पूर्वसूत्रे धातोश्चाधातोर्भवति। तेन धातुसकारस्य सिद्धं भवति। अचकाङ्गवान् अन्वशाङ्गवान्। कथं धातोरेव स्यादेवमर्थं धातुग्रहणम्। किं पुनः कारणं पूर्वसूत्रे धातोरेव न प्राप्नोति। तिप्यनस्तेरित्य् (८। २। ७३) उच्यते। तिप्यनस्तेः सिपि धातो रुर्वेति (८। २। ७३, ७४)। तत्र नञिवयुक्तमन्यसदृशाधिकरणे तथा ह्यर्थ इति अनस्तावस्तिसदृशे तत्कार्यं भवति। कश्चेदानीमस्तिसदृशः। अस्ति वै धातुः। यो ऽन्यो धातुः सो ऽसावनस्तिः अस्तिसदृशो भवति। तेनानया परिभाषया पूर्वसूत्रे धातोरेव स्यात्। अधातोर्न स्यात्। तेनैव धातुग्रहणेन धातोश्चाधातोश्च क्रियते। तदेतद्धातुग्रहणं ज्ञापकं भवति। अञ्चेश्छन्दस्यसर्वनामस्थानमिति (६। १। १७०)। सर्वनामस्थाने तत्सदृशे वासर्वनामस्थानकार्यं भवति॥ ४८॥

1 अन्यसदृशा॰ α : अन्यत्रसदृशा β **2** तदन्यस्मिंस् : तस्मिंस् B **3** यथा : याथ P_2 ‖ यथा [[-1-]] अब्राह्मण॰ P_1 **4** ब्रह्मणसदृशस् B ‖ ॰पाणिनखपादनयन B ‖ नाश्वो गर्दभो वेत्येवं α : नाश्वो न गर्दभ इति एवं β **5** यदपि चायं α : यदयं β ‖ धातो रुर्वेत्य् : धातो भर्वेत्य् J (it is just possible to confuse भ and रु in Śāradā) **6** धातुर्ग्रहणं B **7** After सिपि J repeats धातोभर्वत्यत्र ... ॰अनर्थकम् (dittography through a saut from सिपि in line 000 to सिपि in line 000 **8** ´भ`व´ति $P_1$ **11** `अन्वशाङ्गवान्´ P_1 (m. sec) ‖ स्याद् β : [स्यात् α] ‖ किं om. α ‖ करणं α **12** तिपुनस्तेर् J (possibly Śāradāism, via प्व) ‖ अनस्तर् P_2 a.c. : अनस्तैर् B **13** तिप्य् : [[-1-]]प्य् P_2 a.c. **14** नञिव॰ : नह्रिव॰ J ‖ अन्यसदृशा॰ α : अन्यत्रसदृशा॰ β **15** यो ऽन्यो : यो ऽन्य J : यो ऽन्ये P_1 a.c. ‖ [धातुस् P_2] **16** परिभाषयां J **17** तेनैव : तनै`व´ P_1 : तेनेव P_2 (Abhyankar's तेनेह is wrong) ‖ धातोश्चाधातोश्च : धातोश्च J (haplography) **18** अञ्चेचु J β ‖ ॰छन्दस्य् : छन्⟨?⟩ दस्य P_1 (unclear letter) **19** ॰स्थानं कार्यं J ‖ ४८ om. β

उदित्स्ववर्गमेव गृह्णाति न सवर्णमात्रम् ॥ ४९ ॥

उदिद्वर्णो गृह्यमाणः स्ववर्गमेव गृह्णाति न सवर्णमात्रम्।

कथं ज्ञायते। यदयं न विभक्तौ तुस्मा इत्य् (१। ३। ४) अत्र तुग्रहणादेव सिद्धे सकारस्य ग्रहणं करोति।

किमेतस्या ज्ञापने प्रयोजनम्। चोः कुरित्य् (८। २। ३०) अत्र चुग्रहणेन शकारस्याग्रहणात्कुत्वं न भवति तेन विडिति सिद्धं भवति॥ ४९ ॥

सर्वविधिभ्य इड्विधिर्बलवान् ॥ ५० ॥

सर्वेभ्यो विधानेभ्यो इड्विधिर्बलवान्भवति।

कथं ज्ञायते। यदयं सनि ग्रहगुहोश्चेति (७। २। १२) चकारेण श्र्युको ऽनुकर्षणं करोति।

कथं कृत्वा ज्ञापकम्। अत्र हि चकारो ऽनर्थकः। कस्माल्लूञः सनीण् न। तत्र तावदत्रेण् न भवति इको झलिति (१। २। ९) कित्त्वं तावत्प्रतीक्षते। तत्र कित्त्वे कृते श्र्युकः कितीति (७। २। ११) इट्प्रतिषेधो भविष्यति। नार्थश्चकारेण। पश्यति त्वाचार्यः कित्त्वादपि पूर्वमिडागमः। इटि कृते इको झलिति (१। २। ९) कित्त्वं नास्ति। झलिति वचनात्। तस्माच्चकार इट्प्रतिषेधार्थ इगन्तानाम्।

किमेतस्या ज्ञापने प्रयोजनम्। श्वयित्वेत्यत्र संप्रसारणात्पूर्वमिट् सिद्धो भवति। इटि कृते न क्त्वा सेडिति (१। २। १८) कित्त्वप्रतिषेधः। असति कित्त्वे संप्रसारणं न भवति॥ ५० ॥

2 [गृह्यमानस् P_2] ‖ एव : एवमेव J (dittography) 6 चुग्रहनेन J ‖ ४९ om. β 1 °विधिभ्यो P_2 ‖ बलवा J : बलावान P_1 a.c. 2 विधानेभ्यो β : विधिभ्यो α 3 °गुहश् P_2 a.c. 4 श्र्युको ऽनुकर्षणं : च्र्युको ऽनुकषणं B : श्र्`य्´उको`नुक´र्षणं P_1 (m. sec.) (a.c. : श्रुकेर्षणं) 5 अत्रो हि J ‖ ऽनार्थकः β ‖ लूञः : लूज्ञः J : [लूञस् P_2] ‖ सनीण् : सनीङ् J : [सनि इण् P_2] : संति इण् B 6 अत्रेङ् न J : अत्रेण् न P_1 ‖ झल् : ऊल् J : झाल् P_1 a.c., P_2 a.c. ‖ इति : इत्रि J ‖ प्रतीक्ष्यते P_1 7 कृ`ते´ $P_2$ ‖ च्र्युकः B ‖ [किति इति B] ‖ [कितीतीट्प्रति° $\alpha$] 8 आचार्याः $P_1$ a.c. ‖ पूर्वस् $P_2$ 9 इको झल् : इको ऊल् J : इको झाल् $P_1$ a.c. ‖ कित्त्व B ‖ झल् : ऊल् J : झाल् $P_1$ a.c. ‖ इति : इत J ‖ तस्माश्चकार J, $P_1$ a.c., $P_2$ a.c. ‖ चका[[का]]र $P_1$ 10 [°आर्थः $\beta$] 11 कि`मे´तस्या P_1 12 सेड् : सीड् P_2 ‖ कित्त्व° : किंत्व B (त्त read as न्त ?) 13 ५० om. β

सर्वविधिभ्यो लोपविधिर्बलवान् ॥ ५१॥

इह शास्त्रे सर्वविधिभ्यो लोपविधिर्बलवान्भवति।

कथं ज्ञायते। यदयं प्रत्ययलोपे प्रत्ययलक्षणमित्य् (१।१।६२) आह।

कथं कृत्वा ज्ञापकम्। एतत्सूत्रं नारब्धव्यम्। कथम्। प्रत्ययाश्रयाणि कार्याणि भविष्यन्ति। सर्वाणि कृत्वा पश्चात्प्रत्ययलोपं करिष्यामि। पश्यति त्वाचार्यः लोप एव तावद्भवति। तस्मिन्कृते तदाश्रयाणि न प्राप्नुवन्ति। तस्मात्प्रत्ययलोपे प्रत्ययलक्षणमिति (१।१।६२)।

किमेतस्या ज्ञापने प्रयोजनम्। ते सन्तीत्यत्रादेशात्पूर्वमस्तेरल्लोप इति। तस्मिन्कृते ऽनजादित्वादयादेशो न भवति॥ ५१॥

व्याख्यानतो विशेषप्रतिपत्तिर्न हि संदेहादलक्षणम् ॥ ५२॥

इह शास्त्रे यत्र संदेहस्तुल्यायां संहितायां तत्र व्याख्यानतो विशेषो ऽवगन्तव्यः।

कथं पुनर्ज्ञायते इयमस्ति परिभाषेति। यदयं प्रत्याहारग्रहणे ऽणिति णकारमासजति।

कथं कृत्वा ज्ञापकम्। अत्र हि किलान्यो वर्ण आसक्तव्यः। सन्ति हि बहवो वर्णाः। द्विरनुबध्यमाने चास्मिणणकारे ऽण्ग्रहणेषु संदेहो भवति। किं तु खलु पूर्वेणाहोस्वित्परेणेति। पश्यति त्वाचार्यः अस्त्यत्राण्ग्रहणेषु

3 कथं ज्ञायते β : कथं कृत्वा ज्ञायते α (habitual phrase) ‖ प्रत्ययोलोपे P_1 a.c. 5 भविष्यति J ‖ सेर्वाणि P_1 a.c. ‖ `क´रिष्यामि B 6 पश्यत्याचार्यः α (i.e. om. तु) ‖ लोप : लपो J ‖ एव तावद् : एव वद् J : एतावद् β 7 प्रत्ययोलोपे J : प्रात्ययलोपे P_1 a.c. 8 अत्रादेशात् sic codd. (Abhyankar's reading अत्रायादेशात् and f.n. 4, p. 26, are wrong) ‖ अल्लोप sic codd. : अलोप Abhyankar 9 कृते तेनजादि B (dittography) ‖ ॰आदेश न P_1 (the junction falls across the break between two folios) ‖ ५१ om. β 2 व्या`ख्या`नतो P_2 (saut) 4 [पुनः B] ‖ ज्ञायते [[-2-]]मस्ति P_1 ‖ ऽणिति : ण्णिति β 6 आसक्तव्यः sic codd. (Abhyankar's reading आसङ्क्तव्यः and f.n. 6, p. 26, are wrong) 7 ऽण्ग्रहणेषु : ऽज्ग्रहणेषु J : `ण्ग्र´हणेषु $P_1$ : ज्ग्रहणेषु $P_2$ 8 [पूर्वेण आहो॰ $\beta$] ‖ अत्राण्ग्रहणेषु : अत्राज्ग्रहणेषु J : अत्रा`ण्ग्र´हणेषु P_1 : अत्राज्ग्रहणेष्व P_2

संदेहः। व्याख्यानतो विशेषं प्रतिपादयिष्यामः। अतो ज्ञायते ऽस्तीयं परिभाषेति। व्याख्यानतो विशेषप्रतिपत्तिर्न हि संदेहादलक्षणमिति।

किमेतस्या ज्ञापने प्रयोजनम्। सनीवन्तर्धेत्य् (७। २। ४९) अत्र संदेहः। किं नु खलु इवन्तानामाहोस्विदीवन्तानामिति। अनया स दोषो न भवति। सनि इवन्तानामिति व्याख्यायते॥ ५२ ॥

चानुकृष्टमुत्तरत्र नानुवर्तते ॥ ५३॥

कथं ज्ञायते। यदयमव्यये ऽयथाभिप्रेताख्याने कृञः क्त्वाणमुलावित्य् (३। ४। ५९) अत्र णमुल्ग्रहणं करोति।

कथं कृत्वा ज्ञापकम्। णमुलधिकृतो ऽनुवर्तते। तत्र क्त्वा तावद्वक्तव्यम्। क्त्वा चेति चकारेण णमुलो ऽधिकृतस्यानुकृष्टिर्भविष्यति। नार्थो णमुल्ग्रहणेन। पश्यति त्वाचार्यः यद्यनुकर्षणमिह णमुलः क्रियते तिर्यच्यपवर्ग इत्य् (३। ४। ६०) एवमादिषु सूत्रयोगेष्वनुवृत्तिर्न स्यात्। तस्मात्क्त्वाग्रहणं क्रियते। अयुगपदुभयोरुत्तरत्रानुवृत्तिर्यथा स्यात् इति। चानुकृष्टमुत्तरत्र नानुवर्तते।

किमेतस्या ज्ञापने प्रयोजनम्। वदः सुपि क्यप् चेति (३। १। १०६) यतो भुवो भाव इत्य् (३। १। १०७) अत्रानुवृत्तिर्न भवति॥ ५३॥

9 अतो : अत्रो B 10 °भाषेति : °भाषीति P_1 a.c. ‖ हि om. B ‖ इति om. β 11 °वन्तर्धेत्य् : °बंतर्धेति P_2 : वंतुर्धेति B ‖ अत्र om. β 12 अनया ... सनि om. J 13 भवति : वति P_1 ‖ ५२ om. β 2 कृञः : कृञ्ञः J 3 °णमुलाव् ... अत्र Abhyankar : om. codd. (saut) 4 णमुल् : मुणल् J (metathesis) 5 °आनुकृष्टिर् : °आनुष्टितिर् α ‖ भव्`इ´ष्यति $P_2$  6 णमुल्लग्रहणेन J  ‖ णमुलः : `ण´मुलव् P_2 7 तिर्यश्यप P_1 ‖ एवम् : एवस् P_1 a.c. ‖ स्यत् P_1 a.c. 8 क्त्वा° : का° J : क्क° P_1 a.c. ‖ अयुग[[-1-]]पद् P_2 ‖ इति om. β 9 उत्तरत्र नानु° : उत्तरत्रा नानु° P_2 a.c. 10 [वदस् P_2] ‖ सुपि : स्वपि J 11 [भावे इत्य् β] ‖ इत्य[[त्रा]]त्रानु° P_2 ‖ न om. P_1 ‖ न भवति : भवति न J ‖ ५३ om. β

प्रकृतिग्रहणे यङ्लुगन्तस्यापि ग्रहणम् ॥ ५४ ॥

प्रकृतिग्रहणं यत्र भवति यङ्लुको ऽपि तत्र ग्रहणं भवति।

कथं ज्ञायते। यदयमूदुपधाया गोह इत्य् (६। ४। ७९) उपधाग्रहणं करोति।

कथं कृत्वा ज्ञापकम्। तत्रोपधाग्रहणेनोकारो गृहीतो भवति। तस्मादुकारग्रहणमेवमर्थं कर्तव्यम्। ऊ उतो गोह इति। पश्यति त्वाचार्यः एवमुच्यमाने यो ऽसौ गोहेरभ्यासगत उकारः जोगुहीतीति तस्याप्यूत्वं प्रसज्येत। तस्मादुपधाग्रहणम्। यदि च प्रकृतेर्ग्रहणे यङ्लुको ऽपि ग्रहणं भवति तत एतदुपपन्नं भवति।

किमेतस्या ज्ञापने प्रयोजनम्। जघ्नुरिति यङ्लुको ग्रहणादुपधालोपः सिद्धो भवति॥ ५४ ॥

एकस्मिन्नपि व्यपदेशिवद्भावो ऽप्रातिपदिकग्रहणेन ॥ ५५ ॥

य एकस्मिन्नपि व्यपदेशः सो ऽप्रातिपदिकेन भवति।

कथं ज्ञायते। यदयं पूर्वादिनिः सपूर्वादित्य् (५। २। ८६, ८७) आह।

कथं कृत्वा ज्ञापकम्। अत्र हि सपूर्वादित्येव वक्तव्यम्। कथं पूर्वात्केवलाद्भविष्यति। व्यपदेशिवद्भावेन चैकस्मिन्नपि सह पूर्वेण यः स पूर्वादिनिर्भविष्यति। एवं सिद्धे यत्केवलार्थं पृथक् पूर्वादिनिरित्याह तेन ज्ञायते व्यपदेशिवद्भावो ऽप्रातिपदिकेन।

2 यङ्लको J : यङ्लुके P_1 ‖ तत्र om. J ‖ ग्रहणं भवति α : भवति ग्रहणं β **3** अयं . [[र्थ]] `ऊ´दुपधाया P_2 **5** तत्रोपधा° : तत्रपोधा° J (metathesis) : अत्रोपधा° β ‖ ग्रहणेनोकारो α : ग्रहणेन ऊकारो P_2 : ग्रहणेन ऊकारे B **6** उकार° : उपकार° P_2 ‖ पश्यति त्वोचार्यः P_1 **7** जोगुहीतीति α : जोगुहीति β (i.e. om. इति) **8** तत्तस्माद् J ‖ प्रकृते J ‖ यङ्लोके ऽपि P_1 a.c. **9** भवति ⟨-19-⟩ P_2 **10** [ग्रहणात् P_2] ‖ [°लोपस् P_2] **11** ५४ om. β **1** एकस्मिनपि B ‖ व्यपदेशिवद्° β : व्यपदेशवद्° α **2** य om. J ‖ एकस्मिनपि B ‖ [व्यपदेशस् P_2] : व्यपदेशवद्भावः α **4** आह [[-1-]] कथं P_1 **6** व्यपदेशवद्° α P_2 ‖ चैक° : [च एक° α P_2] ‖ °कस्मिनपि B **7** भविष्यति β : भवति α **8** °भावो : °भावे P_1 a.c.

किमेतस्या ज्ञापने प्रयोजनम्। सूत्रान्ताट्ठग्विहितः (४। २। ६०)। साङ्ग्रहसूत्रिकः। केवलान्न भविष्यति सूत्रमधीते सौत्रः॥ ५५॥

तदेकदेशभूतस्तद्ग्रहणेन गृह्यते ॥ ५६॥

इह यद्यस्यैकदेशभूतं तत्तस्य ग्रहणेन गृह्यते। तद्यथा देवदत्ता गङ्गा यमुनेति। देवदत्तास्थो गर्भो देवदत्ताग्रहणेन गृह्यते। तथानेका नद्यो गङ्गां यमुनां चानुप्रविष्टा गङ्गायमुनाग्रहणेन गृह्यन्ते। एवं तावल्लोके। शास्त्रेऽपि ज्ञापकम्। यदयं नेदमदसोरकोरिति (७। १। ११) प्रतिषेधं शास्ति। इदमदसोः कार्यमुच्यमानं कः प्रसङ्गः यत्सककारयोः स्यात्। नार्थः प्रतिषेधेन। पश्यति त्वाचार्यः तदेकदेशभूतं तद्ग्रहणेन गृह्यते इति। ततः प्रतिषेधं शास्ति।

किमेतस्या ज्ञापने प्रयोजनम्। उच्चकैर्नीचकैरिति सककारयोरव्ययसंज्ञा सिद्धा भवति॥ ५६॥

9 सूत्रान्ताट् : सूत्रांपट् J : सूत्रान्तट् P_1 a.c., P_2 a.c. ‖ ठग् : ग् J 10 °सूत्रिकाः P_1 a.c. ‖ अधीत J : अधीतो P_1 a.c. ‖ सौत्रोः P_1 a.c. ‖ ५५ om. β
2 °ऐक`दे´शभुतं B ‖ `ग्र´हणेन P_1 ‖ देवदात्ता गङ्गा° B 3 देव`द´त्तास्थो $P_1$ ‖ °स्थो : °स्थे $P_1$ a.c. ‖ तथा अनेका $P_1$ ‖ नद्यो गंगा J 4 °प्रविष्ट J ‖ एवं तावल् : एत [[ओ]] त्तावल् $P_1$ 5 नदेमदसरोकारिति J 6 अदसोः : अदसो J : अदसः B ‖ °कारयो`:´ P_1 : [°कारयोस् β] 7 [पश्यत्य् α] ‖ त्वाचार्यः β : आचार्यः α (i.e. om. त्व्) ‖ तदेक° : तादेक° P_1 a.c. ‖ तदेकदेशभुतं β : तदेकभुतं α 8 तत प्रति B 9 [उच्चकैः α] : उच्चकैर् B ‖ °कारयेरोव्ययसंज्ञा P_1 a.c. 10 ५६ om. β

अर्थवशाद्विभक्तिविपरिणामो भवति ॥ ५७॥

अर्थमभिसमीक्ष्य पञ्चमीनिर्दिष्टमपि षष्ठीनिर्दिष्टं भवति अर्थवशात्। तद्यथा उच्चैर्गृहाणि देवदत्तस्यामन्त्रयस्वैनम्। देवदत्तस्य गावोऽश्वाः सुवर्णं चाढ्यो वैधवेयो देवदत्त इति। शास्त्रेऽपि यदयमाह आङो नास्त्रियामिति (७।३।१२०)।

कथं कृत्वा ज्ञापकम्। अत्र घेरुत्तरस्याङो नाभाव इष्यते। अत्र घेरिति षष्ठीवृत्तं सदर्थात्पञ्चमीनिर्दिष्टं भवति। ज्ञापकं च सुप्प्रतिना मात्रार्थ इति (२। १। ९) यस्मान्निपातयति। अत्र सह सुपेति (२। १। ४) तृतीयानिर्दिष्टं सुब्ग्रहणं अनुवर्तते । तेनैवानिर्दिश्यमानेऽपि तृतीयासंप्रत्ययो भविष्यति। न च प्रतेरुत्तरस्या विभक्तेः श्रवणमस्ति। लुकात्र भवितव्यम्। अव्ययादाप्सुपिति (२। ४। ८२)। तदेतज्ज्ञापकं क्रियते। पश्यति तत्र तृतीयानिर्दिष्टमपि सदर्थादन्यविभक्त्यन्तं स्यादिति।

किमेतस्या ज्ञापने प्रयोजनम्। आने मुगित्य् (७। २। ८२) अत्र अत इति पञ्चमीनिर्दिष्टं सत् षष्ठीनिर्देशं भवति। यद्येवमस्येति शास्त्रे ग्रहणानि कर्तव्यानि भवन्ति।

एकवच्चास्यान्यतरस्याम् (१। २। ६९) वश्चास्यान्यतरस्याम् (६। १। ३९) अस्या एव नित्यत्वज्ञापनार्थं क्रियते॥ ५७॥

1 विभक्तिवचनपरिणामो B ‖ °विपरि° : °परि° α 2 अभिसमीक्ष P_1 a.c. 3 उच्चैर् B ‖ °दत्तस्ये आमन्त्र° P_1 : [°दत्तस्य आमन्त्र° B] ‖ स्ववर्णं J 4 [च आढ्यो α P_2] ‖ वेधवेयो B ‖ देवदत्त : दत्तेदत्त α 6 उत्तरम्याङो J ‖ [नाभावः B] ‖ अत्र om. β 7 [सद् α : सत् β] ‖ सुप् : सं J 8 [°आर्थे इति β] ‖ सुपेति : मुपेति J 9 सुब्° : सुब्रु° J 10 प्रतेर् : प्रत्ययेर् J ‖ विभक्ते J : [विभक्तेश् β] 11 लकात्र J ‖ भव्`इ´तव्यं J 12 सद् α : [सत् β] ‖ °भक्तूंतं स्याद् J 13 मुग् : सुग् J 15 भवन्ति : Abhyankar reads न भवन्ति against the MSS and the sense 16 चास्यान्य° : चाद्यान्य° J : चास्यन्य° P_1 : चान्य° β ‖ वश्चा° : वच्चा° J 17 एव नित्यत्व° codd. : एवानित्यत्व° Abhyankar. ‖ ५७ om. P_1 β

पर्जन्यवल्लक्षणप्रवृत्तिः ॥ ५८ ॥

इह शास्त्रे पर्जन्यवल्लक्षणं दृष्टम्। तद्यथा पर्जन्यो यावदूनं पूर्णं चाभिवर्षति †नापूर्णम् ⟨एव⟩ अभिवर्षति†। एवं लक्षणमपि भवति। दीर्घस्य दीर्घत्वं भवति। चिचीषति बुभूषति।

कथं ज्ञायते। यदयं प्रवाहणस्य ढ इति (७। ३। २८) वृद्धस्यापि वाहनशब्दस्य पुनर्वृद्धिप्रतिषेधं शास्ति। पश्यति त्वाचार्यः यत्रापि वृद्धिरस्ति तत्रापि वृद्धिर्भवति। पर्जन्यवल्लक्षणप्रवृत्तेः।

किमेतस्या ज्ञापने प्रयोजनम्। खट्वाढकमित्यत्र दीर्घस्याप्यकः सवर्णे दीर्घत्वं भविष्यति॥ ५८॥

अकृतव्यूहाः पाणिनीयाः ॥ ५९ ॥

व्यूहो नाम रचना। यथाप्राप्तस्य साधनम्। स्थापना व्यूहो लक्षणा रचना पाणिनीयानामाचार्याणां मते ऽकृतवद्भवति। कार्यं दृष्ट्वा यत्कृतं तत्सर्वं निवर्तते।

कथं ज्ञायते। यदयमुर्ऋदित्य् (७।४।७) अत्र उर्ऋदिति ब्रवीति।

कथं कृत्वा ज्ञापकम्। अत्र हि वृतु इत्येवमादीनां णौ चङ्परे ऋदेव भवतीत्युच्यते। तेषां चावश्यमृकारस्य णौ पुगन्तलघूपधगुणवृद्ध्युपधेत्वैर्भवितव्यम्। तेषु कृतेषु नायमृद्भवति। युक्तं

2 [पर्जन्यः β] ‖ पूर्णं : पर्णं B 3 ल[[ल]]क्षणं P_1 4 बभूषति J 5 ढ α : [ढे β] 6 पुन J 8 °आप्यकः : °आपि अकसु B ‖ अकः : अ`क´सु P_2 9 ५८ om. β 1 अकृतः व्यूहः J 2 रचना codd. : Abhyankar's variant (om. नाम) रक्षणां in P_1 (p. 29, f.n. 2) is wrong. ‖ लक्षणा : रक्षणा P_1 (attraction to रचना) 3 पाणिनीयामाम् J ‖ मते om. β ‖ ऽकृतवद् α : [अकृतवद् β] 5 कथं ज्ञायते β : कथं कृत्वा ज्ञायते α (attraction to the phrase in the following paragraph) ‖ उर्ऋद् : तुनूद् J ‖ उऋदित्यत्र om. B (saut) ‖ उर्ऋद् : तुनूद् J : उनूद् B 6 वृतु : वृत्त codd. (तु and त्त are commonly confused in Śāradā; वृतु is used as an example in the *Kāśikā* and sub-commentaries on P.7.4.7) : वृत् Abhyankar ‖ [इति एवं B] ‖ णौ : णो J 7 चङ् : चण् β ‖ ऋद् : ऋचु J ‖ °अवश्यसु J, P_1 a.c. ‖ णौ : णो J 8 पुगन्त° : सुगन्त° P_1 a.c. ‖ लघूपद्रगुण° P_2 : लघूपधस्य गुण° B ‖ °वृद्ध्यु[[-1-]]प° P_2 ‖ °उपधेत्वैर् Wujastyk : उपधेत्वैर् codd. ‖ तेषु [[कृतेषु]] कृतेषु P_2 ‖ कृतेष्व नायम् J

हि तावद्वकुमिरराराम‌ृदिति। तद्यतः उर्ऋदित्य् (७। ४। ७) आह तज्ज्ञापयति गुणवृद्ध्युपधेत्वानि कार्यं दृष्ट्वा निवर्तन्ते।

किमेतस्या ज्ञापने प्रयोजनम्। प्रियं ग्रामणि कुलं यस्य प्रियग्रामणिकः। शेषाद्विभाषेति (५।४।१५४) कपि कृते ह्रस्वत्वं निवर्तते पश्चाद् ह्रस्वो नपुंसक इति (१।२।४७) ह्रस्वत्वं भवति। उच्यते को न्वत्र विशेषः। यावता प्रियग्रामणिक इत्येवं भवति न कश्चिद्विशेषो ज्ञाप्यते। अयमस्ति विशेषः यो ऽयं न कपीति (७।४।१४) प्रतिषेधः के ऽण इति (७। ४।१३) या च प्राप्तिः तस्याः प्राप्तेः स प्रतिषेधः। यद्येतद्ध्रस्वत्वं विधीयते न तस्य प्रतिषेधः।

तेन ह्रस्वो नपुंसके प्रातिपदिकस्येति (१। २। ४७) भवत्येव ह्रस्वत्वम्। न भवति कपीति प्रतिषेधः॥ ५९॥

अतन्त्रं तरनिर्देशः ॥ ६०॥

अप्रधानस्तरनिर्देशो यस्मिन्नर्थे उच्यते तमर्थं ब्रवीति। यस्मात्प्रातिपदिकाद्विधीयते तस्यैवार्थे भवति।

कथं ज्ञायते। यदयं किमेत्तिङव्ययघादाम्बद्रव्यप्रकर्ष इत्य् (५। ४। ११) आह।

कथं कृत्वा ज्ञापकम्। अत्र घादुत्तर आमुर्विधीयते द्रव्यप्रकर्षादन्यत्र। तच्च न संभवति। अयं हि घसंज्ञः तरप्तमप् च। अद्रव्यप्रकर्ष इत्युच्यमाने कः

9 तावद् : ताम J, P_2 a.c., B ‖ इरराराम् Abhyankar : इडराराम् codd. (इड`रा´राम् P_2) ‖ ऋद् codd. : ऋतः Abhyankar ‖ तद्यतः : उद्गतः P_2 a.c. ‖ उर्ऋद् : तुनूद् J 10 उपधेत्वानि Wujastyk : उपधैत्वानि codd. ‖ दृष्ट J 11 प्रियं : प्रिय P_2 , Abhyankar ‖ यस्य α : यस्य स β 12 [पश्चाद्ध्रस्वो P_1 P_2] 13 °स्वो नपुंसक : °स्व नो पुंसक J, P_1 a.c. ‖ नपुंसकेति B 14 °ग्रामणिका J 15 प्रतिषेधः `के ण इति या ... स प्रतिषेधः´ यद्य P_1 (omission by saut) 16 तस्या J ‖ [प्राप्तेसु P_2] ‖ यद्येतद् ... प्रतिषेधः om. J (saut) ‖ [एतद् ह्रस्वत्वं B] 17 न om. P_2 18 हुस्वो J ‖ प्रपदिस्येति J (sheer carelessness) 19 हुस्वत्वं J ‖ न भवति न कपीति α (attraction to P.7.4.14) ‖ प्रतिषेधः om. β ‖ ५९ om. β; in margin of P_1 1 अतन्त्रं : अत्र ⟨?⟩ P_2 a.c. 2 यस्मिनर्थे B 4 किमेतत्तिङ्° J ‖ °तिङ्डव्यय° β ‖ °घादांबद्रप्यप्रकर्ष J : °घादामुद्रव्यप्रकर्ष P_2 6 अत्र : अन्न J ‖ आमुर् : आसुर् J ‖ प्रकर्षा अन्यत्र P_2 7 तच्च : तश्च J ‖ [चाद्रव्य° B]

प्रसङ्गः यदुत द्रव्यप्रकर्षे स्याताम्। एतदाचार्यः पश्यति इमे तरबादयः स्वार्थे विधीयन्ते। प्रातिपदिकार्थे ते परतन्त्रा भवन्ति। अद्रव्यप्रकर्षे घादामुर्भवति।

किमेतस्या ज्ञापने प्रयोजनम्। उच्चैरेव उच्चैस्तराम्। श्रेष्ठ एव श्रेष्ठतम इति सिद्धं भवति॥ ६०॥

प्रधानान्वाचयशिष्टयोः प्रधानशिष्टे संप्रत्ययः ॥ ६१॥

प्रधानं चान्वाचयश्च तौ प्रधानान्वाचयौ। प्रधानं च यच्छिष्टमन्वाचयं च यच्छिष्टं तदुभयं भवति यत्र त्वन्वाचयव्यवस्थापको नास्ति तत्र प्रधानशिष्टं भवति। किं कारणं पुनर्न प्राप्नोति। संनियोगशिष्टानामन्यतरापाये उभयोरप्यभाव इति (परि॰ ३६)। किं पुनः प्रधानं को ऽन्वाचयः। यदर्थो विध्यारम्भस्तत्प्रधानम्। यदन्यस्मिन्विधातव्ये ऽन्यदुच्यते अस्मिन्निदं भवतीति सो ऽन्वाचयः।

कथं पुनर्ज्ञायते अस्त्येषा परिभाषेति। लोके तद्यथा कश्चित्कंचिदाह भिक्षां चर देवदत्तं चानय। स तत्रोभयं करोति। यदि तु देवदत्तं नासादयति तदा भैक्षं भवति।

शास्त्रे ऽपि ज्ञापकं थलि च सेटीडन्तो वेति (६।१।१९६) सेड्ग्रहणम्।

कथं कृत्वा ज्ञापकम्। अत्र सूत्रे सेड्ग्रहणं न कर्तव्यम्। थलीडन्तो वेति वक्तव्यम्। इट एवोदात्तत्वात्सेटि संप्रत्ययो भवति। नार्थः

8 स्यांतां J 11 प्रयोजन P_2 ‖ उच्चैर् B ‖ उच्चैस्तरां B ‖ श्रेष्ठ : श्रष्ट J P_2 ‖ श्रेष्ठंतम : श्रेष्टतम् J P_2 12 ६० om. β 1 °आचयश्रष्टयोः B ‖ प्रधानषष्टे J : प्रधानश्रेष्टो B 2 तौ om. α 3 यत्र β : अत्र α ‖ त्व α : [तु β] (Abhyankar's reading यत्र तत्र (p. 29:25) is wrong ‖ अन्वाचय ⟨-6-⟩ पको नास्ति B ‖ अन्वाचय `शिष्टस्य ज्ञा´पको P_2 (m. sec) ‖ It seems β had a lacuna at this point which was filled in to the best of the scribe of P_2's ability 5 अप्यभाव : अपि भाव J ‖ [प्रधानङ्को B] 6 ऽन्यदुच्यते om. J (saut from ए to ए) ‖ [उच्यते ऽस्मिन्न् P_1] 7 सन्वोचयः P_1 a. c. (metathesis) 8 लोके : लोकं J 9 चर : च`र´ P_2 ‖ स : सु J 10 भैक्षं भवति α : भैक्षं न भवति β 11 च om. codd. ‖ [सेटि इड्° B] ‖ [सेट् ग्रहणं β] 12 [सेट्° β] ‖ थलि डन्तो β (डंतो B) 13 एवोदन्तत्वात् P_2 : एवोदंतत्वात् B ‖ °दात्तत्वत् P_1 a. c. ‖ [नार्थसु P_2]

सेड्ग्रहणेन। पश्यति त्वाचार्यः थलि आद्यन्तो लिट्स्वरश्च प्रधानशिष्टः इट्स्वरश्चान्वाचयशिष्टः। तेन यत्र तावदिडस्ति तत्र चत्वारो भवन्ति। यत्रेदानीमिण्नास्ति तत्र प्रधानान्वाचयशिष्टयोः प्रधानशिष्टमिष्टम्। तेन त्रयः स्वराः स्युः। अनिटि ते मा भुवन्निति सेड्ग्रहणं क्रियते।

किमेतस्या ज्ञापने प्रयोजनम्। अव्ययसर्वनाम्नामकच्प्राक् टेः कस्य च द इति (५। ३। ७१, ७२)। अत्राकच्संनियोगेन कस्य च दकार उच्यते। सो ऽकच्प्रत्ययो भवति। यत्र ककारस्य दकारो भवति तत्रैव स्यात्ततो ऽन्यत्र न स्यात्। अस्यां पुनः सत्यां न दोषो भवति। अकजत्र प्रधानः दकारो ऽन्वाचयशिष्टः। तेन यत्रापि ककारस्य दकारो नास्ति तत्राप्यकच्सिद्धो भवति॥ ६१॥

योगविभागादिष्टसिद्धिः ॥ ६२॥

कथं ज्ञायंते अस्त्येषा परिभाषेति। यदयं तिष्यपुनर्वस्वोर्नक्षत्रद्वन्द्व इत्य् (१।२।६३) अत्र बहुवचनं करोति।

कथं कृत्वा ज्ञापकम्। बहव एव तिष्यपुनर्वसवः। तत्र युक्तं यद्बहुवचनं स्यात्। नार्थो बहुवचनग्रहणेन। पश्यति त्वाचार्यः विभाषा वृक्षमृगेत्य् (२। ४। १२) अत्र योगविभागो ऽस्ति। सर्वो द्वन्द्वो विभाषयैकवद्भवति (परि॰ ६७)। तन्निवृत्त्यर्थं बहुवचनग्रहणं क्रियमाणं ज्ञापकं भवति।

किमेतस्या ज्ञापने प्रयोजनम्। अस्मदो द्वयोश्चेत्य् (१। २। ५९) अत्र योगविभागः सिद्धो भवति। अस्मद एकस्मिन्बहुवचनं सिद्धं भवति।

14 [सेट्॰ B] ‖ प्रश्यत्याचार्यः P_1 a.c. ‖ आद्यन्तो : आस्यन्तो β **15** यत्र om. α **16** यत्रेदानीस् J **17** [त्रयस् P_2] ‖ स्वरा J : [स्वरास् β] ‖ भूवनिति B : भून्निति P_1 P_2 ‖ [सेट्॰ B] **18** अव्ययं॰ B ‖ अकच् : अकं J **19** च : चि P_2 ‖ कस्य च दकार α : कस्यचिदकार β **20** सो ऽकच्॰ : ⟨-2-⟩ सो ऽकं॰ J : सकोच्॰ P_1 a.c. : ऽकच् P_2 (i.e. om. सो) ‖ तत्रेव B **21** अस्या P_1 ‖ [पुनस् P_2] ‖ [[अकजत्र]] J (and omitted) **22** दकारो Wujastyk : चकारो codd. ‖ ऽन्वा`च´य॰ B ‖ `क´कारस्य J **23** अकं सिद्धो J ‖ ६१ : ६२ α : om. β **2** ज्ञायत स्त्येषा α ‖ [॰द्वन्द्वे β] **3** इ`त्य´त्र P_2 **6** सर्वो om. B **7** क्रियमाणा J **9** योगविभागः : [योगविभागस् P_2] : योगः B ‖ सिद्धं om. β

ततश्च द्वयोरर्थयोरस्मदोर्बहुवचनं भवति। तत्र यदुक्तं चकारो विकल्पार्थः क्रियत इति स दोषो भवति॥ ६२॥

प्रातिपदिकविधौ तदन्तविधिर्नास्ति ॥ ६३॥

यत्र प्रातिपदिकं गृहीत्वा कार्यमुच्यते तत्र तदन्तविधिर्न भवति।

कथं ज्ञायते। यदयं सेनान्तलक्षणकारिभ्यश्चेत्य् (४। १। १५२) अत्रान्तग्रहणं करोति।

कथं कृत्वा ज्ञापकम्। अत्रान्तग्रहणं न कर्तव्यम्। सेनालक्षण इत्येव सिद्धम्। येन विधिस्तदन्तस्येति (१। १। ७२) वचनात्। हारिषेण्यः वारिषेण्यः। तदन्तविधिना सेनान्तादपि भविष्यति। तदत्र यदन्तग्रहणं करोति तज्ज्ञापयति अस्तीयं परिभाषेति।

किमेतस्या ज्ञापने प्रयोजनम्। सूत्रनडस्यापत्यं सौत्रनाडिः। तदन्तविधिना फक् न भवति॥ ६३॥

10 ततश्च द्वयोरर्थयोर् : ततश्च योरर्थयोद् J : ततो द्वयोश्चार्थयोर् β (i.e. च and द्वयोः transposed) ‖ अस्मदोर् : अस्मदो J β 11 [क्रियते β] ‖ ६२ om. β
1 प्रतिपदिक॰ P_2 a.c. 2 \`त´दन्त $P_2$ ‖ न भवति : नास्ति B 3 ॰लक्षण॰ $P_2$ a.c. 5 सेना॰ : सेता॰ J : सेनांत B ‖ ॰लक्षणेव J (i.e. om. इति) : ॰लक्षणेत्येव $P_1$ : ॰लक्ष्मण इत्येव $P_2$ a.c. 6 हारिषणाः J 7 वारिषेण्यः om. J : \`वारिषेण्यः´ P_1 ‖ सेनांतास्तदपि J ‖ भविष्यति β : भवति α ‖ तदत्र यद α : तद्यस्माद् β 9 ॰आपत्ये Abhyankar ‖ सौनडिः P_2 a.c. 10 ॰विधिना : ॰विधिनां J : ॰विधिन P_2 a.c. : तदन्तं विधिन B ‖ फक् Wujastyk : च्फञ् P_1 : फञ J : डञ P_2 : इड् B (on the emendation see P.4.1.99) ‖ न om. β ‖ ६३ : ६२ J : om. β

प्रकृतिग्रहणे णिजन्तस्यापि ग्रहणम् ॥ ६४ ॥

कथं ज्ञायते। यदयं हेरचङीत्य् (७।३।५६) आह।

कथं कृत्वा ज्ञापकम्। अत्र हेः कुत्वं विधीयमानं तत्र कः प्रसङ्गो यण्णौ चङ्परे स्यात्। पश्यति त्वाचार्यः प्रकृतिग्रहणे णिजन्तस्यापि ग्रहणं भवतीति तस्मात्प्रतिषेधं करोतीति अचङीति।

किमेतस्या ज्ञापने प्रयोजनम्। सुनोतेः षत्वमुच्यमानं णिजन्तस्यापि भवति अभिषावयतीति॥ ६४ ॥

संज्ञाविधौ तदन्तविधिर्नास्ति ॥ ६५ ॥

यत्र संज्ञा विधीयते तत्र तदन्तविधिर्नास्ति।

कथं ज्ञायते। यदयं सुप्तिङन्तं पदमित्य् (१।४।१४) अत्रान्तग्रहणं करोति।

कथं कृत्वा ज्ञापकम्। अत्रान्तग्रहणं न कर्तव्यम्। केनेदानीं सुप्तिङन्तं पदसंज्ञं भविष्यति। तदन्तविधिना। सुप्तिङ्भ्यामियं संज्ञा प्रारब्धा सुप्तिङन्तस्य भविष्यति। एतत्पश्यत्याचार्यः संज्ञाविधौ तदन्तविधिर्नास्तीति।

किमेतस्या ज्ञापने प्रयोजनम्। तरप्तमपौ घ इति (१। १। २२) तरबित्येतस्य घसंज्ञा तदन्तविधिना तदन्तस्य न भवति गौरितराशब्दस्य। किं च स्यात्। कुमारी गौरितरेत्यत्र घरूपकल्पेत्य् (६।३।४३) अनेन ह्रस्वत्वं स्यात्॥ ६५ ॥

1 णिज्° : णिण् J (possible confusion of Śāradā ज् with Devanāgarī ण्) ‖ °ग्रहणे [[पि]] \`णि´ज° P_1 3 हेः : हे J B ‖ कुत्वं : कंुत्व J (Śāradāism and displaced अनुस्वार) ‖ [प्रसंगः B] 4 चङ्° Abhyankar : चण्° α : चन्° β ‖ णिजन्तस्या° : णंतस्या° J 6 सुनतेः P_1 a.c. : [सुनातेष् P_2] : स्वनोतेः B ‖ णिज्° : निज् P_2 7 अभिभावयति P_2 : अभिषावयति B (i.e. β om. इति) ‖ ६४ om. β 2 \`यत्र ... नास्ति´ $P_1$ m. sec. (omitted by saut from नास्ति) 3 °तिङ्° : °तिट्° $P_2$ a.c. 5 कृत्वा [[ज्ञा]]ज्ञापकम् $P_2$ 6 भविष्यति $\alpha$ : भवति $\beta$ ‖ तदन्त° : यदन्त° $P_2$ ‖ °तिङ्भ्याम् : °तिज्ञाम् J : °तिज्भ्याम् B : °ति\`ङ्भ्या´[[ज्भ्या]]म् P_2 7 °तिङ्न्तस्य P_1 8 [नास्ति इति B] 9 कि\`मे´तस्या P_2 ‖ °तमघौ घ P_1 10 तरपित्य् B 11 गोरितरेत्य् J ‖ घरूपेत्य् α (i.e. om. कल्प) 12 ह्रस्वत्वं J ‖ ६५ om. J β

अभिधानलक्षणाः कृत्तद्धितसमासाः ॥ ६६ ॥

अभिधानं दृष्ट्वा कृत्तद्धितसमासानां प्रयोगो भवति।

कथं ज्ञायते। यदयं प्रे स्त्रो ऽयज्ञ इति (३। ३। ३२) कर्मग्रहणं न करोति।

कथं कृत्वा ज्ञापकम्। अत्र कर्मग्रहणं कर्तव्यम्। प्रे स्त्रो ऽयज्ञकर्मणीति। यथान्यत्र ये यज्ञकर्मणीति (८। २। ८८) ब्रवीति। एतदाचार्यः पश्यति यत्र नाभिधानं तत्र कृत्प्रत्ययानां उत्पत्तिर्न भवति। तेनासत्यपि कर्मग्रहणे अयज्ञकर्मणीव घञ् भवति। तस्मात्कर्मग्रहणं न क्रियते।

किमेतस्या ज्ञापने प्रयोजनम्। यत्राभिधानमाश्रीयते तत्रेयं परिभाषा न वक्तव्या भवति॥ ६६॥

सर्वो द्वन्द्वो विभाषयैकवद्भवति ॥ ६७ ॥

कथं ज्ञायते। यदयं सूत्रे क्वचिद्बहूनामेकवचनं निपातयति गदमदचरयम इति (३।१।१००)।

किमेतस्या ज्ञापने प्रयोजनम्। यो द्वन्द्वैकवद्भावे अपरिगणितानां द्वन्द्व एकवद्दृश्यते तत्रैव परिभाषा वर्तते॥ ६७॥

1 °लक्षणः J 2 दृष्टा J ‖ °तद्धित[[:]] स[[:]] मासानां P_2 ‖ °समासनां B a.c. 3 प्रो स्त्रो J : प्रे स्त्यो β ‖ [ऽयज्ञे β] ‖ न om. P_2 5 कर्मग्रहणं न कतव्यं J ‖ प्रो स्त्रो J : प्रे स्त्यो P_2 : प्र स्त्यो B ‖ °कर्माणीति α ‖ °कर्नणेति P_2 6 ये : प्रे P_1 ‖ यथान्यत्र ... कर्मणीति om. J β (saut) ‖ आ`चा´र्यः B 7 तत्र $\beta$ : ततः $\alpha$ ‖ °प्रत्यया`ना`म् B ‖ न भवति β : भवति न α 9 तत्र यं J 10 न वक्तव्या भवति α : वक्तव्या न भवति β ‖ ६६ om. β 1 द्वन्द्वेर् P_2 a.c. 2 गम्मदयसुचर J : गम्मदयमचर P_1 : गम्मदचरयम P_2 5 ६७ om. β

प्रतिपदविधानाद्योगविभागो गरीयान् ॥ ६८ ॥

प्रतिपदपाठात्सत्यामप्यर्थसिद्धौ योगविभागः क्रियमाणो गुरुतरो भवति।

कथं ज्ञायते। यदयं नेट्यलिटि रधेरित्य् (७।१।६२) आह।

कथं कृत्वा ज्ञापकम्। अत्र सूत्रे रधिग्रहणं न कर्तव्यम्। जभेरचि नुम्भवति। ततो रधेश्च नुम्भवति। अचीत्येव। ततो नेट्यलिटीत्येव रधेरित्येव पुना रधिग्रहणं न कर्तव्यम्। एवं सिद्धे सति यद्रधिग्रहणं करोति तत्पश्यति गुरुतरमेव भवति। कथम्। अक्रियमाणे रधिग्रहणे यो⟨गविभा⟩गो भवति। प्रतिपदविधानाद्योगविभागो गरीयानिति।

किमेतस्या ज्ञापने प्रयोजनम्। पूङः क्त्वा चेत्य् (१।२।२२) अत्र योगविभागे न क्त्वा सेडिति (१।२।१८) क्त्वाग्रहणं प्रत्याख्यातं तद्गुरु भवति। तस्मान्मा भूदिति क्त्वाग्रहणमेव क्रियते॥ ६८ ॥

समासान्तविधिरनित्यः ॥ ६९ ॥

ये समासान्ता विधीयन्ते न ते सर्वकालं भवन्ति।

कथं ज्ञायते। यदयं राजशब्दं प्रतेरंश्वादिषु (c.f. ६। २। १९३) पठति। इदमंश्वादिषु पाठप्रयोजनम्। प्रतेरंश्वादय इत्य् (६। २। १९३) अन्तोदात्तत्वं यथा स्यादिति। प्रतिराज इति।

कथं कृत्वा ज्ञापकम्। अत्रांश्वादिषु पाठो ऽनर्थकः। अयं राजाहःसखिभ्यष्टज् (५। ४। ९१) विधीयते। तत्र च टचो ऽन्तोदात्तत्वं सिद्धं नार्थः पाठेनेति। तत्राचार्यः पश्यति अनित्यष्टच् समासान्त इति।

1 °विधानाद् β : °विभागाद् α ‖ योगविभागो : योगविभादाद्योगविभागो J (saut) 2 °पाठात् : °पादात् J ‖ अप्यार्थ° J 6 अचि [[-4-]] नुम् P_2 ‖ ततो रधेः रधेश्च α B : ततो [[रधे]] रधेश्च P_2 ‖ नुम् : नुग् P_1 7 पुना β (on this form see P.8.3.14 and 6.3.111) : पुन J P_1 (पुना P_1 a.c.)′ 8 गुरु° : पुरु° J ‖ अक्रियमागे ⟨?⟩ P_2 a.c. 9 ⟨ ⟩ Wujastyk (saut) 10 पूङ P_2 ‖ क्त्वा चेत् : क्त्व चेत् P_2 a.c. 11 °विभागो B ‖ क्त्वा सेड् : क्त्व सेड् P_2 a.c. 12 तन्मान् : तस्मात् J : तस्मा`त´ B : तन् Abhyankar ‖ ६८ om. β 2 समासांत J ‖ न ते om. P_2 (confused with °न्ते) ‖ भवन्ति : भवति J B 3 प्रतेरंश्वादिष्व J 4 इदमंश्वादिष्व J 5 अन्तेदात्तंत्वं P_2 a.c. 6 °आदिष्व J ‖ [राजाहस् P_2] 7 °सखिभ्यः β ‖ टज् : ठज् J ‖ टचो ऽन्तो° : टोदंतो° J (i.e. द for च, and vowel metathesis) : ट`चों´[[शों]]तो° B 8 टच् : टश् J

तस्मात्पाठो ऽन्तोदात्तार्थं क्रियते।

किमेतस्या ज्ञापने प्रयोजनम्। पराध्वनि इत्यत्र उपसर्गादध्वनः (c.f. ५।४।८५) समासान्तो न भवति॥ ६९॥

अनित्यमागमशासनम् ॥ ७०॥

य इमे टित्किन्मित आगमाः शास्त्रे शिष्यन्ते ते ऽनित्याः। न सर्वकालमेव भवन्ति।

कथं ज्ञायते। यदयं थो न्थ इत्य् (७।१।८७) आह।

कथं कृत्वा ज्ञापकम्। एतत्सूत्रं थो नुडिति वक्तव्यम्। नुडागमेनापि सिद्धं भवति। ततश्चेयमस्ति परिभाषा अनित्यमागमशासनमिति। पचानः इत्यपि भवति। पचमान इति प्राप्ते आने मुङ् (७।२।८२) न भवति। आगमस्यानित्यत्वात्॥ ७०॥

10 पराध्वनि Wujastyk : शाना ⟨-4-⟩ α : शनाध्वनि ⟨-2-⟩ P_2 : शना ⟨-2-⟩ ध्वनि ⟨-4-⟩ B : Abhyankar's emendation to शताध्वनि misses the point: the example must begin with an उपसर्ग ‖ इत्यत्र Abhyankar : om. α : तु β ‖ उपसर्गाद् : उपर्गाद् B ‖ अध्वनः : अधनः J **11** ६९ om. β **2** य [[-1-]] इमे J ‖ शास्त्रं J ‖ ते om. J (haplography) ‖ [ते अनित्याः β] **4** थो न्थ : था क्तो J : थो [[-1-]] P_1 : थो क्त B ‖ थो `न्थ इत्या´ह P_2 **7** ततश्च … इत्यपि भवति om. β (सिद्धं भवति ⟨-14-⟩ पच्° P_2) (saut) ‖ पचमान इति α : पच्यमानस्येति β ‖ मुङ् B : मुण् α : मुंड् P_2 **8** ७० om. β

शब्दान्तरस्य प्राप्नुवन्विधिरनित्यो भवति ॥ ७१॥

तद्यथा लोलूयतेरचि परतः लोलूय अ इति स्थिते यकारस्य यङो ऽचि चेति (२। ४। ७४) लुक् प्राप्नोति। आर्धधातुके चातो लोप इति (६। ४। ४८) लोपः। किमत्र कर्तव्यम्। परत्वादतो लोप इति (६। ४। ४८)। नित्यत्वाद्यङो लुक् प्राक्। कथं नित्यः। यङ्लुकि कृते ऽतो लोपः (६। ४। ४८) प्राप्नोति अकृते ऽपि। अतो लोपस्त्वनित्यः। न हि यङः सर्वस्य लुकि कृते ऽतो लोपः प्राप्नोति। अनित्यो यङ्लुक्। कथम्। शब्दान्तरस्य प्राप्नुवन्विधिरनित्यो भवति। कथमनित्यः। उपद्रष्टव्यं अतो लोपे कृते ऽनच्कस्य ⟨अ⟩ कृते साच्कस्य। एतदत्र शब्दान्तरम्। अत्र परत्वादतो लोपो भवति। तस्मिन्कृते पश्चादवशिष्टस्य लुक्। अत्र परत्वादतो लोपो भवति। तेन न धातुलोप आर्धधातुके (१। १। ४) एतं विनापि योगं अतो लोपस्य स्थानिवत्त्वाद्गुणो न भवति। लोलुवः पोपुवः॥ ७१॥

1 °आन्तर प्राप्नुवन् P_2 2 अ om. J ‖ `इ´ति P_2 3 अर्ध° P_2 a.c. 4 परत्वद् J ‖ अतो : आतो B 5 नित्यत्वाद् : नित्यचाद् J ‖ Abhyankar's reading in note 1, p. 33̣, of याक् for प्राक् in P_1 and P_2 is wrong ‖ यङ्लुकि sic codd., against the required sense? ‖ ऽतो : त P_1 a.c. : [अतो β] 6 लोपः sic codd., against the required sense : लोपोः P_1 a.c. ‖ प्राप्नोति `अकृतेऽपि ... लोपः प्राप्नोति´ अनित्यो $P_1$ (original saut) 7 यङः : यटः $P_2$ a.c. ‖ प्राप्नोति om. J ‖ अनित्ये $P_1$ a.c. 8 प्राप्नु`वन्´ B ‖ कथंमनित्यः J ‖ उप ⟨-4-⟩ द्रूष्टप[[ङ्लुक्]]व्यं J : उप ⟨-2-⟩ द्रष्टव्यं P_1 : उप ⟨-4-⟩ द्रूष्टव्यं B 9 ऽनच्कस्य : च्छुस्य J : अनच्कस्य β (अनच्छुस्य P_2 a.c.) ‖ ⟨ ⟩ Wujastyk ‖ साच्कस्य : साछ्स्य J : साच्छ्स्य P_2 a.c. ‖ [साच्कस्यैतद् B] 10 अतो : अते P_1 a.c. ‖ अत्र ... भवति om. α β (haplography) 11 धातुलोपा आर्ध° J : धातुलोपे अर्ध B ‖ अर्ध° P_1 12 एतं : यूतं J ‖ योगं Abhyankar : योगः J : योग ⟨-3-⟩ P_1 : योग β ‖ स्थानिवत्त्वाद् β : स्थानित्वाद् α 13 पोपुवः om. P_1 ‖ ७१ om. β

लक्षणान्तरेण प्राप्नुवन्विधिरनित्यः ॥ ७२॥

तद्यथा पा अतुस् इति स्थिते तत्र द्विर्वचनं प्राप्नोति आतो लोपश्च (६।४।६४)। परत्वादातो लोपः। नित्यत्वाद्विर्वचनम्। कथम्। द्विर्वचने चातो लोपो भवति। नन्वातो लोपे कृते द्विर्वचनं न प्राप्नोति। किं कारणम्। अनच्त्वात्। उच्यते द्विर्वचनमपि नित्यम्। कथं द्विर्वचने ऽचीति (१।१।५९) स्थानिवद्भावात्। †उच्यते अन्येन लक्षणेन द्विर्वचनं नित्यं क्रियते। द्विर्वचने चीत्य् (१।१।५९) अनेन कृते† एतस्मिंल्लक्षणे द्विर्वचनस्य प्राप्तिरस्ति। अत एतल्लक्षणान्तरं भवति। यश्च लक्षणान्तरेण प्राप्नोति विधिरसावनित्यो भवति। तस्मादातो लोपस्तावद्भवति। पश्चाद्विर्वचनम्। एवं पपतुः पपुरिति सिद्धं भवति॥ ७२॥

असिद्धं बहिरङ्गमन्तरङ्गे ॥ ७३॥

कथं ज्ञायते। यदयं वाह ऊठं (६।४।१३२) शास्ति।

कथं कृत्वा ज्ञापकम्। अत्रोठ् न वक्तव्यः। वाहः संप्रसारणमित्येव सिद्धम्। पष्ठ उह् अस् इति स्थिते यो ऽसावप्रत्यय उक्तो ण्विन्तस्मिन्प्रत्ययलक्षणेन पुगन्तलघूपधस्येति (७। ३। ८६) गुणे कृते वृद्धिरेचीति (६। १। ८८) सिद्धम्। पष्ठौहः पश्येति। एवं सिद्धे

2 अतुस् : अतुं J : अतुमु β ‖ द्विवचनं β 3 द्विवचनं β ‖ कथं sic codd. Abhyankar's note, p. 33, note 3, is wrong ‖ द्विवचन P_2 4 न : च J ‖ न [[प्रा]] प्राप्नोति P_1 ‖ किं कारणम् β : कथं α (this is the source of Abhyankar's error above) 5 अनच्त्वात् : अनंत्वात् J (Śāradā च् leads to म्, which leads to anusvāra) : अनच्छत्वाद् P_2 a.c. ‖ अपि नित्यम् β : अप्यनित्यम् α 6 लक्षणोन J ‖ नित्यं om. β 7 अनेन कृते sic codd. Abhyankar's suggestion of a lacuna here is unfounded 8 यश्च : यच्च J β 9 विधिरसावनित्यो β : विधिरनित्यो ऽसौ α ‖ तवद् B a.c. ‖ पश्चद् P_2 a.c. : [पश्चात् B] ‖ द्वि`र्व´चनं P_1 10 एवं : एव B ‖ ७२ om. β 1 अन्तराङ्गे P_1 a.c. 2 ऊठं : ऊटं P_1 B 3 अत्रोठ् Abhyankar : अत्रोण् α : अत्रो [[-1-]] ट् P_2 : अत्र ऊट् B ‖ [वाहसु सं॰ P_2] 4 पष्ठ : पृष्ट J : पष्ट β ‖ उह J : ऊह P_1 ‖ अस् : अमु B ‖ प्रत्येयं J 5 ण्विन् : ण्विं J : ण्विंस् P_1 ‖ तस्मिं B ‖ पूगंत J ‖ गुणे om. B 6 पुष्टोहः J : पष्टौहः P_1 (पष्टौहो a.c.) : पष्टौहाः β ‖ पश्यति β

सति यदयं वृद्ध्यर्थं वाह ऊठं शास्ति तज्ज्ञापयति अस्तीयं परिभाषेति। तेन बहिरङ्गलक्षणस्य गुणस्यासिद्धत्वादन्तरङ्गलक्षणा वृद्धिर्न स्यात्। तत्र गुणमाश्रित्य वृद्धिः। बाह्याश्रयत्वाद्बहिरङ्गो गुणः।

किमेतस्या ज्ञापने प्रयोजनम्। ग्रामणि कुलमित्यत्रासिद्धत्वाद् बहिरङ्गलक्षणस्य नपुंसकह्रस्वत्वस्यान्तरङ्गलक्षणस्तुङ् न भवति। अत्रापि हि नपुंसकमाश्रित्य ह्रस्वत्वं तद्बाह्याश्रयं भवति बहिरङ्गम्। ह्रस्वमाश्रित्य तुक् स वर्णत्वादन्तरङ्गम्॥ ७३॥

नाजानन्तर्ये बहिष्प्रकॢप्तिः ॥ ७४॥

अचामानन्तर्यलक्षणे कर्तव्ये बहिरङ्गपरिभाषा नावतरति।

कथं ज्ञायते। यदयं षत्वतुकोरसिद्ध इति (६। १। ८६) तुग्विधिं प्रत्येकादेशस्यासिद्धत्वं शास्ति। अत्राभि प्र इ य इति स्थिते एकादेशं शास्ति। तत्र तुक् च। परत्वान्नित्यत्वाच्च। एकादेशे कृते तुक् दीर्घत्वान्न प्राप्नोति। ततो ऽनेनैकादेशस्यासिद्धत्वात् क्रियते षत्वतुकोरसिद्ध इति (६। १। ८६)। एतच्चानया परिभाषया सिध्यति। कथम्। धातूपसर्गावाश्रित्यैकादेशः वर्णमाश्रित्य तुक्। वर्णत्वादन्तरङ्गतरस्तुक् भवति। तत्रासिद्धत्वाद्बहिरङ्गलक्षणस्यान्तरङ्गलक्षणस्तुग्भविष्यति। नार्थस्तुग्विधिं प्रत्यसिद्धवचनेन। एवं सिद्धे सति यदसिद्धत्वं तुग्विधौ

7 ऊटं J β ‖ [ज्ञापयत्य् P1] ‖ ज्ञापरिभाषेति J (i.e. om. यति अस्तीयं प, by saut from प) **9** गुणम् Wujastyk : ण्विनम् codd. **11** कूलम् J ‖ इत्यासिद्ध॰ J (i.e. om. ॰त्र॰) ‖ ॰लक्षणस्य … ॰आन्तरङ्ग॰ om. J (saut) ‖ ह्रस्वत्वस्या॰ : ह्रस्वांतस्यनुपुंसकह्रस्वांतस्या॰ P1 (probably a saut from the षष्ठी ending of ॰लक्षणस्य earlier in the sentence) ‖ ॰आन्तरङ्गलक्षणस् sic codd. Abhyankar's reading ॰आन्तरङ्गस् is wrong **12** हि om. J ‖ ह्रस्वत्वं J ‖ बहिरंग J B ‖ ह्रस्वम् J **13** अन्तरङ्गम् α : अन्तरङ्गत्वं β ‖ ७३ om. β **1** नाजांतर्ये B ‖ ॰प्रकॢप्तिः : ॰प्रकॢक्त्यप्तिः α **2** अचामांतर्ये B ‖ बहिहिरङ्ग॰ J (dittography) **3** षत्वतुकोर् : षत्वकरो J : षत्वतुकरो P1 a.c. : षद्वुर्तुकरो B ‖ असिद्ध : सिद्ध *codd.* ‖ ॰विधिं : ॰विध्वं J **4** [अत्र अभि P2] ‖ प्र [[-1-]] `इ´ य P2 **5** परत्वानित्य॰ J P2 ‖ नित्यत्वाच्च P1, P2 a.c., B ‖ तुक् : त्वक् P1 **6** ऽनेनैकदेश॰ β ‖ षत्वतुकोर् : षत्वतुकरो J, P1 a.c. : षद्वुर्तुकोर् B ‖ असिद्ध : सिद्ध α **7** एतच्च J, P1 a.c., P2 a.c., B **8** वर्णम् : Abhyankar's reading वर्णमात्रम् is wrong ‖ वर्णत्वाद् : वणत्वाद् P2 **8–9** ॰अङ्गतरस् … स्यान्तर॰ om. B **9** ॰स्यान्तरङ्ग॰ : ॰स्य अन्तरङ्ग P1 P2 ‖ ॰लक्ष`ण´स् B ‖ तुग् : ता J : `तु´वग् P1 **10** [नार्थः B] ‖ प्रत्य् : प्रति J ‖ असिद्धवचनेन : सिद्धवचने J

ब्रवीति तज्ज्ञापयत्याचार्यः अस्तीयं परिभाषेति। अच्यनन्तरे आश्रीयमाणे इयं परिभाषा न भवति। इह चाजनन्तर आश्रीयते। एकादेशे क्रियमाणे बहिष्प्रकॢप्तश्चायम्।

किमेतस्या ज्ञापने प्रयोजनम्। अक्षद्यूरिति। तत्रोठो बहिष्प्रकॢप्तस्यासिद्धत्वादिको यणचीति (६। १। ७७) यणादेशः सिद्धो भवति॥ ७४॥

सकृद्गतौ विप्रतिषेधे यद्बाधितं तद्बाधितमेव ॥ ७५॥

कथं ज्ञायते। यदयं तनादिकृञ्भ्य उरिति (३। १। ७९) पृथक् कृञ्ग्रहणं करोति तनादिकार्यं कृञो मा भूदिति। किं पुनस्तनादिकार्यं यत्कृञो न भवेदिति। अनुदात्तोपदेशवनतितनोत्यादीनामिति (६। ४। ३७) लोपो मा भूदिति। दैवरक्ताः किंशुकाः। नैव कृञो ऽनुनासिको ऽस्ति। इदं तर्हि तनादिभ्यस्तथासोरिति (२। ४। ७९) लुक् सिचो मा भूदिति। किं च स्यात्। विभाषा लुक् प्रसज्येत। नैतदस्ति। अस्त्वन्यत्तनादिकार्यं † लुग्विभाषया। यदा न विभाषा तदा ह्रस्वादङ्गाल्लोपो भविष्यति (c.f. ८। २। २७)। अकृतेति सिद्धम्। एवं सिद्धे यत्करोतेः पृथग्ग्रहणं करोति तज्ज्ञापयति सकृद्गतौ विप्रतिषेधे पुनर्न भवतीति। बाधितं वा सकृत्तद्बाधितमिति। तेन तनादिभ्यस्तथासोरित्य् (२। ४। ७९) अनेन बाधितं ह्रस्वादङ्गादिति (८। २। २७) लोपः पुनर्न स्यात्। अथवा विप्रतिषेधे परमित्य् (१। ४। २) अनेन नियमः क्रियते। विप्रतिषेधे परमेव भवति। तेन गते विप्रतिषेधे पुनः यत्प्राप्नोति

11 अच्य् : अचि P_2 12 चाज् : चाच B ‖ अनन्तर : ऽनन्तर B 13 बहिष्प्रकॢप्तश् : बहिष्प्रक्क्ल्यप्तिः J : बहिष्प्रक्ल्यप्तिः P_1 : बहिष्क्लृप्तश् β ‖ चायम् om. α 14 ज्ञा`प´ने P_2 ‖ तत्रोठो : तत्रोटो J : तत्रोट P_1 a.c. : तत्र ऊटः β 15 बहिष्° : बोहिष° P_1 : बहिः β ‖ °प्रक्क्ल्यप्तस्या° J : °प्रोकॢप्तस्या P_2 a.c. ‖ [°देशसु P_2] 16 ७४ om. β 2 °कृञ्भ्य : °कृञ्भ्यो P_2 a.c., B ‖ प्रृथक् B 3 करोति om. α ‖ तनादि [[-2-]] कार्यं P_2 7 लुक् : लक् J : नुक् P_2 8 नैतदस्ति Wujastyk : नैतदस्ति ज्ञापकम् codd. (inserted by attraction to familiar phrase?) ‖ अस्त्व् sic codd. Abhyankar's अस्त्य् is wrong. 9 ह्रुस्वाद् J ‖ अङ्गालोपो J ‖ भव`इ´ष्यति J 10 करोतेः : करतोः J ‖ पृथङ् B ‖ ग्रहणं om. $\beta$ ‖ `त´ज्ज्ञापयति P_1 ‖ विप्रतिषेधे Wujastyk : विप्रतिषेधः codd. 11 [भवति इति α] ‖ बीधितं वा J ‖ तनादि° : तेनादि° J 12 बाधितं *sic* ‖ ह्रस्वाद् J 13 पुनर्न : पूर्न B 14 [पुनर् P_1]

तन्न भवति।

किमेतस्या ज्ञापने प्रयोजनम्। वृक्ण इत्यत्रापि चोः कुरिति (८।२।३०) कुत्वेन बाधितत्वाद्व्रश्चभ्रस्जेति (८।२।३६) षत्वं न भवति॥ ७५॥

पुनःप्रसङ्गविज्ञानात्सिद्धम् ॥ ७६॥

विप्रतिषेधे कृते यदि पुनरपि किञ्चित्प्राप्नोति तदपि भवति। किं पुनस्तत्। उच्यते विप्रतिषेधे परमित्य् (१। ४। २) अनेन परं तावत्क्रियते। यत्तावत्परं तत्तावत्क्रियते। यदपि पूर्वमपि प्राप्नोति तदपि भवति। तद्यथा पा अतुस् इति द्विर्वचनं प्राप्नोति। आलोपश्च नित्यत्वात्परत्वाच्च विप्रतिषेधे परमित्य् (१। ४। २) अनेन लोपस्तावदौ क्रियते इति पुनःप्रसङ्गविज्ञानाद्द्विर्वचनमपि भवति। एवं पुनःप्रसङ्गविज्ञानात्पश्चाद्द्विर्वचनं भवति। पपतुः सिद्धम्॥ ७६॥

16 चोः क्रुर् J : चो कुर् P_1 17 कुत्वेन : क्रुत्वेन J ‖ व्रश्च° : व्रच्च° α ‖ ७५ om. β 3 [तदुच्यते α] 4 `यत्तावत्परं तत्तावत्क्रियत´ P_1 (omitted by saut) 5 द्विवचनं P_2 ‖ प्राप्नोति : प्राप्तो B 6 परत्वाच् : परताद् J : परत्वाद् P_1 : om. B (reads नित्यत्वाच्च (saut)) ‖ च om. α ‖ विप्रतिषेधेन P_2 ‖ इत्यनेन : इत्येतेन J 7 लोपश्च् om. β ‖ द्विवचनम् B ‖ एवं om. P_2 8 पश्चाद् om. β ‖ द्विवचनं P_1 B ‖ [पपतुस् P_2] ‖ ७६ om. β

अपवादविषये ऽप्युत्सर्गसमावेशः ॥ ७७॥

कथं ज्ञायते। यदयं शेषे विभाषेति (८।४।१८) शेषग्रहणं करोति।

कथं कृत्वा ज्ञापकम्। अत्र शेषग्रहणानर्थक्यम्। अन्तरेणापि शेषवचनं गदादिभ्यो ऽन्यस्मिन्नेव शेषे कार्यं विज्ञास्यते।

एतच्छेषग्रहणं क्रियते। गदादिषु परेषु नेर्णत्वं विभाषया मा भूदिति। तेन गदादिषु पूर्वेणैव नित्यो विधिर्भविष्यति। अयं च गदादिभ्यो यो ऽन्यस्तस्मिन्विभाषा विधिर्भविष्यति। एवं सिद्धे सति यच्छेषग्रहणं करोति तज्ज्ञापयति अपवादविषये ऽप्युत्सर्गसमावेशः। तत इह गदादिष्वपि परेषु स्यादियं विभाषा। तस्माच्छेषवचनम्।

किमेतस्या ज्ञापने प्रयोजनम्।

प्रदीयतां दाशरथाय मैथिली (रामायणे युद्धकाण्डे ९।२२)

इतीञो ऽपवादविषये ऽणपि सिद्धो भवति॥ ७७॥

न विकरणस्वरो लसार्वधातुकस्वरं बाधते ॥ ७८॥

कथं ज्ञायते। यदयं कर्तेत्यत्र तासः परस्य लसार्वधातुकस्य निघातं शास्ति (c.f. ६।१।१८६) तज्ज्ञापयति भवतीयं परिभाषेति।

किमेतस्या ज्ञापने प्रयोजनम्। चिनुते क्रीणीते इत्यत्र विकरणस्वराल्लसार्वधातुकस्वरः सिद्धो भवति॥ ७८॥

समुदायेषु शब्दाः प्रवृत्ता अवयवेष्वपि वर्तन्ते ॥ ७९॥

कथं ज्ञायते। लोकतः। तद्यथा लोके तैलं भुक्तं घृतं भुक्तमिति। शास्त्रे ऽपि ज्ञापकं यदयं वरेस्थानिवद्भावस्य प्रतिषेधं शास्ति।

2 विभाष इति J 3 There is no हि after अपि, *pace* Abhyankar 4 [°आदिभ्यः अन्य° β] ‖ °स्मिनेव B ‖ शेषे β : शेषं α ‖ विज्ञायते J 5 परेषु om. J (saut) ‖ [नेर् α : नेः β] ‖ णत्व B 6 नित्यो : त्यो J 7 तस्मिं B 8 अपवााद° J (*sic*) ‖ परेषु : परेष्वपि परेषु J (saut) 9 [स्यात् β] 12 इतीञो : इतीज्ञा J : इतीञ P_1 a.c. : इञो β (i.e. om. इति) ‖ ऽपोवाद° P_1 a.c. ‖ [ऽपापि α : अणापि β] ‖ ७७ om. β 1 °स्वरो लसार्व° : °स्वर लोसार्व° P_1 a.c. : °स्वर लसाव° P_2 a.c. 4 क्रणीते J 5 लसर्व° P_1 ‖ °धातु`क°´ P_2 ‖ [°स्वरसु P_2] ‖ ७८ om. β 1 शब्दा P_2 ‖ वर्तते J 3 ऽपि om. β ‖ प्रतिषेध J

कथं कृत्वा ज्ञापकम्। इह यायावर इति यो ऽसौ यङो ऽकारो लुप्तो ऽतो लोप इति (६। ४। ४८) तस्य स्थानिवद्भावप्रतिषेधः शिष्टः। आकारलोपो मा भूदिति। आर्धधातुके ऽचि क्ङिति आकारलोपो विधीयते। तत्र कः प्रसङ्गो यदुत यङो ऽवयवे ऽचि लोपः स्यात्। † इह यङः समुदितस्यार्धधातुक⟨त्व⟩मयं यङो ऽवयवः ⟨न⟩ आर्धधातुकं नैवाकारलोपः प्राप्नोति ⟨नार्थो⟩ स्थानिवद्भावप्रतिषेधेन †। एवं सिद्धे सति यद्दूरेस्थानिवद्भावप्रतिषेधं शास्ति तज्ज्ञापयति समुदायेषु प्रवृत्ताः शब्दा अवयवेष्वपि वर्तन्ते इति।

किमेतस्या ज्ञापने प्रयोजनम्। न धातुलोप आर्धधातुक इत्य् (१।१। ४) अत्र धात्ववयवलोपे कृते गुणवृद्धिप्रतिषेधः सिद्धो भवति॥ ७९॥

प्रकृतिवदनुकरणं भवति ॥ ८०॥

कथं ज्ञायते। यदयं क्षियो दीर्घादिति (८। २। ४६) दीर्घग्रहणं करोति।

कथं कृत्वा ज्ञापकम्। अत्र दीर्घग्रहणं न कर्तव्यम्। निर्देशादेव क्षिय इति दीर्घादिति गम्यते। कथं दीर्घस्येयङादेशो विधीयते। यदि हि ह्रस्वत्वं स्यात् क्षेरित्येवं ब्रूयात्। नैतदस्ति। यथैवात्राप्राप्ता सुबुत्पत्तिः एवमियङादेशो ऽप्राप्तः स्यात्। कथमप्राप्ता सुबुत्पत्तिः।

4 यो ऽसौ : यो मा J : य मा P_1 a.c. ‖ यङो : योङ α 5 [लुप्तो α : लुप्तः β] ‖ ऽतो : त α : अतो β ‖ लोप : लोपो P_1 a.c. : `लो´ पः P_2 : [लोपः B] ‖ इति om. β 6 अकार॰ J ‖ ॰लोपे B a.c. ‖ क्विति J ‖ अकार॰ J 7 तत्र कः : तत्राकः P_2 ‖ लोपस्तु P_2 8 यङस्तु P_2 9 आर्धधातुकेनैवा॰ α 10 यद्दूरे॰ : यद्धूरे J 11 शब्दाः J β ‖ वर्तते B ‖ इति om. B 12 अर्ध॰ J a.c., P_1 ‖ [॰धातुके β] 13 ७९ om. β 2 क्षियो : क्षियें J : क्षिये P_1 P_2, B a.c. ‖ दीर्घ॰ : दीत॰ J, P_1 a.c. (possibly a Śāradāism) 4 कर्त`व्यं´ P_1 5 एव हि क्षिय B ‖ दीघस्येयङादेशो : दीघस्येय [[-1-]] ज्ञादेशो J : दीर्घस्येयज्जादेशो P_1 : दीघस्य इयङादेशो β (इयजु a.c.) 6 इत्ये* ब्रूयत् J (Abhyankar's note 8, p. 35, is misleading) ‖ यथैवात्रा॰ : यथैवान्ना॰ J : यत्रैवात्रा॰ P_1 : यथैवा β (i.e. om. अत्र) 7 सुबुत्पत्तिः : स्तव्युत्पत्तिः J : सुव्युत्पत्तिः P_1 ‖ एवमं J ‖ इयङ्॰ : इयज्ञ॰ J : इयजु॰ P_1, P_2 a.c., B a.c. ‖ ऽप्राप्तः : `पि´ प्राप्तस्तु P_2 ‖ कथं स प्राप्ता J ‖ सुबुत्पत्तिः : सव्युत्पत्तिः J : सुव्युत्पत्तिः P_1

अर्थवत्प्रातिपदिकमधातुकम्। अयं च धातुस्तस्मात्सुबुत्पत्तिर्न प्राप्नोति। उच्यते नैष धातुः। धातोरनुकरणमेतत्। † क्षि इति यो ऽधातुस्तस्मादधातुत्वात्प्रातिपदिकसंज्ञा †। प्रातिपदिकात्स्वादयः। तेनात्र प्राप्ता सुबुत्पत्तिः। इयङादेशो न भवति। न चेद्भवति निर्देशादेव क्षिय इति सिद्धम्। नार्थो दीर्घवचनेन। एतत्पश्यत्याचार्यः प्रकृतिवदनुकरणं भवतीति। ततो धातोरेतदनुकरणं भवति। धातुवदेवमत्र सुबुत्पत्तिर्न प्राप्नोति। यथैव नाप्राप्ता सुबुत्पत्तिरियङादेशो ऽप्यप्राप्तः स्यात्। तस्माद्दीर्घवचनं कर्तव्यम्।

किमेतस्या ज्ञापने प्रयोजनम्। इह कश्चिद् द्विः पचत्वित्याह। तत्प्रकृतिवदनुकरणं भवति। † पदद्वया सिद्धा भवति † तेन तिङ्ङतिङ इति (८।१।२८) निघातः। सर्वस्य सुबन्तस्य तिङन्तस्य च पदसंज्ञा एका। तत्र पदादिति न शक्यते वक्तुं तस्मात्समुदायपदत्वमेतेन भवति तस्मादयं यत्नं इति॥ ८०॥

8 धातुस् : धातु`:´ $P_2$ ‖ सुव्युत्पत्तिर् $P_1$ ‖ प्राप्नोति [[र्न प्राप्नोति]] $P_1$ (saut) 10 सुबुत्पत्तिर् ... धातुस्तस्माद् om. J (saut) ‖ धातुस् : [धातुः J] : धातु`:´ B ‖ °त्वात् : °त्वत् J ‖ प्रतिपदिकसंज्ञा P_2 11 प्राप्त J ‖ सुव्युत्पत्तिः J : सुव्युत्पत्तिः P_1 ‖ इयङ्° : इयजु्° J, P_2 a.c. 12 एतत्पश्यत्याचार्यः α : एतदाचार्यः पश्यति β 13 सुबुत्पत्तिर् : सुव्युत्पत्तिर् α 14 सुबुत्पत्तिर् : सुव्युत्तिर् J : सुव्युत्पत्तिर् P_1 : सुबुत्पत्ति β (i.e. om. र्) ‖ इयङ्° : इयञु्° α : इयजु्° P_2 a.c. ‖ [अप्राप्तसु् P_2] 16 द्विः : द्वि α P_2 : द्वि`:´ B 17 पदद्वया सिद्धा codd. (inexplicably): पदद्वयात् सिद्धो Abhyankar 18 तिङतिन् ति J : [तिङतिङ इति P_1] ‖ [निघातसु् P_2] ‖ सुबन्तस्य β : संबन्धस्य α ‖ तिङ्ङन्तस्य B 19 पदादिति : पदानि न B ‖ °त्वमतेन B 20 ८० om. β

अव्यक्ते गुणसंदेहे नपुंसकलिङ्गं प्रयुज्यते ॥ ८१॥

कथं ज्ञायते। यदयमर्धं नपुंसकमिति (२। २। २) नपुंसकग्रहणं करोति।

कथं कृत्वा ज्ञापकम्। अत्र हि अर्धमिति नपुंसकादेव नपुंसकं सिद्धम्। तज्ज्ञापयति अव्यक्ते गुणसंदेहे स्त्रीपुंनपुंसकेष्वपि नपुंसकत्वं नपुंसकलिङ्गं प्रयुज्यते। तेन पुंलिङ्गे ऽपि स्यात्समासः। तस्मान्नपुंसकग्रहणम्।

किमेतस्या ज्ञापने प्रयोजनम्। किं जातमिति निर्देशः सिद्धो भवति। द्वयं चैव हि जायते प्रायेण स्त्री पुमान्वा। अथ चोच्यते किं जातमिति॥ ८१॥

अवयवलोपिनामतो लोपो नास्ति ॥ ८२॥

कथं ज्ञायते। यदयं नलोपः सुप्स्वरसंज्ञातुग्विधिषु कृतीति (८। २। २) तुग्विधिं प्रति नलोपस्यासिद्धत्वं शास्ति।

कथं कृत्वा ज्ञापकम्। वृत्रहभ्यामित्यत्र नलोपे कृते पश्चादतो लोपः प्राप्नोति। तस्मिन्कृते नैव तुक् प्राप्नोति।

कथं कृत्वा। ह्रस्वस्येति तदा न शक्यते वक्तुम्। तस्मान्नार्थो नलोपस्यासिद्धत्वेन। तद्यस्मात्तुग्विधिं प्रति नलोपस्यासिद्धत्वं शास्ति तज्ज्ञापयति अस्तीयं परिभाषेति।

किमेतस्या ज्ञापने प्रयोजनम्। राजीयति राजायते इत्येवमादयः सिद्धा भवन्ति॥ ८२॥

1 अव्यक्ते β : अव्यक्त° α 2 नपुंसक`मिति नपुंसक´ ग्रहणं P_1 (omission by saut) 4 एव α : इति β 5 स्त्रीनपुंसकेष्व् J : स्त्रीपुसकेष्व् P_2 7 जातम् : जेतम् P_2 a.c. ‖ [निर्देशस्̮ P_2] 8 प्रायेण : प्रयोगो B ‖ किं : कि B 9 ८१ om. β
1 अवयबालापिनाम् α 2 [नलोपस्̮ P_2] ‖ °स्वर° : °सुर° B ‖ [कृति इति B] 4 वृत्रहभ्याम् Abhyankar : वृत्रहत्याम् α : वृत्रह`ण´म् P_2 : वृत्रहम् B ‖ नलोपे α : नकारलोपे β 5 तस्मिं B 6 ह्रुस्व° J ‖ तस्यान्नार्थे J 7 नलोप° α : लोप° β ‖ °सिद्धत्वं : °सिद्धतं α 9 ज्ञापने : ज्ञापकं J ‖ राजायते β : राजायती α ‖ इत्य om. β ‖ [आदयस्̮ P_2] 10 ८२ om. β

अन्तरङ्गविधेः प्रतिपदविधिर्बलीयान् ॥ ८३॥

कथं ज्ञायते। यदयं धिन्विकृण्व्योर चेति (३। १। ८०) नुमनुषङ्गयोर्ग्रहणं करोति।

कथं कृत्वा ज्ञापकम्। अत्र हि धिविकृव्योरच्चेति वक्तव्यम्। एवमुच्यमाने अत्वे कृते पश्चान्नुमनुषज्यते। तत्र मिदचो ऽन्त्यात्पर इति (१। १। ४७) वचनादस्थाने नुमः श्रवणं प्राप्नोति। इदमिह संप्रधार्यते। नुम् क्रियतामत्वमिति। अन्तरङ्गो नुम्। अन्तरङ्गत्वान्नुमि कृते पश्चादत्वं भविष्यति। कथमन्तरङ्गो नुम्। प्रकृत्याश्रयत्वात्। कथम्। नुम्विधौ धातोरुपदेशवचनं कर्तव्यम्। धातूपदेशावस्थायामेवेदितो नुम्भवतीति। तेनायमन्तरङ्गः। एवं तर्हि प्रतिपदं धिन्विकृण्व्योरत्वमुच्यते। नुम् सामान्यविहितः। सामान्येनेदितो नुम् विधीयते। तत्र प्रतिपदविधानादत्वे कृते अनिष्टे देशे नुमः श्रवणं प्रसज्येत। तस्मान्नुमनुषङ्गयोर्ग्रहणं क्रियते।

किमेतस्या ज्ञापने प्रयोजनम्। यत्रान्तरङ्गं प्रतिपदं च प्राप्नोति तत्र प्रतिपदं बलीयो भवति॥ ८३॥

1 प्रतिपाद॰ J 2 यदयं om. α ‖ अयं [[-1-]] धिन्॰ P_2 ‖ धिन्॰ : धि॰ J ‖ ॰व्योरश्चेति β 3 ॰षङ्गयो J 4 अत्र हि om. α ‖ अच्चेति : अचेति α : अश्चेति β ‖ वक्तव्य J 5 कृते : कृत्वे J ‖ नुम् : नम् J ‖ अनुषज्येते J ‖ मिदचो : मिदेचा J ‖ पर इ इति J 6 [नुमशु P_2] ‖ ॰प्रधार्येत J 7 [इत्य् P_1] ‖ नुम् : नं J ‖ अंतरगत्वान् J 8 अंतरेगो J ‖ आश्रयात् α 9 धातोरुप॰ : धातरोप॰ P_1 a. c. ‖ ॰आवस्थायास् J ‖ एवेदितो : एवोदितो B ‖ [भवति इति B] ‖ इति om. α 10 धिवि॰ J 11 [॰विहितस् P_2] ‖ सामान्येनेदितो Abhyankar : सामान्ये दितो α : सामान्येनोदितो P_2 : सामान्यनोदितो B ‖ [॰विधानात् α β] ‖ अत्वे : अर्थे J 12 [नुमशु P_2] ‖ प्रसज्यते J ‖ तस्मन्न नुम् B ‖ नुम् : नम् J ‖ षङ्गयो J 13 यत्रा॰ β : अत्रा॰ α 14 ८३ om. β

धातुप्रातिपदिकादनुबन्धप्रातिपदिकं बलीयः ॥ ८४ ॥

कथं ज्ञायते। यदिदं न वृद्भ्यश्चतुर्भ्य इति (७। २। ५९) चतुर्ग्रहणं करोति। अत्र चतुर्ग्रहणं न कर्तव्यम्। यदि न क्रियते कथं चतुर्भ्यः संप्रत्ययो भवति। वृतादींश्चतुरः पठित्वान्ते वृत्करणं करिष्यामः। न कर्तव्यम्। क्रियते न्यास एव। कृपू सामर्थ्ये वृद्यथा तदपि परीक्ष्यते। कृपेरपीट्प्रतिषेधः प्राप्नोति। इष्यते च कृपेः तासि च क्लृप इति (७। २। ६०)। तदेतदन्तरेण चतुर्ग्रहणं चतुर्भ्य एवेट्प्रतिषेधो भविष्यति। नार्थश्चतुर्ग्रहणेन। नैतद्वृत्करणं वृतादिपरिमाणार्थम्। किं तर्हि। द्युतादिपरिमाणार्थम्। कथम्। असत्येतस्मिंश्चतुर्ग्रहणे एतच्छक्यते वक्तुं वृत्करणं वृतादिपरिमाणार्थमिति। † क्रियमाणे हि चतुर्ग्रहणे ऽनन्तरस्य विधिर्वा भवति प्रतिषेधो वेति (परि० १३)। न वृतादिपरिमाणार्थमेव स्यात् †। द्युतादिपरिमाणार्थमेव। एवमपि चतुर्ग्रहणं न कर्तव्यम्। कथम्। द्युतादिभिर्वृतादींन्विशेषयिष्यामः। द्युतादीनां ये वृतादयस्तेभ्यो वृद्भ्य इति। इदं तर्हि प्रयोजनम्। स्यन्दू प्रस्रवणे। स्यन्द् स्य ति इति स्थिते न वृद्भ्यश्चतुर्भ्य इति (७। २। ५९) इट् प्रतिषेधो ऽस्ति। उदितो वेति च (c.f. ७। २। ४४)। तत्रोदित इति तदनुबन्धप्रतिपदकार्यं न वृद्भ्य इति धातुप्रातिपदिकम्। अनुबन्धप्रातिपदिकं बलीय इति कृत्वा वेट्

1 अनुबध० J 2 यदिदं न : यदनेन J β ‖ [वृद्भ्यः β] ‖ चतुग्रहणं J 3 करोति β : भवति α ‖ न om. β ‖ [चतुर्भ्यस् P$_2$] 4 [पठित्वा अंते B] ‖ न : नुम् B 5 करिष्यामः [[नुम् कर्तव्य]] न कर्तव्यम् P$_2$ ‖ न्यास एव β : एव न्यासे α ‖ य`था`P$_2$ ‖ परीक्ष्येत β 6 ०ईट्० : ०ईड्० P$_2$: ०ईज्० B ‖ च α : एव β ‖ कृपे J ‖ क्लृप : क्ल्यप α 7 चतुग्रहणं J ‖ [चतुर्भ्यः P$_2$] 8 [नार्थः α] ‖ ०परिमाणा० Abhyankar : ०परिणामा० codd. 9 ०परिमाणा० Abhyankar : ०परिणामा० codd. ‖ असत्य् α : सत्य् β ‖ [एतच् शक्यते B] 10 ०परिमाणा० Abhyankar : ०परिणामा० codd. ‖ ०आर्थेमिति J ‖ [ऽनन्त० α : अनंत० β] 11 ०परिमाणार्थम् Abhyankar : ०परिणार्थेम् J : ०परिणा`मा´र्थम् P$_1$ : ०परिणामार्थम् $\beta$ 12 ०परिणार्थम् J : ०परिणामार्थम् P$_1$ $\beta$ ‖ एव om. $\beta$ ‖ अपि [[चतुर्गह]] चतुर्ग्रहणं P$_2$ 13 ०आदिभिवृता० J ‖ विशेष्ययिष्यामः J ‖ द्युतादीर्णां J ‖ [वृतादयः $\beta$] 14 प्रस्रवणे : `प्र´स्रवणे P$_2$: स्रवणे B ‖ स्यन्द् स्य ति : स्यद् आस्य ति J : स्यंद स्य ति B ‖ इति om. β 15 उदितो β 16 [तत्र उदित P$_2$] ‖ तद० Abhyankar : वद० codd. ‖ अनुबंधः प्र० J 17 धातुप्रदिपदं P$_2$ ‖ अनुबन्धप्रतिपदिकं B a.c. ‖ [वेट् α : वा इट् β]

प्राप्नोति। चतुर्ग्रहणसामर्थ्याद्धातुप्रातिपदिकं भवति। ततो ज्ञायते अस्तीयं परिभाषेति।

किमेतस्या ज्ञापने प्रयोजनम्। कृत्रिमा क्रिया इति सिद्धं भवति। धातुप्रतिपदविहितः कृञः श चेत्य् (३।३।१००) अनुबन्धप्रतिपदं क्निं न बाधते॥ ८४॥

सामान्यातिदेशे विशेषानतिदेशः ॥ ८५ ॥

कथं ज्ञायते। यदयं गोत्रादङ्कवदित्य् (४।३।८०) आह।

कथं कृत्वा ज्ञापकम्। गोत्रान्तस्येदंवदिति वक्तव्यम्। तेन तस्येदमिति यो विहितः स भविष्यति। कश्च तस्येदमिति विहितः। अङ्कवदेव। एवं सिद्धे सति यदयं गोत्रादङ्कवदित्य् (४।३।८०) आह तज्ज्ञापयति अस्तीयं परिभाषेति। तेन तस्येदमिति (४।३।१२०) सामान्यं तच्छब्देन गृह्यते। षष्ठ्यन्तं तत्रैव स्यात्। तस्मादङ्कवचनमिति॥ ८५॥

18 [॰सामर्थ्यात् J] ‖ प्रातिपदं α : प्रतिपदं B ‖ [ज्ञायते ऽस्तीयं J] **20** कृत्रिमा : कृत्रिमः P_1 β **21** धातु॰ α : धातुः β ‖ अनुबन्धं प्रति॰ J **22** क्निं न Wujastyk : क्तिनं Abhyankar : क्रिन् शं J : क्रिनोर्क्तिन् शं P_1 : क्तिर्न β ‖ बाध्यते β ‖ ८४ om. β **1** ॰आत्`इ´देशे J **3** तस्येद् ति B **4** व्`इ´हितस् P_2 ‖ तस्येदमि वि॰ B ‖ इति [[यो]] विहितः P_1 (original saut.) ‖ विह्`इ´तः P_2 ‖ अंगवद् B ‖ एवैवं B **5** अकंवाद् J **6** तच्छब्देन : त शब्देन J **7** तत्रैव α : तत्रैवं β ‖ ८५ om. β

द्विबद्धं सुबद्धं भवति ॥ ८६ ॥

कथं पुनर्गम्यते इयं परिभाषा विद्यते इति। उच्यते यदयं पेषंवासवाहनधिषु चेति (६।३।५८) धिशब्दे उदकस्य उदभावं शास्ति।

कथं कृत्वा न वक्तव्यम्। उच्यते पूर्वसूत्रेण सिद्धत्वात्। उदकस्योदः संज्ञायामिति (६। ३। ५८)। संज्ञायामुदधिर्भविष्यति। एवं सिद्धे यद्द्वितीयसूत्रे पेषंवासवाहनधिषु चेति (६। ३। ५८) उदकस्योदभावं शास्ति तज्ज्ञापयति अस्तीयं परिभाषा द्विबद्धं सुबद्धं भवति।

किमेतस्या ज्ञापने प्रयोजनम्। यत्सकृद्बद्धं तन्न क्वचिद्भवत्यपि।

यथाचिरप्रकाशका विद्युदिति। प्रत्ययस्थात् कात्पूर्वस्यात इदाप्यसुप इति (७।३।४४)।एवमाद्यन्यदपि विमृश्य योजयितव्यम्॥ ८६ ॥

कृद्ग्रहणे गतिकारकपूर्वस्यापि ग्रहणम् ॥ ८७ ॥

कृदन्तस्य शब्दस्य ग्रहणे गतिपूर्वस्य कारकपूर्वस्य च ग्रहणं भवति।

कथं गम्यते इयं परिभाषास्तीति। यदयं व्याक्रोशीत्यत्र णच् कर्मव्यतिहार इत्य् (३।३।४३) आह।

कथं कृत्वैतज्ज्ञापकं भवति। एतत्किल सूत्रं न वक्तव्यम्। †ननु चानुपदिश्यमाने ऽस्मिन् य्वौ स्यातां न य्वाभ्यां पदान्ताभ्यां पूर्वौ

1 **द्विबद्धं** sic codd. The more usual form is **द्विर्बद्धं**, i.e. with the **सुच्प्रत्यय** signifying **आवृत्ति** 'repetition' **2** [पुनः B] ‖ गगम्यते J : ग[[ग]]म्यते P_1 ‖ यदयं α : यस्मात् β **3** पेषं॰ : पेष॰ β ‖ ॰वासवाहन॰ : ॰वाहनवास॰ α (variant of सूत्र; see below) : ॰वासनवाहन॰ B ‖ उदकस्य उदभावं : उदकशब्दोस्य उभावं J : उदकशब्दोदभावं P_1 (॰शब्दो स्य दभावं a.c.) : उदकस्येदभावं B **4** न om. P_2 **5** उदकस्य उद सं॰ P_2 ‖ ॰कस्योद सं B ‖ संज्ञायाम् : [संज्ञायासु J] : om. β **6** पेषं॰ : पेष॰ β ‖ ॰वासवाहन॰ : ॰वाहनवास॰ α (as above) : ॰वास[[न]]वाहन॰ P_2 : ॰वासनवाहन॰ B ‖ ॰ओदभावं : ॰अदभावं P_2 a.c. **7** परिभाषे P_2 a.c. **8** तन्न क्वचिन्न भव॰ β ‖ भव`त्य´पि P_2 **9** यथाचिर॰ : यथ तु चिर॰ J ‖ यथा अचिकाशिका β (i.e. om प्र) ‖ ॰प्रकाशका P_1: ॰प्रकाशिका P_2 β ‖ त् कात् om. J ‖ सुप : मुप J **10** [इति : इत्य् B] ‖ विमृष्य α P_2 ‖ ८६ om. β **2** ग्रहणे : ग्रहणे सति B **3** व्याक्रोशी[[-1-]]त्यत्र P_1 **4** अत्र णच् कर्म॰ : अत्रेच्छर्म॰ J : अत्र कर्म॰ P_1 : अत्र णः कर्म॰ β ‖ [॰व्यतिहारे इत्य् β] **5** [कृत्वा एतज् α] ‖ भवति : ब्रवीति P_2 : om. B **6** चानुपदिश्॰ : चापदिश्॰ B ‖ ऽस्मिं J ‖ य्वौ : वौ P_1 : ⟨-1-⟩ P_2 : सु⟨-2-⟩ B ‖ पदंताभ्यां J

तु ताभ्यामैजिति (७। ३। ३)।† न दोषः। अङ्गाधिकारादिह यस्मात्प्रत्ययविधिस्तदादि प्रत्यये गृह्यते (c.f. १। ४। १३)। ननु धात्वादिरेवांङ्गम्। व्याङो नैवाङ्गसंज्ञा। तस्मात्कर्मव्यतिहार इति (३। ३। ४३) न वक्तव्यम्। यद्विहितं तत्पश्यति अस्तीयं परिभाषेति। कृद्ग्रहणे गतिकारकपूर्वस्यापि ग्रहणमिति।

किमेतस्या ज्ञापने प्रयोजनम्। प्रयायिणे प्रयायिणः माषवापिणि व्रीहिवापिणीति प्रातिपदिकान्तनुम्विभक्तिषु चेति (८। ४। ११) णत्वं सिद्धं भवति॥ ८७॥

इति श्रीव्याडीयपरिभाषावृत्तिः समाप्ता॥

7 पूर्वौ तु : पूर्वे तु P_2 : (पूर्वो पा a.c.) : पूर्वो पा B ‖ अङ्गादिकारा॰ J **8** प्रत्यये α : प्रत्ययो β ‖ ननु : तत्र P_1 **9** [॰आदिः β] ‖ ॰आङ्गं B ‖ व्याङो : व्याने P_2 a.c. : व्याङेः B ‖ नाङ्गसंज्ञा α (i.e. om. एव) ‖ तस्मान्न P_1 ‖ ॰व्यतिहार इति : ॰व्यातहारेति J : ॰व्यतिहारेनेति P_1 **10** न om. J **11** इति om. α **12** माषवापानि β **13** व्रीहिवापानि इति β ‖ ॰वि`भ´क्तिषु B **14** सिद्धं भवती सिद्धं J : सिद्धं भवती`ति´ सिद्धम् P_1 ‖ ८७ om. codd. **15** श्रीव्यातीय॰ P_1 ‖ [॰वृत्तिस् β] ‖ After समाप्ता : शुभाय भवतात् P_1 : शुभाय भवताच्छ्रोतॄणामोन्तत्सत्। संवत्। शुभम् ⟨and then in Śāradā⟩ भद्रम् कल्याणम् B

Appendix: interpolated text

The following passage on the definition of the *vākya* is interpolated in manuscript J, between fols. 9^{r} and 10^{r} (see edition, notes to 8:4). Diplomatic transcription.

कत्वमेव न स्यात् किं तु मुख्यत्वमेव अथशब्दस्य यो सावर्थो मुख्यस्तेन सह संबंधो लक्ष्यमाणस्यार्थस्य दृष्ट इति तद्वारेण शब्दात्तस्यावगतिरित्यभिधीयते एवं सति यदि निरपेक्षः शब्दः स्वार्थप्रतिपादनद्वारेण लक्ष्यमाणमवगम इति सर्वदा तमर्थमव [end of fol. 9^{r}, start of fol. 9^{v}:] गमयेत् अथ सापेक्षः किं तस्यापेक्षणीयमित्याशंक्याह वक्तुर्वाच्यस्य वाक्यस्वरूपभेदावधारणात्लक्षणा षट्प्रकारैषा विवेक्तव्या सनीषिभिः यः परः प्रतिपत्तये वाक्यमुच्चारयति स वक्ता साकांक्षानां पदानामनेकानां समूहो वाक्यं शब्दे द्विविधमुखं लाक्षणिकं वाभिधाव्यापारमाश्रित्य यद्गोचरी क्रियते तद्वाच्यं एतेषां त्रयाणां वक्तादीनां व्यक्तसमस्तभिन्नानां देशकालावस्था स्वालक्षण्यगतसमस्तवस्तुसंयोजितयोः स्वभावभेदप्रपंचस्ततएषा लक्षणा षट्प्रकारा परामर्शकुशलैर्विवेचनीया तथाविध वक्त्रादिसामग्र्यपेक्षयैव शब्दानां स्वार्थमवगमयतां स्वार्थद्वारेण लक्ष्यमाणे र्थे संबंधस्य वृद्धिव्यवहारेण व्यवधारितत्त्वात् एतदुक्तं भवति न शब्दानामनवधारितलाक्षणिकार्थसंबंधानां लाक्षणिकमर्थं प्रति गमकत्वं नापि च तत्र साक्षादर्थग्रहः किं तर्हि वक्त्रादिसामग्र्यपेक्षया स्वार्थव्यवधानेनेति अत्र हि स्वार्थद्वारेण लक्ष्यमाणार्थाभिनिवेशितशब्दानां उक्ता [end of fol. 9^{v}, start of fol. 10^{r}:] पुनश्चासावेवाह लक्षणा हि लौक्येवेति अत्र हि प्रमाणसापेक्षाणां शब्दानां लक्ष्यमाणे र्थे प्रवृत्तिरुक्ता व्यवहारोपारूढानि प्रत्यक्षादीनि प्रमाणानि लोकशब्देनाभिधीयंते लोकचरितव्यव्यवहारगम्या परिगृहीतसंबंधशब्दनिष्ठेत्यर्थः तदुक्तं भट्टकुमारिलेन निरूढाः लक्षणाः कश्चित्सामार्थ्यादभिधानवत् क्रियंते सांप्रतं कश्चित्लश्चि

Indexes

Alphabetical index of *paribhāṣā*s

*Paribhāṣā*s in parentheses are mentioned in the commentary, but are not discussed explicitly by Vyāḍi. The index is to *paribhāṣā* running numbers.

अकृतव्यूहाः पाणिनीयाः ५९

अङ्गवृत्ते पुनर्वृत्तादविधिर्निष्ठितस्य ३०

अतन्त्रं तरनिर्देशः ६०

अनन्तरस्य विदिर्वा प्रतिषेधो वा १३

अनन्त्यविकारे ऽन्त्यसदेशस्य ..... ४६[b]

अनित्यमागमशासनम् ७०

अन्तरङ्गविधेः प्रतिपदविधिर्बलीयान् ८३

अपवादविषये ऽप्युत्सर्गसमावेशः ७७

अभिधानलक्षणाः कृत्तद्धितसमासाः ६६

अभ्यासविकारेष्वपवादा नोत्सर्गान्विधीन्बाधन्ते १७

अर्थवद्ग्रहणे नानार्थकस्य १

अर्थवशाद्विभक्तिविपरिणामो भवति ५७

अवयवलोपिनामतो लोपो नास्ति ८२

अव्यक्ते गुणसंदेहे नपुंसकलिङ्गं प्रयुज्यते ८१

असति संभवे बाधनं भवति १८

असिद्धं बहिरङ्गमन्तरङ्गे ३२

असिद्धं बहिरङ्गमन्तरङ्गे ७३

इतरेतराश्रयाण्यपि कार्याणि शास्त्रेषु प्रकल्पन्ते २१

इह शास्त्रे व्यवस्थितविभाषा भवति २८

उकार एवैको भाव्यमानो ऽपि सवर्णान्गृह्णाति ..... २७[b]

उक्तार्थानामप्रयोगः ..... ४६[a]

उच्चरितप्रध्वंसिनो ऽनुबन्धाः ८

उदित्स्ववर्गमेव गृह्णाति न सवर्णमात्रम् ४९

उभयत आश्रये नान्तादिवद्भवति ३९

(एकदेशविकृतमनन्यवद्) ३
एकयोगनिर्दिष्टानामप्येकदेशानुवर्तनम् २०
एकस्मिन्नपि व्यपदेशिवद्भावो ऽप्रातिपदिकग्रहणेन ५५
एकानुबन्धकृतमनित्यम् ४०
एकानुबन्धग्रहणे न द्व्यनुबन्धकस्य ४१

औपदेशिकप्रायोगिकयोरौपदेशिकस्य ग्रहणम् ४

कार्यकालं संज्ञापरिभाषम् ४५
कृत्रिमाकृत्रिमयोः कृत्रिमे संप्रत्ययः .... ५[a]
कृत्रिमाकृत्रिमयोरुभयगतिर्भवति .... ५[b]
कृद्ग्रहणे गतिकारकपूर्वस्यापि ग्रहणम् ८७

गौणमुख्ययोर्मुख्ये संप्रत्ययः ३

चानुकृष्टमुत्तरत्र नानुवर्तते ५३

तदेकदेशभूतस्तद्ग्रहणेन गृह्यते ५६
तदङ्गक्तस्तद्ग्रहणेन गृह्यते १४
तन्मध्यपतितस्तद्ग्रहणेन गृह्यते १५
ताच्छीलिकेषु वासरूपविधिर्नास्ति २४

द्विबद्धं सुबद्धं भवति ८६

धातुप्रातिपदिकादनुबन्धप्रातिपदिकं बलीयः ८४
(धातूपसर्गयोरन्तरङ्गकार्यं भवति) ३२

नञिवयुक्तमन्यसदृशाधिकरणं तथा ह्यर्थः ४८
न निमित्तिकार्यं नैमित्तिकस्य १६
न वर्णग्रहणेषु .... १[b]
न विकरणस्वरो लसार्वधातुकस्वरं बाधते ७८
नाजानन्तर्ये बहिष्ट्वप्रक्लृप्तिः ७४
नानुबन्धकृतमनेकाल्त्वम् ९
नानुबन्धकृतमसारूप्यम् १०
निमित्ताभावे नैमित्तिकस्याप्यभावो भवति ३५
निरनुबन्धकग्रहणे न सानुबन्धकस्य ४२

पर्जन्यवल्लक्षणप्रवृत्तिः ५८
पुनःप्रसङ्गविज्ञानात्सिद्धम् ७६

पुरस्तादपवादा अनन्तरान्विधीन्बाधन्ते ६
प्रकृतिग्रहणे णिजन्तस्यापि ग्रहणम् ६४
प्रकृतिग्रहणे यङ्लुगन्तस्यापि ग्रहणम् ५४
प्रकृतिवदनुकरणं भवति ८०
प्रतिपदविधानाद्योगविभागो गरीयान् ६८
प्रत्येकं वाक्यपरिसमाप्तिः २५
प्रधानान्वाचयशिष्टयोः प्रधानशिष्टे संप्रत्ययः ६१
प्रातिपदिकग्रहणे लिङ्गविशिष्टस्यापि ग्रहणम् २२
प्रातिपदिकविधौ तदन्तविधिर्नास्ति ६३

भवति च बहुव्रीहौ तद्गुणसंविज्ञानम् .... ५[c]
भाव्यमानो ऽण् सवर्णान्न गृह्णाति .... २७[a]
भूतपूर्वगतिरिह शास्त्रे संभवति ११

यं विधिं प्रत्युपदेशो ऽनर्थकः स विधिर्बाध्यते ४३
यस्य विदेर्निमित्तं नासौ बाध्यते ४४
येन नाप्राप्ते यो विधिरारभ्यते स तस्यैव बाधको भवति ३७
येन नाव्यवधानं तेन व्यवहिते ऽपि वचनप्रामाण्यात् ३४
योगविभागादिष्टसिद्धिः ६२

लक्षणप्रतिपदोक्तयोः प्रतिपदोक्तस्यैव ग्रहणम् २
लक्षणान्तरेण प्राप्नुवन्विधिरनित्यः ७२
लुग्विकरणालुग्विकरणयोरलुग्विकरणस्यैव ग्रहणम् ३८

वर्णैकदेशा वर्णग्रहणेन गृह्यन्ते २३
वसुप्रवृत्त्या इह शास्त्रे कार्यं भवति १२
(वर्त्स्यत्प्रवृत्त्या इह शास्त्रे कार्यं भवति १२
व्याख्यानतो विशेषप्रतिपत्तिर्न हि संदेहादलक्षणम् ५२

शब्दान्तरस्य प्राप्नुवन्विधिरनित्यो भवति ७१

संज्ञापूर्वको विधिरनित्यः ४७
संज्ञाविधौ तदन्तविधिर्नास्ति ६५
संनिपातलक्षणो विधिरनिमित्तं तद्विघातस्य ७
संनियोगशिष्टानामेकतरापाये उभयोरप्यभावः ३६
सकृद्गतौ विप्रतिषेधे यद्बाधितं बाधितमेव ७५
सकृद्गतौ विप्रतिषेधे यद्बाधितं बाधितमेव तत् ३१
सत्यपि संभवे बाधनं भवति १९
समानाश्रयमसिद्धं व्याश्रयं सिद्धं भवति ३३

समासान्तविधिरनित्यः ६९
समुदाये ऽपि वाक्यपरिसमाप्तिः २६
समुदायेषु शब्दाः प्रवृत्ता अवयवेष्वपि वर्तन्ते ७९
सर्वविधिभ्य इड्विधिर्बलवान् ५०
सर्वविधिभ्य लोपविधिर्बलवान् ५१
सर्वो द्वन्द्वो विभाषयैकवद्भवति ६७
सामान्यातिदेशे विशेषानतिदेशः ८५
स्वरविधौ व्यञ्जनमविद्यमानवत् २९

Page index to *paribhāṣās*

No. 1[a] 1
No. 1[b] 3
No. 2 5
No. 3 7
No. 4 9
No. 5[a] 11
No. 5[b] 12
No. 5[c] 12
No. 6 13
No. 7 14
No. 8 16
No. 9 17
No. 10 17
No. 11 18
No. 12 19
No. 13 20
No. 14 22
No. 15 23
No. 16 24
No. 17 24
No. 18 25
No. 19 26
No. 20 26
No. 21 27
No. 22 28
No. 23 30
No. 24 32
No. 25 33
No. 26 33
No. 27[a] 34
No. 27[b] 35
No. 28 35
No. 29 37
No. 30 38
No. 31 39
No. 32 40
No. 33 41
No. 34 43
No. 35 44
No. 36 44
No. 37 46
No. 38 48
No. 39 49
No. 40 50
No. 41 50
No. 42 51
No. 43 51
No. 44 52
No. 45 52
No. 46[a] 54
No. 46[b] 55
No. 47 55
No. 48 56
No. 49 57
No. 50 57
No. 51 58
No. 52 58
No. 53 59
No. 54 60
No. 55 60
No. 56 61
No. 57 62
No. 58 63
No. 59 63
No. 60 64
No. 61 65
No. 62 66
No. 63 67
No. 64 68
No. 65 68
No. 66 69
No. 67 69
No. 68 70
No. 69 70
No. 70 71
No. 71 72
No. 72 73
No. 73 73
No. 74 74
No. 75 75
No. 76 76
No. 77 77
No. 78 77
No. 79 77
No. 80 78
No. 81 80
No. 82 80
No. 83 81
No. 84 82
No. 85 83
No. 86 84
No. 87 84

Paribhāṣās cross-referenced in the text

No. 13 82
No. 36 65
No. 50 10
No. 59 45
No. 67 66
No. 76 39

Texts cited in the *Vyāḍīyaparibhāṣāvṛtti*

Sūtras of the *Aṣṭādhyāyī*

1.1.1 52
1.1.3 .... 20, 21
1.1.4 .... 47, 72, 78
1.1.5 .... 21, 48
1.1.6 .... 47, 48
1.1.15 .... 8, 9
1.1.22 .... 9, 68
1.1.24 14
1.1.27 12
1.1.28 13
1.1.29 13
1.1.31 13
1.1.42 21
1.1.43 21
1.1.45 27
1.1.47 81
1.1.48 30
1.1.50 34
1.1.52 53
1.1.53 53
1.1.55 .... 17, 53
1.1.59 73
1.1.61 44
1.1.62 58
1.1.66 26
1.1.67 26
1.1.68 2
1.1.69 34
1.1.72 67
1.2.1 3
1.2.4 41
1.2.9 57
1.2.14 41
1.2.18 .... 22, 57, 70
1.2.22 70
1.2.47 64
1.2.59 66
1.2.63 66
1.2.69 .... 29, 62
1.3.1 12
1.3.4 57
1.3.12 36
1.3.14 .... 12, 39
1.3.60 19
1.3.78 36
1.3.90 .... 35, 36
1.4.2 .... 75, 76
1.4.7 53
1.4.13 85
1.4.14 68
1.4.42 12
1.4.45 12
1.4.94 11
1.4.95 11
2.1.4 62
2.1.9 62
2.1.49 7
2.1.61 7
2.1.67 28
2.1.70 28
2.2.2 80
2.3.48 21
2.4.12 66
2.4.13 12
2.4.52 53
2.4.74 72
2.4.77 48
2.4.79 75
2.4.81 15
2.4.82 62
3.1.11 35
3.1.12 35
3.1.13 36
3.1.17 12
3.1.36 15
3.1.37 2
3.1.44 41
3.1.79 75
3.1.80 81
3.1.94 17
3.1.97 .... 18, 26
3.1.100 69
3.1.106 59
3.1.107 59
3.1.120 17
3.1.124 18
3.1.135 18
3.1.143 36
3.2.1 18
3.2.3 18
3.2.56 12
3.2.57 5
3.2.71 50
3.2.112 22
3.2.113 22
3.2.114 22
3.2.121 37
3.2.124 37
3.2.136 6
3.2.149 32
3.2.150 32
3.2.153 32
3.2.167 32
3.3.32 69
3.3.43 .... 84, 85
3.3.100 83
3.3.103 15
3.4.4 21
3.4.59 59
3.4.60 59
3.4.75 21
3.4.77 3
4.1.1 28
4.1.13 21
4.1.26 27
4.1.27 27
4.1.49 51
4.1.92 28
4.1.99 67
4.1.128 29
4.1.152 67
4.2.1 28
4.2.9 .... 50, 51
4.2.24 46
4.2.32 7
4.2.60 61
4.2.67 22
4.2.91 45

4.2.140 53
4.2.142 24
4.3.53 45
4.3.80 83
4.3.97 11
4.3.116 27
4.3.117 27
4.3.120 83
4.3.159 29
5.2.86 60
5.2.87 60
5.3.3 34
5.3.71 66
5.3.72 66
5.4.4 54
5.4.5 54
5.4.11 64
5.4.18 46
5.4.57 35
5.4.69 11
5.4.85 71
5.4.91 70
5.4.127 12
5.4.154 64
6.1.39 62
6.1.64 44
6.1.70 29
6.1.77 75
6.1.79 18
6.1.86 74
6.1.88 73
6.1.95 40
6.1.96 7
6.1.101 40
6.1.102 33
6.1.103 34
6.1.108 42
6.1.123 37
6.1.131 34
6.1.134 47
6.1.162 23
6.1.168 22
6.1.170 56
6.1.177 19
6.1.182 22
6.1.186 77
6.1.196 65
6.1.213 37
6.2.38 6
6.2.44 6
6.2.45 6
6.2.46 6
6.2.156 .... 50, 51
6.2.160 5
6.2.193 70
6.3.26 8
6.3.27 8
6.3.43 68
6.3.58 84
6.3.111 70
6.4.11 31
6.4.16 43
6.4.22 .... 41, 42, 45
6.4.24 .... 16, 41
6.4.35 39
6.4.36 39
6.4.37 .... 41, 75
6.4.48 .... 41, 72, 78
6.4.62 16
6.4.64 .... 42, 73
6.4.79 60
6.4.89 17
6.4.113 34
6.4.120 19
6.4.131 42
6.4.132 73
6.4.134 55
6.4.146 55
6.4.148 .... 50, 51
6.4.153 44
7.1.9 .... 51, 52
7.1.11 .... 23, 61
7.1.12 .... 51, 52
7.1.22 14
7.1.28 34
7.1.34 .... 51, 52
7.1.35 39
7.1.62 70
7.1.75 53
7.1.87 71
7.1.91 33
7.2.1 52
7.2.3 20
7.2.4 20
7.2.5 20
7.2.10 .... 46, 47
7.2.11 .... 9, 46, 47, 57
7.2.12 .... 4, 46, 47, 57
7.2.14 9
7.2.35 .... 46, 47
7.2.38 4
7.2.41 4
7.2.44 .... 46, 47, 48, 82
7.2.49 .... 46, 59
7.2.57 13
7.2.59 82
7.2.60 82
7.2.67 .... 19, 27
7.2.74 4
7.2.75 4
7.2.82 .... 62, 71
7.3.3 85
7.3.28 63
7.3.44 84
7.3.56 68
7.3.64 18
7.3.74 43
7.3.79 38
7.3.83 47
7.3.84 22
7.3.85 22
7.3.86 73
7.3.101 .... 14, 25, 29, 38
7.3.103 .... 23, 25
7.3.113 15
7.3.117 15
7.3.119 .... 15, 16
7.3.120 .... 53, 62
7.4.7 .... 63, 64
7.4.13 64
7.4.14 64
7.4.25 .... 14, 38
7.4.32 12
7.4.41 37
7.4.71 31
7.4.83 .... 24, 25
8.1.4 35
8.1.28 79
8.1.67 11
8.2.1 53
8.2.2 80

8.2.3 53
8.2.20 36
8.2.21 36
8.2.27 .... 41, 75
8.2.30 .... 57, 76
8.2.36 .... 1, 76
8.2.46 78
8.2.56 36
8.2.73 56
8.2.74 56
8.2.80 .... 35, 53, 54
8.2.81 54
8.2.88 69
8.3.14 70
8.3.79 8
8.3.82 7
8.4.1 31
8.4.11 85
8.4.18 77
8.4.46 24
8.4.66 38

Other texts

Kātyāyana *vārttika* 3.1.13.1 36
Kātyāyana *vārttika* 3.1.13.2 36
Kātyāyana *vārttika* 5.4.69.1 11
Kātyāyana *vārttika* 6.1.99.1 35
Padakāra 47
Rāmāyaṇa, yuddhakāṇḍa 9.22 77
Ślokavārttika 3.3.156.2 (= 7.4.41.1) 36
Uṇādisūtra 2.66 8

Metarules of Pāṇinian Grammar

Metarules of Pāṇinian Grammar

The *Vyāḍīyaparibhāṣāvṛtti*

Critically Edited with Translation and Commentary

Dominik Wujastyk

VOLUME II

To my parents, with endless love

Contents

VOLUME II

Abbreviations ix

Introduction to the translation and commentary xi
Paribhāṣās and Pāṇini's grammar xi
The authorship of the *Vyāḍīyaparibhāṣāvṛtti* xiii
The various Vyāḍis xiv
The authorship of the *Saṅgraha* xxiv
Summary xxvii
The *Vyāḍīyaparibhāṣāvṛtti* xxvii
The Translation xxix

Translation 1

Paribhāṣā 1[a] 3
Paribhāṣā 1[b] 11
Paribhāṣā 2 20
Paribhāṣā 3 32
Paribhāṣā 4 42
Paribhāṣā 5[a] 49
Paribhāṣā 5[b] 54
Paribhāṣā 5[c] 58
Paribhāṣā 6 64
Paribhāṣā 7 69
Paribhāṣā 8 83
Paribhāṣā 9 85
Paribhāṣā 10 88
Paribhāṣā 11 91
Paribhāṣā 12 95
Paribhāṣā 13 98
Paribhāṣā 14 103
Paribhāṣā 15 105
Paribhāṣā 16 107
Paribhāṣā 17 109
Paribhāṣā 18 111
Paribhāṣā 19 113
Paribhāṣā 20 115
Paribhāṣā 21 117
Paribhāṣā 22 119
Paribhāṣā 23 125
Paribhāṣā 24 127
Paribhāṣā 25 129
Paribhāṣā 26 130
Paribhāṣā 27[a] 132
Paribhāṣā 27[b] 133
Paribhāṣā 28 134
Paribhāṣā 29 137
Paribhāṣā 30 139
Paribhāṣā 31 141
Paribhāṣā 32 144
Paribhāṣā 33 149
Paribhāṣā 34 154
Paribhāṣā 35 157
Paribhāṣā 36 159
Paribhāṣā 37 163
Paribhāṣā 38 166
Paribhāṣā 39 168
Paribhāṣā 40 169

Paribhāṣā 41 . . . 171
Paribhāṣā 42 . . . 173
Paribhāṣā 43 . . . 174
Paribhāṣā 44 . . . 176
Paribhāṣā 45 . . . 178
Paribhāṣā 46[a] . . . 181
Paribhāṣā 46[b] . . . 183
Paribhāṣā 47 . . . 184
Paribhāṣā 48 . . . 186
Paribhāṣā 49 . . . 188
Paribhāṣā 50 . . . 190
Paribhāṣā 51 . . . 192
Paribhāṣā 52 . . . 194
Paribhāṣā 53 . . . 196
Paribhāṣā 54 . . . 198
Paribhāṣā 55 . . . 200
Paribhāṣā 56 . . . 203
Paribhāṣā 57 . . . 205
Paribhāṣā 58 . . . 208
Paribhāṣā 59 . . . 211
Paribhāṣā 60 . . . 214
Paribhāṣā 61 . . . 217
Paribhāṣā 62 . . . 220
Paribhāṣā 63 . . . 222
Paribhāṣā 64 . . . 224
Paribhāṣā 65 . . . 226
Paribhāṣā 66 . . . 228
Paribhāṣā 67 . . . 230
Paribhāṣā 68 . . . 231
Paribhāṣā 69 . . . 233
Paribhāṣā 70 . . . 235
Paribhāṣā 71 . . . 236
Paribhāṣā 72 . . . 238
Paribhāṣā 73 . . . 240
Paribhāṣā 74 . . . 243
Paribhāṣā 75 . . . 246
Paribhāṣā 76 . . . 248
Paribhāṣā 77 . . . 250
Paribhāṣā 78 . . . 252
Paribhāṣā 79 . . . 254
Paribhāṣā 80 . . . 256
Paribhāṣā 81 . . . 259
Paribhāṣā 82 . . . 261
Paribhāṣā 83 . . . 263
Paribhāṣā 84 . . . 265
Paribhāṣā 85 . . . 268
Paribhāṣā 86 . . . 270
Paribhāṣā 87 . . . 272

Bibliography **275**

Citation indexes **283**
Sūtras of the *Aṣṭādhyāyī* . . . 283
Vārttikas from the *Mahābhāṣya* . . . 289
Prose citations from the *Mahābhāṣya* . . . 290
Citations from the *Kāśikāvṛtti*, and the commentaries *Nyāsa* and *Padamañjarī* . . . 295
Citations from the *Siddhāntakaumudī*, and the commentaries *Bālamanoramā* and *Tattvabodhinī* . . . 296
Other commentators' *paribhāṣās* . . . 297
Other texts cited . . . 300
Citations from the *Dhātupāṭha* . . . 301
Index of word forms discussed . . . 302

Abbreviations

For the text editions used, see the bibliography.

ABORI	*Annals of the Bhandarkar Oriental Research Institute*
BORI	Bhandarkar Oriental Research Institute
Ca.	*Cāndravyākaraṇa*
Dhp.	*Dhātupāṭha*
K.	Kātyāyana's *vārttikas*
KV.	*Kāśikāvṛtti*
Mbh.	*Mahābhāṣya*
NCC	*New Catalogus Catalogorum* (Raghavan 1968)
P.	Pāṇini's *Aṣṭādhyāyī*
PK.	*Prakriyākaumudī*
SK.	*Siddhāntakaumudī*
VP.	*Vākyapadīya*

Introduction to the translation and commentary

Paribhāṣās and Pāṇini's grammar

Paribhāṣās are auxiliary hypotheses which seek to improve or explain the procedures of Pāṇini's grammar.

Pāṇini provides four thousand rules, plus a list of roots and some nominal stems. With this equipment he accounts for the correct utterances of the Sanskrit language. Either we may use his system to make predictions of those sentences which will correctly express the intention of the speaker, or we may apply the system the other way around and use if to assign a structural analysis to a sentence which already exists and is before us as an abstract object. Thus, if we wish to express 'I shall go', Pāṇini's grammar leads us through a series of selections to the forms *gamiṣyāmi* or *gantāsmi*. Alternatively, if we find a form *abhavat* and are in doubt as to its construction and meaning we can turn to the grammar and from it classify the form as *tiṅanta, laṅ, ekavacana* and so on. This is in no way to deny that meaning resides primarily in sentences: a grammar may be viewed as the abstraction of the results of examining many sentences.

If we consider Pāṇini's grammar as a theory of the Sanskrit language (just as Newton's mechanics is a theory of the dynamics of physical objects), we shall immediately wish to test it, to find out how good it is. There are multitudes of words and sentences which corroborate the theory. But in a few cases the predictions of the theory are wrong. Thus, for example, if a speaker wishes to express the plural of the word *śata* 'hundred', he will find that the strict application of Pāṇini's rules predicts the form **śatan* (see argument § 7.2, p. 73). We know that this is a wrong form because it does not correspond to language as it exists, i.e., to usage which contains the form *śatāni* in this meaning.

Rather than giving up Pāṇini's grammar as wrong in such cases, it is natural to try to improve the theory. The tradition introduces extra rules to correct the situation. These are the *paribhāṣās*, a term which may be translated as 'metarules', 'principles', 'theorems' or 'auxiliary hypothesis'. In the above example, if we introduce the auxiliary hypothesis no. 7 about concomitant items then we get the correct prediction of the form *śatāni* 'hundreds'. In this way many shortcomings of the grammar can be rectified.

There is a nucleus of about one hundred such extra-*Aṣṭādhyāyī paribhāṣās* which is generally accepted; our Vyāḍi commentator discusses eighty-seven and incidentally cites two others. It is a moot point whether or not Pāṇini actually had some of these *paribhāṣās* in mind as he composed his grammar; probably he did have at least some of them in mind, whether explicitly or not. A study of the earliest *mīmāṃsā* from this point of view might throw some light on this question. About fifty *paribhāṣās* are given explicitly by Pāṇini, but these are straightforward instructions for the correct reading of his grammar, and are non-controversial.[1]

Kātyāyana has used a number of *paribhāṣās*, or *paribhāṣā*-like statements, but has not normally entered into arguments for or against them.[2]

It is with Patañjali that we find the first really developed discussions of *paribhāṣās*. His *Mahābhāṣya* is full of short passages in which a possible redundancy or fault of some kind is identified in a *sūtra*, and then this irregularity is shown to intimate some general principle which renders the *sūtra* efficient and furthermore is of use in other situations too. These passages are very formulaic; again and again the following phrases occur:

*ācāryapravṛttir jñāpayati ... [paribhāṣā] ... bhavati yad ayam ... [sūtra] ... karoti [*or *śāsti]*	The teacher's procedure intimates that ... (*paribhāṣā*) ... exists, because he teaches the following ... (*sūtra*).
kathaṃ kṛtvā jñāpakam ...	How come this is an intimation? ... (the irregularity)?
paśyati tv ācāryaḥ ... [paribhāṣā]	But the teacher observes that ... the (*paribhāṣā*).

This approach has been formalized by the tradition into a series of four steps which lead to the acceptance of a *paribhāṣā*. They are:

1. *(ādau) vaiyarthyam*
2. *(paścāt) iṣṭārthajñāpanam*
3. *(tataḥ) svāṃśe cāritārthyam*
4. *anyatra phalam*

The starting point, *vaiyarthyam* 'redundancy', means that there must be something in one of Pāṇini's rules which is redundant or inconsistent, be it a word or even a syllable. *Iṣṭārthajñāpanam* 'suggesting a desired sense' means that the redundancy must intimate some desired meaning. The statement of this meaning is the *paribhāṣā* itself, which is formulated at this stage. *Svāṃśe cāritārthyam* 'efficacy on its own behalf' means that the suggestion which arose at stage two must remove or resolve the redundancy of stage one, rendering Pāṇini's statement operationally meaningful to the highest degree. *Anyatra phalam* 'additional effect' means that the suggestion must not only satisfy the requirements

[1]See Abhyankar, *Paribhāṣāsaṃgraha* (Poona: BORI, 1967), pp. 4–5.
[2]Ibid., p. 6.

of its genesis; it must also be of use in solving problems elsewhere. This is the *prayojana* term. Argument § 9.1 (page 86) gives a particularly clear and simple example of this procedure.

The fourth stage in the above scheme is particularly important as it ensures that the overall information content of the grammatical theory is not reduced.[3]

Patañjali did not separate the discussion of *paribhāṣās* from his other grammatical discussions, but in later times a separate literature grew up around the *paribhāṣās*. Authors would select a list of these maxims and argue the pros and cons of accepting each one, giving examples and counter-examples. The *Vyāḍīyaparibhāṣāvṛtti* is one such work, and may be the earliest surviving one.

The authorship of the *Vyāḍīyaparibhāṣāvṛtti*

The argument about Vyāḍi's identity has up to the present time has been for or against one single candidate. Wezler did briefly mention a lexicographer Vyāḍi,[4] but otherwise only the ancient philosopher of language mentioned by Kātyāyana in the *Mahābhāṣya* has been considered.

Furthermore, there has been no real examination of whether the name Vyāḍi which appears in the manuscript colophons should be taken as applying to the author of the *vṛtti* or of the *paribhāṣās* themselves. The most natural way of reading the title *Vyāḍīyaparibhāṣāvṛtti* – which appears in all the manuscripts – is, I would argue, 'A commentary on the *paribhāṣās* of Vyāḍi'. In other words, it is the rules which are by Vyāḍi, not the commentary. This impression is underlined by the fact that one of the manuscripts of the text, P_2, is accompanied by a listing of the *paribhāṣās* alone, entitled *Vyāḍīyaparibhāṣāpāṭha*, which can only be translated, 'The list of Vyāḍi's *paribhāṣās*'. Such bare listings of *paribhāṣās* ascribed to Vyāḍi are not rare in other manuscripts too.[5] It could, at a stretch, be argued that this title means 'Vyāḍi's listing of [someone else's] *paribhāṣās*', thus leaving the door open to interpreting the commentary as also being by Vyāḍi, but this is an unnatural reading of the compound.

This leaves us with 'Vyāḍi' as the name of a compiler of a list of *paribhāṣās*, and a commentary on these by an anonymous author. As Abhyankar pointed out, there is a living tradition amongst *vaiyākaraṇas* that a Vyāḍi was the first writer of *paribhāṣās*,[6] a tradition also mentioned by Haribhāskara at the end of his *Paribhāṣābhāskara*.[7] But this tradition concerns the *paribhāṣās* themselves; it says nothing of a commentary.

There is, therefore, no strong evidence that even the manuscript scribes of the *commentary* before us thought it was by Vyāḍi. Rather, the evidence points

[3] See D. Wujastyk, "Do Paribhāṣās Wrongly Immunize Pāṇini's Theory Against Criticism?", in *Proceedings of the International Seminar on Studies in the* Aṣṭādhyāyī *of Pāṇini* (Poona: Univ. of Poona, 1983), pp. 97–103, for a fuller discussion of this point.

[4] A. Wezler, *Paribhāṣā IV, V und XV. Untersuchungen zur Geschichte der einheimischen indischen grammatischen Scholastik* (Berlin, Zürich: Gehlen, 1969), p. 23.

[5] V. Raghavan *et al*, *New Catalogus Catalogorum* (Madras: Univ. of Madras, 1968–), volume 11, p. 219b, lists over a dozen such MSS.

[6] Abhyankar, *Paribhāṣāsaṃgraha*, p. 11.

[7] Ibid., p. 374.

to the ascription of the *paribhāṣā* list itself to Vyāḍi, while the commentary remains anonymous.

But even if we were to accept the idea that the commentary was by an author called Vyāḍi, as Abhyankar does, there are many references to this name in Sanskrit literature and most of these references must be to different people. There is no *a priori* reason to think that the *paribhāṣās* or the commentary before us are by the ancient Vyāḍi mentioned in the *Mahābhāṣya*.

The various Vyāḍis

Before plumping for a particular identity for our author or authors, let us summarize the information we have on the various Vyāḍis. As far as possible the following sections are arranged chronologically.

Kātyāyana's Vyāḍi (before *ca.* 250. BC)

This is the best known and earliest Vyāḍi. He is a philosopher of language mentioned in *vārttika* 45 on P.1.2.64: *dravyābhidhānaṃ vyāḍiḥ* 'the signification [of a word] is a [particular] thing, [says] Vyāḍi.' This view is opposed to that of Vājapyāyana, mentioned earlier in *vārttika* 35, who argues that the prime signification of a word is a generic form, or type. These two viewpoints have been very important in the development of the Sanskrit philosophy of language and have been discussed clearly by Matilal.[8] Vyāḍi's view is closer to that of ordinary-language philosophers, while Vājapyāyana's is more bizarre, but better suited to the assumptions of the *mīmāṃsā* theorists.

Prātiśākhya Vyāḍi (between Pāṇini and Patañjali, i.e., before 140 BC?)

A Vyāḍi is mentioned in five of the *sūtras* of the *Ṛgvedaprātiśākhya*.[9] His views cover certain usages of accent and *abhinidhāna*, a phonetic 'implosion'[10] which, according to Vyāḍi, disappears in most cases. He is classed with Śākalya and Gārgya as using the term *samāpādya* for various *sandhis* and finally he regards *anusvāra* either as pure nose sound (*nāsikya*) or as a nasalized vowel (*anunāsika*).

Apart from enlarging a little on these matters, the commentator Uvaṭa (11th century, Gujarat) also ascribes to Vyāḍi some views on the nature of the *svarita* accent (*sub sūtras* 3.8, 3.18). One suspects that Uvaṭa is not meaning to be too specific here; by mentioning Vyāḍi's name he is only name-dropping. On the other hand, this may be a reference to a tradition from *Vedavikṛti* circles

[8]B. K. Matilal, *Epistemology, Grammar and Logic in Indian Philosophical Analysis* (The Hague, Paris: Mouton, 1971), pp. 106–22.

[9]M. D. Shastri (ed)., *The Ṛgveda-Prātiśākhya with the commentary of Uvaṭa ... vol. II, text in sūtra form ....* (Allahabad: The Indian Press, 1931), nos. 3.23, 3.28, 6.43, 13.31, and 13.37.

[10]Cf. W. S. Allen, *Phonetics in Ancient India* (London: OUP, 1953), pp. 71–75.

(see p. xxiii below), in which case the chronology of that Vyāḍi would have to be revised back by several centuries.

In these sources Vyāḍi's name appears in the variant form Vyāḷi.

Patañjali's Vyāḍi (before 140 BC)

Patañjali mentions the name Vyāḍi only once, in paraphrasing Kātyāyana's *vārttika* as mentioned above.

Patañjali also mentions the derivative word Vyāḍīya, in a list of names including Āpiśala, Pāṇinīya and Gautamīya.[11] The names refer to boarding students of Apiśali etc., and when compounded in a *dvandva* the first member retains its normal accent (P.6.2.36). All we learn here is that a Vyāḍi had live-in students.

The *Gaṇapāṭha* Vyāḍi (between Pāṇini and 7th cent. AD).

The name Vyāḍi arises three times in connection with the *Gaṇapāṭha*.

In the *krauḍyādi* list the name Vyāḍi occurs (67.3) as forming the feminine Vyāḍyā (cf. P.4.1.80). In the *gahādi* list, the name Vyāḍi occurs (74.34) as forming the derivative Vyāḍīya (cf. P.4.2.138). In the *chāttryādi* list the name Vyāḍi occurs (91.4) as receiving an acute on its first syllable when followed by *śālā*. Thus: *vyā́ḍiśālā* 'the hall or abode of Vyāḍi' (cf. P.6.2.86).

Apart from these citations, the *Gaṇapāṭha* mentions the word *vyāḍa* 'cunning' (231.4) which makes a *tatpuruṣa* with an accompanying word in the locative: *akṣeṣu vyāḍaḥ akṣavyāḍa* 'cunning at dice' (cf. P.2.1.40). The word *saṃvyāḍa* occurs in the same context (231.14). Finally, the word *avyaḍa* occurs in the *svāgatādi* list (256.6) as forming the derivative Vyāḍi and not Vaiyāḍi, as P.7.3.3 would otherwise prescribe (see P.7.3.7).

From these examples we deduce that the *Gaṇapāṭha* knows a descendant of Vyaḍa called Vyāḍi, who has followers called Vyāḍīyas, a home called a *śālā*, and a feminine relative Vyāḍyā.

Bṛhatkathā Vyāḍi (before AD 600).

The *Bṛhatkathā* of Guṇāḍhya (before 600 AD) was written in a language called *paiśācī bhāṣā* and contained a series of adventure stories, probably of Buddhist origin.[12] It has even been conjectured that the work was composed as early as the first of second century AD. The work is no longer extant, but is best known from several collections of stories which are reworkings of translations of the original *Bṛhatkathā*. Two of these representations are from Kashmir: the *Bṛhatkathāmañjarī* by Kṣemendra (*ca.* AD 1037), the *Kathāsaritsāgara* by Somedeva (*ca.* AD 1070).[13] Another version, the *Bṛhatkathāślokasaṅgraha* by

[11] Mbh. III.125:11.

[12] On the *Bṛhatkathā* and its descendants, see A. B. Keith, *A History of Sanskrit Literature* (Oxford: OUP, 1920), chapter 12.

[13] The *Haracaritacintāmaṇi* by Jayadratha (*ca.* AD 1203–26) is partly based on these two works, and chapter 27 reproduces the Vyāḍi material that interests us.

Budhasvāmin (8th or 9th cent.), is known from Nepalese manuscripts.[14] It is the Kashmiri version that is of interest to us, for it opens with an episode involving a grammarian Vyāḍi.

The central figure of the episode is Vararuci, also known as Kātyāyana. He is involved in various escapades which result in his becoming the pupil of the teacher Varṣa in Pāṭaliputra. His co-students are Vyāḍi, Indradatta, and eventually even Pāṇini. All this occurs in the reign of the king Nanda. Vyāḍi is depicted as an elder contemporary of Kātyāyana and Pāṇini, being the son of a brāhmaṇa called Karamba or Karambaka, from the city of Vitāsī or Vetasa. After studying grammar from Varṣa, Vyāḍi becomes peripherally involved in some adventures concerning the king, and eventually announces that he is leaving to perform austerities. He vanishes from the story for good. Legend has it that Nanda was the predecessor, or one of the predecessors of Candragupta Maurya (*fl.* 321 BC). It is noteworthy that this whole episode is missing from the Nepalese version of the tale. This could mean that the story is a Kashmiri addition, and did not form part of the original *Bṛhatkathā* at all. However, it is more likely that we are dealing here with two recensions of the *Bṛhatkathā*, and that Kṣemendra and the others were faithfully representing the work as it had reached them, and that the Vararuci episode was part of the work from an early time.

Bhartṛhari's Vyāḍi (before 5th cent.)

Bhartṛhari does not mention Vyāḍi's name in the *Vākyapadīya*, or *Prakīrṇakāṇḍa* but he does in the *Dīpikā*, his commentary on the *Mahābhāṣya*. Bhartṛhari is very important in this context as being the first author to link the name Vyāḍi with the legendary grammatical compendium called the *Saṅgraha*.

In the *Dīpikā* Bhartṛhari twice refers to Vyāḍi's opinion that words signify *dravya* 'particular things':[15]

> *kiṃ punar ākṛtiḥ padārtha āhosvit dravyam| ācāryāṇāṃ vipratipatteḥ saṃdehaḥ| vājapyāyanasyākṛtiḥ| vyāḍes tu dravyaṃ*
>
> 'Is the referent of a word a form or a substance?' There is uncertainty because the ācāryas do not agree: a form, according to Vājapyāyana; a substance according to Vyāḍi

and again:[16]

> *tathā dravyam api abhidhīyate upalakṣaṇaṃ gotvādaya iti vyāḍimatam|*
>
> But from Vyāḍi's point of view, the substance too is [directly] denoted, while 'being a cow' etc., is a subsidiary qualification.

---

[14] As well as Keith, *A History*, see E. P. Maten, *Budhasvāmin's Bṛhatkathāślokasaṃgraha* (Leiden: Brill, 1973).

[15] J. Bronkhorst (ed. and tr.), *Mahābhāṣyadīpikā of Bhartṛhari. Fascicule IV: Āhnika I* (Poona: BORI, 1987), p. 15:3–4, the commentary on Mbh.I.6:8. The translations are my own.

[16] Ibid., p. 16:17–18, the commentary on Mbh.I.6:9.

These views are entirely derivable from the *vārttika* which mentions Vyāḍi, and therefore do not imply access to any special textual tradition of Vyāḍi's work.

The third mention of Vyāḍi's name, however, introduces a new association. In the course of a discussion of the precise meaning of the word '*siddha*', Bhartṛhari says:[17]

> *kāryatvapratiṣedhāt siddhatvāpratiṣedhāc ca niścitaṃ saṃgrahe nityaparyāyavācinaḥ| ihāpi tad eva| kutaḥ| saṃgraho py asyaiva śāstrasyaikadeśaḥ tatraikataṃtratvād Vyāḍeś ca prāmāṇyād ihāpi tathaiva siddhaśabda upāttaḥ|*
>
> — And because '*kāryatva*' is prohibited and '*siddhatva*' is not prohibited, the latter's mention in the *Saṅgraha* is certainly as a synonym for *nitya* 'permanent'. It is the same here as well.
>
> — Why?
>
> — The *Saṅgraha* too is a part of this same discipline. So because it is a single system, and because of Vyāḍi's importance, the word *siddha* 'valid' is used in just the same way.

For Bhartṛhari, Vyāḍi was clearly the author of a work called *Saṅgraha* which discussed, according to Patañjali, whether or not words are eternal or manufactured, and decided that grammar must be written in either case.[18]

The fact that Bhartṛhari feels the need to assert strongly that the *Saṅgraha* really must be counted as a grammatical work suggests that its real sphere was probably not pure grammar. Perhaps it was a philosophical or logical treatise.

From this point onwards grammarians use the name Vyāḍi in two distinct contexts: as the proponent of the *dravya* theory of signification, mentioned in the *vārttika*, and as the author of the *Saṅgraha*, usually expressing ideas concerning the eternality of words, and the relationship between word and sense. We may refer, for clarity's sake, to *vārttika*-Vyāḍi and *Saṅgraha*-Vyāḍi. There are also many references throughout the literature to 'the author of the *Saṅgraha*', who is assumed by most scholars to be identical with *Saṅgraha*-Vyāḍi. The *Saṅgraha* question will be discussed below (p. xxiv).

Bhartṛhari is traditionally taken to be the author of the commentary called the *Vṛtti* on the *Vākyapadīya* (*kāṇḍas* one and two). There has been some debate about his authorship but it seems that in the light of present evidence the traditional view is acceptable.[19] The *Vṛtti* is preserved in only two manuscripts and the text is fragmentary towards the end.[20] The *Vṛtti* on the first *kāṇḍa* mentions the *Saṅgraha*, the Saṅgrahakāra, but not the name Vyāḍi. I have not had access to the fragmentary *Vṛtti* on the second kāṇḍa.

[17] Ibid., p. 19:29–20:2, commenting on Mbh.I.6:21.

[18] Mbh.I.6:12–14.

[19] See G. Cardona, *Pāṇini: A survey of research* (The Hague: Mouton, 1976), pp. 297 f.

[20] Ibid., note 502.

The *Kāśikā*'s Vyāḍi (before 650)

Our earliest recension of the *Gaṇapāṭha* is embedded in the *Kāśikā*, so the remarks above on *Gaṇapāṭha*-Vyāḍi have their *terminus ad quem* with this text.

Apart, then from citations in the *Gaṇapāṭha*, the authors of the *Kāśikā*, mention the name Vyāḍi in two places. In commenting on P.2.4.21 Jayāditya (*d.* 661) gives us the cryptic example: *vyāḍyupajñaṃ daśahuṣkaraṇam* 'the making of ten *huṣ*s, invented by Vyāḍi' (KV.II.266). This is meant to illustrate something originally invented by Vyāḍi, but no commentator, ancient or modern, has any clear idea what the 'making of ten *huṣ*s' might be. A variant appears in Vāmana's remarks on P.6.2.14 (KV.IV.18), where he speaks not of *daśahuṣkaraṇa* but of *duṣkaraṇa*, 'doing *duṣ*' or 'doing with difficulty', an achievement attributed by Jayāditya to Apiśali, instead of Vyāḍi (comment on P.4.3.115, KV.III.698). In the Devanāgarī script *duṣ* (दुष्) and *huṣ* (हुष्) can be confused, and *duṣ* (दुष्) could easily be a scribal contraction of *daśahuṣ* (दशहुष्). But this brings us no closer to understanding what is meant. The commentators Jinendrabuddhi and Haradatta (see below) are interesting but not illuminating.

One fact can be salvaged from these curious statements of the *Kāśikā*. The Vyāḍi they are referring to cannot in any obvious way be identified with *vārttika*-Vyāḍi or *Saṅgraha*-Vyāḍi.

The grammar of Candra (*ca.* 450), which stands in some sort of relationship with the *Kāśikā*, does not have any mention of these examples. It mentions the name Vyāḍi only in the commentary on the rule which derives 'Vyāḍi' from the ancestral name 'Vyaḍa' (Ca.6.1.18; cf. P.7.3.7), and *Gaṇapāṭha*-Vyāḍi above).

The lexicographer Vyāḍi (before *ca.* 6th cent. to *ca.* 1100)

With the lexicographer Vyāḍi we move on to slightly, but only slightly, firmer ground. The information on this Vyāḍi has been summarized by Vogel and Birwé.[21]

The lexicographer Vyāḍi was the author of a synonymic verse dictionary called the *Utpalinī* (or sometimes *Utpala*(*mālā*)). It is only known now from citations. It may have been a large work, and regarded highly, since it is said by several classical authors to have been among the sources of Amara's *Nāmaliṅgānuśāsana*, and is fairly widely quoted by other lexicographical authors, especially Hemacandra (*b.*1089). It is still possible that manuscripts of the work may come to light.

From the available quotations, the work seems to show a close acquaintance with Tantric Mahāyāna Buddhism. A reference to the śakti Tārā, the feminine consort of the Bodhisattva Avalokiteśvara, may point to a terminus a quo of

[21] C. Vogel, *Indian Lexicography*, vol. V, part II, fasc. 4. of *A History of Indian Literature*, ed. by Jan Gonda (Wiesbaden: Harrassowitz, 1979), pp. 306–8; R. Birwé, "Fragments from three lost Kośas: Vyāḍi's Utpalinī II", *Journal of the American Oriental Society* **87** (1967), pp. 39–52.

about the sixth century when, according to the Tibetan historian Tārānātha (*b.*1575), the tantric Avalokiteśvara cult was introduced.[22]

Vyāḍi's *Utpalinī* is quoted by Hemacandra (*fl.* 1089–1172/73) which fixes his upper limit, but if it is true that the *Utpalinī* was known to Amara, this would push its date closer to the lower limit.

An examination of the surviving verses from the *Utpalinī* shows no particular concordances with the *Vyāḍīyaparibhāṣāvṛtti*.[23]

Jinendrabuddhi's Vyāḍi (before *ca.* 700)

Jinendrabuddhi, commenting on the *Kāśikā*, has given us what may be the first clear reference to a Vyāḍi who propounded *paribhāṣās*. Under P.2.4.21, where the *Kāśikā* has referred to *daśahuṣkaraṇa*, Jinendrabuddhi explains:[24]

> *Vyāḍir apy atra yugapatkālabhāvinām̐ vidhīnām̐ madhye daśa huṣkaraṇāni kṛtvā paribhāṣitavān pūrvam̐ pūrvam̐ kālam iti*
>
> Vyāḍi too, having made ten *huṣkaraṇas* here amongst rules which apply simultaneously, explained (*paribhāṣ°*) that the time is one before another.

The passage is far from clear, but the sense seems to be that by sometimes using *huṣkaraṇas*, Vyāḍi was able to decide the order of simultaneously applicable rules. Jinendrabuddhi's use of the verb *paribhāṣitavān* can only be meant to indicate that this Vyāḍi was the author of *paribhāṣās*.

Jinendrabuddhi mentions Vyāḍi again under P.7.2.11 where he glosses the *Kāśikā*'s *kecit* 'some people' as *śvabhūtivyāḍiprabhṛtayaḥ* 'Śvabhūti, Vyāḍi *et al.*'.[25] These scholars are said to read the marker *g* into P.7.2.11 which, through *sandhi*, makes no apparent difference to the final form of the rule. (By this means they include forms derived by P.3.2.139 in the sphere of P.7.2.11, thus accounting for *bhūṣṇu* and proscribing **bhaviṣṇu*.)

In a third reference, under P.7.3.7, the *Kāśikā* derives 'Vyāḍi' from 'Vyaḍa' and Jinendrabuddhi takes the derivation a stage further, saying that 'Vyaḍa' is so called because his *aḍa* has gone away (*vigata*).[26] It is only with Haradatta (see below) that we find out what an *aḍa* is.

Helārāja's Vyāḍi (before *ca.* 10th cent.)

Helārāja's date is not absolutely certain, but he is probably the teacher of Abhinavagupta (*ca.* 1000). He precedes Kaiyaṭa (*fl.* 11th century) and is probably

---

[22]Tārānātha, *Tārānātha's History of Buddhism in India*, tr. Lama Chimpa and Alaka Chattopadhyaya (Calcutta: Bagchi, 1980), chapter 24 (esp. p. 209), connects the spread of the Tārā and Avalokiteśvara temples with Candragomin.

[23]These verses are collected in Birwé, "Fragments", cited above.

[24]*Nyāsa*, KV.II.266:26–27.

[25]*Nyāsa*, KV.V.679:28.

[26]*Nyāsa*, KV.VI.11:27.

the same Helārāja who, according to Kalhaṇa (born *ca.* 1100), wrote a work of 12,000 ślokas on the Kings of Kashmir.[27]

In his commentary on the third *kāṇḍa* of Bhartṛhari's work, Helārāja mentions Vyāḍi's name seven times.[28] In all cases the reference is to *vārttika*-Vyāḍi. It has been argued that the commentary on the second *kāṇḍa* of the *Vākapadīya* is also by Helārāja, and not by Puṇyarāja as asserted in many manuscript colophons.[29] One reference is made to Vyāḍi in this part of the commentary, and it is of importance as repeating the legend that Vyāḍi is the author of the *Saṅgraha*. Commenting on verse 476, Helārāja (Puṇyarāja?) says:[30]

> *ihá purā pāṇinīye 'smin vyākaraṇe vyāḍyuparacitaṃ granthalakṣaparimāṇaṃ saṅgrahābhidhānaṃ nibandhanam āsīt*||
>
> In the past there used to be a work on this Pāṇinian grammar, composed by Vyāḍi. It was called the *Saṅgraha* and was 100,000 *granthas* long.[31]

This could be an amalgam of the statement of Bhartṛhari quoted above, that Vyāḍi composed the *Saṅgraha*, and his remark about this text:[32]

> *caturdaśa sahasrāṇi vastūni asmin saṃgrahagranthe*|
>
> There are fourteen thousand subjects [discussed] in this book, the *Saṅgraha*.

Kaiyaṭa's Vyāḍi (before early 11th cent.)

Kaiyaṭa is very restrained in the matter of referring to Vyāḍi. I can find only one mention of the name, in his commentary on the famous *vārttika* 45 on P.1.2.64 (*Pradīpa* II.94^b).

Although Kaiyaṭa says that he owes a great deal to [Bhartṛ]hari's book (presumably the *Dīpikā*),[33] yet he does not follow Bhartṛhari when the latter links the *Saṅgraha* with Vyāḍi's name (see above). When Patañjali first speaks of the *Saṅgraha*,[34] Kaiyaṭa is content with the laconic gloss: *granthaviśeṣa* 'a certain book'.[35]

---

27 Cf. Cardona, *Pāṇini: a survey*, p. 299.

28 K. A. Subrahmania Iyer, *Vākyapadīya of Bhartṛhari with the Commentary of Helārāja; kāṇḍa III, part 1* (Poona: Deccan College, 1963), pp. 9:9:14, 15:2, 82:10, 106:2:11, 188:2, 190:2.

29 See A. N. Aklujkar, 'The Authorship of the Vākya-kāṇḍa-ṭīkā', in *Charudeva Shastri Felicitation Volume* (Delhi, 1974), pp. 165–88.

30 R. Sharma (ed), *Vākyapadīyam, Part II, with the commentary Ambākartrī by Raghunātha Sharmā* (Varanasi: Vārāṇaseya Saṃskṛta Viśvavidyālaya, 1968), p. 570:1.

31 A *grantha* is a section of text, verse or prose, 32 syllables long.

32 Bronkhorst, *Mahābhāṣyadīpikā*, p. 17:27, commenting on Mbh.I.6:12.

33 *Pradīpa*, I.5:6.

34 Mbh.I.6:12.

35 *Pradīpa*, I.55^a:3.

Haradatta's Vyāḍi (before *ca.* 1000–1100)

We saw that Jinendrabuddhi derived the name Vyaḍa (Vyāḍi's ancestor) from *vi* + *aḍa* explaining it as 'one whose *aḍa* is gone'. Haradatta now tells us that an *aḍa* is a *vṛścikalāṅgūlam* 'scorpion's tail',[36] and by extension *taikṣṇyam* 'sharpness'. So Vyāḍi is the descendant of Vyaḍa the Mild.

It is worth noting here, as an example of independent thought, that Viṭṭhala (14th cent.) accounts for the name Vyaḍa quite differently. While commenting under P.7.2.7 in the *Prakriyākaumudī* (PK.I.814) Viṭṭhala says:

> *viśeṣeṇāḍaty udyamaṃ karotīti vyaḍaḥ*
>
> He exerts himself especially, i.e., he makes an effort, so he is Vyaḍa.

This is simply in line with the *Dhātupāṭha* which records (Dhp.1.380): *aḍa udyame*.

Haradatta also tries in the same place (*ad* P.2.4.21), to throw some light on the perplexing question of the ten *huṣkaraṇas*, first raised in the *Kāśikā* (see p. xviii above). However Haradatta obviously had a variant text before him; he reads *duṣkaraṇa*, not *daśahuṣkaraṇa*.[37] He claims that *duṣ* is a conventional term, like Pāṇini's *vṛt*. Later on, *ad* P.4.3.115 (KV.III.698), he again tries to explain *duṣkaraṇa*. After repeating the *vṛt* analogy, he adds: *kāmaśāstram ity anye* 'according to others it is [to do with] erotics.'

I think it is fair to say Haradatta is floundering on this issue.

Puruṣottamadeva's Vyāḍi (before *ca.* 1150)

Puruṣottamadeva's citation of Vyāḍi's name is of interest since it shows clearly the development of the *Saṅgraha*-Vyāḍi idea.

Abhayanandin (8th cent.), in his commentary *Mahāvṛtti* on the Jainendra grammar, has quoted a view from the *Saṅgraha*. He says:[38]

> *bhuvādīnāṃ vakāro 'yam lakṣaṇārthaḥ prayujyate|*
> *iko yaṇbhir vyavadhānam ekeṣām iti saṃgrahaḥ|*

Thus, Abhayanandin is quoting a verse in which the *Saṅgraha* is said to declare the opinion of some [other] grammarians about the separative function of the semivowel in this unusual *sandhi*. Puruṣottamadeva then quotes this opinion and attributes it to Vyāḍi (or Vyāḷi) and Gālava:[39]

> *ikāṃ yaṇbhir vyavadhānam vyāḍigālavayor iti vaktavyam|*

Obviously there is some confusion here. If Vyāḍi is the author of the *Saṅgraha* in question, he cannot also be the holder of an opinion cited in that text as

---

36 *Padamañjarī*, KV.II.266:13.

37 See *Padamañjarī*, KV.II.266:15; this variant is the same as that of Vāmana (*ad* P.6.2.14) mentioned above, where it is Apiśali, not Vyāḍi who is responsible for '*duṣkaraṇa*.'

38 *Mahāvṛtti*, p. 23, on *sūtra* 1.2.1.

39 *Bhāṣāvṛtti*, p. 387, *ad* P.6.1.70.

held by 'some [others]'. Perhaps Puruṣottamadeva saw '*Saṅgraha*' and the urge to produce the name 'Vyāḍi' overcame him.

In his dictionary *Trikāṇḍaśeṣa* Puruṣottamadeva also records a tradition that Vyāḍi lived in the Vindhyas, was the son of Nandinī and was learned (*medhavī*).[40] These traditions may go back to the *Bṛhatkathā* legends.

Haribhāskara's Vyāḍi (before 17th cent.)

Haribhāskara's *Paribhāṣābhāskara* is late and largely derivative from Sīradeva, but he records a tradition which is of interest to us. Near the close of his work he remarks:[41]

> *kecit tu vyākhyānato viśeṣapratipattir ityādisarvaparibhāṣā vyāḍimuninā viracitā ity āhuḥ| vastutas tu nānācāryāṇām imāni vacanāni pūrvodāhṛtalaṇsūtrādigataṇakārādy-upadānatātparyajñāpakebhya iṣṭasiddhaye kevalam pāṇinyādimunitrayeṇa urarīkriyante*
>
> Some, however, say that all the *paribhāṣās*, from *vyākhyānato viśeṣapratipattir* onwards, were composed by the sage Vyāḍi. In actual fact, though, these statements of various authorities – which are made because of the intimations which are the significance of using items such as the letter *ṇ* in the *sūtra laṇ*, previously exemplified, in order to fulfill desiderata – are completely accepted by the three sages, Pāṇini etc.

This is another clear reference to a tradition about a Vyāḍi who composed *paribhāṣās*, albeit rejected by Haribhāskara. Abhyankar, himself a traditionally trained *paṇḍita*, has mentioned that this belief that Vyāḍi was the first writer on *paribhāṣās* is a living tradition amongst traditional scholars.[42]

Nāgeśa's Vyāḍi (before *ca.* 1755)

I refer to Nāgeśa not because he is in receipt of a different, or more ancient tradition, but purely because his views have been uniquely influential. In fact a great deal of his writing on *paribhāṣās* is heavily influenced by Nīlakaṇṭhadīkṣita (early 17th cent.) and Sīradeva (12th cent.) in both style and content.

In his commentary *Uddyota* on Kaiyaṭa's *Pradīpa*, he glossed Kaiyaṭa's restrained remark *granthaviśeṣa* mentioned above, with:[43]

> *saṃgraho vyāḍikṛto lakṣaślokasaṃkhyo grantha iti prasiddhiḥ|*
>
> It is well known that the *Saṅgraha* was a book by Vyāḍi numbering one hundred thousand verses.

---

[40] Y. Mīmāṃsaka, *Saṃskṛta Vyākaraṇa-śāstra kā Itihāsa (tīn bhāgoṃ meṃ pūrṇa)* (Sonīpat: Rāma Lāla Kapūra Ṭrasṭa, 1973), I.275 f.

[41] Abhyankar, *Paribhāṣāsaṃgraha*, p. 374.

[42] Ibid., p. 11.

[43] *Uddyota*, I.55^{a}:4.

It is probably this statement more than any other that is responsible for the widespread assumption that any Vyāḍi is identically equal to *Saṅgraha*-Vyāḍi. His comment is of course to be traced to Helārāja (see p. xx above).

Vedavikṛti Vyāḍi (before *ca.* 18th cent.)

It is well known that the Vedic hymns are traditionally recited in a variety of complex syllabic rearrangements called *vikṛtis*. There are eight standard rearrangements, which are called *jaṭā, mālā, śikhā, rekhā, dhvaja, daṇḍa ratha* and *ghana*, in ascending order of complexity.

A number of short texts and commentaries exist explaining this subject and its intricacies, and in this literature the name Vyāḍi looms large. Several of these texts have been collected by Abhyankar and Devasthali.[44]

The basic work in this literature is the *Vikṛtivallī*, which consist of twenty-eight verses.[45] Its opening verses pay homage to God in the form of Nārāyaṇa and to teachers such as Śaunaka, Śākala, Śākalya and Bharadvāja. The author names himself Maharṣi Vyāḍi, and belongs to the Śaiśirīya branch of the Ṛgveda.

There are several commentaries and derivative texts.[46] One of the commentators, Anantācārya, flourished in 1625, which gives a *terminus ad quem* for this Vyāḍi. Furthermore there is evidence that Vyāḍi knew a text called *Upalekhasūtra*. This text is not finally dated, but its earliest citation is by Mahidāsa in 1557.[47]

Another work basing itself on Vyāḍi's *Vikṛtivallī* is Madhusūdana Maskari's *Aṣṭavikṛtivivṛti* (or *-vivaraṇa*). This has a commentary by one Purogama. The date of both authors is unknown, but the earliest dated MS is 1790, and Purogama quotes widely from the *purāṇas*.[48] Purogama has a short disquisition in which he argues that there is no contradiction in the fact that Vyāḍi is called both an *ṛṣi* '[superhuman] seer' and an *ācārya* '[human] professor'.[49] Its only interest is that he refers to the *Ṛgvedaprātiśākhya* (13.31) where Vyāḍi is classed with Śākalya and Gārgya as an *ācārya*. Clearly, for Purogama, the *Prātiśākhya* Vyāḍi and the present Vyāḍi are one.

Other than this instance, there is surprisingly little reference to any Vyāḍi outside the *vikṛti* literature. There appears to be no mention of *vārttika*-Vyāḍi or *Saṅgraha*-Vyāḍi.

---

[44] K. V. Abhyankar and G. V. Devasthali (eds), *Vedavikṛti-lakṣaṇa-saṃgraha (A Collection of Twelve Tracts on Vedavikṛtis and allied topics)* (Poona: BORI, 1978).

[45] Ibid., pp. 1–3.

[46] Ibid., texts 2–4, 8.

[47] Ibid., pp. xiv–xv.

[48] Ibid., pp. 75 ff.

[49] Ibid., p. 81:7–11.

The poet Vyāḍi (before early 13th cent.)

A single verse is attributed to a Vyāḍi in the collection *Saduktikarṇāmṛta* by Śrīdharadāsa (early 13th cent.).[50] It betrays no particular affiliations with any other Vyāḍi.

Alchemical Vyāḍi

The name Vyāḍi (or Vyāḷi) occurs frequently in the literature on alchemy, *rasaśāstra*. In the sixteenth century the Tibetan historian Tārānātha (*b.* 1575) wrote of a Vyāḷi from eastern India who failed, after twelve years of striving, to gain magical powers and to make gold and thence set off on a series of extraordinary adventures. He eventually learned true (Buddhist) spirituality from one Carpaṭi.[51]

Before this, Sāyaṇa (14th cent.) in his famous *Sarvadarśanasaṅgraha* had mentioned Vyāḷi in his chapter on *Raseśvaradarśana*. Here, Vyāḷi is amongst several sages (including Carvaṭi and Govindabhagavatpāda) who gained liberation while embodied.[52]

Perhaps the earliest secure references to an alchemical Vyāḍi are those of the *Garuḍapurāṇa* which may date from the tenth century (although the text is composite).[53] In this text Vyāḍi is said to have achieved marvellous powers, and to be an expert in jewellery and the cleaning of pearls.[54]

Vyāḍi's name is also cited in texts such as the *Rasaratnasamuccaya* and the *Rasaratnapradīpa*, but the literature on *rasa* is as yet unclassified and chronologically chaotic, so one cannot at present assess the historical value of these citations.[55]

The authorship of the *Saṅgraha*

Clearly an important philosopher of language called Vyāḍi lived between Pāṇini and Kātyāyana. However, there is no *early* evidence that he wrote a work called the *Saṅgraha*. Our first testimony to this is a single phrase in Bhartṛhari's *Dīpikā*, written at least six hundred years later, and most other statements seem derivable from this.

A work called the *Saṅgraha* did exist before 140 BC, because Patañjali refers to it four times.[56] He also refers to the qualification *sāṅgrahasūtrika* 'one

[50] See L. Sternbach, *A Descriptive Catalogue of Poets quoted in Sanskrit Anthologies and Inscriptions*, (Wiesbaden: Harrassowitz, 1978), volume II, p. 488 for further references.

[51] A. Grünwedel, *Tāranātha's Edelsteinmine, das Buch von den Vermittlern der Sieben Inspirationen* (Petrograd: L'Académie Impériale des Sciences, 1914), p. 116 ff.

[52] *Sarvadarśanasaṅgraha* (Poona: Anandasrama, 4th ed. 1977), p. 81:8.

[53] See L. Rocher, *The Purāṇas*, in *A History of Indian Literature*, edited by Jan Gonda (Wiesbaden: Harrassowitz, 1986), p. 177.

[54] See references in Mīmāṃsaka, *op. cit.*, volume I, pp. 280–81, and *The Garuḍa Purāṇa* (Delhi: Motilal Banarsidass, 1978), volume I, p. 69.35.36–37.

[55] P. C. Rây, *A History of Hindu Chemistry* (London: Williams and Norgate, 1907, 1909), volume II, p. lix, notes that a Vyāḍi is mentioned in the *Rasarājalakṣmī* which cannot be later than the 14th cent.

[56] Mbh. I.6:12:21, 468:11:12.

who has studied the *Saṅgrahasūtra*,' suggesting that the *Saṅgraha* may have been cast in *sūtra* form.[57] But two facts suggest that, for Patañjali, Vyāḍi was not the author of this work. The most important is that in two of his citations he actually says that the *Saṅgraha* is by one Dākṣāyaṇa. Now several authors have asserted that Dākṣāyaṇa must be the familial name of Vyāḍi, but there is no evidence whatsoever for this. Such assertions are based on reasoning backwards from the assumption that Vyāḍi wrote a *Saṃgraha*.

The second fact arises from the context in which Patañjali first cites the *Saṅgraha*. In his introduction to the *Mahābhāṣya* he is discussing one by one a series of basic questions:

- *keṣāṃ śabdānām* (Mbh. I.1:3),
- *kaḥ śabdaḥ* (1:6),
- *kāni śabdānuśāsanasya prayojanāni* (1:14),
- *kiṃ śabdopadeśaḥ kartavya āhosvit* ... (5:13),
- *kiṃ punar ākṛtiḥ padārtha āhosvit dravyam* (6:8), and finally,
- *kiṃ punar nityaḥ śabda āhosvit kāryaḥ* (6:12).

He cites the *Saṅgraha* on the last question (6:12), but the immediately preceding issue (6:8) is actually the one associated with the name Vyāḍi in the famous *vārttika*. It seems most unlikely that if Patañjali thought Vyāḍi was the author of the *Saṅgraha* he would at this point not mention Vyāḍi's name or at least refer to the *vārttika*. Both those arguments are, of course, *ex silentio*, but they are nevertheless strong.

The other source of information about the ancient *Saṅgraha* brings us back once again to Bhartṛhari. At the end of the second *kāṇḍa* of his *Vākyapadīya* is the well known and much discussed passage on the history of grammar.[58] In brief, the passage says that the *Saṅgraha* was eclipsed because it met mainly with grammarians who were fond of abridgements and of little learning (*Vākyapadīya* II, verse 481). Patañjali then recast the work incorporating the chief points of logic in his *Mahābhāṣya* (482). Even this work, however, was beyond many untutored wits, and through the dry logic of three particular scholars, Vaiji, Saubhava and Haryakṣa, the sage's book, which was the *Saṅgraha* thinly disguised (*saṅgrahapratikañcuka*), was ruined (483–84). With time that grammatical tradition slipped away from the students of Patañjali's system and remained amongst Southerners as a mere book (485). Then, through the efforts of Candra and others, who received the tradition from Parvata (or 'from the mountain') and followed the logical seeds sown in the *Mahābhāṣya*, that tradition blossomed once again (486). Finally, Bhartṛhari's own teacher pondered those logical developments and his own philosophical views and produced the present compendium of traditions (487).

---

[57] Mbh. II.284:4.

[58] The various points at issue have been summarized by Cardona, *Pāṇini: a survey*, pp. 247–50. Cf. also G. Cardona, "Still again on the history of the Mahābhāṣya", *ABORI* **58–59** (1978), pp. 79–99 and J. Bronkhorst, "On the History of Pāṇinian Grammar in the early centuries following Patañjali," *Journal of Indian Philosophy* **11** (1983), pp. 392 ff.

This paraphrase is somewhat free, but one point is particularly deliberate: the translation of *granthamātro vyavasthitaḥ* (485) as 'remained ... as mere book'.[59] This phrase has caused great confusion in the past. It seems to me that the author cannot mean, as is generally thought, that the *Mahābhāṣya* came to exist in the South in manuscript form alone (i.e., with no living tradition of interpretation) because he has, in the previous verse (484), already referred to the *Mahābhāṣya* as a *grantha* 'book'. The point is not that the oral tradition failed, leaving only written texts. After all, Candra seems to have found the tradition all right, in Parvata. Rather, the *Mahābhāṣya* went from being an *ārṣo granthaḥ* 'a holy sage's book' (484) to being a *granthamātraḥ* 'just a book' (485). In other words, through inadequate exposition the *Mahābhāṣya* lost its high prestige and came, among Southerners (and also in Kashmir, according to Kalhaṇa's *Rājataraṅgiṇī*[60]), to be regarded as a book like any other.

This interpretation of Bhartṛhari's words might seem uninteresting until one realizes that there are at least two known authors who seem to take exactly this attitude to the *Mahābhāṣya*: Śabarasvāmin and *paribhāṣā*-Vyāḍi (see below). Devasthali gathered convincing evidence that Śabara knew and used the *Mahābhāṣya*, and yet did not treat it as an authority and never mentioned Patañjali's name.[61] Devasthali concluded that Śabara must have written before 100 BC, that is at a time when the *Mahābhāṣya* was a newly written text and had not yet won acclaim. But as Bronkhorst has argued, Śabara's attitude to the *Mahābhāṣya* could be explained equally well if he wrote at any time when that text was not highly regarded.[62] Matilal tentatively places Śabara between *ca.* 300 and AD 400, which would agree well with Bhartṛhari's statement.[63] Thus we would, with Bronkhorst, postulate a period preceding Bhartṛhari and Candra (*ca.* 400–450) when the *Mahābhāṣya* was not particularly revered, and was freely used without acknowledgement by authors such as Śabara. And as Bronkhorst has pointed out, it is in this period that we might locate the author of the *Vyāḍīyaparibhāṣāvṛtti*.[64]

Later grammatical literature abounds with quotations from a text called the *Saṅgraha*. These all occur after Bhartṛhari and require careful study in their own right. Many have been collected by Mīmāṃsaka.[65] In almost all cases the author is called merely *Saṅgrahakāra*, and it may well be that, as

---

[59]'*Grantha*' may, of course, mean 'work' as well as 'book'. The present argument is not materially affected by this distinction.

[60]*Rājataraṅgiṇī*, 1.176; 4.488.

[61]G. V. Devasthali, "On the probable date of Śabara-Svāmin", *ABORI*, **23** (1942), pp. 84–97, "Positive data for the date of Śabarasvāmin", *The Journal of the Gaṅganāth Jhā Research Institute*, **6** (1949), pp. 231–40, and "Śabara and Patañjali", *Journal of the University of Bombay* **20** (1951), pp. 101–6. Cited in Bronkhorst, "On the History of Pāṇinian Grammar", pp. 402–404.

[62]Bronkhorst, "On the History of Pāṇinian Grammar," pp. 402–404.

[63]Matilal, *Epistemology*, p. 19. See also J-M. Verpoorten, *Mīmāṃsā Literature*, in *A History of Indian Literature* edited by Jan Gonda (Wiesbaden: Harrassowitz, 1987), p. 8.

[64]Bronkhorst, "On the History of Pāṇinian Grammar", p. 391 and again in "*Vārttika*", *Wiener Zeitschrift für die Kunde Südasiens* **34** (1990), p. 139.

[65]*Saṃskṛta-vyākaraṇa śāstra kā itihāsa*, I.282–90.

Scharfe has suggested,[66] the many *Saṅgraha* references by Bhartṛhari and his commentators in fact refer to the *āgamasaṅgraha* 'collection of teachings' made by Bhartṛhari's own teacher, Vasurāta.[67]

Summary

As we have seen, the name Vyāḍi arises in no less than eighteen literary contexts. There are other citations, mostly late, but these can be traced to one or other of the above sources. It is tempting to amalgamate at least some of these, to say for instance that the *Gaṇapāṭha* Vyāḍi is the same as Patañjali's, which in turn is certainly the same as Kātyāyana's. But not enough material survives of any of these Vyāḍis to make any probative identifications on grounds either of content or style. Until further evidence is forthcoming it is wisest to withhold judgment.

There are, however, two important points which do emerge. First, the reference by Jinendrabuddhi, though it concerns the problematic *huṣkaraṇas*, really does seem to be a reference to a *paribhāṣā* writer. This, if it is a true reference to our Vyāḍi, would place him earlier than *ca.* 700. Secondly, for the reasons given in the discussion on the *Saṅgraha*, it is conceivable that there was a period just preceding Bhartṛhari and Candra when the *Mahābhāṣya* was not highly regarded (at least in the South and Kashmir), and that our commentary was written in this intellectual climate.

The *Vyāḍīyaparibhāṣāvṛtti*

The *Vyāḍīyaparibhāṣāvṛtti* is an odd work for several reasons. In the first place it is almost devoid of any reference to other authors. In two places the Vyāḍi commentator refers to the *Vārttikakāra* (5:18, 28:20) and quotes *vārttikas*, proving that he had at least Kātāyana's work before him. He also quotes a *vārttika* without referring to its author (28:6). (This particular *vārttika* appears as a *sūtra* in the *Kāśikā*.[68]) The only other name he cites is 'Padakāra', 'word maker' (37:23). This name is used in the plural in a passage by Patañjali,[69] to refer to the authors of the *Padapāṭha*, the analyzed version of the Vedic hymns. Kātyāyana, the author of the *vārttikas* also wrote the *Vājasaneyiprātiśākhya* and might therefore be thought of as a Padakāra. There is some confusion in the tradition as to whom the name Padakāra refers to. Some authors use it to mean Patañjali, while others mean Kātyāyana.[70] The Vyāḍi commentator's reference, at any rate, is almost certainly to Kātyāyana's first *vārttika* on P.1.1.6. It is important to note, however, that the Vyāḍi commentator is here using an expression for which our first testimony is the *Mahābhāṣya*.

[66] H. Scharfe, *Grammatical Literature*, vol. V., part II, fasc.2 of *A History of Indian Literature* edited by Jan Gonda (Wiesbaden: Harrassowitz, 1977), pp. 125 f.

[67] Cf. *Vākyapadīya*, II.487.

[68] P.6.1.100, KV.IV.569.

[69] Mbh.II.85:5, repeated III.117:18, 398:9.

[70] See Mīmāṃsaka, *Saṃskṛta Vyākaraṇa*, III, pp. 332 f.

Apart from these references to Kātyāyana, the Vyāḍi commentator's only other clear external reference is the quotation of a verse from the *Rāmāyaṇa* (77:11). This does not help us at all.

Thus the Vyāḍi commentator appears to have worked largely in intellectual isolation, with only his wits and the *Mahābhāṣya* to guide him (see commentary § 31.1).

This brings us to the second oddity of the text. The *Vyāḍīyaparibhāṣāvṛtti* is overflowing with parallel passages and even direct quotations from the *Mahābhāṣya* (*pace* Abhyankar). This can be proved conclusively by the several diagnostic instances where the Vyāḍi commentator's argument is logically and textually later than the same argument in the *Mahābhāṣya*. Such instances have been frequently pointed out in the commentary; some particularly clear examples are the commentaries on § 2.4, § 4.5, § 5^a.5, § 5^c, § 6.2, § 7, § 31.1, and § 30.1. There are very many other instances where the Vyāḍi commentator is using the *Mahābhāṣya* without saying so: see commentaries on § 1^a.6, § 2.1, § 31.2, § 32.1, § 33, § 61.3, § 62.1 *et passim*. This feature of the text could be accounted for by the conjecture, made above (p. xxvi), that the Vyāḍi commentator was writing in a period when the *Mahābhāṣya* was not thought important. This would also explain the fact that the *Vyāḍīyaparibhāṣāvṛtti* often displays a cavalier attitude to the arguments of the *Mahābhāṣya*; the latter's arguments will be acknowledged, but discarded, or ignored altogether; see, for example, the commentaries on § 2.19, § 3.11, § 5^b.1, § 5^b.2, § 22.1, *et passim*. No author later than Bhartṛhari would maintain such an attitude to the *Mahābhāṣya*.

A very simple fact about the *Vyāḍīyaparibhāṣāvṛtti* which should not be overlooked is that it contains a shorter list of *paribhāṣās* than any other work on this subject. Puruṣottama discusses 120 *paribhāṣās*, Sīradeva 130, Nīlakaṇṭha 140, Haribhāskara (who closely follows Sīradeva) 132 and Nāgeśa 132. If the Vyāḍi commentator had before him a longer list and were trying to minimize the number of *paribhāṣās* he would surely have presented arguments for rejecting certain ones (cf. his rejection of no. 2). Although an argument *ex silentio*, the fact that the Vyāḍi commentator's list is shorter than anyone else's is at least consonant with the conjecture that he is the earliest extant writer on *paribhāṣās*.

A few of the arguments in the *Vyāḍīyaparibhāṣāvṛtti* seem to show that the Vyāḍi commentator did not know the *Nyāsa* (e.g., commentaries § 1^b.5 and § 6, § 5^c), that he preceded the *Kāśikā* (e.g., commentary § 11), and that he preceded the other *paribhāṣā* commentators, including Puruṣottamadeva (e.g., commentaries § 2, § 7.4, § 10.1). Sometimes, too, the Vyāḍi commentator uses arguments that seem to align him with Candra (e.g., commentaries § 7.6, § 11, and § 86.1).

Any one of these pieces of evidence alone would not be sufficient grounds for asserting anything more than a faint guess about the date of the *Vyāḍīyaparibhāṣāvṛtti*. But when all these small facts are taken together the case is a little stronger. Abhyankar cannot be right in putting the Vyāḍi commentator before Patañjali; there is overwhelming evidence in the text that he knew and used the *Mahābhāṣya*. But we may with some justification place him before Bhartṛhari, that is, in the fifth century AD. And even if some lucky future discovery enables us to determine that this is not his physical date, it is without doubt his intellectual date.

The Translation

The translation of any technical language poses special problems, and Sanskrit linguistics is no exception. Isadore Pinchuck has clarified a number of important issues in her book *Scientific and Technical Translation*, and I have tried to put her suggestions into practice.[71]

I have tried to minimize interference, defined as the persistence in the target language (English) of usage peculiar to the source language (Sanskrit).[72] I have also tried to some extent to follow Pinchuck's hierarchy of units of translation, equating concepts where possible, then lexical and syntactic units on the level of sentence, and only then the smaller units of words and morphemes.[73] In practice, as Pinchuck also points out, the substitution of sentence for sentence is most effective.[74]

In my use of square brackets I have tried to ensure always that the sentence would be *syntactically whole if read without the brackets*. If the phrases in brackets are removed, the text should still read meaningfully, if perhaps cryptically. It is wholly unacceptable for a translator to place syntactially essential parts of the sentence within parentheses, unless the Sanskrit text itself is genuinely incomplete. I consider this an important practical consequence of the belief that the prime unit of meaning, and therefore translation, is the sentence, and not the word. Constant violation of this principle may be found in most English translations of Sanskrit technical literature including, for example, Kielhorn's translation of the *Paribhāṣenduśekhara*. If Kielhorn meant us to believe that the parenthetical suppletions were his own words and the text outside the parentheses a faithful translation of Nāgeśa's, then the underlying text would have to be virtually meaningless. I leave it as a hilarious exercise for the reader to read the translation while omitting the parenthetical matter. Although Nāgeśa's Sanskrit is notoriously elliptical, it is nevertheless grammatically whole. Any English translation, without suppletions, must reflect this fact.

To move to specifics, I have throughout been consistent in translating technical terms and phrases. Thus 'subsequence' translates *paratva*, 'invariance' *nityatva*, and so on.

As is well known, Pāṇini operates with several types of linguistic zero. I have not attempted to translate them all differently, but the broad distinction between *lopa* on the one hand and *luk*, *ślu*, *lup* on the other has been preserved in English by using the terms 'elision' and 'deletion' respectively. Thus, the 'elision' of an affix is taken to mean that the affix is replaced by zero, but that

[71] I. Pinchuk, *Scientific and Technical Translation* (London: A. Deutsch, 1977). There are many other good books on this subject.

[72] Ibid., p. 47.

[73] Ibid., p. 48.

[74] Ibid., p. 51.

the environmental effects of that affix remain in force;[75] 'deletion' (which is always deletion of an affix[76]) is taken to mean the same, except that the effects of the deleted affix on a pre-affixal base (*aṅga*) also disappear.[77]

The word 'item' is repeatedly used in a completely neutral sense for the referent of a Sanskrit pronoun or an adjective.

The terms *siddha* and *asiddha* are rendered 'valid' and 'invalid'. This is not perfect, but is at least close. The word 'virtual' is used in its technical sense, as in the disciplines of contemporary science, meaning 'present in effect, though not in fact'.

'Intimation' was chosen to translate *jñāpaka*, as supplying verbal derivatives more easily then 'clue' or other possible translations.

It was often necessary to translate *ca* with adversative force as 'but',[78] and such idiomatic phrases as *kathaṃ kṛtvā* have been rendered 'how come', etc., which carries the same slightly idiomatic flavour in English.[79]

There are several idioms specific to technical grammatical writing. These often involve carrying the conventions of the grammatical *sūtra* into prose. For example P.1.1.49 teaches that the genitive is to be construed with *sthāne*. Thus, in *sūtras*, 'of x' means 'in place of x'. This convention is carried over into the commentarial literature, and it is common in grammatical prose to find the genitive used in this technical way, with ellipsis of *sthāne*. Similarly, *hrasva* is translated 'short vowel', not just 'short', because of P.1.2.28.

Finally, the dashes are meant to separate the various interlocutors. Like the *Mahābhāṣya*, the *Vyāḍīyaparibhāṣāvṛtti* is a series of propositions, refutations, examples and counter-examples which read almost like a play. The arguments are separately numbered for ease of reference.

The loci

A serious attempt has been made to locate other occurrences of most of the Vyāḍi commentator's arguments, and the *paribhāṣās*. These references have generally been placed in the footnotes to the translation. I have not treated them as testimonia to the main edition because of the uncertainties surrounding the Vyāḍi commentator's date, and the lines of transmission within the tradition of grammar.

These loci show how very close the Vyāḍi commentator normally is to the *Mahābhāṣya*, while conversely, the occasional absence of any parallels throws

---

[75] P.1.1.60, 1.1.62.

[76] P.1.1.61.

[77] P.1.1.63. On these distinctions, cf. G. Cardona, *Pāṇini: His Work and its Traditions* (Delhi: Motilal Banarsidass, 1988) vol. 1, p. 53 f. (§ 79).

[78] See J. S. Speijer, *Sanskrit Syntax* (Leyden: Brill, 1886), § 441. For the disjunctive use of *ca* in the *Aṣṭādhyāyī* see S. D. Joshi and S. Bhaṭe, "The Role of the Particle *ca* in the Interpretation of the *Aṣṭādhyāyī*", in *Proceedings of the International Seminar Studies in the Aṣṭādhyāyī of Pāṇini*, edited by S. D. Joshi and S. D. Laddu (Pune: Univ. of Poona, 1983), pp. 174 ff., *et passim*.

[79] G. Cardona points out that *kathaṃ kṛtvā*, being related to the phrase *iti kṛtvā*, might perhaps more appropriately be translated in American English as 'on what basis' (private communication, 2/5/1986). This is the sense to be understood by 'how come'.

light on the Vyāḍi commentator's independence and originality (e.g., § 58.3, § 59, § 60.1, § 62.2, § 63, etc.).

Explanation and comments

In the sections entitled 'Explanation' I have expounded the lines of reasoning of the Vyāḍi commentator's text, in his own terms, normally without trying to correct or supplement his arguments. I have presented my own comments and reflections to the sections entitled 'Comments'. Between them, these sections embody much of the oral commentary on the text which I received from Pt. V. B. Bhāgavat and Dr. S. Bhaṭe when I read the text with them in 1979, as well as the results of my subsequent reflection and research. With his usual bravura style, Housman says:[80]

> The apparatus criticus is embedded in the commentary and the two are closely interwoven; and that is as it should be. The usual separation of inseparable things, interpretation and criticism, is injurious to both, but especially the latter. It is the expedient of editors who wish to shirk discussion of their text because they fear that they could not defend it. Criticism apart from interpretation does not exist; and 'critical edition' is the most inappropriate of all names for the thing to which custom applies it, an edition in which the editor is allowed to fling his opinions in the reader's face without being called to account and asked for his reasons.

I have tried not to separate the inseparable. The commentary in volume II was written as the text was translated and expounded, and this is how it should be read. I have explained the readings of the manuscripts, wherever possible, in the critical apparatus to the text in volume I, but there are also several textual notes in the comments in volume II.

The Vyāḍi commentator's remarks on the *paribhāṣās* become sparser towards the end of the work. This accords with the common practice of traditional commentators, and I too have taken a similar line. I have had more to say in my analysis and discussion of the earlier *paribhāṣās* and arguments. For the reasons outlined at the end of the Foreword to volume I, once the position of the *Vyāḍīyaparibhāṣāvṛtti* relative to the rest of the Sanskrit grammatical tradition became more or less clear, I restricted my explanation and comments to the more interesting or difficult passages.

[80] A. E. Housman (ed.), *M. Manilii, Astronomicon, recensuit et enarravit A. E. Housman* (London: Grant Richards, 1903–30), vol. 5, p. xxxiii.

The *Vyāḍīyaparibhāṣāvṛtti*

— Now I shall discuss the indication of *paribhāṣās*.

This 'now' is meant as a heading. One is to understand that the discipline by which *paribhāṣās* are indicated has been headed, since from here on we shall proceed saying 'this [*paribhāṣā*] is validated in this rule'.

— Why is the reason for [saying], 'this one is validated in this'?

— Because he who has got to know the *paribhāṣās* becomes capable of teaching the discipline himself. Indeed, he gets to know the *paribhāṣās* easily. So an explanation is to be consulted.

So, to begin with there is this *paribhāṣā*:

Explanation The points being made in this introductory paragraph are not very clearly stated, but they seem in general terms to be as follow: First a partial analysis and explanation of the phrase *atha paribhāṣāsūcanaṃ vyākhyāsyāmaḥ* is given. Then the rationale for studying the *paribhāṣās* is given: it renders one capable of teaching grammar by oneself, and helps one to get to know the *paribhāṣās* easily. Therefore *paribhāṣās* do necessarily have to be explained.

Comments Abhyankar likened the style of the opening phrases to the *Mahābhāṣya*.[81] However it is a common enough beginning in *śāstric* literature. It lends to the first sentence the status of an initial rule, and indeed the following sentences do gloss it in a manner. But there is no doubt that, in common with the whole introductory paragraph, this first sentence reads a little strangely. Belvalkar took it to mean 'we shall now explain the *Paribhāṣāsūcana*', taking the last word as the title of the work.[82] Abhyankar followed him in this,[83] although he seems to have realized that the correct title of the work, as given in the colophon, is simply (*Vyāḍī*)*yaparibhāṣāvṛtti*.[84]

The word '*sūcana*' is translated literally as 'indicated', although 'listed' (cf. *sūcī*) might be possible. With these introductory phrases the Vyāḍi commentator is clearly

[81] Abhyankar, 1967.11.

[82] Belvalkar 1938.230.

[83] Abhyankar 1967, *passim*.

[84] Abhyankar 1967.11. For further discussion of the work's title in the introduction above, p. xiii.

suggesting a parallellism with such famous phrases as *atha śabdānuśāsanam*, *atha yogānuśāsanam*, and *athāto darśapūrṇamāsau vyākhyāsyāmaḥ*.[85]

The reasons given for taking up the study of *paribhāṣās* are decidedly odd, given the many substantial reasons that the author might have chosen. It may be that a portion of the text has been lost at this point: particularly in the sentence beginning *sa tāvat sukham* ... one might suspect ellipsis of a phrase taking up the correlative *tāvat*. In the last sentence too, *tatrādita* ..., we get the odd, isolated use of *tāvat*. On the other hand, this usage is fairly typical of the *Mahābhāṣya*, where it often precedes an example, and means 'thus, such as, for example' (Mbh.I.1:3; 8:10; 19:18; 20:17, etc.).

[85] *Mahābhāṣya*, *Yogasūtra*, and *Āpastambaśrautasūtra* respectively.

Paribhāṣā 1^a

When a meaningful item is mentioned, that item should not be mentioned without meaning.[86]

Explanation Grammatical rules apply to items such as letters, morphemes, inflected works, or groups of words. This *paribhāṣā* tells us how to rank these items. First, if one item could be considered either to have meaning or not to have meaning, then the former case should be chosen (argument § 1^a.1). Secondly, if there are two identical items available for an operation, one with meaning, and the other without, the former should be chosen (argument § 1^b.1).

Comments The translation of *grahaṇa* as 'mentioned' is not intended to suggest the use/mention distinction. What it means here is the 'taking' of a linguistic item, in the sense of its use or utterance.

Argument 1^a.1[87] [1^a:2

— Where, then, is this *paribhāṣā* intimated?
— In the rule *vraścabhrasja* ... etc. (P.8.2.36).

[86] This *paribhāṣā* is well known to Kātyāyana, who justifies several arguments by referring to it with the catch-phrase *arthavadgrahaṇāt* (Mbh.I.70:6, 74:26, 496:20; II.181:13, 346:12; III.45:16, 180:17, 238:12, 417:20, 438:15, 458:13). It is also well known to Patañjali who often uses it (Mbh.I.74:28, 496:17:17 (*sic*):19:21; II.44:16, 181:12:14, 346:16; III.417:21, 438:14:16, 458:14, *et passim*). He also quotes it frequently in the same form as that used by the Vyāḍi commentator (Mbh.I.70:9, 81:25, 175:23; II.181:15, 202:20). When quoting the *paribhāṣā* in full, Patañjali often follows it with the set phrase *ity evam asya na bhaviṣyati*, 'and so this will not happen to it', referring to a previous argument (Mbh.II.411:13, 437:10; III.103:19, 169:2, 180:18 (no negative), 184:9, 266:22, 447:11). Finally, he twice considers the *paribhāṣā* inapplicable (Mbh.III.76:17, 266:22).

The *paribhāṣā* is discussed by all the *paribhāṣā* commentators: Puruṣottamadeva (no. 1), Nīlakaṇṭha (no. 11), Haribhāskara (no. 9), Nāgeśa (no. 14), Śeṣādrisudhī (no. 14).

[87] This argument is not found in Kātyāyana or Patañjali. It is common in the *paribhāṣā* literature: Puruṣottamadeva (no. 1), Sīradeva (no. 9), Nīlakaṇṭha (no. 11), Haribhāskara (325:17) and Śeṣādrisudhī (397:21) acknowledge that they take the argument from Sīradeva, while Nīlakaṇṭha, who normally follows the *Mahābhāṣya* absolutely, takes it from the *Śabdakaustubha* (on P.1.1.68). Sīradeva's phraseology is virtually identical to that of Puruṣottamadeva, who is thus likely to be his source.

Bhaṭṭojī Dīkṣita, in his *Śabdakaustubha* (on P.1.1.68) also accepts this argument as proof of the existence of *paribhāṣā* 1^a, adding that it is also *nyāyasiddha* 'validated as being an adage'.

— How come?
— Because the words *rāj* and *bhrāj* are read in it. After all, it is possible to do without the mention of the word *rāj* here, because that one word *bhrāj* alone [will do].

But the teacher observes that this should be a mention of the word *rāj* as a meaningful item. So the word *rāj* is included in order to establish this *paribhāṣā*, namely, 'when a meaningful item can be chosen an item not having meaning should not be [chosen]'.

Explanation This first attempt to derive this *paribhāṣā* from a Pāṇinian rule bases itself on P.8.2.36. This rule specifies seven roots and also includes those ending in *-ch* and *-ś*, saying that their final consonants become *ṣ* under certain conditions. Among the roots mentioned are *rāj* and *bhrāj*. We know that they are roots because they appear in the *Dhātupāṭha* (P.1.3.1, Dhp.1.194, 874, 875), but suppose for a moment that we were viewing these roots as mere groups of letters, without meaning. It would then be sufficient to cite *bhrāj* in the rule (but see below), and unnecessary cite both: since the two items share a common final element *r-ā-j*, a rule for one will suffice for both.

By stating both, the argument goes, Pāṇini is intimating that we cannot consider them as mere concatenations of letters, trying to apply the rule when ever we see that concatenation, in any context. The rule applies specifically to those two roots, as distinct meaningful items. It is not any group of letters ending in *-r-ā-j* or *-bh-r-ā-j* which suffers its final letter to be replaced by *ṣ*, but only the meaningful roots *rāj* 'shine' and *bhrāj* 'shine'.

Comments Without exception, all other authors using this argument take the word *bhrāj* to be the redundant one (*vyartha*) and therefore the intimation. This makes sense because, as Puruṣottamadeva and others say, *rāj* is a part of *bhrāj*, and so reference to the first would include the second too, if they are taken as mere word-final groups of letters.

In contrast to this, the *Vyāḍīyaparibhāṣāvṛtti* manuscripts are unanimous in reading the word *rāj* as being the redundant one. This is not reasonable because if *bhrāj* is meant to cover *rāj* then it could cover just *-j*, or anything ending in any combination of the letters of *bhrāj*. The rule would apply too widely; the fault of *atiprasaṅga* would arise.

The Vyāḍi commentator's strange view here is not just a manuscript error, but is embedded in the logic of his argument. If another author can be found who takes the same view about the redundancy of *rāj*, it might prove a crux for dating our text. The common reproduction of false reasoning is more likely to signal intellectual contact than the common reproduction of a correct result.

Argument 1^a.2[88] [1^a:7

— This is not an intimation, because there is another reason for stating this [word *rāj*].
— 'What?'
— There are two [different] words *bhrāj* [involved] here. One is read in the list beginning with *phaṇ*, the other in the list beginning with *varc*. [The word *rāj* is mentioned] so that it [*bhrāj*] should be taken as the one read in the list beginning with *phaṇ*; it should not be taken as the one read in the list beginning with *varc*. And *vibhrāj* 'radiant' is [derived] from the latter.

Explanation Another explanation is possible for the mention of both *rāj* and *bhrāj* in the rule. It starts from the fact that there are two different roots *bhrāj* mentioned in the *Dhātupāṭha*. Pāṇini framed the *sūtra* (P.8.2.36) as he did in order to distinguish between them. One *bhrāj* (Dhp.1.194) is read in the *Dhātupāṭha* on its own, as it were,[89] while the other immediately follows the root *rāj* (Dhp.1.874, 875). Therefore, saying not just *bhrāj* but *rāj* + *bhrāj* in the *sūtra* is like saying 'I mean the *bhrāj* which goes with *rāj*'. This use of contiguity (*sāhacarya*) as a method of distinguishing isomorphous items is a recognized device in Sanskrit grammar (see Laddu 1973; also argument § 4.5). It is this principle which the Vyāḍi commentator is implicitly using.

Thus, having supposedly accounted otherwise for the mention of both roots in the rule, we need not accept argument § 1^a.1, and the *paribhāṣā* needs to be established by other means.

Comments This argument is unsatisfactory. If we consider that the *paribhāṣā* has not been established, then *bhrāj* is a meaningless group of letters and it cannot possibly matter which *bhrāj* in the *Dhātupāṭha* is meant. If we consider that the *paribhāṣā* is established then we have to say that Pāṇini mentions *rāj* and *bhrāj* simply because he wishes to account for forms from those roots (e.g., *virāṭ*, *vibhrāṭ*). Omitting either root would leave his description of Sanskrit incomplete.

The manuscripts all read *ardharcādi* instead of *varcādi*. The later is a subgroup of the *Dhātupāṭha* containing *rāj* and *bhrāj*.[90] The *ardharcādi* list is a much better

---

[88] Bhaṭṭojī Dīkṣita applies the contiguity principle to P.8.2.36 in the *Siddhāntakaumudī* (SK.I.392 (378) = P.8.2.30 and SK.III.195 (2354) = P.6.4.125). But he ignores this argument in the *Śabdakaustubha* on P.1.1.68 (see footnote 87, p. 3).

Sāyaṇācārya also uses the principle in this context in the *Mādhavīyadhātuvṛtti* (1964 ed., 88:26), and refers on this point to Maitreya, Kṣīrasvāmin and Sammatākāra. The *Kṣīrataraṅgiṇī* of Kṣīrasvāmin does indeed have the principle applied to P.8.2.36 (1957 ed., 73, no. 111). The other two references are untraced. Kṣīrasvāmin, in 8th century Kashmir, is therefore our earliest testimony for this argument.

None of these authors, however, takes the step of using the contiguity argument in this context to refute the *paribhāṣā*. This step is taken by the *paribhāṣā* commentators Haribhāskara (no. 9) and Śeṣādrisudhī (no. 14). Vaidyanātha (*Gadā* p. 32, on pbh. 15) refers to their arguments concerning the marker *ṛ*.

[89] On the *phaṇādi* list and its particular functions see Abhyankar (1961.261a) and P.6.4.125. It is a subgroup of the *Dhātupāṭha* containing *bhrāj*.

[90] See Sāyaṇa's *Mādhavīyadhātuvṛtti* (1964.84–89, nos. 98–113) and Böhtlingk 1887 (on Dhp.1.175–197).

known group of words which may decline both in the masculine and neuter genders; but neither *rāj* nor *bhrāj* appear in it.[91]

Argument 1ᵃ.3[92] [1ᵃ:11

— In that case, this is an intimation: *kās* is established because of the mention of *āsi* in *dayāyāsaś ca* (P.3.1.37); this being the case, the fact that he makes mention of *kās* [in P.3.1.35] is an intimation of this [*paribhāṣā*].

Explanation In P.3.1.35 Pāṇini allows the suffix *-ām* after the roots *kās* etc., in forming the periphrastic perfect: *kāsāṃ cakre*. Then in P.3.1.37 he says that *-ām* may also follow the roots *day*, *ay* and *ās*. Now, if the *paribhāṣā* did not hold then having said *ās* in P.3.1.37, it would not be necessary to say *kās* separately, because, meaning apart, the unit *ā-s* is present in *k-ā-s*. A rule for the former would work for the later. Therefore Pāṇini's purpose in stating *kās* separately must be to give us a clue to the existence of the *paribhāṣā*. The root *as* by itself, and the unit *ā-s* in *kās* must differ in some essential way which makes it necessary to mention both. They differ in meaning: the *ās* in *kās* does not mean 'sit'. Therefore we must, if possible, take (grammatically) meaningful items into consideration when applying Pāṇini's rules.

Comments Here we have the same reasoning as in argument § 1ᵃ.1, and it seems cogent. Neither the contiguity principle, nor any other apparent way of explaining Pāṇini's mention of *kās* is satisfactory. The only resolution of the difficulty is to accept the *paribhāṣā* (see argument § 1.4).

In the sentence *āsigrahaṇāt* ... (1ᵃ:11), the *asya* is not feminine in agreement with *paribhāṣā*. We must therefore consider some such phrase as *paribhāṣāvidhāna* 'laying down of the *paribhāṣā*' to be implicit.

Note also here the method of quoting the root with a suffix *i*, common in Pāṇini, but first codified by Kātyāyana (*vārt.* 2 on P.3.3.108).

Argument 1ᵃ.4[93] [1ᵃ:12

— That [mention of *kās* in P.3.1.35] should be for the purpose of preventing over-application.

In that case [i.e., if *kās* were not mentioned] it (P.3.1.35) would wrongly apply also to such items as *nāsṛ*. Because *kās* is mentioned the problem does not arise.

---

[91] See Abhyankar (1961.38ᵇ) and P.2.4.31.

[92] This argument is not found in the *Mahābhāṣya*, nor in any of the *paribhāṣā* commentaries, the *Kaumudī*, *Kāśikā*, *Nyāsa*, or *Padamañjarī*. It seems unique to the Vyāḍi commentator.

In the *Mahābhāṣya*, the application of the suffix *-ām* after both *ās* and *kās* is considered an intimation, but of a different fact (Mbh.III.259:8–16).

Exactly the same reasoning as this argument is applied to the forms *kās* and *cakās* in Patañjali's commentary on P.3.1.35, *vārt.*1 (Mbh.II.44:13 ff.), in order to show that the separate mention of *cakās* in the *vārttika* is necessary.

[93] Like argument § 1ᵃ.3, this argument seems to be unique to the Vyāḍi commentator.

Explanation There is another possible explanation for mentioning *kās* separately, which obviates the need to treat its mention as a clue to the *paribhāṣā*.

If *kās* were not mentioned and *ās* were taken without reference to its meaning, then any root ending in *ā-s* would qualify for the periphrastic perfect suffix by P.3.1.35. This would make the rule's application far too general, and the fault of *atiprasaṅga* 'over application' would arise. To avoid this Pāṇini says *kās*. He is saying, as it were, 'among all the roots ending in *ā-s* which you might be thinking of, only consider *kās* for this rule'.

Comments The term *atiprasaṅga* is an older term than the more common *ativyāpti* used by the later grammatical writers under the influence of Nyāya. *Atiprasaṅga* occurs twenty three times in the *Mahābhāṣya*; *ativyāpti* is not used once. Thus the Vyāḍi commentator demonstrates yet again the closeness of his vocabulary to that of the *Mahābhāṣya*.

The root *nās* is given the marker *ṛ* by the Vyāḍi commentator, in common with all the major editions of the *Dhātupāṭha*.[94] In the Pathak and Chitrao 1935 edition, however, it is erroneously given as *ṇāsu*, both in the index and list.[95]

The root *ṇāsṛ* follows *kāsṛ* in the Pāṇinīya *Dhātupāṭha*, with *bhāsṛ* intervening (Dhp.1.654–656). But in the Cāndra *Dhātupāṭha*, *ṇāsṛ* follows *dāsṛ* immediately.[96] This situation would make the Vyāḍi commentator's argument (marginally) more cohesive.

The Vyāḍi commentator does seem to accept this argument, because in argument § 1ᵃ.5 he goes on to offer another way of establishing the *paribhāṣā*.

Unlike argument § 1ᵃ.3, this argument does not deny the fact that a rule which applies to a group of letters (*ās*) can also be applied to anything containing that group (*kās*). It is just that in the cases quoted Pāṇini limits our choice by saying *kās* and *day*. But this leaves very many cases wide open. For example, in the very next rule, P.3.1.38, the root us is mentioned as optionally forming the periphrastic perfect. Can we then freely make periphrastic perfects of *duṣ*, *tuṣ*, *puṣ*, etc. by this rule? Clearly not. Therefore the whole of argument § 1ᵃ.4 suffers from *atiprasaṅga* and does not seem a cogent refutation of argument § 1ᵃ.3.

Argument 1ᵃ.5 [1ᵃ:14

— Hence this mention of *day*, when it is established [already] because of the mention of *ay*, is answered. It too is for the purpose of disqualifying such items as *ay, ray, pay, may, cay, tay*, and *nay*.

Explanation The same reasoning as that of argument § 1ᵃ.4 is applied to Pāṇini's mention of both *day* and *ay* in P.3.1.37. He says *day* only to disqualify all other words ending in *a-y*.

[94] Böhtlingk 1887, Dhp.1.656; *Mādhavīyadhātuvṛtti* (1964), Dhp.1.404, etc.
[95] Pathak and Chitrao, 1935.654, no. 625.
[96] Liebich 1902, 15*, no. 457.

Comments The group of roots mentioned, *ay–nay*, corresponds almost exactly to Dhp.1.503–509, which runs: *aya-vaya-paya-maya-caya-taya-ṇaya gatau*, and immediately precedes *daya dānagativakṣaṇahiṃsādāneṣu*. It is certain, then, that the Vyāḍi commentator had this group in mind. The variant *daya* for *caya* is explicable through the similarity of *c* and *d* in *Śāradā*. And the text's *nay* for the *Dhātupāṭha's ṇay* is simply the root after the action of P.6.1.65 *ṇo naḥ*.[97]

This leaves the question of the text's reading of *ray* for the *Dhātupāṭha*'s *vay*. The root *ray* does appear in the *Dhātupāṭha* immediately after *day*, also in the sense *gatau* (Dhp.1.510–511).

In the Cāndra *Dhātupāṭha*, *ray* is included in the group, being placed immediately after *ṇay*,[98] but *vay* is there too. The *Kātantra Dhātupāṭha* reads *aya-vaya-paya-taya-caya-raya*, then *naya*, then *daya*,[99] and thus reads both *ray* and *vay*, with Candra but omits *may*, and treats *nay* separately. This type of question cannot be finally settled in the absence of a thoroughly critical edition and study of the Pāṇinīya *Dhātupāṭha*. But a first attempt at clarification seems to indicate that the Vyāḍi commentator's version comes after the Pāṇinian version, reading *ray* for *vay*. Then Candra compromises by following Pāṇini but adding *ray* on the end of the list. The *Kātantra* reading seems only to indicate that the list was being tampered with. All these suggestions are tentative in the extreme.

The Vyāḍi commentator's use of *pratyukta* which I have translated as 'answered' is slightly odd, but I think what he means is clear: we don't need to consider *day* as a *jñāpaka*.

Argument 1[a].6[100] [1[a]:16

— In that case this is the intimation: *svaṃ rūpaṃ śabdasya aśabdasaṃjñā* (P.1.1.68). Here he mentions *rūpa* 'form'.

— How come it is an intimation?

— In this rule it is not necessary to mention *rūpa* 'form'. To say just *svaṃ śabdasya*... 'an expression's own' is valid, because an expression has nothing that is its own except its form.

— But the teacher observes that an expression does have something else which is its own.

— And what is that?

— That something else is meaning. Therefore, *rūpa* 'form' is not what is being referred to here [in P.1.1.68, by the word *sva*]. And in other places too it is a meaningful item which is referred to, not one which has no meaning.

— What does this accomplish?

— The *paribhāṣā* 'when an item having meaning can be taken an item not having meaning should not be taken' becomes necessary.

---

[97] See Abhyankar 1961, *sub nopadeśa*; P.8.4.14.

[98] Liebich 1902, 14*, no. 424.

[99] Palsule 1955, *passim*.

[100] This argument appears in the *Mahābhāṣya* on P.1.1.68 (Mbh.I.175:20–23).

It is also mentioned by all the *paribhāṣā* commentators, who all refer the argument back to the *Mahābhāṣya*.

Explanation The Vyāḍi commentator's reasoning here is straightforward. In *svaṃ rūpaṃ śabdasyāśabdasaṃjñā* (P.1.1.68) Pāṇini says 'An expression has its own form ....'. In Sanskrit the word *sva* 'own' could be used alone, exocentrically, to mean something like 'own essential property'. This being so, the fact that in P.1.1.68 Pāṇini uses the word *rūpa* 'form' in apposition to *sva* means that he must consider that *rūpa* is not the word's 'own essential property'. Otherwise he could have read the rule without the word *rūpa*, and *sva* would by itself have expressed the expression's 'own essential property', that is, its form.So Pāṇini's usage in P.1.1,68 shows that he felt there was something other than form which constituted an expression's 'own essential property'. This must, by elimination, be meaning. This is the only other thing which could be called an expression's *sva*.

Thus it is established that for Pāṇini the 'essential property' or dominant feature of an expression, that which is apprehended first, is its meaning. And if the word *rūpa* were omitted from P.1.1.68, as the Vyāḍi commentator at first suggested it could be, we would cease to understand that the rule concerns an expression's form, and take it to be about an expression's meaning.

Finally, the Vyāḍi commentator says that elsewhere too Pāṇini (or the world?) prefers the item which bears meaning to that which does not. This is taken to be the very principle embodied in the *paribhāṣā*, which is thus shown to be at work in Pāṇini's system.

Comments This argument is the same as that of the *Mahābhāṣya*, down to the very phraseology. There are two points in the language of the *Mahābhāṣya* which need clarifying. These lie in the first and last sentences of the passage. The opening sentences say:

> What is the point of mentioning *rūpa* 'form'?
>
> Because saying *svaṃ śabdasyāśabdasaṃjñā* by itself will not make the *rūpa* an expressions's technical name..

These statements imply two things. First Patañjali considers that P.1.1.68 means 'the technical name for an expression is its own form'. This amounts to reading the rule with the word *saṃjñā* instead of *saṃjñin* as the *Siddhāntakaumudī* does (SK.I.35:2 (25)). This is confirmed by Patañjali's comments on the 11th *vārttika* on P.1.1.62 (Mbh.I.163:15) where he argues that the form *hanti* is a technical name for itself, and invokes P.1.1.68 to prove it.

The second point of style to be considered briefly is the use of the phrase *na kartavyā* in the last sentence of the argument (Mbh.I.175:23).

At first glance it would seem to mean 'this *paribhāṣā* is not to be made'. That is, the *paribhāṣā* is unnecessary, does not exist, and is not at work in Pāṇini's grammar. Actually it means the opposite. A careful reading of the passages where Patañjali says of a *paribhāṣā* that it is *na kartavyā* shows that he means rather 'we do not have to make up, to invent, this *paribhāṣā*.' The *paribhāṣā* is as good as stated by Pāṇini and need not be framed by us later grammarians. This meaning of Patañjali's emerges particularly clearly in passages where *na kartavyā* is contrasted with *bhavati*, for example in the discussions on P.6.1.223, P.7.2.114, and P.7.4.82 (Mbh. III.120:23, 313:21, 357:18). The *paribhāṣā* need not be made up; the teacher shows us that it already exists.

In traditional terms, the distinction being made is between on the one hand a *vācanikī paribhāṣā* which we ourselves propose and justify by trial and error in examples, and on the other hand a *jñāpakasiddha paribhāṣās* which already exists and is at work in the grammar, as we know from Pāṇini's intimations (see Kielhorn

1874.iv-xvi). This is well understood by later writers who quote the mention of *rūpa* in this rule (P.1.1.68) as a *jñāpaka* or intimation for the existence of the *paribhāṣā* (see Nāgeśa 32:5). Some question arises, however, as to whether the rule P.1.1.68 itself should be rejected because of the arguments in *vārttikas* 2 to 4. If it is rejected than the *paribhāṣā* remains to be established (see Nīlakaṇṭha (no. 11) and Haribhāskara (no. 9)).

The Vyāḍi commentator does not follow the above outlined usage of *kartavyā* and means by it simply 'necessary'. This can be seen from his immediately following phrase (1^a:23) 'what is the point of intimating this *paribhāṣā*?'.

Regarding the text of the *Vyāḍīyaparibhāṣāvṛtti* at this point (1^a:20), it might be argued that the adopted text readings should be altered to conform more exactly with the text of the *Mahābhāṣya*, which is so obviously the source of this part of the text. Thus: '*kiṃ punas tadanyat| arthaḥ*', with correspondingly different translation. However, the manuscript readings at this point show unambiguously that the text was always read as printed here. There are no *sandhi* variants which would allow us to construe with the *Mahābhāṣya* phraseology. Variants of *sandhi* are not strong evidence for the original state of a text, but in cases like the present one they nevertheless show us the sentence boundaries that were understood by readers of the text.

Argument 1^a.7[101] [1^a:23

— What is the point of intimating it?

— So that *kāśe* 'on the grass', *kuśe* 'on the *kuśa* grass' and *babhruśe* 'on the one with speckles' should not be termed *pragṛhya*.

The above *paribhāṣā*, which is too wide in its application, is prohibited wherever it is not desirable:

Explanation What is the purpose of the *paribhāṣā*? In P.1.1.13 Pāṇini rules that *śe* be termed *pragṛhya*. *Śe* is a suffix, realized as *e* (P.1.3.8), which can replace the normal nominal endings (*sup*) in Vedic Sanskrit (*chandas*). terming it *pragṛhya* means that it will not combine with following vowels by the normal processes of *sandhi* (P.6.1.125).

If the *paribhāṣā* did not hold good, the question would arise as to whether the *-śe* in the words *kāśe*, *kuśe*, *babhruśe* should, by the same rules, be exempted from *sandhi*. By applying the *paribhāṣā* the doubt is solved: if we take meaning into account then the two *śes* are clearly different. One means a Vedic suffix (nom. pl.) while the other is just the (grammatically) meaningless last two letters of a word. So there is no question of a *sandhi* prohibition for the latter.

Comments It is worth noting that, by citing the examples *kāśe*, *kuśe* and *babhruśe* (*babhru* + *śa*, *matvarthe*, by P.5.2.100), the assumption is being made that *artha* can be *kṛtrimārtha*, i.e., that 'meaning' in this context quite definitely includes 'technical meaning', or 'grammatical meaning' (see Lyons 1968.435 ff.).

---

[101] The examples *kāśe*, *kuśe* and *babhruśe* all occur in the *Mahābhāṣya* in the commentary on P.1.1.13 (Mbh.I.70:5–8). The added problem that *śe* in *babhruśe* might be considered meaningful since it is a *matvarthīya* secondary suffix is there dealt with.

The examples are taken up by Puruṣottamadeva (no. 1) and, following him, by Sīradeva (no. 9).

Paribhāṣā 1^b

Not when letters are mentioned.[102]

Explanation This *paribhāṣā* exempts letters from the application of the first *paribhāṣā*, pbh. 1^a. That is to say, the meaningfulness or otherwise of letters does not furnish any criterion for which of several occurrences of the letter is to be taken.

Comments The Vyāḍi commentator is alone in using the arguments which follow to establish this *paribhāṣā*. On the approaches taken by other authors see Kielhorn (1874.84 note 1).

Later grammarians held that this *paribhāṣā* does not apply to letters with markers (*anubandhas*), see Sīradeva (no. 10), or when a group of letters are mentioned together: see Haribhāskara (no. 10), quoting Kaiyaṭa.

Argument 1^b.1[103] [1^b:2

— How is this known?

— Since here in *iṭ-vahimahiṅ* (P.3.4.78) he gives one item the marker *ṭ*.

— Giving it the marker *ṭ* is apparently to distinguish it.

— But it is possible to do without that. We shall say *er at*, '*ă* instead of *ĭ*' [and not *iṭo 't* (P.3.4.106)]. And the *ă* will not wrongly replace the letter *i* in *vahi* and *mahi* too, because it is a meaningful

---

[102] This *paribhāṣā* is explicitly known to Kātyāyana as being an exception to pbh. 1^a: see *vārt.* 2 on P.3.4.77 (Mbh.II.181:13).

In the same passage, the *paribhāṣā* is paraphrased by Patañjali. It is also accepted by all the *paribhāṣā* commentators, including Nāgeśa who includes it in his discussion of pbh. 1^a. See Puruṣottamadeva (no. 2), Sīradeva (no. 10), Nīlakaṇṭha (no. 12), Haribhāskara (no. 10) and Nāgeśa (on no. 14).

[103] The argument as such does not occur in the *Mahābhāṣya*. The idea of changing the reading of P.3.4.106 does occur, however, in the commentary on *vārt.* 2 on P.3.4.79 (Mbh.II.182:17). It is there proposed to change the marker of *ị* from *ṭ* to *ṭh*. Then the rule 3.4.106 would read *iṭho 't*.

Argument § 1^b.1 is summarized in one sentence by Puruṣottamadeva (no. 2), according to the old printed edition of the text by Bhaṭṭāchārya (1946) (Abhyankar's P) although the B.O.R.I. manuscript (Belvalkar 1938, no. 294. Abhyankar's M) omits this sentence. He is quoting the *Nyāsa* on P.3.4.78 (KV.III.215; see argument § 2.1).

The other *paribhāṣā* commentators do not mention this argument, although Sīradeva (no. 10) does mention the next one, argument § 2.2.

letter *i* which is concerned, and the letter *i* in *vahi* and *mahi* has no meaning. Because of its [the *i*'s] meaninglessness, it [the *a*] will not arise.

Given that the statement 'when a meaningful item is mentioned, that item should not be mentioned without meaning (pbh. 1^a)' is valid, then by giving the letter *ṭ* in order to make the distinction he [the teacher] is intimating that it is a letter which is being mentioned here, and this *paribhāṣā* does not apply where letters are mentioned.

Explanation When Pāṇini enumerates the verbal suffixes in *tiptasjhi ... iḍvahimahiṅ* (P.3.4.78) he gives the indicative 1st. sg. middle suffix *i* the marker letter *ṭ*. Why should he do this?

There is a rule, *iṭo 't* (P.3.4.106) by which Pāṇini substitutes *a* for the suffix *i* in the optative (*liṅ*). In this rule too he marks the *i* with *ṭ*. Thus the marker *ṭ* specifies that it is the same suffix *i* being dealt with in both rules. In particular, the rule P.3.4.106 is not meant to apply to the final *i* of the dual and plural suffixes *vahi* and *mahi* which also appear in P.3.4.78. The marker *ṭ* distinguishes the 1st. sg. middle *i* from all other *i*-s.

However, it could be argued that given the previous *paribhāṣā*, this *ṭ* is superfluous. If we discarded the *ṭ* in both places, reading just *i* in P.3.4.78 and *er at* instead of P.3.4.106, then the substitution would work equally unambiguously. There would be no confusion with the *i*-s of *vahi* and *mahi* because those *i*-s have no meaning by themselves. By contrast, the *i* of the sg. middle does have (grammatical) meaning, and pbh. 1^a would make us prefer this.

Therefore the marker *ṭ* which, given the first *paribhāṣā*, could be dispensed with, is deliberately put there by Pāṇini to tell us that the first *paribhāṣā* does not apply in cases like the present one, where only letters are mentioned.

Comments The *Kāśikā* on P.3.4.78 (KV.III.215 f.) says the marker *ṭ* has the function of distinguishing the *i* of the 1st sg. middle (see P.3.4.106) from the *i* in the other suffixes like *mahi*. Furthermore, the *ṭ* has no positional function (see P.1.1.46), because of the governing rules *pratyayaḥ* (P.3.1.1) and *paraś ca* (P.3.1.2).

Then, on P.3.4.106 (KV.III.233), the *Kāśikā* says that the *i* in question cannot be confused with the augment *i*, which also has the marker *ṭ*, because the latter has no meaning and is therefore disqualified by *paribhāṣā* 1^a.

Two things are strange about this. First it is surprising that the *Kāśikā* does not invoke *paribhāṣā* 1^b to prevent 1^a from applying to P.3.4.106, the more so since pbh. 1^b is given in a *vārttika* and is accepted by all *paribhāṣā* commentators.

Secondly, the reasoning given on P.3.4.106 could be brought to bear in the context of the discussion on P.3.4.78 with the result that the marker *ṭ* would be shown to be superfluous, just as the Vyāḍi commentator argues in argument § 1^b.1.

Exactly this point is taken up by Jinendrabuddhi in the *Nyāsa* on P.3.4.78 (KV.III.215). After showing that in fact the *ṭ* is not necessary, as the *Kāśikā* would have us believe, to distinguish the two *i*-s mentioned above, he asks if we are to believe that this *ṭ* is really unnecessary after all? He answers, delightfully, that for one who has been capable of following the above arguments the *ṭ* is not necessary, but for others it is!

On another point, in 1ᵇ:2, the Vyāḍi commentator says *kila*, 'apparently', which may imply reference to a traditionally held view (*kila āgame*), and he may thus be referring to an earlier text. Like the Vyāḍi commentator, the *Kāśikā* (on P.3.4.78, KV.III.215) uses the expression '*viśeṣaṇārtha*' to describe the *ṭ* in question: perhaps this signals a common source for the authors at this point.

Argument 1ᵇ.2[104] (same speaker) [1ᵇ:32

— And this is not a common reference both to the [augment] *iṭ* which comes before an *ārdhadhātuka* suffix [by P.7.2.35] and to the one which is an inflectional ending, and is made in order that it be replaced by the letter *a* [in both situations, by P.3.4.106]:

[egs.] *laviṣīya* 'may I cut'
paviṣīya 'may I purify'.

— But here it is not desirable [that P.3.4.106 apply].
— Even if it is not desirable, nevertheless it would still apply.
— It would not wrongly apply.
— How so?

Explanation To refute argument § 1ᵇ.1 it is necessary to show that the mention of *ṭ* in P.3.4.78 and P.3.4.106 has some function.

There is another letter *i* which has the marker *ṭ*: the augment *i* which applies before *ārdhadhātuka* suffixes by P.7.2.35. It might therefore be thought that the marker *ṭ* is given to the suffix *i* so that operations designed for it will also apply to the augment *i*.

Thus, while forming *laviṣīya*, the benedictive (*āśirliṅ*) 1st sg. middle of the root *lū* (Dhp.9.13) we go through the following steps:

i)	*lū*				+	*liṅ*	by P.3.3.173
ii)	*lū*				+	*iṭ*	by P.3.4.77, 78 etc.
iii)	*lū*				+	*a*	by P.3.4.106
iv)	*lū*			+ *sīyuṭ*	+	*a*	by P.3.4.102 suffix is *ārdhadhātuka* by P.3.4.116, so
v)	*lū*	+	*iṭ*	+ *sīyuṭ*	+	*a*	by P.7.2.35

followed by *lo-i-sīy-a* → *lav-i-sīy-a* → *lav-i-ṣīy-a*. Going purely by the rules (*lakṣaṇaikacakṣuṣkapākṣa*), it should be possible to apply P.3.4.106 also to the augment *iṭ* introduced at stage v). And this would give the mention of the *ṭ* with the suffix some purpose, i.e., generality. It widens the scope of P.3.4.106.

---

[104] This argument is not found in the *Mahābhāṣya*, but the examples *laviṣīya* and *paviṣīya* are quoted together under the seventh *vārttika* on P.3.1.3 (Mbh.II.8:6) in the course of an argument about accentuation.

Sīradeva (no. 10) mentions the arguments, but does not get involved in all the following intricacies. He avoids them by invoking a principle that pbh. 1ᵇ does not apply when a marker is used with the letter in question (see also footnotes to argument § 2.5). The Vyāḍi commentator would seem to be unaware of this principle.

But this will generate the wrong forms **lavasīya* and similarly **pavasīya* (from *pū*).

The point is pressed that regardless of the wrong results, rules are rules and these are the forms we get. At least the *ṭ* has been given a function and saved from redundancy.

In response, it is argued that if we really apply the rules carefully, mentioning *ṭ* with both the suffix and the augment is still not enough to ensure that P.3.4.106 applies to both. This is argument § 1^b.3.

Argument 1^b.3

[1^b:35

— The *iṭ* [in P.3.4.106] is qualified as being *ṅit*, [i.e.,] as being the *iṭ* that relates to an item with the marker *ṅ* [cf. P.3.4.99]. And the one which occurs in an *ārdhadhātuka* pertains both to what is marked with a *ṅ* and to other things as well. So the latter will not be replaced [by *a*, according to P.3.4.106].

Explanation The *iṭ* referred to in P.3.4.106 is qualified as being *ṅitaḥ* 'related to an item with marker *ṅ*', because *ṅitaḥ* is read into P.3.4.106 from P.3.4.99. The *iṭ* as suffix is always a replacement of an item with marker *ṅ* because the general form of the benedictive verbal suffixes before replacement is *liṅ*, in which the *ṅ* is a marker.

The *iṭ* as augment belongs to an *ārdhadhātuka* suffix by P.7.2.35. In the benedictive it sometimes belongs to an item marked with *ṅ*.

The *iṭ* augment also sometimes belongs to an item not marked with *ṅ*. For example when the verb has the mediopassive endings (*ātmanepada*) the augment *iṭ* precedes the augment *sīyuṭ* which is not marked with *ṅ* nor leads to anything else so marked.

The argument is that since the suffix *iṭ* is always a replacement of an item marked with *ṅ*, and the augment *iṭ* only sometimes belongs to an item marked with *ṅ*, P.3.4.106 will apply to the former rather than the latter. This is because being *ṅitaḥ* 'of an item marked with *ṅ*' is a permanent characteristic (*viśeṣaṇa*) of the suffix, rather than an impermanent characteristic (*upalakṣaṇa*), as it is for the augment.

In sum, the marker letter *ṭ* is not capable of causing P.3.4.106 to apply to both the suffix *i* and the augment *i*. Therefore argument § 1^b.2 is refuted and the mention of the marker *ṭ* is an intimation of the existence of *paribhāṣā* 1^b.

Comments The argument can only be understood if the difference between a *viśeṣaṇa* and an *upalakṣaṇa* is brought out, and a kind of *paribhāṣā* is assumed, giving the former more weight. But none of this is explicit in the text. (In this connection the famous crows on the rooftop (Mbh.I.84 f.) are *upalakṣaṇas*, whereas the colour of the roof would be a *viśeṣaṇa*.)

It is perhaps worth noting that the entire *ārdhadhātuka* suffix in *laviṣīya* (and *paviṣīya*) is not marked by *ṅ*, even though the substituend of the personal endings is the *ṅ*-marked *liṅ*. For the reasoning see the *Kāśikā* on P.3.4.103 (KV.III.231) which draws the general conclusion that although *l*-suffixes may be marked by *ṅ*, this qualification does not carry over to their substitutes.

The genitive *ṅitaḥ*, it will be noted, has to be interpreted as a *sthānaṣaṣṭhī*, meaning 'in place of', in the case of the suffix *iṭ*. In the case of the augment *iṭ* it has to be taken as an *avayavaṣaṣṭhī*, meaning 'belonging to' or 'part of'. The Vyāḍi commentator is silently exploiting this difference, one feels, deliberately.

Argument 1^b.4 [1^b:37

— Even so, it [P.3.4.106] would still apply in *puṭiṣīya* 'may I combine together', because it [the *ārdhadhātuka*] is marked with a *ṅ* according to the rule *gāṅkuṭādibhyo ñṇit ṅit* (P.1.2.1).

Explanation In argument § 1^b.3 the action of P.3.4.106 was said not to apply to the augment *i* because it did not permanently belong to an item marked with *ṅ*. P.1.2.1 rules that all suffixes which follow *gāṅ*, *kuṭ,puṭ*, etc. in the *Dhātupāṭha* (Dhp.6.73–108) have the marker *ṅ*, on condition that they do not have the marker *ñ* or *ṇ*. So after these roots the augment *i* does always belong to an item marked with *ṅ*.

Therefore in, say, *puṭiṣīya* the distinction we had established between the augment and the suffix is lost, and P.3.4.106 could wrongly apply to the augment.

Therefore, the marker letter *ṭ* serves the function of making P.3.4.106 apply to both the suffix and the augment of the roots enumerated in P.1.2.1. Although the forms thus produced will be wrong, it will not be necessary to assume that by giving the marker *ṭ* Pāṇini is hinting at the existence of *paribhāṣā* 1^b.

Argument 1^b.5 [1^b:38

— In that case, then, the distinction [between *iṭ* augment and *iṭ* suffix] is effected by the rule *lasya* (P.3.4.77), which also subsists [in P.3.4.106].

— How so?

— Because it is the *iṭ* which replaces an *l*-suffix marked with a *ṅ* [which is concerned]. And if that *iṭ* replaces an item marked with a *ṅ* then the letter *a* replaces it.

Argument 1^b.6[105] (summing up) [1^b:40

— Therefore this use of the marker *ṭ* [in P.3.4.78] is for the purpose of making an intimation, not for the purpose of making a common reference [to *iṭ* augment and *iṭ* suffix].

Explanation Another distinction between the augment *i* and the suffix *i* is proposed, which will hold even in the case of *puṭiṣīya*, where both are 'of an item marked with *ṅ*'.

The suffix *i* is a replacement for the general form of the verbal endings, *l*, by P.3.4.77, 78. Furthermore, *lasya* (P.3.4.77) is carried forward into P.3.4.106. So by this rule *a* replaces an *i* which is itself a replacement of both an item marked with *ṅ* and the

[105] Sīradeva (no. 10) sums up the entire argument from § 1^b.2 to the present conclusion in one sentence. He dismisses the confusion about *iṭ*-s saying that one could not possibly think that P.3.4.106 applied to the augment *i* because it is out of context, while the suffix *i* is in context. This is, of course, essentially the point the Vyāḍi commentator has been labouring to make.

The *Nyāsa* arguments referred to previously (argument § 1^b.1) deal with essentially the same question, but there is a subtle difference in treatment.

general suffix. Only the suffix *i* has both these qualifications. In no circumstances can the augment *i* have both these qualifications. In no circumstances can the augment *i* be said to replace or belong to the general *l*-suffix.

Finally, therefore, the marker *ṭ* given to the suffix *i* is shown to have no function. Therefore it is a clue to the existence of the *paribhāṣā* 1^b.

Comments The difference in treatment between the *Nyāsa* and the Vyāḍi commentator is as follows: the latter is willing to consider that both the suffix *i* and the augment *i* are *liṅaḥ* 'of *liṅ*'. This ignores the fact that the suffix and the augment have different types of genitive relationship to *liṅ* (see argument § 1^b.3). Therefore arguments § 1^b.4 and § 5 are necessary. The *Nyāsa* (on P.3.4.78, KV.III.215) on the other hand, uses the fact that there are two different types of genitive at work here to distinguish between an augment and a suffix. The argument is therefore considerably shorter.

It would seem, then, that the Vyāḍi commentator does not know the *Nyāsa* (eighth century) arguments on this point.

The Vyāḍi commentator's argument would read much more fluently, and be clearer, if the *ṅitaḥ* (1^b:39) in *lasya ṅito ya iḍ iti* were omitted. This would also solve the problem that the following phrase apparently repeats what has already been said.

Two MSS (β) have the variant *tiṅo* at this place. This does not make sense, since the suffix *i* does not *replace* a *tiṅ*; it *is* a *tiṅ*.

Argument 1^b.7

[1^b:41

— If this is intimated, then here too, in *smipūṅrañjvaśāṃ sani* (P.7.2.74) a letter *ṛ* is mentioned. It [the augment *i*, by P.7.2.74] applies, in that case, to *ṛ* as a mere letter. But it is *ṛ* as a verb for which it is required.

Explanation If the *arthavatparibhāṣā* (pbh. 1^a) does not hold where letters are concerned, then a problem arises in the interpretation of P.7.2.74. This rule prescribes the augment *i* after certain roots, including *ṛ*. According to *paribhāṣā* 1^b we shall have to treat this as any letter *ṛ*, not as a meaningful root.

Argument 1^b.8[106]

[1^b:42

— This is not so. This [*i* in P.7.2.74] is a reference to the verb *ṛ* alone, not the letter *ṛ*.

— How is that known?

— Because he states *kiraś ca pañcabhyaḥ* (P.7.2.75). For if in this rule (P.7.2.74) it is the letter *ṛ* which is meant then there would be no need to say 'and also after the five [roots] *kṝ (gṝ, dṛ, dhṛ and prach)*' (P.7.2.75), because *kṝ* and the others end in the letter *ṛ* and that [augment] would be sanctioned by the previous rule [P.7.2.74] alone.

[106] Arguments § 1^b.7 and § 8 do not appear in the *Mahābhāṣya*, nor in any of the *paribhāṣā* commentaries.

Explanation The answer proposed is that in fact Pāṇini has guarded against this possibility and has hinted to us that *ṛ* is a meaningful root by framing the next rule, P.7.2.75. Here he extends the scope of the first rule to cover the roots *kṝ*, *gṝ*, *dṛ*, *dhṛ*, and *prach*. As can immediately be seen, four of these roots end in *ṛ*, two long and two short. If *ṛ* in the previous rule, P.7.2.74, were just a meaningless letter than the augment would already apply after the four roots and P.7.2.75 would be largely redundant. So *ṛ* in P.7.2.74 must be interpreted as a meaningful root.

Argument 1^b.9

[1^b:47

— This is not what it [P.7.2.75] is for. Actually, *prach* has necessarily to be mentioned there [in P.7.2.75], in order to prohibit *ekāca (upadeśe 'nudāttāt)* (P.7.2.10).

Furthermore the augment *iṭ* which belongs to an *ārdhadhātuka* suffix is:

1. Applied in the case of *kṝ* and the others [by P.7.2.35].
2. It is [then] prohibited for roots ending in *u*, *ṛ*, or *ḷ* by *sani grahaguhoś ca* (P.7.2.12).
3. It is once again made applicable by the mention of the letter [*ṛ*] in *smipūṅrañjvaśāṃ sani* (P.7.2.74).
4. It is [then] made optional by *iṭ sani vā* (P.7.2.41), which follows *vṝto vā* (P.7.2.38).
5. Therefore this rule [P.7.2.75] serves the purpose of making that [augment] permanent.

Explanation The objection is now raised that even if we interpret *ṛ* as a meaningless letter, P.7.2.75 can still be shown to serve a useful function. So we need not assume, with argument § 1^b.8, that P.7.2.75 is only there to hint that the *ṛ* in P.7.2.74 is meaningful.

First of all P.7.2.74 has to be extended to explicitly cover the root *prach*, because the application of the augment after roots like *prach*, which have one vowel and an acute accent in the *Dhātupāṭha* (Dhp.6.120), was prohibited by P.7.2.10. To undo this prohibition in the case of *prach* we have to mention it now.

Secondly, with respect to the other four roots ending in *ṝ̆*, a series of rules come into play, first prescribing, then prohibiting and finally making optional the augment *i*. The important part of this for us is that once the augment has been applied in the desiderative, after the meaningless letter *ṛ*, by P.7.2.74, it is made optional again by P.7.2.41. So P.7.2.75 is given to cancel the optionality for these four particular roots.

But, as specifically stated by the Vyāḍi commentator, the optionality prescribed in P.7.2.41 takes place in the special context of P.7.2.38. That means that this optionality applies only to items ending in long *ṝ*. This leads to the next argument.

Comments According to this view, the augment *i* is optional, in the desiderative, after all roots ending in *ṝ* (except *kṝ* and *gṝ*), and permanent after all roots ending in *r̥̆*. This resulting over-application of the rule is ignored by the Vyāḍi commentator. It would seem that had he wished, the Vyāḍi commentator could have solved this problem (however unsatisfactorily) with the same arguments as those used in argument § 1^a.4.

Argument 1^b.10 [1^b:52

— If so, then this rule [P.7.2.75] should not be stated as *kiraś ca pañcabhyaḥ* 'and after the five [roots] *kir* [etc.].'

— How?

— One should say [instead] *kṝ-gṝ-pracchām* 'after the roots *kṝ*, *gṝ* and *prach*', because by mentioning the letter *ṛ* there [in P.7.2.74] he intimates that items ending in *ṛ* are included. And not all the roots *kir* etc. end in *ṛ*.

— But surely he says 'five'?

Therefore [by stating P.7.2.75] the teacher is intimating that when in the previous rule [P.7.2.74] the letter *ṛ* is mentioned, it is the mention of a meaningful item.

Explanation This argument attempts to re-establish the position of argument § 1^b.7 that the *ṛ* in P.7.2.74 is a meaningful root.

As we saw in argument § 1^b.8, P.7.2.41 only makes the augment *i* optional after items ending in long *ṝ*, not those ending in short *r̥̆*. So if the augment *i* needs to be made permanent after any roots, it is only those ending in long *ṝ*. The augment is already permanent after those ending in short *r̥̆*. So if argument § 1^b.8 be accepted, then P.7.2.75 – as Pāṇini states it – has too much in it. The roots *ṛ* and *dhṛ*, which end in the short vowel, could be left out of the *sūtra*: P.7.2.75 might be justifiable for *kṝ* and *gṝ*, but not for *dṛ* and *dhṛ*. The fact that they are there indicates that argument § 1^b.8 must be wrong, and the *ṛ* in P.7.2.74 must be a meaningful root.

Prach in P.7.2.75 will still be necessary for the reasons given in argument § 1^b.7.

Comments Manuscript P$_1$, and probably the β MSS, read a long vowel *ṝ* in the last sentence of this argument (1^b:54 *ṛkārāntānāṃ*). If this reading is maintained, the sense is that the short *ṛ* in P.7.2.74 also signifies long *ṝ*. In other words the vowel *ṛ* stands for itself and letters homorganic with it.

It would seem unnecessary to say this in view of the fact that it is already taught in P.1.1.69. However it would be necessary to say it if in that rule the Vyāḍi commentator takes the *ṇ* of the abbreviation *aṇ* as the first one in the *Śiva sūtras*. In that case *aṇ* would only stand for *a*, *i* and *u*, but not *ṛ* and *ṝ* would not be homorganic. See argument § 49.

Argument 1^b.11 [1^b:56

— And if it [*ṛ* in P.7.2.74] is taken as a letter then the augment *iṭ* is correctly validated for [the roots] *dṛ* and *dhṛ*.

So 'not when letters are mentioned (pbh. 1^b)' is not omitted.

And there exist no problems

Of the derived and the explicitly stated it is only the explicitly stated which is taken [into consideration].[107]

Explanation This *paribhāṣā* which, as will be seen, has a lot in common with pbhs. 3 and 4, lays down that if we have a choice between an item explicitly stated in a fully fledged form and the same item produced by the application of a series of rules, the former is preferred.

Comments As mentioned, this *paribhāṣā* is accepted by all the *paribhāṣā* commentators. However, their reasons for accepting it undergo a change with time.

Puruṣottamadeva (no. 3) and Sīradeva (no. 39) give the *paribhāṣā* as being intimated in P.3.2.57. Sīradeva quotes a *kārikā* from the *Kāśikā* (KV.II.581) – a variant of that given in the *Mahābhāṣya* on P.3.2.57 – which summarizes the arguments. Both agree that the *paribhāṣā* is *anityā*, not always applicable.

Next, Nīlakaṇṭha (no. 102), following Kaiyaṭa, says that the *paribhāṣā* is established purely on the basis of the worldly experience that something explicit is apprehended by the mind more quickly than something inexplicit.

Haribhāskara (no. 41) gives Sīradeva's arguments for the intimation of the *paribhāṣā* in P.3.2.57, but adds that 'really' (*vastutaḥ*) it is established from worldly experience, as Nīlakaṇṭha says.

Nāgeśa (no. 105) drops the idea that the *paribhāṣā* is intimated by Pāṇini and simply follows Nīlakaṇṭha, as elsewhere, adding that it is *anityā*.

Śeṣādrisudhī (no. 97) follows Nāgeśa, also saying that the *paribhāṣā* is *anityā*.

Thus we see, in successive writers, a movement away from the idea that this *paribhāṣā* is established on the basis of Pāṇini's intimation in P.3.2.57, and towards the idea that it is adapted from common daily experience, i.e., from *jñāpakasiddhatva*

[107] The *paribhāṣā* is stated in full in one *vārttika*, the second on P.6.2.2 (Mbh.III.123:8). It is also used, though not stated in its full form, in a *kārikā*, number three on P.6.2.46 (III.160:17).

The maxim is used very frequently throughout the *Mahābhāṣya* (I.70:8, 71:16, 74:2:21, 90:17:19, 139:5, 402:20, 444:24; II.61:22, 106:8, 439:8; III.73:19, 83:20, 123:9, 145:5, 160:19, 194:7, 204:14, 246:1, 266:24, 272:20, 329:8, 331:12, 342:3, 375:4, 427:20). In one instance only (III.375:4) the *paribhāṣā* is rejected because it would lead to a wrong result. In another case (III.272:19–22 and 342:2–5) two passages exemplify the formulaic style of the *Mahābhāṣya* by repeating, in identical phrases, an argument concerning this *paribhāṣā* and *sthānivadbhāva*.

All the *paribhāṣā* commentators accept this *paribhāṣā*; see Puruṣottamadeva (no. 3), Sīradeva (no. 39), Nīlakaṇṭha (no. 102), Haribhāskara (no. 41), Nāgeśa (no. 105), Śeṣādrisudhī (no. 97).

to *lokanyāyasiddhatva*. The demonstrable historical development of the proof of this *paribhāṣā* gives us a scale of reference against which we can judge other authors who discuss the same problem. Authors taking the first point of view should – in the absence of contrary evidence – be considered prior to those arguing from daily experience, since the latter argument presupposes knowledge of the former, and its rejection. The Vyāḍi commentator shares the more archaic approach. There are some related questions concerning the interpretation of the compound *lakṣaṇapratipadokta*. The earlier writers, from Puruṣottamadeva and Sīradeva to Haribhāskara, all consider that the compound is a *dvandva* 'co-ordinate compound', meaning '*lakṣaṇa* and *pratipadokta*'. Then they interpret *lakṣaṇa* to mean *lākṣaṇika* 'arising from rules'. *Lakṣaṇa* is said to mean *lākṣaṇika* because of *upacāra*, in other words, just by implication. So the *paribhāṣā* in this interpretation is about the difference between an item explicitly stated, and the same item arrived at step by step through the application of rules (see Puruṣottamadeva (113:13): … *lākṣaṇikasya khaṇḍaśo vyutpāditasya*). In a brief aside, Sīradeva (209:18) notes that not everyone is of this view.

Nāgeśa, however, interprets the compound as being a *dvandva* of two *tatpuruṣas*, reading *ukta* with both the other words. So to him the compound means '*lakṣaṇokta* and *pratipadokta*'. This is all clarified in the commentary by Vaidyanātha (*Gadā* 215:17)), which also rejects Sīradeva's statement that, by implication, *lakṣaṇa* means *lākṣaṇika*. (Vaidyanātha adds that anyway *lakṣaṇa* could itself be a *matvarthīya taddhita* derived by *arśa ādibhyo 'c* (P.5.2.127). The *arśa ādi* group is an *ākṛtigaṇa* 'sample list', so *lakṣaṇa* could theoretically be included in it. It would them mean 'having rules in it[s formation]'.)

By interpreting the compound in this way, Nāgeśa is able to get double mileage from the *paribhāṣā*. *Lakṣaṇokta*, explains Vaidyanātha, means not just 'stated by a rule' but 'stated by a general rule'. This is in contrast to *pratipadokta* 'stated by a specific word'. Thus two classes of problem can be solved by the *paribhāṣā*. First those arising from the classical situation exemplified by the *khiṣṇuc* argument from P.3.2.57. As stated above, the conflict here is between an item directly stated in a rule *pratipadokta* and the same item (*lākṣaṇika*). Thus *iṣṇuc* in P.6.2.160 can only refer to *khiṣṇuc* in P.3.2.57 and not to *ksnu*, even though the latter becomes *kniṣṇuc* after the application of a few rules.

The second type of problem concerns the conflict between deriving an item from a rule which explicitly states the item by name, or from a rule which covers a more general category of which the item in question is a member. Thus the *diksamāsas* 'directional compounds' mentioned in P.1.1.28 can only be the compounds formed by P.2.2.26 in which the term *dik* actually occurs. They are not compounds formed by the general rule P.2.2.24. For further examples of these two types of problem see Kielhorn (1874.486 notes 2 and 3).

Since the *paribhāṣā* is being used to solve two distinct types of problem, the use of either type of situation to provide the intimation of its existence would be asymmetrical and partial. This may explain the movement away from considering the *paribhāṣā* to be *jñāpakasiddha* and towards it being considered *lokanyāyasiddha*.

One may note, however, that in establishing the *bahiraṅgaparibhāṣā*, Nāgeśa (no. 50) is content to use two diverging methods of proof, one based on a *jñāpaka*, the other on a worldly maxim. On this and the resulting two-fold interpretation of that *paribhāṣā* see Bronkhorst 1986, part I, section 3, and *passim*.

Argument 2.1–2.10 [2:2

Explanation The series of arguments which follows below forms a unit. The main drift of the arguments can be summarized as follows. Pāṇini mentions the suffix *iṣṇu* in P.3.2.57. (Ignore the marker letters for the moment.) It is prescribed after the root *bhū*. Why does Pāṇini do this, when *bhū* is *seṭ* root (it is marked with an acute accent in the *Dhātupāṭha*, Dhp.1.1; see P.7.2.10, P.7.2.35) and would thus have the augment *i* of *iṣṇu* and perhaps also the retroflex *ṣ* and *ṇ*. So Pāṇini could apparently have discarded the initial *i* of *iṣṇu* and perhaps also the retroflex *ṣ* and *ṇ*, and called the suffix simply *snu*.

The answer given is that if the suffix were just *snu* then P.6.2.160, which adjusts the accent when *nañ* (alpha privative) precedes the compound, would not apply to a word formed with *snu*, when it should. The reason is that P.6.2.160 applies to a word ending with the suffix *iṣṇu*. *Snu* may well become *iṣṇu*, but as it stands it is not *iṣṇu*. Therefore by saying *iṣṇu* and not *snu*, or even *ṣṇu*, in P.3.2.57, Pāṇini is implying the underlying principle that the explicitly mentioned item (*iṣṇu* in P.6.2.160) cannot refer to the same item in another rule if the latter has first to be derived (*snu* → *iṣṇu*).

Certain secondary questions arise when the marker letters are taken into consideration.

Comments The argument as presented by the Vyāḍi commentator is essentially the same as that given in the *Mahābhāṣya* on P.3.2.57. There is a *kārikā* given there which summarizes the argument, while the commentary of Patañjali explains the *kārikā* as well as raising some additional points. The *kārikā* is as follows:

> *iṣṇuca ikārāditvam udāttatvāt kṛtaṃ bhuvaḥ*
> *nañas tu svarasiddhyartham ikārāditvam iṣṇucaḥ*

Which may be translated as:

> *Iṣṇuc* is made to begin with the letter *i* because *bhū* is acute.
> But *iṣṇuc* begins with the letter *i* so that the proper accent is achieved after *nañ*.

The *Mahābhāṣya* comments on the *kārikā* as follows (Mbh.II.105:22):

> — 'Why is *khiṣṇuc* made to begin with the letter *i*, and not stated just as *ksnu*? There would be the added advantage that the letter *c*, which is for the accent, would be unnecessary.[108]
> — By what [rule], in that case, is it made to have to have an initial *i*?
>
> *Iṣṇuc* is made to begin with the letter *i* because *bhū* is acute.
>
> — There will be an initial *i* because *bhū* [in the *Dhātupāṭha*] is acute (P.7.2.10; P.7.2.35).
> — In that case this is the purpose: that [suffix] has the marker *kh*. When it has been de-aspirated (P.8.4.55) there would be a doubt as to whether it [the suffix] has the marker *k* or *kh*.[109]
> — This is nothing but a doubt, and in all cases of doubt the following applies: 'Particulars are clarified through explanation. There is no lack of definition just because there is doubt'.

---

[108] Cf. arguments § 2.1 to § 2.3.
[109] Cf. arguments § 2.4, § 2.5.

> But *iṣṇuc* begins with the letter *i* so that the proper accent is achieved after *nañ*.

— In that case the purpose is that the accent should be according to *kṛtyokeṣṇuccādayaś ca* (P.6.2.160).[110]
— This too is not the purpose. This [*ksnu*] will also become *iṣṇuc* when the augment *i* and retroflexion have taken place.
— This does not work, because 'Of the derived and the explicitly stated it is the explicitly stated which is taken [into consideration]'.
— Or, on the other hand, the retroflexion is actually invalid. That [*iṣṇuc* produced by P.8.3.59 and P.8.4.1] is just *isnuc* [as far as P.6.2.160 is concerned].[111]

Argument 2.1 [2:2

— The intimation of this is the mention of [the suffix] *khiṣṇuc* in *kartari bhuvaḥ khiṣṇuckhukañau* (P.3.2.57).
— How come it is an intimation?
— On this it is said:

'Why is this *khiṣṇuc* made to begin with the letter *i*, and not stated just as *ksnu*? This would also have the advantage that it would not be necessary to use the marker *c*. It is pointless to give a monosyllable the marker *c* because it [the correct accent] is produced by the [general rule about the] accent on a suffix [P.3.1.3].'
— What would be the derivation of a form?
— *Āḍhyaṃbhaviṣṇu* 'prospering' is derived after the augment *i*, *guṇa*, its substitute *av*, and retroflexion have taken place.
— This is quite right.

Explanation Initially (arguments 2.1 to 2.6), the attempt is made to show that P.3.2.57 intimates the existence of this *paribhāṣā*.

Kartari bhuvaḥ khiṣṇuckhukañau (P.3.2.57) contains the explicit mention of the suffix *khiṣṇuc*. It can, however, be demonstrated that if we took the suffix just as *ksnu*, rejecting both the initial *i* and the marker *c*, we would get perfectly good results in deriving forms.

Derivation of *āḍhyaṃbhaviṣṇú* with Pāṇini's *khiṣṇuc*:

i)	*āḍhya*	+	*bhū*	+	*khiṣṇuc*	by P.3.2.57
ii)	*āḍhyaṃ*	+	*bhū*	+	*iṣṇuc*	by P.6.3.67
iii)	*āḍhyaṃ*	+	*bho*	+	*iṣṇuc*	by P.7.3.84
iv)	*āḍhyaṃ*	+	*bhav*	+	*iṣṇuc*	by P.6.1.78
v)	*āḍhyaṃbhaviṣṇú*					by P.6.1.163

[110] Cf. argument § 2.6.
[111] Cf. arguments § 2.11, § 2.12.

Derivation with the hypothetical suffix *ksnu*:

i)	*āḍhya*	+	*bhū*	+		+	*k(h)snu*	by new rule 3.2.57
ii)	*āḍhyaṃ*	+	*bhū*	+		+	*snu*	by P.6.3.67
iii)	*āḍhyaṃ*	+	*bhū*	+	*i*	+	*snu*	by P.7.2.35
iv)	*āḍhyaṃ*	+	*bho*	+	*i*	+	*snu*	by P.7.3.84
v)	*āḍhyaṃ*	+	*bhav*	+	*i*	+	*snu*	by P.6.1.78
vi)	*āḍhyaṃ*	+	*bhav*	+	*i*	+	*ṣṇu*	by P.8.3.59 and P.8.4.1
vii)	*āḍhyaṃbhaviṣṇú*							by P.3.1.3 (and 1.1.21)

Comments The phrase 'on this it is said' (2:4 *atrocyate*), while it could be taken simply as a preamble to the statement of an opponent (*uttarapakṣin*), could also be taken as an opening for a quotation. And indeed the following phrases are virtually *verbatim* the same as the opening comment of the *Mahābhāṣya* on P.3.2.57. This suggests very strongly that the Vyāḍi commentator is quoting the *Mahābhāṣya* here.

Argument 2.2

[2:8

— But there is a problem with the accent. Because it refers to *iṣṇuc*, the rule *kṛtyokeṣṇuccārvādayaś ca* (P.6.2.160) would fail to apply to the occurrence [of that suffix] in [*an*]*āḍhyaṃbhaviṣṇu*.
— For what reason?
— This latter occurrence is not *iṣṇuc*.
— What is it then?
— *ksnu*.

Explanation It has been shown that, as far as derivation is concerned, *ksnu* works just as well as *khiṣṇuc* as a suffix in the derivation of *āḍhyaṃbhaviṣṇu*.

However, if we want to form the negative compound *anāḍhyaṃbhaviṣṇúḥ* 'one who does not become rich', we run into difficulties in getting the correct accent.

P.6.2.160 rules that the final syllable of the second word in a compound be acute, if the compound has *nañ* (alpha privative) as its first member and the suffix *iṣṇuc* (*inter alia*). Otherwise *tatpuruṣe tulyārthatṛtīyāsaptamyupamānāvyayadvitīyākṛtyāḥ* (P.6.2.2) would cause the accent to fall on the first word if the compound, the *nañ* (see P.2.2.6). This would give the wrong form **ánāḍhyaṃbhaviṣṇuḥ*.

Now, if we have formed *āḍhyaṃbhaviṣṇu* with *ksnu* instead of *khiṣṇuc*, then since P.6.2.160 only mentions the latter the rule cannot be applied to the negative compound, or indeed any other word formed with the modified suffix *ksnu*.

Argument 2.3

[2:10

— But does it not become *iṣṇu* once the augment and retroflexion have taken place?

Explanation P.6.2.160, the rule which would give the correct accent to the negative compound *anāḍhyaṃbhaviṣṇúḥ*, mentions the suffix *iṣṇu*, not *snu*. But the latter suffix, after a few steps of derivation, does become *iṣṇu* (see argument § 2.1). So may we not say that P.6.2.160 applies to *snu* also, with the rider that it should first undergo a few operations?

Argument 2.4[112] [2:11

— That is true. However *guṇa* fails to apply in this case because it [*ksnu*] has the marker *k*.

Explanation *Kṅiti ca* (P.1.1.5) prohibits *guṇa* before a suffix which has the marker *k*. Therefore, since *ksnu* apparently has this marker, will not the *guṇa* of *bhū* in *āḍhyaṃbhaviṣṇu* (see argument § 2.1, stage 4) be prevented?

Comments This is a diversionary argument with no bearing on the main discussion. The Vyāḍi commentator answers it with argument § 2.5.

However, in the form in which it appears in the *Mahābhāṣya*, it does indeed have a bearing on the main question. This question is about the necessity or otherwise of the initial *i* of *iṣṇu*. This *i*, the argument has so far proposed, is unnecessary (see discussion, p. 22 ff.). Then it is suggested that the *i* is there to prevent the *sandhi* rule *khari ca* (P.8.4.55) from acting. This would act if the *kh* came into contact with the *s* (or *ṣ*) of *snu* (or *ṣṇu*), and the result would be an ambiguous *k*.

This argument is then rejected as not being a sufficient motive for having the *i*.

Clearly argument § 2.4 is more relevant to its context as it appears in the *Mahābhāṣya*. We may thus suspect that this was the Vyāḍi commentator's source for this particular argument, but that he failed to integrate it properly into the flow of his own ideas.

Argument 2.5 [2:12

— This is not a *k*.
— What is it then?
— It is the letter *kh* which is [first] given; it has turned into a non-aspirate [by P.8.4.55]. So this [*ksnu*] does become *iṣṇu*.

Explanation The *k* in *ksnu* is the result of applying the *sandhi* rule P.8.4.55 to *kh* + *snu*. Since this rule falls in the *tripādī* section of the *Aṣṭādhyāyī*, its outcome cannot feed the earlier rule, P.1.1.5, which prevents *guṇa*.

[112] This argument and its reply in argument § 2.5 occur in the *Mahābhāṣya* on the first part of the *kārikā* under P.3.2.57 (Mbh.II.106:2; see loci 2.1–2.10, general). In that context, the answer given is that argument § 2.4 is a mere doubt, and in such cases *paribhāṣā* commentators mention this argument.

Comments It appears that this argument based on *asiddhatva* 'invalidity' did not occur to Patañjali as a solution to argument § 2.4, because he invokes the *vyākhyāna-paribhāṣā* (no. 52) as his solution. This is not such a strong argument as that from *asiddhatva*.

The final sentence of this argument 'so this [*ksnu*] does become *iṣṇu*' is picks up argument § 2.3 and returns to the main line of the discussion.

Argument 2.6 [2:13

— But in that rule [P.6.2.160] it is *iṣṇuc* [with a *c*] which is mentioned.

Argument 2.7 [2:13

— In that rule [P.6.2.160] as well I shall say *iṣṇucārvādayaś ca* [i.e., with a single *c*].

Explanation P.6.2.160 mentions the suffix *iṣṇu* with the marker *c*. Referring implicitly back to argument § 2.1 where it was said that this *c* could be dispensed with, these two arguments now propose that if we do finally opt for calling the suffix in P.3.2.57 *ksnu* then we should drop the marker *c* in P.6.2.160 as well. In this way there will be no danger of P.6.2.160 not applying to words formed with *ksnu* just because the suffix differs in its marker.

Argument 2.8 [2:14

— On the other hand, he should, at least, be asked:

Now if this is being made *khiṣṇuc* [in P.3.2.57] what [else] could that [P.6.2.160] refer to?

— To the one read in *alaṃkṛñ* ... etc. (P.3.2.136) which means 'having such and such a behaviour.' This too is actually *iṣṇu*, according to the explanation.

Explanation Going back to the *khiṣṇuc* in P.3.2.57, perhaps we should ask whether this *khiṣṇuc* is necessary in order to harmonize with some other referent of the accent rule P.6.2.160? So what else can that rule refer to? Those words formed by P.3.2.136. So the *iṣṇuc* in P.6.2.160 has to cover *khiṣṇuc* in P.3.2.57 and *iṣṇuc* in P.3.2.136 (ignoring for the moment the question of the marker *c*). Finally, the Vyāḍi commentator suggests, the *iṣṇuc* in P.3.2.136 can also be derived from *snu* by the same arguments as before. So the *i* really is redundant.

On another interpretation, argument § 2.8 may be simply a continuation of the discussion in § 2.6 and § 2.7 about the marker *c*. Would this *c* be necessary to the suffix of rule P.3.2.136? No, for the reasons given.

This interpretation does not solve the problem that if P.3.2.136 still reads the suffix as a disyllable then omitting the *c* will throw out the accent on the words formed by this rule.

Comments Abhyankar's reading of *ksnuci* for *khisnuci* (2:14) would lead to a more common-sense argument. Although *ksnau* (loc. sg.) would be even better, since the *c* has been rejected in argument § 2.1.

The reasoning would then be that, if Pāṇini reads *ksnu* in P.3.2.57, might not P.6.2.160 refer to some other rule altogether? After all, P.3.2.136 has *iṣṇuc* in it, just as P.6.2.160 has. The answer is that P.3.2.136 can have its *iṣṇuc* reduced to *iṣṇu* as has been explained for *khiṣṇuc*. It is left to us to add the further step that this *iṣṇu* is derivable from the simpler *snu* (but see argument § 2.10).

Even this reading of the argument is somewhat forced. It is to be suspected that better manuscript readings might clarify this argument.

Argument 2.9 [2:16

— Therefore there is no point in mentioning the item beginning with *i* [*iṣṇuc*, in P.3.2.57 etc.].

This being established, the fact that he [Pāṇini] does mention the item beginning with this is an intimation that,

> Of the derived and the explicitly stated it is the explicitly stated which is taken [into consideration].

Argument 2.10 [2:18

— And [the suffix] *iṣṇuc* is read explicitly with items such as *alaṃkṛñ*- etc. (P.3.2.136).
— But this [suffix], if it is not [at first] made to begin with an *i*, is made into *iṣṇuc* by a process of derivation (P.7.2.35 etc.).
— Only that item which is explicitly stated [i.e. *khiṣṇuc* in P.3.2.57] would be referred to [by P.6.2.160], not this one [i.e. the suffix without *i* in 3.2.136].

Therefore this too is made *iṣṇuc*.

Explanation This seems to be an attempt to repeat the argument for *iṣṇuc*, with initial *i*, in P.3.2.136 (cf. argument § 2.8). It does not work, of course, because *alaṃkṛñ* etc., are not all *seṭ* roots. They do not get the *i* 'by a process of derivation'. Note that P.3.2.138 gives the *tācchīlika iṣṇu* after the root *bhū*. Not all authorities agree that *chandasi* is read into 3.2.138 from 137: see Sāyaṇa's reference to the fact that followers of Candra's system apply this rule to ordinary usage (Sāyaṇa 1964.41:22; Candra Ca.1.2.93. Note also the *laukika* 'mundane' example *bhrājiṣṇu* quoted in the *Kāśikā* on P.3.2.138 (KV.II.652).

Argument 2.11 [2:21

— This is not an intimation. Even if the *paribhāṣā* does not exist, this item with an initial letter *i* [*iṣṇuc*, P.3.2.57] is still necessary.

Argument 2.12

[2:22

— I shall present that [suffix] with a retroflex [i.e., *-*ṣṇu*-*]. Because once the augment *i* is added, the retroflexion which is brought about by a process of derivation [P.8.3.59 and 8.4.1] is invalid [w.r.t. any prior rule] because of [the rule] *pūrvatrāsiddham* (P.8.2.1). Because of that, this [suffix] becomes *isnu* [as far as P.6.2.160 is concerned]. But that [mentioned in P.6.2.160] is stated to be *iṣṇu*.

Explanation One issue which the Vyāḍi commentator seems to neglect altogether is that in any suffix an initial *ṣ* will count as a marker by P.1.3.6 and is thus liable to be elided by P.1.3.9. So his readiness to read the suffix as *ṣṇuc* is quite mistaken.

The problem of the invalidity of the retroflexion with respect to P.6.2.160 is a real one, and is perhaps the very reason why Pāṇini reads the suffix as he does.

Argument 2.13

[2:24

— But is it not made to be *iṣṇuc* in the rule *alaṃkṛñ* ... etc. (P.3.2.136)? Why is that?

— It is read with the retroflex to intimate that the retroflexion is not invariably the case.

— That [retroflexion] too would be intimated. And this being so, the derivative retroflexion is invalid.

Explanation This argument is not clearly put. It seems that, thinking he has satisfactorily dealt with *khiṣṇuc* in P.3.2.57, the Vyāḍi commentator now turns to *iṣṇuc* in P.3.2.136, and tries to explain it. But, however the steps in the Vyāḍi commentator's logic may be construed, the central claim that the retroflexion in the suffix *iṣṇu* is not invariable is false, and the argument falls down.

However, as will be seen in argument § 2.14, the Vyāḍi commentator seems to draw a conclusion quite unrelated to this or the preceding argument.

Argument 2.14

[2:26

— Therefore this [suffix in P.3.2.57] must necessarily be *khiṣṇuc*, and it is not so as an intimation [of the *paribhāṣā*] but in order that there be a common reference [by P.6.2.160 to the suffixes in both P.3.2.57 and P.3.2.136].

Explanation The *Kāśikā* (*sub* P.6.2.160, KV.V.153) is of the opinion that although *khiṣṇuc* in P.3.2.57 has two markers, and *iṣṇuc* in P.6.2.160 only has one (cf. pbh. 41), the latter rule still applies to *khiṣṇuc* because it has the initial *i*. This implies the point of view that the initial *i* in *khiṣṇuc* has no other function, i.e., it is there for the sake of generality (*sāmānyagrahaṇārtham*). This is exactly the point of view finally accepted by the Vyāḍi commentator, who then moves on to other strategies to establish *paribhāṣā* 2.

However, although the Vyāḍi commentator finally accepts this argument, it was not his starting point in argument § 2.11, where this line of objection to argument § 2.1 begins. So his confident 'therefore' is somewhat misleading.

Argument 2.15 [2:28

— In that case this is the intimation: the mention of *pravṛddha* amongst *vrīhi*... etc. (P.6.2.38), because of [the form] *mahāpravṛddha*.

— How come it is an intimation?

— The mention of *pravṛddha* should not be included here [in rule P.6.2.38].

— How about the form *mahāpravṛddha*?

— It will have the original accent on the first word by *karmadhāraye 'niṣṭhā* (P.6.2.46). Because there [in P.6.2.46] the [past passive participle suffix] *kta* recurs, having started from *arthe kte ca* (P.6.2.44, 45). And the word *pravṛddha* does end in *kta*, and the word *mahat* [→ *mahā*] is not a past participle.

This being the case, the fact that he reads the word *pravṛddha* amongst *vrīhi* ... etc. is the teacher's intimation that this operation [of P.6.2.38] takes place where the first and last words [of compounds] are explicitly mentioned.

Argument 2.16 [2:35

— And where are the first and last words explicitly mentioned?

— In *śreṇyādayaḥ kṛtādibhiḥ* (P.2.1.59). Because here the first words do not have past participle endings, and the last words do end in *kta*.

However, regarding *mahāpravṛddha*, only the first word is explicitly stated, here in *sanmahatparamottama* ... (P.2.1.61), and not the last word. Then again a compound of qualifier and qualificand [P.2.1.57] comes about with neither [member] being [explicitly] mentioned.

— This being so, what is accomplished?

— The *paribhāṣā* 'Of the derived and the explicitly stated only the explicitly stated [is considered]' becomes necessary.

Argument 2.17[113] [2:41

— What is the point of intimating it?
— In this [example]:

kā usrā 'what cow?' → *kosrā*

there is no latter form [substitution, i.e., to **kusrā*] by *usy apadāntāt* (P.6.1.96).

Explanation In the *Mahābhāṣya*, this argument runs as follows. The purpose of the word *apadāntāt* in P.6.1.96 is queried. It is there to prevent *kā usrā* becoming **kusrā* instead of *kosrā*. Then it is proposed that even so it is possible to do without the word, and the form **kusrā* will be prevented by *paribhāṣā* 1[a]. This is shown to have unwanted side effects. Then *paribhāṣā* 2 is proposed instead of 1[a]. The reasoning (given by Kaiyaṭa, *Pradīpa* V.107[b]) is that the *us* in *usrā* is a derivative form. The derivation is as follows:

	vas	+	*rak*	by *Uṇādi* 170
→	*us*	+	*ra*	by P.6.1.15
(↛	*us*	+	*ra*	by P.8.3.60, because of P.8.3.110)

The effect of *paribhāṣā* 2 is that the *us* in *usrā*, because it is derivative, will always be passed in favour of any *us* explicitly stated. Thus the *paribhāṣā* does have a function.[114]

Note, however, that this function exists if and when we try to do without the word *apadāntāt* in P.6.1.96. So if we leave Pāṇini's *sūtra* as it is, this *paribhāṣā* does not come into play. The Vyāḍi commentator seems to ignore this fact in presenting argument § 2.17, although it forms the basis of his rebuttal of the argument in § 2.18. It thus seems clear that the Vyāḍi commentator has here lifted an argument from the *Mahābhāṣya*, just because it happens to quote the *paribhāṣā*. But in trying to use it in a context which makes nonsense of the reasoning, he proves his posteriority to the *Mahābhāṣya* text as we know it.

Argument 2.18 [2:42

— This is no purpose. Here [in P.6.1.96] it says *apadāntāt* 'not after the end of a word', and this [*usrā*] does come after the end of a word. And in this [example, *usrā*] there is no explicitly stated *us*. The prior item [i.e., the *ā* of *kā*] too is replaced [cf. P.6.1.87].

[113]This argument is present in the *Mahābhāṣya* (Mbh.III.76:16–19).

[114]The *Mahābhāṣya* immediately passes on from this argument to say that *apadāntāt* is necessary in the rule because of what will follow. Nothing is said to refute the argument based on *paribhāṣā* 2: it is just pushed aside. Indeed on purely contextual and logical grounds it could be omitted without altering the flow of ideas in the least. It could conceivably have been inserted into the text.

Explanation The Vyāḍi commentator here takes note of the real point of argument § 2.17 as it appears in the *Mahābhāṣya* and correctly states that since *kā* and *usrā* are separate words, and the condition of P.6.1.96 is that the prior item *a* should not be at the end of a word, the rule will not apply in the first place.

The interpretation of the text at 2:43–44 is that *us* is derivative (see argument § 2.17), not explicitly stated, and so P.6.1.87 applies and the final *ā* of *kā* and the initial *u* of *usrā* are both replaced by *o*. This would seem to be a retrenchment to the position of argument § 2.17, ignoring the fact that this has been refuted.

Argument 2.19 [2:44

— Therefore, because there is no purpose for this *paribhāṣā* it does not exist. The intimations have to be refuted.

Comments This is an extraordinary statement, following as it does after the intricate arguments above. It is especially remarkable since, as has been mentioned (see discussion above, p. 20), the *paribhāṣā* is evidently accepted by Kātyāyana and Patañjali. The easy dismissal of the convention speaks of a very self-assured attitude to the tradition. Obviously the Vyāḍi commentator felt free enough to make bold independent assertions, in the teeth of the *Mahābhāṣya*. The latter text became absolutely authoritative for the tradition after Candragomin and the *Kāśikā* authors.

Paribhāṣā 3

Of the secondary and the primary, the primary is meant.[115]

— When both a secondary and primary [sense] are understood, the primary one is taken.

Explanation When an operation is ruled for a word which has two senses, a primary and a secondary, then the operation only takes place when the word is being used in its primary sense.

Comments The *paribhāṣā* is broadly accepted by the tradition, though with reservations. It is commonly said to be *anityā* 'not invariably the case', or only applicable to finished words, and rules concerning these.

The more common reading of the *paribhāṣā* is with the word *kārya* compounded with *saṃpratyaya*, thus making clearer that fact that the rule is not a mere general dictum about the primacy of direct sense over indirect, but is a regulative principle in derivational chains of operations. The *Mahābhāṣya* is still vacillating about whether to read *kārya* or not. In the first and third citations of the *paribhāṣā* it does (see footnote 115, p. 32) whilst in the second and fourth it does not. (In the last case *saṃpratipattiḥ* is read for *saṃpratyayaḥ*.) The later *paribhāṣā* commentators all read *kārya*. Thus it seems that the older form of the *paribhāṣā* is without the word *kārya* while the later is with it. This may be a sign of the grammarians appropriating a maxim which was originally of more general application, a *nyāyokti* 'well known phrase or saying', and making it more suitable to a grammatical context (cf. Kaiyaṭa on P.8.3.82, vārt. 2 (*Pradīpa* VI.201): *laukika evāyaṃ nyāyaḥ śāstre āśrīyate...*).

[115]This *paribhāṣā* appears four times in the *Mahābhāṣya* (Mbh.I.71:18, 354:12; III.161:2, 445:20) and in Kaiyaṭa and Nāgeśa's *Uddyota* on P.8.3.82.

It is accepted by all the *paribhāṣā* commentators: Puruṣottama (no. 5), Sīradeva (no. 100), Nīlakaṇṭha (no. 14), Haribhāskara (no. 102), Nāgeśa (no. 15), and Śeṣādrisudhī (no. 15).

Argument 3.1 [3:3

— How is that known?

— Since here in: *dyāvāpṛthivīśunāsīra* ... [etc.] (P.4.2.32) he reads the irregular retroflex *ṣ* in *agnīṣoma*.

Here in *agneḥ stutstomasomāḥ* (P.8.3.82) the retroflexion of *s* is laid down after a short vowel [*i*]. So how is it possible that *s* should be made retroflex after the word *agni* when it ends in a long vowel [*ī*]?

Explanation In P.4.2.32 Pāṇini cites the form *agnīṣoma*, with a retroflex *ṣ* in the word *soma*. The trouble is that P.8.3.82, which teaches this retroflexion, specifies that it takes place 'after [the word] *agni*'. This *agni* has a short final *i*. But the one in *agnīṣoma* has a long *ī* (by P.6.3.26). Strictly, then, P.8.3.82 cannot apply to *agnī* + *soma*, and the cited form *agnīṣoma* is irregular.

Argument 3.2 [3:6

— But will it not happen because of the assertion [of P.8.3.82]? He speaks of the retroflexion of *s* following *agni*, but there is no word *agni* with a short vowel [*ĭ*, before *soma*]. So it will happen because of the assertion [of P.8.3.82].

Explanation In grammar it is axiomatic that every rule of Pāṇini must have a function. Pāṇini has stated P.8.3.82, but, as far as we can see, the conditions for its application are never met. Therefore, since it must work, we shall say that does indeed cause the retroflexion of *s*, even if the initial conditions are not precisely met. And the citation of the form *agnīṣoma* in P.4.2.32 can be taken as confirmation of this argument.

Comments This type of statement, that a certain state of affairs is so 'because of the assertion' of some other item, is common from the arguments of Kātyāyana onwards. See the numerous references under *vacana* and *vacanaprāmāṇya* in Pathak and Chitrao (1935, p. 162).

Argument 3.3 [3:7

— The assertion [of P.8.3.82] does have scope [elsewhere]. The scope is this: Agni is [some]one with the qualities of fire (*agni*), Soma is [some]one with the qualities of *soma*. Agni and soma [together] make *agnisomau* 'Agni 'n Soma'.

Explanation We can only justify 'forcing' a rule in the above way if there really is no other situation where it might work normally. The disputant now claims there is such situation.

When 'Agni' and 'Soma' are the proper names of two people, named so because they display the qualities of the real *agni* and the real *soma*, then their names may be compounded to give *agnisoma*. The *i* is now short, so P.8.3.82 can apply normally.

Argument 3.4 [3:9

— But should not the *i* be lengthened by *devatādvandve ca* (P.6.3.26)?
— The above is not a *devatādvandva* 'copulative compound of divinities'.

Explanation Why will not the *i* be lengthened by the rules P.6.3.26 and 27? Because these rules only apply when a *devatādvandva* is being formed, i.e., a compound of the names of gods. But we were careful in argument § 3.3 to make clear that we were talking about two people, not two gods.

Argument 3.5 [3:10

— Since this scope does exist, the fact that he reads *agnīṣoma* is the teacher's intimation that the mention [in P.4.2.32] is of that word *agni* which is primary [in sense], and so it is long here [by P.6.3.26]. Thus it is that

> Of the secondary and the primary, the primary is meant.

Explanation Finally, we cannot say that P.8.3.82 causes retroflexion after long *i* just because it has nothing else to do (argument § 3.2). It could indeed apply to *agnĭsoma* 'two people called Agni and Soma'. So the retroflex *ṣ* in *agnīṣoma* is, ultimately, illegal. Therefore, by citing this form, Pāṇini is telling us that, though apparently illegal, it is legalized once we adopt the *paribhāṣā*. The *paribhāṣā* is thus validated, and P.8.3.82 takes place when the sense of *agni* and *soma* are primary (as made clear by the long *ī*), but not when secondary (as shown by the short *ĭ*).

Comments It is interesting to note that the argument implies an identity between fire the God and fire the incandescent carbon particles.

Argument 3.6 [3:13

— What is the point of intimating this *paribhāṣā*?
— There is no retroflexion of *s* here in *agnisomau māṇavakau* 'the two lads Agni and Soma'.

Explanation The retroflexion (P.8.3.82) is barred because the words *agni* and *soma* have their secondary senses in this example (see argument § 3.3) and the *paribhāṣā* thus applies to prevent the operation.

Comments In this and the following argument, attempts are made to give the *paribhāṣā* some purpose. At first these purposes are accepted, but ultimately they are refuted (see arguments § 3.13 and § 3.14) and the *paribhāṣā* is discarded (see argument § 3.16).

Argument 3.7[116] [3:14

— Now, of someone who was not a cow but turned into a cow we say *go 'bhaṿat* 'he became a cow' [cf. P.5.4.50]. The term *pragṛhya* is not applied by *ot* (P.1.1.15) [to the *o* of *go*].

Explanation Another purpose for the *paribhāṣā* is proposed. The argument so briefly characterized in the text concerns the derivation of the phrase *go 'bhavat* 'he became a cow'. This is formed thus:[117]

i)	*gaur*		*abhavat*	
ii)	*gaur*	*cvi*	*abhavat*	by P.5.4.50
iii)	*go*	*cvi*	*abhavat*	by P.2.4.71
iv)	*go*		*abhavat*	by P.6.1.67 (and P.1.3.9)
v)	*g*	*o*	*bhavat*	by P.6.1.109 (note option by P.6.1.122)

The crucial point concerns steps iv) and v). If at stage iv) we were to think that since *go* ends in *o* it might be termed *pragṛhya* by P.1.1.15, then we could not go on to stage v). We would have to stop derivation because of P.6.1.125.

However, if by saying 'he became a cow' we are speaking figuratively, for example if the man under discussion is stupid or a Vāhīka,[118] then we may say that the word *go* is being used to express a secondary sense. The man has assumed cow-like qualities.

Then the *paribhāṣā* can be appealed to. Since the sense is secondary and, by pbh. 3, only words with their primary sense are meant, P.1.1.15 is not applicable to *go*. Then we go on to state v) and the desired result, *go 'bhavat*. So the *paribhāṣā* is shown to have a use.

Comments Two problems are outstanding with this argument. First, in order for *go* to be subject to P.1.1.15 it must be a *nipāta* or particle. The Vyāḍi commentator tries to solve this problem in argument § 3.8.

The second problem is that if the *paribhāṣā* effectively blocks P.1.1.15, why should it not equally block all other operations? The *Padamañjarī* (paraphrasing Kaiyaṭa (*Pradīpa* I.251^{b})) answers that while the word *go* is being derived, and up to the moment its inflexional suffixes are added, it has its own proper meaning. The secondary meaning is a result of its context in a sentence, once it formation is over. In the sentence it is seen to be co-referential with something which is not a cow, so we have to interpret it figuratively. And it is *after* this has happened that *cvi* is added and the *paribhāṣā* is applied. In other words, it adds, *paribhāṣā* 3 is applicable only to words (*padas*), not to stem forms (*prātipadikas*).[119]

---

[116] The basic argument occurs four times in the *Mahābhāṣya*, with each occurrence of pbh. 3 (Mbh.I.71:18, 354:12; III.161:2, 445:20). The example *go 'bhavat* is only used in the first of these references.

Expositions in Kaiyaṭa's *Pradīpa* (I.251^{b}) and Nāgeśa's *Uddyota ad loc* (I.252^{a}); *Padamañjarī* on P.1.1.15; *Bālamanoramā* on P.5.4.50 (SK.II.654 (2117)). See also Puruṣottamadeva (no. 5), Sīradeva (no. 100), Haribhāskara (no. 102), Nāgeśa (no. 15), Śeṣādrisudhī (no. 15).

[117] Nearly all commentators introduce *cvi* after the stem (*prātipadika*). It should be introduced after an inflected word (*pada*), since it is a *taddhita* suffix: see *Nyāsa*, *Padamañjarī*, *Bālamanoramā*, etc., on P.5.4.50 (KV.IV.361 ff., SK.II.654 (2117)).

[118] A tribe of dolts.

[119] See *Padamañjarī* on P.1.1.15 (KV.I.114–15); cf. Mbh.I.71:19–20, Kaiyaṭa *ad loc* and *Uddyota ad loc*. Cf. also Bronkhorst 1986 (pp. 129 ff.).

Argument 3.8[120] [3:15

— But then how is this word *go* a particle (*nipāta*)?
— It [*cvi*] is mentioned in *cvir avyayam* (*Uṇādi* 223). Therefore because of its [*cvi*] being a particle [cf. P.1.4.61] it [*go*] may indeed by [a particle].

Explanation Once again the Vyāḍi commentator's argument is not very explicit. The problem at least is clear (see commentary on argument § 3.7). The form *go* at stage iv) has to be a particle for P.1.1.15 to be a threat.

Perhaps the Vyāḍi commentator is thinking that since the word-stem (*prātipadika*) *go* is formed by an *Uṇādi* suffix (*Uṇādi* 225) it is not normally liable to be an indeclinable (*avyaya*).[121] But *Uṇādi* 223 specifies that an *Uṇādi* formation can indeed be an indeclinable, if it ends in *cvi*.[122] This being said, by the ordinary application of P.1.4.61 we arrive at the fact that *go* at stage iv) is a particle. Thus argument § 3.8 holds and is apparently a valid purpose for the *paribhāṣā*.

Comments The explanation offered above may be over-sophisticated. The Vyāḍi commentator returns to the particle problem in argument § 3.14 in terms which suggest that for him the difficulty still stands. In the present argument he may simply be glossing over the distinction between a particle and an indeclinable. If *go*, as a *cvi* formation, is an indeclinable then in very broad terms it is a particle as far as P.1.1.15 is concerned.

Argument 3.9 [3:17

— This *paribhāṣā*, 'when a secondary and a primary [sense] are understood, the primary one is taken,' does not exist.
— Why?
— Because the Agni who is secondary is an Agni who is similar to the real *agni*; [likewise] a Soma who is similar to the real *soma*. Or else it points to some other sense.

This being so, it [the word in its secondary sense] is either derivative or else an element of usage. And the one which is primary is either explicitly stated or else an initial element.

Therefore this [*paribhāṣā* 3] is answered for by one or other of these *paribhāṣās*: 'of the derived and the explicitly stated ...' (pbh. 2), 'of an initial element or an element of usage ...' (pbh. 4)

---

120 This particular argument, with its appeal to the *Uṇādisūtras*, does not appear elsewhere as part of the discussion, although Kaiyaṭa (*Pradīpa* I.251^b:5) does mention that *go* is an *Uṇādi* formation.

121 See *Tattvabodhinī* on *Uṇādi* 223 (SK.IV.198:25). Originally this seems to be meant to apply only to *glauḥ* and *nauḥ*, formed by *Uṇādi* 222. But Bhaṭṭojī makes it clear that he considers that all *Uṇādi* formations are covered (SK.IV.198:1 (*Uṇādi* 223)).

122 Particles are a subset of indeclinables (P.1.1.37). So the fact that an item is the latter does not logically entail its being the former. This problem is not faced.

— Even if an intimation of this *paribhāṣā* is stated, it is still not a real intimation.

Argument 3.10 [3:22

— If the *paribhāṣā* does not exist, whilst the scope [for P.8.3.82] does exist, then the retroflexion of *ṣ* said to follow a short vowel [*i*, P.8.3.82] fails to apply after a long vowel [*ī*]. For that reason this [*paribhāṣā*] should exist.

Explanation This argument simply reverses argument § 3.5. There we said that the strict application of P.8.3.82 without the *paribhāṣā* would yield **agnĭṣoma* and **agnīsoma*. This state of affairs was rectified by applying the *paribhāṣā*. Now, in argument § 3.10, the Vyāḍi commentator is objecting that if we do not accept the *paribhāṣā* we shall be stuck with the hypothetical forms **agnĭṣoma* and **agnīsoma*.

Comments On the use of neuter *etad* to refer to the feminine *paribhāṣā* compare the *Mahābhāṣya* on K.6.4.174.4 (Mbh.III.234:21): *napuṃsakaṃ liṅgasarvanāma* 'the neuter is the common denominator of the genders.'

Argument 3.11 [3:24

— Alternatively, this retroflexion of *s* is not irregular because the word *agni* does have a long vowel [*ī*]. It is still the word *agni* because 'an item altered in part does not behave like something else (cf. Nāgeśa 37).'

Explanation The notion here is that although P.8.3.82 contains *agnĭ*, we can shut one eye to it and treat it as *agnī*. It is, after all, the same word, for all the difference of its last letter.

Comments The *ekadeśavikṛtanyāya* quoted here is accepted by all the *paribhāṣā* commentators of all schools (see Abhyankar 1961.88b; Abhyankar 1967 *passim.*). It is obviously accepted by the Vyāḍi commentator too. It is surprising, then, that he does not treat it separately, or give any justification for it. It is generally taught as a worldly maxim: a dog is a dog (is a dog) even if its ear is cut off; it does not thereby turn into a horse or a donkey.[123]

The fact that the rule is taken for granted by Kāṭyāyana and Patañjali[124] makes it all the more strange that the Vyāḍi commentator does not explain it independently.

Argument 3.12 [3:25

— In that case, the very same rule will make retroflexion of *s* wrongly apply after both the short vowel and the long vowel!

---

[123]See, e.g., Sīradeva no. 40, p. 210:6.

[124]See, for example vārt. 4 on *Śivasūtra* 2, and *bhāṣya* thereon (Mbh.I.21:13).

Argument 3.13[125] [3:26

— Alternatively, because of Suṣeṇa, the optionality which is contextual from *vibhāṣeṭaḥ* (P.8.3.79) recurs [in P.8.3.82]. It [the option] is there [in P.8.3.79] taken to be a determined option. By that means it [the retroflexion of *ṣ*] will never take place after short vowel, and will only take place after a long vowel, [*ī*].
— Having dealt with the matter like this, that [example] *Agnĭsomau* 'the two lads Agni 'n Soma' will cease to be a purpose [for the *paribhāṣā*].

Explanation The proposal is that we read *vibhāṣā* 'optionally' from P.8.3.79 into P.8.3.82. Then, having made the operation of P.8.3.82 optional, we specify that this option is not a free option, but that the rule always applies in certain cases, and never in others. This is technically called a *vyavasthitavibhāṣā* 'determined option' (see Abhyankar 1961, p. 349a, *s.v.*). By this means we can get what we want from the rule, i.e., *agnĭsoma* without retroflexion, and *agnīṣoma* with it, and there is no necessity of invoking the *paribhāṣā*. It is redundant.

Comments The mention of *suṣeṇa* is something of a problem. Note also that two manuscripts read this alone, omitting the following *sūtra* (see apparatus on 3:26).

The word Suṣeṇa is a name and is formed by the first *gaṇasūtra* on P.8.3.98: *eti saṃjñāyām agāt.*[126] The rise of this *gaṇasūtra* from oblivion to a mere addition in an *ākṛtigaṇa* 'sample list', to a full Pāṇinian *sūtra* can be traced in the literature (Mbh.III.448:11; Candra Ca.6.4.89, and 85, 86; *Kāśikā* on P.8.3.98, KV.VI.586; cf. *Nyāsa* and *Padamañjarī*; finally most modern editions).

It is not clear what bearing the formation of *suṣeṇa* has on the ensuing argument. It seems unnecessary to see here any reference to Suṣeṇa Kavirāja Miśra, a sub-sub commentator on the Kātantra system of grammar.[127] The name Suṣeṇa is known from epic and medical literature. Nor will any obvious Śāradāism give us a better reading than Suṣeṇa. It remains a puzzle.

Argument § 3.13 is cogent enough, in scholastic terms; the determined option is a well known device. But there is of course no question of Pāṇini himself having intended the optionality of P.8.3.79 to extend to the following rules.

---

[125]The argument is first used in the *Nyāsa* on P.8.3.82 (KV.VI.571:30). It then appears in Sīradeva (no. 100), who notes that Puruṣottamadeva (no. 5) does not use it: *puruṣottamadevena na vyākhyātam*. It then seems to sink without trace.

[126]*Kāśikā* VI.586:2. Wrongly printed as a separate rule in Vasu 1891, Böhtlingk and other editions. See *Kāśikā*, loc. cit., f.n. 1. On verbal formations cf. P.8.3.65.

[127]See NCC, III.224, *sub Kalāpacandra*.

Argument 3.14

[3:30

— And that [example] *go 'bhavat* 'he became a cow' which was mentioned [argument § 3.8] is also not a purpose.

— Just how does the term *pragṛhya* not apply here [cf. argument § 3.8]?

— The postposition of the *t* in *ot* (P.1.1.15) is refuted because there exists no homorganic letter. Since the letter *o* is not being narrowed down to items of the same length, it is being restricted to being defined as a particle. The term *pragṛhya* applies only to that letter *o* which is a particle.

So that one letter *o* which is both a particle and not a particle must not be so termed.

Explanation It will be recalled that the *paribhāṣā* was of use in the formation of *go 'bhavat* because it prevented *go* from being termed *pragṛhya* (argument § 3.7). The Vyāḍi commentator now challenges this by saying that the term *pragṛhya* could not apply to *go* in the first place. For *go* to be termed *pragṛhya* it must be a particle, according to P.1.1.15. The Vyāḍi commentator takes the *t* in P.1.1.15, which is otherwise redundant, as a sign that not only must *go* be a particle, but it must never have any other classification (see commentary § 3.14). And since *go* is sometimes classified as something else, and not always as a particle, it cannot fulfill the requirements of P.1.1.15. Therefore it is not termed *pragṛhya*, and therefore the *paribhāṣā* is unnecessary.

The subsidiary argument about the letter *t* is as follows. A general rule obtains in Pāṇini's system that when a vowel is cited it stands for itself and also for those vowels homorganic with it (P.1.1.69). That is to say, the same vowel bearing the three different accents, nasalization or not, and the three time measures of utterance: short, long or prolonged. When, however, it is desired to specify the particular time measure of a vowel it is cited with a *t* next to it (P.1.1.70). Thus the *t* in P.1.1.15 being cited with a *t* next to it stands only for the long time measure. But *t*, being a diphthong, is naturally long, and has no short version. And its prolonged version is *pragṛhya* anyway, by definition (P.6.1.125). So the *t* has no function.

But nothing in Pāṇini's system can be allowed to remain redundant, so in the *t* we see a function of another sort: it is specifying that the particle qualifying as *pragṛhya* by P.1.1.15 must be only a particle and never anything else. It is not made clear quite how the *t* is expected to indicate all this.

Comments The Vyāḍi commentator's argument here that the letter *t* in Pāṇini's rule *ot* (P.1.1.15) is redundant is interesting. The argument seems to be cogent: there is no sound homorganic with *o* which should not be termed *pragṛhya*. The vowel *o* does not have a short value in Sanskrit.[128] And if it be argued that the *t* should exclude the prolonged measure of *o*, this too can be refuted on the grounds that a prolonged vowel is for all intents and purposes *pragṛhya* in practice, being declared

[128] But see the practice of the Chāndogyas mentioned under *Śivasūtra* 4, vārt. 4, and the rejoinder.

invariable along with *pragṛhya* items in P.6.1.125. So the *t* really seems superfluous. Or at least it is reasonable to argue so. This makes it very interesting to find that the point has been ignored by all the major classical commentators, i.e., in the *Mahābhāṣya*, *Pradīpa*, *Uddyota*, *Kāśikā*, *Nyāsa*, *Padamañjarī*, *Kaumudī*, *Bālamanoramā*, *Tattvabodhinī*, *Mahābhāṣyadīpikā* (Bhartṛhari), *Prakriyākaumudī* and *Prasāda*. The translator Vasu alone saw something wrong and said 'the final *t* is a surplusage.' Even Candragomin's sharp eye saw no fault (*ot* Ca.5.1.128).

When the Vyāḍi commentator uses the verb *pratyākhyāyate* 'is refuted' it may be that he is simply speaking of himself, with a modest passive. However, elsewhere he has no hesitation in using the active, first person form of verbs (e.g., 2:13 etc.). So it may well be that he is here referring to some other author who proposes the rejection of *t* in P.1.1.15. Since the argument is so rare, it would be interesting if it could be identified in another text, as it might help to place the Vyāḍi commentator some sort of relation to the tradition.[129]

However, when the Vyāḍi commentator goes further and assigns the function of demarcation to the *t* as he does, he is over-stepping the bounds of logic. And his subsequent argument that an item which is only sometimes a particle cannot be subject to a rule about particles itself requires a tacit *paribhāṣā*. Note the play on the word *avadhāraṇa* and the particle *eva* in the next sentence. This is an echo of P.8.1.62 where Pāṇini speaks of *eva* having the sense of *avadhāraṇa* 'demarcation'.

Argument 3.15 [3:34

— And this one [letter *o*] which ends in a *cvi* is a particle here because of *cver* [P.1.4.61?].

Explanation This statement is not clear. It would appear from the context that *cver* must be a reference of some sort to P.1.4.61, the rule by which an item ending in *cvi* can be termed a particle. This same rule also assigns the term *gati* to the same items. Perhaps this is the 'particle and not a particle' which the Vyāḍi commentator referred to in argument § 3.14.

At any rate this statement is meant to cap the reasoning of argument § 3.14, rendering the example *go 'bhavat* useless as a purpose for the application of the *paribhāṣā*.

Argument 3.16 [3:36

— Because of this, and because there is no intimation, because it is answered for in either case, this *paribhāṣā* does not exist.

Explanation The form *agnīṣoma* in P.4.2.32 was meant to be the intimation of this *paribhāṣā*, and the expression *go 'bhavat* was meant to be its purpose (see arguments § 3.5 and § 3.7). Both these examples have been explained without recourse to the *paribhāṣā* (see arguments § 3.9, 13 and 14). Therefore the *paribhāṣā* is untenable.

[129] For arguments which are along the lines of argument § 3.14, though not the same, see *Kāśikā* and commentaries on P.7.1.90, KV.V.635 ff.; *Nyāsa* and *Padamañjarī* on P.6.1.93, KV.IV.561.

Comments The arguments are slightly confused by the introduction in argument § 3.6 of *agnisoma* as a purpose for the *paribhāṣā*. In argument § 3.9 the Vyāḍi commentator argues that this is not a purpose, for he suddenly ends up saying that *agnīṣoma* is not an intimation. The two issues are of course interdependent.

However his general sense seems to be clear. This use of *pratyukta* 'answered for' is not common.

Finally, the Vyāḍi commentator stands alone in the tradition in rejecting this *paribhāṣā*.

Paribhāṣā 4

Of an initial element [in a derivation], and an element of usage, it is the initial element which is taken [into consideration].[130]

— When an item is mentioned both as an initial element and as an element of usage, it is the initial element which is meant and not the element of usage.

Explanation Suppose that in the course of a derivation a rule refers to some item which has two possible referents: first that item as directly stated by Pāṇini in some other rule, as a prime element of an initial string, and secondly that same item as part of a formed word, as a segment of discourse. Which of the two possible referents is to be understood? The present *paribhāṣā* teaches that the first must be understood.

Comments This *paribhāṣā* does not arise directly from the *munitraya* – Pāṇini, Kātyayana and Patañjali – although the earliest *paribhāṣā* commentators argue that it is *jñāpaka-siddha*. The earlier writers, Puruṣottamadeva and Sīradeva, are disposed to accept the *paribhāṣā*. The Vyāḍi commentator does not, and after Nīlakaṇṭha's categorical rejection it is also rejected, after much argument, by all later commentators.

In general terms, the arguments for and against the *paribhāṣā* are the same through all the authors, the differences being in emphasis and regard for the authority of the *Mahābhāṣya*: Nīlakaṇṭha and, following him, Nāgeśa, both object to the *paribhāṣā* initially on the simple grounds that it is not used in the *Mahābhāṣya*.

On the Sanskrit grammarians' understanding of the distinction between metalanguage and object language see Palsule (1970), *inter alia*.

The phrase 'initial element' translates *aupadeśika*. This is the general adjectival term for items occurring in Pāṇini's *upadeśa*. *Upadeśa* means 'teaching', but it is traditionally glossed as *ādyoccāraṇa* 'initial utterance'. The *upadeśa* comprises all those grammatical elements which form the starting point of a derivation, the 'initial

---

[130]This *paribhāṣā* does not appear in Kātyāyana's *vārttikas*, nor in the *Mahābhāṣya*. Both sources use the term *aupadeśika* 'belonging to the initial elements; but although both are perfectly familiar with the concept of object language, and refer to it as *prayoga* 'usage, object language', (see Palsule 1970) neither source actually employs the secondary derivative *prāyogika* 'existing in the object language', 'part of usage'.

The main *paribhāṣā* commentators all deal with this *paribhāṣā*: Puruṣottamadeva (no. 4), Sīradeva (no. 81), Nīlakaṇṭha (no. 15), Haribhāskara (no. 84), Nāgeśa (no. 120.2).

string of auxiliary symbols' or 'non-terminal strings' (cf. Lyons 1978.50, 162), such as roots, suffixes, case terminations, in the form in which they are first given by Pāṇini in a rule or list. This rather generalized characterization is summarized in the following ubiquitous verse:[131]

> *dhātusūtragaṇoṇādivācyaliṅgānuśāsanam*
> *āgamapratyayādeśā upadeśāḥ prakīrtitāḥ*

The phrase 'an element of usage' translates *prāyogika*. This simply means a phonetic unit as it is in actual speech, a terminal element or 'acoustic blast'.

These contrastive terms, *aupadeśika* and *prāyogika*, are very close in sense to the terms 'auxiliary symbol' and 'terminal symbol' used by Chomsky and others when describing phrase structure grammars. Terminal symbols are items which 'actually occur in sentences'. Auxiliary symbols comprise 'all other terms or symbols that are employed in the formulation of grammatical rules ...' (Lyons 1978.50). Thus a *prāyogika* item is indeed a terminal symbol. But *aupadeśika* items are a subset of auxiliary symbols; they are those which precede any grammatical process. They form the initial string of a derivation. They are selected by rules with a predominantly semantic input, but have not themselves undergone change.

Argument 4.1[132] [4:4

— How is that known?

— Since in *śvīdito 'niṣṭhāyām* (P.7.2.14) he makes mention of *śvi*. For once vocalisation has taken place there [in *śvi*] it [the prohibition of the augment *i*] is validated by *śryukaḥ kiti* (P.7.2.11) alone.

But the teacher observes that it is one of the initial elements *u*, *ṛ*, or *ḷ* which meant. Therefore he makes mention of *śvi* [in P.7.2.14].

Explanation The argument is based on the derivational history of forms from the root *śvi* 'swell'. The standard Pāṇinian derivation of the past passive participle *śūna* 'swollen' (a *niṣṭhā*) is as follows:

i)	*śvi*		+	*kta*	by P.3.2.84, 3.4.70
ii)	*śu*	*i*	+	*kta*	by P.6.1.15
iii)	*śu*		+	*kta*	by P.6.1.108
iv)	*śū*		+	*kta*	by P.6.4.2
v)	*śū*		+	*na*	by P.8.2.45

At stage iv) the augment *i* might have applied by the general rule P.7.2.35. It is prohibited by P.7.2.14 which is applicable because *śvi* is followed by *kta* which is called *niṣṭhā* by P.1.1.26. In P.7.2.14 *śvi* is explicitly mentioned.

The argument of the Vyāḍi commentator is that since P.7.2.11 already prohibits the augment for roots ending in *ū* (among other things), and since at stage iv) *śvi* has indeed come to end in *ū*, surely this rule is sufficient to prevent the augment, and P.7.2.14 is superfluous.

---

[131] Cited, for example, by Vāsudevadīkṣita in the *Bālamanoramā* on P.1.3.2 (SK.I.9 (3)).

[132] Kātyāyana on P.7.2.14 (Mbh.III.286) raises the question as to why this *sūtra* is necessary, for the same reasons as the Vyāḍi commentator's argument § 4.1. But Kātyāyana and Patañjali both assume the recurrence of *upadeśe* 'amongst the initial elements' from P.7.2.10. So for them the *paribhāṣā* is not necessary at this point.

The problem is resolved by the assumption that Pāṇini has the *paribhāṣā* at the back of his mind. *Śvi* in P.7.2.14 is explicitly mentioned as an initial element whereas the *śū* of stage iv), to which P.7.2.11 would apply, is already a product of derivation and is thus ready for use in the object language. Therefore by assuming the existence of the *paribhāṣā* only *śvi* can be taken into consideration, and not *śū*. To put it another way, the *ū* referred to by P.7.2.11 can only be an initial auxiliary symbol. The *ū* at stage iv) is part of the object language and therefore cannot be the referent of P.7.2.11. So P.7.2.14 is necessary.[133]

It is interesting to note that although the *Padamañjarī sub* P.7.2.14 recites Kātyāyana's argument, the *Nyāsa* (KV.V.688:25) does not refer to it.

All the *paribhāṣā* commentators on this *paribhāṣā* mention this argument, giving Kātyāyana's solution (see references in footnote 130). Nāgeśa generalizes the point by saying that Pāṇini and Kātyāyana often use the word *upadeśa*, which would be unnecessary if the *paribhāṣā* existed for them (Nāgeśa, 229–30).

Comments The Vyāḍi commentator shows no evidence of being aware of the obvious argument used by Kātyāyana, that the word *upadeśa* is read into P.7.2.14 from P.7.2.10. Even if he did not think it valid, he should have given it some attention; the fact that he does not strongly suggests that he did not know it, and understood a different *anuvṛtti* at this point.

Argument 4.2[134] [4:8

— What is the point of intimating this?

— In *taraptamapau gha* (P.1.1.22) it is the initial element which is meant, not the element of usage. It [the term *gha*] does not apply here in *nadītara* 'one who crosses a river'.

Explanation P.1.1.22 assigns the technical name *gha* to the items *tarap* and *tamap* (introduced by P.5.3.57 and 55 in the sense *atiśāyana* 'extreme' and 'the more extreme of two' respectively). A *gha* has the property of shortening the final *ī* of *nadī*, when suffixed to this word (P.6.3.44). This is an optional operation.

Thus if the *tara* in *nadītara* is termed *gha*, we might have the wrong form **nadĭtara*. However, the -*tara* in *nadītara* is derived from *tṝ* 'cross over' (Dhp.1.1018; P.3.3.57). So as an initial element it is *tṝ*, and not *tara*. So by the application of the *paribhāṣā* it cannot be the object of P.1.1.22, and cannot be termed *gha*.

---

[133]Note that in the discussion on P.7.2.14 Patañjali uses the old term *prasāraṇa* (seventeen occurrences in Mbh.) for the more usual *saṃprasāraṇa* (169 occurrences).

[134]The problem of *nadītara* is first raised by Kātyāyana, in the *vārttikas* on P.1.1.22 (Mbh.I.79), and discussed there by Patañjali. The argument is the same as the one given here, although the *paribhāṣā* is not explicitly used. The argument is based rather on the fact the *tarap* has a marker, and must therefore be considered an initial element. But then the argument is brushed aside (Mbh.I.79:21–22) and another line of enquiry pursued. See also *Padamañjarī* on P.1.1.22 (KV.I.125; but not *Nyāsa*), and the *paribhāṣā* commentators (see footnote 130, p. 42).

Comments This is a straight attempt to reinterpret pbh. 4 in terms of phb. 3, and thereby to discard it as a separate rule.

It is proposed that to say *aupadeśika* 'initial element' is the same as saying *pratipadokta* 'explicitly stated'. Likewise the term *prāyogika* 'being an element of usage' and *lākṣaṇika* 'being derived' are equated, though less clearly. These equated terms are, of course, those of pbh. 2. So pbh. 4 is ruled out of court as being unnecessary.

Argument 4.3[135] [4:10

— This *paribhāṣā* does not exist.

— How so?

— The 'set of initial elements' comprises the list of rules and the appendices. What exists 'in it' is 'an item of the initial elements'. Being 'an item of the initial elements' means, in other words, being explicitly stated.

Being 'an element of usage' means either being suitable for use, or being usage.

So this *paribhāṣā*: 'Of the derived and the explicitly stated' is here possible (pbh. 2).

Comments This somewhat shaky line of argument is not entirely objectionable in theory, but it would take the careful examination of limiting cases to prove anything, and not the rough equation of terms which the Vyāḍi commentator attempts. It is especially inappropriate for him to take this line since he never defines his technical terms. This is in contrast to other writers, for example Puruṣottamadeva (114:7). Notice in particular that Puruṣottamadeva glosses *prāyogika* as *prayoge bhavaḥ*. This is a correct gloss of the secondary suffix *ika* (i.e., *ṭha*; see P.7.3.50) in the sense *tatra bhavaḥ* (P.4.3.53). The Vyāḍi commentator glosses *aupadeśika* in this way, and offers *prayogam arhati* as one gloss for *prāyogika*. This is valid too, by P.5.1.64. But where we would expect a statement like Puruṣottama's we get *prayogo bhavati*. The suffix *ika*, however, is not used in this sense (*svārthe*). We may, then, have here a mistaken transmission of *prayogo* for *prayoge*. Superscript *o* and *e* are conceivably alike in Śāradā.

[135] This exact argument is not known in the later commentators, although from Sīradeva onwards (see footnote 130, p. 42) the commentators do say that the *tarap* argument (argument § 4.2) can be solved with the help of pbh. 2, and the contiguity argument. While the Vyāḍi commentator uses the latter (argument § 4.5) he does not introduce pbh. 2 in this context.

Argument 4.4 [4:13

— And the intimation which was stated has yet another purpose.
— What?
— If *ukaḥ kiti* [part of P.7.2.11] is stated then both vocalisation and the augment *i* apply to *śvi* + *ta*. In that situation the augment *i* will take place because of subsequence.
— The vocalisation is invariant: if the augment *i* is applied [first] it [vocalisation] applies, while if the vocalisation is applied [first] the augment *i* does not apply. It is prohibited by *ukaḥ kiti* [part of P.7.2.11].

This being so, this [mention of *śvi* in P.7.2.14] is an intimation.
— But if [the *paribhāṣā*] 'a rule about the augment *i* takes precedence over all rule (pbh. 50)' prevents vocalisation, and the augment *i* does arise, then then the prohibition *ukaḥ kiti* [in P.7.2.11] would have nothing to do.

In that situation, when vocalisation does not take place, how would the augment *i* be prohibited? For this reason the mention of *śvi* [in P.7.2.14] is not for the sake of intimation.

Explanation If we are to do away with pbh. 4, then its logical basis, the intimation, must be shown to have some other function. The intimation is the inclusion of *śvi* in P.7.2.14 (argument § 4.1).

Argument § 4.4 is concerned with contrasting the following two possible lines of derivation:

śvi + *kta*

śu + *ta* by P.6.1.15 and 108 | **svi* + *i* + *ta* by P.7.2.35

The left-hand path takes vocalisation as operating first; the right-hand has the augment *i* obtaining first.

In the initial part of the argument the Vyāḍi commentator invokes the principles of subsequence (*paratva*) and invariance (*nityatva*) (see comments on argument § 4.4). The augment *i* is introduced by a rule subsequent to that which introduces vocalisation. So by the principle of subsequence the augment should take place first: the derivation should follow the right-hand path.

But the vocalisation operation is invariant: it takes place whether or not the augment is introduced. An invariant rule takes precedence over a subsequent one, so vocalisation takes place first: the derivation follows the left-hand path. This is the basic position assumed in argument § 4.1, which leads us to say that *śvi* in P.7.2.14 is an intimation of pbh. 4, because otherwise P.7.2.11 would be quite adequate to prohibit the augment *i*. Now the Vyāḍi commentator takes a new line by introducing yet another principle: *paribhāṣā* 50. This makes all rules subsidiary to rules about the augment *i*. Thus we are brought back to the right-hand path of derivation. Once we have

**śvi* + *i* + *ta*

as a possibility we have to act fast to prevent this application of the augment *i*. The only rule applicable here is P.7.2.14, which mentions *śvi*. P.7.2.11 is simply inapplicable.

Thus the mention of *śvi* in P.7.2.14 is vindicated, without assuming pbh. 4.

Comments The rule ordering principles of subsequence and invariance are pervasive in Pāṇini's grammar.

According to P.1.4.2 an operation stated later in the grammar takes precedence over one stated earlier, if they both apply at once. (On the sphere of application of this rule see, e.g., Cardona 1970a, 1988.§ 3.5.) This is the principle of subsequence.

If two rules apply at once, but one of them applies regardless of whether the other is applied or not, then the former is called invariant (see Nāgeśa no. 46, Cardona 1988.§ 3.3; Mbh.I.194–95 defines invariance as *kṛte 'pi prāpnoty akṛte 'pi*.)

Where the two principles clash, a rule which is invariant takes precedence over one which is subsequent (see Nāgeśa, nos. 38, 42).

It is important to note here that while the Vyāḍi commentator employs the principles and also assumes their hierarchical ranking, he does not give them explicitly in his own work.

Argument 4.5[136] [4:20

— And if it be said that *nadītara* is a purpose [argument § 4.2], this is no purpose, because of contiguity. The *tara* which is contiguous with *tama* is the one expressing 'extremity'. Therefore the *tarap* which ends in a primary suffix will not be meant.

— Thus, because there is no intimation, no purpose, and because of the absence of another, this *paribhāṣā* just does not exist.

Explanation As previously, in argument § 1^a.2, the Vyāḍi commentator appeals to the principle of contiguity. By this principle, if there are several occurrences of an item, the contexts helps us to decide which occurrence is relevant to any specific issue. In the present case we have to decide whether or not to apply the technical term *gha* to the *tara* in *nadītara*.

In P.1.1.22, where *tara* is termed *gha*, it is read along with *tama* (see argument § 4.2). Later, when meanings are assigned to these suffixes, they are again read together. So by the principle of contiguity it is the same *tara* in each case. So the *tara* which is termed *gha* is the one which means 'extremely'. But the -*tara* in *nadītara* does not have this meaning, so it cannot be termed *gha*. The problem raised in argument § 4.2 is thus solved without recourse to the *paribhāṣā*. The reference to the

[136]This argument from contiguity is alluded to by Sīradeva (p. 241:29) and Haribhāskara (p. 357:14), but not by Puruṣottamadeva (no. 4). It is not used by Patañjali as part of his *nadītara* discussion on P.1.1.22. But Kaiyaṭa's *Pradīpa* and Nāgeśa's *Uddyota* on Mbh.I.79:13 do mention it, as does the *Padamañjarī* on P.1.1.22 (KV.I.125:10).

'*tarap* which ends in a primary suffix' means the -*tara* at the end of *nadītara* which is formed with the primary suffix *ap* from the root *tṝ* by the rule P.3.3.57.

The Vyāḍi commentator then rejects the *paribhāṣā*. It is not clear what he means by 'another' (but see below).

Comments According to one study of the occurrences of the contiguity principle, none of the classical authors use the principle to solve this particular *tara* problem (Laddu 1973). As shown above (footnote 136) this argument is used by a few authors, but is by no means common. In particular it is not used by Puruṣottamadeva, but does appear in Sīradeva and Kaiyaṭa. Note too that the principle is not explicitly known to Kātyāyana, and is only used implicitly by Patañjali, without the typical expression *sāhacaryāt* being used in the sense here understood (Laddu 1973.168–69). The Vyāḍi commentator's usage on this point thus places him after Patañjali.

In his final sentence, the Vyāḍi commentator rejects the *paribhāṣā* partly because of 'the absence of another'. All manuscripts concur on the reading *asaṃbhavāt*. However, if it could be shown that the reading was originally *saṃbhavāt*, then the reference would clearly be to argument § 4.3, where it is shown that the functions of this *paribhāṣā* can be met by pbh. 2. Then 'because of the possibility of another' would indeed be a reason to discard pbh. 4.

Paribhāṣā 5^a

Of the technical and the non-technical, the technical is meant.[137]

— When both a technical and a non-technical [sense] are understood, the technical one is there taken.

Explanation Pāṇini defines many technical terms. Often these terms are words which already have meanings in ordinary usage. If a situation arises where either the defined sense or the ordinary language sense could apply, the former is to be taken.

Comments Most of the *paribhāṣā* commentators take pbh. 5^a to be a worldly maxim, being reapplied to grammar (*lokanyāyasiddha*). The Vyāḍi commentator is alone in attempting to prove it by intimation. The other authors simply exemplify its application (see comments on pbh. 5^b below).

Most commentators from Puruṣottamadeva on state that the *paribhāṣā* is not invariant, and that it alternates with pbh. 5^b. Nāgeśa goes so far as to reject pbh. 5^a altogether, in favour of pbh. 5^b.

Argument 5^a.1 [5^a:3

— How is that known?

Since he gives *mahārājāṭ ṭhañ* (P.4.3.97) in its final form. For in this case the compound-final suffix *ṭac* is prohibited by *na pūjāyām* (P.1.4.94) and *atir atikramaṇe ca* (P.1.4.95) it is those items reverenced by *su* and *ati* alone which are meant. There is no prohibition [of *ṭac*] here [in *mahārāja*].

---

[137] Both the terms *kṛtrima* and *akṛtrima* are known to Kātyāyana (Mbh.III.176:9; I:80:11). His argument in the latter context suggests strongly that the idea behind this *paribhāṣā* was present to him, though perhaps not in its finished form.

Patañjali quotes the *paribhāṣā* explicitly six times (Mbh.I.80:13:16:21, 81:2, 277:23, 330:21).Note that only in the first instance does he say *kāryasaṃpratyayaḥ*. In all other instances it is just *saṃpratyayaḥ*. The Vyāḍi commentator follows this latter form, while all other commentators follow the former.

All the *paribhāṣā* commentators discuss this rule: Puruṣottamadeva (no. 7), Nīlakaṇṭha (no. 88), Haribhāskara (no. 103), Nāgeśa (no. 9) (to reject it), Śeṣādrisudhī (no. 9).

See also *Bālamanoramā* on P.1.1.23 (SK.I.257:10 (258)) and *Tattvabodhinī ad loc.* (SK.I.258:12 (258)), and on P.3.2.4 (SK.IV.46:24 (2916)), the *Padamañjarī* on P.3.2.1 (KV.II.540:8), etc., etc.

Explanation In rule P.4.3.97, Pāṇini explicitly uses the form *mahārāja*, thus showing that he considers it correct. It is formed with the compound-final suffix *ṭac*, by P.5.4.91. If it were not so we should expect a form **mahārājñaḥ* with *rājan* behaving as an ordinary *-an* stem with an ablative suffix.

The first member of the compound, *mahat*, is clearly a word expressing praise or reverence of the king. But the rule *na pūjanāt* (P.5.4.69) prohibits the use of *ṭac* after any compound whose first member expresses reverence. So why does not this rule block P.5.4.91?

This would indeed happen if *pūjana* in P.5.4.69 meant just 'praise' or 'reverence', as it does in ordinary usage. But in P.1.4.94 and 95 Pāṇini has laid down that *su* and *ati* are termed *karmapravacanīyas* 'prepositions' when and if they express *pūjā*. This is the only place where Pāṇini links any words which could take first place in a compound with the work *pūjā*. Therefore we should understand him to mean that *pūjā* has a technical use which refers not to *any* word expressing 'reverence t only to *su* and *ati*. Therefore *mahārāja*, beginning as it does with *mahat*, may receive the suffix *ṭac* because Pāṇini uses the word *pūjana* on P.5.4.69 with its technical sense 'only *su* and *ati*'.

Thus from this assumption we can extrapolate the general principle that when a term has a technical as well as a non-technical sense, the former is what Pāṇini means.

Comments Pāṇini says, in P.1.4.94 and 95, that *su* and *ati* are prepositions (*karmapravacanīyāḥ*) when they signify *pūjā*. The Vyāḍi commentator apparently turns this right round to mean: the prepositions *su* and *ati* (and only these two) are signified by the term *pūjā*. This does violence to Pāṇini's intention.

Note that at this point the Vyāḍi commentator is ignoring the existence of Kātyāyana's *vār* a 1 on P.5.4.69: *pūjāyāṃ svatīgrahaṇam*, which says exactly what the Vyāḍi commentator is trying to extract illicitly from P.1.4.94 and 95.

The use of the past participle dual form in the phrase *svatyor eva pūjitayor grahaṇaṃ bhavati* (5^a:6) is a little odd. A plural would read more smoothly, with *svatyor* taken as a subjective genitive (P.2.3.65).

Argument 5^a.2 [5^a:7

— This is not an intimation, because *su* and *ati* are not prescribed only in the sense *pūjā* 'reverence'.

Explanation The looseness of argument § 5^a.1 is checked. *Su* and *ati* only mean *pūjā* when being designated prepositions. This is not their exclusive meaning.

Comments The problem is still not quite solved because, this argument depends on *pūjā* having a technical sense of *su* and *ati*, and vice versa.

Argument 5^a.3 [5^a:7

— In that case, then, the reason why when *na pūjanāt* (P.5.4.69) is mentioned only and *ati* are meant is that the mention of an inherent item implies mention of that in which it inheres.

Therefore it [*mahārāja* in P.4.3.97] is an intimation.

Explanation The same limitation of *pūjana* in P.5.4.69 to *su* and *ati* is attempted, but this time for a different reason. A maxim is involved according to which the mention of *pūjana* (or *pūjā*) implies the mention of *su* and *ati* because *su* and *ati* inhere in, or are located in *pūjana* (or *pūjā*).

Comments The relationship of *āśraya* 'residence' and *āśrayin* 'resider' is central and primitive in Nyāya (see Potter 1977.49 and *passim*). Although the term *āśraya* does appear in the *vārttikas* and *Mahābhāṣya*, the maxim as such does not. Nor is it normally considered one of the grammatical *paribhāṣās*.

Regarding the whole of arguments § 1–3, there are so many excellent and straightforward examples for this *paribhāṣā* (e.g., Pāṇini's use of *karman*), at least in the first instance, that it seems extraordinary to pick such an abstruse and unclear line of argument.

Argument 5^a.4 [5^a:10

— What is the point of intimating this?
— The compound-final suffix [*ṭac*] in *mahārāja* is validated because: 'of the technical and the non-technical the technical is meant'.

Argument 5^a.5 [5^a:11

— Those who do not have this rule [P.4.3.97] do have the *paribhāṣā*.
— What do they say?
— What is the point of mentioning *kalyāṇa* 'excellent' in [the phrase] *svatī kalyāṇe*,'*su* and *ati* in the sense "excellent" ', in the list beginning with *kāṣṭha*? As long as [the words] *kāṣṭha* etc. are introduced when there is a word for something being reverenced, according to *pūjanāt pūjitam* (P.8.1.67), then it is these words *kāṣṭha* etc., which mean 'reverencing'. It is only when *su* and *ati* are synonyms for *kalyāṇa* 'excellent' that there is reverence. So there is no point in mentioning *kalyāṇa*.

They state the purpose of the refutation [of *kalyāṇa*] thus:
— How?
— *Pūjana* should be a technical term for *su* and *ati* as synonyms of *kalyāṇa* 'excellent'.
— What is accomplished?
— The author of the *vārttikas* has stated, on *na pūjanāt* (P.5.4.69), that *su* and *ati* should be mentioned. It becomes unnecessary to state this.

This being the case, the prohibition [of the compound-final suffixes] does in no way apply after those words which express reverence [in general].

Therefore there is no point to the *paribhāṣā*. And there is no further purpose [to it].

And so:

Explanation This is a very vexed passage. It is all the more difficult since the argument seems to be unique to the Vyāḍi commentator, and we have no comparative material.

In the previous arguments, the Vyāḍi commentator used the mention of *mahārāja* in P.4.3.97 as his starting point for proving the *paribhāṣā*. Now he turns to those who do not accept this *sūtra* and asks what arguments they can use.

They start from the reading *svatī kalyāṇe* which appears in the *kāṣṭhādi* list (but see comments below). It is argued that, judging from the wording of P.8.1.67, the *kāṣṭhādi* words must always mean 'reverencing' because the word *pūjana* 'reverencing' in the rule itself is like a gloss on them. So to further gloss the words *su* and *ati* as *kalyāṇa* 'excellent' is quite unnecessary.

Since it is unnecessary, it must be a sign that *pūjana* is a technical term meaning only *su* and *ati*, which are synonyms for *kalyāṇa*.

This being so, we could do away with Kātyāyana's *vārttika* on P.5.4.69 which restricts *pūjana* in the rule to just *su* and *ati*. We have shown that this is so already. But the fact that the *vārttika* is there shows that, at least as far as Kātyāyana was concerned, the *sūtra* still needed definition. This in turn means that although the term *pūjana* was a technical term for *su* and *ati*, it could still have its ordinary sense of 'reverencing'. Thus, Kātyāyana shows that he did not accept the *paribhāṣā*. If we accept his *vārttika*, the *paribhāṣā* has no purpose.

Comments There are several disparate points of interest in this passage.

The first is the reference to 'those who do not have this *sūtra*'. It appears that the Vyāḍi commentator is aware of some grammarians who do not accept a certain *sūtra*. The context seems to make it clear that he means P.4.3.97. It is a fact that this *sūtra* is not mentioned, quoted, or even referred to throughout the *Mahābhāṣya*. And although it is included by the *Kāśikā*, the *Nyāsa* argues that on face value the *sūtra* is not necessary, and is only of use in as much as it gives the correct accent for the word *mắhārājikaḥ* 'a devotee of the great king' (KV.III.681 f.). By P.4.3.97 the suffix of this word, with the wrong accent, would be formed by the suffix *ṭhak*. It is interesting then to see that Candragomin does in fact use *ṭhak* to form this word (Ca.3.3.63). Of course he was not concerned with accentuation in writing his grammar. He may here be preserving for us a trace of a tradition of deriving *māhārājika* with *ṭhak* rather than *ṭhañ*, and therefore omitting P.4.3.97. Candragomin does know the suffix *ṭhañ*, and indeed uses it after *mahārāja* in another place (Ca.3.1.32, cf. P.4.2.35).

Rāmacandra also does not read P.4.3.97, presumably because it concerns accent, which he does not treat in his *Prakriyākaumudī*. His commentator Viṭṭhala does, however, mention it (PK.I.778:19).

The second point to note is the Vyāḍi commentator's reading of the *kāṣṭhādi* list. Evidently for him it ends: ... *śvatī kalyāṇe*. This conflicts with all the known readings of this list. All have *su* and *ati*. Some have *su*, *ati* and *kalyāṇa*. But none read *kalyāṇa* as a meaning gloss. (See *Kāśikā* 1970 edition, II.901:5 and note 9.)

Finally, it seems that the Vyāḍi commentator reads the *sūtra* P.8.1.67 as *pūjanāt pūjitam anudāttaṃ kāṣṭhādibhyaḥ*. However the last word was not part of the *sūtra* as composed by Pāṇini, but was added by writers after the *Mahābhāṣya* in accordance with Kātyāyana's recommendation (*vārt.* 1 on P.8.1.67). Thus the Vyāḍi commentator has the text in a form later than the *Mahābhāṣya.*[138]

Concerning the language of this passage, note the use of the archaic *bhūyiṣṭhā* (nine occurrences in the *Mahābhāṣya*) and the use of *prayojana* in the singular, a feature more typical of Kātyāyana than Patañjali.

[138] For a fuller discussion of these points and some very interesting conclusions which may be drawn from them, see Bronkhorst 1983, section 6.2.

Both the technical and the non-technical are recognised.[139]

Explanation A word which has one sense in common usage, but to which Pāṇini has assigned a specific technical sense, may be taken either way.

Comments The maxim means, as Vaidyanātha makes clear (p. 15:13), that a term may have its ordinary meaning in one place, its technical meaning in another, and both at once in a third place.[140]

Although dignified as an independent maxim by Nāgeśa, this *paribhāṣā* is scarcely more than a rebuttal of the *kṛtrimākṛtrimaparibhāṣā* (pbh. 5^a). The four times it is mentioned by Patañjali under P.1.1.23, *vārt.* 4[141] it seems to be no more than an ordinary statement made in the course of an argument, i.e., that 'such and such a term can be taken both ways'. It is not given as a quotation with *iti*, and its phrasing varies slightly:

I.81:5 *ubhayagatis tasya bhavati ...*
I.81:8 *ubhayagatiḥ punar iha bhavati*
I.81:12 *... ubhayagatir bhavati*
I.81:15 *... ubhayagatir bhavati*

Furthermore, in its only other appearance in the *Mahābhāṣya* it again appears as an ordinary statement, rather than as a quoted maxim:

I.278:4–5 *evam ubhayoḥ kṛtrimayor ubhayagatiḥ prasajyeta*

It would seem, then, from its non-formulaic use by Patañjali, that this was originally not a *paribhāṣā* at all, but just a recurring phrase in Patañjali's argument against the *kṛtrimākṛtrimaparibhāṣā* (pbh. 5^a). This latter *paribhāṣā* however, certainly is a fixed formula.

---

[139] The *locus classicus* for the *ubhayagatiparibhāṣā* (pbh. 5^b) is Patañjali's discussion under *vārttikas* 3 and 4 on P.1.1.23. (see especially Mbh.I.81:5:8:12:15). See also the use of the idea, if not the actual form of the Paribhāṣā, under P.1.3.14 (I.278:3–4).

The *paribhāṣā* is treated also by Puruṣottamadeva (no. 7), Sīradeva (no. 101), Nīlakaṇṭha (no. 88), Nāgeśa (no. 9) and Śeṣādrisudhī (no. 9). These authors, like the Vyāḍi commentator, do not treat it as a separate maxim, but treat it as a corollary to pbh. 5^a.

[140] For examples and a paraphrase of Vaidyanātha see Kielhorn 1874.48, note 1.

[141] Mbh.I.81:5:8:12:15.

However, fixed though pbh. 5[a] may be, it is eminently unsuited for the interpretation of Pāṇini's rules in general, as the arguments for the *ubhayagati* position show. This fact, in addition to the fact that the tradition felt the necessity of refuting pbh. 5[a] and of eventually putting the *ubhayagati* principle in its place, would seem to point to a non-Pāṇinian origin for this maxim. And dealing as it does with the use of technical terminology, it is unlikely to have been drawn from any popular adage. This is in spite of Kātyāyana's statement that unless something is done about it, people will not immediately think of the non-technical sense, 'just as in the world' they do not.[142] Rather it may have been a *paribhāṣā* from an earlier, or at least different, grammatical school, or from another formal discipline altogether.

A problem which faces those who accept both the *kṛtrimākṛtrima* and the *ubhayagati* principles is, of course, when to apply which? Puruṣottamadeva (116:8–13) expresses this very dilemma nicely when he says:

> Well now, how does one judge between these two mutually contradictory statements? If a technical term is mentioned, how can it be taken both ways? And if a term is taken both ways, how can a non-technical term be mentioned. It is said that 'one should not kill any creature' and 'animals were created to be sacrificed'. In these sorts of situations, by virtue of the authoritativeness of the masters' works, both [are accepted]. As [Varāha]mihira has said, 'When the statements of the wise conflict, who can work out what is right?'
>
> Alternatively these two statements are to be harmonised by means of [the distinction between] a generalisation and a special case.
>
> In this or some other way the removal of the conflict has to be thought out.

Nāgeśa (p. 15:1–2) is terser but more practical when he suggests:

> In that case, in deciding where something can be taken both ways, or only in the non-technical sense, or only in the technical sense, our only recourse is to an interpretation which accords with correct forms.

We are referred to correct usage to decide issues of derivation (the *lakṣyaikacakṣuṣka* view).

In short, the problem stands.

Argument 5^b.1[143] [5^b:23

— *Sādhakatamaṃ karaṇam* (P.1.4.42) is a case of the technical [sense of *karaṇa*]; *śabdavairakalahābhrakaṇvameghebhyaḥ karaṇe* (P.3.1.17) is a case of the non-technical [sense of *karaṇa*].

---

[142] Mbh.I.80:11 *itarathā hy asaṃpratyayo 'kṛtrimatvād yathā loke.*

[143] These examples are found in the *Mahābhāṣya* on P.1.1.23, *vārt.* 4 (Mbh.I.81:12–14). The rule given there to illustrate the technical sense of *karaṇa* is however P.2.3.18 *kartṛkaraṇayos tṛtīya*. P.1.4.42 is given earlier to demonstrate that the term *karaṇa* is technical (I.81:11).

Puruṣottamadeva (no. 7) also gives this argument and follows the *Mahābhāṣya* in giving P.2.3.18 instead of P.1.4.42.

Nīlakaṇṭha (no. 88) refers us to these arguments in the *Mahābhāṣya*. Nāgeśa (no. 9) gives P.3.1.17 as an example of the non-technical use of *karaṇa*.

Explanation This and the following arguments scarcely need elaboration. In P.1.4.42 *karaṇa* means 'most effective means'. This is its technical sense as a *kāraka*.

On the other hand, in P.3.1.17 *karaṇa* simply means 'doing'. So in some rules *karaṇa* has a technical sense, in others not.

Argument 5^b.2[144] [5^b:25

— *Ādhāro 'dhikaraṇam* (P.1.4.45) is a case of the technical [sense of *adhikaraṇa*]; *vipratiṣiddhaṃ cānadhikaraṇavācī* (P.2.4.13) [and] here in *ic karmavyatihāre* (P.5.4.127) are cases of the non-technical [senses of *adhikaraṇa* and *karma*].

Explanation In P.1.4.45 *adhikaraṇa* means 'location'. This is its technical sense as a *kāraka*. On the other hand in P.2.4.134 *adhikaraṇa* simply means 'thing, item'. So in some rules *adhikaraṇa* has its technical sense, in others not.

Part of the argument, I would suggest, has been lost here through a *saut de même au même*. The missing part might read:

> ... *akṛtrimasya*|
> *karmaṇi dvitīyā* (P.2.3.1) [or *kartur īpsitatamaṃ karma* (P.1.4.49)] *iti kṛtrimasya*| ....

The full argument, as reconstructed would then be:

> In P.2.3.1 (or P.1.4.49) *karman* means 'most desired to be reached by the agent'. This is its technical sense as a *kāraka*.
>
> On the other hand, in P.5.4.127, *karman* means simply 'action'. So in some rules *karman* had its technical sense, in others not.

Comments Note that, in illustrating the technical uses of terms, the Vyāḍi commentator consistently chooses their definitions as *kārakas*. This is in contrast to the practice of the *Mahābhāṣya* and all later commentators, who give *vibhakti* rules in this context.

---

[144]These examples also occur in the *Mahābhāṣya* on P.1.1.23, *vārt.* 4 (Mbh.I.81:15–16 and 10–11). The rule given to illustrate the technical sense of *adhikaraṇa* is, however, *saptamy adhikaraṇe ca* (P.2.3.36). P.1.4.45 is given earlier to demonstrate that the term *adhikaraṇa* is technical (Mbh.I.81:14). The rule given in the *Mahābhāṣya* to illustrate the non-technical sense of *karman* is, however, *kartari karmavyatihāre* (P.1.3.14) (but see reading of MS β on *Vyāḍīyaparibhāṣāvṛtti* 5:26).

Puruṣottama (no. 7) follows the *Mahābhāṣya* on these points. As before, Nīlakaṇṭha (no. 88) refers us to the *Mahābhāṣya*. Nāgeśa (no. 9) gives P.2.4.13 as an example of the non-technical use of *adhikaraṇa*, and P.1.3.14 as one of *karman*. Śeṣādrisudhī (no. 9) reiterates the arguments about the sense of *karman* which occur in the *Mahābhāṣya* under P.1.4.31, in the *Kārakāhnika*.

Argument 5^b.3[145] [5^b:27

— And in operations concerning *ṣaṃkhyās* 'numerals' an item which is not technically a numeral can also be involved.

Explanation Having given examples where either the technical or the non-technical senses of a word are applicable, the Vyāḍi commentator now gives a case where both are applicable at once.

Saṃkhyā 'numeral' is technically defined in P.1.1.23 as the term for *bahu, gaṇa* and words formed with the suffixes *vatu* and *ḍati* (e.g., *tāvat, kati*). However in the very next rule, P.1.1.24, where the word *saṃkhyā* is still in force, items ending in *s* and *n* are mentioned as being included. But none of the items covered by P.1.1.23 ends in *s* or *n*. But several ordinary numerals do, e.g., *ṣaṣ* 'six' *pañcan* 'five'. So *saṃkhyā* here must have its non-technical meaning, in spite of the fact that it has just been defined technically.

Furthermore, in *saṃkhyāyā atiśadantāyāḥ kan* (P.5.1.22) the suffix *kan* is prescribed after *saṃkhyās* 'numerals' with the exception of those ending in *ti* or *śat*. Once again, none of the technical *saṃkhyās* ends in *ti* or *śat* (*kati* ends in *ati*). But several ordinary numbers do, e.g. *saptati* 'seventy' and *catvāriṃśat* 'forty'. The forms *bahuka* 'expensive' and *gaṇaka* 'which costs a *gaṇa*', also derived by this rule, show that the technical sense of *saṃkhyā* is also to be understood.

Thus, in P.5.1.22, *saṃkhyā* has both its technical and non-technical senses.

Comments It would seem natural to account for this double role of the term *saṃkhyā* by saying that P.1.1.23 is an *atideśa* 'extension' rule, expanding the normal meaning of *saṃkhyā* to cover the extra items. This is ultimately, of course, what using the *ubhayagati* principle comes to.

The only difficulty is that Pāṇini usually signals an *atideśa* rule by marking the item to be included by the extension with the suffix *-vat* 'like'. E.g., *sthānivad ādeśo 'nalvidhau* (P.1.1.56). In the case of P.1.1.23 he would thus have said ... *saṃkhyāvat*.

Patañjali mentions this proposal (Mbh.I.81:16–20) and his answer to the difficulty is to appeal to common usage. If we say someone who is not called Shakespeare (Brahmadatta in Patañjali's example) 'he is a Shakespeare' or 'this Shakespeare', we do not mean that the person literally *is* Shakespeare. We mean he is *like* Shakespeare, at least in his writing. In the same way, we should accept that when Pāṇini says '*bahu* etc. are numerals', he only means us to understand that they are *like* numerals.

Patañjali seems to accept this argument from common sense, although he goes on to give a different explanation, based on an intimation from P.5.1.22, and a third based on the fact that *saṃkhyā* is a *mahatī saṃjñā* 'big term', and big terms arebig because they mean what they say.

Whichever explanation one chooses has its drawbacks. It is characteristic of Patañjali to present several suggestions, and leave us to decide. But it is important to recognise that there are several ways of explaining Pāṇini's use of the term *saṃkhyā* which do not require us to accept the *ubhayagati* principle.

---

[145] This conclusion, together with the reasons leading to it, is found in the *Mahābhāṣya* at P.1.1.23 (Mbh.I.80–81).

It recurs in Puruṣottamadeva (no. 7), Nīlakaṇṭha (no. 88), Nāgeśa (no. 9), Śeṣādrisudhī (no. 9). The last mentioned reiterates Patañjali's arguments on P.1.1.23 *vārts.* 3 and 4, without referring to P.5.1.22.

Paribhāṣā 5[c]

In an exocentric compound its constituents [too] are comprehended.[146]

Explanation Pāṇini has defined a *bahuvrīhi* as two or more syntactically related words in composition whose referent is other than the referents of the constituents of the compound (P.2.2.24). This criterion has led to their being called 'exocentric compounds' in modern literature.[147] Thus 'bird-brain' refers to someone stupid; the compound is not talking about a brain (or a bird). A 'four-door' is a car, not a 'four' type of door.

The present *paribhāṣā* is modifying this situation. It teaches that although an exocentric compound refers to some item other than those referred to by its constituents, it may also include these. Thus if we say 'the green-berets are coming' not only do the soldiers come, but their berets come with them.

Comments The terms 'exocentric' and 'endocentric' were introduced by Leonard Bloomfield in 1933.[148] Since Bloomfield was familiar with Pāṇini's grammar it is ar-

---

[146]This *paribhāṣā* is used by Kātyāyana, though not quoted as a maxim (Mbh.III.3:21), and he attributes this interpretation of *bahuvrīhis* to Pāṇini, saying that it is the same in worldly usage (cf. also I.207:24 ff.).

Patañjali uses the *paribhāṣā* explicitly three times (Mbh.I.86:6, 405:23, 426:22). In commenting on Kātyāyana's passage (III.3:22) Patañjali uses the phrase *tadguṇasaṃvijñānam* (as does Kātyāyana) and produces examples which are elsewhere used to illustrate the *paribhāṣā* (I.405:24, 426:23). But the *paribhāṣā* itself is not here quoted, and it is not specified that *bahuvrīhis* in particular are being referred to. The argument has more in common with that on P.1.2.31; *vārt*. 3 (Mbh.I.207:24), in that the suggestion is that in general when Pāṇini mentions an item he intends its constituents, or qualities, to be taken with it.

The *paribhāṣā* is treated by all the *paribhāṣā* commentators: Puruṣottamadeva (no. 6), Sīradeva (no. 42), Haribhāskara (no. 44), Nīlakaṇṭha (no. 56), Nāgeśa (no. 77) and Śeṣādrisudhī (no. 66).

See also *Nyāsa* on P.1.1.27 (KV.I.130 f.) and *Padamañjarī ad loc.* (KV.I.130:21), as well as *Bālamanoramā ad loc.* (SK.I.207:20 (213)) and *Tattvabodhinī* (SK.I.207:25 (213)).

Interestingly, although it is the main thrust of the argument in Patañjali's first paragraph on P.1.1.27, this question is not raised by Viṭṭhala on P.1.1.27 (PK.I.134), who prefers to start with the problem raised in Kātyāyana's first *vārttika* (see argument § 5[c].3).

[147]See, for example, Coulson 1976.117 ff. and Bubenik 1978.192 f.

[148]See Bloomfield 1933.235–37; see also Lyons 1968.231 f. and p. 486 section 6.4.

guable that he derived the terms from Pāṇini's words *anyapadārtha* and its correlative *svapadārtha*, used by Patañjali (Mbh.I.382:16 etc.).[149]

The standard examples used by Patañjali to illustrate this *paribhāṣā* are these (Mbh.I.86:7; 405:24; 426:23; III.3:23):

śuklavāsasam ānaya 'bring the white-robed one'
lohitoṣṇīṣā ṛtvijaḥ pracaranti 'the red-turbaned priests set out'

The exocentric compounds translated as 'white-robed' and 'red-turbaned' refer to the person and the priests respectively. Yet when the person arrives, so does his white robe, and when the priests leave, so do their red turbans. So the compounds' constituents are also comprehended.

The counter-example given is this (Mbh.I.86:5; III.3:20):

citragur ānīyatām 'bring Speckleneat'

The cowherd Speckleneat is so called because his neat (cows) are speckled. However, when he is brought his neat are left behind. This exemplifies an exocentric compound in which the constituents are not comprehended along with the exocentric referent.

Obviously this discussion is incomplete without some theory of inherence or concomitance that can account for why the *paribhāṣā* does not invariably apply. And such a theory would rest on the distinction between permanently inherent attributes ('pale-face') and separable attributes ('green-berets').[150]

It is interesting to reflect briefly on the fundamental issue at stake in this discussion of *bahuvrīhi*-inclusiveness. (The issue is particularly clearly illustrated in argument § 5^{c}.2 below.) Through a purely grammatical inquiry into the inclusiveness of endocentric compounds the ancient Indian linguists arrived at the problem of whether a class name includes itself as a member of the class it names. It is a small (but of course momentous) step from this to the question which has proved so fruitful in modern logical and mathematical theory: whether the class of all classes which are not members of themselves is or is not a member of itself. This problem, Russell's Paradox, was discovered by Bertrand Russell in 1901 while studying Cantor's proof that there is no greatest number.[151] It has been said that considerations of this problem have 'stimulated some of the most important developments in mathematical logic in this century'.[152] There are other related famous modern paradoxes of semantics which bear an even closer likeness to the *bahuvrīhi*-inclusion problem: Berry's paradox and Grelling's paradox, for example.[153]

---

[149] I have developed this argument in the article 'Bloomfield and the Sanskrit origin of the terms "Exocentric" and "Endocentric" ', *Historiographia Linguistica*, vol. 9 (1982), pp. 179–184.

[150] Such a discussion is adumbrated in Puruṣottamadeva's use of the phrase *upalakṣaṇatvād eva* (115:14), and taken up in greater detail by Sīradeva (210:26–31), Nīlakaṇṭha (304:2–5), Nāgeśa (170:5 ff.) and Śeṣādrisudhī (435:17). See Kielhorn (1874.388 note 2 and 389 notes 1, 2, 4,). The discussion appears also in Kaiyaṭa on *vārt.* 15 on P.6.1.1 (V.7.1 ff.), and in the *Nyāsa ad loc.* (KV.IV.435:27 ff.) where the *paribhāṣā* is alluded to (435:32). Jinendrabuddhi here suggests that the same reasoning is being used in the *Kāśikā*, but this is doubtful. Although the *Kāśikā* is making basically the same point about the *bahuvrīhi ekāc* in P.6.1.1, the language and phrasing suggest a simpler approach, without appeal to the *paribhāṣā* directly.

Thus, the Vyāḍi commentator once again shows ignorance of arguments common from the *Nyāsa* onwards.

[151] Cf. Ayer 1972.49, Sainsbury 1979.308 ff.

[152] Sainsbury 1979.309.

[153] Sainsbury 1979.311 f.

It is noteworthy that such questions were approached in modern times primarily through an examination of the foundations of mathematics, while in ancient India they arose in the province of grammar.

Argument 5ᶜ.1[154]

[5ᶜ:29

— How?

— Because after saying, '[the suffix *khyun* applies] when the words *āḍhya* etc. are *cvi*-expressive' (P.3.2.56), he [Pāṇini] then makes the prohibition 'not when *cvi* is there'.

— How?

— *Cvi* is the meaning of these co-occurring words [*āḍhya* etc.]: they are *cvi*-expressive. 'When they are there' means [in other words] 'when they are *cvi*-expressive'. Because it [the compound '*cvi*-expressive'] refers to something else it is an exocentric compound. That [suffix *khyun*] will arise when those items whose meaning is *cvi* are co-occurring words. It [the suffix] does in no way apply to *cvi* [itself]. There is no point in the prohibition.

He [Pāṇini] is observing that this *paribhāṣā* does exist; what applies to items which are *cvi*-expressive potentially applies to *cvi* too.

That is why there is a prohibition.

Explanation In P.3.2.56 Pāṇini prescribes the suffix *khyun* (→ *ana* by P.7.1.1) after the root *kṛ* (Dhp.8.10) when it co-occurs with certain words like *āḍhya* etc. which stand as its logical objects. The sense of the suffix is then *karaṇa* 'means of making'. There is one stipulation, however, on the meanings of the words *āḍhya* etc. They should have the sense of the suffix *cvi* without actually having the suffix itself. Pāṇini expresses this by using the *bahuvrīhi: cvyartheṣu* 'having the meaning of *cvi*' or '*cvi*-expressive', and following it by the negation of the actual suffix itself: *acvau* 'not when *cvi* is there'. The fact that Pāṇini makes this negation necessarily implies that he felt that the *bahuvrīhi* compound *cvyartheṣu* could refer not only to its exocentric qualificands *āḍhya* etc., but that it could also have an endocentric reference to *cvi*

[154]Kātyāyana does question the need for the prohibition *acvau* in his *vārttika* 1 on P.3.2.56 (Mbh.II.105:3). However he does not come to the Vyāḍi commentator's conclusion, and eventually suggests that the prohibition is not directly relevant to the *sūtra* itself, but is put in for the sake of what follows (*vārt.* 3). Thus argument § 5ᶜ.1 does not appear in Kātyāyana or Patañjali. Nor is it used by the *Kāśikā* on P.3.2.56, nor by *Nyāsa* or *Padamañjarī ad loc.* (See the *Siddhāntakaumudī* (SK.IV.65:8 (2973)) for the views of *Kāśikā* contrasted with those of the *Bhāṣya*.). Nor in the *Kaumudī* on P.3.2.56 SK.IV.65 (2973), nor in the *Prakriyākaumudī* (II.530).

The argument appears in Puruṣottamadeva (no. 6), Sīradeva (no. 42) and Haribhāskara (no. 44). Nāgeśa (no. 77) does not mention it, but his commentator Vaidyanātha does briefly (*Gadā* 170:28 f.).

Thus this argument seems to have a life restricted to the earlier *paribhāṣā* commentators only.

itself. So for Pāṇini the compound meant both 'when those items which have the meaning of *cvi* are present' and 'when *cvi* is present'.

Thus Pāṇini held that when a *bahuvrīhi* is used, its constituents also are understood.

Comments The meaning of the suffix *cvi* is *abhūtatadbhava* 'becoming what it was not before', i.e., a change of state (see P.5.4.50, *vārt.* 1). Thus: *stambhī karoti* 'he makes [what was not a post] into a post'. Here the *ī* of *stambhī* is the final replacement of *cvi*. In P.3.2.56 Pāṇini is accounting for such forms as *āḍhyaṃ karaṇaṃ* 'a means of becoming rich'. The sense is of a change of state (from poverty) but the suffix on *āḍhyaṃ* is the ordinary accusative inflection, not *cvi*.

The lack of prominence of argument § 5^c.1 in later literature may be due to the simple but convincing approach of the *Kāśikā* to the interpretation of the expression *cvyartheṣu acvau* in P.3.2.56. It says (KV.II.578:2 f.):

> The suffix *cvi* is prescribed as an option. So there are two kinds of items which have the meaning of *cvi*: those ending in *cvi* and those not ending in *cvi*. In this rule those ending in *cvi* are excluded.

This is so simple and so obviously true to Pāṇini's intention that it is hard to see any problem. It is not that *cvyartheṣu* somehow teaches *cvi*, and so has to be negated; *cvi* is an option (by P.4.1.82).[155] And as an option it may or may not apply, even when an utterance has the meaning which it expresses. Thus *acvau* is stated in P.3.2.56 merely to ensure that *cvi* is not chosen.

This common-sense approach may have dampened any later attempts to preserve argument § 5^c.1.

It may be noted that when, later in the commentary on P.3.2.56 (KV.II.579:1 f.), the *Kāśikā* questions the necessity of the expression *acvau* it is on general grounds, quite different from those of argument § 5^c.1.

Much of the Vyāḍi commentator's prose in argument § 5^c.1 is cast in the typical commentarial style adopted when glossing exocentric compounds (see Coulson 1976.175, Filliozat 1988.175). There is no equivalent idiom in English: the point being made is simply that *cvyartha* is a *bahuvrīhi* and so has an exocentric sense.

[155] On the *anuvṛtti* of *vā* beyond P.5.2.140 see *Kāśikā* on P.5.3.1 (KV.IV.241:1 f.): *vāvacanāṃ tu varttate eva.*

Argument 5ᶜ.2[156] [5ᶜ:35

— What is the point of intimating this?

— The the term 'pronoun' is defined thus: 'the *sarva*-initial items are pronouns' (P.1.1.27) and the term 'root' is defined thus: 'the *bhū*-initial items are roots' (P.1.3.1).

Because 'in an exocentric compound its constituents [too] are comprehended', the word *sarva* is [itself] termed a pronoun.

Explanation This argument is the *locus classicus* for the *paribhāṣā*.

When a class of items is referred to using the standard *bahuvrīhi* construction with *ādi* 'beginning', the question arises as to whether the item in the *bahuvrīhi* itself is part of the class. Thus in P.1.1.27 Pāṇini refers to the items 'headed by *sarva*'. Does he mean to include *sarva* itself among the items? Likewise in P.1.3.1, he refers to the items 'headed by *bhū*'. Is *bhū* itself included as one of these items?

The answer to both questions is 'yes' because of the application of the *paribhāṣā*.

Comments If another author were found who linked this *paribhāṣā* with the interpretation of P.1.3.1 it might throw light on the Vyāḍi commentator's position in the tradition.

[156] The argument occurs in Patañjali's commentary on P.1.1.27, before he discusses the first *vārttika* (Mbh.I.86:2–8). He actually quotes the *paribhāṣā* to solve the problem. The later phrases of this argument, where Patañjali generalizes the maxim, recur in three other places in the *Mahābhāṣya* (see footnote 146, p. 58). The particular application of the argument to P.1.1.27 does not recur, nor does the application of the argument in the context of P.1.3.1 occur in the *Mahābhāṣya*.

The *Kāśikā* does not mention the argument under P.1.1.27 or under P.1.3.1, but the *Nyāsa* does take it up in the former context (KV.I.130:29) and quotes the *paribhāṣā*, no doubt following the *Mahābhāṣya*. This sparks off an extended discussion of the topic in the *Padamañjarī.ad loc.*, which sees the entire argument as implicit in the *Kāśikā's* phrasing and use of relative pronouns. This may well be apt: it is at least plausible that the authors of the *Kāśikā* took care to steer around an issue which involved a lot of detailed analysis, the introduction of a *paribhāṣā*, and a result which was perfectly obvious in the first place, especially if this could be achieved by the careful phrasing of the analysis of a *bahuvrīhi*. The *paribhāṣā* is quoted briefly by Viṭṭhala on P.1.1.27 (PK.I.134:9) and the argument in full appears in the *Bālamanoramā* (SK.I.207:9 ff. (213)) and the *Tattvabodhinī* (SK.I.207:25 (213)). None of these texts, however, refers to P.1.3.1 in this connection, nor do they mention argument § 5ᶜ.2 in their comments on P.1.3.1.

The argument using P.1.1.27 is mentioned by all the *paribhāṣā* commentators up to Haribhāskara (no. 44) who alone does not mention P.1.1.27 as an example of the maxim, but quotes P.1.3.13 and P.6.1.6 instead. Nāgeśa (no. 77) quotes both P.1.1.27 and P.6.1.6 as examples, and argues a case for P.4.2.11 being a counter-example.

Once again, none of these authors uses P.1.3.1 as an example of the *paribhāṣā's* application. Nor does Kaiyaṭa.

This, then, seems to be a unique, if obvious, idea of the Vyāḍi commentator.

Argument $5^c.3$[157] [5^c:37

— And the retroflexion which applies to the *n* in the term *sarvanāma* does not take place because it is given in its final form.

Explanation This argument is purely technical and of secondary relevance to the *paribhāṣā* itself.

By P.8.4.3, a dental *n* in the second word of a compound is replaced by a retroflex *ṇ* under the normal conditions of retroflexion (see P.8.4.1, 2; Whitney 1889 § 189, also § 193), as long as the compound is a conventional name, or proper noun (*saṃjñā*; cf. Palsule 1966). Thus:

vardhrī + nasaḥ	'leather' + 'nose'
vardhrīṇasaḥ	'rhinoceros'

But *sarvanāma* 'pronoun' is a conventional term, so its *n* too should be liable to retroflexion by the preceding *r*, in spite of the word-boundary.

This does not take place because by using the very word itself in P.1.1.27 Pāṇini has demonstrated explicitly its correct form, and this demonstration supersedes any oddities arising through derivation (see Abhyankar 1961.205 *sub nipātana*).

Comments The distribution of this argument in the literature is quite definite: it occurs regularly in the commentaries on P.1.1.27 (occurrences under P.8.3.4 may by grouped with these) and never in the commentaries on *paribhāṣā* 5^c. This is perfectly reasonable, as the argument concerns the word *sarvanāma*, which occurs in P.1.1.27 and should be different according P.8.3.4. The *paribhāṣā* has absolutely nothing to do with this question. Their only connection is spatial – and that only in the *Mahābhāṣya*; this argument happens to by physically next after arguments which do concern the *paribhāṣā* (Mbh.I.86:2–8, and 9 onwards).

Thus, since argument § 5^c.3 in no way logically follows from argument § 5^c.2, we must assume that the Vyāḍi commentator was here drawing his material from the *Mahābhāṣya* directly and, becoming engrossed in the discussion, copied too much.

---

[157] This argument is exactly that of *vārt.* 1 on P.1.1.27 (Mbh.I.86:11). The issue, and consequential issues, are debated by Patañjali *ad loc.* Later on, in *vārt.* 6 on P.8.4.3 itself, Kātyāyana refers back to *vārt.* 1 on P.1.1.27 and again Patañjali summarises the argument (Mbh.III.455:1 ff.).

The *Kāśikā* does not pick up the argument in either place though its commentaries do: the *Nyāsa* on P.1.1.27 (KV.I.134:30), but not the *Padamañjarī*; The *Padamañjarī* on P.8.4.3 (KV.VI.608:8), but not the *Nyāsa*.

The argument is not cited by any of the *paribhāṣā* commentators in the context of this *paribhāṣā*.

The argument is put forward by Viṭṭhala on P.1.1.27 (PK.I.134:12).

Precursory exceptions block immediately adjacent rules.[158]

Explanation Normally a general rule (*utsarga*) is stated first, and then the exception to it (*apavāda*) follows. However, in some cases the exception precedes the general rule in the sequence of *sūtras* of the *Aṣṭādhyāyī*. It is then called a precursory exception (*purastādapavāda*). The present *paribhāṣā* teaches that precursory exceptions only preempt those (general) rules which are nearest to them. The effect of the exception then ceases.

Comments The wording of the *paribhāṣā* would lead one to think that an exception only preempted an *immediately* following rule. However the examples given universally show that what is meant in the *nearer* of two following rules.

The principle is usually linked to another, complementary *paribhāṣā: madhye 'pavādāḥ pūrvān vidhīn bādhante* 'interjacent exceptions preempt preceding rules'. This principle is given by all the *paribhāṣā* commentators except the Vyāḍi commentator: Puruṣottamadeva (no. 9), Sīradeva (no. 47), Nīlakaṇṭha (no. 50), Haribhāskara (no. 49), Nāgeśa (no. 60) and Śeṣādrisudhī (no. 51). It is also known to Patañjali, who sometimes contrasts it with *paribhāṣā* 6 (Mbh.II.327:3–6, III.80:6–9). It is not clear why the Vyāḍi commentator does not give this *paribhāṣā*.

[158] This principle is not quoted by Kātyāyana, but is frequently used by Patañjali (Mbh.I.90:14; II.54:22, 95:14, 152:14, 184:22, 224:16, 322:9:14, 327:5; III.69:5, 80:8, 233:3, 308:20, 450:6).In all cases Patañjali refers to the *paribhāṣā* with the air of its being a fundamental law of grammar which needs no proof or justification.

It is widely accepted in the tradition, and is commented on by Puruṣottamadeva (no. 8), Sīradeva (no. 44), Nīlakaṇṭha (no. 49), Haribhāskara (no. 46), Nāgeśa (no. 59) and Śeṣādrisudhī (no. 50).

Argument 6.1[159] [6:2

— How is that known?

— Since in: *se 'sici kṛtacṛtacchṛdatṛtaḥ* (P.7.2.57) he teaches the optional prohibition of the augment *i* after [the root] *nṛt* when *s* follows. After *nṛt* there is an exception to the [fourth class] thematic affix *śyan*. The thematic affix *śyan* in no way applies to it [*nṛt*]; there is no point in prohibiting the augment *i*.

So the teacher is observing that the precursory exception [?] blocks [the class 1 thematic affix] *śap*, which is the [more] immediately adjacent one, and not the thematic affix *śyan*.

Thus, 'precursory exceptions block immediately adjacent rules'.

Explanation This argument, as transmitted by the manuscripts, is not perfectly clear.

In general a root with a verbal suffix is liable to receive the thematic affix *śap*, realized as *a*.

Thus, to form the present tense *bhavati* 'it is' we have:

i)	*bhū*			+	*laṭ*	by P.3.4.69 and 3.2.123
ii)	*bhū*			+	*ti*	by P.3.4.77, 78 ff.
						ti is a *sārvadhātuka* (P.3.4.113)
						and so to express agency we get:
iii)	*bhū*	+	*śap*	+	*ti*	by P.3.1.68

This is the rule for all roots in general. Roots which behave otherwise are presented as variations from this norm. Thus *nṛt*, a root of the *divādi* group (class four) does not take the thematic affix *śap*, but instead *śyan* by P.3.1.69. So instead of stage iii) above, we will have:

nṛt	+	*śyan*	+	*ti*	by P.3.1.69

The rule P.3.1.69 is an exception (*apavāda*) to P.3.1.68 which immediately precedes it, and it takes precedence since its sphere of operation lies entirely within that of P.3.1.68. This is the simple, normal situation. However, there is another rule, P.3.1.33, which is also an exception. It is designed to insert the future stem morphemes between the root and the general verbal suffixes of the future (or conditional) tense.

Thus to form the simple future of *nṛt* we would begin:

i)	*nṛt* + *lṛṭ*	by P.3.3.13 (cf. P.3.3.133)
ii)	*nṛt* + *ti*	by P.3.4.77, 78 ff.
		(N.B. *ti* is *sthānivat* 'like *lṛṭ*' by P.1.1.56)
iii)	*nṛt* + *sya* + *ti*	by P.3.1.33

[159] It may well be that in composing this passage the Vyāḍi commentator had one eye on Patañjali's commentary on P.3.1.33 (Mbh.II.42–43). This is an involved treatment of the relations of general rule and exception as applied to P.3.1.33, 67, 68 and 69,the very group the Vyāḍi commentator is looking at. However the *Mahābhāṣya* is extremely clear on all the issues involved, and at no point introduces the *paribhāṣā*.

I have not been able to locate this argument elsewhere either. It is not used by any of the *paribhāṣā* commentators.

Here, at stage iii), the future stem morpheme *sya* has preempted the general thematic affix *śap* (see *Siddhāntakaumudī* SK.III.29:4 (2186) *śabādyapavādāḥ* [*idaṃ sūtram*]). So P.3.1.33 is a precursory exception to P.3.1.68.

To sum up then, we are concerned with three rules, which we can label $\mathcal{A}$, $\mathcal{B}$ and $\mathcal{C}$.

$\mathcal{A}$ = P.3.1.33
$\mathcal{B}$ = P.3.1.68
$\mathcal{C}$ = P.3.1.69

The rule $\mathcal{C}$ is an exception to $\mathcal{B}$, and $\mathcal{A}$ also is an exception to $\mathcal{B}$. The argument in the Vyāḍi commentator circles around the relationship between $\mathcal{A}$ and $\mathcal{C}$.

The Vyāḍi commentator begins by citing P.7.2.57. This rule teaches the optionality of the augment *i* after several roots (given in alphabetical order) when a suffix with initial *s* follows. Among the roots specified is *nṛt*, which normally takes the augment. Thus, for *nṛt*, P.7.2.57 means that before a suffix with initial *s* the augment may optionally be omitted. The Vyāḍi commentator then states that the normal fourth class thematic suffix *śyan* which follows *nṛt* by P.3.1.69 is preempted. He does not say by what, but we deduce he must have P.3.1.33 in mind. Thus the Vyāḍi commentator is suggesting that $\mathcal{A}$ is an exception, a precursory exception, to $\mathcal{C}$.

This being so, he concludes, there is no point in (optionally) prohibiting the augment *i* in P.7.2.57. The thinking behind this statement remains obscure. But it leads the Vyāḍi commentator on to say that Pāṇini is, in this set up of rules, showing us that the precursory exception $\mathcal{A}$ preempts only the nearer of the two rules which it could preempt; it is an exception only to $\mathcal{B}$, not to $\mathcal{C}$. And this is but an instance of the general *paribhāṣā*.

It is possible that when the Vyāḍi commentator says that *śyan* is preempted after *nṛt* he has in mind P.3.1.67, not P.3.1.69 as suggested above.

P.3.1.67 *sārvadhātuke yak* provides the passive-stem morpheme *ya* between the root and a verbal suffix. It could, at a pinch, be considered a precursory exception to P.3.1.68 and 69 (but see Mbh.II.42:20). In this case, if it preempted the *śyan* of P.3.1.69 in all situations, then since all fourth class roots would now be followed by a suffix beginning with *y* and not *s*, P.7.2.57 could have no possible application to *nṛt*. So by including *nṛt* in P.7.2.57, Pāṇini is showing that *nṛt* can sometimes precede a suffix with initial *s*, which in turn means that P.3.1.67 cannot always preempt P.3.1.69: it is at least sometimes preempted by P.3.1.33.

Both these arguments are unsound; see below.

Comments The two approaches outlined above both have serious flaws. In the first, where rule $\mathcal{A}$ is taken to be P.3.1.33, the flaw is that this rule really only applies when the future or conditional tenses are to be formed. In all other cases it is irrelevant. Thus it cannot lead to any general conclusions since there are plenty of other verbal suffixes both with *s* and without, which apply in other circumstances. An added difficulty is that even if P.3.1.33 is considered a permanent exception to *śyan*, it is not at all clear why this renders P.7.2.57 unnecessary. An option between the two future forms *nartsyati* and *nartiṣyati* seems very proper.

In the second approach, where $\mathcal{A}$ is taken to be P.3.1.67, a similar problem applies: P.3.1.67 does not have the same domain of application as P.3.1.68 or 69. They do not overlap at all, so how can they have any relationship as general and exceptional rules. As Patañjali says (Mbh.II.42:20): '*yak* is prescribed in the impersonal and passive, and *śap* in the active; how could *yak* ... possibly block *śap* ...?' Without any better text of the *Vyāḍīyaparibhāṣāvṛtti* and in the absence of any other version of this argument than the Vyāḍi commentator's, it is impossible to take the matter further.[160]

One other measure, though extreme, might make more sense of the passage. If we assume that the Vyāḍi commentator turned the whole discussion upside down and was not talking about precursory exceptions at all, but ordinary following ones, then we get the following argument: among the rules $\mathcal{A}$, $\mathcal{B}$ and $\mathcal{C}$ it is $\mathcal{C}$ which is the exception and the question is whether it is preempting $\mathcal{A}$, or only $\mathcal{B}$. If it preempts $\mathcal{A}$ (say P.3.1.33), then indeed one might question the point of mentioning *nṛt* in P.7.2.57, for no future stems would be possible. And the solution would then be that $\mathcal{C}$ blocks $\mathcal{B}$ (i.e., *śap*), the rule nearer to itself, and not the more remote $\mathcal{A}$.

However, this interpretation would require an upheaval in the manuscript readings as well as an interpretation of the *paribhāṣā* quite different even to that assumed by the Vyāḍi commentator himself in argument § 6.2. It thus has very little to recommend it.

Argument 6.2[161] [6:7

— What is the point of intimating this?

— Here in *vibhāṣā diksamāse* (P.1.1.28) the mention of [the word] *bahuvrīhi* is rejected. The prohibition in the statement which immediately follows it, *na bahuvrīhau* (P.1.1.29), is made optional. It is not made optional further on in *dvandve ca* (P.1.1.31): witness *dakṣiṇottarapūrvāṇām* 'of the south, the north and the east'.

Explanation With this argument we return to surer ground. In P.1.1.28 Pāṇini prescribes that the words of the *sarvādi* group are only optionally termed *sarvanāma* 'pronoun' when they are in a directional compound. In practice this means that Sanskrit compounds of the type 'north-east', 'south-west' can optionally take the pronominal instead of the nominal inflexions.

These directional compounds are classified as *bahuvrīhis* 'exocentric compounds' by Pāṇini (P.2.2.26), and Pāṇini's formulation of P.1.1.28 has the word *bahuvrīhau* 'in an exocentric compound' in it. A lengthy argument in the *Mahābhāṣya* (Mbh.I.90:9–26) establishes that it is not necessary to have this word *bahuvrīhau* in the rule, and it is rejected. The Vyāḍi commentator takes this as his starting point. With the word *bahuvrīhau* rejected, P.1.1.28 becomes an exception to the following rule P.1.1.29. This much is fine; the directional compounds may optionally receive either the pronominal or nominal inflexions, as desired. The only change is that, now that P.1.1.28 stands as an exception, it might extend its influence to P.1.1.31 which prohibits words of the *sarvādi* group being termed *sarvanāma* when in a copulative compound (*dvandva*). The effect of P.1.1.28 on P.1.1.31 would be to make pronominal inflexions optional

[160] It may be mentioned that the text of the *Vyāḍīyaparibhāṣāvṛtti* is here not altogether wholesome. At 6:4 there is a variant in the α MSS which might be simple dittography. On the other hand it might hide a reference to the thematic future morpheme *sya* (... *syavikaraṇa*...). Taking this into account does not help our arguments at all, however.

[161] This argument is directly related to the *Mahābhāṣya* discussion on P.1.1.28 (Mbh.I.90:9–10 and 90:14–16) where the identical ideas are proposed, and even the same example, *dakṣiṇottarapūrvāṇām*, is used. It does not appear elsewhere in the *Mahābhāṣya*.

The argument is not used by any of the *paribhāṣā* commentators. Nor does it appear in the *Kāśikā* or *Kaumudī*, or commentaries, on P.1.1.28.

in copulative compounds of direction. Thus the compound *dakṣiṇottarapūrvāṇām* 'of the south and north and east', which has the nominal genitive plural inflexion, would be liable, wrongly, to get the pronominal inflexion *-eṣām*.

The *paribhāṣā* averts disaster. By its application, the precursory exception P.1.1.28 may only block the rule nearest to it, P.1.1.29, and may not affect any later rule. So P.1.1.31 stands free and unaffected.

Comments It is very interesting to find the Vyāḍi commentator here using the same arguments as the *Mahābhāṣya*, where the rest of the tradition does not. The reason would seem to be that, although the tenor of Patañjali's discussion on P.1.1.28 seems to be in favour of rejecting the word *bahuvrīhau*, his final point of view is not totally clear. The last stated view is that of an *ekadeśin*, one who half understands. This is a typical feature of the *Mahābhāṣya*, which often presents several arguments and leaves the reader to choose.

Thus, since it is not absolutely clear that Patañjali wants to reject *bahuvrīhau* in P.1.1.28, most authors prefer not to do so and for them argument § 6.2 cannot arise. The Vyāḍi commentator, in his bold way, is willing to base an argument on the rejection of *bahuvrīhau*.

It seems perfectly clear here that when the Vyāḍi commentator says (6:8) *pratyākhāyate* '... is rejected' he is definitely referring to the *Mahābhāṣya* discussion of P.1.1.28.

Concerning the viability of the argument itself, some question remains as to whether a *dvandva* of the type quoted (6:10) can truly be a *diksamāsa*. The rule P.2.2.26 would suggest that *diksamāsas* are necessarily *bahuvrīhis*. This would, however, completely undermine argument § 6.2, both for the Vyāḍi commentator and for the *Mahābhāṣya*, as well as proving the *bahuvrīhau* of P.1.1.28 redundant.

Paribhāṣā 7

An operation occasioned by a concomitance does not cause it to be disrupted.[162]

— That operation which is occasioned by a concomitance is not the cause of the disruption of it [the concomitance].

Explanation If two items, say A and B, by coming together cause a third item C to arise, then C may not cause any further operation which would obliterate A or B (and thus their conjunction).

The precise nature of A and B, and their relationship, becomes a question of some debate.

Comments This *paribhāṣā* has presented problems since the time of Patañjali. Fundamentally, it has to be admitted that while perhaps necessary in some instances, it leads to wrong results in others: it is *anityā* 'not invariably the case'. The Vyāḍi commentator goes so far as to say it has no apparent purpose at all (7:38 *prayojanaṃ mṛgyam*). This bold statement is particularly interesting in the context of Patañjali's discussion of the *paribhāṣā* under P.1.1.39.

Patañjali's discussion, the *locus classicus* for the *paribhāṣā*, is divisible into three main parts. First, when it has been decided that this *paribhāṣā* should be made (Mbh.I.97:13), six purposes for it are proposed. These are stated in *vārttikas* 4–9 and amplified in Patañjali's comment. Each time it is shown that the situation can be handled without recourse to the *paribhāṣā*. Just as it is beginning to look as though the *paribhāṣā* might have to be discarded for want of use, three new purposes for it are proposed (98:20–25). These are not given as *vārttikas* (but cf. I.83:18; III.346:4; II.46:8) and form a unit by themselves. Most important of all, they are not refuted.

[162] This *paribhāṣā* is known to Kātyāyana. It is mentioned once in full as *vārt.* 3 on P.1.1.39 (Mbh.I.97:10), and once in brief as *vārt.* 6 on P.7.3.118–119 (Mbh.III.343:5).

Patañjali's discussion takes place in the context of P.1.1.39. It is actually quoted there twelve times (Mbh.I.97:11:17:21, 98:1:6:11:16:21:23:24, 99:3:23). It also occurs in the contexts of P.1.1.4 *vārt.* 8 (Mbh.I.53:15), P.1.1.20 *vārt.* 6 (I.75:22), P.1.1.24 *vārt.* 3 (I.83:18), P.2.4.81 *vārt.* 4 (I.496:23), P.3.1.16 *vārt.* 5 (II.46:9), P.7.2.101 (III.309:9:12), P.7.3.118–119 *vārt.* 6 (III.343:6:6) and P.8.2.7 *vārt.* 3 (III.387:16). Cf. footnote 386, p. 261 below.

The *paribhāṣā* is accepted by all the *paribhāṣā* commentators: Puruṣottamadeva (no. 10), Sīradeva (no. 64), Nīlakaṇṭha (no. 75), Haribhāskara (no. 66), Nāgeśa (no. 85) and Śeṣādrisudhī (no. 73).

It is also accepted in the commentaries: see *Kāśikā* on P.7.1.13 and *Nyāsa ad loc.* (KV.V.544), *Siddhāntakaumudī* on P.7.1.13 (SK.I.198 (204)), etc.

The *vārttikas* resume, and seven situations are enumerated (*vārttikas* 10–16) where the *paribhāṣā* cannot be applied.

The Vyāḍi commentator, after supposedly establishing the *paribhāṣā* by means of an intimation, picks precisely those three purposes which were not refuted in the *Mahābhāṣya*, and refutes them. He ends by stating that there is no apparent purpose for the *paribhāṣā*. Plainly, the Vyāḍi commentator's version of the three purposes must be later than the *Mahābhāṣya* passage, because the argument is one step more developed in the Vyāḍi commentator's case. And had the refutations been known when the *Mahābhāṣya* passage was written, some attention would surely have been given to them.

It seems irrefutable, then, that the Vyāḍi commentator had the *Mahābhāṣya* before him at this point. But one fact is slightly disturbing. This passage fits so ill in the sequence of arguments in the *Mahābhāṣya*, and so conspicuously lacks any justification in the *vārttikas* in this sequence, that one cannot but wonder if it is not an interpolation. Perhaps the Vyāḍi commentator took the passage from a third work not known to us? Without further evidence it would be prudent to stay with the most obvious hypothesis, that the Vyāḍi commentator is here re-working material he found in the *Mahābhāṣya*.

With regard to the interpretation of the *paribhāṣā* itself, the main problem is raised indirectly by Kātyāyana. In P.1.1.39, *vārt.* 10 (Mbh.I.99:1), he poses the problem that if the *paribhāṣā* held good, a suffix occasioned by a letter might wrongly destroy that letter. Patañjali gives as an example of this situation the word *dākṣi*. Here the suffix *iñ* ($\rightarrow i$) is prescribed after the final *a* of *dakṣa* by P.4.1.95 *ata iñ*. Then P.6.4.148 *yasyeti ca* causes this *a* to disappear because it is before an *i*. I.e.,

dakṣa	+	*iñ*	by P.4.1.95
dakṣ	+	*iñ*	by P.6.4.148

Ostensibly the *i* is caused by only one item, the preceding *a*. But Kātyāyana, if he really had this example in mind, must have considered that the suffix *i* was somehow the result of a *saṃnipāta* 'concomitance'. Clearly he must have meant something other than a juxtaposition. Nāgeśa suggests that he means the concomitance of qualificand and qualifier (Nāgeśa 177:7 *viśeṣyaviśeṣaṇasaṃnipāta*), in this case the stem (*prātipadika*) *dakṣa* and its qualification 'ending in *a*'. Then the suffix *i*, arising from the concomitance of these two, would not be able to destroy the preceding *a*.

This sounds rather far-fetched, and Patañjali thinks so too: he remarks that the suffix (*pratyaya*) is not the outcome of any concomitance as far as its dependence on a letter is concerned (Mbh.I.99:3). He suggests instead that the true concomitance lies in the fact that *dakṣa* is technically termed an *aṅga* 'pre-suffixal base'. The definition of an *aṅga* in P.1.4.13 involves the concomitance of two items, *dakṣa* and *i*. The required concomitance is achieved and P.6.4.108, which is caused by the *aṅga*, is not allowed to destroy the *a*, because of the *paribhāṣā*. This seems fine, if unlikely. But one difficulty remains: why did Kātyāyana not say this?

Nāgeśa takes this difficulty one step further. If Kātyāyana really means items termed *aṅga* to be included when he says *varṇāśraya* 'occasioned by a letter', then we shall have to reckon with examples like '*śaiva*'. The suffix here is not 'occasioned by a letter' at all. It is prescribed directly for the word '*śiva*' by P.4.1.112 *śivādibhyo 'ṇ*. Once again, are we to conclude that Kātyāyana was wrong? Nāgeśa sweeps aside the whole suggestion about *aṅga* and avoids admitting that he is contradicting Patañjali by saying that the *aṅga* argument is the work of an *ekadeśin* 'one with partial understanding' (Nāgeśa 178:7–10). Instead he makes his own suggestion about qualifier and qualificand, vindicating Kātyāyana but infinitely complicating the interpretation of the *paribhāṣā*.

We know for certain that the Vyāḍi commentator did not have this interpretation in mind because he proves the *paribhāṣā* by intimation from a *sūtra*. And the *sūtra* does not involve a concomitance of the *viśeṣyaviśeṣaṇa* 'qualifier and qualificand' type (see Kielhorn 1874.411, fn. 1). By *saṃnipāta* the Vyāḍi commentator means concomitance in the simplest sense of 'conjunction' of 'juxtaposition'.

Argument 7.1.[163] [7:3

— How?

— Since he states *ato dīrgho yañi* (P.7.3.101). This rule *ato dīrgho yañi* is not really necessary. [Formations such as]

vṛkṣāya	'for the tree'
plakaṣāya	'for the fig-tree'

will come about by *akṛtsārvadhātukayoḥ* (P.7.4.25). This being valid, by *yañi* [in P.7.3.101] he is observing that there will be no lengthening of items with this sort of [derivational] background.

— And what sort of [derivational] background has this formation?

— It is an item ending in the letter *a* whose [derivational] background is concomitance; it does not become the cause of the loss of the *a*. By virtue of this statement [of *yañ* in P.7.3.101] there is lengthening [of the *a* of *vṛksa*].

— What is accomplished?

— 'An operation occasioned by a concomitance does not cause it to be disrupted.'

Explanation The Vyāḍi commentator's logic is not explicit here, but we can attempt a reconstruction of his argument. He starts by criticising the normal derivation of dative singular forms like *vṛksāya*. This derivation is as follows:

i)	*vṛkṣa*	+	*ṅe*	by P.2.3.13
ii)	*vṛkṣa*	+	*ya*	by P.7.1.13
iii)	*vṛkṣā*	+	*ya*	by P.7.3.101 and 102

The Vyāḍi commentator says that the rule leading to stage iii), P.7.3.101 (taken with 102), is not necessary. The same form could be achieved by applying P.7.4.25. This latter rule prescribes that a long vowel replace the final vowel of the pre-suffixal base (*aṅga*) when the suffix begins with *y* and has the marker *k* or *ṅ*. (The suffix must not be a primary nominal suffix or a *sārvadhātuka* one; see Discussion below). The suffix

[163] The argument in this precise form is not found elsewhere in the literature, either in the *Mahābhāṣya*, the *paribhāṣā* commentators, the *Kāśikā* or *Siddhāntakaumudī*. Rule P.7.2.101 is drawn into discussions on this *paribhāṣā*, but the point being made is different from the Vyāḍi commentator's.

at stage ii) satisfies these conditions: it begins with *y* and is considered to have the marker *ṅ* which appeared in stage i) (*sthānivadbhāva*). So we would have

iii)* *vṛkṣā* + *ya* by P.7.4.25

So why, the Vyāḍi commentator asks, has Pāṇini given the rule P.7.3.101?

The answer is that the *paribhāṣā* prevents P.7.4.25 from applying, but does not interfere with P.7.3.101.

The reason is as follows: the suffix *ya* which appears at stage ii) is the result of a concomitance. This is between the final *a* of *vṛkṣa* and the suffix *ṅe*. When these two come together, *ya* is born. Therefore, by the *paribhāṣā*, *ya* cannot be responsible for the demise of either itself or the preceding *a*. Therefore a rule based on *ya*, like P.7.4.25 may not cause the replacement of the *-a*.

However, P.7.3.101 (with 102), it may be argued, depends to an equal degree on the following *ya*. After all, does not the abbreviation *yañ* mean, in this case, 'when *y* follows'?

The answer to this objection is not recorded in the Vyāḍi commentator's text, but is given by Sīradeva (30:9–10) and Śeṣādrisudhī (44:16). It is that by reason of the fact that *y* is given as one member of a *pratyāhāra* 'abbreviation' it does not count as far as the *paribhāṣā* is concerned. In P.7.4.25, by contrast, the *y* is explicitly mentioned.

Since derivation by P.7.4.25 could potentially take place, but Pāṇini also frames P.7.3.101 (and 102), there must be a principle which distinguishes them, and disqualifies the former. The *paribhāṣā* is that principle.

Comments This argument is not strong. It depends on the fact that P.7.3.101 (with 102) is not affected by the *paribhāṣā*. Although Sīradeva and Śeṣādrisudhī do bring forward arguments for this position, as mentioned, they are alone in doing this. The majority view in the tradition is just the opposite: P.7.3.101 (with 102) is cited as a case where the *paribhāṣā* would prevent the correct formation of a word by this rule. The usual conclusion from this is that the *paribhāṣā* must therefore by *anityā* 'not invariably so', and must not be applied to P.7.3.101. This view is found in Puruṣottamadeva (117:25), Nīlakaṇṭha (308:10), Haribhāskara (351:9), Nāgeśa (181:2), *Kāśikā* on P.7.1.13 (KV.V.544:5) and *Siddhāntakaumudī* on the same (SK.I.198:2 (204)).

The greatest stumbling block for the Vyāḍi commentator's argument is that rule P.7.4.25 is specifically aimed at verbal derivation, '*akṛt*...', and would therefore normally not be considered for application to the present case.

The term *evaṃjātīyaka* is typical of Patañjali's vocabulary. He uses it forty-five times, normally in the more general meaning 'of this kind', but several times with the just-discernibly more specific sense of 'of this origin, background' (e.g., I.4:13).

It is strange that the Vyāḍi commentator only refers to P.7.3.101 and not directly to 7.3.102. It is, in fact, only the latter rule which applies to nouns, although the term *yañ*, around which his argument revolves, does come from P.7.3.101. For the same usage see *vārt.* 7 on P.1.1.39 (Mbh.I.98:4).

The *Laghuśabdenduśekhara* on P.7.1.13 does speak of the possibility that P.7.4.25 could apply to the formation of the dative sg. form *kaṣṭāya* (*Laghuśabdenduśekhara*, V.70).

In 7:7 the Vyāḍi commentator uses the word *akārānta* 'ending in the letter *a*' where all others authors use the more precise *adanta*, thus specifying that a short measure *ă* is meant. On the Vyāḍi commentator's views of homorganic letters see *paribhāṣā* 49.

Argument 7.2[164] [7:10

— What is the point of intimating this?

— In *śatāni* 'hundreds' and *sahasrāṇi* 'thousands', the [augment] *num* is appropriate before a strong stem suffix [by P.7.1.72]. When this is done, the term *ṣaṭ* wrongly applies [to *śatan*, and *sahasran*,] by *ṣṇāntā ṣaṭ* (P.1.1.24). Then, by *ṣaḍbhyo luk* (P.7.1.22) [the suffixes] *jas* [nom. pl.] and *śas* [acc. pl.] would wrongly be deleted.

Because 'an operation occasioned by a concomitance does not cause it to be disrupted' the problem does not arise. For in this case, the final letter *n* [in *śatan*, and *sahasran*], which comes because of the strong stem suffix, cannot lead to the destruction of that strong stem suffix.

Explanation The formation of the nominative plural neuter of *śata* 'hundred' is as follows:

i)	*śata*			+	*jas*	by P.4.1.2, 2.3.1 etc., 1.4.102, etc.
ii)	*śata*			+	*śi*	by P.7.1.20
iii)	*śata*	+	*num*	+	*śi*	by P.7.1.72
iv)	*śata*	+	*n*	+	*i*	by P.1.3.9

At state iv) we have the stem *śatan* with suffix *i*. By P.1.1.24 anything ending in *ṣ* or *ṇ* is liable to be termed a *ṣaṭ* 'six'. And by P.7.1.22 the nominative and accusative plural suffixes are deleted after a *ṣaṭ*. This would mean the loss of the *i* in stage iv) and the consequent wrong form **śatan* for the plural.

However the *num* of stage iii) arose as a result of the concomitance of the final *a* of *śata* and the following *i*. By the *paribhāṣā*, therefore, the *num* may not cause the destruction of this concomitance: it may not cause the *a* or the *i* to disappear. Thus the suffix is preserved and the correct form *śatāni* is achieved.

---

[164]The difficulty with *śata* is as old as Kātyāyana (Mbh.I.83:13). This argument is found after *vārt.* 9 on P.1.1.39 in the *Mahābhāṣya* (Mbh.I.98:20). See discussion under *paribhāṣā* 7. Cf. also the *Mahābhāṣya* on P.1.1.24, *vārt.* 2, (Mbh.I.83:14).

It is also used by all the *paribhāṣā* commentators, with the exception of Śeṣādrisudhī. See also Kaiyaṭa and Nāgeśa on Mbh.I.98:20, under *vārt.* 1.1.39.9. (*Pradīpa* and *Uddyota*, I.328–29).

See discussion on *paribhāṣā* 7 above, (Cf. Kielhorn 1874.410 fn. 1.) for comment and other occurrences.

Argument 7.3[165] [7:16

— This is no purpose. The term *ṣaṭ* in no way applies to this case. After rejecting the use of *-anta* 'end' in *ṣṇāntā ṣaṭ* (P.1.1.24) he teaches the purpose which is that it is [only] those numbers which invariably end in the letter *ṣ* and *n* that have that [term *ṣaṭ* applied to them]. And this [number] does not invariably end in *n*, so the term *ṣaṭ* does not arise, let alone the deletion (*luk*) which depends upon the term *ṣaṭ*.

Explanation The Vyāḍi commentator argues that *śatan* + *i* (see argument § 7.2, stage iv)) is not a *ṣaṭ* because this latter term only applies to numbers like *pañcan* or *ṣaṣ* whose final letter is always and invariably an *ṣ* or an *n*. In *śata*, though, the *n* is adventitious and is not invariably present. Furthermore, if *śatan* does not qualify as a *ṣaṭ* it cannot suffer the operations proper to a *ṣaṭ*. So the threat of losing the final *i* is obviated. The correct form *śatāni* is then derivable (using P.6.4.8) without recourse to the *paribhāṣā*.

Comments The puzzling point in this argument is the Vyāḍi commentator's clear reference to the rejection of the word *-anta* in P.1.1.24, and the subsequent statement that the purpose – presumably of accepting *-anta* after all – is to teach the invariability of the final *-ṣ* and *n* in items to be termed *ṣaṭ*.

The *Mahābhāṣya* does not make such a rejection. Candra has omitted *-anta* form his version of this rule, Ca.2.1.21, but gives no argument for doing so in the commentary.

The discovery of a work giving this particular suggestion, that *-anta* be rejected from P.1.1.24, might shed light on the Vyāḍi commentator's antecedents. (It must be clearly noted, however, that this suggestion of the Vyāḍi commentator's is not the same as Kaiyaṭa's and others' suggestion that the use of *-anta* suggests reading *upadeśe* into the rule.[166])

---

[165]This argument does not appear in the *Mahābhāṣya*. On P.1.1.24 Patañjali does argue, following Kātyāyana, that the word *upadeśe* should be added to the rule, in which case the difficulty with *śata* is solved in a way very similar to the Vyāḍi commentator's (Mbh.I.83:14). But the terms are different. The Vyāḍi commentator does not read the extra word and takes the meaning 'invariable' as suggested by the word *-anta*. Patañjali does not do this, although *Kaiyaṭa* does take the word *upadeśa* as suggested by *-anta* (*Pradīpa* I.328^b). This idea is taken up by the *Kāśikā* on P.1.1.24 (KV.I.128:5). Cf. also *Nyāsa* (KV.I.129:19 f.) and *Padamañjarī* (KV.I.128:18 f.). It might be argued that taking the word *upadeśa* as suggested by *-anta* is a mere notational variant of the Vyāḍi commentator's argument, and that he used the term *nitya* loosely.

Note that while the *Kāśikā* tradition accepts the *upadeśa* argument, the *Siddhānta-kaumudī* tradition takes the other solution to the *śata* problem, accepting the *paribhāṣā* (see SK.I.383:1 (369)). Jñānendrasarasvatī makes the observation that the *upadeśa* argument is only used by those who feel that the *paribhāṣā* is not invariably applicable (*Tattvabodhinī*, SK.I.383:26 (369)). This view is sheer recklessness (*sāhasamātram*), says Jñānendrasarasvatī, for if one may not apply a *paribhāṣā* where it is needed, where can it be applied? He further offers a refutation of the argument that *upadeśe* is suggested by *-anta* in P.1.1.24.

[166]See footnote 165 above.

Argument 7.4[167] [7:20

— In that case this is the purpose:

iyeṣa 'he desired',
uvoṣa 'he burned'

For here when the 3rd sg. perfect suffix (*ṇal*) follows [the root] *uṣ*, and *guṇa* has taken place, then by *ijādeś ca gurumato 'nṛcchaḥ* (P.3.1.36) [the suffix] *ām* would wrongly be applied. And once *ām* is there then the perfect suffix (*li*) would be wrongly deleted (*luk*).

This problem does not arise, because 'an operation occasioned by a concomitance does not cause it to be disrupted'. Thus here, the heaviness of the syllable, which is caused by the concomitance with the perfect suffix (*liṭ* see P.7.3.86), cannot cause the destruction of that perfect suffix (*liṭ*).

Explanation The derivation of *uvoṣa* (identical to that of *iyeṣa*) is as follows:

i)	*uṣ*			+	*liṭ*	by P.3.2.115
ii)	*uṣ*	+	*uṣ*	+	*liṭ*	by P.6.1.8
iii)	*u*	+	*uṣ*	+	*liṭ*	by P.7.4.60
iv)	*u*	+	*uṣ*	+	*ṇal*	by P.3.4.77, 78, 82; 1.3.78; 1.4.101, 102, 108, etc.
v)	*u*	+	*oṣ*	+	*ṇal*	by P.7.3.86
vi)	*uv*	+	*oṣ*	+	*ṇal*	by P.6.4.78

This stage (with the elision of the markers *ṇ* and *l*) is the final, correct form. However the problem arises if we try to continue derivation:

vii) **uvoṣ* + *ām* + *ṇal* by P.3.1.36.

One of the conditions which triggers this rule is that the root contains a heavy syllable (the *o* in *uvoṣ*).

The immediate corollary is the deletion of the perfect suffix:

viii) **uvoṣ* + *ām* by P.2.4.81

---

[167] Like argument § 7.2, this argument is found after *vārt.* 9 on P.1.1.39 in the *Mahābhāṣya* (Mbh.I.98:23). See the discussion under *paribhāṣā* 7. Cf. too *Mahābhāṣya* on P.1.1.8, *vārt.* 7 (Mbh.I.59:13). This argument, or one very similar to it, was known to Kātyāyana, who frames a *vārttika* (no. 1 on P.3.1.36) to avoid the difficulty, without having recourse to the *paribhāṣā* (Mbh.II.44:20). Patañjali glosses Kātyāyana with this very argument (Mbh.II.44:21), using the examples *iyeṣa* and *uvoṣa*. It is curious, then, to find that a few lines further on Patañjali quotes the *paribhāṣā* as the solution to the problem (Mbh.II.46:7–9). It may be that in saying *uktam vā* in *vārt.* 5 on P.3.1.36 Kātyāyana is actually just referring back to his first *vārttika* on that *sūtra*, and not to *vārt.* 3 on P.1.1.39, i.e., the *paribhāṣā*.

See also the *Cāndravṛtti* on Ca.1.1.52 where the *uvoṣa* problem is referred to. The *paribhāṣā* is not used, however.

See also the *Nyāsa* on P.3.1.36 (KV.II.417–18) and *Padamañjarī* on the same (KV.II.417:9 ff.).

Among the *paribhāṣā* commentators this argument is cited by Puruṣottamadeva (no. 10) alone.

and the final wrong form:

ix) **uvoṣām cakāra* by P.3.1.40.

The problem is, then, that the heavy syllable which appeared at stage v) (by P.7.3.86) as a result of the concomitance of the root and the perfect suffix has gone on, in stages vii) and viii), to cause that very perfect suffix to disappear.

If we invoke the *paribhāṣā*, this turn of events will be prohibited and stage vi) will be the final and correct form of the verb. The heavy syllable which resulted from a concomitance may not turn and disrupt that concomitance by causing one of its elements to be deleted.

Comments It appears that the Vyāḍi commentator, and Patañjali in some moods, are unaware of *vārt.* 1 on P.3.1.36. This *vārttika* specifically excludes the operation of this rule when the heavy syllable has arisen as a result of a following perfect tense suffix. This also means that, *pace* Patañjali on *vārt.* 5, Kātyāyana did not here wish to treat the problem as amenable to the *sannipāta paribhāṣā*.

There is some justification for this view, because if the stages of the *uvoṣa* derivation are observed closely it will be seen that the concomitance of stage v) does not cause the disappearance of the perfect suffix directly. The concomitance brings in the *-ām* suffix (stage viii). So the disruption is not direct, but at one remove; as the *Nyāsa* puts it (KV.II.418:16), ... *·liṭsannipāto gurumattāyā hetuḥ*. It could be argued, then, that the *paribhāṣā* is powerless here because the result of the concomitance is only a contingent cause of the disruption. It would seem that Kātyāyana may have had this, or some similar, objection to the use of the *paribhāṣā* (which he certainly knew – see footnote 162, p. 69) and therefore chose to dispose of the problem by explicit prohibition.

Thus, while the *iyeṣa/uvoṣa* problem was known to Kātyāyana, it seems to have been Patañjali's idea to solve it using the *sannipāta paribhāṣā*. And in instances like Mbh.II.46:8, Patañjali is wrongly putting his own argument into Kātyāyana's mouth. The Vyāḍi commentator is thus following Patañjali more closely than Kātyāyana at this point.

It is interesting to note that the *Cāndravyākaraṇa* resolves the *uvoṣa* problem in a manner more akin to Kātyāyana's. The commentary on Ca.1.1.52 says:

> *naiṣa lavidhānakāle gurumān*
> This (*uvoṣa*) does not have a heavy syllable at the time when the verbal suffix is introduced.

Thus he is suggesting that the move to stage vii) should be considered immediately after stage i). This is like the Vyāḍi commentator's argument § 7.4: the heavy syllable is not original, and therefore cannot trigger the operation. This, of course, implies another convention or *paribhāṣā* of sorts, in its turn.

The fact that Puruṣottamadeva is the only other *paribhāṣā* commentator to mention this argument yields another case where the Vyāḍi commentator aligns himself with the oldest commentarial stratum.

Argument 7.5[168] [7:25

— This is no purpose either. Here too, in *ijādaś ca gurumato 'nṛcchaḥ* (P.3.1.36) it is said that the presentation [of the word *gurumat* in P.3.1.36] with the suffix *-mat* (*matun*) is not necessary. For example *guroś ca halaḥ* (P.3.3.103) [does not have it].

He teaches the purpose of that [*matup*], which has been rejected, by saying, '*matup* is used to mean invariable connection.' And this syllable in *iyeṣa* is not invariably heavy. Therefore that problematic deletion will not arise here.

Explanation The Vyāḍi commentator's argument for using the *paribhāṣā* to solve the difficulty (argument § 7.4) is that, because of its very phrasing, the rule in question, P.3.1.36, cannot apply to *iyeṣa* and *uvoṣa*. He deduces this from the fact that in P.3.1.36 Pāṇini uses the word *gurumat* to refer to a heavy syllable. The Vyāḍi commentator questions the need for the suffix *mat* (technically called *matup*). Would it not be enough to say '*guru*', as in fact Pāṇini does in P.3.3.103? The meaning of the rule would apparently not be changed.

The Vyāḍi commentator then refers to an unidentified commentator whose explanation of the presence of *-mat* is that it indicates permanence, or invariance. That is to say, the rule only affects those items which have a permanent heavy syllable, not items like *uvoṣa* which get a heavy syllable in the course of derivation. (This is, of course, very similar to pbh. 2.)

Thus, P.3.1.36 cannot properly apply to *iyeṣa* and *uvoṣa* and so the *paribhāṣā* is not needed to resolve the difficulty. It is therefore still purposeless.

Comments The Vyāḍi commentator is plainly referring here to some commentary on the rules of Pāṇini which, he says, first rejects the suffix *matup*, and then reinstates it to avoid problems with forms like *iyeṣa* and *uvoṣa*.

Although Kātyāyana comes close to this statement in his *vārttikas* 2 and 3 on P.3.1.36 (Mbh.II.45:1, 4) it is nevertheless not quite what he is saying. In *vārt.* 2 Kātyāyana is questioning the need for the word *gurumat* as a whole, in the *sūtra*. It is necessary, he says, because otherwise roots like *yaj* which, in the 1st. sg. perfect, satisfy all the other criteria of the rule, would wrongly get the *-am* suffix. Saying *gurumata* stops this. In *vārt.* 3 Kātyāyana is suggesting that because the word *upadeśa* (cf. p. 42 above) is expressed, everything is satisfactory.

But the word *upadeśa* is nowhere explicit, so we must assume that it is suggested in some way by the word *gurumat*; in Patañjali's words, *upadeśe gurumata iti vaktavyam* (Mbh.II.45:5). But it is Kaiyaṭa who first suggests just how this might take place. And he does this precisely by singling out the suffix *matup*, just as the Vyāḍi commentator does, and considering that it expresses invariance: *tasmān nityayoge matupa āśrayaṇād ...* (*Pradīpa* III.83^b:28). So this seems to be the first instance of the Vyāḍi commentator's argument § 7.5, although it is not applied to *iyeṣa* and

[168] The *Siddhāntakaumudī* tradition does not raise the question addressed in this argument at all on P.3.1.36. *Gurumat* is implicitly assumed to mean *upadeśe gurumat* (*Tattvabodhinī*. SK.III.53:26 (2232)).

uvoṣa by Kaiyaṭa. (Nāgeśa, in his *Uddyota* at this point quotes a verse which gives *nityayoga* as one of the senses of *matup*.)

Furthermore, if we look at *vārt*. 3 without Patañjali's comments, it would seem that Kātyāyana is either suggesting that the word *upadeśa* be added to the *sūtra*, or else he read the *sūtra* with the word already in it, or read it from some previous rule.

Candra seems to understand *gurumat* in the sense of 'invariably heavy' or 'heavy in the metalanguage', for as we have seen, he glosses it as *lavidhānakāle gurumān* 'heavy at the time the verbal suffix is applied' (*vṛtti* on Ca.1.1.52).

Kaiyaṭa's argument is repeated in the *Nyāsa* on P.3.1.36 (KV.II.418:17 ff.), where it is indeed invoked to solve the *uvoṣa/iyeṣa* problem. See also *Padamañjarī* (KV.II.417:8–14) for the same.

In arguing that *gurumat* in P.3.1.36 would be perfectly well replaced by *guru*, the Vyāḍi commentator refers to P.3.3.103 where indeed *guru* alone is used, without *mat*, in much the same meaning. This latter rule is not commented on by Patañjali or Kātyāyana. But in the *Kāśikā guru* is glossed as *gurumān* (without comment) and the *Nyāsa* clarifies the point. It asks how *gurumān dhātuḥ* can be understood, when all Pāṇini said was *guru* (*Nyāsa* at KV.III.75:21 f.). The answer is *sāmarthyāt* 'because the senses are connected'. After all, it adds, *guru* is not a proper term for a root, but for a syllable. So if we call a root 'heavy' we mean 'it has a heavy syllable in it'.

Thus, although the Vyāḍi commentator's reference to P.3.3.103 is not traceable in the context of argument § 7.5, the use of *guru* in that rule was clearly a debated issue at an early time.

Argument 7.6[169] [7:29

— In that case, this is the purpose:

śakaṭau 'in the cart',
paddhatau 'on the footpath'

Here, at the stage of *śakaṭi* and *paddhati*, when the letter *au* has been produced by *iduḍbhyām* (P.7.3.117) and *ac ca gheḥ* (P.7.3.119), [the suffix] *ṭāp* might, by *ataḥ* (P.4.1.4), wrongly apply after the words *śakaṭi* and *paddhati*, which [at this point] end in the letter *a*. And once *ṭāp* is there, *yāṭ* might appear by *yāḍāpaḥ* (P.7.3.113). Then an undesired form would arise.

But because 'an operation occasioned by a concomitance does not cause it to be disrupted', there is no problem. Because here, the

[169]This argument, though perhaps not with these very examples, was known to Kātyāyana, who sums it up and quotes the *paribhāṣā* in *vārttikas* 5 and 6 on P.7.3.119 (Mbh.III.343:3, 5). For Kātyāyana, the problem is simply the appearance of the suffix *ṭāp*. He considers that the *paribhāṣā* prevents this. Therefore it follows that, for Kātyāyana, *vighāta* means the simple interruption of the contiguity or juxtaposition of stem and suffix. Patañjali's commentary on this brings in the specific examples *śakaṭau* and *paddhaṭau*, adding little else (Mbh.III.343:4–7). He has quoted the same argument elsewhere (Mbh.I.98:22 f.). In both places Kaiyaṭa has commented (*Pradīpa* I.329^a:10 ff.; V.240:15 ff.).

Among the *Paribhāṣā* commentators the argument is used by Puruṣottamadeva (no. 10) and Sīradeva (no. 64) (who rejects it).

See also *Tattvabodhinī* I.247:17, etc.

fact of ending in *ă*, which is brought about by concomitance with the letter *au*, may not straight away cause the destruction of the letter *au*.

Explanation The Vyāḍi commentator's phrasing is confusing here. It is tempting to think that he is reproducing an argument which does not perfectly fit the context. His presentation of the difficulty in forming *śakaṭau* is as follows:

i)	*śakaṭi*					+	*ṅi*	The loc. sg. suffix is added to the stem (P.4.1.2, etc.)
ii)	*śakaṭa*					+	*au*	by P.7.3.117, 119
iii)	*śakaṭa*	+	*ṭāp*			+	*au*	by P.4.1.4
iv)	*śakaṭa*	+	*ṭāp*	+	*yāṭ*	+	*au*	by P.7.3.113

This is certainly a wrong form, but the *au* has not actually been destroyed, as the Vyāḍi commentator seems to suggest (7:34), unless *vighāta* is taken to mean 'separation' (cf. Kaiyaṭa's *Pradīpa* I.39[a]:11 … *ānantaryaṃ vihanyeta*).

The appearance of the final *a* of *śakaṭa* at stage ii) is caused by the concomitance, at stage i), of the stem (a *ghi*) and the locative suffix. Therefore, the Vyāḍi commentator argues, this final *a* may not trigger an operation which leads to the *vighāta* of the suffix, and thus the destruction of the original concomitance.

For a clearer statement of this argument as put by Patañjali see below.

Comments The Vyāḍi commentator's argument seems to be a version of the one which arises in the *Mahābhāṣya* when discussing P.7.3.116–119. However, the situation here is complicated because it is not at first clear what the original reading of these *sūtras* was. The rules in question are concerned with the locative singular endings of feminines (and masculines in -*nī*) with final *ā*, *i*, *ī*, *u* and *ū*. It seems that Pāṇini formed two rules: *ṅer ām nadyāmnībhyaḥ* (P.7.3.116) and *aud ac ca gheḥ* (P.7.3.118 and 119). Kātyāyana proposes making each of these rules into two, thus producing four in all. He splits the second into *aut* (P.7.3.118) and *ac ca gheḥ* (P.7.3.119). But although he says he is splitting the first into two, what he actually does is add a postscript of his own, as a second rule: *idudbhyām* (P.7.3.117). This does not appear to have been part of Pāṇini's rule 7.3.116 originally. Thus we must consider that Kātyāyana is being somewhat loose in his terminology. When he says *yogavibhāga* in *vārt.* 2, he does not mean 'splitting the rule', but 'creating two rules'. In proposing rule 7.3.117, Kātyāyana is accounting for feminine stems in short *i* and *u* which may thereby optionally follow the long *ī* and *ū* declension in forming their locative singular. Thus *gati* has the normal locative *gatau*, but by 7.3.117 may also have the form *gatyām*.

The reason an extra rule is necessary is as follows. Pāṇini divides *i* and *u* stems into two main classes: feminines in long *ī* or *ū*, and stems in short *i* or *u*. The former he calls generically *nadī*, the latter *ghi*. (P.1.4.3–7). Some qualifications are made about what counts as a *nadī*, and among other things it is said that feminine stems in short *i* and *u* which would normally be termed *ghi* may optionally be termed *nadī* if a suffix marked with a *ṅ* follows (P.1.4.6). The locative singular is such a suffix. Now in forming the locative, P.7.3.116 accounts for the *am* ending of *nadī* type stems. While P.7.3.118–119 accounts for the *au* ending of *ghi* type stems: *nadyām*, *agnau*.

It would seem simple enough that those *ghi* stems mentioned above which have the option of being *nadī* stems in the locative could take either form of ending. However the rules teaching the terms *nadī* and *ghi* are in the one-name-section (P.1.4.1–2.2.38) where only one name at a time may apply to any item, and in cases of conflict the subsequently taught name prevails (P.1.4.2). In this case, *ghi* is taught after *nadī*. Therefore if both are applicable, the stem would have to be counted as a *ghi*, not a *nadī*. Therefore Kātyāyana has to create a separate rule specifically for these stems as *nadīs*, for unless he did so they would automatically revert to being *ghis*. Thus, rule 7.3.117 is framed such that it specifically refers to those, and only those, short *i* and *u* stems as are termed *nadī*. Since the rule has no other scope (*avakāśa*) it cannot be preempted by the following rule about *ghis*. Such a preemption would leave this new rule without any function whatsoever, and redundancy is not tolerated in the grammar.

The second split, of P.7.3.118 and 119 into two rules, is not at all problematic. It merely allows for the correct forms of the words *sakhi* and *pati* which are neither *nadī* nor *ghi* (P.1.4.7–9). The same effect as splitting the rule can be attained without doing so if it is read with – as it were – a semi-colon after *aut*. The part of the rule concerning a *ghi* would then have the status of a postscript. Kātyāyana suggests this procedure for those who do not wish to split the rule, and compares this usage to P.3.1.11 where a similar 'phrasing' takes place (*vārt.* 4 on P.7.3.118–119, Mbh.III.34:22). He lets the matter rest here, and this accounts for the *Kāśikā's* comment that, 'those who read just one *sūtra* describe the *aut* coming after *ĭ* and *ŭ* as the main prescription and the substitution of *a* for the final letter of the *ghi* as an appended prescription' (KV.VI.123:7 f.).

It is at this point that Kātyāyana presents the argument used by the Vyāḍi commentator in argument § 7.6. In *vārttika* 5 Kātyāyana prohibits the suffix *ṭāp* once the *ă* has replaced the final of the *ghi*. This would normally take place by P.4.1.4 (see stage iii in argument § 7.6. above). Then, in *vārttika* 6, he decides that a specific prohibition is not necessary since *ṭāp* would be prohibited by *paribhāṣā* 7 anyway. This is exactly the point made by Vyāḍi.[170]

It is necessary to understand the train of Kātyāyana's reasoning, given above, to see that the Vyāḍi commentator's argument is a little odd. First of all he says that the suffix *au* arises through the action of P.7.3.117. This is quite wrong on any Pāṇinian interpretation, for this rule only extends the application of the suffix *ām* to nouns like *śakaṭi*; it is really to be read as a rider to P.7.3.116. The suffix *au* is assigned by the following rule, P.7.3.118. However, the Vyāḍi commentator's mistake assumes a more interesting aspect when we turn to Candra and find the rule *idudbhyām aut* (Ca.6.2.61). If the Vyāḍi commentator were looking at such a rule then his statement makes perfect sense. It is common practice to quote only the beginning of a rule, so his omission of *aut* is not a serious objection. Candra's rule does exactly what the Vyāḍi commentator says: it prescribes *au* after stems in *ĭ* and *ŭ*. Candra's next rule – and also Pāṇini's – prescribes an *a* as the replacement of the final letter of the stem. (Candra naturally avoids using the term *ghi*.)

It would be difficult, on so little evidence, to posit any definite historical relationship here between Kātyāyana, Candra and the Vyāḍi commentator. Obviously Kātyāyana comes first, since P.7.3.117 is really his composition. To my knowledge, no one in the Pāṇinian tradition ever suggests the fusion of P.7.3.117 and 118, although these rules, together with P.7.3.116 and 119, were subject to much debate and rearrangement from an early time. The fact that Candra does fuse them suggests

[170] Kātyāyana does not stop here, though. He goes on to suggest that even the *paribhāṣā* need not be invoked. The suffix *ṭāp* could be prevented by using the marker *ḍ*. This involves, however, rewriting the rule.

that the debate concerning these rules did not stop with Patañjali, and that either the Vyāḍi commentator knew Candra's grammar or else was privy to the same arguments which led Candra to frame his rule Ca.6.2.61 as he did.[171]

A final note on another feature of the Vyāḍi commentator's argument may be made. The Vyāḍi commentator sees the difficulty in forming *śakaṭau* as the introduction of *yāṭ* subsequent to that of *ṭāp* (argument § 7.6, stage iv above). However most other commentators see the crucial difficulty as the introduction of *ṭāp* in the first place. A reference to this point of view, though not to the Vyāḍi commentator personally, is found in Kaiyaṭa's comment under *vārt.* 7.3.118–119.5: *anye ṭāpi yāṭprasaṃgam āhuḥ* (*Pradīpa* VI.231:22).

Argument 7.7[172] [7:36

— This too is no purpose. For here in *ac ca gheḥ* (P.7.3.119) too, having rejected making a conjunction [of two rules into one] the purpose [of so doing] is stated: it is that things being as they are, nothing else should be allowed to wrongly apply.

— And what might wrongly apply?

— *Ṭāp*. Therefore a purpose [for the *paribhāṣā*] still has to be sought.

Explanation The Vyāḍi commentator's phrasing here is somewhat vague, and this makes interpretation hard. Once again he is referring to some source which he does not name. If we attempt to reconstruct the point of view of this source it would seem to be as follows. It is proposed that P.7.3.119 be read as one rule, presumably with the previous rule P.7.3.118. This proposal is rejected. The reason given is that the derivation may be as it properly is, and that nothing untoward, such as *ṭāp*, should be prescribed. Thus that fact that P.7.3.119 is read as a separate rule makes *paribhāṣā* unnecessary.

Comments The variant readings of the manuscripts on 7:37 are of interest. Instead of *samuccaya-* they give *attā-* or *atā-*. this would shift the argument squarely to that given by the *Kāśikā*, mentioned in footnote 172, p. 81, concerning the marker *t*. It is not clear quite how the readings *attā-* or *atā-* are to be interpreted, but their relation to the argument mentioned seems indubitable.

It would then appear that the Vyāḍi commentator is referring to a source which rejects the marker *t*, but then accepts it since it prevents *ṭāp* being prescribed. This

---

[171] For another discussion of the above points, reaching a slightly different conclusion, see Bronkhorst 1983, § 6.3.

[172] This argument does not appear in the *Mahābhāṣya*. The discussion there about whether P.7.3.118 and 119 should be read as one or two rule revolves around the correct derivation of *sakhi* and *pati*, and not *śakaṭi* and *paddhati*. The *ṭāp* issue is a separate one, raised in *vārt.* 5 on P.7.3.119 (Mbh.III.343:3). For an outline of this see argument § 7.6 above.

The *Kāśikā* implicitly rejects argument § 7.6 too, but not by using the Vyāḍi commentator's argument § 7.7. The *Kāśikā* sees the use of the marker *t* in the rule as evidence that *ṭāp* cannot apply (KV.VI.123:6). For an explanation of why this is so see the *Nyāsa* at KV.VI.123:24–29.

Any source or parallel for this argument seems to be lacking.

interpretation in its turn requires the somewhat idiosyncratic sense of *pratyākhyāya* as 'challenged' rather than 'rejected'. This sense has been suggested in other cases of the Vyāḍi commentator's use of the word (see argument § 7.5, etc.).

Since this particular argument about the marker *t* is used in the *Kāśikā*, but not in the *Mahābhāṣya*, it must have arisen in the intervening period of which we have no trace, except perhaps for the *Vyāḍīyaparibhāṣāvṛtti* itself.

Paribhāṣā 8

Marker letters are produced and disappear.[173]

— No sooner are marker letters produced than they disappear.
— How is that known?

Explanation Pāṇini teaches most linguistic elements such as roots, suffixes etc. as having attached to them certain marker letters. These specify which operations the element is to undergo. The present *paribhāṣā* teaches that these marker letters do not persist in time. That is to say, once they have been noted they immediately disappear, and do not have any further influence on grammatical events.

Comments The fact that the Vyāḍi commentator accepts this *paribhāṣā*, when no one else in the Pāṇinian tradition even discusses it, is very puzzling. It also suggests something of the isolation which the Vyāḍi commentator's work has experienced, for if other scholars had encountered his arguments for the *paribhāṣā* they would surely have made some remarks.

One of the reasons why this convention was not accepted generally could be because it conflicts with the two following *paribhāṣās* (nos. 9 and 10), which are widely accepted.

[173]This *paribhāṣā*, in a slightly different and more generalized form, was known to Kātyāyana. In *vārt.* 10 on P.1.4.109 (Mbh.I.356:4) he makes the point that speech consists of a sequential string of single sounds, and each of these sounds disappears once it has been produced. This point is made while discussing some of the difficulties in defining the term *saṃhitā* 'juxtaposition'.

Patañjali glosses this argument of Kātyāyana's and in the process produces a formulation very close to that of the *paribhāṣā: uccaritapradhvaṃsino khalv api varṇāḥ* (Mbh.I.356:7).

In another place too, Patañjali produces this same formulation with the same surrounding argument. This time, though, he is commenting directly on a *sūtra*, P.6.3.59, and there is no *vārttika* (Mbh.III.163:18). (This suggests that the latter passage is a simple transplantation of the former to a new context.)

However, neither Kātyāyana nor Patañjali use the *paribhāṣā per se*, though it is clear that its phrasing arose from their usage. The *paribhāṣā* is much more specific and grammatically oriented. Its meaning is not the same.

The *paribhāṣā* is not discussed by any of the Pāṇinian *paribhāṣā* commentators. It is, however, given in the *paribhāṣā* lists of the heterodox schools, the Śākaṭāyana (no. 13), the Candra (no. 14) and the *Kātantra* (no. 55).

It is not mentioned in the sub-commentaries on P.1.4.109, 6.3.59 or 6.4.62 in the *Mahābhāṣya*, *Kāśikā* or *Siddhāntakaumudī*.

The Vyāḍi commentator seems to be alone among Pāṇinians in accepting this *paribhāṣā*, aligning himself rather with the heterodox schools of grammar.

The paribhāṣā would also seem to be redundant since markers are satisfactorily elided by *tasya lopaḥ* (P.1.3.9). However is should be borne in mind that the rule which the Vyāḍi commentator invokes to demonstrate the *paribhāṣā*, P.6.4.62, contains the word *upadeśe* 'amongst the initial elements'. Thus, the *paribhāṣā* concerns the very initial stage of derivation, before any rule whatsoever, even P.1.3.9, has applied. Against this it could further be argued that we do not even know which letters are markers until we have applied a rule of Pāṇini which defines these letters (P.1.3.2–8). To this objection there appears to be no answer.

Thus, it seems that the *paribhāṣā* is a somewhat general and imprecise measure, not perfectly fitted to Pāṇini's system, but very appropriate for those schools who do without the rule *tasya lopaḥ* (P.1.3.9).

Argument 8.1[174] [8:3

— Because *syasicsīyuṭtāsiṣu bhāvakarmaṇor upadeśe*... (P.6.4.62) is valid, and this being so, he includes [the root] *hana* in it by mentioning the vowels (*ac*). For here, *hana* and *graha* end in vowels, and so saying just 'the vowels (*ac*)' in that [rule] is perfectly adequate. But the teacher observes that 'marker letters are no sooner produced than they disappear'.

Here, the letter *a* [at the end of *hana*] is no sooner produced than it is elided. So there [in the rule] the mention of the vowels is not adequate. And for that reason *hana* and *graha* are included.

Explanation In rule P.6.4.62, Pāṇini prescribes certain rather involved operations which are to apply to, among other things, items given as initial elements (*upadeśe*) with a final vowel, as well as to the roots *hana* and *graha*. But surely *hana* and *graha* both have final vowels, so would they not be included by the former criterion? This would indeed be so, were it not for the fact that in Pāṇini's mind, when he formulated this rule, was the postulate that 'marker letters are no sooner produced than they disappear'. And the final *a* of the two roots is a marker letter, so it is necessary to mention them separately in the rule.

Comments The fact that the final letters of *hana* and *graha* are markers (*it*) is inferred from their positions in the *Dhātupāṭha* (Dhp.2.2, 9.61). Strictly, they should be pronounced *hanã*; *grahã*. The nasalization of the final *a* in each item would then signal the fact that they are markers (P.1.3.2). The uniqueness of this argument is curious. If it were traced elsewhere, some link with the Vyāḍi commentator might be established. Since this *paribhāṣā* is not generally accepted by the Pāṇinīyas, it is most likely that an argument corresponding to argument § 8.1, if it is to be found at all, would appear in the commentarial literature of the heterodox grammar schools.

---

[174] This argument appears to be unique to the Vyāḍi commentator.

A marker letter does not make an item polyliteral.[175]

— A polyliteral item does not become so by the addition of a marker letter.
— How is that known?

Explanation Many grammatical elements are presented by Pāṇini together with one or more marker letters. Furthermore, there are operations in the grammar which depend on whether the item in question has one or more than one letter. The present *paribhāṣā* teaches that for the purposes of assessing whether any particular item has one or more than one letter, markers do not count. Thus the familiar thematic vowel of first conjugation verbs is given by Pāṇini as *śap*. But *ś* and *p* are markers, so technically speaking *śap* is one letter.

Comments This postulate is widely accepted throughout the tradition, and presents no special difficulties of interpretation.

The text of the Vyāḍi commentator's commentary is somewhat corrupt at the end (9:9–10): see discussion below.

[175] Kātyāyana does not give any evidence that he knows this *paribhāṣā*. In fact his comment in *vārt.* 3 on P.1.1.26 (Mbh.I.84:20) suggests that he would not consider the *paribhāṣā* necessary. He says: *anubandho 'nyatvakara iti cen na lopāt* 'if it be thought that a marker makes any difference, this is wrong, for it is elided'. Thus, for Kātyāyana, the rule P.1.3.9, which elides markers, acts before the item marked can be said to be qualitatively or quantitatively altered in any way.

Patañjali uses the *paribhāṣā* twice (Mbh.I.132:5, 267:3). The context is the same in both cases, and is essentially that of argument § 9.1. The first use is in the course of Patañjali's own comments on P.1.1.55, when he is trying to justify the use of *śit* in that rule. The second use is in his comment on P.1.3.9, *vārt.* 15, and he explicitly refers back to the first discussion: *yad apy uktaṃ sarvādeśa iti* (Mbh.I.267:2).

The *paribhāṣā* is discussed by all the *paribhāṣā* commentators: Puruṣottamadeva (no. 11), Sīradeva (no. 6), Nīlakaṇṭha (no. 6), Haribhāskara (no. 6), Nāgeśa (no. 6) and Śeṣādrisudhī (no. 7). They all accept the *paribhāṣā*, and reproduce the same argument for it.

The *Kāśikā* does not quote the *paribhāṣā* on P.1.1.55 or 1.3.9, but the commentary of Jinendrabuddhi does so on the first of these rules (*Nyāsa* KV.I.182:27 f.), as well as under P.6.4.127 (*Nyāsa* KV.V.479:22) and elsewhere.

Bhaṭṭojī Dīkṣita uses the *paribhāṣā* in discussing P.7.1.17 (SK.I.209:3 (214)).

Argument 9.1[176] [9:3

— Since in *anekāl śit sarvasya* (P.1.1.55) he mentions *śit* 'an item with the marker *ś*'. For in that context, a substitute which has the marker, when taken together with the marker, is indeed polyliteral. So it will be a valid total substitute, solely on account of [the phrase] *anekāl* 'polyliterate' [in the rule]. There is no need to add *śit* [to the rule]. But the teacher observes that a substitute which, together with its marker, is polyliteral, really only consists of one letter. And that item is not a total substitute. It is because of this that *śit* is mentioned.

Explanation The general rule in Pāṇinian substitution rules is that the substituend is given in the genitive case (P.1.1.49), and the substitute replaces only its initial or final letter (P.1.1.54, 52). However, in P.1.1.55 Pāṇini teaches how he deals with circumstances when it is not just the first or last letter of an item which is to be altered, but the whole if it. Substitutes which are to replace the whole of the substituend are distinguished either a) by having more than one letter, or b) by carrying the marker *ś*. The Vyāḍi commentator notes, however, that any item fulfilling condition b) will automatically also fulfill condition a). So condition b) is strictly unnecessary. Therefore, when Pāṇini deliberately included condition b) in the rule he must have been working on the supposition that the addition of a marker letter does not count when assessing how many letters a particular item consists of. This is the *paribhāṣā*.

Comments No comment is needed on this simple and common argument. However a word may be said about the Vyāḍi commentator's use of the two particles *sārdham* (9:4) and *sākam* (9:6), both meaning 'together with', defining the sociative use of the instrumental suffix. These adverbs are less common than *saha* in this context and may reflect a usage of the Vyāḍi commentator's time or dialect. In the absence of comparative or historical linguistic statistics, nothing more can be said at this stage.

Argument 9.2[177] [9:8

— What is the point of intimating this?

— *Ūd upadhāyā gohaḥ* (P.6.4.89). This *ūd* is not polyliteral; it does not become a total substitute.

But ⟨...⟩ because the substituend is specified [...] *ūd* does not become the total substitute for the penultimate letter.

---

[176] The *locus classicus* of this argument, to which all the writers mentioned in footnote 175, p. 85, refer, is Patañjali's discussion on P.1.1.55 (Mbh.I.132:4–5). He repeats the argument under P.1.3.9, *vārt.* 15 (Mbh.I.267:3–4). For further citations of the argument see footnote 175 above.

[177] This argument does not appear in the *Mahābhāṣya*, although some other problems concerning P.6.4.89 are recognised and discussed (e.g., Mbh.I.118:16 and III.178:20; I.121:21 etc.). Nor is it raised in the *Kāśikā* or subcommentaries on P.6.4.89, nor in the *Siddhānta-kaumudī* texts on the same, nor by any of the *paribhāṣā* commentators. The argument seems unique to the Vyāḍi commentator.

Explanation In P.6.4.89 Pāṇini is teaching that the vowel *-o-* of *goh-* is to be replaced by long *-ū-*, before certain suffixes. Thus forms like *gūhati* and *gūhia* are accounted for. To signify that he means *-ū-* itself, and not any of the vowels homorganic with it, he uses the marker *t*, according to the well known *tapara* convention (P.1.1.70). Thus the form *ūt* appears in the rule. But this form arguably consists of two letters. Therefore, applying P.1.1.55, the possibility arises of *-ū-* replacing not just the vowel of *goh*, but the whole of the word preceding the *-o-*, giving the wrong form *ūh* (but see below).

However, by applying the *paribhāṣā* we may not count *ūt* as more than one letter; P.1.1.55 may not apply, and thus the correct forms in *gūh-* are ensured.

Comments There are several excellent examples which could be cited to show the reworking of the *paribhāṣā* (see e.g., *Sīradeva* (no. 6); Kielhorn 1874.33 f. etc.), and so it is extraordinary that the Vyāḍi commentator should choose P.6.4.89 as his example, when there are such difficulties associated with the argument. The problem with his argument is this: it is true that *ūt* might be taken to have two letters. But P.1.1.55, which would then teach that *ūt* replace the *whole* of the substituend, cannot apply to P.6.4.3. This is because the rule explicitly states which part of the substituend is to be replaced: the *upadhā* 'penultimate letter'. Since this is explicitly stated, there can be no doubt whatsoever as to just what *ūt* replaces. So the *paribhāṣā* is irrelevant. This may be what the Vyāḍi commentator was saying in the last lines of his commentary (9:9–10), but they are too corrupt now to be sure.

The central point is that in P.6.4.89 *upadhāyāḥ* is a *sthānaṣaṣṭhī* 'a genitive of place' while *gohaḥ* is an *avayavaṣaṣṭhī* 'a partitive genitive'. Thus *ūt* replaces the *upadhā* which is part of *goh*. It would be quite wrong to interpret *gohaḥ* as a genitive of place, although this would make more sense of the Vyāḍi commentator's argument. He could then claim that *ūt* would replace the whole of *goh*, instead of just its last letter. But this interpretation of the rule is nonsensical, and has been explicitly rejected by Kātyāyana and Patañjali when discussing genitives of place (P.1.1.49; Mbh.I.118:14 ff.).

Since the Vyāḍi commentator has apparently gone badly wrong in this argument, it forms a useful text for identification. Any other author found using argument § 9.2 is likely to be directly related to the Vyāḍi commentator in some way.

A marker letter does not make an item non-isomorphic.[178]

— Suffixes taken together with markers are not [thereby made] non-isomorphic.

Explanation Many grammatical elements, such as suffixes, are presented by Pāṇini together with marker letters. Furthermore, there are certain operations which depend upon whether two given items have the same form or not, whether they are isomorphic. The present *paribhāṣā* teaches that for the purposes of deciding whether or not two items have the same form, markers do not count. Thus Pāṇini teaches two different suffixes, *ṇyat* and *kyap*. However, stripped of their markers, both have the form *ya*. So by the application of this *paribhāṣā* they may be called isomorphic.

Comments As may have already been apparent from footnote 178 below, there is a definite relationship between this *paribhāṣā* and the *anekānta paribhāṣā* (*anekāntā anubandhāḥ*: Nāgeśa no. 4). These two postulates really do the same job, and in tacit acceptance of this fact the *paribhāṣā* commentators up to Nāgeśa do not use the

[178]It appears definite that Kātyāyana did not know this *paribhāṣā* as such, because he raises the very problem which the *paribhāṣā* is designed to solve, and solves it by other means. In *vārt.* 4 on P.3.1.94 (Mbh.II.79:20) Kātyāyana asks whether suffixes which differ due to having different markers would thereby be potentially optional. P.3.1.94 allows such optionality only for suffixes which are dissimilar in form. In the next *vārttika*, no. 5, he answers that the problem does not arise, since markers are not an intrinsic part of what they mark. As Patañjali explains, it is the suffixes as they are in actual usage which must be considered (Mbh.II.79:25 . . . *prayoge 'sarūpāṇām vāvidhir nyāyyaḥ*). It is worth noting in passing that Kātyāyana's postulate that markers are not an intrinsic part of what they mark is itself a widely accepted *paribhāṣā* (*anekānta anubandhāḥ*); the Vyāḍi commentator, however, does not mention it at all.

Patañjali does know the *paribhāṣā*. He mentions it twice, later in the discussion referred to above, and on *vārt.* 6 on P.1.3.10 (Mbh.I.267:1). The two cases where he establishes the *paribhāṣā* as an intimation are the same, and based on P.3.1.39 (Mbh.II.80:7; I.267:1. See Kielhorn 1874.40 fn. 1).

The *paribhāṣā* is discussed by the following *paribhāṣā* commentators: Puruṣottamadeva (no. 12), Sīradeva (no. 38), Nīlakaṇṭha (no. 8), Haribhāskara (no. 40), Nāgeśa (no. 8), Śeṣādrisudhī (no. 6).

The *paribhāṣā* is cited by the *Kāśikā* on P.3.1.94 (KV.II.493–94), though not by the *Siddhāntakaumudī*. It is left to Vāsudevadīkṣita (SK.IV.3:8 (2830)) to do so in his *Bālamanoramā* on this rule. But Bhaṭṭojī Dīkṣita does quote the *paribhāṣā* when discussing P.3.1.68 (SK.IV.10:2 (2844)).

anekāntā paribhāṣā, but instead prefer the present *paribhāṣā* (*Vyāḍīyaparibhāṣāvṛtti* no. 10).

It is Nāgeśa who first introduces the *anekānta* postulate and discusses it, thereby making it famous. It must be added, however, that he ultimately rejects it, preferring the view that markers are indeed an intrinsic part of what they mark.[179] The situations where this view is troublesome are then dealt with piecemeal in the three *paribhāṣās* which begin *nānubandhakṛtam*... (Nāgeśa nos. 6, 7, 8).

Argument 10.1[180] [10:3

— How is that known?

— Since in *vibhāṣā kṛvṛṣoḥ* (P.3.1.120) he prescribes [the suffix] *kyap* as an option, in order that *ṇyat*, taken together with the markers, are non-isomorphic. And so this [option between them] is validated by *vāsarūpo 'striyām* (P.3.1.94) alone; there is no point in stating the optionality [separately in P.3.1.120].

But the teacher observes that items taken together with markers are not [thereby] non-isomorphic. It is such items as are non-isomorphic when the markers have been elided which are covered by the *vāsarūpa* rule (P.3.1.94). And in this case, once the markers of *ṇyat* and *kyap* are elided, they are isomorphic. Therefore the option is proposed [in P.3.1.120].

Explanation The argument is straightforward. In P.3.1.120, Pāṇini teaches that the suffix *kyap* may optionally take the place of *ṇyat*, which he gives four rules later on, in P.3.1.124. He teaches this optionality in spite of the general maxim given in P.3.1.94 which states that a suffix taught after a root in this section may freely alternate with any non-isomorphic suffix. It seems, then, that for Pāṇini *kyap* and *ṇyat* are isomorphic. In fact, *k*, *p*, *ṇ* and *t* are markers here, and once they are elided the suffixes do indeed have the same form, *ya*.

Therefore the general conclusion is drawn that Pāṇini does not pay heed to marker letters when deciding whether two items are isomorphic or not.

Comments In stating that this argument is also found only in Puruṣottamadeva (footnote 180, p. 89) it should be emphasized that it is the particular use of P.3.1.120 which is meant. The outer form of the argument is common to most discussions of the application of this *paribhāṣā*.

Two points are of special interest here. First, the fact that P.3.1.120 is not even mentioned in the *Mahābhāṣya*. This conclusively establishes the fact that argument

[179] Nāgeśa p. 11:1–3; 12:1–2.

[180] This argument does not appear in the *Mahābhāṣya*. In fact P.3.1.120 is one of those rules which do not appear in the *Mahābhāṣya* at all, not even incidentally, or as part of the derivation of an example (see Lahiri, p. 23).

The argument is not found in the *Kāśikā* or *Siddhāntakaumudī* traditions under P.3.1.120.

The only use of this argument found so far is in Puruṣottamadeva's discussion of this *paribhāṣā* (p. 118:10 ff.).

§ 10.1 is completely independent of the *Mahābhāṣya*, and must either be an original idea of the Vyāḍi commentator, or it must come from some other commentarial tradition, not based on Patañjali. Secondly, the fact that the Vyāḍi commentator and Puruṣottamadeva alone share this argument points once again to a close relationship between these two early authors. The great divide here comes after Puruṣottamadeva, with Sīradeva. This scholar, in his true fundamentalist style, returns to the argument twice used by Patañjali, which establishes the *paribhāṣā* by intimation from P.3.1.139 (Mbh.I.267:1 and II.80:7). All following authors do likewise.

The discovery of any other citation of this argument in the literature would be interesting for comparison.

Argument 10.2[181] [10:10

— What is the point of intimating this?

— The *vāsarūpa* rule (P.3.1.94) does not apply to *karmaṇy aṇ* (P.3.2.1) and *āto 'nupasarge kaḥ* (P.3.2.3), because 'a marker letter does not make an item non-isomorphic.'

Explanation The purpose of the *paribhāṣā* is to avoid the problem that P.3.1.94, by which non-isomorphic suffixes may alternate with each other, might apply to the two suffixes *aṇ* and *ka*, given in P.3.2.1 and 3. If this were the case, *aṇ* and *ka* would be valid alternatives: *ka* would apply in the circumstances described by P.3.2.1 and *aṇ* would apply in those of P.3.2.3, leading to wrong forms.

If we apply the *paribhāṣā*, then *aṇ* and *ka* are seen to be isomorphic, because the *ṇ* and *k* are mere markers. Both suffixes have the final form *a*. Therefore they may not alternate freely, and are restricted to their proper domains.

Comments The fact that this argument is not used by any *paribhāṣā* commentator between Puruṣottamadeva and Nāgeśa would suggest that Nāgeśa had access to Puruṣottamadeva's work, when composing his own.

---

[181] This argument is fairly common the commentarial literature, though not completely formulated in the *Mahābhāṣya*.

The problem of *aṇ* and *ka* appearing to be non-isomorphic is raised by Patañjali four times. These two suffixes seem to furnish the standard example of two items distinguished only by their markers. Patañjali's comments arise in discussion of *vārt.* 6 on the first *śivasūtra*, *vārt.* 10 on P.1.3.9, *vārt.* 1 on P.3.1.32 and *vārt.* 4 on P.3.1.94 (Mbh.I.16:26, 265:23; II.42:10, 79:21). The phrasing of the first and third, as the second and fourth instances, are the same. In each of these cases Patañjali recognizes the difficulty, but in none of them does he solve it using the present *paribhāṣā*.

The argument is presented by the following *paribhāṣā* commentators: Puruṣottamadeva (no. 12), Nāgeśa (no. 8) and Śeṣādrisudhī (no. 6).

It is not mentioned in the *Kāśikā* or *Siddhāntakaumudī* traditions on P.3.2.1 or 3.

Paribhāṣā 11

Here in the discipline [of grammar] the previous state [of an item] may prevail.[182]

— Here in the discipline, operations are performed with regard to a stage which occurred earlier.

Explanation A Pāṇinian derivation is a series of steps, each consisting of a grammatical operation. Normally the output of one step provides the input for the next, in the sense that the output contains the conditions which trigger the next operation.

It may happen that an impasse is reached. The latest stage of the derivation does not provide the appropriate conditions for the next operation to begin. But the word being derived is still incomplete. It may be that the particular conditions needed to continue have been present at an earlier stage, but were obscured by intermediate operations. The present *paribhāṣā* sanctions reference back to an earlier stage of derivation in such situations.

Comments The *paribhāṣā* is common throughout the tradition, from the time of Patañjali. It is quoted in two distinct forms, however. These are:

> *bhūtapūrvagatir iha śāstre bhavati*, and
> *sāṃpratikābhāve bhūtapūrvagatiḥ*

(with minor variants). The textual distribution of these two forms is quite definite. The first form is used by Patañjali (with one exception, Mbh.III.109:9) and by Candra (no. 82), Śākaṭāyana (no. 18) and, of course, by the Vyāḍi commentator. The other form exclusively is used by Puruṣottamadeva and all the following authors, and also in the *Kāśikā* (by implication). Thus the Vyāḍi commentator once again demonstrates an affiliation with the *Mahābhāṣya* and Candra, as opposed to the post-*Kāśikā* tradition.

---

[182]The *paribhāṣā* is not used by Kātyāyana. Patañjali refers to the principle twelve times (Mbh.I.76:10:11, 139:14; III.109:8:9:19, 165:23, 181:25, 184:2, 294:16, 300:24, 335:12). Although the *paribhāṣā* is not quoted explicitly in the *Kāśikā*, Vāmana evidently has it in mind commenting on P.6.1.177, and this is brought out in the subcommentaries on this rule (KV.IV.660:7–8:14 ff.:30). The same is true of Jayāditya's remarks on P.3.1.97, which are not much amplified in the subcommentaries.

It is discussed by all the major *paribhāṣā* commentators: Puruṣottamadeva (no. 15), Sīradeva (no. 37), Nīlakaṇṭha (no. 55), Haribhāskara (no. 39), Nāgeśa (no. 76), Śeṣādrisudhī (no. 65).

Argument 11.1 [11:3

— How is that known?
— Since he says *oka ucaḥ ke* (P.7.3.64).
— How come this is an intimation?
— Because of the fact that ... the suffix *ka* is the one characterized as following an item with a penultimate *i, u, ṛ* or *ḷ* ... [?] is termed *it*. ... In that connection it is improper to say 'when *ka* follows' ... the substitute *ka* follows *uc*, after ascertaining that this *ka* is prior. ...

Explanation This passage is so textually corrupt that it is difficult to extract any clear argument from it. This difficulty is compounded by the fact that no other authors use an argument based on P.7.3.64. Indeed this *sūtra* does not appear at all anywhere in the *Mahābhāṣya*, even incidentally.

Argument 11.2[183] [11:7

— What is the point of intimating this?
— In *pavyam* 'to be purified', before the suffix has been applied, there is the *guṇa* appropriate before an *ārdhadhātuka*, that is to say, an *ārdhadhātuka* in general [P.7.3.84]. Once this is done, there is the substitution [of *av*] for an item ending in *v*, appropriate before a suffix beginning with *y* [P.6.1.79]. Once this is done, *ṇyat* would wrongly apply because it now follows a consonant [P.3.1.124].

Having noted that this did, at a previous stage, end in a vowel, [the suffix] *yat* applies [by P.3.1.97].

Explanation This argument revolves around the piecemeal derivation of *pavyam* 'to be purified'. The sequence is as follows:

i)	*pū*	+	some *ārdhadhātuka*	
ii)	*po*	+	some *ārdhadhātuka*	by P.7.3.84
iii)	*pav*	+	some *ārdhadhātuka* with initial *y*	by P.6.1.79
iv)	**pav*	+	*ṇyat*	by P.3.1.124

[183] This argument, adumbrated by Kātyāyana in *vārt.* 3 on P.2.4.35, is given by Patañjali in exactly the same words as the Vyāḍi commentator, in his comment on this *vārttika* (Mbh.I.483:14–16), and later, on P.3.1.97 (Mbh.II.82:7–9).

The same argument, though not the example *pavyam*, is given by Puruṣottamadeva (no. 15), Sīradeva (no. 37) and Haribhāskara (no. 39).

The reasoning is rejected by Vaidyanātha Pāyaguṇḍa in his commentary on Nāgeśa's treatment of the *paribhāṣā* (Vaidyanātha 169:28 ff.).

Stage ii) gives the *guṇa* of the base (*aṅga*) appropriate to most suffixes in general. Then we narrow things down by assuming our suffix begins with the letter *y*. This leads to the form *pav*, which is consonant-final. And by P.3.1.124, all consonant-final roots get the suffix *ṇyat*, not *yat*. This would lead to the undesired form **pāvyam*.

However, if we apply the *paribhāṣā* we can see that at a previous stage, ii), the root did indeed end in a vowel. We can act on this, then, and apply the suffix *yat* by P.3.1.97, giving the desired form *pavyam*.

Comments It is extraordinary that such a bizarre argument has persisted for so long in the tradition, being rejected only with the *navyavaiyākaraṇas*. It is impossible to consider seriously the piecemeal addition of a suffix which this argument requires, the *lakṣaṇaikacakṣuṣka* view taken to absurd lengths.

Argument 11.3[184] [11:10

— It is just the same with

vāyū́nā́m 'of the winds'
ikṣūṇā́m 'of the sugar-canes'.

By understanding the short vowel which existed at a previous stage [the rule] *nām anyatarasyām* (P.6.1.177) gives the correct accent. Because 'the previous stage is recognised'.

Explanation Pāṇini teaches, in P.6.1.177, that an item ending in a short, acutely accented vowel may optionally shift the accent to the inflectional suffix in the genitive plural. Thus the noun *vāyú* may have genitive plural forms *vāyū́nām* or *vāyūnā́m*.

It may be objected that in the genitive plural the noun would no longer have a short final vowel, the *ŭ* having been replaced by *ū*, according to P.6.4.3 *nāmi*. This is indeed the case, and so strictly speaking the optional form *vāyūnā́m* is illegitimate.

However, if we invoke the *paribhāṣā*, we can say that P.6.1.177 should be applied with reference to the earlier stage of the derivation, when the final vowel was still short. Thus, in the derivation:

i)	*vāyú*	+	*nām*	P.2.3.50 etc.
ii)	*vāyū́*	+	*nām*	by P.6.4.3
iii)	*vāyú*	+	*nā́m*	optionally by P.6.1.177

stage iii) proceeds with reference to stage i).

[184]This difficulty is first put forward by Kātyāyana in *vārt.* 1 on P.6.1.177, but his solution, in the same *vārttika*, is different. He urges the *anuvṛtti* of *matup* from the previous rule, P.6.1.176, and interprets the rule to mean that only a stem which has a short vowel before *-mat* is subject to the accent variation. It is Patañjali, commenting on the *sūtra* and *vārttika*, who introduces the *paribhāṣā* as the solution (Mbh.III.109:8–9), giving the same argument as the Vyāḍi commentator.

None of the other *paribhāṣā* commentators give this argument.

The *Kāśikā* accepts Kātyāyana's suggestions that *matup* is read into this rule, but takes this fact as an indication that the *paribhāṣā* is to be applied. This is clarified in the *Nyāsa* and *Padamañjarī* (KV.IV.660). The *Bhāṣāvṛtti* does not comment on P.6.1.177, nor does Candra, since the rule concerns accent.

Comments The use of the word *ikṣūṇām* in this context seems to be unique to the Vyāḍi commentator, and might identify his sources if traced elsewhere. Otherwise his argument seems to be closer to Patañjali than anyone else, and does not try to blend the two approaches of Patañjali and Kātyāyana, the *paribhāṣā* and *matup*, as does the *Kāśikā*.

Paribhāṣā 12

Here in the discipline [of grammar] an operation takes place by the application of *vasu*.[185]

Explanation The proper reading of this *paribhāṣā* (see below) provides a 'look-ahead' feature for derivations: operations may take place on the basis of what will be, but is not yet, the case.

Comments The reading *vasu-pravṛttyā*, given as the archetypal reading by the canons of textual criticism, renders the *paribhāṣā* senseless. However, it seems that the mistake is more than scribal since it is repeated in argument § 12.1. The correct reading of the *paribhāṣā* is, of course, *vartsyatpravṛttyā iha śāstre kāryaṃ bhavati* 'here in the discipline [of grammar] an operation takes place according to the future behaviour [of an item]'. The Vyāḍi commentator seems to have erred by confusing the first word of the maxim, *vartsyat*, with the first word of the rule which is invariably invoked to derive the *paribhāṣā*: *vasu* in P.7.2.67 (see argument § 12.1). Since this argument revolves around the use of the suffix *vasu*, it seems to have slipped into the *paribhāṣā* itself, by mistake. The question is, of course, 'whose mistake?' Since the *vasu*- readings are both archetypal and reasonably explicable as mental slips, it is justifiable to leave them in the text and attribute them to our author.[186]

The arguments presented by the Vyāḍi commentator all make sense if one reads *vartsyat* 'future' or 'what is to come' for *vasu* '-*vas*', and the author himself reverts to the correct form later in the text (12:6, 8). However, it is worth noting that, even there, the manuscripts are unanimous in reading *vatsyaty* for *vartsyaty*, though this certainly does seem explainable as a scribal slip.

The correct form of the *paribhāṣā* (as discussed by the commentators mentioned in footnote 185) is the natural twin of the preceding *paribhāṣā*, no. 11. Whereas that rule taught that an earlier stage of a derivation may be relevant to the present operation, this *paribhāṣā* teaches that an operation may have reference to some future stage of the derivation.

---

[185] The *paribhāṣā* as it stands is of course unique to the Vyāḍi commentator (see comments), but the corrected *paribhāṣā* is discussed by Puruṣottamadeva (no. 16), Sīradeva (no. 84), Nīlakaṇṭha (no. 140, his last), and Haribhāskara (no. 87). Puruṣottama's discussion is almost identical to the Vyāḍi commentator's.

The *paribhāṣā* is not mentioned in the *Mahābhāṣya* nor in the *Kāśikā* nor *Siddhānta-kaumudī* nor commentaries under P.7.2.67.

[186] Housman says even of Bentley that, '...many a time when he feigned and half fancied that he was correcting the scribe, he knew in his heart ... that he was revising the author' (*Astronomicon* I, p. xviii.).

It is interesting to note that although this *paribhāṣā* has a fairly secure place in the commentarial literature on *paribhāṣās*, it is not used by Kātyāyana or Patañjali, and does not appear in either the *Kāśikā* or the *Siddhāntakaumudī*.

Argument 12.1[187] [12:2

— How is that known?
— Since in *vasvekājādghasām* (P.7.2.67) he says *iṭ*.
— How come this is an intimation?
— In this context the inclusion of *ekāc* 'monosyllable' is rejected.
— How?
— Because nothing exists which is monosyllabic before [the suffix] *vasu*, because in this context there must be reduplication. But the teacher observes that this becomes monosyllabic because of the application of *vasu* [or: because of the future behaviour of the item].
— How?
— Once [the augment] *iṭ* is applied, there is elision of the reduplicative syllable by *ata ekahalmadhya* ... (P.6.4.120).

He prescribes *iṭ* knowing that this will become monosyllabic.

Explanation In P.7.2.67, Pāṇini rules that the participial suffix ***vas*** only gets the initial augment ***i*** in certain circumstances, to give such forms as ***ād-i-vān*** 'one having eaten' (reduplicated perfect participle). One of these circumstances is 'after a monosyllabic theme (***aṅga***)'. But nothing which is monosyllabic precedes ***vas***. But items which are polysyllabic do indeed *become* monosyllabic after some transformations. So the ***ekāc*** in P.7.2.67 suggests that we can look to the future state of a derivation to justify present operations. We can add the ***i*** augment first, and later make the theme monosyllabic by applying P.6.4.120, even though P.7.2.67 relys on this monosyllabicism for its action.

Argument 12.2[188] [12:7

— What is the point of intimating this?
— The *ātmanepada* taught by *śadeḥ śitaḥ* (P.1.3.60) is valid because the item with the marker *ś* will be present here.

[187] Patañjali does question the need for ***ekāc*** in P.6.2.67 (Mbh.I.300:17), but he does not invoke the present ***paribhāṣā***. Rather, he considers pbh. 11, the ***bhūtapūrvagati*** rule.

This argument from a ***jñāpaka*** is used by Puruṣottamadeva (no. 16), Sīradeva (no. 84), and Haribhāskara (no. 87). Nīlakaṇṭha (no. 140) considers the ***paribhāṣā*** to be ***nyāyasiddha***, and Sīradeva actually give ***lokanyāyas***.

[188] All the ***paribhāṣā*** commentators who treat this ***paribhāṣā*** also use this argument.

Explanation P.1.3.60 teaches that after the rood *śad* 'decay', when it has a suffix with the marker *ś*, there are *ātmanepada* verbal suffixes. An example derivation with *śad* is as follows:

i)	*śad*			+	*laṭ*	by P.3.2.123
ii)	*śad*	+		+	*te*	by (P.3.4.78), P.1.3.60
iii)	*śad*	+	*śa*	+	*te*	by P.3.1.77
iv)	*śīy*	+	*śa*	+	*te*	by P.7.3.78

The affix *śa* is added by P.3.1.77 to root which is already followed by a *tiṅ* suffix (such as the *parasmaipada tip* by P.3.4.78). But it is P.1.3.60 tells us which kind of *tiṅ* to choose in the first place. So P.1.3.60 has to act with foreknowledge of stage iii) of the derivation, when the *śa* will be present.

A prescription or a prohibition applies to the nearest item.[189]

Argument 13.1[190] [13:2

— How is this known?
— Since he teaches the prohibition in connection with *ṇi* and *śvi* [i.e., P.7.2.5].
— How come this is an intimation?
— The prohibition in connection with *ṇi* and *śvi* does not have to be stated. For, once the prohibition by *neṭi* (P.7.2.4) has applied [countermanding the *vṛddhi* applicable by P.7.2.1], and *guṇa* has taken place, and with the substitution of *ay*, the required form would be achieved.

But the teacher observes [that] the prohibition [in P.7.2.4] applies to the immediately preceding *vṛddhi*, which is specifically that of an item ending in a consonant. It is not just any *vṛddhi*. Thus he teaches the prohibition connected with *ṇi* and *śvi*.
— Why?
— Because otherwise there would be prohibition also of the *vṛddhi* of *ṇi* and *śvi* before *sic* [the aorist *s*].
— This being so, what is the outcome?

[189]This *paribhāṣā* is cited by Patañjali in a recurring passage (Mbh.I.101:11, 167:11, 216:3, 277:12, 278:16, 319:15) and elsewhere (I.225:6, 284:22, II.59:17; III.248:6, 279:20, 336:9).

It is discussed by Puruṣottamadeva (no. 17), Sīradeva (no. 48), Nīlakaṇṭha (no. 51), Haribhāskara (no. 50), Nāgeśa (no. 61) and Śeṣādrisudhī (no. 52).

It is cited also in the *Siddhāntakaumudī* on P.8.4.22 (SK.I.368:2 (359)).

[190]P.7.2.5 is not commented on in the *Mahābhāṣya*.

The problem of *ṇi* and *śvi* in P.7.2.5 is discussed in the *Kāśikā* on this rule, and in the *Nyāsā*, *ad loc* (KV.V.659 f.), but a solution is achieved through applying the *antaraṅga* principle.

A similar, but not identical, argument, using P.7.2.4, is advocated by Puruṣottamadeva (no. 16), Sīradeva (no. 48), Haribhāskara (no. 50), and Śeśādrisudhī (no. 52). None of these authors starts from P.7.2.5.

— It is necessary to state the *paribhāṣā* 'a prescription or a prohibition applies to the nearest item'.

Explanation This argument revolves around the interpretation of a short sequence of rules at the beginning of the second *pāda* of the seventh *adhyāya* of the *Aṣṭādhyāyī*. In treating the vowel grade of aorist forms, Pāṇini first of all frames the general rule 7.2.1 *sici vṛddhiḥ parasmaipadeṣu* which teaches that a base vowel *i u ṛ* or *ḷ* is replaced by *vṛddhi* before the active aorist suffixes. In P.7.2.3 *vadavrajahalantasyācaḥ* he extends this *vṛddhi* substitution to cover all bases ending in consonants, whatever their vowel. The roots *vad* and *vraj* are mentioned specifically to forestall an optionalization given later in P.7.2.7 which could apply to them. Next, in P.7.2.4 *neṭi*, Pāṇini prohibits this *vṛddhi* substitution before the augment *iṭ*.

The question is, which *vṛddhi* is being prohibited: that just mentioned in P.7.2.3, or the original, general *vṛddhi* substitution of P.7.2.1? How do we decide which is meant?

Fortunately for us, in P.7.2.5 *hmyantakṣaṇaśvasajāgṛṇiśvyeditām*, which extends the *vṛddhi* prohibition, Pāṇini mentions the two items *ṇi*, the causal suffix, and *śvi*, a root. These give us a crux, because both are liable to *vṛddhi* by P.7.2.1, but not by P.7.2.3. Therefore the prohibition of P.7.2.4 only covers the immediately preceding rule, and should not be taken as a prohibition of the more removed rule P.7.2.1, since Pāṇini separately mentions items whose *vṛddhi* by this rule is to be prohibited.

And if we were to think that P.7.2.4 *neṭi* could be applied to P.7.2.1, it can be shown that a redundancy would be created. If P.7.2.4 prohibits *vṛddhi* in the formation *aśvayīt* 'he swelled', from *aśvi* + *īt*, then *guṇa* will apply giving us *aśve* + *īt* and then *aśvay* + *īt*. Now any further *vṛddhi* for such a form is prohibited by the first part of P.7.2.5 which deals in general with forms ending in *y*. So the later mention of *ṇi* and *śvi* in the same rule is redundant. This redundancy is obviated by assuming the *paribhāṣā*.

Comments The most obvious fact here is that this argument says nothing to justify including prescriptions in the *paribhāṣā*; it establishes Pāṇini's usage only in the case of a prohibition. The deduction overreaches the evidence. Moreover, a *paribhāṣā* which deals with two distinct types of rule, as this one does, cannot strictly be established by intimation from any one rule. At best it must be presented as an amalgam of two *paribhāṣās*, each intimated by its own type of rule.

Nāgeśa takes the most natural course here and says the *paribhāṣā* is rooted in the maxim about proximity (*Nāgeśa*, p. 149: *pratyāsattimūlako 'yam*). In saying this he is, as so often, following Nīlakaṇṭha (*Nīlakaṇṭha*, p. 302: *iyam upasthitinyāyamūlā* ...). Sīradeva before them declared the same, hedging his bet by adding, 'they say an intimation too' (*Sīradeva*, p. 216: *ayaṃ cārthaḥ pratyāsattinyāyalabdhaḥ paṭhyate | jñāpakam apy āhuḥ* ...). This ambivalence goes right back to Puruṣottamadeva who also gives both approaches, first of all basing the *paribhāṣā* on the maxim about proximity, and then giving two types of intimation, one for prescriptions and one for prohibitions (Puruṣottama, p. 12): *ayaṃ cārthaḥ pratyāsattinyāyasiddha eva* ...). The continuity of phrases from author to author through the literature is very apparent here.

The second point to be noted is that in the process of deriving a correct form from *ṇi* or *śvi* it is assumed in this argument that *vṛddhi* is applicable before *guṇa*. The following argument, § 13.2, arises from querying this assumption.

Argument 13.2[191]

[13:10

— This is not an intimation. Even if this *paribhāṣā* were intimated elsewhere, it would still be possible to account for the prohibition connected with *ṇi* and *śvi*.

Both *guṇa* and *vṛddhi* apply to *ṇi* and *śvi* when *sic* follows.

— What is there to say about this?

— There is *guṇa* by virtue of subsequence, there is *vṛddhi* by virtue of invariance. *Vṛddhi* is invariant because it would apply whether or not *guṇa* is applied.

— It would not apply even when *guṇa* is applied. *Iko guṇavṛddhī* (P.1.1.3) is stated.

— In that case, then, it is stated that *vṛddhi* before *sic* is *antaraṅga*.

— *Guṇa* is even more *antaraṅga*.

— How?

— Because *sic* is not the only cause of *vṛddhi*.

— What [else] is, then?

— *Parasmaipada* is too. *Sic* is, however, the only cause of *guṇa*.

Once *guṇa* has been done, because it is *antaraṅga*, and *ay* has been substituted, then the *vṛddhi* proper to an item ending in a consonant is prohibited by *hmyante* ... (P.7.2.5, first part). [So] the mention *ṇi* and *śvi* is pointless.

This being established, the fact that *ṇi* and *śvi* are mentioned is the teacher's way of observing that there is no *antaraṅga* before *sic*. And therefore the fact is that the inclusion of *vṛddhi* in *iko guṇavṛddhī* (P.1.1.3) is for the sake of *sic*, in order that the *vṛddhi* before *sic* be specifically of *ĭ, ŭ, ṛ̆* or *ḷ*, and so that it should be prohibited by *kṅiti ca* (P.1.1.5).

Once it [*vṛddhi*] is prohibited, the substitution of *uvaṅ* [*uv* for *u*] in *nyanuvīt* 'he sounded' is valid.

Therefore it [the mention of *ṇi* and *śvi*] is not an intimation [of the *paribhāṣā*].

Explanation The Vyāḍi commentator argues that the prohibition of *ṇi* and *śvi* in P.7.2.5 does not intimate this *paribhāṣā*, but another one about an *antaraṅga* rule not applying before *sic*.

[191] Cf. the argument in the *Kāśikā* on P.7.2.5 (footnote 190 above).

Argument 13.3[192] [13:24

— In that case, this is the intimation: the mention of *ubhābhyām* 'after both' in *ḍāb ubhābhyām* (P.4.1.13); the mention of *tābhyām* 'than these two' in *tābhyām anyatroṇādayaḥ* (P.3.4.75); the mention of *pūrva* 'prior' in *yathāvidhy anuprayogaḥ pūrvasmin* (P.3.4.4).

The rule [in each case] would wrongly apply to the nearest one it would not apply only to the one prior to that.

And it is desirable [that it should]. Therefore this [stipulation in each rule] is stated.

Comments The first of these three extra *jñāpakas* cited by the Vyāḍi commentator, P.4.1.13, is interesting because Patañjali questions the purpose of *ubhābhyām* in the rule, and rejects it as unnecessary. He then goes on to discuss the purpose of *anyatarasyām*, which makes the rule optional. This latter argument is rehearsed by later commentators, but Patañjali's initial rejection of *ubhābhyām* seems to have been picked up elsewhere only by the learned Jñānendrasarasvatī (*Tattvabodhinī*, P.4.1.13 (SK.I.507 (461))), who refers to the opinion of 'some' (*eke*) and 'others' (*anye*). Even Candra maintains a reference to the two preceding *sūtras* (Ca.2.3.14). Here again, the Vyāḍi commentator demonstrates his close adherence to Patañjali.

Argument 13.4[193] [13:28

— What is the point of intimating this?

— In *suḍ anapuṃsakasya* (P.1.1.43) the mention of *anapuṃsakasya* 'not of a neuter' prohibits [only] that application which is nearest. It does not prohibit *śi sarvanāmasthānam* (P.1.1.42). Therefore the technical term *sarvanāmasthāna* is valid here in *kuṇḍāni tiṣṭhanti* 'the pitchers are standing'.

Explanation The Vyāḍi commentator provides a purpose for the *paribhāṣā*.

---

[192] Patañjali queries the utility of *ubhābhyām* in P.4.1.13 (Mbh.II.204:10). P.3.4.75 is not mentioned anywhere in the *Mahābhāṣya*, but the purpose of *tābhyām* is queried in the *Kāśikā* and subcommentaries(KV.III.211). The use of *pūrvasmin* in P.3.4.4 does not appear to be taken up by any commentators.

None of the *paribhāṣā* commentators uses these rules as *jñāpakas*.

[193] This argument is the locus classicus for the *paribhāṣā*, used by Patañjali in the recurring passage mentioned above (Mbh.I.101:11, etc.; see footnote 189 above).

It is repeated up by Puruṣottamadeva (no. 17) and Śeṣādrisudhī (no. 52), and referred to in passing by Nāgeśa (no. 61).

Argument 13.5[194] [13:31

— If this *paribhāṣā* does exist, what is the point of mentioning *sā* in *sāmantritam* (P.2.3.48)? Surely if 'a prescription or a prohibition applies to the nearest item' then the technical term *āmantrita* will only apply to that first class inflection which is characterized as being appellative [cf. P.2.3.47], not to one characterized as [conveying solely the sense of] a nominal stem [cf. P.2.3.46].

So, since this is the case, the fact he mentions *sā* intimates that this *paribhāṣā* is not invariant.

Explanation The Vyāḍi commentator argues for the *anityatva* of the *paribhāṣā*.

Argument 13.6[195] [13:36

— What is the point of intimating that variability?

— So that *na gośvansāvavarṇa* ... (P.6.1.182) is a prohibition of the section starting *sāv ekāc* ... (P.6.1.168) and not [just] of the nearest item.

Explanation Here and in the next argument, the Vyāḍi commentator proposes purposes for the *paribhāṣā*.

Argument 13.7[196] [13:38

— Similarly *vibhāṣā sākāṅkṣe* (P.3.2.114) applies only to *abhijñāvacana* ... (P.3.2.112) and not to the nearest rule, *na yadi* (P.3.2.113).

Argument 13.8[197] [13:40

— Rules like this [P.4.2.71?] etc. apply to all four of the rules starting with *tad asminn sati* ... (P.4.2.67), not [just] to the nearest one.

Comments This passage is corrupt in the manuscripts, but its interpretation as here is probably not wrong in essence.

---

[194] P.2.3.48 is not commented on in the *Mahābhāṣya*, and this argument is not used by the *paribhāṣā* commentators.

The *paribhāṣā* is mentioned in the *Nyāsa* and thence in the *Padamañjarī sub* P.2.3.48 (KV.II.208).

[195] This argument is not used by the *paribhāṣā* commentators.

Jinendrabuddhi points out in his commentary on P.6.1.182 (KV.IV.663:21) that this rule is not to be taken as a prohibition only of what immediately precedes, and this seems to be an indirect reference to the *paribhāṣā*.

[196] This argument is not used by the *paribhāṣā* commentators.

[197] Once again, this argument is not used by the *paribhāṣā* commentators.

The *anuvṛtti* of the group of *sūtras* has been the subject of discussion since Patañjali (see the notes in Joshi and Bhaṭe 1984.20–25), but not in the particular context of the present *paribhāṣā*.

The mention of an item includes what has been annexed to it.[198]

— That which is annexed to an item is present with the mention of that item.

Argument 14.1 [14:3

— How is that known?
— Since in *na ktvā seṭ* (P.1.2.18) he teaches the prohibition of the marker *k*.
— How come this is an intimation? For there will not be any prohibition here [of *vṛddhi*, by P.1.1.5] before an item marked with *k*, solely because of the separation [of the item and the marked suffix by *i*]. Therefore there is no point in this prohibition [i.e., P.1.2.18].

However, the teacher observes that this augment *i*, being annexed to the item marked with *k*, is included with the mention of the item marked with *k*. The statement [of P.1.2.18] is for this reason.

Explanation The argument is that in, say, *div* + *iṭ* + *ktvā*, the *iṭ* added by P.7.2.35 intervenes between root and suffix. This prevents – *prima facie* – the possibility of the suffix causing strengthening of the root vowel, since the suffix no long strictly follows the root. This suggests that Pāṇini had the *paribhāṣā* in mind, and framed P.1.2.18 to suggest this to us.

[198] This maxim does not appear in the *Mahābhāṣya* and is not discussed by the commentators. But see discussion of pbh. 56, p. 203 below.

Argument 14.2 [14:8

— Others say that the intimation is the assertion of the prohibition *na seṭ* 'not [so *ktvā*] having the augment *i*' [i.e., P.1.2.18], the very assertion of the prohibition.

— How so?

— *Sārvadhātukārdhadhātukayoḥ pugantalaghūpadhasya ca* (P.7.3.84–85) is stated in the context of the examples *devitvā* 'having played', *sevitvā* 'having sewn'.

But this augment *i* is neither an *ārdhadhātuka* nor is it a *sārvadhātuka*. And that which is an *ārdhādhatuka* [i.e., *tvā*] is separated off by the augment *i*. Therefore, even if the marker *k* be not there, there is no *guṇa*. There is no point in the prohibition [i.e., P.1.2.18].

However, the teacher observes that this augment which is appended to the *ārdhadhātuka* suffix is included by mentioning the *ārdhadhātuka*, because 'the mention of an item includes what has been appended to it'. This being the case, the *guṇa* which would apply before the augment *i* is prohibited before an item marked with *k*.

Therefore the prohibition of the marker *k* is for the purpose of intimation.

Explanation This repeats the idea of argument § 14.1.

Argument 14.3[199] [14:15

— What is the point of intimating this?

— The augment *s* in *sarveṣām* 'of them all.' What is appended to the inflection is included by the mention of the inflection. Therefore the [substitution of] *e* [for final *a* of *sarva*] by *bahuvacane jhaly et* (P.7.3.103) is valid.

Explanation The derivation of the gen. pl. form *sarveṣām* of the pronoun *sarva* includes the following:

i)	*sarva*			+	*ām*	
ii)	*sarva*	+	*s*	+	*ām*	by P.7.1.52
iii)	*sarve*	+	*s*	+	*ām*	by P.7.3.103

Stage iii) requires that the final short *a* of the *aṅga* be replaced by *e* when followed by *ām*, but the *s* gets in the way, interfering with the contiguity which is the condition for the change. But by invoking the *paribhāṣā*, the mention of *ām* can be taken to include the augment *s*, and the problem is solved.

---

[199] P.7.1.52 and the immediately succeeding rules are the occasion for quite a lot of discussion in the *Mahābhāṣya* and the *Kāśikā*, but the present *paribhāṣā* is not invoked in this context.

The mention of an item includes what has been added to it internally.[200]

— That which has been added internally to an item is included by the mention of that item.

By mentioning a nominal stem, what has been added to the nominal stem internally is included.

Explanation This *paribhāṣā* is thematically similar to the previous one.

Argument 15.1[201] [15:4

— How is that known?
— Because he teaches the prohibition *nedamadasor akoḥ* (P.7.1.11).
— How come this is an intimation?
— The mention of *idam* and *adaṣ* includes *k*. Therefore the prohibition *akoḥ* has to be stated.

Explanation In P.7.1.11, Pāṇini teaches that the normal pronominal instr. pl. suffix *ais* does not occur after *idam* and *adas*, except when they have *k*. This *k* is the suffix *akac* added by P.5.3.71 in certain defined senses. But the fact that Pāṇini mentions this *k* suggests that by saying *idam* he also intends us to understand *imaka* and other such forms which include the *k*. In other words, he has the present *paribhāṣā* in mind.

---

[200] The phrase *tanmadhyapatitatvam* is used twice by Patañjali (Mbh.I.89:15; III.259:12), but the maxim is not cited as such.

It is, however, cited in the *Kāśikā* on P.6.1.132, 6.1.135, and 7.1.11 (KV.IV.607, VI.602, and V.541).

It is discussed by Puruṣottamadeva (no. 19), Sīradeva (no. 75), Nīlakaṇṭha (no. 81), Haribhāskara (no. 77), Nāgeśa (no. 89) and Śeṣādrisudhī (no. 77).

Patañjali does have a related maxim: *tadekadeśabhūtaṃ tadgrahaṇena gṛhyate* (Mbh.I.184:13:21:24, repeated at I.316:18:26, 317:3), which does much the same job as the present *paribhāṣā* and which is derived from Kātyāyana's *vārt.* 7 on P.1.1.71 (repeated as *vārt.* 4 on P.1.4.13). See Vyāḍi *paribhāṣā* 56, p. 203 below.

[201] This argument does not appear in the *Mahābhāṣya* or its main commentators, but does occur in the *Kāśikā* tradition on P.7.1.11, where it is explicitly cited (KV.V.541).

Argument 15.2[202]

[15:7

— What is the point of intimating this?
— [The derivation of the following examples:]

bhinátti 'he splits',
chinátti 'he cuts'.

By mentioning the root (in P.6.1.162), the *śnam* [the thematic affix of the seventh conjugation] which has been added internally to the root is included. It is established that the final of the root is acute (P.6.1.162).

Bhinátti and *chinátti* do have the acute on the middle [vowel].

Explanation By P.6.1.162, a root like *pac* has the acute on its final syllable: *pácati*. By invoking the *paribhāṣā* we can take this mention of the root to include the thematic affix which becomes part of it, and thus the acute accent falls on the thematic affix, which is the final part of the root+affix unit.

[202] This argument is not used in the commentaries on P.6.1.162.

An operation on a contingent item does not apply to the causal [*sic*].[203]

— An operation stated for a contingent item does not apply to the cause.

Explanation If item A is a contextual cause for item B, then an operation which applies to B may not apply to A.

Comments The manuscripts let us down here. P_2 and B attest *nimitti-*, but none *nimittasya*. Both have been accepted on the strength of the commentary's paraphrasing gloss, and the repetition of the *paribhāṣā* at the end of argument § 16.1.

Argument 16.1[204] [16:2

— Here [in P.8.4.46], after *r* and *h* [preceded by a vowel], there is said to be gemination of a following consonant (excepting *h*). *R* and *h* are the cause; the consonant for which the gemination is stated is the contingent item. Therefore the gemination of consonants (excepting *h*) does not apply to *r* and *h*, which are causes.

Explanation P.8.4.46 is the rule which accounts for such changes as *arka* → *arkka*, *brahmā* → *brahmmā* and so on (a form of *sandhi* common in manuscripts, but discarded in modern printed editions). The argument here is that because the letters *r* and *h* cause the gemination, they are not themselves subject to it; forms like **arrkka*, **brahhmmā* are thus illegal.

[203] This *paribhāṣā* is not found in the *Mahābhāṣya*, nor does it appear in the *Kāśikā* under P.4.1.112, 4.2.142 or 8.4.46. The only *paribhāṣā* commentator who treats it is Puruṣottamadeva (no. 94).

[204] See Mbh.I.28:13–15, Sīradeva (no. 107), and other discussions of the *śrutānumiti paribhāṣā*. This argument is used by Puruṣottamadeva (no. 94).

Argument 16.2[205] [16:6

— How is that known?

— Because he reads the word *kṣīrahrada* 'Milkpond' in the list beginning with *śiva*. The gemination which would wrongly apply to the *r* here in *hrada* does not take place.

The teachers read just the rule ... *grāmahradottarapadāc ca* (P.4.2.142). They give *hrada* in its final form because 'an operation on a contingent item does not apply to the cause'.

Argument 16.3[206] [16:10

— What is the point of intimating this?

— There is no gemination of the letter *r* in *spardhate*.

Comments This would seem to be a poor example, since the letter *r* here does not meet the conditions of P.4.2.142: it does follow a vowel, but not *r* or *h*. Nāgeśa cites the form *mahāhrada* which does make the point correctly.

[205] This argument is also used by Puruṣottamadeva (no. 94) as a *jñāpaka* for the *paribhāṣā*.

[206] This is given by Puruṣottamadeva, *loc. cit.* not as a purpose, but as an intimation. See also Nāgeśa's remarks on this issue in his discussion of the *śrutānumiti paribhāṣā* (no. 104).

In mutations concerning reduplicative syllables exceptions do not block general rules.[207]

— In mutations concerning reduplicative syllables, exceptions do not block generalities.

Argument 17.1[208] [17:3

— How is that known?
— Because he teaches the prohibition in *dīrgho 'kitaḥ* (P.7.4.83).
— How come this is an intimation?
— Because the prohibition *akitaḥ* 'not having the marker *k*' is made in it. Thus, in *jaṅgamyate* 'he keeps going', once the argument *nuk* is applied there must be no lengthening [cf. P.7.4.85]. And even without that [i.e., P.7.4.83] the prohibition is valid.
— How?
— This [augment] *nuk* is an exception to lengthening. In this case the lengthening will be blocked by *nuk*, because it is an exception. There is no lengthening at all here. There is no point in the prohibition.

But the teacher observes that this exception, *nuk*, will not block the general rule, lengthening.

Therefore the prohibition *akitaḥ* 'not having the marker *k*' is there [in P.7.4.83], so that there must be no lengthening before an item with the marker *k*.

[207]This maxim is derived from Kātyāyana: *vārt.* 2 on P.3.1.6 (Mbh.II.11:15), repeated as *vārt.* 2 on P.7.4.82 (Mbh.III.357:1). It is glossed by Patañjali at these places, and discussed nearby (Mbh.II.11:22; III.357:12:17).

It is discussed by Puruṣottamadeva (no. 20), Sīradeva (no. 96) and Haribhāskara (no. 98), and cited in the *Kāśikā* on P.7.4.66 and 7.4.83 (KV.VI.186, VI.198).

[208]See Patañjali on *vārttika* V.7.4.83.4 (Mbh.III.358:11–18), and the *Kāśikā* on P.7.4.83 (KV.VI.198). This argument and the next (§ 17.2) are used by all the *paribhāṣā* commentators who discuss this *paribhāṣā*. See also argument § 18.2, below.

Explanation The derivation involved is as follows:

i)				+	*gam*	+	*yate*	
ii)	*ja*			+	*gam*	+	*yate*	
iii)	*ja*	+	*n*	+	*gam*	+	*yate*	augment *nuk* by P.7.4.85
iv)*	*jā*	+	*n*	+	*gam*	+	*yate*	by P.7.4.83

The *k* of *nuk* prevents the lengthening threatened by P.7.4.83. But this is not necessary: P.7.4.83 only teaches lengthening of a final vowel of the reduplicate syllable (*abhyāsa*), and once *nuk* is added, the *abhyāsa* becomes *jan*, and no longer ends in a vowel. The redundancy of P.7.4.83 suggests the present *paribhāṣā*.

Argument 17.2[209] [17:11

— What is the point of intimating this?
— In *mīmāṃsate* 'he considers', both [substitution by] *i* and lengthening would apply. Because of its being an exception, the lengthening alone would take place. Therefore, by means of the *paribhāṣā* 'in mutations concerning reduplicative syllables exceptions do not block general rules', the [substitution by] *i* is performed first, then there is the lengthening.

Explanation The derivation involved is as follows:

i)	*mān*			+	*san-*	by P.3.1.6
ii)	*mān*	+	*mān*	+	*san-*	by P.6.1.9
iii)	*man*	+	*mān*	+	*san-*	by P.7.4.59
iv)	*ma*	+	*mān*	+	*san-*	by P.7.4.60
v)	*mi*	+	*mān*	+	*san-*	by P.7.4.79
vi)	*mī*	+	*mān*	+	*san-*	by P.3.1.6

After stage iv), two rules might apply, P.7.4.79 or P.3.1.6.

Paribhāṣā 18

Where there is no possibility, blocking occurs.[210]

— Where no possibility exists, there is blocking.

Comments This is, of course, closely related to the *paratva* principle (P.1.4.2), which is more usually invoked to solve some of the conflicts mentioned below.

Argument 18.1[211] [18:2

— In *vṛkṣebhyaḥ* 'to the trees', *plakṣebhyaḥ* 'to the fig trees' both the lengthening before a nasal, semivowel, *jh* or *bh* [by P.7.3.102 and also] the substitution of *e* before a stop of sibilant [by P.7.3.103] would apply. There is no possibility of them both applying there at once: the lengthening is blocked by the [substitution of] *e*.

Explanation In the derivation

i)	*vṛkṣa*	+	*bhyaḥ*	by P.2.3.13 etc.
ii)*	*vṛkṣe*	+	*bhyaḥ*	by P.7.1.103
iii)	*vṛkṣā*	+	*bhyaḥ*	by P.7.3.102

the possibility of ii) is blocked by the rules leading to iii).

[210] Patañjali's cites this maxim eleven times (Mbh.III.6:5:22, 98:4, 121:23, 232:16:22, 263:18, 264:13, 315:6, 354:8:17).

It is treated by Puruṣottamadeva (no. 21), Sīradeva (no. 35), Nīlakaṇṭha (no. 45) and Haribhāskara (no. 36).

This maxim is normally discussed together with the next, no. 19.

[211] This argument is not part of the early commentarial discourse on this *paribhāṣā*; it is usually derived from P.3.1.23. Nīlakaṇṭha and Haribhāskara do use this argument, however.

Argument 18.2[212] [18:5

— But how, then, is it known that when there is no possibility, blocking occurs?
— Because he teaches the prohibition *akitaḥ* 'not having the marker *k*' in *dīrgho 'kitaḥ* (P.7.4.83).
— How come it is an intimation?
— In *jaṅgamyate* 'he keeps going', the possibility does exist that both things might happen: the augment *nuk* and also lengthening. The augment *nuk* applies to the reduplicative syllable, and the lengthening to the vowel.

But the teacher observes that when there is a possibility, there is no blocking. Therefore, because of the prohibition *akitaḥ* 'not having the marker *k*', while there is the possibility, the blocking which is given by implication, does not occur. Blocking occurs when there is no possibility.

Argument 18.3 [18:11

— What is the point of intimating this?
— So that in *kāryam* 'to be done', *aco yat* (P.3.1.97) should not apply. Because there is not possibility that [both] *ṇyat* [by P.3.1.124] and *yat* could apply.

[212] See argument § 17.1 above. This argument is not usually part of the discussion of the present *paribhāṣā*.

Even when there is a possibility, blocking occurs.[213]

Comments This maxim would appear to contradict the preceding one, rendering them both pointless.

Argument 19.1[214] [19:2

— How so?

— Because it is observed in the world. For it is observed in the world as follows: 'Give curds to the *brāhmaṇas*, buttermilk to Kauṇḍinya.' Here, even when there is the possibility of giving curds, the giving of buttermilk forestalls it. And the possibility does exist of curds as well as buttermilk being given to Kauṇḍinya.

Even when there is a possibility, blocking occurs.

Explanation Though banal, this ubiquitous example does nicely illustrate the rules of scoping. Kauṇḍinya is, of course, a brāhmaṇa.

Argument 19.2[215] [19:6

— What is the point of intimating this?

— The *akac* which is prescribed for a pronoun [cf. P.5.3.71] blocks the *ka* which governs [that section; cf. P.5.3.70]. And [yet] the possibility does exist that they might be applied alternately.

[213] This maxim is cited by Patañjali (I.115:2; III.6:23:25, 121:24, 232:22:24, 264:14, 315:9, 354:18).

It is discussed by Puruṣottamadeva (no. 23), Sīradeva (no. 86), Nīlakaṇṭha (no. 47) and Haribhāskara (no. 89).

[214] This argument, doubtless of 'hoary' antiquity, has been used to justify the maxim since Patañjali (Mbh.I.115:3; III.6:24, 121:24, 232:23, 264:15, 315:9, 354:18); he calls it a *laukiko dṛṣṭāntaḥ*.

[215] This is not normally given as a purpose for the maxim. But see the *Pradīpa* and *Uddyota* (IV.395^b) on *vārttikas* V.5.3.72.1 and 2. See also the *Nyāsa* and *Padamañjarī* on P.5.3.71 (KV.IV.292 f.).

Comments The *Nyāsa* discussion on P.5.3.71 (KV.IV.292 f.) argues that although the two affixes *ka* and *akac* do not apply in the same places, they do apply in the same senses, and this the basis upon which one can be treated as an exception to the other. Such bizarre formas as **idakaṃka* or **adakaska* are thus avoided. It would seem likely that the Vyāḍi commentator was aware of some such argument.

Even if items are presented in a single rule, only some recur.[216]

— Even if items are presented in a single rule, part of them continues on, and part of them is cancelled.

Comments This maxim, as used by Patañjali, is judged by Joshi and Bhaṭe to be *ad hoc* and "neither consistent nor logical" (1984.28).

Argument 20.1[217] [20:3

— How is that known?
— Since he says *tasmād ity uttarasya* (P.1.1.67)
— How come this is an intimation?
— In this rule it is not necessary to put *iti*, because it is presented contextually.
— Where is it presented contextually?
— In *tasminn iti nirdiṣṭe pūrvasya* (P.1.1.66).

Alternatively, it does not recur. [But then] *nirdiṣṭa* must be mentioned as well [as *iti*].

Since this is the case, by mentioning *iti* the teacher is intimating that the use of *iti* does not recur, while the mention of *nirdiṣṭa* does recur.

— This being so, what is the outcome?
— It is intimated that, 'even if items are presented in a single rule, only some recur.'

[216]This maxim is cited by Patañjali three times (Mbh.II.212:24, 375:12; III.74:20).

It is discussed by Puruṣottamadeva (no. 25), Sīradeva (no. 8), Nīlakaṇṭha (no. 10), and Śeṣādrisudhī (no. 18).

It is used in the *Kāśikā* on P.5.2.25 (KV.IV.143).

[217]The non-recurrence of *iti* in P.1.1.67 is discussed in the *Nyāsa* on that passage (KV.I.237) and it is said to imply the present *paribhāṣā*.

Puruṣottamadeva and Sīradeva give the present argument as a *jñāpaka* for the *paribhāṣā*.

Explanation The word *nirdiṣṭa* is normally held to recur in P.1.1.67 from the preceding rule (*Kāśikā* on P.1.1.67, KV.I.236). But the word *iti*, which is also present in P.1.1.66, is repeated in P.1.1.67 by Pāṇini in order to teach the *paribhāṣā*.

Argument 20.2[218] [20:10

— What is the point of intimating this?

— *Kṛte granthe* (P.4.3.116) is made a heading. Then in *saṃjñāyām* (P.4.3.117), *granthe* is cancelled.

Likewise with *saṃkhyāvyavāder ṅīp* (P.4.1.26) [and] *dāmahāyanāntāc ca* (P.4.1.27). Here, *saṃkhyādeḥ* recurs while *avyayāder* is cancelled.

[218]The example of P.4.1.26–27 is cited by all the *paribhāṣā* commentators, but that of P.4.3.116–117 seems to be the Vyāḍi commentator's alone.

In the disciplines, mutually dependent operations are acceptable.[219]

Argument 21.1[220] [21:2

— How is that known?

— Because he says *vasv ekājādghasām* (P.7.2.67). The augment *i* is caused by a monosyllable; the fact of being monosyllabic is caused by the *i*. So this is mutual dependence. Mutually dependent operations are acceptable.

Comments It is not clear how the augment *i* could be said to cause *ekāctva* (i.e., *abyāsalopa*, P.6.4.20). In a derivation such as that of *pecivas* there might be said to be a mutuality between the change of *pac*→*pec* (depending on *vas*) and *vas*→*ivas* (depending on *pac*). But this does not seem to be the point being made.

Argument 21.2[221] [21:5

— What is the point of intimating this?

— Vocalisation is *i, u, ṛ, ḷ* in place of *y, v, r, l* (P.1.1.45). Now, by means of the term 'vocalisation' the letters *i, u, ṛ, ḷ* replace *y, v, r, l*. By the same token, the term 'vocalisation' applies to the *i, u, ṛ, ḷ*. Thus the mutual dependence is valid.

[219]This maxim and its opposite are known to Patañjali (Mbh.I.40:21:22, 60:18, 94:23, 95:4, 111:12, 158:4, 257:22, 274:24:26, 275:1, 393:24, 449:10; II.11:8, 113:5, 126:13:16, 139:8, 197:18, 240:10; III.174:6, 273:8). In almost every case Patañjali cites the negation of the maxim.

It is discussed by Puruṣottamadeva (no. 96), Sīradeva (no. 3), Nīlakaṇṭha (no. 3) and Haribhāskara (no. 3).

[220]The Vyāḍi commentator is alone in citing this argument as evidence for the *paribhāṣā*.

[221]Patañjali notes the *paribhāṣā* under P.1.1.45, but argues that it should not be allowed (Mbh.I.111:11–12).

The *Kāśikā* on P.1.1.45 (KV.I.160f.) discusses the problem of the two meanings of *saṃprasāraṇa*, but not in the context of the *paribhāṣā*.

All the *paribhāṣā* commentators use this as the main argument for the maxim.

Explanation The word *saṃprasāraṇa* in P.1.1.45 can be taken in one of two ways: as a term designating a process (the replacing of *yaṇ* by *ik*) or as a term designating a substitute (the *ik* which has replaced *yaṇ*). So when, say, *vac*→*uc*, we rule a *saṃprasāraṇa* in place of *vac*; but *saṃprasāraṇa* is only there after the substitution has taken place. The interpretations of the term depend on each other.[222]

[222]The issue concerning the interpretation of *saṃprasāraṇa* in P.1.1.45 as discussed in the *Mahābhāṣya* and the *Kāśikā* has been well described by Ojihara and Renou (1960–67, 2nd fascicule, pp. 1 ff.).

When a nominal stem is mentioned, its differentiation by genders is also meant.[223]

— When a nominal stem is mentioned, that stem differentiated into the feminine, masculine and neuter genders is meant as well.

Argument 22.1[224] [22:3

— How is that known?
— Because he says *kumāraḥ śramaṇādibhiḥ* (P.2.1.70).
— How come that is an intimation?
— A compound is here made of the word *kumāra* with [the words] *śramaṇā*, etc. This word *kumāra* is masculine gender. *Śramaṇā* etc., though, are feminine gender. And yet the heading rule about co-referentials is in force [P.2.1.49]. In this case co-reference would fail to obtain.

But the teacher observes that when *kumāra* is mentioned its differentiation by gender is also meant. Therefore *kumāraśramaṇā* 'a girl ascetic' is a correct compound of the word *kumāra* with *śramaṇā*, etc. So when a nominal stem is mentioned its differentiation by genders is also meant.

[223]This *paribhāṣā* is first mentioned by Kātyāyana in *vārt.* 4 on P.4.1.1 (Mbh.II.192:3). He also refers to it in *vārttikas* V.5.2.52.1, V.6.1.85.9, and V.7.1.1.12 (Mbh.II.385:1, III.61:13, and 238:17). It is discussed by Patañjali at these places and elsewhere (Mbh.I.402.4, II.258:22, III.157:2, 223:12:16), in a manner which shows he accepted it as a standard maxim.

The *Kāśikā* and its commentaries discuss the *paribhāṣā* under P.2.1.67 and P.4.1.1 (KV.II.88 f., III.253 ff.).

It is discussed by all the main commentators: Puruṣottamadeva (no. 26), Sīradeva (no. 28), Nīlakaṇṭha (no. 38), Haribhāskara (no. 28), Nāgeśa (no. 71) and Śeśādrisudhī (no. 61).

Cardona gives critique of recent discussions of this *paribhāṣā* (1976.170).

[224]P.2.1.70 is one of those rules neither discussed nor even mentioned in the *Mahābhāṣya*.

This argument is used by Nīlakaṇṭha, Nāgeśa, and Śeṣādrisudhī amongst the *paribhāṣā* commentators.

Explanation The stem *kumāra* must also imply *kumārī*: only the latter form is allowed to form a compound with words from the *śramaṇādi gaṇa*.

Argument 22.2[225] [22:10

— What is the point of intimating this?

— In *yuvā khalatipalitavalinajaratībhir* (P.2.1.67), a compound [of the word *yuvā*] is stated. And that compound may also be of the word *yuvati*. From *yuvatiḥ palitā* comes *yuvapalitā* 'a girl prematurely grey.'

Explanation The two arguments above are as follow. P.2.1.70 *kumārāḥ śramaṇādibhiḥ* teaches that *kumāra* and *śramaṇā* etc., when co-referential (2.1.49), may (11) be compounded (3, 4) to form a *tatpuruṣa* compound which is a *karmadhāraya* (1.2.42). Half the *śramaṇādi* list consists of feminine words. How can a masculine noun, *kumāra*, and a feminine noun, from the *śramaṇādi* list, be co-referential? They cannot, of course, and this is just Pāṇini's way of telling us that *kumāra* counts as *kumārī* as well. In other words, the *paribhāṣā* is true.

The purpose given for this *paribhāṣā* is the formation of the compound *yuvapalitā* 'a girl grey in youth'. P.2.1.67 teaches that *yuvan* and *khalati*, etc., may be compounded in the same circumstances as *kumāra* and *śramaṇā* etc. The words listed in P.2.1.67 are collectively given a feminine suffix. How can they be co-referential with the masculine noun *yuvan*? The present *paribhāṣā* solves the difficulty by allowing that *yuvan* 'young man' also counts as *yuvati* 'young woman'.

Comments The two cases, P.2.1.70 and 2.1.67 are really identical situations. That one should be a *jñāpaka* and the other a *prayojana* is an arbitrary choice. In fact, the *Kāśikā* takes them contrariwise; P.2.1.67 is the *jñāpaka* and 2.1.70 an example of the application of the *paribhāṣā* (KV.II.88 f., II.92). In this the *Kāśikā* is following the *Mahābhāṣya*, which, commenting on P.2.1.67, says that by stating the rule assymetrically, in terms of gender, and yet holding that the items to be compounded are co-referential, Pāṇini is hinting that the first and second words of the resulting compound should be of the same sort. And the purpose of this hint is that we should know that the present *paribhāṣā* is at work in the system. This is differently put, but it is essentially the same point.

The *Mahābhāṣya* does not comment on P.2.1.70. It is curious, then, that the Vyāḍi commentator uses P.2.1.67 and 70 as he does, in the teeth of the tradition of the *Mahābhāṣya*.

---

[225] Patañjali mentions this argument under P.2.1.67 (Mbh.I.402:1–5) in a manner which shows he accepts the *paribhāṣā*. For translation and discussion see Joshi and Roodbergen 1971.184 f.

The argument also appears in the *Kāśikā* and its commentaries on P.2.1.67 (KV.II.88 f.).

Puruṣottamadeva is the only *paribhāṣā* commentator to use this argument, which is surprising, given its prominence in the *Mahābhāṣya*.

Argument 22.3[226] [22:13

— However, if this [*paribhāṣā*] is intimated, then the mention of *ṅī* and *āp* in *ṅyāpprātipadikāt* (P.4.1.1) becomes pointless. For if it [the rule] were *prātipadikāt* then since there is mention of a nominal stem, its differentiation by genders would be valid too.

Explanation The existence of the *paribhāṣā* raises a problem with respect to P.4.1.1. This is a heading rule which teaches that the suffixes (3.1.1) taught subsequently are applied after (3.1.2) a nominal stem, or what ends with (1.1.72) the feminine suffixes *ṅī* and *āp*. This much seems plain.

But if the *paribhāṣā* really does hold good, surely it is unnecessary to make a special point of mentioning the feminine suffixes *ṅī* and *āp*? Are they not covered by saying 'after a nominal stem' and invoking the *paribhāṣā* to indicate that the scope of 'nominal stem' includes feminine stems?

Comments This problem, first posed by Kātyāyana (*vārt.* 4 on P.4.1.1), presupposes a particular interpretation of the *paribhāṣā*. Thus, *prātipadikagrahaṇena* must be taken to mean both 'by mentioning a nominal stem' and 'by mentioning that an item is a nominal stem'. There seems to be some confusion here between a class member and the class name.

Without this confusion, the question as to why *ṅī* and *āp* are mentioned in P.4.1.1 would not arise, because if the natural sense of the *paribhāṣā* were taken, whereby a nominal stem which is mentioned in a rule stands for itself in all the genders, then the *paribhāṣā* would not apply in P.4.1.1. If it were applied, P.4.1.1 would strictly speaking mean, 'suffixes are applied after a *prātipadika*, a *prātipadikam* and a *prātipadikī*.' This is, of course, nonsense. So, if we admit the problem with *ṅī* and *āp*, we admit also this confusion, or double sense, of the *paribhāṣā*.

Patañjali takes this course, following Kātyāyana, but the *Kāśikā* does not. Instead it sensibly interprets the *paribhāṣā* in only the first of the two above senses, saying that 'the *paribhāṣā* applies in the situation where a rule applies to the actual form of a word' (KV.III.255). As a rationale for this interpretation, the *Kāśikā* gives the example of P.2.1.67 (see argument § 25.1). The *Nyāsa* explains for us here that apart from proving the existence of the *paribhāṣā*, the fact that this *paribhāṣā* is proved from a case where an actual word (*śabdasvarūpa*) is mentioned shows that this is how it is to be interpreted (KV.III.256).

The *Nyāsa* further enlarges on this point from another angle, namely that a *prātipadika* cannot be modified by a feminine suffix and still be a *prātipadika*. This emerges from the definition of this term in P.1.2.45. It is, among other things, not a suffix, nor anything that ends in a suffix. This is modified in the next rule so that a *prātipadika* may legitimately end in a *kṛt* or a *taddhita* suffix. But this still does not include the feminine suffixes. So even if the *paribhāṣā* were thought to be applicable in the case of P.4.1.1, it could not apply to those technically termed *prātipadika* because, by assuming feminine suffixes, they would cease to be *prātipadikas*.

In spite of the clarification brought to this issue by the *Kāśikā* and the *Nyāsa*, through disproving the second, general meaning of the *paribhāṣā*, it is regrettable that

---

[226] This argument is used by Kātyayana, Patañjali, the *Kāśikā* authors and commentators, Bhaṭṭojī Dīkṣita and commentators (SK.I.179 f. (182)), and Nāgeśa (no. 71) alone amongst the *paribhāṣā* commentators. See the comments, p. 121.

later *paribhāṣā* writers, from Puruṣottamadeva to Nāgeśa, all take the old positions, and leave themselves in great difficulty as to the correct interpretation of P.4.1.1. Bhaṭṭojī Dīkṣita sums up *this* tradition in the *Siddhāntakaumudī* on P.4.1.1 by saying that indeed since the *paribhāṣā* is valid and applicable to P.4.1.1 the mention of *ṅī* and *āp* in the rule is unnecessary (except for deriving *taddhitas* with feminine endings) (SK.I.179 f. (182)).

Argument 22.4 [22:15

— It is for the sake of what follows. He will say *tasyāpatyam* (P.4.1.92). Here, *tasyāḥ* 'of her' would fail to be included. [Similarly] in *tena raktam* (P.4:2.1.), *tayā* 'by her' would fail to be included. In order that *ṅī* and *āp* should recur here [in these examples], it [P.4.1.1] is 'after a nominal stem, and after *ṅī* and *āp*'. Thereby, the selection of a [secondary] suffix is validated both for what is covered by the co-significative inflection [i.e., *tasya, tena*] and also for what is followed by *ṅī* or *āp*.

Explanation This argument presents a *prima facie* purpose for the *paribhāṣā*. The rule cited apparently applies only to masculine pronouns, to suffixes indicating the family descendants of males: the *paribhāṣā* extends the usage to apply to feminine ones too.

Comments Rules like P.4.1.92 are usually interpreted in the light of P.1.2.69 which should account adequately for neuter suffixes being used to cover the other genders too; see § 22.5 below.

Argument 22.5[227] [22:20

— This is not the purpose [of the *paribhāṣā*], because as far as the co-significative inflections are concerned, they are being presented as sole remainders. By *napuṃsakam anapuṃsakenaikavac cāsyānyatarasyām* (P.1.2.69) that [word *tasya* 'its'] is the sole remainder of 'his, hers, and its'. Thereby the selection of a [secondary] suffix is valid after everything: there is no point in mentioning *ṅī* and *āp* [in P.4.1.1.].

Explanation So the previous argument for the purpose of the rule is refuted.

[227] Note that Kātyayana does reject the presence of *ṅī* and *āp* in P.4.1.1, in his *vārt.* 4 on this rule (Mbh.II.192:3).

Argument 22.6[228] [22:24

— In that case, the purpose is this. † It is to give purpose to just this. †

The statement he will there make, [i.e., the present *paribhāṣā*] that when a nominal stem is mentioned its differentiation by genders is also meant, this statement is proper as long as there is no feminine suffix.

— In that case, if an item with a feminine suffix, being mentioned, does not include its differentiation by genders then here in *caṭkāyā airak* (P.4.1.128) it the suffix *airak* will fail to apply after *caṭaka*.

Similarly in *eṇyā ḍhak* (P.4.3.159) it [the suffix *ḍhak*] will fail to apply after *eṇa*.

Explanation The argument here is essentially trying to save a role for both the present *paribhāṣā* and also P.1.2.69.

Comments The transmitted text is not completely clear at the beginning of this passage, but it is probably referring to the feminine suffix of the third person pronoun. It also appears that the Vyāḍi commentator is referring to someone else's text. Perhaps the reference is to the *Mahābhāṣya*?

Argument 22.7[229] [22:28

— These two words are not being presented as feminine.

— How?

— *Yā* is substituted for *ṅasi* after an item ending in *caṭaka* [cf. P.7.1.39]. One lengthening has been performed by *ato dīrgho yañi* (P.7.3.101), the form *caṭakāyā* is established.

— If this is so, then why is *vṛddhi* not applied thus, by *caṭakāyairak* [cf. 4.1.128]?

— For clarity's sake. If one said *caṭakāyairak* there would doubt as to whether it were *erak* or *airak*.

— There is no doubt. If it were *erak* he would just say *ḍhrak* [= *era*. Cf. P.7.1.2, 4.1.129]. There would be the added benefit that the subsequent mention [of *ḍhrak* in P.4.1.129] would be unnessary.

— In that case, then, *bahulam* 'frequently' recurs.

— Where is it introduced?

— In *śeś chandasi bahulam* (P.6.1.70). Thereby the whole prescribed rule is applied 'frequently'. Thus *kāraḥ* 'doer' *prakāraḥ* 'method' and the like are established.

---

[228] On the *caṭakā* discussion, see the *Mahābhāṣya* under P.4.1.128, (Mbh.II.258:18–22).

[229] Cf. footnote 228 above.

The [form] *eṇyā* is established by replacing *ṅasi* after the word *eṅa* with *ḍyā* [cf. P.7.1.39]. Then the last vowel and what follows it [in *eṇa*] is elide [cf. P.6.4.143]. And it is for this reason that this [*paribhāṣā*] is not dropped. And there is nothing wrong with saying 'except when there is a feminine suffix.'

Explanation Kātyāyana's first *vārttika* on P.4.1.128 argues that the word *caṭakā* in the *sūtra* should be changed to *caṭaka* in the masculine, and then the *paribhāṣā* would be invoked to get the full interpretation we want across all genders. Patañjali concurs. The Vyāḍi commentator is here going by a different route, and trying to argue that *caṭakā* (and similarly *eṇī*) is actually a masculine form, by some tricky manipulations including an appeal to special vedic usage:

caṭaka	+	*ṅaś*	
caṭaka	+	*yā*	by P.7.1.13
caṭaka	+	*yā*	by P.7.1.39
caṭakā	+	*yā*	by P.7.3.101

Furthermore, the commentator is attempting to recast this section of the *Aṣṭādhyāyī*. The suffix *ḍh* → *ey* by P.7.1.2, and so *ḍhrak* becomes *eyrak*. Then by P.6.1.66 this becomes *erak*. And *bahulam* 'in some cases, frequently' – properly meant only for vedic usage – is read back into the preceding rules from P.6.1.70 (*apakarṣa*, the converse of *anuvṛtti*).

The mention of a letter includes the parts of the letter.[230]

— By mentioning letters, the parts of the letters are included.

Argument 23.1 [23:3

— How is that known?
— He proposes the rule *eca ig hrasvādeśe* (P.1.1.48)
— How come it is an intimation?
— This rule does not have to be formulated. When there is a short substitute of *i, u, ṛ,* or *ḷ* in place of *e, o, ai*, or *au*, then it will be the letters *i* or *u*. *I* and *u* will replace the letters *e* and *o* because they have the same place [of articulation, and] *ai* and *au* because the latter [part of these vowels] is the more important.

'Prior' and 'latter' are words for parts. This being so, the letters *i* and *u* are words for *e, o, ai* and *au*. If 'the mention of a letter includes the parts of the letter,' then the abbreviation including them is justified.

And furthermore a purpose is stated for this rule. *Ai* and *au* are diphthongs: a measure of the letter *a* plus a measure of the letters *i* and *u*. When short vowels are prescribed [as substitutes] for them, the letter *i* or the letter *u* should replace *ai* or *au*, and the letter *a* should never do so. The rule is proposed so that this might be so. And if this *paribhāṣā* exists then this purpose is justified.

Explanation This argument addresses a genuine problem in P.1.1.48.

[230]This maxim arises from Kātyāyana's *vārttika* 6 on the third and fourth *Śivasūtras* (Mbh.I.24:1), and is also cited by Patañjali (I.23:24, 24:2, 26:5–6, 63:21:23; III.26:22 (rejected), repeated at 200:9 (rejected), 452:11 (rejected)). It is not taken up by other authors in the Pāṇinian tradition.

Argument 23.2[231] [23:12

— And also because he pronounces the retroflexion of the *ṇ* in [in the *-tṝṇām* of] ... *hotṛ[potṛ]praśāstṝṇām* (P.6.4.11).
— How come this is an intimation?
— The retroflexion of the *ṇ* is here stated because it follows a *r* or a *ṣ* (cf. P.8.4.1). But we do not see *r* or *ṣ* here [in *tṝṇām*]. However, the teacher observes that there is an *r* in the letter *ṛ* and because of this he pronounces the retroflex *ṇ*.
— If the mention of a letter includes the parts of the letter [? then this argument is valid].

Explanation Pāṇini makes the *n* in the gen. pl. suffix of P.6.4.11 retroflex, because of the preceding *ṝ*. But the retroflexion rule, P.8.4.1, only mentions preceding *r* and *ṣ*, not the vocalic *ṛ*. But because, by the present *paribhāṣā*, there is an 'element' of *r* in *ṝ*, the retroflexion still takes place.

Argument 23.3[232] [23:16

— And since he prescribes *ĭ* and *ŭ* to replace the letters *ai* and *au* (cf. P.8.2.106).
— How come this is an intimation?
— Prolation is being specified for *ai* and *au*. How could *i* and *u* possibly ever come about where *i* and *u* themselves do not [previously] exist?

The teacher, however, observes that *ai* and *au* do have *i* and *u*, if these two are included by the mention of the letters. If the mention of a letter includes the parts of the letter, then this is justified.

Argument 23.4[233] [23:21

— What is the point of intimating this?
— In *ānṛdhuḥ* 'they increased' the *r* is noted and then the augment *nuṭ* [i.e., *n*] which is due because of the two consonants [i.e., *r* and *dh*, cf. P.7.4.71] is validated.

---

[231] The need to augment P.8.4.1 to deal with vocalic *ṛ* is seen by Kātyāyana (Mbh.III.452:2). But in the same context Patañjali explicitly negates the present *paribhāṣā* (Mbh.III.452:6).
The *ṇ* in P.6.4.11 is queried by Jinendrabuddhi in the *Nyāsa* on that rule (KV.V.340) but he does not infer the present *paribhāṣā*; rather, he sees it as a general prescription which rules *vārttika* V.8.4.1.1 unnecessary.

[232] This argument does not appear in the main commentators.

[233] This argument, with the same example '*ānṛdhuḥ*', is given by Patañjali when discussing *vārt.* 11 on the fourth *śivasūtra* (I.25:19), and it is repeated in the *Kāśikā* on P.7.4.71 (KV.VI.190).

Paribhāṣā 24

The rule about the optionality of isomorphs does not apply to those [suffixes] of habit [etc].[234]

— As far as the suffixes of habit are concerned the instruction of the rule on the optionality of isomorphs does not exist.

Explanation The 'rule about the optionality of isomorphs' is rule P.3.1.94 *vāsarūpo 'striyām*. This an *adhikāra* rule, governing, with P.3.1.91, the rules up to the end of the third *adhyāya*. The present maxim argues that this *sūtra* does not apply to the so-called *tācchīlika* 'suffixes of habit' rules, i.e., P.3.2.134–177.

Argument 24.1 [24:3

— How is that known?
— Because in the rule *jucaṅkramy* ... (P.3.2.150) he prescribes the suffix *yuc* after [the root] *pad*.
— How come that is an intimation?
— This [root] *pad* has an acute accent on its marker. [The suffix] *yuc* is valid for it by *anudāttetaś ca halādeḥ* (P.3.2.149). There is no point in mentioning [the root] *pad* once again.

This being the case, by mentioning *pad* the teacher is intimating that the rule about the optionality of isomorphs does not apply to those suffixes of habit [etc.].

[234]This maxim is derived by Patañjali (II.133:16, 134:5 and cf. III.234:7).
It is discussed by Puruṣottamadeva (no. 28), Sīradeva (no. 43), Nīlakaṇṭha (no. 53), Haribhāskara (no. 45), and Nāgeśa (no. 67).
It is cited in the *Kāśikā* on P.3.2.150, 153, and alluded to under P.3.2.146 (KV.II.660 f., 662 f., 658).

Argument 24.2 [24:8

— What is the point of intimating this?
— In *bhāsate bhāsvaraḥ* 'the sun shines', in spite of the rule about the optionality of isomorphs, the [suffix] *yuc*, appropriate to an item [like *bhās*] with a grave accent on its marker [cf. P.3.2.149], does not arise.

Argument 24.3 [24:9

— If this [maxim] is intimated, then the mention of *dīp* in *sūdadīpadīkṣaś ca* (P.3.2.153) is redundant. After this [root] *dīp*, [the suffix] *yuj* is prescribed [? by the general rule P.3.2.149].

By *namikampismyajasakamahiṃsadīpo raḥ* (P.3.2.167) [the suffix *ra* comes after *dīp*]. This specifically prescribed item [*ra*] will block the [suffix] *yuc* which is prescribed in general. This being the case, the fact that he makes mention of *dīp* under the heading of prohibition [i.e., *na* in P.3.2.152] is the teacher's intimation that *yuc* and *ra* are co-extensive.

Argument 24.4 [24:14

— What is the point of intimating this?
— *Kamrā* 'loving', and *kamana* 'loving' are [both] valid.

Paribhāṣā 25

A sentence is complete with respect to each single one [of its constituents].[235]

Argument 25.1 [25:2

— How is that known?
— From the world. Thus, for example, 'let Devadatta, Yajñadatta and Viṣṇumitra eat'. And one does not say it individually: the [root] *bhuj* 'to eat' is completed with each single one [of the names].

Argument 25.2 [25:4

— This *paribhāṣā* is also present in the discipline [of grammar].
— How is that known?
— He says *ṇal uttamo vā* (P.7.1.91)
— How come this is an intimation?
— Because here the term *uttama* 'first person' is applied to the combined triplet [of singular, dual and plural endings]. *Uttama* 'first person' cannot qualify just *ṇal* alone in that [triplet].

But the teacher observes that 'a sentence becomes complete with respect to each single one [of its constituents]'. Thereby the expression *uttama* 'first person' applies to each single item in the triplet.

Argument 25.3 [25:9

— What is the point of intimating this?
— It is not necessary to state that the terms *guṇa* and *vṛddhi* have reference to each individual one [of the letters they name].

---

[235] This maxim is originally Kātyāyana's *vārt.* 12 on P.1.1.1. It is cited by Patañjali several times in a few recurring passages (Mbh.I.41:11, 57:21, 212:17, 369:16, 378:3, 461:12; II.142:12; III.10:26, 439:2, 453:13).

It is discussed by Puruṣottamadeva (no. 29), Sīradeva (no. 78), Nīlakaṇṭha (no. 104), Haribhāskara (no. 80), Nāgeśa (no. 107) and Śeṣādrisudhī (no. 99).

A sentence is also complete with respect to the aggregate [of its constituents].[236]

— A sentence is completed with respect to the aggregate [of its constituents] too.

Argument 26.1 [26:2

— Thus, for example, if one says 'fine the Gargas a hundred', they are not fined individually, even though kings are greedy for gold. And this *paribhāṣā* is present in the discipline too.

Argument 26.2 [26:4

— The intimation is the fact that he says *prathamayoḥ pūrvasavarṇaḥ* (P.6.1.102).
— How come it is an intimation?
— This word *prathamā* 'first' is the technical term for the whole combined triplet [of singular dual and plural endings]. So here, [P.6.1.102] the two first triplets are mentioned, the first and the second. This is because of the assertion 'of two first ones'.

But how does one know that it is the two triplets which are meant, and not the first items beginning with a vowel [i.e., the dual and plural nominative endings *au, as, akaḥ* recurs from P.6.1.101].

The teacher's procedure intimates that it is the triplets which are meant, because by saying *tasmāt* in *tasmāc chaso naḥ puṃsi* (P.6.1.103) he is referring specifically to an item homorganic with

---

[236]This maxim is the reflection of the previous one, no. 25. It too is referred to first by Kātyāyana, in *vārt.* 4 on P.1.1.10 (Mbh.I.66:10). It is found in Patañjali's recurring passages mentioned in footnote 235, p. 129, and elsewhere (Mbh.I.41:13, 57:22, 378:4, 461:9; III.5:1:8:15, 10:27, 364:17, 439:4, 453:14).

It is discussed by Puruṣottamadeva (no. 30), Sīradeva (no. 79), Nīlakaṇṭha (no. 105), Haribhāskara (no. 81), Nāgeśa (no. 108) and Śeṣādrisudhī (no. 100).

what preceded it. So he is intimating that by this rule there is an item homorganic with what preceded it also for *śas* [the acc. pl. suffix]. And this is justified if it is the two triplets which are meant [in P.6.1.102].

Thus the mention of *prathamayor* 'of the two first ones' [in P.6.1.102] is the intimation. A sentence is also complete with respect to the aggregate [of its constituents].

Argument 26.3 [26:12

Thus, rules like *ṅe prathamayor am* (P.7.1.28), and so on, are validated.

Paribhāṣā 27ᵃ

A vowel or semivowel which is being generated does not include letters homorganic with it.[237]

Argument 27ᵃ.1 [27ᵃ:2

— How is that known?
— Because he prescribes the long letter *ī* in *ī haly aghoḥ* (P.6.4.113).
— How come it is an intimation?
— This rule ought to be stated thus: *ĭ haly aghoḥ*.
— How, if that is so, will the letter *ī* come about?
— The letter *i* is mentioned in *aṇudit savarṇasya* ... (P.1.1.69). While in that situation [i.e., P.6.4.113] all [the kinds] of the letter *i* are potentially applicable in place of that [substituted], there will be a long [*ā* of the original] by *sthāne 'ntaratamaḥ* (P.1.1.50). [So] there is no point in mentioning the long [*ī*].

But the teacher observes that a vowel or semivowel which is being generated does not include letters homorganic with it, and so he does pronounce it [the *ī*] as a long vowel.

Argument 27ᵃ.2 [27ᵃ:9

— What is the point of intimating this?
— Here in *idama iś* (P.5.3.3.), short, long and prolated [vowels] are not synonymous as substitutes for *idam*.

[237] This maxim is known to Patañjali (Mbh.I.123:26, 177:24, 178:7; III.110:16:17, 230:22). It is discussed by Puruṣottamadeva (no. 31), Sīradeva (no. 11), Nīlakaṇṭha (no. 16), Haribhāskara (no. 11).

Argument 27^a.3

[27^a:10

— If this is intimated, then the *t* which is put next to the letter *u* in *diva ut* (P.6.1.131) is not necessary.
— How so?
— This letter *u* will be generated in place of the letter *v*. Therefore, because a vowel or semivowel which is generated will not include letters homorganic with it, only the short will arise, not the long and prolated. So there is no point in putting the *t* there.

The teacher observes:

[Paribhāṣā 27^b]

The single letter *u* alone, even if it is being generated, includes letters homorganic with it.[238]

Argument 27^b.1

[27^b:15

— What is the point of intimating this?
— Because the letter *u* in *adaso 'ser dād u do maḥ* (P.8.2.80) includes the letters homorganic with it. Here in *amŭṣmin, amūbhyām* it is a short which replaces a short, a long which replaces a long.

[238] See footnote 237, p. 132, and Mbh.III.110:19 for the distribution of this *paribhāṣā*.

In this discipline the determined option exists.[239]

Argument 28.1

[28:2

— How is that known?
— Because he say *vā kyaṣaḥ* (P.1.3.90).
— Apparently this rule need not have been framed.
— If it is not framed, how will the optional mediopassive suffix come about? [E.g.,]

paṭpaṭāyati 'it patters',
paṭpaṭāyate 'it patters'.

— By *nityavīpsayoḥ* (P.8.1.4) there is reduplication: *paṭat paṭat*. [Then the suffix *ḍāc* is added by] *avyaktānukaraṇād dvyajavarārdhād amitau ḍāc* (P.5.4.57). By *nityam āmreḍite ḍāci* (K.6.1.99.1 or P.6.1.100) the letter *p* replaces the letter *t* as the form of the preceding and following [letter]. Once *paṭapaṭā* is established, either *kyaṣ* or *kyaṅ* arises.
— How?
— We shall split a rule here [i.e., P.3.1.13]. [The rules] *kartuḥ kyaṅ salopaś ca* (P.3.1.11) and *bhṛśādibhyo bhuvy acver lopaś ca halaḥ* (P.3.1.12) generate only the suffix [suffix] *kyaṅ*. Therefore let us say only *lohitādiḍājbhyaḥ* (cf. P.3.1.13) [omitting *kyaṣ*].

Thus, when *kyaṅ* is there, then the mediopassive applies because 'something with the marker *ṅ* precedes' (P.1.3.12). When *kyaṣ* is there, then the active applies, because of *śaṣāt* ... (P.1.3.78).

There is no point in the rule *vā kyaṣaḥ* (P.1.3.90). Therefore this rule is framed in order to make a determined option.

---

[239]The concept of *vyavasthitavibhāṣā* starts with Patañjali (I.488:14; II.127:12; III.260:15), but he does not actually cite the *paribhāṣā*.

It is discussed by Puruṣottamadeva (no. 62), Sīradeva (no. 124), Nīlakaṇṭha (no. 93), Haribhāskara (no. 125) and Nāgeśa (no. 99).

— How?
— Some items in the list beginning with *lohita* take the mediopassive only, some take both voices. But by splitting the rule [P.3.1.13] all of them take both voices. By that means [i.e., P.1.3.90] only the mediopassive applies to *nīla* and the rest. The word *lohita* takes both [voices].

What the *vārttikakāra* says about this is not necessary, namely that *kyaṣ* is stated to follow *lohita* and *ḍāc* [only] while the other are [to be included] in the list beginning with *bṛśa* (Kāt.V.3.1.13.1–2).

Argument 28.2[240] [28:19

— What is the point of intimating this?
—

> The following are not optional alternatives:
> Devatrāta [proper name], *galaḥ* 'throat', *grāha* 'crocodile',
> the rule about present and future participles when *iti* is used,
> *gavākṣa* 'window' and *saṃśitavrata* 'firm in vow'.

In '*Devatrāta* ...' the mention of *anyatarasyām* 'alternatively' in *nudavidoṇdatrāghrā* ... (P.8.2.56) means that the non-nasalization [of the *t* in *trāta*] is only when it is a name; when it is other than a name both [*n* and *t*] are possible: *trāhḥ*, *trāṇaḥ*.

The same goes for *gala* 'throat'. *Gṝ* too receives *guṇa* [P.7.3.84 → *ga*] and the subsequent *r* [P.1.1.51 → *gar*]. Then by *gro yaṅi* and *aci vibhāṣā* (P.8.2.20, 21) the *l* is produced. This resulting [form] *gala* occurs only when a part of the body is meant. When it is other than part of the body it is *gara*. The suffix *ṇa*, by *vibhāṣā grahaḥ* (P.3.1.143), gives *grāha*, but *grāha* means only an aquatic creature. For anything other than an aquatic creature, only the suffix *ac* is used, giving *graha* 'planet', etc.

The rule about present and future participles, when *iti* is used:

> *varṣati iti* 'it rains',
> *dhāvati iti* 'it runs',
> *hanti iti* 'it strikes',
> *palāyate iti* 'it runs off'.

[240]The verse beginning '*devatrātā* ...' (28:20–21) is a *ślokavārttika* found twice in the *Mahābhāṣya* (Mbh.II.165:4; III.350:10).

Elsewhere the [participle suffixes] *śatṛ* are always used. The rules *nanvor vibhāṣā* (P.3.2.121) and, in the present tense [cf. P.3.2.123], *laṭaḥ śatṛśānacāv* ... (P.3.2.124) apply, but because it is a determined option, they [the two participle suffixes] do not occur when the word is present.

The same goes for *gavakṣa* which is always formed by *avaṅ sphoṭāyanasya* (P.6.1.123), when meaning 'window'. Elsewhere there is an option.

In *saṃśitavrata* 'firm in vow', the substitution of *i* by *śāchoḥ anyatarasyām* (P.7.4.41) is invariably performed. Apart from this [i.e., when reference is not to a vow] the option exists:

saṃśitavrata 'firm in vow',
saṃśātavrata 'honest'.

In an operation concerning accent a consonant is treated as non-existent.[241]

— When an accent is being generated, any intervening consonant is treated as non-existent.

Argument 29.1 [29:3

— How is that known?

— Because he teaches the prohibition *anāvaḥ* 'not of *nau*' in *yato 'nāvaḥ* (P.6.1.213).

— How come it is an intimation?

— *Yato 'nāvaḥ* (P.6.1.213) is a prohibition in this [word] *nāvyâm* 'navigable'. If this is the purpose, then that mention of *anāvaḥ* has no purpose.

— How?

— 'Acute', 'grave' and 'circumflex' are said of a vowel. But there is not one here at the beginning [of *nāvyam*]. Therefore, because one [vowel] just does not exist here at the beginning [of nāvyam] there will no acuteness. There is no point in prohibiting [it].

Since this is the case, the teacher, by teaching the prohibition, is intimating that 'in an operation concerning accent a consonant is treated as non-existent.'

[241]This maxim goes back to Kātyāyana's *vārt.* 4 on P.1.1.73 (Mbh.I.189:20). See too *vārt.* 2 on P.6.1.223 (Mbh.III.119:18) and *vārt.* 3 where its purposes are listed.

It is used by Patañjali (I.128:16:19, 145:20, 206:14–15; III.119:20:21, 120:6:9:15, 389:4).

It is discussed by Puruṣottamadeva (no. 32), Sīradeva (no. 53), Nīlakaṇṭha (no. 67), Haribhāskara (no. 55) and Nāgeśa (no. 79).

It is cited in the *Kāśikā* on P.6.1.135, 6.1.176, 6.1.223 and 8.2.4 (KV.IV.612, 659, 691, VI.359).

Argument 29.2 [29:10

— What is the point of intimating this?
— Here in Gā́rgyâḥ and Vā́tsyâḥ [proper names] the letter *a* is not the initial letter, but the acute is still valid for it [*garga* + *yañ*. cf. P.6.1.197].

The same goes for *pácâti* 'he cooks' and *páṭhâti* 'he reads'. The circumflex is valid by *udāttād anudāttasya svaritaḥ* (P.8.4.66) even in spite of the intervening letters *c* and *ṭh* [*pác* + *ati* → *pácâti*].

Once it has happened to the pre-suffixal base an operation does not apply to the finished form, † because it has happened again.[242]

— Once it has happened to the pre-suffixal base, [i.e.,] when an operation on the pre-suffixal base has been done, † because the operation has happened again, any other rule which might apply does not arise.

Comments I might initially be thought that the odd ablative reading *punarvṛttād* in the maxim might be a simple Devanāgarī reading error between द and त. But this does not explain enough, since the error is compounded with the reading *punarvṛttāt-kāryasya* in the commentary which does not admit of any obvious scribal error.

Argument 30.1 [30:4

— How is that known?
— Because he states *jñājanor jā* (P.7.3.79). Apparently this rule ought to be stated thus: *jñājanor ja*.
— What would be the derivation of a form?
— *Jānīte* 'he knows' *jāyate* 'he is born'. Once the existence of *jă* has been generated [by the modified rule above] there there will be lengthening by *ato dīrgho yañi* (P.7.3.101).
— Since this is the case, by prescribing the long substitute [*jā* in P.7.3.79] he is intimating that once the substitution of *ja* has taken place, caused by the pre-suffixal base, there may not be another lengthening.

---

[242]This *paribhāṣā* is accepted first by Patañjali (Mbh.III.230:17, 252:11, 334:19, 335:4, 349:10).

It is discussed by Puruṣottamadeva (no. 71), Sīradeva (no. 91), Nīlakaṇṭha (no. 86), Haribhāskara (no. 94), Nāgeśa (no. 92) and Śeṣādrisudhī (no. 80).

The *Kāśikā* cites the maxim three times: under P.7.1.30, 7.1.90, and 7.3.78 (KV.V.563, 635 f., VI.87).

Argument 30.2

[30:9

— What is the point of intimating this?

— In *kriyate* 'it is done', once the substitution of *ri* [for *r* in *kṛ*] has been done [P.7.4.27] the lengthening proper before a suffix [such as the passive *yak*] which is neither primary nor *sārvadhātuka* [cf. P.7.4.25] does not occur because 'once it has happened to the pre-suffixal base an operation does not apply to the finished form † because it has happened.'

If there is conflict when two apply simultaneously then the one which is blocked is blocked for good.[243]

— Where two [operation] might apply at once, the maxim 'when there is a conflict the latter prevails' is applied. Then, once the latter has been done, if the former should again have the potential of applying, it does not do so.
— For what reason?
— Because what is blocked once is blocked for good. It does not arise again.

Argument 31.1[244] [31:5

— How is that known?
— Because here in *kartari karmavyatihāre* (P.1.3.14) he makes mention of *kartṛ* 'in the active voice'.
— How come it is an intimation?
— One should say here [just] *karmavyatihāra*. There is no point in mentioning *kartṛ*.

[243]This *paribhāṣā* is very well known to Patañjali, who uses it a dozen times (Mbh.I.140:12:17:24, 305:17:23; III.158:18, 177:10, 207:2, 250:17, 258:10, 260:10, 266:11). In almost every case it is quoted as a reason not to apply the *punaḥprasaṅga* maxim (*Vyāḍīyaparibhāṣāvṛtti* no. 76).

It is discussed by all the *paribhāṣā* commentators: Puruṣottamadeva (no. 39), Sīradeva (no. 20), Nīlakaṇṭha (no. 25), Haribhāskara (no. 20), Nāgeśa (no. 40) and Śeṣādrisudhī (no. 39).

It is quoted in the *Kāśikā* on P.6.3.139, 7.1.77 (KV.V.320:6, 586:6, 624:1) and in the *Siddhāntakaumudī* on P.6.4.119 (SK.III.291:8 (2471)).

Finally, the Vyāḍi commentator repeats the maxim as no. 75 (p. 246 below), with differing arguments.

[244]Though not set out as a proof of this *paribhāṣā*, the presence of *kartari* in P.1.3.14 is questioned, and justified as above, in the *Mahābhāṣya* (Mbh.I.277:14–16) and indeed in *vārttikas* 1 and 2 on P.1.3.14 (Mbh.I.278:8:10). However it is *paribhāṣā* 13 which finally solves the problem in this context.

None of the *paribhāṣā* commentators use this argument.

— But surely the mediopassive inflection would then potentially apply in the impersonal and passive to express *karmavyatihāra* 'reciprocal action'.
— What is the problem with this?
— None at all at this point; but later on there would be a prohibition.

Just as there is a prohibition [of the mediopassive inflections] in the active, so in the same way there would potentially be a prohibition in the impersonal and passive voices as well [by P.1.3.15, 16].

vyatigamyante grāmāḥ 'the villages are being mutually visited.'
vyatihanyante dasyavaḥ 'the Dasyus are being mutually killed.'

[Such examples would wrongly be disallowed].
— So be it. It [the correct mediopassive inflection] will come about because re-applicability is recognised (*paribhāṣā* 76) [as legitimate in derivation]. There is no point in mentioning *kartṛ* [in P.1.3.14].

This being the case, by mentioning *katari* 'in the active voice', he is intimating that if there is a conflict where two apply simultaneously, then the one which is blocked is blocked for good. The mediopassive inflection proper to the impersonal voice, being once blocked by the simultaneous mediopassive suffixes proper to reciprocal action, may not recur again.

Explanation In P.1.3.14 Pāṇini teaches that the *ātmanepada* terminations are to be used. There are two conditions: that there be reciprocal action and that the agent be expressed, that is to say, the verb be active.

The point is raised that this last stipulation is unnecessary. And to the counter argument that the *ātmanepada* terminations would then apply in the other voices of the verb with the sense of *karmavyatihāra* 'reciprocal action', the disputant asks why this should be a problem. The crux of the argument then follows. In the subsequent rules, P.1.3.15 and 16, the *ātmanepada* is proscribed for certain usages. As it stands, this proscription applies to active verbs only, because *kartari* recurs for P.1.3.14. Should it be removed, however, then the proscriptions would be more general, and this is not desirable. The examples quoted would not be legitimate; they are cases of the *ātmanepada* occurring after the passive stems of exactly those verbs explicitly mentioned in P.1.3.15, with prefixes *vyati* demonstrating that they express *karmavyatihāra*. So *kartari* must be present.

In an attempt to salvage the point, the disputant appeals to *paribhāṣā* 76, which teaches that rules may be reapplied, even if previously blocked. Therefore even without *kartari* in P.1.3.14, the correct *ātmanepada* terminations can be applied in the other voices, even though they were once blocked by P.1.3.15 or 16. So by this maxim *kartari* can be omitted.

And yet Pāṇini has nevertheless read the word *kartari* in P.1.3.14. Therefore we finally have to conclude that he does not accept the *paribhāṣā* 76, and holds its opposite to be true, namely that once an operation is blocked by another simultaneous operation, it may not reapply. And so the present maxim is shown to be one of Pāṇini's presuppositions.

Comments This argument typifies our author in two respects. The lines of reasoning and indeed a number of phrases, are modelled on the *Mahābhāṣya* discussion of P.1.3.14; yet the Vyāḍi commentator takes an independent line, turning Patañjali's arguments to a new purpose. Secondly, the argument is not very well expressed, and is intrinsically weak. The whole give the impression of an author working alone, without the benefit of criticism or dialogue.

Argument 31.2[245] [31:15

— What is the point of intimating this?
— At the stage of *śās* + *hi* or *han* + *han* the substitution of *tātaṅ* [for *hi*] is applicable by *tuhyos tātaṅ āśiṣy anyatarasyām* (P.7.1.35), as well as the appearance of *śā* [for *śās*, by P.6.4.35] and the appearance of *ja* [for *han*, by P.6.4.36]. *Tātaṅ* is the substitute, because of subsequent. Once this is done, the appearance of *śā* and *ja* by virtue of re-applicability does not take place. They do not appear because 'if there is conflict when two apply simultaneously then the one which is blocked for good'. The form *śiṣṭāt* [cf. P.6.4.34] etc. is validated.

Explanation In forming the imperative singular of *śās* or *han* we reach a stage *śās* + *hi* or *han* + *hi*. At this point a choice opens up. Either *hi* is changed for *tāt* by P.7.1.35, or *śās* and *han* become *śā* and *ja* respectively by P.6.4.35 and 36. These two possibilities are simultaneous. The principle of subsequence selects the former operation. Once it has taken place, we might try to apply the latter operation as well (since by *sthānivadbhāva* the *tāt* could be taken as a virtual *hi*, allowing P.6.4.35 and 36 to operate). This reapplication is forbidden by the present *paribhāṣā*.

Comments Once again the Vyāḍi commentator uses the same argument as the *Mahābhāṣya*. In this case the argument seems sound and clear, and recommends itself as an illustration of the maxim; yet the rest of the tradition ignores it.

---

[245] This difficulty is recognised in *vārt.* 25 on P.1.1.56, and the present solution is given by Patañjali in his subsequent comments (Mbh.I.140:10–12).

A similar, though not identical, argument is offered by Haribhāskara (no. 20).

The external is invalid with respect to the internal.[246]

— An external rule is invalid when an internal rule is to be performed.

Comments This is, of course, the best known and most discussed of the *paribhāṣās*. The terms *antaraṅga* and *bahiraṅga* have been neutrally translated here as 'internal' and 'external', although they are such common and crucial terms in the Sanskrit grammatical system that it could be argued that they should not be translated at all.

The theory behind this maxim is clearly a form of bracketing, to establish a hierarchy of precedence among the operations to be performed in deriving a form (see Crystal 1980.47). However, a great deal of commentarial discussion, particularly stemming from Nāgeśa's treatment of the maxim, has been devoted to elucidating the criteria by which operations are classed as external or internal. The discussion has become extremely sophistical in an effort to broaden the applicability of the maxim, and remove genuine difficulties. As a result the entire interpretation of the maxim since Nāgeśa has become overburdened with obfuscating scholasticism. A number of issues and misunderstandings amongst the commentators have been explained and clarified by Bronkhorst (1986). Two of his main theses are that Vaidyanātha Pāyaguṇḍa misunderstood a crucial part of his teacher Nāgeśa's exposition of this maxim, and that Kielhorn has mistranslated the maxim.

[246]This maxim is frequently used by Kātyāyana, in particular in the recurring phrase *na vā bahiraṅgalakṣaṇatvāt*, which occurs twenty-three times as a *vārttika*. It is always glossed by Patañjali with the explicit statement of the *paribhāṣā* (Mbh.I.117:1; II.9:3, 185:16; III.44:19, 50:6, 64:18, 68:10, 70:22, 74:8, 85:17, 88:23, 93:3, 117:3, 124:19, 246:19, 255:4, 271:16, 278:15, 312:24, 401:9, 407:6, 407:6, 426:7:13:14:16:17:17), except in one case (Mbh.III.434:9) where, although Patañjali does not actually spell out the maxim, it is obviously intended. Kātyāyana also refers to the *paribhāṣā* in other words (Mbh.I.223:15) and in a *ślokavārttika* (Mbh.I.145:18). In both cases Patañjali supplies the explicit statement of the maxim (Mbh.I.145:22, 223:16).

Furthermore, Patañjali frequently uses the maxim himself, without special reference to a *vārttika* (Mbh.I.26:14, 51:9, 54:12, 55:4, 97:18, 161:10, 223:21, 316:7; III.33:7, 167:11, 346:15, 347:22, 389:12, 452:18). He calls it the *asiddhaparibhāṣā* (Mbh.III.85:24).

It is discussed by Puruṣottamadeva (no. 41), Sīradeva (no. 69), Nīlakaṇṭha (no. 58), Haribhāskara (no. 71), Nāgeśa (no. 50), Śeṣādrisudhī (no. 42), and again by the Vyāḍi commentator (no. 73).

It is quoted five times in the *Kāśikā*, on P.6.4.19, 6.4.22, 6.4.132, 8.2.78, and 8.3.15 (KV.V.358, 369, 484, KV.VI.441, 497). It is mentioned once in the *Siddhāntakaumudī*, (SK.I.52–53 (47)).

Note that Patañjali himself did not expect the *paribhāṣā* to be universally applied: in his discussion under *vārttika* 5 on P.6.3.68 he clearly states that the maxim cannot be applied in the *uttarapada adhikāra*, i.e., *pāda* 3 of *adhyāya* 6 (Mbh.III.167:12–14).

Argument 32.1[247] [32:3

— How is that known?

— Because he says *om āṅoś ca* (P.6.1.95). There is no point in stating that when *āṅ* follows the latter form comes about [in place of both letters]. Thus, for the stage *adya ā ūḍha* the lengthening of the vowel before a homorganic letter [cf. P.6.1.101] would apply [first], followed by *guṇa*. Firstly it [long ā] will be the single substitute for them [the -*a* and *ā*]; once that has occurred it the final form is arrived at by the *guṇa*: *adyoḍhaḥ* 'brought today'.

This being the case, by saying this [i.e., *āṅ* in P.6.1.95] he is intimating that the root and prefix have the internal operation. The single substitute [of *ā* for *a* + -*ā*] is external; because it is invalid even when that [*sandhi* of root and prefix: *adya oḍhaḥ*] has been done. The post-*a guṇa* [P.6.1.81] comes next. It is invariant. After it, however, *vṛddhi* would wrongly apply [P.6.1.88]. Therefore the introduction [of *āṅ* in P.6.1.96] is for this reason.

Explanation The argument is made unclear by the phrasing of 32:6–7. But this aside, the reasoning is as follows.

From the string *adya–ā–ūḍha* two lines of derivation are possible. If the left junction is performed first then we have:

i)	**adyā*	+	*ūḍha*	by P.6.1.101
ii)	*adyoḍha*	+		by P.6.1.87

If the right junction is performed first, we have:

a)	*adya*	+	*oḍha*	by P.6.1.87
b)	*adyoḍha*	+		by P.6.1.95

[247] This argument is presented *in nuce* in *vārt.* 9 on P.6.1.108 (Mbh.III.83:25). See also Patañjali's discussion preceding and following this, from *vārt.* 7 onwards (Mbh.III.83:10–84:3). The reasoning there is that the presentation by Pāṇini of P.6.1.95 proves the *antaraṅga/bahiraṅga* principle, because of the example *adyoḍhaḥ*. What is *antaraṅga* and what is *bahiraṅga*? The operation between root and suffix is *antaraṅga*. How do we know that? Patañjali's words suggest that it is more or less self evident. The subcommentators attempt to make this last point more rigorous (*Pradīpa* and *Uddyota* V.120–21), but are forced to introduce notions which Patañjali was not using at this point.

The *paribhāṣā* commentators in general do not use this argument. Amongst them the standard argument for intimating this *paribhāṣā* is based on P.6.4.132 (see Kielhorn 1874.235 ff.). Nāgeśa (no. 50) does mention it, however, but does not treat it as a *jñāpaka*, but as a *prayojana* (Nāgeśa 93:5 ff.).

The fact that Pāṇini teaches 6.1.95 shows that he believes the second option will occur, giving stages a) and b). That is to say, for Pāṇini, the operation between root and prefix takes precedence over that between one word and another.

The reasoning which follows seems to be aimed at establishing, on independent grounds, that the first junction is external and the second is internal. And it would follow from this that Pāṇini's presentation of P.6.1.95 shows he considers the external operation invalid when the internal one can be performed.

However, the Vyāḍi commentator appears to say instead that the first junction is external because it is invalid. This is, of course, circular. And he goes on to make some unclear statements to the effect that the second junction is invariant, and therefore would take precedence. The danger would then arise of *vṛddhi* replacing *-a* + *o-*. So P.6.1.95 is necessary. The three possible derivations may be represented as follows:

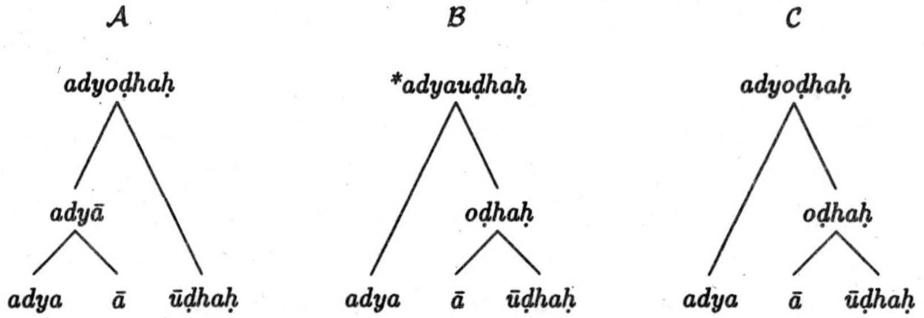

Case *A* ignores both the *paribhāṣā* and P.6.1.95; *B* applies the *paribhāṣā* but not P.6.1.95; *C* applies the *paribhāṣā* and P.6.1.95, showing that the existence of the form *adyoḍhaḥ* and the existence of P.6.1.95 together predicate the existence of the *paribhāṣā*.

Comments A number of confusions in this passage would be clarified by conjecturing the substitution of the *paribhāṣā* itself for the reading *dhātūpasargayor antaraṅgakāryam bhavati* in line 32:7, and altering the reading *asiddhatvāt* of line 32:8 to *anityatvāt*. But in the complete absence of any MS evidence whatsoever for these changes we must assume that the difficulties are archetypal.

Plainly, as it stands, this argument does not establish the *paribhāṣā*, but rather the *dhātūpasarga* maxim. It is equally plain that the argument derives from the *Mahābhāṣya* passage referred to in footnote 247, p. 145, and is an attempt to make that argument rigorous by deriving the *antaraṅgatā* or *bahiraṅgatva* from considerations of *nityatva*. Unfortunately the argument has become confused. It is nevertheless clear that the Vyāḍi commentator's treatment here presupposes that of the *Mahābhāṣya*, and attempts to improve upon it.

Argument 32.2[248] [32:10

— What is the purpose of intimating this?
— In [the examples:]

paṭvyā 'with the sharp one (f.)' and
mṛdvyā 'with the soft one (f.)'

there is a latter semivowel substitution [possibility]; because this is invalid, the former semivowel substitution being internal, occurs.

Explanation The starting point of this argument is the string *paṭu-ī-ā*. (The *ī* is the feminine suffix (*ṅīp*) and the *ā* is the instrumental singular inflection (*ṭā*)). As before, we have a choice as to which of the two junctions is performed first. Thus we might generate:

i) *paṭu* + *ya* by P.6.1.77

or, performing the first junction first, we generate:

a) *patvī* + *a* by P.6.1.77
b) *paṭvyā* by P.6.1.77 again

By applying the *paribhāṣā* we find that the left junction, being *antaraṅga*, takes precedence over the right junction, which is *bahiraṅga*. So the form *paṭvyā* is correctly generated.

Comments The Vyāḍi commentator does not mention the question which becomes all important in the later literature, as to what criteria decide whether a particular operation is *antaraṅga* or *bahiraṅga*. In Patañjali, in his statement of the argument, does not make clear why he considers the first junction to be *antaraṅga*; he just states that it is so (Mbh.I.145:7). In a subsequent passage, after giving an appealingly familiar, mundane analogue (Mbh.I.145:23 ff.) he proposes, without argument or reasons, a scale of descending *antaraṅgatā* (Mbh.I.145:25–28). It is proposed that operations on a *prātipadika* concerning type (*sāmānya*,) the individual (*vyakta*), gender, number and case be performed in that order. Nāgeśa notes perceptively that this presupposes the *vibhajyānvākhyāna* view of derivation, that is, a word is built up by successive additions of grammatical units (as opposed to the *pada*- or *vākyānvākhyāna* views; see Joshi and Roodbergen 1980.i–ii, and *passim*). As his commentator Vaidyanātha Pāyaguṇḍa makes explicit, this view amounts to choosing a left-branching derivational tree. Vaidyanātha Pāyaguṇḍa says:

> ... *antaraṅgatvāt, pūrvopasthitanimittakatvāt,* ... *bahiraṅgeti, paścād-upasthitanimittakatvenety arthaḥ.*[249]

---

[248] As stated by Patañjali, the examples *paṭvyā*, *mṛdvyā* are sanctioned by tradition, or *mūrdhābhiṣikta* (Mbh.I.144:8).

This particular argument is presented by Patañjali in his discussion on the *ślokavārttikas* on P.1.1.57 (Mbh.I.145:6–8). In fact the argument as a whole is given in the *ślokavārttika* which immediately follows (Mbh.I.145:11:14:16:18), but without particular reference to our examples.

Once again this argument is quoted by Nāgeśa alone amongst the *paribhāṣā* commentators (Nāgeśa 103:6), with direct reference to the *Mahābhāṣya* as his source.

[249] *Gadā*, 103:25–26.

and to make his concept of *upasthiti* even clearer he says:

> *laukikaprāyogikoccāraṇakrameṇa pūrvaśrutanimittakatvam ity arthaḥ.*[250]

In diagram form, the options are:

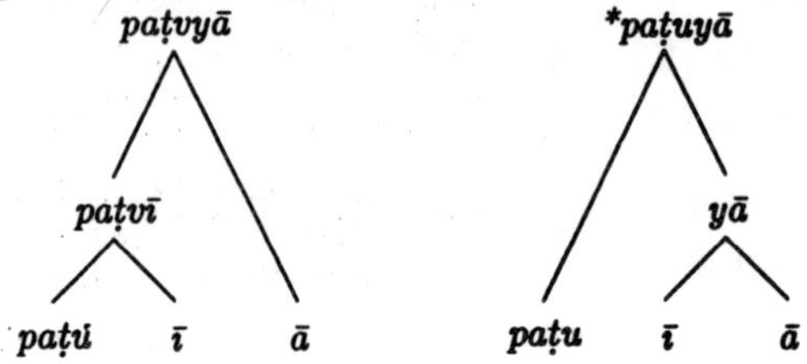

[250] *Gadā*, 103:13–14.

Paribhāṣā 33

What has a common basis is invalid, what has divergent bases is valid.[251]

Comments It is interesting to note that although this maxim seems to have *paribhāṣā* status in the *Mahābhāṣya*, none of the commentators treat of it. The Vyāḍi commentator alone discusses it as a separate principle, again showing his independence of all sources but the *Mahābhāṣya* and his own wits (see footnote 252, p. 149).

Argument 33.1[252] [33:2

— How is this *paribhāṣā* known to exist?
— Because *sic* [the aorist sibilant] is marked with a *k* by *hanaḥ sic* (P.1.2.14). Once this is done, the nasal is elided on the basis of the *sic*, by *anudāttopadeśa* ... (P.6.4.37). On the basis of the letter *t* the letter *t* [i.e., *sic*] is elided by *hrasvād aṅgāt* (P.8.2.27). Thus *āhata* 'he hit' is established. Even if this rule [P.1.2.14] did not exist, having generated *sic* by *cleḥ sic* (P.3.1.44), then at the stage *han-s-ta* it [the suffix *ta*] would have the marker *ṅ* by *sārvadhātukam apit* (P.1.2.4). Once the letter *t* is marked with *ṅ* there is elision

[251]This idea is known to Kātyāyana, who uses it in *vārt.* 12 on P.6.4.22 (Mbh.III.190:22). The same wording printed by Kielhorn as a statement of Patañjali's (Mbh.III.212:7) may be suspected of being in fact the voice of Kātyāyana again, by analogy with the first mentioned occurrence. Patañjali quotes the maxim in a more stereotyped form (if the preceding be true) in five places (Mbh.II.52:4; III.190:23, 197:22, 212:7, 213:2).

None of the *paribhāṣā* commentators discuss the maxim.

It is stated by the *Kāśikā* as being intimated by the word *atra* in P.6.4.22 (KV.V.364–65). The same is said in the *Siddhāntakaumudī* on the same rule (SK.III.25–26 (2183)). The subcommentaries in both places take up the issue.

For one of the very few mentions of this maxim by a modern author see Geiger 1909:259.

[252]This difficulty about deriving *āhata* is as old as Kātyāyana. He mentions it as part of his discussion on P.3.1.44, in *vārt.* 5 (Mbh.II.51:22). He there proposes that P.1.2.14 exists to intimate that the *n* of *han* appears not to be elided (Kātyāyana actually says 'is not elided', but the reference can only be to *asiddhavadbhāva*). But he says no more than this. It is Patañjali who quotes the *paribhāṣā*, in giving a rationale for Kātyāyana's statement (Mbh.II.52:4). However he goes on to supersede this statement by invoking the *antaraṅga paribhāṣā*. This probably accounts for the absence of the *samānāśraya* maxim amongst traditional commentators.

Patañjali's arguments are repeated by Haradatta *ad* P.1.2.14 (*Padamañjarī* I.287:5–14).

[of final *n*] on the basis of this letter *t*, according to *aniditāṃ hala upadhāyāḥ kṅiti* (P.6.4.24). And by *hrasvād aṅgāt* (P.8.2.27) the *s* is elided. In this way *āhata* 'he hit' is established.

There is no point in the rule *hanaḥ sic* (P.1.2.14).

— Not so! If the rule [P.1.2.14] is not framed then once the letter *s* has been elided the letter *a* in *ha* may potentially elide by *ato lopaḥ* (P.6.4.48) since on the basis of the letter *s* [cf. P.1.1.62] it [the *a*] precedes an *ārdhadhātuka*.

— Then why does this not happen as well when the rule is framed?

— By *asiddhavad atrābhāt* (P.6.4.22) the [elision of the] letter *n* is invalid. Because of this, it [the *a*] is separated [from the *ārdhadhātuka*] by the letter *n*.

— The *ābhāt* ruling [P.6.4.22] covers *aniditāṃ halaḥ* (P.6.4.24) too. Therefore, because the elision of the letter *n* is invalid from both points of view, the letter *a* will not be elided. So the rule [P.1.2.14] has no point.

This being the case, by framing the rule he is observing that what has a common basis is invalid, what has divergent bases is valid. For if the rule is framed then the elision of the letter *n* is based on the letter *n*, and the elision of the letter *n* is also [based] on the same letter *s*.

So they have a common basis. If the rule is not framed, then the elision of the letter *n* is based on the letter *n*, the elision of the letter *n* only on the letter *n*. These have divergent bases. But he frames the rule and observes that the one with the common basis is invalid.

Explanation The reasoning is a little involved here, and it is well to have before one the two suggested derivations of *āhata*. (The form of the verb with prefix *ā* is used since by P.1.3.28 this ensures the use of the *ātmanepada* inflection *-ta*).

The first (and ultimately correct) derivation is:

i)	*ā*	+	*han*			+	*ta*	
ii)	*ā*	+	*han*	+	*sic*	+	*ta*	by P.3.1.44
iii)	*ā*	+	*han*	+	*sic*[k]	+	*ta*	by P.1.2.14
iv)	*ā*	+	*ha*	+	*sic*[k]	+	*ta*	by P.6.4.37
v)	*ā*	+	*ha*			+	*ta*	by P.8.2.27
[vi) ↛	*ā*	+	*h*			+	*ta*	by P.6.4.48]

The second derivation, omitting P.1.2.14, is:

a)	*ā*	+	*han*	+			*ṫa*	
b)	*ā*	+	*han*	+	*sic*	+	*ta*	by P.3.1.44
c)	*ā*	+	*han*	+	*sic*	+	*ta[ṅ]*	by P.1.2.4
d)	*ā*	+	*ha*	+	*sic*	+	*ta[ṅ]*	by P.6.4.24
e)	*ā*	+	*ha*	+			*ta[ṅ]*	by P.8.2.27
[f)	*ā*	+	*h*			+	*ta*	by P.6.4.48]

The point at issue is this: in the first derivation, at stage iv), the *ā* of *han* is elided on the basis of the following *sic* which has the marker *k*. Then the possibility might arise of a stage vi) where the *k* of the remaining *ha* would be elided by P.6.4.48. This operation too is triggered by the presence of the *sic*. (The elision of the *sic* by P.8.2.27 is invalid w.r.t. P.6.4.48 since it is in the *Tripādī*.) Thus, in this derivation the elision of *n* and of *n* are both caused by, or based on the same element, namely *sic*.

In the second derivation, at stage d) the *n* of *han* is elided, this time on the basis of the suffix *ta* with the marker *ṅ*. Then the possibility arises, as before, of stage f), where the *a* of the remaining *ha* is elided on the basis of the following *sic*. In this derivation, then, the elision of *n* and of *n* are caused by, or are based on, different elements.

The Vyāḍi commentator argues that in fact neither stage vi) or f) will arise, since both the rules which elided the *n* of *han* are in the *ābhīya* section. Since the rule for eliding the *a* is also in this section, these rules should be virtually invalid with respect to each other. So as far as P.6.4.48 is concerned, the *a* is still present, and the *a* cannot therefore be elided. So no problem seems to exist. And yet Pāṇini presents the rule P.1.2.14, whose only purpose can be to show that he prefers the first derivation to the second, and that without P.1.2.14 the second would take place, and stage f) would indeed arise, in spite of the *ābhīya* context.

Therefore Pāṇini is intimating that operations based on separate items are in fact valid with respect to each other, in spite of the *ābhīya* ruling. And only operations arising from the same basis or condition are *asiddha* with respect to each other.

Comments The translation of '... *nakārasyāsiddhatvāt* ...' (33:13) as:

> By *asiddhavad atrābhāt* (P.6.4.22) the [elision of the] letter *n* is invalid.

is, strictly, unwarranted, since the sense has been inverted. But the text as it stands is plainly wrong.

Argument 33.2[253] [33:21

— What is the point of intimating this?

---

[253]Like the previous argument, this one goes back to Kātyāyana, who gives its outline in *vārts.* 9–12 on P.6.4.22 (Mbh.III.190:11 ff.). The full detail is filled in by Patañjali (esp. Mbh.III.190:23–25). This whole passage has been translated by Geiger (1909:233 ff.).

The argument is reproduced in the *Kāśikā* on P.6.4.22 (KV.V.368–69), and is discussed by the subcommentators. See also the *Bālamanoramā* on P.6.4.22 (SK.III.26:3–6 (2183)) where Jinendrabuddhi puts the argument with his characteristic clarity, concision and intelligibility. See also *Tattvabodhinī* (SK.III.25:28 ff. (2183)).

Nāgeśa, in discussing the *antaraṅga paribhāṣā* (106:2–3), mentions that it is not valid in the *ābhīya* section, and Vaidyanātha gives the present argument (upon which this conclusion is based) in his commentary (*Gadā* 106:12 ff.). See also Kielhorn's translation (1874:256–66, especially footnote 2).

— *Papuṣaḥ* 'those who have drunk (acc. pl.).' When the second [i.e., accusative] plural [suffix] follows, at the stage *pap-i vas* [actually *papā-vas śas*] there is vocalisation [of *vas*] on the basis of the *śas* [acc. pl. suffix] by *vasoḥ samprasāraṇam* (P.6.4.121) and the substitution of the former for the latter [and former letters, i.e., *vas* → *u-as* → *us* by P.6.1.108]. Once this is done, at the stage *pap-us* [actually *papā-us-ś*], then on the basis of the *us* there is elision of the latter *ā* [in *pā*] by *ato lopa* ... (P.6.4.64) because of the initial vowel [of *us*] and because an item marked with *ṅ* [or *k*] follows [*us* again, originally *kvasu*]. If this is being carried out [however], the vocalisation will be invalid by *asiddhavad atrābhāt* (P.6.4.22). Because of this there is no vowel at all [at the beginning of *us*: it is *vas* still], so how can there be elision of the latter *ā*?

However, if this *paribhāṣā* exists, then this vowel *u* is valid because of the divergence of bases: the vocalization of *vas* here is based on *śas*; the elision of the letter *ā* is based on the *us*. So there is a divergence of the bases. And because we have shown that 'what has divergent bases is valid' the letter *ā* is elided and once this is done *papuṣaḥ* 'those who have drunk' is established.

Explanation The derivation under discussion is this:

i)	*pā*	+	*liṭ*	+	*śas*	
ii)	*papā*	+	*liṭ*	+	*śas*	by P.6.1.8, 7.4.59
iii)	*papā*	+	*kvasu*	+	*śas*	by P.3.2.107
iv)	*papā*	+	*us*	+	*śas*	by P.6.4.131, 108
v)	*pap*	+	*us*	+	*śas*	by P.6.4.64

The vocalization of *vas* at stage iv) is based on the *śas* which follows. And the elision of a stage v) is based on the *us* which follows, because the latter begins with a vowel.

The problem arises, however, that both these operations are prescribed in the *ābhīya* section (P.6.4.22–175). Therefore they should in principle be virtually invalid with respect to each other. But this would mean that the *us* generated at stage iv) would still appear to be *vas* as far as P.6.4.64 is concerned. This rule could not than apply, since it depends upon the item having an initial vowel.

The problem is solved by applying the *paribhāṣā*. The bases of the two operations are different: one is *śas* and the other *vas*, or *us*. Furthermore, 'what has divergent bases is valid'. In other words, since the two operations are based on different items as causes, they are valid with respect to one another, in spite of being in the *ābhīya* section.

Comments There seems to be some confusion in the text about the forms quoted to represent the derivation of *papuṣaḥ*. The Vyāḍi commentator quotes *papivas* as the first stage, when he must be talking about *papā-vas-śas*. The augment *i* is certainly applicable (cf. *papivān*), but in this form it disappears when its cause, the *valādi* suffix *vas* (cf. P.7.2.35) is changed to *us* (cf. *paribhāṣā* 35 esp. argument § 2). One must assume that the Vyāḍi commentator had in mind the fuller derivation: ***pā-liṭ-śas*** → ***papā-liṭ-śas*** → ***papā-vas-as*** → ***papā-ivas-as*** → ***papā-us-as***, etc.

Paribhāṣā 34

By virtue of the assertion, in spite of the intervention of an item which never fails to intervene.[254]

— An operation which has an application, and whose statement has an intervention by an adjacent letter or conjunct, such an operation does take place, purely by virtue of its assertion, even if there is intervention.

Explanation If a rule is prescribed to apply to a certain item, but that item is invariably separated from the provenance of the rule by some other item, then the rule will apply nevertheless. This is because of the sheer fact that it has been given and would otherwise be purposeless.

Comments The word 'assertion' translates *vacana*. This term has a special sense in Sanskrit grammar: by stating a rule, making the assertion that it is so, Pāṇini is taken to be intimating that this rule does indeed function, even if it appears not to in some situations. This idea is at the root of the whole notion of *jñāpana*. The double negation in the *paribhāṣā* signifies additional certainty or emphasis: *dvau nañau dārḍhyam gamayataḥ*. It is a common stylistic feature of *paribhāṣās*; cf. *nāprapta* (no. 36), etc.

[254]This maxim occurs several times in the *Mahābhāṣya* (Mbh.III.281:3, 324:11, 330:10, 344:18, 359:21) being quoted by Patañjali in exactly the same form as that given by the Vyāḍi commentator. The general notion of *vacanaprāmāṇya* is common throughout the *vārttikas*.

The maxim is quoted three times in the *Kāśikā*, *sub* P.7.3.54, 7.4.1, 8.2.19, (KV.VI.69, 130, 379) and in the *Siddhāntakaumudī* on P.7.3.86 (SK.III.30:2 (2189)).

Argument 34.1[255] [34:4

Thus, for example, the lengthening in *śāmyati* 'he becomes quiet', due by *śamān aṣṭānāṃ dīrghaḥ śyani* (P.7.3.74), would fail to apply.
— For what reason?
— That which would have become long [the *a* in *śam*] is separated off by another consonant [the *m*]. And not a single one of the eight items from *śam* on ends in a vowel, or could give point to the assertion [of P.7.3.74]. And yet this lengthening is stated. In this case, by virtue of the assertion the lengthening does occur, even though of the non-final item.
— How?
— Because apart from the one separated off, there is no vowel here which would become long. In this way this *paribhāṣā* should be known to be intimated.

Explanation The lengthening prescribed by P.7.3.74 applies to a final vowel because of P.1.1.52.

Argument 34.2[256] [34:11

— What is the point of intimating this?
— In *adhijigāṃsate* 'he studies hard' lengthening is prescribed for the final of *gam* by *ajjhanigamāṃ sani* (P.6.4.16). This being so, the lengthening applies to the root with the intervening letter *m*, and not to the reduplicative syllable, when separated off by the root.

Explanation The rule P.6.4.16 teaches lengthening of *gam* in the desiderative. Of course P.1.1.52 applies here, but *gam* has no final vowel. So the *paribhāṣā* applies to give point to the prescription, and the *a* of *gam* is lengthened.

Comments Note the Vyāḍi commentator's variant reading of P.6.4.16, and see the first sentence of the *Kāśikā's* comment on the rule; *ajantānām aṅgānām hanigamyoś ca* ... (KV.II.352:2).

The argument is rendered unclear by the last statement, *nābhyasasya dhātuvyavāye* (34:13). It is not obvious what this contributes to the reasoning. Probably it means

[255]The problem with P.7.3.74 and the roots *śam* etc., which do not end in vowels, is recognised in *vārt.* 1 on P.1.2.28 (Mbh.I.205:5) and in Patañjali's comment thereon. But the present *paribhāṣā* is not invoked as a solution.

This argument seems to have sunk without trace in the later literature. The general attitude to P.7.3.74 in all later authors is '*spaṣṭam*' (e.g., *Bālamanoramā*, SK.III.338:24 (2519)). While true, the problem of *vyavadhāna* certainly deserves to be mentioned.

[256]This argument is not found elsewhere, it seems, as a purpose for the *paribhāṣā*. But *han* and *gam* are included in the same *vārttika* as *śam* etc. (see footnote 255, p. 155).

that *-ji-* in *adhijigāṃsate* is not lengthened even though it is *always* (cf. *na avyavadhāna*) separated from the proper sphere of action of the rule, P.6.4.16.

When the cause ceases to exist the effect also ceases to exist.[257]

Argument 35.1[258] [35:2

— Thus for example the shade, which is caused by the umbrella, disappears when the umbrella goes away. In the discipline too there is an intimation inasmuch as he states *stauti* 'he praises' in the list beginning with *sunoti* 'he squeezes out' [in P.8.3.65].
— How come it is an intimation?
— This word *ṣṭu* is read amongst the initial elements [Dhp.2.34]. The letter *ṣ* in it is changed to the letter *s* by *dhātvāder* ... (P.6.1.64). And the retroflexion of the *ṭ* [by P.8.4.41] is caused by the retroflex *ṣ*. When that [*ṣ*] ceases to exist then the retroflexion of the *ṭ* [by P.8.4.41] disappears. Therefore it becomes *stauti*.

Thus 'when the cause ceases to exist ...' is validated.

Comments Note that *ṣṭutva* (35:6) is grammatical idiom for the application of *ṣṭunā ṣṭuḥ*, P.8.4.61, and must not be confused with the root *ṣṭu* under discussion.

[257] This *paribhāṣā* is not quoted as such in the *Mahābhāṣya*, although the notion it embodies was known. Kātyāyana frequently speaks of *nimittābhāva* (e.g. *vārts.* 8 on P.2.3.46 and 2 on P.3.3.132). Patañjali also speaks of an item disappearing when its cause disappears (Mbh.I.164:7, 462:22; II.118:5:11, 139:11, 158:22).

The maxim is discussed by Puruṣottamadeva (no. 113), Sīradeva (no. 99), Nīlakaṇṭha (no. 64) and Haribhāskara (no. 101). See the discussion of the Vyāḍi commentator's *paribhāṣā* no. 59, (p. 211 below).

[258] This simile does not appear in the *Mahābhāṣya*, or amongst the *paribhāṣā* commentators.

The *stauti* argument, that when the *ṣ* becomes *s* then the *ṭ* which it caused becomes *t*, does not appear in these sources either. However, an identical argument based on *sthā* in P.8.4.61 (which is *ṣṭhā* in the *Dhātupāṭha*, Dhp.1.975) is given as the intimation of the maxim by Puruṣottamadeva (no. 113), Sīradeva (no. 99) and Haribhāskara (no. 101).

Argument 35.2 [35:8

— The purpose for its intimation is *papuṣaḥ* 'those who have drunk (acc. pl.)', *tasthuṣaḥ* 'those who have stood (id.)'. Here the augment *i* which is caused by a consonant (except *y*) [cf. P.7.2.35] disappears once that consonant disappears [cf. P.6.4.131].

Explanation See analysis § 33.2 and discussion thereon.

Of items taught in conjunction, if one of the two disappears, both of them cease to exist.[259]

Explanation Suppose two items, A and B, are taught together, simultaneously and in conjunction, in a single rule. Then if A disappears then B will also disappear.

Argument 36.1[260] [36:2

— How is this known?
— From the world. Thus, for example: something is meant to be done by Devadatta and Yajñadatta. If Devadatta has gone off, Yajñadatta does not do it by himself.

Argument 36.2[261] [36:3

— And there is also an intimation in the discipline, since he states *bilvakādibhyaś chasya luk* (P.6.4.153).
— How come it is an intimation?
— Because he makes mention of *cha* [= the suffix *īya*] in this rule. Suppose one said *bilvakādibhya luk* 'there is deletion after items in the list beginning with *bilvaka*'. Then by the *paribhāṣā: pratyayasya lukślulupaḥ* (P.6.1.61) there is no other suffix at all, except for *cha*, which follows the items in the *bilvaka* list, when a secondary suffix

[259] This maxim appears three times in the *Mahābhāṣya* (Mbh.II.215:23, 357:18–20; III.229:13).

It is discussed by all the *paribhāṣā* commentators: Puruṣottamadeva (no. 65), Sīradeva (no. 72), Nīlakaṇṭha (no. 77), Haribhāskara (no. 74), Nāgeśa (no. 86), Śeṣādrisudhī (no. 74). Cf. the arguments under the Vyāḍi commentator's *paribhāṣā* no. 61 (p. 217).

It is quoted in the *Kāśikā* on P.6.4.153 (KV.V.504), and in the *Siddhāntakaumudī* on the same rule (SK.II.384:1 (1311)).

[260] This worldly illustration is used by Patañjali (Mbh.II.216:1, 357:19–20).

[261] The main argument is presented by Patañjali in his commentary on P.6.4.153 (Mbh.III.229:7–14). It is echoed in the *Kāśikā* (KV.V.504:1–3), *Siddhāntakaumudī* (SK.II.383:8 (1311)), their commentaries, and in the *paribhāṣā* commentaries mentioned in footnote 259 above.

follows. Therefore, without mentioning *cha* [P.6.4.153], only the *cha* is deleted. So there is no point in mentioning *cha* [in P.6.4.153].

Thus, for example, when the analytical form is 'the town near the Bilva trees', the suffix *cha* and the augment *kuk* are applied after the word *bilva* by *naḍādīnāṃ kuk ca* (P.4.2.91). [Then the secondary suffix] *aṇ* applies by *tatra bhavaḥ* (P.4.3.53) giving *bilvakīyā*, which means 'being in this [town of] Bilvakīyā'. In this situation, 'Pāṇinians do not have fixed arrangements' (*paribhāṣā* 59), so at the stage **bilva-k-cha* the *cha* is deleted, even without stating *cha* [in P.6.4.153].

— If this is done the *aṇ* too could potentially be elided [by P.6.4.153], because it too would then be following the word *bilvaka*.

— Surely it says 'before a secondary suffix' [in P.6.4.153]. And *aṇ* does not have a secondary suffix after it.

— This is not a problem. When the analytical form is 'that which belongs to a Bailvaka [i.e., one who lives in Bilvakīyā]' then the *cha* appropriate after a word with initial *vṛddhi* [by P.4.2.114] is generated; then *aṇ* is followed by a secondary suffix. Therefore *cha* is mentioned [in P.6.4.153] to exclude [application to] *aṇ*.

— This is not so. For if the *aṇ* here were going to be deleted then by *asiddhavad atrābhāt* (P.6.4.22) the deletion of *cha* is invalid, and thereby there is no deletion of the *aṇ*. Therefore there is no point in mentioning *cha* [in P.6.4.153].

This being so, by mentioning *cha* he is observing that the exclusion of a suffix also applies to it with its augment.

— Then how could this [P.6.4.153] apply here to the *cha* alone?

— How could it fail to do so?

— Because the [augment] *kuk* is taught in conjunction with the *cha* [in P.4.2.91].

— This being established, what is the ouctome?

— The *paribhāṣā* 'of items taught in conjunction, if one of the two disappears both of them cease to exist' is necessary.

Explanation In P.6.4.153, Pāṇini teaches the deletion by *luk* of the suffix *cha* before a *taddhita*, after the words *bilvaka* etc. Now *cha* is the one and only suffix which ever appears after *bilvaka* and before a *taddhita*. And *luk* cannot delete anything other than a suffix, because of P.1.1.61. So there is no reason to mention *cha* specifically in P.6.4.153, since nothing else could possibly be affected by the rule: saying just 'there is deletion' would unambiguously refer to deletion of *cha*.

At this point the Vyāḍi commentator enters into some skirmishing about whether this is really the case (see below). The outcome is that the mention of *cha* is indeed superfluous, and must therefore be an intimation. What does it intimate? That if

Pāṇini had not been specific in P.6.4.153 about what was to be deleted, then the argument *kuk* would have disappeared along with the suffix *cha*. And why should this happen? Because the suffix *kuk* is taught 'in conjunction' with *cha*. Thus the principle emerges that if items are taught in conjunction and one of them subsequently disappears, the other goes with it.

The 'skirmishing' mentioned above concerns arguments about whether *cha* really is the only item liable to be deleted by P.6.4.153, or whether another secondary suffix, *aṇ* might not also be a candidate.

To be deleted by P.6.4.153 a suffix must be:

i) preceded by *bilvaka*, etc.,

ii) followed by a secondary suffix

First the Vyāḍi commentator presents '*Bilvakīya*', the name of a town, and then proposes to add *aṇ* to it. Naturally the *cha* (=*īya*) is deleted by P.6.4.153 giving '*Bailvaka*'. We cannot delete the *aṇ* because criterion ii) above is unfulfilled. The opponent then proposes to fulfill it by adding *aṇ* again to make a further derivative: *Bailvaka* + *aṇ*. Now surely i) and ii) are specified. No, replies the Vyāḍi commentator, because by P.6.4.22 the processes being discussed are prescribed in the *ābhīya* section of the *Aṣṭādhyāyī*, and are therefore as if not performed with respect to one another, i.e., they are virtually invalid. In particular, the *cha* is as if it were still present as far as the new *aṇ* is concerned: *bailvak* [*īya*]*a* + *aṇ*. Therefore the *aṇ* does not follow the word *bilvaka*, and condition i) is violated.

Thus there really is no other suffix than *cha* to which P.6.4.153 could apply.

Comments This passage is rather rambling and in places a little unclear. The phrase *tatra bhava iti bilvakīyā* in 36:11 is unclear, but is supported in all MSS. And in the passage 36:19–21 particularly, slightly differing interpretations are possible. It is also possible that the reading *kuto mā bhūd* (36:21) might be read as *kuko* ..., since *k* and *t* can be confused in Śāradā. But none of the MSS preserves such a reading. Note that the statement *na sa bilvakāt* (Mbh.III.229:10–11) which is attributed to Patañjali in Kielhorn's edition, is read as a probable *vārttika* in the Nirṇaya Sāgara Press edition (*Mahābhāṣya* with commentaries, V.360[a]).

Argument 36.3 [36:24

— Others say, 'But it is not the case that the form *cha* is prounced so that only the form *cha* might be deleted, and not the letter *ka*.[262] Deletion is said to apply to a suffix; how could it possibly apply to what is not a suffix? How could it apply to the front part of an item [i.e., to -*k* of -*kīyā*]?'

But the teacher observes that this *paribhāṣā* does exist, since he makes mention of the form *cha* [in P.6.4.153].

Explanation The point here seems to be that some 'others' do not accept argument § 36.2, but hold instead that P.6.4.153 cannot apply to *kuk* because this is not a suffix, but an augment. And P.6.4.153 only applies to suffixes. The outcome is the same: *cha* is unnecessary in that rule.

[262] It is unfortunately not obvious whom the Vyāḍi commentator means by 'others'.

Comments The final statement here is odd. The argument just given would establish not the *paribhāṣā*, but rather the statement at 36:27–28, that 'the exclusion of a suffix also applies to it with its augment'.

Argument 36.4[263] [36:28

— What is the point of intimating this?
— *Pañcendra* and *daśendra*, mean 'of [the goddess] Pañcendrāṇī' [etc.], because it is something belonging to the deity (cf. P.4.2.24). Once the feminine suffix has been deleted, the [augment] *ānuk* [which is taught in conjunction with it in P.4.1.49] is also proved to be excluded.

Explanation In P.4.1.49 the augment *ānuk* [→ *ān*] is prescribed after words like *Indra* before the feminine suffix *ī*. In other words, the augment and the suffix are taught in conjunction and the resulting form is 'Indrāṇī'. From this is formed the name of the goddess Pañcendrāṇī. If we take the further step of making a secondary derivative of Pancendrāṇi by adding *aṇ* by P.4.2.24, then by P.4.1.88 the *an* is deleted. This causes the deletion of the feminine suffix *i*, by P.1.2.49. And here the process would stop, were it not for the *paribhāṣā* which allows the feminine suffix to take the augment with it when it disappears. The correct form *pañcendra* thus results.

[263]The example is used by Patañjali, though as part of a different argument, concerning *sthānivadbhāva* (Mbh.I.153:22).

This very argument is given by Puruṣottamadeva (no. 65), Nāgeśa (no. 86) and Śeṣādrisudhī (no. 74). Another similar argument, using a different example, is presented by Puruṣottamadeva, and this is reproduced by Sīradeva (no. 72) and Haribhāskara (no. 74).

Paribhāṣā 37

A rule $\mathcal{X}$ which is introduced when [another rule] $\mathcal{Y}$ cannot fail to apply, blocks that very $\mathcal{Y}$.[264]

— The double negation in 'when $\mathcal{Y}$ cannot fail to apply' signifies the original: 'cannot fail to apply' means 'perforce applies'. If, when a rule $\mathcal{Y}$ is applicable, another rule $\mathcal{X}$ is framed, the $\mathcal{X}$ blocks the $\mathcal{Y}$.

But if $\mathcal{Y}$ sometimes applies and sometimes does not apply then $\mathcal{X}$ does not block it.

Explanation If a rule $\mathcal{Y}$ has the domain of operation **Y** and a second rule $\mathcal{X}$ has a smaller domain **X** then if $\mathbf{Y} \cap \mathbf{X}$ then $\mathcal{Y}$ is barred from applying in **X**. The antithesis of this situation is $\mathbf{X} \cup \mathbf{Y}$. In this case $\mathcal{X}$ does not necessarily block $\mathcal{Y}$. This is perhaps more clearly expressed using Venn diagrams (see Figure).

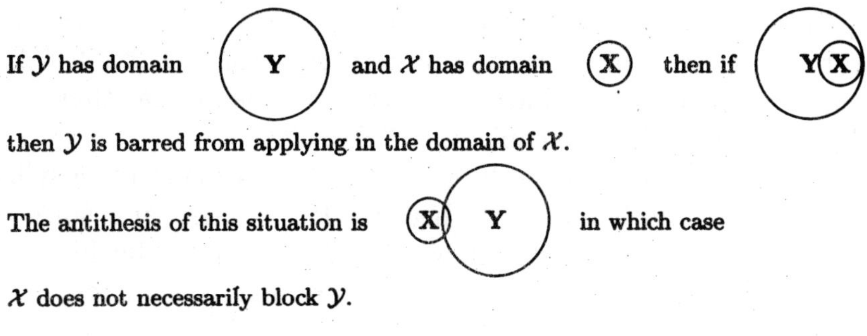

Scoping rules.

---

[264]This *paribhāṣā* is prefigured in several places in the *Mahābhāṣya* (Mbh.I.457:2, III.104:17, 107:15, 218:6, 232:21, 315:11) and in four cases it is stated explicitly almost as distinct maxim (III.69:4, 233:1, 295:20, 296:1). It is quoted in the *Kāśikā* on P.6.1.89 (KV.IV.556) and is discussed by the following *paribhāṣā* commentators: Nīlakaṇṭha (no. 48), Nāgeśa (no. 57) (see Kielhorn 1874.320 note 2), Śeṣādrisudhī (no. 49).

Comments The general principle here is the same as that obtaining between *utsarga* and *apavāda*, in relation to *avakāśatva*. For discussion see Cardona 1970, in particular p. 62.

The Vyāḍi commentator's paraphrase of the double negation in *na aprāpta* calls to mind the common but undatable maxim: *dvau nakārau prākṛtārthasya dārḍhyam gamayataḥ*.

Argument 37.1 [37:6

— How is this *paribhāṣā* known to exist?

— Because in *sanīvantardha* ... (P.7.2.49) he reads the word *svṛ*, to make an option.

— How come it is an intimation?

— According to *ārdhadhātukasya* ... (P.7.2.35) the [augment] *iṭ* is applicable to exactly this [*svṛ*] before *ārdhadhātuka* suffixes. It is [then] prohibited by *ekāca upadeśe 'nudāttāt* (P.7.2.10). Then again, to block this [rule], *svaratisūti* ... (P.7.2.44) is stated.

However the [augment] *iṭ* which belongs to an *ārdhadhātuka* before *san* [the desiderative] is prohibited by *sani grahaguhoś ca śryukaḥ kiti* (P.7.2.12, 11). This [prohibition] too could [in theory] be blocked by that [rule P.7.2.44].

So by making mention of *svṛ* in *sanīvantardhau* (P.7.2.49) the teacher is observing that if $\mathcal{Y}$ cannot fail to apply, $\mathcal{X}$ blocks it.

— How so?

— Because this option rule [P.7.2.44] is introduced both when the prohibition [of *iṭ*] after *svṛ* due to its being monosyllabic [P.7.2.10] cannot fail to apply, and also when the one due before other *ārdhadhātuka* suffixes is applicable [i.e., P.7.2.12].

Thus, because that [prohibition] due to its being monosyllabic is not applicable before *san*, [because P.7.2.12 is,] and since [the prohibition by] *sani grahaguhoś ca* (P.7.2.12) is applicable before *san*, but not applicable elsewhere, the optionality is introduced by *svaratisūti* ... (P.7.2.44).

But it does not block that which is applied and not applied [i.e., P.7.2.12]. Therefore mention is made of *svṛ* [in P.7.2.49]. Thus, then, the formulation [of P.7.2.49] is for what is both applied and not applied. By *ārdhadhātukasya* ... (P.7.2.35) it is applied; by *ekāca* ... (P.7.2.10) it is prohibited. On the non-option point of view, though, it is prohibited by *sani grahaguhoś* (P.7.2.12) because it [*svṛ*] is an item ending in *ŭ* or *r̥̆*. It is to block this that mention is made of *svṛ*. Because of the mention of *svṛ* [in P.7.2.49] this [*paribhāṣā*] is intimated.

Argument 37.2

[37:23

— What is the point of intimating this?
— From the Padakāra's [i.e., Kātyāyana's] point of view, which is one of refutation, the example *adīdhayur* 'they shone' is proper [cf. *vārt.* 1 on P.1.1.6].
— How
— The *guṇa* which precedes *jus* [the 3rd pl. *-us*: cf. P.7.3.83] is introduced in the province of a prohibition, [by P.1.1.5; cf. P.1.2.4]. This prohibition, which always applies, is blocked by this [*guṇa*].

It [the *guṇa*] blocks that which applies and which does not fail to apply. It [the *guṇa*] is prohibited by *kṅiti* ... (P.1.1.5), and applied before *jus* [by P.7.7.3.]. For there is no *jus* such that this prohibition would not apply to it.

However, by *dīdhīvevīṭām* (P.1.1.6) the prohibition [of *guṇa*] is applicable when *jus* follows specifically after *dīdhī* and *vevī*. For any other root before jus, that [rule $\mathcal{X}$] applies which is present both when that [rule $\mathcal{Y}$] applies and does not apply [where $\mathcal{X}$ = P.1.1.5 and $\mathcal{Y}$ = P.1.1.6].

Thus, the *guṇa* which precedes *jus* [by P.7.3.83] blocks that [rule, i.e., P.1.1.5] which makes the prohibition of this [*guṇa*] applicable everywhere: and it does not block that [i.e., P.1.1.6] which applies in some cases and not in others. Thus it [P.7.3.83] blocks *kṅiti* ... (P.1.1.5) and does not block *dīdhīvevīṭāṃ* (P.1.1.6).

Therefore the *guṇa* of this [i.e., *adīdhayuḥ*] is different; it is not the *guṇa* which occurs when *jus* follows.

Paribhāṣā 38

Of an item whose thematic affix is deleted and one whose thematic affix is not deleted it is the one whose thematic affix is not deleted which is taken [into consideration].[265]

Comments The text is correct enough (though not entirely satisfying) up to the end of argument § 38.2. The subsequent arguments are jumbled, in the wrong context, and wrong. However, the problem existed already in the archetypal manuscript and will only be fully solved by the discovery of an earlier exemplar.

The readings *tibnirdeśa* are given instead of *dvirnirdeśa*, as *præstat difficilior lectio*.[266]

— When an item whose thematic affix is deleted or whose thematic affix is not deleted is mentioned, it is only the one whose thematic affix is not deleted which is taken [into consideration].

Argument 38.1[267] [38:3

— How is this known?
— Because in *svaratisūti* ... (P.7.2.44) he makes mention of *sūti* [class 2] and *sūyati* [class 4].
— The purpose of specifying these two is to obviate [any reference to] *suvati* [class 6].
— This is not so. *Sūti* means only the one with the marker *ṅ*; this is required for *sūyati*. Thereby it [P.7.2.44] will not apply to *suvati* [which does not have marker *ṅ*].

[265] This *paribhāṣā* is suggested in the *Mahābhāṣya* on P.2.4.77 (Mbh.I.495:14).

It is discussed by Kaiyaṭa and Nāgeśa in their commentaries on the *Mahābhāṣya* on P.7.2.44 (*Pradīpa* and *Uddyota* VI.134): Kaiyaṭa accepts that the *paribhāṣā* is suggested by this *sūtra*; Nāgeśa is not happy with it ('*cintyam etat*').

The *paribhāṣā* is discussed by the commentators Puruṣottamadeva (no. 67), Sīradeva (no. 83), Nīlakaṇṭha (no. 83), Haribhāskara (no. 86), Nāgeśa (no. 90), Śeṣādrisudhī (no. 78).

[266] Cf. West 1973, p. 51.

[267] For explanation of this and subsequent arguments see Keilhorn 1874.432 ff.

This being the case, by specifying these two he is intimating that this *paribhāṣā* does exist. *Ṣūṅ* only refers to *sūyati*, which does not have its thematic affix [*ya*] deleted. Therefore mention is made of *sūti*, in order that an item with its thematic affix deleted should also be [included].

Argument 38.2[268] [38:9

— What is the point of intimating this?
— In *gātisthāghupā* ... (P.2.4.77), when *pā* is mentioned it is only the one which does not have its thematic affix deleted: *apat* 'he drank' [and not 'he protected']. It should not be the one with its thematic affix deleted: *apāsīt* 'he protected'. In that context it is only the one which does not have its thematic affix deleted [which is meant].

Argument 38.3 [38:11

If *ṣūṅ* were stated, it would not be the one whose thematic suffix is elided [which would be meant].

Therefore, in *sūtisūyati* ... (P.7.2.44), the specification of the *tip* [3rd sg. suffix] is done to make sure it is not the one which has its thematic affix deleted.

The teacher's procedure intimates that only the one with its thematic affix deleted is meant.

Argument 38.4 [38:14

By specifying the *tip* [3rd sg. suffix *-ti*] here in *gātisthāghupā* ... (P.2.4.77) he is intimating that this *paribhāṣā* does exist.

268 This argument is used by Patañjali under P.2.4.77 (see ref. in note 265 above).

An item does not behave like the final and the initial when it is the basis for [operations on] both.[269]

— Where it would apply to both, to the final and the initial, the status of being like the initial and final does not apply [cf. P.6.1.85].

Argument 39.1 [39:2

Thus for example, in the world, if two equally forceful men have on servant, he does their work by turns. And when they approach him simultaneously, and they are not in conflict with one another, then he does the work consecutively. But when they are in conflict then he does not do the work of even one of them. It is the same here [in grammar] too: if an item is like a final it is not like an intial.

Argument 39.2 [39:7

— What is the point of intimating this?
— *Palāyate* 'he flees' is from *ayati* with preceding *parā* [cf. P.8.2.19]. When it [the single substitute, *ā*, in *par-ā-yate*] is not behaving like the initial of the root, then it behaves like the final of the prefix [i.e., *parā-yate*].

When it is not behaving like the final of the prefix then it is behaving like the initial of the root [i.e., *par-āyate*]. So once the single substitute has been made [*parā* + *ayate* → *parāyate*] it is possible to state that [*l* replaces final *r*] 'of a prefix when *ayati* follows' [cf. P.8.2.19].

---

[269]This maxim is quoted nine times by Patañjali (Mbh.I.151–52, 224:17; III.48:18 (a passage repeated at 259:12, 292:10, 324:16 and 399:10), 60:1, 62:17).

It is discussed by Puruṣottamadeva (no. 51), Sīradeva (no. 60), Nīlakaṇṭha (no. 120) and Haribhāskara (no. 62).

It is cited in the Kāśikā on P.7.1.80 (KV.V.626).

What is done by a single marker is not invariable.[270]

— Here in the discipline, what is done by a single marker, be it *ñ* or *ṇ*, is not invariable.
— How is that known?

Argument 40.1[271] [40:3

— Because in *mantre śetavahokthaśas* ... (P.3.2.71) he says '*ṇvin*'. The marker *ṇ* in it is put there for the purpose of *vṛddhi*. The marker *n* is put there for the purpose of accent. But it is possible to get [all] this with a single marker: one should here say [just] *ñi*. Both the accent and the *vṛddhi* will come about [by P.7.2.115 and P.6.1.197].

This being the case, by using two markers he is intimating that the *paribhāṣā* 'what is done by a single marker is not invariable' does exist.

Argument 40.2 [40:8

— What is the point of intimating this?
— If a book is composed on the subject of a luminary it is [called] *jyotiṣam* 'astronomical' [cf. P.4.3.116].

Soma and Indra are the divinity of the pulse oblation, [which is therefore called] the Somendra pulse oblation [by P.4.2.24].

Because the effect of the [marker] *ṇ* [of the prescribed suffix *aṇ* in each case] is not invariable the *vṛddhi* does not occur.

Explanation The point here is that according to P.4.3.116 the suffix after *jyotir* 'luminary' would be *aṇ*. This causes *vṛddhi* of the first syllable by P.7.2.115, giving **jyautiṣam*. This does not take place because it is only triggered by the single marker *ṇ*, and according to the *paribhāṣā* this makes it occasional.

---

[270] This *paribhāṣā* is not discussed in the *Mahābhāṣya* or by other commentators.
[271] This argument does not occur in the *Mahābhāṣya*.

Likewise by P.4.2.24 the application of *aṇ* might have given **saumendra*, were it not for the *paribhāṣā*.

Comments From Kātyāyana's comments on P.4.3.116 (Mbh.II.316–17) we see that for him the rules 116 to 118 constitute a single rule. It is he who proposes to split this into three rules, giving us the text we have today.

Furthermore, since the suffix is given at the end of the original single rule, by splitting it into three the first two new rules give conditions for the application of an unstated suffix. The commentators, say *yathāvihitaṃ pratyayaḥ bhavati* 'the suffix is as ordained', that is *aṇ* by P.4.1.83. But in his *vārttikas* on P.4.3.116, Kātyāyana tells us that the suffix *aṇ* is to be used after the words of the *Makṣika* list. We do not have this list. This comment of Kātyāyana's only makes sense if it is an aside on the whole original rule because, having once split the rule up, the suffix *aṇ* would apply anyway by P.4.1.83.

In short, then, Kātyāyana has mutilated Pāṇini's text at this point, in order to introduce the suffix *aṇ* where only *vuñ* would have applied.

The fact that the Vyāḍi commentator gives the present argument shows that he has the later form of the text before him, i.e., later than Kātyāyana and almost certainly later than Patañjali.

Of course, reading the rules as Pāṇini wrote them – in a single rule – there is no possibility of *jyotir* getting the suffix *aṇ* by this rule in the first place.

Comments An overall question remains regarding the Vyāḍi commentator's sources for this *paribhāṣā* and the related arguments.

Paribhāṣā 41

When an item is mentioned having one marker, it is not [the same as] that item with two markers.[272]

— When an item having one marker is mentioned, it does not include that item with two markers.

Comments The maxim as it appears in the *Mahābhāṣya* is more general than the Vyāḍi commentator's version: *tadanubandhakasya grahaṇe 'tadanubandhakasya*. Where the Vyāḍi commentator specifies 'one marker', 'two markers'. Patañjali says only 'so many'; 'different from that many'.

Note that the other *paribhāṣā* commentators use the Vyāḍi commentator's form of the maxim, suggesting a tradition of its formulation not derived from the *Mahābhāṣya*. (They give Patañjali's version too.)

Argument 41.1[273] [41:3

— How is that known?

— Because although the elision of *i* or *a* before an *ī* [or a secondary suffix] is valid [by P.6.4.148: *yasyeti ca*] he [nevertheless] uses the marker *ḍ* in *vāmadevyāḍ ḍyaḍḍyau* (P.4.2.9), in order to elide the letter *a*. By doing this he intimates that when an item having one marker is mentioned, it does not include that item with two markers.

Explanation The marker *ḍ* causes elision of the last vowel of an item and whatever follows it, by P.6.4.143. Thus:

vāmadeva	+	*ḍya*	by P.4.2.9
vāmadev	+	*ya*	by P.6.4.143

[272]The maxim is used several time by Patañjali (Mbh.II.16:6, 208:8, 274:4; III.183:24). See also *Kāśikā* on P.7.1.36 (KV.V.571), and Puruṣottamadeva (no. 37), Sīradeva (no. 51), Haribhāskara (no. 53) and cf. Nāgeśa (no. 82).

[273]This argument, in a fuller form, is given by Patañjali in his comment on P.4.2.9 (Mbh.II.274:2–6). (See also *Kāśikā* on P.4.2.9 (KV.III.515), etc.)

The argument is encapsulated in a *ślokavārttika* (Mbh.II.274:7–8), which would seem to postdate Kātyāyana, because of the absence of any *vārttika* on this *sūtra*.

But this same effect would be achieved by the action of P.6.4.148.

Therefore the only reason the *ḍ* is there is to distinguish the suffixes *ḍya* and *ḍyat* from *ya* and *yat* (cf. P.6.2.156). The suffix *yat* has but one marker: *t*. The suffix *ḍyat* has two: *ḍ* and *t*. By legislating separately for the second, Pāṇini is showing that for him they are not equivalent: they are differentiated by their markers, and a rule for *yat* will not apply to *ḍyat*.

Comments This argument is used to prove both the present *paribhāṣā* and the next one (no. 42). This exactly follows Patañjali's procedure in the the passage referred to in footnote 273, p. 171.

Argument 41.2 [41:6

— What is the point of intimating this?

— In *yayatoś cātadarthe* (P.6.2.156) it is *yat* which is meant [and not *ḍyat*]. Thus it gives *ávāmadevyam* 'not a descendant of Vāmadeva' [by P.6.2.2].

Explanation P.6.2.56 teaches the acute accent for the final syllable of words formed with *ya* and *yat*, under certain conditions. This would lead to the form **avāmadevyám*.

However P.4.2.9 teaches that the suffix after *vāmadeva* must be *ḍya* or *ḍyat*. This being so, because of the *paribhāṣā* these suffixes will not be liable to the effect of P.6.2.156, and the word is accented normally by P.6.2.2: *ávāmadevyam*.

Paribhāṣā 42

When an item is mentioned without a marker, that item with a marker is not meant.[274]

— When an item having no marker is mentioned, it does not include that item with a marker.

Argument 42.1 [42:3

— How is that known?

— Because in *vāmadevyāḍ ḍyaḍḍyau* (P.4.2.9) he marks the letter *y* with a *ḍ*, so that the last vowel and whatever follows it will be elided [by P.6.4.143]. For this is already achieved here by the elision of final *i* and *a* before *ī* [or a secondary suffix, by P.6.4.148: *yasyeti ca*].

So in this case he is intimating that when the letter *y* is mentioned without a marker, the reference does not include it with a marker.

Argument 42.2 [42:7

— What is the point of intimating this?

— When the letter is mentioned in *yayatoś cātadarthe* (P.6.2.156), this accent [i.e., on the final syllable] will not thereby apply to *ávāmadevyam* [because it is formed with *ḍya*].

Comments Note once again, throughout these arguments, the use of *-kāra* to refer to what is clearly a suffix (42:5:8). Cf. 36:8 etc.

[274]This maxim is originally Kātyāyana's, being presented by him in *vārt.* 2 on P.4.1.15 (Mbh.II.208:5).

See also Patañjali's use of the *paribhāṣā* (Mbh.I.254:8; II.274:4; III.169:3, 183:22:23, 274:11, 254:8, 259:3:21, 271:2), and Kātyāyana's reference back to his own statement of it, in *vārt.* 3 on P.7.1.84 (Mbh.III.271:1).

If an instruction serves no purpose for a certain rule, that rule is blocked.[275]

Argument 43.1 [43:2

— For example, the pronounciation of the letter *e* serves no purpose for a rule about the letter *e*. The prounciation of the letter *o* serves no purpose for a rule about the letter *o*.

Therefore the rule about the letter *e*, the rule about the letter *a* and the rule about the letter *o* is read.

He will say *ato bhisa es* (cf. P.7.1.9). In the rule about *indra* and *varuṇa* [etc.] one should say *ănuk* (cf. P.4.1.49). And the substitute for *ṅasi* [abl. sg. suffix] should be stated as *ăt* (cf. P.7.1.12). One should say *āta o ṇalaḥ* (cf. P.7.1.34).

Then afterwards,once *vṛddhi* and the long substitution for two homorganic letters has been done, the latter form [substitution, by P.6.1.97] would apply in

vṛkṣaiḥ 'with the trees',
Indrāṇī 'wife of Indra',
vṛkṣāt 'from the tree' and
papau 'he drank'.

These rules serve no purpose for the latter form [substitution], and therefore the latter from [substitution] is blocked.

Explanation The four rules, P.7.1.9, 4.1.49, 7.1.12 and 7.1.34, could theoretically be altered, in the way the Vyāḍi commentator suggests, without impairing the derivations they control.

Taking as the starting point the modified rules, the possibility of a wrong result arises, because P.6.1.97 might apply. The *paribhāṣā* stops this happening, and so the modified rules are vindicated.

[275]This maxim, and the next (no. 44), do not appear in the Pāṇinian tradition, but are used in the Kātantra (no. 50) and Cāndra (no. 37) systems.

Thus, in the first case, the Pāṇinian derivation is:

vṛkṣa	+	*bhis*	
vṛkṣa	+	*ais*	by P.7.1.9.
vṛkṣais			by P.6.1.88

The modified derivation:

i)	*vṛkṣa*	+	*bhis*	
ii)	*vṛkṣa*	+	*es*	by *ato bhisa es*
iii)	*vṛkṣais*			by P.6.1.88

But at ii), P.6.1.98 might apply, giving **vṛkṣes*. The *paribhāṣā* prevents this. The other examples are:

- Pāṇinian:

indra	+	*ān*	+	*ī*	P.4.1.49
indrānī					by P.6.1.101
indrāṇī					by P.8.4.2.

- Modified:

i)	*indra*	+	*an*	+	*ī*	by *indravaruṇa... anuk*
ii)	*indrānī*					by P.6.1.101
iii)	*indrāṇī*					by P.8.4.2

Difficulty: stage ii) might generate **indranī* by P.6.1.97.

- Pāṇinian:

vṛkṣa	+	*ṅasi*	
vṛkṣa	+	*āt*	by P.7.1.12
vṛkṣāt	+		by P.6.1.101

- Modified:

i)	*vṛkṣa*	+	*ṅasi*	
ii)	*vṛkṣa*	+	*at*	by *ṭāṅasiṅasām ina – atsyāḥ*
iii)	*vṛkṣāt*	+		by P.6.1.101

Difficulty: stage ii) might generate **vṛkṣat* by P.6.1.97.

The point seems to be that the three modified rules contain a redundancy. The new version of rule P.7.1.9 could get the same result by teaching *is* instead of *es* (*vṛkṣa* + *is* → **vṛkṣes* by P.6.1.87). Likewise a new rule 6.1.101 could teach *n* instead of *an*, and a new rule 7.1.12 could teach *t* instead of *at*.

Since these rules have nothing to gain by containing the redundancy, it serves to block P.6.1.97 which would otherwise apply.

A rule of which it [the instruction] is the condition, is not blocked.[276]

Argument 44.1 [44:2

— Thus, for example, in the world, if a statement is considered as a condition with respect to a certain purpose, then that statement is what brings about the achievement of that purpose.

Thus one says 'eat!' [only] when a person has not eaten.

Argument 44.2 [44:3

The same applies here [in grammar]: the utterances of the letters *a* and *e* which are the condition for the rule are what bring about that rule; the utterance of the letter *a* [brings about] the lengthening of the homorganic letter [modified P.6.1.101], and the utterance of the letter *e*, the rule about *vṛddhi* [modified P.6.1.88].

— How is it that these rules do apply when the letters *a* and *e* do not fail to apply, as in *vṛkṣaiḥ* 'with the trees', etc.

— Here, the letter *e* or the letter *a* are the only condition for these rules. Therefore those rules do arise. And the latter form [substitution] does not occur [cf. P.6.1.97].

Comments Although the general meaning of the above two arguments is obvious, it is not clearly expressed. The whole discussion is an extension to the previous *paribhāṣā*, forming an *apavāda* to it.

[276] See footnote 275, page 174 above.

Argument 44.3

[44:8

† In rules such as *ato bhisa ais* and *āta au ṇala* ((P.7.1.9, 34), the contrast of the rules is understood because of the contrast of the assertions.

atijarasaiḥ 'from the very aged' [cf. P.7.1.12],
dadaridrau 'he got poor' [cf. P.7.1.34].

A rule of which it [the instruction] is the condition, is not blocked.

Ato bhisa ais (P.7.1.9), *ṭāṅasiṅsām inātsyāḥ* (P.7.1.12), *āta au ṇalaḥ* (P.7.1.34).

Comments This is opaque as it stands. Furthermore, the examples chosen are too highly specific; they are normally used to illustrate quite other points (cf. P.7.2.101).

Technical terms and *paribhāṣās* are operation-timed.[277]

— What is the meaning of this?

— *Kāryakālam* 'operation-timed' means 'whose time is the operation'. 'Time' means 'reading'. Another meaning is 'location'. The time of technical terms and *paribhāṣās* is just where they are read. Wherever the operation is, is where it is to be done.

Argument 45.1 [45:4

— Thus, for example, once *sici vṛddhi parasmaipadeṣu* (P.7.2.1) has appeared, *vṛddhir ādaic* (P.1.1.1) arises. This [latter rule], being placed at the head of the discipline arises after that rule [i.e., P.7.2.1].

Likewise *aden guṇaḥ* (P.1.1.2) arises after the prescriptions for *guṇa*.

Likewise *alo 'ntyasya* (P.1.1.52) arises after [the rule] *rājñaḥ ka ca* (P.4.2.140).

Likewise *ṅic ca* (P.1.1.53) and *anekālśit sarvasya* (P.1.1.55) arise after *asthidadhisakthyakṣṇām anaṅ udāttaḥ* (P.7.1.75), and *aster bhū* (P.2.4.52).

In this way, 'technical terms and *paribhāṣās* are operation-timed'; it [the term or *paribhāṣā*] is seen to arise where the operation is.

[277]This *paribhāṣā* is used fifteen times by Patañjali (Mbh.I.54:17, 55:1, 66:11:26, 68:22, 274:22, III.21:24, 98:21, 165:23, 274:3, 385:8:10:20, 418:18, 426:13), with acceptance.

Note that the *yathoddeśaparibhāṣā*, which is normally coupled with the present *paribhāṣā*, is only mentioned once by Patañjali (Mbh.I.67:1), and then only as an extreme measure. The Vyāḍi commentator is again in consonance with Patañjali when he gives only the *kāryakāla* view.

Argument 45.2

[45:12

— But how is it known that this *paribhāṣā* exists?
— Becuse he states *na mu ne* (P.8.2.3).
— How come it is an intimation?
— Because when the substitution of *nā* for the *ṭā* which follows the word *adas* is taking place, by *āṅo nāstriyām* (P.7.3.120), the presence of *mu* [in *amu* by P.8.2.80], which is defined as a *ghi* [by P.1.4.7] is valid. In this contect, when *pūrvatrāsiddham* (P.8.2.1) applies, while *nā* is being generated, then *mu* is declared to be valid by *na mu ne* (P.8.2.3).

But although that *nā* is generated, it fails to apply in this rule [i.e., P.1.4.7].
— How?
— Even if the presence of *mu* [by P.8.2.80] is valid with respect to the rule about *nā* [P.7.3.120], it is still invalid with respect to the term *ghi* [P.1.4.7]. *Mu* is not at all present there. How [then] can the term *ghi* apply? And if the term *ghi* does not exist, how can *nā* arise?

Therefore *ghisaṃjñāyāṃ ca* 'and also when the term *ghi* [is being defined]' should be added to [the rule] *na mu ne* (P.8.2.3). But this is not stated. So the teacher is observing that technical terms and *paribhāṣās* are operation-timed. That [term or *paribhāṣā*] appears where the operation is.

This [i.e., P.1.4.7] appears in *adaso 'ser dā du do maḥ* (P.8.2.80). And by *śeṣo ghy asakhī* (P.1.4.7) it [the term *ghi*] comes after the generation of *mu* [i.e., P.8.2.80]. Therefore once the term *ghi* is valid, the existence of *mu* is valid [w.r.t. P.7.3.120], so the validity of this *mu* is generated by this [i.e., by P.8.2.3]. This *paribhāṣā* is intimated by the framing of this rule [P.8.2.3].

Explanation The sequence of operations in question is as follows:

i)	*adas*	+	*ṭā*	
ii)	*amu*	+	*ṭā*	by P.8.2.80
iii)	*mu*		is not *asiddha*	by P.8.2.3 (w.r.t. P.7.3.120)
iv)	*amu*		is a *ghi*	by P.1.4.7
v)	*amu*	+	*nā*	by P.7.3.120

Stage iv) could not take place were it not for P.8.2.3 which declares that the *asiddha* principle of the *tripādī* does not apply to *mu* when *nā* is involved.

Comments In P.7.3.120 Pāṇini uses the term *āṅ* to refer to the instrumental suffix *ā* which is normally given the marker *ṭ* thus: *ṭā* (cf. P.4.1.2). this same *āṅ* appears also in P.6.4.141 and 7.3.105. The marker *ṅ* serves no apparent purpose whatsoever. The term is said by Bhaṭṭojī Dīkṣita to belong to the Easterners (or ancients): *āṅ iti ṭāsaṃjñā prācām* (SK.I.245:1 (244)). The problem is not discussed in the *Mahābhāṣya*.

The argument is clear, but towards the end of this passage its expression becomes somewhat tangled, and it seems that somehow the readings *nābhāva* (see text edition 45:25) have become ubiquitous in the manuscripts when clearly the notion of technical *siddhatva* can only be relevant to *mu*.

Argument 45.3 [45:27

— What is the point of intimating this?

— It is also stated here on *adaso' ser dā du do maḥ* (P.8.2.80). The term *pragṛhya* is said to apply to the *ī* and the *ū* [of *ami* and *amū*, by P.1.1.11]. That [term *pragṛhya* from P.1.1.11] will arise after this [rule] *eta īd bahuvacane* (P.8.2.81).

It is correct to say that technical terms and *paribhāṣās* are operation-timed.

Paribhāṣā 46[a]

Things that have been stated are not expressed [again].[278]

— Something that has been stated once is not express again.

Explanation This *paribhāṣā* is a generalized version of the *anabhihita* principle (P.2.3.1).

Comments The text of the arguments here is corrupt even in the archetype. The two examples are conflated and the problems raised are not solved.

Argument 46[a].1 [46[a]:2

— Why?
— Because this is observed in the world. Thus, for example, once one has said 'man' [there is no need to express] the same again; and a second [example] is 'duty must be performed' in which there is no repeated expression ....

Argument 46[a].2[279] [46[a]:4

— If this is so then the prohibition *na sāmivacane* (P.5.4.5) is not proper.
— How come?
— Because once the suffix *kan* has been applied by *anatyantagatau ktāt* (P.5.4.4) ....

[278]The distribution of this *paribhāṣā* is interesting. It is frequently used by Patañjali, appearing fourteen times in the *Mahābhāṣya* (Mbh.I.105:3, 227:3, 238:11, 240:25, 241:24, 252:8, 348:19, 370:19, 390:16, II.15:15, 23:15, 199:3, 392:22; III.417:3).

It is generally accepted by the heterodox grammatical schools, but completely ignored by the Pāṇinian *paribhāṣā* commentators, with the exception of the Vyāḍi commentator. Once again his principal allegiance is to Patañjali.

[279]The objection to P.5.4.5, though not this whole argument, is given by Kātyāyana in his *vārttika* on P.5.4.5. He uses the expression *prakṛtyabhihita*, rather than *uktārtha* (Mbh.II.431:2). It seems that he and Patañjali would indeed reject P.5.4.5, thus showing their implicit adherence to the present *paribhāṣā*.

Explanation The argument is only partially stated here, but its point seems to be this: in P.5.4.4 the suffix *-ka* is taught after a past participle in the sense of an uncompleted process. Thus *bhinnaḥ* 'split', but *bhinnakaḥ* 'partly split'. The next rule, P.5.4.5, proscribes the suffix *-ka* when a word meaning 'half' precedes the participle. Thus *sāmikṛtam* 'half done' but not **sāmikṛtakam*.

But if the *paribhāṣā* were at work in Pāṇini's system then P.5.4.5 would be unnecessary since the words meaning 'half' would already have expressed the idea of incompletion, and so it would not need to be expressed a second time in the suffix *-ka*.

Argument 46^a.3[280] [46^a:6

— And this word *lopa* elision must definitely recur; it is stated like this, so there is no purpose in the word *ca* 'and' [?in P.6.4.20]. But the teacher observes that the *ŭ* which is really being stated [as a replacement] for the one which goes in the same position as the final, is also [a replacement] for the letter *v* which is not a final. Not merely for the one which is not a final. And the letter *v* in *jvar* and *tvar* [cf. P.6.4.20] is not in the same position as the final.

It [i.e., *ū*] does not replace what is separated by the letter *a*. That is done perforce because of the word *ca*. Therefore this word *ca* is for the purpose of intimation.

Explanation This argument seems unconnected with the *paribhāṣā* in question. It might be better placed in the discussion of *paribhāṣā* 46^b – although even this is not certain – or again *paribhāṣā* 74.

Neither the problem nor the intended solution are clear. The issues seem to revolve around the use of *ca* in P.6.4.20, and the fact that *u* is prescribed by that rule to replace the *v* in *jvar* and *tvar*, when this *v* is neither final nor an *upadhā*. The *ca* would make the rule apply to these *roots*.

[280] The *Mahābhāṣya* does not comment directly on rule P.6.4.20, and this argument does not appear.

Paribhāṣā 46^b

When a modification does not apply to a final, it applies to what is in the same position as the final.[281]

Argument 46^b.1[282] [46^b:2

— What is the point of intimating this?
— In *anastakṣṇaḥ* 'cartmakers' the *a* is elided [by P.6.4.134]. Thus, it is the non-final letter *a* which is elided; this being said, it is that which has the same position as the final [which is elided], not the final itself.

Explanation In *anastakṣan* the last *a* must be elided to form the acc. pl., etc. This takes place by P.6.4.134. However this rule might be interpreted to mean that other vowels in the word should be elided. For example, P.6.4.134 might be read to stipulate that it is the *a* of an *aṅga* ending in *an* which is elided. But the word *anas* qualifies for this. Similar arguments would lead to difficulties with the other vowels.

However, by adopting the *paribhāṣā* it can only be the *a*, which occupies (virtually) the same position as the final *n*, which is meant.

[281]This *paribhāṣā* is known to and used by Patañjali (Mbh.I.48:4; III.21:2:7:11:20, 22:5:10:15:21, 23:19, 31:11, 414:16), but is originally stated by Kātyāyana in *vārt*. 5 on P.6.1.13 (Mbh.III.21:1).

It is generally discussed by the commentators: Puruṣottama (no. 107), Sīradeva (no. 112), Nīlakaṇṭha (no. 94), Haribhāskara (no. 114), Nāgeśa (no. 95), Śeṣādrisudhī (no. 89).

It is used in the *Kāśikā* on P.8.2.80 (KV.VI.445:2).

[282]This argument does not appear as such in the *Mahābhāṣya*, as a proof of the *paribhāṣā*. However, all the elements of the reasoning, and the example *anastakṣṇaḥ* are there (Mbh.III.21:23).

The argument is standard amongst the *paribhāṣā* commentators on this *paribhāṣā*.

A rule with a technical term is not invariable.[283]

— Here, a rule which is framed with a technical term in it is not, it seems, invariably the case.

Argument 47.1[284]

[47:3

— How is that known?

— Since he says *or guṇaḥ* (P.6.4.146). Because when *guṇa* is generated here in place of *u*, it is *o*. For brevity's sake one should say *or ot* there [instead of P.6.4.146]: *o* goes in place of the letter *u*.

This being the case, by mentioning *guṇa* the teacher is observing that a rule with a technical term is not invariable.

Therefore it is so that the *guṇa* would not be invariable here too [in P.6.4.146], because a rule with a technical term is not invariable.

[283]This *paribhāṣā* is discussed by Puruṣottamadeva (no. 83), Sīradeva (no. 71), Nīlakaṇṭha (no. 78), Haribhāskara (no. 73) Nāgeśa (93.1) and Śeṣādrisudhī (no. 81). See also *Kāśikā* on P.6.4.146 (KV.V.494:8) and *Siddhāntakaumudī* on P.6.4.146 and P.2.4.79 (SK.II.159:2 (847), III.374:1 (2547)).

[284]The following two arguments are standard throughout the *paribhāṣā* commentaries. For argument § 47.2 see Kielhorn 1874:441, footnote 1.

Argument 47.2 [47:8

— What is the point of intimating this?
— In Svāyambhuva 'descendant of Svayambhu' there is no *guṇa* [by P.6.4.146].

Comments The particular example *svāyambhuva*, though common enough as a word, is cited by Puruṣottamadeva (149:6) in the context of a verse from Kālidāsa's *Kumārasambhava* (verse 1, ch. 2). Sīradeva (235:27) quotes the same verse, but thenceforth the word alone is quoted.

The Vyāḍi commentator's citation of the form, with its analytical phrase equivalent does not suggest that he is quoting, and it would be wrong to suggest any particular relationship to Kālidāsa from his use of this example.

The *Kāśikā* also cites this example under P.6.4.146 (KV.V.495:1), without reference to Kālidāsa. It seems therefore that this literary reference was Puruṣottamadeva's idea. He repeats it in his gloss on P.6.4.146 in his *Bhāṣāvṛtti*.

An object linked with *nañ* 'not' or *iva* 'like' is similar yet different, because that is the sense [of it].[285]

— Whatever thing is observed linked with *nañ* 'not' or *iva* 'like' intimates an operation on something which is different from that, but similar to it.

Argument 48.1[286] [48:3

Thus, for example, when one says 'brings a non-*brāhmaṇa*' it is someone like a *brāhmaṇa* who is brought, having just the same belly, hands, feet and eyes, and not a horse or an ass. This is how it is in the world.

Argument 48.2[287] [48:5

[This holds] in the discipline too, since he mentions *dhātu* 'root' in *sipi dhāto rur vā* (P.8.2.74).

— How come it is an intimation?

— Because the mention of *dhātu* 'root' is pointless here. It is said [in P.8.2.74], 'when *sip* follows after a root'. *Sip* [2nd sg. inflection] only comes after a root, not a nominal stem. There is no point in mentioning *dhātu* in that [rule, P.8.2.74].

This being the case, by mentioning *dhātu* he is intimating that in the previous rule [P.8.2.73] it is after a root and after a non-root.

---

[285]This maxim is used seven times by Patañjali (Mbh.II.22:13, 145:18; III.34:12, 51:2, 94:16, 153:13, 255:17).

It is discussed by Puruṣottamadeva (no. 97), Sīradeva (no. 31), Nīlakaṇṭha (no. 41), Haribhāskara (no. 31), Nāgeśa (no. 74) and Śeṣādrisudhī (no. 63).

[286]This illustration is regularly given by Patañjali to illustrate the present *paribhāṣā* (Mbh.II.22:15, 145:20; III.34:14, 51:4, 94:18, 153:15, 255:19).

[287]The argument as such does not appear in the *Mahābhāṣya*.

The examples *acakād bhavān* and *anvaśād bhavān* do occur in the *Kāśikā* on P.8.2.73, 74 (KV.VI.437:4:10) and, interestingly, in the *Cāndravṛtti* too, on the equivalent rules, Ca.6.3.105, 106.

Thereby it is established [that the substitution applies] for the letter *s* of the root. [Egs.:],

acakād bhavān 'your Honour was radiant',
anvaśād bhavān 'your Honour commanded'.

— How can the mention of *dhātu* 'root' [in P.8.2.74] have the meaning 'only after a root'? And for what reason would it not apply only after a root in the previous rule?
— It is stated thus: *tipy anasteḥ* (P.8.2.73). In *tipy anasteḥ sipi dhāto ru vā* (P.8.2.73, 74) the operation applies to something which is not *asti* [but] which is similar to *asti* 'an object linked with *nañ* or *iva* [i.e., *an-asti* in P.8.2.73] is similar yet different because that is the sense [of it]'.
— And what, in that case, is similar to *asti*?
— *Asti* is in fact a root. Something else which is a root, which is not *asti*, is similar to *asti*.

Therefore, by the present *paribhāṣā*, it would be only a root [which would be meant] in the previous rule. A non-root would not be meant. So by this mention of *dhātu* 'root' [in P.8.2.74] it is made to cover both a root and a non-root. Thus this mention of *dhātu* is an intimation.

Argument 48.3[288] [48:18

— In *añceś chandasy asarvanāmasthānam* (P.6.1.170) the operation appropriate to a non-*sarvanāmasthāna* [non strong case stem] happens either to a *sarvanāmasthāna* or to what is similar to one.

Explanation Pāṇini's rule 6.1.170 as framed has the *anuvṛtti* of the word *vibhakti* from P.6.1.168. Thus, on a literal interpretation it would mean that the acute accent would be prescribed after *añc* for any *vibhakti* that is not a *sarvanāmasthāna*. The fault is *ativyāpti*, because the term *vibhakti* covers also the verbal inflections. Thus we have to assume that the rule is about inflections which are not *sarvanāmasthānas*, but are like them, that is, nominal inflections.

Comments The argument is better put by Puruṣottamadeva and Sīradeva. Vyāḍi's phrasing is not accurate, as it implies that an operation for a non-*sarvanāmasthāna* may also occur to a *sarvanāmasthāna*.

It is also ambiguous from the manuscripts whether the reading in 48:19 is to be *vāsarvanāma-* (← *vā asarva-*) or *vā sarva-*. The former has been preferred since the latter would merely compound the error and seems more unlikely (see West 1973.51).

[288] This argument is given by Puruṣottamadeva (no. 97) and Sīradeva (no. 31), but not in the *Kāśikā*, *Siddhāntakaumudī* or *Mahābhāṣya*.

Paribhāṣā 49

An item with the marker *ŭ* includes only its own class, not all the items homorganic with it.[289]

— An letter which is mentioned with the marker *ŭ* includes only its own class, not all the homorganic items.

Explanation P.1.1.69 teaches that a letter with the marker *u* stands for itself and all the letters *savarṇa* with it. And *savarṇa* is defined in P.1.1.9 as *tulyāsyaprayatnam* 'having the same effort at a position in the mouth' (cf. Deshpande 1975.8 ff.).

The present *paribhāṣā* modifies the teaching of P.1.1.69: the letter with marker *u* stands for its *varga* 'class' and not in fact the whole group of *savarṇa* letters.

Comments Vyāḍi seems to be alone in presenting this maxim, and his arguments for it show that he has a totally different notion of *sāvarṇya* from the mainstream of the Pāṇinīya tradition.

A *varga* is the set of five stops produced at a particular place of articulation (*sthāna*), e.g., *k*, *kh*, *g*, *gh*, *ṅ* (cf. Allen 1953:46–47). The letters *savarṇa* with each other, on the other hand, share the same point of articulation and internal effort (Deshpande 1975:11). Thus, for example, the letters *savarṇa* with *k* would traditionally be considered to be the *kaṇṭhyāḥ sparśāḥ* 'velar stops', i.e., *kh*, *g*, *gh*, *ṅ*.

Plainly this is the same as the *varga*. So Vyāḍi must have some other notion of *sāvarṇya* in mind. And indeed his examples make it clear that he believes that *ś* is *savarṇa* with *t* (argument § 49.1) and that *ś* is *savarṇa* with *c* (argument § 49.2). Now *s* and *ś* certainly share the same place of articulation as *t* and *c* respectively, but their *prayatna* 'effort' is normally considered to be different. The sibilants are pronounced with openness (*vivṛta*) while the stops are pronounced with contact (*spṛṣṭa*) (cf. *Siddhāntakaumudī* on P.1.1.9 (SK.I.19:1 (10)), and Allen 1953.25).

Thus, for Vyāḍi *sāvarṇya* is equivalent to *sasthānatva* 'identity of place of articulation'. His interpretation of P.1.1.69 is thus unique. For him it means that a letter

[289]This maxim is not given in the *Mahābhāṣya*, or elsewhere. A different but related maxim is discussed by Puruṣottamadeva (no. 89), Sīradeva (no. 17), Nīlakaṇṭha (no. 131) and Haribhāskara (no. 17). They read *savarṇam eva* for Vyāḍi's *svavargam eva*. It does seem, however, that they have the same notion in mind as Vyāḍi: where he distinguishes *vargam* from *savarṇamātram* they distinguish *savarṇam* from *savarṇamātram*. Vyāḍi's position is clearer. Nīlakaṇṭha rejects the maxim because it is not found in the *Mahābhāṣya*. He also disagrees with the particular notion of *sāvarṇya* that it implies, i.e., *sthānamātratulyam* (Nīlakaṇṭha 315:18), showing thus that he takes it to have the same meaning as Vyāḍi's maxim.

marked with *u* would (were it not for the *paribhāṣā*) stand for itself and all the letters sharing its place of articulation, regardless of type of effort.

For further discussion, interesting though somewhat unclear, see Deshpande (1975.79–82). Deshpande's views on Vyāḍi's relationship to the *munitraya* (1975.77) is not reasoned and, I believe, wrong.

Argument 49.1[290] [49:3

— How is this known?
— Because in *na vibhaktau tusmāḥ* (P.1.3.4) he mentions the letter *s* seven though it is valid from the mention of *tu*.

Argument 49.2[291] [49:5

— What is the point of intimating this?
— The mention of *cu* in *coḥ kuḥ* (P.8.2.30) does not include the letter *ś*. Therefore *viḍ* 'the people' [← *viś*] is validated.

Explanation The derivation of *viḍ* 'the people' is:

viś	
[**vik* or **vih*	by P.8.2.30, prevented by *paribhāṣā*]
viṣ	by P.8.2.36
viḍ	by P.8.2.39.

[290] This argument is given by those *paribhāṣā* commentators mentioned in footnote 289, with the exception of Nīlakaṇṭha (no. 131).

[291] This argument is found in the same places as the previous one (see footnote 290), although the example *viḍ* is Vyāḍi's alone.

A rule about the augment *i* is stronger than any other rule.[292]

— A rule about the augment *i* it is stronger than all other prescriptions.

Argument 50.1[293] [50:3

— How is that known?
— Because he draws *śryukaḥ* [from P.7.2.11] into *sani grahaguhoś ca* (P.7.2.12) by the use of the word *ca* 'and'.
— How come this is an intimation?
— Because the word *ca* here is redundant.
— How would the augment *i* [*iṭ*] not appear before the aorist *s* [*san*] after *lūñ* 'to cut'?
— He observes, after all, that the augment *i* will not occur since it [the *san*] has the marker *k* by virtue of *iko jhal* (P.1.2.9). Once the marker *k* is generated there the augment *i* will be prohibited by *śryukaḥ kiti* (P.7.2.11). There is no point in the word *ca* 'and' [in P.7.2.12].

But the teacher observes that the augment *i* precedes the existence of the marker *k*.

Once the augment *i* is generated *iko jhal* (P.1.2.9) does not give the marker *k*, because of the assertion of *jhal* 'beginning with a stop'.

---

[292] This maxim is accepted by the earlier commentators and rejected by the later, on the grounds that it is not used by Patañjali (Nīlakaṇṭha 316:5: *bhāṣyāvyavahṛtā nirmūlā ca*). It is accepted by Puruṣottamadeva (no. 90), Sīradeva (no. 82) and Haribhāskara (no. 85) and rejected without argument by Nīlakaṇṭha (no. 136) and following him, Nāgeśa (no. 93.8).

It is not used in the *Kāśikā* or *Siddhāntakaumudī*.

[293] This argument is presented by Puruṣottamadeva (no. 90), Sīradeva (no. 82), and Haribhāskara (no. 85).

Therefore the word *ca* [in P.7.2.12] is there in order to prohibit the augment *i* for items ending in *ĭ*, *ŭ*, *ṛ̆*, and *ḷ*:

Explanation . The word *ca* in P.7.2.12 intimates the existence of this *paribhāṣā*. If the augment *i* were not the first item prescribed in the derivation of the aorist of a root such as *lu*, then the root would be directly followed by the aorist sibilant, *san*. This *s* is a member of the *pratyāhāra jhal*. Therefore P.1.2.9 would apply, and the marker *k* would be prescribed. This being done, P.7.2.11 by itself would prevent that augment applying.

As it is, the use of *ca* in the next rule, P.7.2.12, shows that for Pāṇini the former rule does not prevent the augment. This assumption must be, then, that the augmentation is the first operation to be prescribed.

Argument 50.2[294] [50:11

— What is the point of intimating this?

— Here in *śvayitvā* 'having swollen' the augment *i* is established before the vocalization: Once the augment *i* is generated, the marker *k* is prohibited by *na ktvā seṭ* (P.1.2.18). If the marker *k* does not exist there is no vocalization.

Explanation The correct derivation of *śvayitvā* is:

i)	*śvi*			+	*ktvā*	
ii)	*śvi*	+	*i*	+	*ktvā*	by P.7.2.35
iii)	*śvi*	+	*i*	+	*tvā*	by P.1.2.18
iv)	*śve*	+	*i*	+	*tvā*	by P.7.3.84
v)	*śvayitvā*					by P.6.1.78

The augment *i* is introduced right at the beginning, by virtue of the present *paribhāṣā*. Were this not so, then we might get the following sequence:

a)	*śvi*	+	*ktvā*	
b)	**śui*	+	*ktvā*	by P.6.1.15
c)	**śu*	+	*ktvā*	by P.6.1.108

Here, vocalization has preceded the augmentation and the wrong form results. With the correct derivation, however, the marker *k* is nullified at stage ii) because of the presence of the augment, and thenceforth vocalisation cannot take place. (N.B. *śvi* is a member of the *yajādi gaṇa* and is thus liable to the action of P.6.1.15.)

---

[294] As for previous argument (see footnote 293, p. 190).

Paribhāṣā 51

A rule about elision is stronger than any other rule.[295]

— Here in the discipline a rule about elision is stronger than any other rule.

Argument 51.1[296] [51:3

— How is that known?
— Because he says *pratyayalope pratyayalakṣaṇam* (P.1.1.62).
— How come this is an intimation?
— This rule need not be framed.
— How so?
— Operations dependent on suffixes will occur. After they have all taken place I shall perform the elision of the suffixes.

But the teacher observes that it is the elision which in fact takes place [first]. Once it is done those [operations] which depend on it [i.e., the suffix] fail to apply. Therefore *pratyayalope pratyaylakṣaṇam* (P.1.1.62) exists.

[295]This maxim does not appear in the *Mahābhāṣya*, but is discussed by Puruṣottamadeva (no. 91), Sīradeva (no. 111), Nīlakaṇṭha (no. 137), Haribhāskara (no. 113) and Nāgeśa (no. 93.7). Only the Vyāḍi commentator accepts it; the others reject it because it has no purpose which cannot be explained some other way and because it is not found in the *Mahābhāṣya*.

It is not used in the *Kāśikā* or *Siddhāntakaumudī*.

[296]This argument is presented by Puruṣottamadeva (no. 91) and Sīradeva (no. 111). Nīlakaṇṭha (no. 137) and Haribhāskara (no. 113) mention it only to reject it.

Argument 51.2[297] [51:8

— What is the point of intimating this?
— In *te saṇti* 'they are' The *a* of *asti* is elided [by P.6.4.111] before substitution occurs [by P.6.1.78]. So once this has been done there will be no substitution [of the -*e*] by *ay* because there is no initial vowel.

Explanation The derivation the Vyāḍi commentator wishes to avoid is:

i) *te asanti*
ii) **tay asanti* by P.6.1.78

The proper process being:

a) *te asanti*
b) *te santi* by P.6.4.111.

[297] This argument is quoted by Puruṣottamadeva (no. 91) and Sīradeva (no. 111) only. They use *kāni santi* instead of *te santi* as their example. Haribhāskara (no. 113) mentions this argument, attributing it to Sīradeva, only to refute it (369:11 … *iti Sīradeva tan na*), explaining the facts with reference to *paratva* and *nityatva*.

The understanding of particulars comes from exposition, for the existence of doubt does not imply any lack of definition.[298]

— Here in the discipline, where there is doubt concerning an equivalent conjunction, then the difference is to be understood from the exposition.

Explanation This is perhaps the best known of all *paribhāṣās*, partly from its appealing catholicity of meaning, and partly because it has since the time of Sīradeva been taken as the first of the *paribhāṣās*, because it is the first to be discussed in the *Mahābhāṣya*.

For a clear idea of what Patañjali has in mind by *vyākhyāna* see Mbh.I.11:23:

> *udāharaṇam pratyudāharaṇaṃ vākyādhyāhāra ity etat samuditaṃ vyākhyānaṃ bhavati*
>
> 'A commentary (*vyākhyāna*) is a combination of example, counter-example and a filling out of the sentence'.

Argument 52.1[299] [52:4

— How is it known that this *paribhāṣā* exists?
— Because when mentioning the abbreviations he attaches the letter *ṇ* to *aṇ*.
— How come this is an intimation?
— Because a different letters should, it seems, be attached in this case. There are, after all, many letters. And since this letter *ṇ* is appended twice there is doubt whenever a *ṇ* is mentioned as to whether it is actually the former one or the latter one.

---

[298] Patañjali quotes the maxim twelve times (Mbh.I.6:26, 7:5, 35:16, 42:13, 119:24, 266:16, 271:16, 272:27, 273:4; II.106:4, 106:18; III.246:3).

It is discussed by all the *paribhāṣā* commentators: Puruṣottamadeva (no. 120), Sīradeva (no. 1), Nīlakaṇṭha (no. 1), Haribhāskara (no. 1), Nāgeśa (no. 1), and Śeṣādrisudhī (no. 1).

[299] This famous argument is given by Patañjali while discussing *śivasūtra* 6 (Mbh.I.34–35, especially 35:15–18). It is reiterated by all the *paribhāṣā* commentators (see footnote 298, p. 194).

But the teacher observes, 'doubt exists whenever a *ṇ* is mentioned here; we shall understand the difference from exposition'. Thus one knows that this *paribhāṣā* exists: The understanding of particulars comes from exposition, for the existence of doubt does not imply any lack of definition.

Argument 52.2[300] [52:6

— What is the point of intimating this?
— There is doubt here in *sanīvantardha* ... (P.7.2.49). Is it in fact items ending in *-iv* or items ending in *-īv* which are meant?

Because of this *paribhāṣā* the problem does not exist. It is explained as *sani ivantānām*.

300 **This argument is not given in the *Mahābhāṣya* nor by any of the *paribhāṣā* commentators. P.7.2.49 is not commented on directly in the *Mahābhāṣya*, and the *Kāśikā* records a variant reading of the rule (KV.V.729). The Vyāḍi commentator seems to be alone in using this rule to illustrate the present *paribhāṣā*.**

Paribhāṣā 53

An item drawn in by *ca* 'and' does not recur further on.[301]

Comments All the authors who discuss this *paribhāṣā*, with the exception of the Vyāḍi commentator, agree that it is *anityā* 'not invariably true'.

Argument 53.1[302] [53:2

— How is this known?
— Because he mentions *ṇamul* [the suffix -*am*] in [the rule] *avyaye 'yathābhipretākhyāne kṛñaḥ ktvāṇamulau* (P.3.4.59).
— How come it is an intimation?
— *Ṇamul* has been made a heading, and recurs [from P.3.4.26]. In that context [i.e., P.3.4.59] it is in fact only necessary to state *ktvā*. By saying *ca*, thus: ... *ktvā ca* [instead of ... *ktvāṇamulau*], the *ṇamul* which has been made a heading will be drawn in [from P.3.4.26 into 59]. There is no point in mentioning *ṇamul* [in 59].

But the teacher observes that if *ṇamul* were drawn in here then it would not recur in rules and regulations such as *tiryacy apavarge* (P.3.4.60). Therefore *ktvā* [*sic*] is mentioned, in order that the two of them should not recur at once, further on. An item drawn in by *ca* 'and' does not recur further on.

Comments The statements about *ktvā* and the non-simultaneity of *ktvā* and *ṇamul* are puzzling (53:8). The underlying idea seems to be related to the *Kāśikā*'s proposition (KV.III.193:7–8) that *ṇamul* is mentioned so that *ktvā* and *ṇamul* should recur

---

[301] This *paribhāṣā* does not appear in the Mahābhāṣya. It is, however, discussed by all the *paribhāṣā* commentators: Puruṣottamadeva (no. 87), Sīradeva (no. 46), Nīlakaṇṭha (no. 57), Haribhāskara (no. 48), Nāgeśa (no. 78), Śeṣādrisudhī (no. 67).

It is not quoted in the *Kāśikā* or *Siddhāntakaumudī*.

[302] This argument is presented as the *jñāpaka* for the maxim by all the commentators mentioned in footnote 301, p. 196.

Although the *Kāśikā* does query the mention of *ṇamul* in P.3.4.59 it does not resort to the maxim explicitly (KV.III.192).

later with equal force. Unfortunately, the Vyāḍi commentator seems to be saying the opposite of this. There is no manuscript evidence to suggest emending the text (the readings would have to be ***tasmāt ktvā'ṇamulor' grahaṇaṃ kriyate||.[a]yugapad...***).

The ***Nyāsa's*** comments on the ***Kāśikā*** at this point are almost a paraphrase of the present ***paribhāṣā***, though it is not actually quoted (KV.III.193–94).

Argument 53.2[303] [53:10

— What is the point of intimating this?
— So that because of [the *ca* in] *vadaḥ supi kyap ca* (P.3.1.106) *yat* does not recur in *bhuvo bhāve*(P.3.1.107) [from P.3.1.97].

Comments Note that at the end of his commentary on this maxim Nīlakaṇṭha (304:13) refers to a commentary which he has written on the ***Aṣṭādhyāyī*** called the ***Pāṇinīyadīpikā***:

> ... ***asmatkṛtapāṇiniyadīpikā.***

According to Mīmāṃsaka (1973.I.494), this commentary is no longer extant, and this reference seems to be the only mention of it in the literature.

[303] This argument is given by all the commentators mentioned in footnote 301, p. 196, except Nīlakaṇṭha and Haribhāskara.

Paribhāṣā 54

When a theme is mentioned, that item with deleted *yaṅ* is included too.[304]

— Where a theme is mentioned, the item with deleted *yaṅ* [i.e., the active intensive theme] is mentioned as well.

Explanation 'Theme' is here being used in its technical sense to translate the non-Pāṇinian term *prakṛti*.

Yaṅluk 'having deletion of *yaṅ*' refers to the intensive formed with strong reduplication and the *parasmaipada* suffixes (cf. Whitney 1889.362–63).

When a theme alone is mentioned, reference to this intensive stem is also to be understood.

Argument 54.1[305] [54:3

— How is this known?
— Because in *ūd upadhāyā gohaḥ* (P.6.4.89) he mentions *upadhā* 'penultimate letter'.
— How come this is an intimation?
— By mentioning *upadhā* there, the letter *u* is meant. So the letter *u* [itself] should be used for this purpose, thus: *ū uto gohaḥ*. But the teacher observes that if it were stated in this way then the long *ū* [substitution] would also be potentially applicable to the letter *u* in the reduplicative syllable of *goh* in *joguhīti* 'he keeps very secret'. For this reason *upadhā* 'penultimate letter' is mentioned. And if, when the theme is mentioned, that item with deleted *yaṅ* is also meant then this is proper.

---

[304] This maxim is not used in the *Mahābhāṣya*.

All the *paribhāṣā* commentators treat of it: Puruṣottamadeva (no. 72), Sīradeva (no. 68), Nīlakaṇṭha (no. 76), Haribhāskara (no. 70), Nāgeśa (no. 93.9) and Śeṣādrisudhī (no. 86).

It is used in the *Siddhāntakaumudī* on P.7.3.94 (SK.III.480:1 (2651)).

[305] This argument is repeated by Puruṣottamadeva (no. 72), Sīradeva (no. 68), and Haribhāskara (no. 70).

Explanation The Vyāḍi commentator proposes rephrasing P.6.4.89, to omit the apparently unnecessary word *upadhā*.

However, if an *ū* simply replaced any *u* in *guh* which would otherwise become *o*, then it might apply to the first syllable of the intensive *joguhīti*. (Here the form was **juguhīti*. The *guṇa* is brought about by P.7.4.82). So it is after all necessary to specify that *ū* replaces only the *upadhā*.

But surely *gohaḥ* in P.6.4.89 is not the same thing as the *joguh-* of our example? Obviously, for Pāṇini the mention of *upadhā* in P.6.4.89 can only be justified if *gohaḥ* included *joguh-*. And this is a special case of our present *paribhāṣā*.

Argument 54.2 [54:10

— What is the point of intimating this?

— In *jaghnur* 'they slew' the elision of the penultimate letter is valid because of the inclusion of that item with deleted *yaṅ*.

Comments This argument is not given by any other author and is opaque.

The quotation of a perfect tense as an example of a *yaṅluk* situation seem extraordinary. It may be that the Vyāḍi commentator's example was mistaken, or altered in transmission. If it read *jaṅghan-* then some sense might be made of it, along the lines of the argument presented by Nāgeśa and others (cf. Gokhale 1913.197:2, Kielhorn 1874.446) involving intensive benedictive forms from *han* which might be liable to substitution by *vadh*, according to P.2.4.42, were it not for the *paribhāṣā*.

The mention of a nominal stem does not mean that, though alone, an item is as if it were what is denoted.[306]

— A nominal stem does not bring it about that a denotation applies also to what is alone.

Explanation This maxim is an exception, for the case of nominal stems, to a more general maxim, the *vyapadeśivadbhāva paribhāṣā*. This more general maxim teaches that when a rule applying to an item specifically designates that item, for example by reference to its context or concomitants, then the rule applies equally to that item when it is isolated.

The present *paribhāṣā* notes that this procedure does not apply when the denotation or designation is made by a nominal stem.

Comments This somewhat abstrusely expressed general maxim would seem to be non-Pāṇinian in origin, for otherwise Pāṇini could have avoided framing P.1.1.21, or could at least have simplified it.

It is odd that the Vyāḍi commentator presents the exception while not giving the general maxim first.

---

[306] The general *vyapadeśivadbhāva* maxim is known to Kātyāyana, who invokes it thrice (Mbh.I.76:23; II.75:7; III.1:8). He does not make the present exception for nominal stems.

Patañjali also uses the general maxim frequently. He mentions the present *paribhāṣā* six times as a limitation to the general maxim (Mbh.I.185:22:23, 186:5, 224:19; II.202:2:8).

This *paribhāṣā* is discussed by all the *paribhāṣā* commentators: Puruṣottamadeva (no. 79), Sīradeva (no. 56), Nīlakaṇṭha (no. 72), Haribhāskara (no. 58), Nāgeśa (no. 32), Śeṣādrisudhī (no. 32).

It is also quoted in the *Kāśikā* on P.5.2.87 (KV.IV.197).

Argument 55.1[307] [55:3

— How is that known?
— Because he says *pūrvād iniḥ* (P.5.2.86) [and also] *sapūrvāc ca* (P.5.2.87).
— How come this is an intimation?
— Because here it is only necessary to say *sapūrvāt*.
— How will it [the suffix *ini*] arise after *pūrva* when it is by itself?
— That [suffix] *ini* which arises [after an item that is] together with *pūrva* [by P.5.2.87] will arise after *pūrva* [when it is alone] because, though alone, an item is as if it were what is denoted. This being the case, because he states separately that *ini* comes after *pūrva*, so that it applies to that by itself [i.e., by stating P.5.2.86], one knows a nominal stem does not mean that an item is as if it were what is denoted.

Explanation Pāṇini gives P.5.2.86 and 87 as two separate rules. By the first the suffix *ini* may follow the word *pūrva*; by the second *ini* may follow *pūrva* when *pūrva* itself is compounded with some preceding item. The two rules generate the forms *pūrvī* and *kṛtapūrvī* respectively.

The Vyāḍi commentator argues that only the second rule is really necessary because by the general principle of *vyapadeśivadbhāva* the prescription which applies to *pūrva* when preceded by some item also applies to it when it is alone. (This is somewhat akin to the reverse of the *tadanta* principle.)

However, Pāṇini has given us the two rules separately, so he cannot, we infer, accept this proposition. Since *pūrva* is a *prātipadika*, in contrast with the examples normally used to establish the general maxim (see for example Nāgeśa pp. 59–62, on no. 30), we must deduce that the *vyapadeśivadbhāva* maxim is inoperative where *prātipadikas* are concerned.

Argument 55.2[308] [55:9

— What is the point of intimating this?
— [The suffix] *ṭhak* is prescribed after the *sūtra* [P.4.2.60]. Thus: *sāṅgrahasūtrikaḥ* 'one who knows or has studied the *saṅgrahasūtra*'. It will not arise after that [word *sūtra* when it is] by itself. Thus, he who studies a *sūtra* is a *sautra*.

---

[307] Patañjali presents this argument, though not in detail, in his discussion on *vārt.* 15 on P.1.1.72 (Mbh.I.186:5–6).

See also the *Nyāsa sub* P.5.2.87 (KV.IV.197:21–25).

It is also presented by all the *paribhāṣā* commentators mentioned in footnote 306, p. 200.

[308] Again, this argument is given by Patañjali (Mbh.I.185:22–186:1) and all the *paribhāṣā* commentators mentioned in footnote 306, p. 200, with the exception of Nīlakaṇṭha who merely refers us to the *Bhāṣya*.

Explanation This is clear. When the word *sūtra* is alone, P.4.2.60 is disqualified from applying to it, in spite of the *vyapadeśivadbhāva* principle. Thus the word *sūtra* gets the suffix *aṇ* by P.4.2.59, rather than *ṭhak* by P.4.2.60 where the suffix is applied to 'what ends in -*sūtra*'.

Mention of an item includes what is a part of that item.[309]

— If something is here part of some item then mention of that item includes it.

Comments Strangely, although this *paribhāṣā* is obviously part of Patañjali's world of discourse, it is not used by the later tradition. Its job is done by the *tanmadhyapatita paribhāṣā* (*Vyāḍīyaparibhāṣāvṛtti* no. 15). Thus, while commenting on passages where Patañjali uses the present maxim, Kaiyaṭa says: *tadekadeśavijñānād iti madhyapātino 'kajādayas tadekadeśā iti tattvabuddhiṃ na vighnanti* (*Pradīpa* I.525^b:18–19), and later Nāgeśa says: *ekadeśasadṛśyam ca madhyapātitvena bodhyam* (*Uddyota* I.526^a:20).

Argument 56.1[310] [56:2

Thus, for example, take [the names] Devadattā, Gaṅgā, Yamunā. Mention of Devadattā includes the womb which is within Devadattā. Likewise the mention of Gaṅgā or Yamunā includes the many rivers which flow into the Gaṅgā and the Yamunā. This, then, is the case in the world.

---

[309] This *paribhāṣā* is known to Patañjali, who quotes it six times, first in the context of his discussion on *vārt.* 7 on P.1.1.72 (Mbh.I.184:13:21:24) and then while discussing *vārt.* 4 on P.1.4.13 (Mbh.I.316:18:26, 317:3).

Kātyāyana is certainly using the same idea as that embodied in the *paribhāṣā* when he uses the phrase *tadekadeśavijñāna* (Mbh.I.184:12, 316:17), though for him it does not yet seem to have become a fixed *paribhāṣā* as such.

[310] This passage is identical to Patañjali's gloss on *vārt.* 7 on P.1.1.72 (I.184:13–15), even to the alternation *tadekadeśabhūtas/-bhūtam*. It is found again under *vārt.* 4 on P.1.4.13 (Mbh.I.316:19–20) in identical terms.

Argument 56.2[311] [56:4

In the discipline too it is intimated. Because he teaches the prohibition *nedam adasor akor* (P.7.1.11). How could an operation stated for *idam* and *adas* possibly apply to them when they have the letter *k* attached to them? There is [surely] no point in the prohibition. But the teacher observes that mention of an item includes what is a part of that item. So he teaches the prohibition.

Comments Note that in order to consider *imakam* and *amukam* as subject to the present maxim we must take a more active sense for *-bhūta* in the *paribhāṣā*, translating, '... includes what has become part of that item'.

Argument 56.3[312] [56:9

— What is the point of intimating this?
— The technical term 'indeclinable' is valid for *uccakaiḥ* 'high' and *nīcakaiḥ* 'low', which have the letter *k* attached to them [cf. P.1.1.37].

Explanation *Uccais* and *nīcais* are included in the *sarvādi* group which are termed 'indeclinable' by P.1.1.37.

By the present *paribhāṣā* the term 'indeclinable' may also cover the terms when the infix *akac* has become part of them.

[311] This argument is given generally as the *jñāpaka* for the *tanmadhyapatita paribhāṣā*. See footnote 200, p. 105, for references.

[312] This argument is implicit in Patañjali (Mbh.I.184:3 ff.), though not spelt out.

It is given explicitly by Nāgeśa under the *tanmadhyapatita paribhāṣā* (Nāgeśa no. 89), and similarly by Śeṣādrisudhī (no. 77).

Paribhāṣā 57

Inflectional endings change to comply with the meaning.[313]

— Having regard to the meaning, an item, though presented with the fifth [inflection] becomes a presentation with the sixth [inflection], to comply with the meaning.

Comments Note that in the wording of this *paribhāṣā*, Patañjali reads simply '*arthāt* ...' where the Vyāḍi commentator and Haribhāskara read '*arthavaśāt* ...'.

The Vyāḍi commentator's opening statement on this maxim seems needlessly specific; the inflection change from fifth to sixth is the subject of argument § 57.4. Perhaps the text has somehow come to be transposed?

Argument 57.1[314] [57:3

Thus, for example, 'Devadatta's house is tall; call him.' 'The horses and cows and the gold are Devadatta's, Devadatta, the rich son of a widow'

Explanation The point here is, of course, that the genitive 'Devadatta's' is changed to an accusative in the second half of the first sentence. In the second sentence the genitive becomes a nominative.

Comments Sharfe has offered an interesting observation on Patañjali's use of the word *vaidhaveya* 'son of a widow' (1977.160). According to him the reference is to a custom whereby a rich widow would adopt a son to avoid her inherited property falling into the hands of her late husband's family.

[313] This maxim is used five times by Patañjali, each time being accompanied by the *laukika* examples of argument § 57.1 (Mbh.I.264:14, 274:7; II.418:1; III.9:3, 328:15).

It is not quoted in the *Kāśikā* or *Siddhāntakaumudī*. It does appear in the *Nyāsa* (KV.VI.124:26–27).

It is discussed by Puruṣottamadeva (no. 88), Sīradeva (no. 120) and Haribhāskara (no. 122).

[314] These examples appear wherever the *paribhāṣā* is quoted. See footnote 313, p. 205.

Argument 57.2[315]

[57:4

It is so here in this discipline too, since he says *āṅo nāstriyām* (P.7.3.120).

— How come this is an intimation?

— Here, *nā* is required to replace the *āṅ* which follows a *ghi*. The use of the sixth [inflection] in *gheḥ* [in P.7.3.119] turns into a presentation of the fifth [inflection], because of the meaning which is present.

Explanation The word *gheḥ* in P.7.3.119 is genitive. It appears by *anuvṛtti* in P.7.3.120, but here it must be construed as an ablative of succession: 'after *ghi*'.

Comments Both this argument and the next seem to be presented as *jñāpakas*, though somewhat unclearly. There may well have been some disruption of the text here.

Argument 57.3[316]

[57:7

And the intimation comes from the fact that he presents [*pratinā* as] a final form, in *sup pratinā mātrārthe* (P.2.1.9). The mention of *sup*, which has been presented with the third [inflection], recurs here from *saha supā* (P.2.1.4). This alone would be enough to specify the third [inflection], even if it were not presented explicitly.

But no inflection would be audible after *prati*; deletion has to occur here by *avyayād āpsupaḥ* (P.2.4.82). So this intimation is generated. He observes that because of the meaning which is present, that which is presented with the third [inflection] should nevertheless end in another inflection.

Explanation The precise import of this argument is not clear, but the general drift is as follows. In P.2.1.4, Pāṇini introduces the word *supā* 'with an inflectional termination'. By the *tadanta* principle this can also mean 'with an inflected word'. This word *supā* then may recur in P.2.1.9. In that rule the word *pratinā* is stated, with the same third inflection as *supā*. In actual use this inflection after *prati* will be deleted. Somehow this suggests the *paribhāṣā*.

Comments Note that this argument is quite distinct from the common discussion about the necessity of *sup* in P.2.1.9, which could apparently be understood by *anuvṛtti* from P.2.1.2 (e.g., in the second half of the post-*Bhāṣya kārikā* in *Kāśikā* II.26:4). It is hard to escape the impression that the Vyāḍi commentator knew that P.2.1.9 involved some problem about *anuvṛtti*, but that he went off on the wrong tack.

---

[315] This argument appears in the *Nyāsa sub* P.7.3.120 (KV.VI.124:26–27). It is also quoted by Puruṣottamadeva (no. 88) and Sīradeva (no. 120).

[316] This argument appears to be unique to the Vyāḍi commentator.

Argument 57.4[317] [57:13

— What is the point of intimating this?
— In *āne muk* (P.7.2.82) *ataḥ* [from P.7.2.80] is present. It was presented [originally] with the fifth [inflection], but comes to be presented [here] with the sixth [inflection]. If this be so, the citations in the discipline are to be made 'of it' [i.e., 'of the *at*' of P.7.2.80].

Comments The slightly obscure statement at the end of this argument (57:14–15) seems simply to be emphasizing the genitive character of *ataḥ* when imported into in P.7.2.82, and broadening it to apply to all cases where P.7.2.82 applies. Abhyankar has emended the text to reverse the sense, but this is not necessary.

Argument 57.5[318] [57:16

— ... *ekavac cāsyānyatarasyām* (P.1.2.69) and *vaś cāsyānyatarasyām* ... (P.6.1.39) are stated in order to intimate the invariance of this [*paribhāṣā*].

Explanation The reason why the Vyāḍi commentator thinks that these two rules should show the *nityatva* of this *paribhāṣā* is not absolutely clear.

Certainly the presence of the word *asya* in each rule could be challenged:[319] in P.6.1.39 particularly, it merely refers to *vayas* (P.6.1.38) which is already genitive. Perhaps, therefore, the idea is that, had it not been for *asya*, the case of *vayas* would have changed to something else.

Comments The text would read more easily with Abhyankar's tempting emendment, which reverses the sense: because of *asya* in these sūtras, the *paribhāṣā* is *not* invariant. But there is no manuscript evidence for such a reading, and the general problems of interpreting the text on this *paribhāṣā* suggest that a piecemeal patching of the text is not a proper solution to the difficulties. Either the Vyāḍi commentator simply got it wrong at this point, or some more pervasive problem has arisen in the transmission of the text.

---

[317] This argument is adumbrated in the *Mahābhāṣya* on P.7.2.82 (Mbh.III.303:18–23). However, the *paribhāṣā* itself is not invoked to solve the *ataḥ* problem, but instead a rather vague assertion with reference to P.1.1.66. Neither the *Pradīpa* nor the *Uddyota* mention the *paribhāṣā* here either.

The *Kāśikā* and its subcommentaries present essentially the same argument as the *Mahābhāṣya*, again without quoting the *paribhāṣā* explicitly (KV.V.764). Similarly, see the subcommentaries on the *Siddhāntakaumudī* (SK.IV.116–117 (3101)).

This argument, in the Vyāḍi commentator's form, is used by Puruṣottamadeva (no. 88).

[318] The Vyāḍi commentator seem to be unique in quoting these rules for this purpose. The *asya* in P.1.2.69 is questioned by Jinendrabuddhi (KV.I.385:23–28) and Jñānendrasarasvatī (SK.II.210:28–30 (935)), and Viṭṭhala (PK.I.642:13–16), but it is decided that it is there for clarity's sake; it is nothing to do with the *paribhāṣā*.

Patañjali queries the necessity of *vaś cāsya* in P.6.1.39 (Mbh.III.33:19 ff.). But it is not until Haradatta that the presence of *asya* is specifically queried (*Padamañjarī* KV.IV.495:14–16). And Rāmacandra drops *asya* from P.6.1.39 altogether (PK.II.173:9), without comment. (It is restored in *Siddhāntakaumudī* etc., SK.III.250 (2414).) None of these authors mentions the *paribhāṣā*.

[319] See footnote 318, p. 207 above.

The application of rules is like the rain.[320]

— Here in the discipline a rule appears like the rain.

Argument 58.1[321] [58:2

Thus for example, the rain falls just as much on the empty as on the full; it does not rain only on what is not full.

Argument 58.2[322] [58:3

The same goes for a rule: a long vowel gets lengthened. [For example:]

cicīṣati 'he wants to pile up',
bubhūṣati 'he wants to become'.

Explanation The root *ci* has short *i*. This is lengthened in the desiderative by P.6.4.16. The root *bhū* already has a long vowel, but is not excluded from the action of P.6.4.16. There is, of course, no apparent effect in this case.

[320]This maxim goes back to the *Mahābhāṣya* where Patañjali twice quotes a different form of it (Mbh.I.196:15; III.89:16): *kṛtakāri khalv api śāstraṃ parjanyavat*.

It does not appear in the *Kāśikā* or *Siddhāntakaumudī*.

It is discussed by all the *paribhāṣā* commentators: Puruṣottamadeva (no. 86), Sīradeva (no. 87), Nīlakaṇṭha (no. 111), Haribhāskara (no. 90), Nāgeśa (no. 111) and Śeṣādrisudhī (no. 103).

[321]This worldly example is given twice in the *Mahābhāṣya*, when the *kṛtakāri* maxim is presented (see footnote 320, p. 208). All the commentators either quote it or refer to it; Nāgeśa (no. 111) and Śeṣādrisudhī (no. 103) however keep to *śāstric* arguments.

[322]This argument, simple as it is, seems unique to the Vyāḍi commentator.

Argument 58.3[323] [58:5

— How is this known?

— Because in *pravāhaṇasya dhe* (P.7.3.28) he teaches the prohibition of another *vṛddhi* for the word *vāhana* which has *vṛddhi* anyway. But the teacher observes the *vṛddhi* applies even where *vṛddhi* already exists, because the application of rules is like the rain.

Explanation In P.7.3.28, Pāṇini teaches that *vṛddhi* is optional for the first part of *pra-vāhana*, but prohibited for the second (*na* from P.7.3.27). But *vāhana* already has *vṛddhi*. So by prohibiting it Pāṇini is demonstrating his belief that the rule would apply in any case, whether or not *vṛddhi* were there. In general terms, that is, a rule applies irrespective of its target.

Comments This argument is based on a reading of the *anuvṛtti* in P.7.3.28 which is totally different from the rest of the tradition. Everything revolves around the *na* in the previous rule, P.7.3.27. For the Vyāḍi commentator, this *na* is read into P.7.3.28. Thus *vṛddhi* is optional for the first part of the word, *pra*, as it would be anyway (*na vā* being taken as identical to *vā*), while a new *vṛddhi* is negated for *-vāhana*. Given this, the Vyāḍi commentator's argument makes perfect sense. But the rest of the tradition does not give this. Everyone else agrees that the *na* is not read into P.7.3.28. For them, *vṛddhi* is prescribed for *vāhana* in spite of the redundancy (*piṣṭapeṣaṇam*).

The whole question can be traced back to Patañjali who, in discussing P.7.3.28 (Mbh.III.322), raises just this question about the *anuvṛtti* of *na*. The discussion involves P.6.3.39, whose application is desired. But it can only apply if the *vṛddhi* is prescribed in P.7.3.28. But then another argument is put forward which would allow *na* to be read in P.7.3.28 after all (Mbh.III.322:4–6). (Note that the discussion assumes the *prāptāprāpta* theory of negative options.)

Thus, the *Mahābhāṣya* itself would appear to support the Vyāḍi commentator's interpretation of P.7.3.28, while all other available commentators, as well as Candragomin and Devanandin, rest with the first half of Patañjali's little dialogue.

Confusingly, Kaiyaṭa seems to draw the wrong conclusion from Patañjali's discussion (*Pradīpa* VI.195). Jinendrabuddhi and Haradatta struggle with this (KV.VI.32–33) coming to yet another solution, that *na* intimates the non-invariance of the prohibition in P.6.3.41, and Nāgeśa echoes Haradatta's conclusion in his *Uddyota* on Kaiyaṭa (*Uddyota* VI.195).

Of course, to know whether Pāṇini himself intended to read *na* in P.7.3.28 one would need an objective test of the kind used by Kiparsky (1979). Unfortunately Kiparsky does not discuss P.7.3.28, although one would have expected him to do so, since it is a testable option rule. In general terms, Kiparsky argues persuasively that *vā* and *na vā* mean different things in the Aṣṭādhyāyī. *Vā* means 'preferably', while *na vā* means 'preferably not' (1979:11 *et passim*). In the present case the *anuvṛtti* of *na* in P.7.3.28 would thus make *pravāhaṇeyaḥ* the favoured option, and *prāvāhaṇeyaḥ* the rarer form. This is not the place for a word frequency investigation; the fact that Monier Williams quotes the first form only from grammatical sources, the second

[323] The Vyāḍi commentator seems alone in using this precise argument (see the discussion). Different but related arguments, based on P.7.3.28, are presented by Puruṣottamadeva (no. 86), Sīradeva (no. 87) and Haribhāskara (no. 90).

also from '*Pravara* texts', is inconclusive. Patañjali uses only the first form, in the feminine. It is enough here to point out that the problem is theoretically soluble.

The main point, to sum up, is that the Vyāḍi commentator stands over against the rest of the tradition in considering *na* to be read in P.7.3.28 by *anuvṛtti* form P.7.3.27.

Note that although an almost identical argument is proposed by several of the commentators (see footnote 323, p. 209) it is in fact based on the premise that *vṛddhi* alone recurs, and is therefore being prescribed in P.7.3.28. The argument is far less clear or convincing than the Vyāḍi commentator's. It is tempting to see here a traditional argument from P.7.3.28, with *anuvṛtti* of *na*, being fudged to work in the opposite circumstance.

Argument 58.4[324] [58:8

— What is the point of intimating this?
— In *khaṭvāḍhakam* 'half a stone of bed [?]' there is a long [vowel] in place of the preceding *a*, *i*, *u*, *ṛ* or *ḷ* and the following homorganic vowel [by P.6.1.101] even though they are long already.

Explanation The example is made up of *khaṭvā* + *āḍhakam*. The rule P.6.1.101, which applies here, prescribes a long substitute for the junction vowels. But they are both long already. By the *paribhāṣā*, the rule applies notwithstanding.

[324]The expression *khaṭvāḍhakam* is Patañjali's (Mbh.I.16:1), but this argument seems to be the Vyāḍi commentator's.

Paribhāṣā 59

Pāṇinians do not have fixed arrangements.[325]

— *Vyūha* 'arrangement' means *racanā* 'organizing', the accomplishment of what is generally applicable. In the opinion of the Pāṇinian teachers, establishing, arrangement, definition, organizing are as if they were not done. Having once seen an operation then all that has been done is waived.

Explanation The sense of this *paribhāṣā* as interpreted by the Vyāḍi commentator is that in Pāṇinian derivations the order of the application of rules is not fixed.

Comments As expounded by the Vyāḍi commentator, this maxim teaches an extreme *lakṣyaikacakṣuṣka* position: word derivations are goal-driven. Also implicit is the *siddha* principle, as propounded by Joshi and Kiparsky (1979), whereby all rules potentially apply, or compete for application, unless otherwise stated (1979.228: *sarvatra siddham*).

The meaning of the *paribhāṣā* changes in the hands of other interpreters: the intermediate position, held up to the time of the *Siddhāntakaumudī*, is that the maxim means 'when the cause disappears, so does its effect' (*kāraṇanāśe kāryanāśaḥ*). This is equivalent to *Vyāḍīyaparibhāṣāvṛtti* no. 35. In some circumstances, with this interpretation, the form which is sought can affect the derivation which leads to it, as a sort of Aristotelian final cause. Eventually, with Nāgeśa, even this compromise is rejected. The pure *lakṣaṇaikacakṣuṣka* view is upheld: language is produced through the operation of perfect grammatical rules, with no element of feedback. The collocation *yathāprāpta* (*Vyāḍīyaparibhāṣāvṛtti* 59:2) is typical of the *Mahābhāṣya*'s style, and occurs a dozen times. Joshi and Roodbergen (1975.126, note 357) interpret it to mean that a form is to be derived according to the general rule, if a special rule is not applied.

[325]This maxim is not used in the *Mahābhāṣya*.

It is explained by all the *paribhāṣā* commentators: Puruṣottamadeva (no. 104), Sīradeva (no. 49), Nīlakaṇṭha (no. 61), Haribhāskara (no. 51), Nāgeśa (no. 56) and Śeṣādrisudhī (no. 48).

It does not appear in the *Kāśikā*, but is quoted in the *Siddhāntakaumudī* three times, under P.1.3.11, 6.3.138, 6.4.131 (SK.I.53:1 (46), 424:3, 444:4). It is also glossed by the *Bālamanoramā* (SK.I.54:8 ff. (46)) and the *Tattvabodhinī* (SK.I.54:18 ff. (46)).

Argument 59.1[326] [59:5

— How is this known?
— Because in *ur ṛt* (P.7.4.7) he says that *ṛ* replaces *ṛ*.
— How come this is an intimation?
— Because on this, it is said that items such as *vṛt* etc., before *ṇi*, when *caṅ* follows [i.e., in the causative aorist] get just *ṛ*. But before *ṇi* it is necessary that the letter *ṛ* in them must undergo the *guṇa* due for a light penultimate letter [by P.7.3.86] or the *vṛddhi* [by P.7.2.115], or have their penultimate letter replaced by *i* [by P.7.1.101]. Once these have been generated, this *ṛ* does not arise.

It would be proper, in this case, to say 'replace *ir*, *ar* and *ār* by *ṛ*' [instead of P.7.4.7]. So by saying *ur ṛt* (P.7.4.7) he is intimating that once the operations of *guṇa*, *vṛddhi* and the replacement of the penultimate letter by *i* have been seen, they are waived.

Comments The problem here raised by P.7.4.7 is recognised in the *Kāśikā*, and solved there by invoking *vacanaprāmāṇya* (KV.VI.136:3–4 and subcommentaries).

Since this argument does not appear elsewhere, one does not know what to make of the Vyāḍi commentator's '*ucyate*' (59:7).

Argument 59.2[327] [59:11

— What is the point of intimating this?
— One whose village has a benevolent leading family is a *priyagrāmaṇikaḥ*. Once [the *bahuvrīhi* suffix] *kap* has been generated by *śeṣād vibhāṣā* (P.5.4:154) then the shortening [of the *i* in *grāmaṇi*, from *grāmaṇī*] is waived; next the shortening is brought about by *hrasvo napuṃsake* ... (P.1.2.47).
— It is said, what is the difference here? No difference is suggested as far as *priyagrāmaṇikaḥ* is concerned.
— A difference does exist. It is this: there is a prohibition [of the shortening] by *na kapi* (P.7.4.14), and a prescription [of it] by *ke 'ṇaḥ* (P.7.4.13). This prohibition is of this [particular] prescription. If the shortening is prescribed [by P.1.2.47] the is will not be prohibited. Therefore the shortening comes about by *hrasvo napuṃsake prātipadikasya* (P.1.2.47).

The prohibition *na kapi* (P.7.4.14) does not arise.

---

[326] This argument seem unique to the Vyāḍi commentator as a *jñāpaka* for the *paribhāṣā*.

[327] The problem is raised first by Patañjali under *vārt.* 7 on P.1.2.49 (Mbh.I.225:4–12), although it is not solved using the *paribhāṣā*.

This argument is not presented by any of the *paribhāṣā* commentators in their discussion of this maxim.

Explanation The derivation of the form *priyagrāmaṇika* with the removal of the inflections is:

priya-s	+	*grāmaṇī-s*	
priya	+	*grāmaṇī*	by P.2.4.71
priyagrāmaṇī	+	*kap*	by P.5.4.154

At this point the *ī* may be shortened by two different rules: P.1.2.47 or P.7.4.13. In general terms the latter would normally be chosen because of *paratva*, although the Vyāḍi commentator does not make this explicit. If P.7.4.13 is chosen, however, the immediately subsequent rule, P.7.4.14, causes problems. By applying the *paribhāṣā* we may choose the option that suits us, which is P.1.2.47. Thus the *ī* is shortened and the desired form attained.

Comments This particular problem of *priyagrāmaṇikaḥ* is normally solved by adopting the *kramānvākhyānapakṣa*, i.e., deriving the form by gradually adding on its elements, in conjunction with the *antaraṅga* principle.

Paribhāṣā 60

The specification of *-tara* is not the main point.[328]

— The specification of *-tara* [the comparative suffix] is not of principal importance; it signifies that meaning which is present when it is stated. It has the sense of that nominal stem after which it is prescribed.

Explanation Pāṇini prescribes the suffix *-tara* to express the superiority of one item over a second (P.5.3.57). The present *paribhāṣā* allows the suffix to be used in some cases without special reference to its prescribed function, but simply to express the sense of the base to which it is attached, as what might be called a semantic enclitic.

Comments The Vyāḍi commentator's use of *apradhāna* to gloss *atantra* is interesting since *pradhāna* is the first meaning given to *tantra* in the *Amarakośa* (Amara 1969, line 2705). This does suggest that the Vyāḍi commentator knew a *kośa*, but takes us no further than that.[329]

The opening sentences are not very well expressed. The point is, of course, that *tara* is *svārthe*.

[328]This maxim is known to Kātyāyana who quotes it in *vārt.* 1 on P.2.2.34. This *vārttika* is then discussed by Patañjali (Mbh.I.435–36). This whole section of the *Mahābhāṣya* has been translated and discussed in some detail by Roodbergen and Joshi (1974.lxvii–lxviii, 206–11). The idea behind the maxim is discussed in another passage which occurs, almost verbatim, four times in the *Mahābhāṣya* (Mbh.I.211–12; II.144:13, 172:20, 245:20). This passage is full of the homely metaphor which makes the *Mahābhāṣya* so enjoyable. Finally the maxim is quoted twice, explicitly, in Patañjali's discussion of P.1.2.33 (Mbh.I.210:6:9). Its opposite, *tantram taranirdeśaḥ* is quoted a few lines later (210:12).

The *paribhāṣā* is not discussed by any of the *paribhāṣā* commentators, and is not mentioned in the *Kāśikā* on P.2.2.34 (although *Haradatta* makes the point without actually citing the *paribhāṣā* (KV.II.145:10 ff.)).

[329]See Introduction, p. xviii.

Argument 60.1[330] [60:4

— How is that known?
— Because he says [the rule] *kimettiṅavyayaghād āmv adravya-prakarṣe* (P.5.4.11).
— How come this is an intimation?
— Here, *āmu* [the suffix *ām*] is prescribed after a *gha* in cases other than when a thing is superior. And that is not possible. Because this term *gha* means *tarap* and *tamap* [the comparative and superlative suffixes]. And if it says 'not when a thing is superior' how can it [P.5.4.11] possibly apply, since those two mean the superiority of a thing?

Thus the teacher is observing that these two, *tara* etc., are prescribed in the sense of the item [i.e., the stem] itself. They are dependent on the meaning of the nominal stem.

[The suffix] *āmu* occurs after a *gha*, when a thing is not superior.

Comments The Vyāḍi commentator's argument seems to be based on a very idiosyncratic interpretation of P.5.4.11. The main tradition takes *adravyaprakarṣe* in that rule to mean that the suffix in question, -*ām*, can apply only in adverbial circumstances, not in adjectival ones. The Vyāḍi commentator seems to forget the word *dravya*-, and interprets the rule as a prescription of -*ām* in situations where no *prakarṣa* 'excellence' is denoted. This is not the standard explanation of the rule.

Alternatively, one might think the Vyāḍi commentator is taking *atiśayana* in P.5.3.57 as being specifically *dravyātiśayana*. But this seems highly improbable, since *tiṅaḥ* recurs in P.5.3.57 from 56.

Argument 60.2[331] [60:11

— What is the point of intimating this?
— It is established that *uccaistarām* 'high(-er)' means just 'high'; *śreṣṭhatama* means just 'best'.

Explanation The point in these two examples is that the addition of -*tara* and -*tama* makes no difference to the sense of the words without these suffixes.

[330]In his discussion on *vārt.* 2 on P.6.2.139 (Mbh.III.136:1–3) Patañjali recognizes that -*ām* prescribed after -*tara* is *svārtha*. But the Vyāḍi commentator's argument as such does not appear in the *Mahābhāṣya*.

[331]This argument, with the first example, is used by Patañjali in his comment on P.1.2.33 (Mbh.I.210:6–7). The example of *śreṣṭhatama* is used by Kātyāyana in *vārt.* 3 on P.5.3.55 (Mbh.II.416:3) as part of a quotation illustrating that a word which is already superlative may have a further superlative suffix, which carries no special sense of its own (it is *svārthika*).

Comments Note the interesting derivation of *śreṣṭha* from the root *śaṃs* (Dhp.1.764):

praśasya	+	*iṣṭha*	by P.5.3.55
śra	+	*iṣṭha*	by P.5.3.60
śreṣṭha			by P.6.1.87

Of similar interest are the derivations of *jyeṣṭha* and *jyāyān* from *praśasya* (P.5.3.61) and several others in these rules and in P.6.4.154–163.

Paribhāṣā 61

Of two items taught, one principal and one appended, that taught as principal is meant.[332]

— 'One principal and one appended' means a principal item and an appended item. ['Two items taught' means] what is taught as a principal item and what is taught as an appended item, not together. And where there is nothing to prove that it is the appended item [which is meant] then the item taught as principal is [assumed to apply].

Argument 61.1 [61:4

— Why, though, would it fail to apply?
— Because 'of items taught in conjunction, if one of the two disappears, both of them cease to exist (*paribhāṣā* 36)'.

Argument 61.2 [61:5

— What, then, is the principal item, and what the appended?
— The principal item is that for the sake of which the rule is framed; when something else has to be prescribed, then whatever else is stated, as 'this being so, this occurs', is the appended item.

[332]This *paribhāṣā* does not appear as such in the *Mahābhāṣya* or in the *paribhāṣā* commentaries. However the notion of *anvācaya* 'appending' was known to Kātyāyana (*vārttikas* 16 on P.1.1.44 and 4 on P.7.3.119) and in three places Patañjali draws a distinction between items which are *pradhānaśiṣṭa* and others which are *anvācayaśiṣṭa* (Mbh.II.20:22, 21:21; III.343:1). The first of these passages is clearly the source of the other two: the second is identical to the first, while the third refers back explicitly to the first. (Curiously, *vārt.* 4 on P.7.3.119 appears to refer back to Patañjali's discussion on P.3.1.11.) The present *paribhāṣā* is clearly a formalization of Patañjali's procedure. The *paribhāṣā* commentators discuss a maxim which is similar to the present one, *pradhānāpradhānayoḥ pradhāne kāryasaṃpratyayaḥ*. However the examples and intimations given are different.

Otherwise this maxim, as given by the Vyāḍi commentator, appears only amongst the non-Pāṇinian schools, where it is common.

Argument 61.3[333] [61:8

— How is it known that this *paribhāṣā* exists?
— In the world it is like this: one person says to another 'go for alms, and [while you are about it] bring back Devadatta'.

He then does both. But if he cannot find Devadatta then the alms round [still] takes place.

Argument 61.4[334] [61:11

— In the discipline too there is an initiation: the mention of *seṭ* in *thali ca seṭīḍ anto vā* (P.6.1.196).
— How come this is an intimation?
— It is unnecessary to mention *seṭ* in this rule. One should [just] say *thalīḍ anto vā*. Because of the acute accent specifically on *iṭ*, it is certain that it [the root] is *seṭ*. There is no point in mentioning *seṭ*. But the teacher observes that before *thal* [2nd sg. perfect inflection] the initial, final and perfect tense accents [P.6.1.193, 195, 196] are the principally taught item, and the accent on *iṭ* is taught as an appendix. So wherever there is *iṭ* there are four [syllables liable for acute accent]. Where, though, there is no *iṭ* then 'of two items taught, one principal and one appended, that taught as principal is desirable.' So three accents are possible. *Seṭ* is mentioned [in P.6.1.196] so that they should not apply when there is no *iṭ*.

Explanation This argument is not as complicated as it at first appears. In P.6.1.196 Pāṇini teaches the accentuation of *iṭ* for a word which has *iṭ*. This seems an unnecessary repetition until we realize that this accentuation also applies to three other vowels in the word. And these are what are in fact being principally taught: the prescription of the *iṭ* accent is merely an appendix. So the rule is really teaching that the three other accents are possible for a word with *iṭ* in it, and also that that very *iṭ* may also be accented. It is the primary burden of the rule which is really meant. Given that, the word *seṭ* in P.6.1.196 is not redundant.

Comments In 61:2 of the Vyāḍi commentator's text there is some confusion of genders. If *anvācaya* is masculine, *pradhāna* should take an adjectival function too, and be masculine. Or if left neuter, then *tau* should be changed to *te* in accordance with P.1.2.69. Cf. *pradhānaḥ* in 61:22, *pradhānam* elsewhere.

---

[333] This little story goes back to Patañjali, who quotes it in the first of the three contexts mentioned in footnote 332, p. 217 (Mbh.II.20:23–24).

[334] This question about *seṭ* in P.6.1.196 is found in the *Mahābhāṣya*, in Patañjali's comments on that rule (Mbh.III.115–16), although the *paribhāṣā* is not explicitly invoked there. The same question is echoed in the *Kāśikā* (KV.IV.676:8) and in the *Padamañjarī* (KV.IV.676:21 ff.) and by Nāgeśa (*Laghuśabdenduśekhara* IV.525:30–526), and Kaiyaṭa (*Pradīpa* V.174^b). None of these authors refers to the *paribhāṣā*.

In 61:14 the reading of all the MSS is *liṭsvara*. A reading *litsvara*, if available, would be preferred. *Liṭ* is not wrong, since *liṭ* is *lit*. But the reference is clearly to P.6.1.193. Cf. *Laghuśabdenduśekhara* IV.526:17 and Kaiyaṭa's *Pradīpa* V.174[b]:6.

The usual examples quoted to show the working of P.6.1.196 are *lulavitha*, where the acute accent may be on any one of the vowels, and *yayắthâ* which is *aniṭ* and is therefore exempt from the action of P.6.1.196. In Jayakṛṣṇa's *Subodhinī* subcommentary on this issue there seems to be a misprint: for *yathā thali svaraḥ* (SK.IV.525:11 (3732)) read instead *yayātha litsvaraḥ*. The mistake is an easy one in Devanāgarī.

Finally, let us note that if we follow Nāgeśa, this *paribhāṣā* could not possibly apply here in any case. The Vyāḍi commentator has told us (61:4–5) that this maxim is given to counteract *paribhāṣā* 36. But in the *Uddyota* on P.6.1.196 (V.174[b]:14) Nāgeśa notes that these accents are not *sanniyogaśiṣṭa*: they are taught *paryāyeṇa*, one after another. So *paribhāṣā* 61 has no scope here.

Argument 61.5[335] [61:18

— What is the point of intimating this?

— Because here in *avyayasarvanāmnām akac prāk ṭeḥ, kasya ca daḥ* (P.5.3.71 and 72), the letter *d* is taught in conjunction with *akac* and as a replacement for [the letter] *k*. That *akac* is a suffix. It would only arise where the letter *d* replaces the letter *k*. However, if this [*paribhāṣā*] exists then there is no problem. *Akac* is the principal item here, the letter *d* the appended. So *akac* is also valid wherever the letter *d* does not replace the letter *k*.

Explanation The argument really only makes sense if we assume that P.5.3.71 and 72 are a single rule. On this assumption, the rule teaches that pronouns and indeclinables may take the infix *akac*, and their final *k* is replaced by *d*. Applying *paribhāṣā* 36, these two operations would have to go together, and if one failed to occur, the other would also not occur. This would mean that *akac* could only apply to words whose final *k* was being replaced by *d*. This is absurd. The present *paribhāṣā*, no. 61, solves the problem. The replacement is subsidiary to the infixation, so the latter is what is meant primarily. The replacement may or may not take place once the infixation has occurred.

Comments The word *saṃniyogena* used by the Vyāḍi commentator in glossing P.5.3.71–72 (61:19) does not appear in the *Mahābhāṣya*'s discussion of these rules, but it does occur in almost all the *sūtra vṛttis*: see the *Kāśikā* (KV.IV.293:6) and the *Cāndravṛtti* (on Ca.4.3.57). This suggests that the Vyāḍi commentator did have some gloss on the *sūtras*, other than the *Mahābhāṣya*, before him.

On the question of taking P.5.3.71 and 72 as one rule, it is of interest to note that the *Mahābhāṣya* comments on these rules together as one statement (Mbh.I.422). Although the first rule is several times quoted alone by Patañjali, this does not entirely rule out the possibility of there being originally a single rule. The *Bhāṣāvṛtti* also comments on P.5.3.71–72 as one statement.

---

[335] This argument does not appear in the *Mahābhāṣya*, nor in the *Kāśikā* or *Siddhāntakaumudī* on P.5.3.71–72.

What is required is obtained by splitting the rule.[336]

Explanation Although not perfectly clear from the Vyāḍi commentator's treatment, this maxim normally means that *only* what is required is obtained by splitting the rule: any unwanted side-effects are ignored.

Comments The Vyāḍi commentator seems to take this maxim to mean that one can use *yogavibhāga* to get what one wants.

Argument 62.1[337] [62:2

— How is it known that this *paribhāṣā* exists?

— Because he mentions *bahuvacana* 'plural' in *tiṣyapunarvasvor nakṣatradvandve* ... (P.1.2.63).

— How come this is an intimation?

— There are in fact several *tiṣyas* and *punarvasus* [i.e., stars in the constellations]. So it is correct that it [the *dvandva*] should be plural. There is no point in mentioning 'plural' [in P.1.2.63]. But the teacher observes that the splitting of a rule takes placed in *vibhāṣā vṛkṣamṛga* ... (P.2.4.12), so that 'all *dvandvas* may optionally be singular (*paribhāṣā* 67)'. To avoid this the mention of 'plural' is made, [and] it is an intimation.

---

[336]This principle is not used in the *Mahābhāṣya*, although the idea of *yogavibhāga* is very common.

It is discussed by all the *paribhāṣā* commentators: Puruṣottamadeva (no. 100), Sīradeva (no. 121), Nīlakaṇṭha (no. 115), Haribhāskara (no. 123), Nāgeśa (no. 114).

[337]While discussing *vārt.* 5 on P.2.4.12 Patañjali makes some remarks which resemble this argument (Mbh.I.476–477:2). But they are not quite the same: he is suggesting that *paribhāṣā* 67 is intimated by P.1.2.63, but he does not take the next step of deducing *paribhāṣā* 62. The same remarks are reproduced in the *Kāśikā* on P.1.2.63 (KV.I.372:1–4). The same view is repeated by the *paribhāṣā* commentators on the *dvandvaikavadbhāva paribhāṣā:* Puruṣottamadeva (no. 50), Sīradeva (no. 16), Nīlakaṇṭha (no. 22), Haribhāskara (no. 16), Nāgeśa (no. 34) and Śeṣādrisudhī (no. 34).

Explanation The only reason for specifying *bahuvacana* 'plural' in P.1.2.63 is that *dvandvas* could conceivably be something else, i.e., singular. But as the *sūtras* stand there is not general rule permitting *dvandvas* to be singular. If, however, P.2.4.12 is split into two parts then singular *dvandvas* are indeed a possibility in all cases and it becomes necessary to specify 'plural' in P.1.2.63 to exclude these singular forms. Thus, *bahuvacana* in P.1.2.63 intimates that *yogavibhāga* is an accepted method and is used by Pāṇini to provide singular dvandvas.

Comments The Vyāḍi commentator seems to be alone in using this argument to prove *paribhāṣā* 62. All other authorities use this argument to prove *paribhāṣā* 67.

Argument 62.2[338] [62:8

— What is the point of intimating this?

— The splitting of the rule *asmado dvayoś ca* (P.1.2.59) is valid.

After *asmad* [1st person pronoun] the plural is valid when there is one item. And then after *asmad* the plural is valid when there are two objects.

It is wrong to say about that [i.e., P.1.2.59] that the word *ca* 'and' is put there in order to make an option.

Explanation This argument is somewhat unclear, unless we assume that *ekasmin* 'when one item is present' does not recur in P.1.2.55 from the previous rule, P.1.2.58. In that case, the rule *asmado dvayoś ca* would mean that the first person pronoun can optionally be pluralized when two items are present. (cf. Kielhorn 1874.171 fn.2). To get the required inclusion of the pluralization when only one item is present it would then be necessary to split P.1.2.59 into *asmadaḥ*, with *ekasmin* recurring from 58, and *dvayoś ca*. The *paribhāṣā* makes this possible.

Comments One again the Vyāḍi commentator seems to be on his own. It is particularly puzzling that in his last sentence (62:10–11) he appears to be quoting someone's opinion that *ca* in P.1.2.59 is *vikalpārtha*. I can trace no mention of this point of view. No other authors seem to use the technique of *yogavibhāga* to interpret P.1.2.59. The general consensus is that the *ca* indicates the *anukarṣa* 'concatenation' of *dvayoś* to *ekasmin* etc. (e.g. *Bālamanoramā* SK.II.122:17–18 (818): *cena dvayor ity anukarṣaḥ*).

[338] I can find no trace of an argument along these lines in the standard sources, except perhaps for Jñānendrasarasvatī's statement that because of *ca*, *ekasmin* etc., recurs in P.1.2.59 from 58 (*Tattvabodhinī* SK.II.122:26–27 (817)). But this is not linked with the *paribhāṣā*.

The *tadanta* rule does not apply to a rule about a nominal stem.[339]

— Where a nominal stem is mentioned and then an operation is stated, the *tadanta* rule [P.1.1.72] does not exist.

Explanation The *tadanta* rule is of course P.1.1.72, which prescribes that an operation ordained with respect to some item X also applies to items ending in X. The present *paribhāṣā* teaches that this general maxim does not apply to rules about whole nominal stems.

Comments The Vyāḍi commentator's simple phrasing is unique. From Patañjali onwards all other authors quote the maxim as beginning with *grahaṇavatā*, a form which causes commentators some difficulty (see Kielhorn 1874.160 fn.2).

Argument 63.1[340] [63:3

— How is that known?
— Because here in *senāntalakṣaṇakāribhyaś ca* (P.4.1.152), he makes mention of *anta* 'end'.
— How come this is an intimation?
— It is not necessary to mention *anta* here; *senālakṣaṇa* is sufficient by itself, because of the assertion *yena vidhis tadantasya* (P.1.1.72). [Thus]

Hāriṣeṇya 'descendant of Hariṣena',
Vāriṣeṇya 'descendant of Variṣena'.

---

[339] This maxim is known to Kātyāyana who assumes it in *vārt.* 1 on P.4.1.14. It is known to Patañjali in a slightly different phrasing (*grahaṇavatā prātipadikena* ...). He quotes it thus nine times (Mbh.II.201:13:21, 202:5, 205:12, 345:11:16, 370:1, 385:18, 401:7).

It appears in the *Kāśikā* on P.4.1.4, 5.1.20, 5.2.56, 5.2.87 (KV.III.276, KV.IV.30, 176, 197.).

It is discussed by all the *paribhāṣā* commentators: Puruṣottamadeva (no. 78), Sīradeva (no. 55), Nīlakaṇṭha (no. 71), Haribhāskara (no. 57), Nāgeśa (no. 31), Śeṣādrisudhī (no. 31).

[340] This argument does not appear in the *Mahābhāṣya*, nor in the *Kāśikā*. But in his commentary on the latter, Jinendrabuddhi does cite the *grahaṇavatā prātipadikena paribhāṣā* as an explanation for the word *anta* in P.4.1.152.

The *paribhāṣā* commentators do not argue from P.4.1.152.

Because of the *tadanta* rule it [the suffix *ṇya*] will apply after what ends in *sena*, as well. So by mentioning *anta* here [in P.4.1.152] he is intimating that this *paribhāṣā* does exist.

Argument 63.2[341]

[63:9

— What is the point of intimating this?
— The descendant of Sūtranaḍa is Sautranāḍi. The *tadanta* rule does not make [the suffix] *phak* apply [by P.4.1.99].

Explanation P.4.1.99 prescribes the suffix *phak* after *naḍa* etc., to express 'descendant of'. Thus *naḍa* + *phak* → *nāḍāyana* (cf. P.7.2.118 and 7.1.2.). But because of the present *paribhāṣā*, P.4.1.99 does not apply to items *ending* in the nominal stem *naḍa*. So a descendant of Sūtranaḍa is named by adding the suffix *iñ* (P.4.1.95), not *phak*.

[341] This example is common as an illustration of the suspension of *tadantavidhi*. But it is usually linked with *vārt.* 3 on P.1.1.72, which prohibits *tadantavidhi* in rules about suffixes (Mbh.I.183:17). The example itself, 'Sautranāḍi', is Patañjali's (Mbh.I.183:20). It is quoted thereafter by most commentators on P.1.1.72 *Kāśikā (KV.I.253:3)*, *Nyāsa* (KV.I.254:18–20), *Bālamanoramā* (SK.I.38:14–16 (26)). It is the regular *prayojana* for the *paribhāṣā* cited by the commentators: Puruṣottamadeva (no. 78), Sīradeva (no. 55), and Haribhāskara (no. 57).

Paribhāṣā 64

When a root is mentioned, that item ending with the causative suffix (*ṇic*) is also meant.[342]

Comments The word *prakṛti* in this *paribhāṣā* refers exclusively to verbal roots, and is therefore translated thus, as if it were the word *dhātu*.

Argument 64.1[343] [64:2

— How is this known?

— Because he says *her acaṅi* (P.7.3.56).

— How come this is an intimation?

— Here, a velar substitute is being prescribed for [the *h* in] *hi*; how could this possibly occur before *ṇi* [the causative suffix] when *caṅ* [the reduplicated aorist suffix] follows? But the teacher observes that when a root is mentioned that item ending with the causative suffix [*ṇic*] is also meant, and so he makes the prohibition 'not when *caṅ* follows'.

Explanation The suffix *caṅ* is a replacement for the general aorist tense suffix *cli*, which arises after roots which end in the causal suffix *ṇi* (cf. P.3.1.48). In P.7.3.56 Pāṇini teaches a velar substitute for *h* of the root *hi* when reduplicated, and make the specific exclusion of this when *caṅ* follows. But this implies that Pāṇini assumes that the mention of *hi* includes the derivative from *hi* made with *ṇi*. Generalizing this we get the *paribhāṣā*.

---

[342]This maxim is not quoted in the *Mahābhāṣya*, in spite of the assertions of Nīlakaṇṭha (no. 85) and Nāgeśa (no. 91) that it is. It is, however inferable from *vārt.* 2 on P.7.3.56, and this is no doubt what the distinguished authors are referring to.

It is discussed by the following *paribhāṣā* commentators: Puruṣottamadeva (no. 73), Sīradeva (no. 90), Nīlakaṇṭha (no. 85), Haribhāskara (no. 93), Nāgeśa (no. 91) and Śeṣādrisudhī (no. 79).

[343]This is the standard intimation of the maxim, and is presented by all the *paribhāṣā* commentators (see footnote 342, p. 224). The same idea is present in *vārt.* 2 on P.7.3.56, though it is not there generalized into a principle; the application is restricted to the root in question, *hi*.

Argument 64.2[344] [64:6

— What is the point of intimating this?
— The retroflexion of *s* which is prescribed for *sunoti* 'he squeezes out' is also for that [verb] ending with the causative suffix. Thus:

abhiṣāvayati 'he causes to be squeezed out'.

Explanation In P.8.3.65 Pāṇini teaches the replacement of *s* by *ṣ* for certain verbs, including *sunoti*, after a prefix ending in *i* or *u*: thus *abhiṣunoti*. By the present maxim we may also account for the *ṣ* in the causative form *abhiṣāvayati*.

Comments The *Mahābhāṣya* accounts for the form *abhiṣāvayati* differently. In *vārttikas* 3 and 4 on P.8.3.65, and the *bhāṣya* thereon, it is proposed that the retroflexion still applies to the causative form because a part of it – namely the root – is the same as in the non-causative (Mbh.III.442:22–443:4). A rather woolly solution this, it is echoed in the *Kāśikā* on P.8.3.65 (KV.VI.559:3), where it is made more explicit that the prefix and consequent retroflexion of *s* apply before the causal suffix is added.

In the *Vyāḍīyaparibhāṣāvṛtti* here, we have an argument which seems to be independent of the *Mahābhāṣya*. It surfaces here and with Puruṣottamadeva, but is generally superseded by the weaker, though more prestigious, argument from the *Mahābhāṣya*.

344 Puruṣottamadeva (no. 73) presents the same argument as the Vyāḍi commentator, but Sīradeva (no. 90) says the *paribhāṣā* is not needed to account for *abhiṣāvayati*, and argument § 64.2 then drops out of use.

The *tadanta* rule does not apply to a rule giving a technical term.[345]

— The *tadanta* rule [P.1.1.72] does not exist where a technical term is being prescribed.

Comments The Vyāḍi commentator's reading of the *paribhāṣā* is anomalous in omitting the expression *pratyayagrahaṇe,* which the other commentators and the *Mahābhāṣya* include. This limits the sphere of the maxim to technical terms denoting suffixes only.

Argument 65.1 [65:3

— How is this known?
— Because he says *anta* 'end' in *suptiṅantaṃ padam* (P.1.4.14).
— How come this is an intimation?
— The mention of *anta* in it is not necessary.
— In that case how will the term *pada* apply to an item ending in *sup* or *tiṅ*?
— By the *tadanta* rule. This technical term which is presented with respect to *sup* and *tiṅ*, will apply to items ending in *sup* and *tiṅ*. The teacher is observing that the *tadanta* rule does not apply to a rule giving a technical term.

[345] In the *ślokavārttika* on P.4.2.45 it is stated that *tadantavidhi* does not always apply: its sphere of action is defined by enumeration and the teacher must intimate that it is to be applied in specific cases (Mbh.II.280–81).

The maxim is explicitly stated by Kātyāyana in his first *vārttika* on P.1.4.14. The following discussion by Patañjali is identical in sense, and often in word, to the Vyāḍi commentator's discussion. The Vyāḍi commentator's arguments 1 and 2 are the same as Mbh.I.318:20–25 and 319:1–2 respectively.

The maxim is generally accepted: see *Siddhāntakaumudī* on P.7.1.52 (SK.I.215:3 (217)), and Puruṣottamadeva (no. 81), Sīradeva (no. 27), Nīlakaṇṭha (no. 34), Haribhāskara (no. 27), Nāgeśa (no. 27) and Śeṣādrisudhī (no. 27).

Argument 65.2

[65:9

— What is the point of intimating this?

— The word *gauritarā* 'whiter', which ends in the suffix *tarap* from *taraptamapau gha* (P.1.1.22), does not come to be termed a *gha* by the *tadanta* rule.

— And what would happen?

— In *kumārī gauritarā* 'the whiter girl' there would be shortening [of the *ī* of *kumārī*] by *gharūpakalpa* ... (P.6.3.43).

Primary and secondary nominal forms, and compounds are defined according to usage.[346]

— Primary and secondary nominal forms and compounds are employed after their usage has been observed.

Explanation This teaches a *lakṣyaikacakṣuṣka* position with regard to *kṛt* and *taddhita* suffixation and compounding. These formations take place only if usage warrants them.

Argument 66.1 [66:3

— How is this known?

— Because he makes no mention of *karman* 'action' in *pre stro 'yajñe* (P.3.3.32).

— How come this is an intimation?

— *Karma* should be mentioned here. Thus: *pre stro 'yajñakarmaṇi*, just as elsewhere he says *ye yajñakarmaṇi* (P.8.2.88). The teacher is hereby observing that primary nominal suffixes do not arise where usage does not warrant them. Therefore, although *karma* is not mentioned [in P.3.3.32, the primary suffix] *ghañ* arises, as it were, *ayājñakarmaṇi* 'not when there is sacrificial action.' Therefore no mention of *karma* is made [in P.3.3.32].

---

[346]This *paribhāṣā* seems to have been known to Kātyāyana, though perhaps not as a set formula. In *vārt.* 3 on P.3.3.19 (Mbh.II.146:5) he states that the rule does not apply too widely (*atiprasaṅga*) because a suffix is valid if it accords with usage.

Patañjali's comment on this *vārttika* gives the *paribhāṣā* as a paraphrase of Kātyāyana's statement (Mbh.II.146:7). The wording used by Patañjali is identical to the Vyāḍi commentator's. Elsewhere the general principle of *abhidhānatva* is frequently applied by both Patañjali and Kātyāyana. For further references see Joshi and Roodbergen 1969.vii, and Kielhorn 1887.245–46.

The maxim is not discussed as a separate *paribhāṣā* by any of the *paribhāṣā* commentators, nor is it quoted in the *Kāśikā* or *Siddhāntakaumudī*.

Argument 66.2 [66:9

— What is the point of intimating this?
— Where usage is referred to, this *paribhāṣā* does not have to be stated.

All copulative compounds are optionally singular.[347]

Comments Note that in argument § 62.1 the Vyāḍi commentator claimed to establish this *paribhāṣā* by *yogavibhāga*; here he attempts to derive it differently, by *jñāpaka* from P.3.1.100.

On the use of the singular in the phrase *sarvo dvandvaḥ* in the *paribhāṣā*, note the adage*anudbhūtāvayavavivakṣayā ekavacanam* 'the singular may be used to express the fact that that the parts [of the item referred to] have not become apparent.' Note also that any *dvandva* which does become singular must also become neuter by *sa napuṃsakaṃ* (P.2.4.17).

The Vyāḍi commentator's treatment of this maxim is noticeably simpler and more primitive than that of the other *paribhāṣā* commentators.

Argument 67.1 [67:2

— How is this known?

— Because in some places in the rules he gives, in its final form, a singular for many items: thus, *gadamadacarayamaḥ* ... (P.3.1.100).

Argument 67.2 [67:4

— What is the point of intimating this?

— The *paribhāṣā* applies only in cases such that when there is singularization of a copulative compound, then that which appears in the singular is seen to be a copulative compound of innumerable items.

Comments The words *tatraiva* (67:5) here are confusing. If a reading such as *tatreyam* were available instead, it would make more sense of the passage, which is not cogent as it stands.

[347] This maxim is common in the tradition. Patañjali states it thrice (Mbh.I.232:4–5, 435:1–2, 476–77), it appears in the *Kāśikā* on P.1.2.63 (KV.I.372), and is discussed by all the *paribhāṣā* commentators: Puruṣottamadeva (no. 50), Sīradeva (no. 16), Nīlakaṇṭha (no. 22), Haribhāskara (no. 16), Nāgeśa (no. 34) and Śeṣādrisudhī (no. 34).

Splitting a rule is more cumbersome than prescribing a specific word.[348]

— Even if the sense is thereby established, the splitting of a rule is more cumbersome than reading a specific word.

Argument 68.1[349] [68:4

— How is that known?
— Because he says *neṭy aliṭi radheḥ* (P.7.1.62).
— How come it is an intimation?
— The mention of *radh* in the rule is unnecessary. *Jabh* has [the augment] *num* before a vowel [cf. P.7.1.61]. Next, *radh* too has *num*, only before a vowel. Then by [saying] just *neṭy aliṭi*, it will only apply to *radh*; no further mention of *radh* is necessary. This being the case, by mentioning *raḍh* he is observing that it [the splitting of rules] is in fact more cumbersome.
— How?
— If *radh* is not mentioned there is splitting of a rule. Thus, splitting a rule is more cumbersome than prescribing a specific word.

Explanation The opponent is proposing to amend the *sūtrapāṭha* to read:

jabher aci	for P.7.1.61
radeś ca	(for P.7.1.61)
neṭy aliṭi	(for P.7.1.62)

Instead of:

radhijabhor aci	P.7.1.61
neṭy aliṭi radheḥ	P.7.1.62

Although the former formulation saves a word, the latter saves a rule. We infer that the latter procedure was considered a greater saving by Pāṇini.

[348] This maxim does not occur as such in the *Mahābhāṣya*, *Kāśikā* or *Siddhāntakaumudī*. It is discussed by the following *paribhāṣā* commentators: Puruṣottamadeva (no. 98), Sīradeva (no. 110), Nīlakaṇṭha (no. 138), Haribhāskara (no. 112).

[349] Discussed in the places mentioned in footnote 348, p. 231.

Argument 68.2[350] [68:10

— What is the point of intimating this?
— If there is splitting of the rule *pūṅaḥ ktvā ca* (P.1.2.22) the mention of *ktvā* may be rejected because of *na ktvā seṭ* (P.1.2.18); this [splitting] is cumbersome. Therefore, so that it does not happen this *ktvā* [in P.1.2.22] is mentioned.

Explanation The point here is not perfectly clear, but seems to be as follows. If instead of P.1.2.22 we read:

1. *pūṅaḥ*
2. *ktvā ca*

then we can assume that *ktvā* will be read into 1 from P.1.2.18. Then 2 is altogether superfluous. But since splitting a rule is cumbersome, we do not do it, and prefer to mention *ktvā* in P1.2.22.

Comments The mention of *ktvā* in P.1.2.22 has caused trouble since before the time of Patañjali. He records the view of the Bhāradvājīyas that it is put there for the sake of what is to follow (Mbh.I.201:16). This view is repeated in the *Kāśikā* on P.1.2.22 (KV.I.297 f.).

The Vyāḍi commentator seems to be trying to solve the problem of the presence of *ktvā* in a circuitous way, by first assuming that to remove the *ktvā* the rule must be split, and then invoking the *paribhāṣā* to show that Pāṇini prefers mentioning a word (here *ktvā*) to splitting a rule.

---

[350] A variant of this argument, without reference to the *paribhāṣā*, occurs in Patañjali's exposition of the last part of the *ślokavārttika* on P.1.2.18 (Mbh.I.200:17–20). The idea of splitting P.1.2.22 is present here.

A rule about a compound-final suffix is not invariable.[351]

— Compound-final suffixes which are prescribed do no apply the whole time.

Argument 69.1[352] [69:3

— How is this known?
— Because he reads the word *rāja* 'king' in the list of items, beginning with *aṃśa*, which follow *prati*. It is in the list beginning with *aṃśa* for the purpose of reading, so that by *prater aṃśvādayaḥ* ... (P.6.2.193) it can have a final acute. Thus:

pratirājá 'enemy king'.

— How come it is an intimation?
— It is unnecessary to read it here in the list beginning with *aṃśa*. The [compound-final suffix] *ṭac* is prescribed after *rāja, aha* and *sakhi* [by P.5.4.91]. And the fact that *ṭac* has a final acute is established [by P.6.1.163], so there is no point in reading it [*rāja*]. The teacher is here observing that the compound-final *ṭac* is not invariable. So the reading [of *rāja* in the *aṃśa* list] is done in order to make the final acute.

---

[351]This maxim is first worked out by Patañjali in his discussion on P.6.2.197 (see especially Mbh.III.140:6). This is echoed in the *Kāśikā* on P.6.2.197 (KV.V.184) and in the *Siddhāntakaumudī* on the same (SK.IV.597 (3931)).

It is discussed by Puruṣottamadeva (no. 82), Sīradeva (no. 63), Nīlakaṇṭha (no. 74), Haribhāskara (no. 65), Nāgeśa (no. 84) and Śeṣādrisudhī (no. 72).

[352]This argument for the *paribhāṣā* is distinct from Patañjali's, and appears in the *Śabdakaustubha*, from where it is quoted by Nīlakaṇṭha (no. 74). Neither Puruṣottamadeva nor Sīradeva mention it, but it reappears, as one would expect, in Nāgeśa (no. 84) and Śeṣādrisudhī (no. 72).

Several *jñāpakas* for this maxim are offered by different authors. As Haribhāskara (no. 65) remarks: *jñāpakāntaram api granthāntarād avagantavyam*.

Comments This argument seems to be independent of the *Mahābhāṣya* but, being based on an accent rule, it must have been developed within the orthodox grammatical tradition, without the influence of the Buddhist or Jaina grammarians.

Argument 69.2[353] [69:10

— What is the point of intimating this?
— In *parādhvani* 'on the highest path' the compound-final [suffix *ac*] which follows *adhvan* when the latter follows a preverb [by P.5.4.85], does not occur.

Comments This argument only makes sense if the example begins with an *upasarga*. Hence the readings, which are very faulty, cannot be accepted as they appear to stand.

[353] As allusion to this argument appears in Sīradeva (no. 63), but not elsewhere.

Paribhāṣā 70

An instruction about an augment is not invariable.[354]

— These augments which are taught in the discipline with the markers *ṭ*, *k*, and *m*, are not invariable. They do not apply the whole time.

Argument 70.1[355] [70:4

— How is this known?
— Because he says *tho 'nthaḥ* (P.7.1.87).
— How come this is an intimation?
— This rule should be stated thus: *tho nuḍ*. It [the correct form] would also be achieved by means of the augment *nuḍ*. So this *paribhāṣā* does exist: an instruction about an augment is not invariable.

Comments This argument is very strange in that no *vaiyarthya* is demonstrated in P.7.1.87, and the suggested revision of the *sūtra* does not save any syllables.

Argument 70.2 [70:6

It is also so in *pacānaḥ* 'cooking'. Once *pacamānaḥ* is obtained the [augment] *muk* which precedes the *āna* does not apply [by P.7.2.82], because the augment is not invariable.

[354] This maxim is not used by Patañjali (although he does argue that *āgamā avidyamānavad bhavanti*).

It is quoted in the *Kāśikā* on P.7.1.1 (KV.V.526). The following commentators discuss it: Puruṣottamadeva (no. 84), Sīradeva (no. 98), Nīlakaṇṭha (no. 87), Haribhāskara (no. 100), Nāgeśa (no. 93.2) and Śeṣādrisudhī (no. 82).

[355] This argument seems unique to the Vyāḍi commentator.

Paribhāṣā 71

A rule which would apply to a different expression is not invariant.[356]

Argument 71.1[357]

[71:2

— Thus, for example, when [the suffix] *ac* follows the intensive form of *lū* 'cut', at the stage *lolūya* + *a* the letter *y* might be deleted by *yaṅo ci ca* (P.2.4.74). But when an *ārdhadhātuka* follows there is elision by *ato lopaḥ* (P.6.4.48). What is to be done here? According to subsequence it is *ato lopaḥ* (P.6.4.48). According to invariance it is the earlier deletion of *yaṅ* (P.2.4.74).

— How is it invariant?

— Once *yaṅ* is deleted [by P.2.4.74], then the *a* would be elided [by P.6.4.48]; and it is the same even if that [deletion of *yaṅ*] doesn't happen. But the elision of the *a* [by P.6.4.48] is not invariant. Because once the whole of *yaṅ* has been deleted [by P.2.4.74], the *a* cannot be elided [by P.6.4.48].

— The deletion of *yaṅ* [by P.2.4.74] is not invariant.

— How so?

— A rule which would apply to a different expression is not invariant.

— Observe closely: if the elision of the *a* is performed [by P.6.4.48] then it [deletion by P.2.4.74] is of an item with no vowel; if it [elision]

[356]This maxim is apparently not known to Kātyāyana, but is very frequently used by Patañjali (Mbh.I.53:4, 68:2, 286:5, 502:5; II.7:24, 10:12, 28:7:8, 169:23:24, 263:7, 385:9; III.4:7, 10:6, 14:24, 214:6, 221:17, 345:16, 360:13, 390:10.)

Strangely, considering its frequency in the *Mahābhāṣya*, the maxim is not used in the *Kāśikā* or *Siddhāntakaumudī*, nor is it discussed by any of the *paribhāṣā* commentators, with the exception of Nāgeśa (no. 43). He accepts it.

[357]This argument, including the use of the *paribhāṣā*, occurs in the Patañjali's discussion under *vārt.* 7 on P.1.1.4. The point of the *vārttika* is that P.1.1.4 is unnecessary, and the *paribhāṣā* is not proven, but rather used as a self-evident principle (Mbh.I.52–53).

is not performed it [deletion] is of an item with a vowel. This is a different expression.

In this case elision of *a* [by P.6.4.48] arises first because of subsequence. Once that is done then afterwards there is deletion of what is left. Therefore even without the rule *na dhātulopa ārdhadhātuke* (P.1.1.4), there will be no *guṇa* [of the *ū* in *lolū-*] because the elision of the *a* is like the original. [Thus:]

loluvaḥ 'a terrific cutter',
popuvaḥ 'a terrific cleaner'.

Explanation The derivation in question begins thus:

i)	*lū*	+	*yaṅ*			by P.3.1.22
ii)	*lūlū*	+	*yaṅ*			by P.6.1.9
iii)	*lolū*	+	*yaṅ*			by P.7.4.82
iv)	*lolū*	+	*yaṅ*	+	*ac*	by P.3.1.134

At this point two rules are simultaneously applicable:

a)	*lolū*			+	*ac*	by P.2.4.74
b)	*lolū*	+	*y*	+	*ac*	by P.6.4.48

The *prima facie* view is that operation a) is *nitya*, while b) is *para*. (Being *nitya* is defined as *kṛtākṛtaprasaṅgī*; in this case a) is *nitya* if it applies whether or not b) applies.) According to the general understanding, a *nitya* rule supersedes a *para* one (cf. *parān nityaṃ balavat*, Nāgeśa no. 42), although the Vyāḍi commentator does not make this explicit.

The opponent then argues that the operation a) is not really *nitya* because the object of the operation is different before and after the action of b). Therefore b) should act first, followed by a). So the final stages of the derivation are:

v)	*lolū*	+	*y*	+	*ac*	by P.6.4.48
vi)	*lolū*	+		+	*ac*	by P.2.4.74
vii)	*loluva*					by P.6.4.77

Comments This argument is not a proof or intimation of the *paribhāṣā*, but rather an argument for dropping P.1.1.4, which incidentally involves the *paribhāṣā*. This is most inappropriate for a *paribhāṣā* commentary, but makes perfect sense in the context of *vārttika* 7 on P.1.1.4. It thus seems certain here that the Vyāḍi commentator has copied the argument from the *Mahābhāṣya* rather blindly.

The only other commentator to give the *paribhāṣā* is Nāgeśa. He and the Vyāḍi commentator share a close dependence on the *Mahābhāṣya* and an original approach and this has caused them both accept this maxim which is so common in the *Mahābhāṣya*, but so rare elsewhere.

Paribhāṣā 72

A rule which would apply by virtue of some other rule is not invariant.[358]

Explanation This maxim is related to the previous one. It teaches that the idea of invariance (*nityatva*) is limited in the following way: If rules $\mathcal{A}$ and $\mathcal{B}$ apply simultaneously, and if $\mathcal{A}$ could apply both before and after the application of $\mathcal{B}$, then $\mathcal{A}$ is normally said to be invariant. However, if, once $\mathcal{B}$ has applied, some third rule $\mathcal{C}$ must apply before $\mathcal{A}$ can apply, then $\mathcal{A}$ is not invariant.

Argument 72.1[359] [72:2

— Thus, for example, at the stage *pā + atus* [perfect, 3rd dual suffix] reduplication [by P.6.1.8] would apply, also elision of the *ā* [by P.6.4.64]. According to subsequence it is elision of the *ā*. According to invariance it is the reduplication.
— How so? The elision of *ā* takes place also when there is reduplication. Surely too the reduplication would not apply once the elision of *ā* has been performed.
— For what reason?
— Because there is no vowel [cf. P.6.1.1].
— It is said [that] the reduplication too is invariant.
— How?
— Because of [the elided *ā*] being like the original, by *dvirvacane 'ci* (P.1.1.59); it is said that the reduplication is made invariant by another rule. Once this rule [P.6.4.64] has been performed, then

---

358 This rule is not quoted as such in the *Mahābhāṣya*, though the concept of the intervention of a third rule having a bearing on *nityatva* is known (cf. Mbh.II.97:3–4 etc.).

It is discussed by Nāgeśa alone (no. 45) amongst the *paribhāṣā* commentators. He accepts it, noting that it is mentioned by Kaiyaṭa in the latter's discussion of P.6.4.22 (*Pradīpa* V.290^b:33).

359 The derivation of *papatuḥ* is named by Patañjali as one of the purposes of P.1.1.59 (Mbh.I.157:1), but the *paribhāṣā* is not explicitly mentioned. The same is true of the *Kāśikā* on the same rule (KV.I.215:2).

See also argument § 76.1 below, and footnote 368, p. 248.

by virtue of *dvirvacane 'ci* (P.1.1.59), the reduplication [by P.6.1.8] does apply.

— So this [P.1.1.59] is another rule. And a rule which applies by virtue of some other rule is not invariant.

Therefore first the *ā* [of *pā*] is elided [by P.6.4.64], and afterwards there is reduplication. Thus *papatuḥ* 'they two drank' and *papur* 'they drank' are validated.

Explanation The derivation under discussion is as follows:

i)	*pā*	+	*liṭ*	by P.3.2.115 etc.
ii)	*pā*	+	*tas*	by P.3.4.78 etc.
iii)	*pā*	+	*atus*	by P.3.4.82 etc.

At this point two rules are simultaneously applicable:

$\mathcal{A}$	*pā pā*	+	*atus*	by P.6.1.8
$\mathcal{B}$	*p*	+	*atus*	by P.6.4.64

The *prima facie* view is that $\mathcal{A}$ is *nitya*, while $\mathcal{B}$ is *para*. The opponent argues that the reverse is true. Although it might appear that $\mathcal{A}$ is *nitya*, because of P.1.1.59, the fact that this third rule has to be mentioned invalidates this *nityatva*. Thus the proper sequence of derivation is $\mathcal{B}$ followed by $\mathcal{A}$.

Comments Note that, as with the previous maxim, the arguments presented are not intimations, but just examples of the *paribhāṣā* in use.

The text is not entirely satisfactory here, and this may account for the rather involved look of this essentially simple argument.

The external is invalid with respect to the internal.[360]

Explanation See notes on *paribhāṣā* 32. The examples given here, however, show that the Vyāḍi commentator is taking the *paribhāṣā* this time to refer to non-simultaneous operations.

Argument 73.1[361] [73:2

— How is that known?
— Because he prescribes *ūṭh* in place of [the *v* of] *vāha* (P.6.4.132).
— How come this is an intimation?
— It is not necessary to mention *ūṭh* here. It [the correct form] is established by saying just 'there is vocalization of *vāha*' [cf. P.6.4.131]. At the stage *paṣṭa* + *uh* + *as*, the non-suffix *ṇvin* has been stated [by P.3.2.64]. Before this [*ṇvin*], *guṇa* is generated by the suffix rule *pugantalaghūpadhasya* (P.7.3.86). Once this is done, it [the final correct form] is established by *vṛddhir eci* (P.6.1.88):

paṣṭauhaḥ paśya 'look at the young bull'.

This being the case, by prescribing *ūṭh* in place of *vāha* , in order to get the *vṛddhi*, which is the internal rule, would not take place because the *guṇa*, which is an external rule, is invalid. Thus, the *vṛddhi* depends on the *guṇa*; the *guṇa* in external because it depends on an item outside [i.e., *ṇvin*].

Explanation The derivation of the acc. pl. form *paṣṭauhaḥ* 'young bulls' is:

---

[360]See footnote 246, p. 144.

[361]This argument about the ancient word *paṣṭauha* is given by Kātyāyana in *vārt.* 1 on P.6.4.132 and the following (Mbh.III.222–23), and it is explicitly said by Patañjali to be an intimation of the *paribhāṣā* (II.223:5–6).

See also Kielhorn's discussion of *viśvauhaḥ* (Kielhorn 1874.235–37).

i)	*paṣṭa*	+	*vah*			+	*as*	
ii)	*paṣṭa*	+	*vah*	+	*ṇvin*	+	*as*	by P.3.2.64
iii)	*paṣṭa*	+	*vāh*	+	*ṇvin*	+	*as*	by P.7.2.116
iv)	*paṣṭa*	+	*vāh*			+	*as*	by P.6.1.67 etc.
v)	*paṣṭa*	+	*ūh*			+	*as*	by P.6.4.132, and 6.1.108.
vi)	*paṣṭauhas*							by P.6.1.89

The present argument proposes the alternative derivation:

a)	as for i)							
b)	as for ii)							
c)	as for iii)							
d)	*paṣṭa*	+	*uh*	+	*ṇvin*	+	*as*	by modified 6.4.132
e)	*paṣṭa*	+	*oh*	+	*ṇvin*	+	*as*	by P.7.3.86
f)	*paṣṭa*	+	*oh*	+		+	*as*	by P.6.1.67 etc.
g)	*paṣṭauhas*							by P.6.1.88

The fact that Pāṇini has framed P.6.4.132 as he has shows that he rejected the latter derivation. The grounds for this are that the operation giving the *vṛddhi* at stage g) is *antaraṅga*, while the operation giving the *guṇa* at stage e) is *bahiraṅga*. And Pāṇini must have assumed that as far as g) is concerned, e) had not taken place. In other words, a *bahiraṅga* operation is invalid when an *antaraṅga* one is to be performed.

Argument 73.2[362] [73:10

— What is the point of intimating this?
— In *grāmaṇi kulam* 'the leading family of the village', the augment *tuk*, being an internal rule [i.e., P.6.1.71] does not apply because the external rule [P.1.2.47] giving the shortening of a neuter is invalid. Because here too the shortening depends on the [fact that *kula* is] neuter, so being dependent on an outside item it is external. The [augment] *tuk*, depending on the short [*i* of *grāmaṇi*] is internal because it is a letter.

Explanation The derivation here is :

i)	*grāmaṇī*	+	*kulam*			
ii)	*grāmaṇī*	+	*kvip*	+	*kulam*	by P.3.2.76
iii)	*grāmaṇĭ*	+	*kvip*	+	*kulam*	by P.1.2.47

The problem now arises that *tuk* might apply by P.6.1.71, giving:

**grāmaṇĭ* + *tuk* + *kvip* + *kulam*

[362]This precise argument, with the same example, is given by Patañjali in his comments concerning *paribhāṣā* no. 7 (which is *vārt.* 3 on P.1.1.39). He first suggests there that the *grāmaṇikulam* problem with *tuk* can be solved by *paribhāṣā* no. 7, and then refutes this, saying that the *asiddhaparibhāṣā* will do the job (Mbh.I.97:16–18).

The same solution for the same problem, though in a different context, is supplied by Patañjali in discussing P.1.1.62 (Mbh.I.161:5–10).

This operation, however, is *antaraṅga* because it is triggered by the *-i* of *grāmaṇī* (and the *kvip*), while the shortening of the *-i* at stage iii) is relatively *bahiraṅga* because it is triggered by the neuter word *kulam*. Thus, the *tuk* is prevented from applying because of the *paribhāṣā* which states that an external operation is not valid with respect to an internal one. Thus, as far as P.6.1.71 is concerned, *grāmaṇī* still has a long final *i*. Therefore P.6.1.71 cannot apply.

Comments It is certain that the first *Mahābhāṣya* passage mentioned in footnote 362, p. 241, is the Vyāḍi commentator's source for this argument.

The final comment that *tuk* is *antaraṅga* 'because it is letter' is not explicable as it stands. *Tuk* does indeed depend on the letters *i* and *p*; but then a reading *varṇatvād* would have been better. But even though P.6.1.71 is a *varṇa* rule in this sense, this is not the reason for it being *antaraṅga*.

It is not counted as external when there is vowel juxtaposition.[363]

— The *bahiraṅga paribhāṣā* [no. 73] does not come into play if there is a rule about the juxtaposition of vowels.

Explanation This is an *apavāda* to the previous maxim, the *antaraṅga paribhāṣā*.

An operation which would normally be considered *bahiraṅga* (and therefore *asiddha* with respect to *antaraṅga* operation) is not counted as such when the *antaraṅga* operation in question involves the juxtaposition of vowels.

Argument 74.1[364] [74:3

— How is that known?
— Because in *ṣatvatukor asiddhaḥ* (P.6.1.86) he prescribes the invalidity of a single substitute with respect to an operation concerning [the augment] *tuk*. Here, at the stage

abhi + pra + i + ya

he prescribes that the single substitute is generated; once this is done, *tuk* fails to apply because of the length [of the resulting -*e*-]. So therefore *ṣatvatukor asiddhaḥ* (P.6.1.86) is given, because the single substitute is invalid. And this is established because of this *paribhāṣā*.
— How?
— The single substitute refers to root and prefix; the [augment] *tuk* refers to a letter. Because of being [based on] a letter, *tuk* is

[363]This maxim is suggested by Patañjali as a rider to *paribhāṣā* 73 in his comment on *vārt.* 21 on P.1.4.2 (Mbh.I.310:7). He accepts that Pāṇini tacitly uses this maxim.

It occurs in the *Kāśikā* on P.6.4.19, where it is also discussed by Jinendrabuddhi and Haradatta (KV.V.358).

It is discussed by all the *paribhāṣā* commentators: Puruṣottamadeva (no. 42), Sīradeva (no. 70), Nīlakaṇṭha (no. 59), Haribhāskara (no. 72), Nāgeśa (no. 51) and Śeṣādrisudhī (no. 43).

[364]This argument is given by Patañjali (Mbh.I.310:8) and by all the other commentators on this maxim.

more internal. So the *tuk*, whose rule is internal, will come about because the external rule is invalid.

There is no point in asserting the invalidity [of the single substitute] with respect to a rule about *tuk*.

This being so, by saying that it [the single substitute] is invalid with respect to a rule about *tuk*, the teacher is intimating that this *paribhāṣā* [no. 74] does exist. When having reference to the juxtaposition of vowels, this *paribhāṣā* [no. 73] does not apply. And here there is reference to a juxtaposed vowel. When the single substitute is being generated, this [*tuk* rule] is counted as external.

Explanation The derivation in question here is:

i)	*abhipra*	+	*i*	+	*ya*	by P.7.1.37 etc.
ii)	*abhipre*			+	*ya*	by P.6.1.87
iii)	the -*e* is invalid w.r.t. *tuk*					by P.6.1.86
iv)	*abhipre*	+	*tuk*	+	*ya*	by P.6.1.71

Note that at stage i) the addition of prefixes to the root counts as a *samāsa*, so P.7.1.37 can act. Also, *ya* has the marker *p*, being *lyap* in full, so P.6.1.71 can act.

For the addition of *tuk* by P.6.1.71, the base to which it is added must have a short final vowel. But after stage ii) this is no longer the case. So by P.6.1.86, stage ii) is made invalid with respect to stage iv). However, by normal criteria, *tuk* is *antaraṅga* with respect to the *ekadeśa* of *e* for -*a* + *i*, so by *paribhāṣā* 73 the *ekadeśa* would already be *asiddha*, and P.6.1.86 would be unnecessary. But since Pāṇini gave the rule he must have thought that *paribhāṣā* 73 was not applicable here. And the reason is that we are dealing with vowel junction.

Argument 74.2[365] [74:14

— What is the point of intimating this?

— *Akṣadyūḥ* 'a gambler'. In this, the *ūṭh*, which is considered to be external, is invalid; because of this [we have to apply the *paribhāṣā*. Then,] the substitution of *yaṇ* by *iko yaṇ aci* (P.6.1.77) is established.

Explanation The derivation here is:

i)	*akṣa*	+	*div*			+	*kvip*	by P.3.2.178 etc.
ii)	*akṣa*	+	*di*	+	*ūṭh*	+	*kvip*	by P.6.4.19
iii)	*akṣa*	+	*di*	+	*ūṭh*			by P.6.1.67 etc.
iv)	*akṣa*	+	*dy*	+	*ūṭh*			by P.6.1.77

If *paribhāṣā* 73 applied then *ūṭh* would be *asiddha* with respect to the change of *i* to *y*, because *ūṭh* is *bahiraṅga* while *i* to *y* is *antaraṅga*. But because of the present *paribhāṣā*, this is not the case and the derivation can proceed.

---

[365] This example too is Patañjali's (Mbh.I.310:5). It is common thereafter (see footnote 363, p. 243).

Comments The last sentence of this passage (74:14–16) seems to say the opposite of what is meant, but there is no trace of any variant reading which would help. The translation given assumes the ellipsis of an explanatory phrase.

Paribhāṣā 75

If there is conflict when two apply simultaneously then the one which is blocked is blocked for good.[366]

Argument 75.1 [75:2

— How is this known?
— Because he makes separate mention of *kṛñ* in *tanādikṛñbhya uḥ* (P.3.1.79), in order that an operation for *tan* etc., should not apply to *kṛñ*.
— But what operation is there which applies to *tan* etc., but should not apply to *kṛñ*?
— The elision of the nasal by *anudāttopadeśavanatitanotyādīnām* ... (P.6.4.37) must not take place: e.g.,

daivaraktāḥ kiṃśukāḥ 'the *kiṃśuka* flowers crimsoned by fate'

[*rañj* + *ta* → *rakta*].
— *Kṛñ* does not in fact have a nasal.

Argument 75.2 [75:6

— In that case this is it: the deletion of *sic* [the aorist sibilant] by *tanādibhyas tathāsoḥ* (P.2.4.79) must not take place.
— What would happen?
— The deletion would potentially be optional [when or *kṛñ* it should be invariable].
— It is not so! There must be some other operation for *tan* etc., than the deletion option [of P.2.4.79]. [Because] when there is no option [i.e., P.2.4.79 does not apply to *kṛñ*] then the elision will occur by *hrasvād aṅgāt* (P.8.2.27). Thus *akṛta* 'he did' is validated [either way].

366 See footnote 243, p. 141, and the discussion of *paribhāṣā* 31, p. 141 ff.

This being the case [i.e., there being no demonstrable reason for reading *kṛñ* separately in P.3.1.79], by mentioning *kṛ* separately [in P.3.1.79] he is intimating that if there is a conflict when two apply simultaneously there is no reapplication. In other words, once something is blocked it is blocked [for good].

Therefore the elision [of the aorist sibilant in *kṛ*] which is blocked by *tanādibhyas tathāsoḥ* (P.2.4.79) may not recur because of *hrasvād aṅgāt* (P.8.2.27).

Argument 75.3 [75:13

— Alternatively, the restriction is generated [implicitly] by *vipratiṣedhe param* ... (P.1.4.2): in a conflict *only* the latter [rule] occurs. Once the conflict has thereby gone, that which could apply again does not do so.

Argument 75.4 [75:16

— What is the point of intimating this?

— Here in *vṛkṇa* 'chopped' the retroflexion of the *s* by *vraścabhrasja* ... (P.8.2.36) does not take place because it is blocked by the velar substitute from *coḥ kuḥ* (P.8.2.30).

Explanation The point being made here is that the correct derivation is:

vraśc	+	*na*	
vrask	+	*na*	by P.8.2.30 blocking 8.2.36

and not:

vraśc	+	*na*	
**vrasṣ*	+	*na*	by P.8.2.36

It is valid because reapplicability is recognised.[367]

— When there has been a conflict, if something might then apply again it too occurs.
— But what is it?
— It is said that by *vipratiṣedhe param* ... (P.1.4.2), what is subsequent is as such, performed; what is actually subsequent is, as such, performed. And if what was prior might apply, it too occurs.

Comments This maxim is a direct contradiction of *paribhāṣā* 75. They are applied as appropriate to produce the desired form. Their existence side by side implies an extreme *lakṣyaikacakṣuṣka* view. See Sīradeva's comment: ... *lakṣyasthityaiva hy etayor vyavastheti* (Sīrådeva 184:27).

Argument 76.1[368]

[76:5

— Thus, for example, in *pā* + *atus* [perfect 3rd dual suffix] reduplication would apply [by P.6.1.8]. But the elision of *ā* applies [by P.6.4.64] because of invariance and subsequence, by *vipratiṣedhe param* ... (P.1.4.2), and elision is performed first. Thus, the reduplication takes place too because reapplicability is recognised. So the reduplication occurs afterwards too because reapplicability is recognised. [The form] *papatuḥ* 'those two drank' is established.

---

[367] This maxim is known to Kātyāyana who mentions it in three *vārttikas* (Mbh.III.270:7, 278:9, 348:3).

Patañjali, in addition to commenting on these instances, uses it several times (Mbh.I.140:11:17:23, 305:18:26, 500:11, 502:8:13; II.385:12; III.158:17, 177:9, 207:1, 258:10, 347:4), and also uses the simple phrase *punaḥ prasaṅga* several times (e.g. Mbh.III.264:8:12); cf. footnote 243, p. 141.

The maxim is not quoted in the *Kāśikā* or *Siddhāntakaumudī*, but the *paribhāṣā* commentators all discuss it: Puruṣottamadeva (no. 40), Sīradeva (no. 21), Nīlakaṇṭha (no. 26), Haribhāskara (no. 21), Nāgeśa (no. 39) and Śeṣādrisudhī (no. 40).

See also *Vyāḍīyaparibhāṣāvṛtti* 31:11, p.141 above.

[368] See footnote 359, p. 238. There is one passage in the *Mahābhāṣya* where the present *paribhāṣā* is used in the context of perfect tense reduplication, but different examples are used (Mbh.III.270:7 ff.).

Explanation See argument § 72.1 above. It is possible for rule $\mathcal{A}$ to arise, be superseded by $\mathcal{B}$, and then to apply once again, by virtue of the present *paribhāṣā*.

Comments Although the ideas being presented here by the Vyāḍi commentator are very simple, the passage is somewhat garbled and repetitive.

A general rule applies simultaneously, even in the province of an exception.[369]

Argument 77.1[370] [77:2

— How is this known?
— Because he makes mention of *śeṣa* 'the rest' in *śeṣe vibhāṣā* ... (P.8.4.18).
— How come it is an intimation?
— The mention of *śeṣa* here is unnecessary. Even without saying *śeṣa*, the operation will be understood to apply only to what is other than *gad* etc. [cf. P.8.4.17], that is, the rest.
— This mention of *śeṣa* is made so that the retroflexion of *n* should not apply before [the verbs] *gada* etc., as an option. So by the former [rule, P.8.4.17,] the operation will be invariant before *gad* etc. And when everything other than *gad* etc., follows, then the operation is optional. This being so, by mentioning *śeṣa* [in P.8.4.18] he is intimating that a general rule applies simultaneously, even in the province of an exception. Thus the option [P.8.4.18] would here apply before *gad* etc., as well.

So *śeṣa* is stated.

---

[369]This *paribhāṣā* is not used as such in the *Mahābhāṣya*, although the concepts it embodies are present there (cf. Mbh.II.79:12 ff., 178–79) in the *vārttikas* and in Patañjali.

The maxim is not used in the *Kāśikā* or *Siddhāntakaumudī*, or commented on by the *paribhāṣā* commentators. It is common in the Kātantra *paribhāṣā* texts.

[370]This argument is as rare as the *paribhāṣā* itself. Haradatta thinks the word *śeṣa* in P.8.4.18 is unnecessary, but takes the discussion no further.

Argument 77.2[371] [77:10

— What is the point of intimating this?
— In *pradīyatāṃ dāśarathāya maithilī* 'give the girl from Mithilā to the son of Daśaratha' (*Rāmāyaṇa, yuddhakāṇḍa* 9.22), the [suffix] *aṇ* is validated even in the province of the exception by *iñ*.

Explanation The point here is that the suffix *aṇ*, which forms *Dāśaratha* from *Daśaratha*, is taught as a general rule (P.4.1.83), while *iñ* is taught as an exception to it (P.4.1.95). Thus we would expect *Dāśarathi*. The *paribhāṣā* solves this problem.

371 The quotation from the *Rāmāyaṇa* is interesting, as it is also used by the *Kāśikā* on P.4.1.95. However, it is not the *paribhāṣā* that is invoked there, but *vivakṣā*; *Dāśaratha* means not 'son of' but 'belonging to' (see the *Nyāsa*'s comments, KV.III.434:22–24).

It seems to me that Abhyankar (1967.13) makes too much of this quotation from the *Rāmāyaṇa*; it does not help us at all in dating the Vyāḍi commentator. But it does establish some common ground with the *Kāśikā*: either one borrowed from the other, or both borrowed from an unknown third source which used this phrase in the context of P.4.1.95.

The accent on a thematic affix does not block the accent on a verbal inflection which is a *sārvadhātuka*.[372]

Explanation By P.6.1.158, only one of the syllables of a word is acutely accented; all the rest are grave, or *anudātta*. Various rules teach which syllable is acute, and these rules sometimes conflict.

The present *paribhāṣā* teaches that if one rule prescribes that the acute accent falls on a verbal thematic affix, while another teaches it falls on the final inflection, the latter wins.

Argument 78.1[373]

[78:2

— How is that known?

— He intimates that this *paribhāṣā* exists by teaching [in P.6.1.186] the lowering of [the accent on] a verbal inflection which is a *sārvadhātuka*, following [the periphrastic future suffix] *tās*. Thus:

kártā 'he will do'

Explanation The derivation of the periphrastic future *kártā* is as follows:

i)	*kṛ*			+	*luṭ*	by P.3.3.15
ii)	*kṛ*			+	*tip*	by P.3.4.77, 78
iii)	*kṛ*	+	*tā́s*	+	*tip*	by P.3.1.33
iv)	*kṛ*	+	*tā́s*	+	*ḍā*	by P.2.4.85
v)	*kṛ*	+	*t*	+	*ā*	by P.7.4.143
vi)	*kár*	+	*t*	+	*ā*	by P.7.3.86

At stage iii) the accent on thematic affix *tā́s* (by P.3.1.3) might be expected to block the earlier applicable accent on the inflectional suffix (P.3.1.3). But we can deduce that this is not the case by the fact that Pāṇini has to teach the suppression of the suppression of suffixal accent in P.6.1.186. If the *paribhāṣā* did not exist, P.6.1.186 would not be necessary.

[372]This maxim appears twice in the *Mahābhāṣya* (Mbh.II.110:14–15, III.100:9–11). It is not separately discussed by any of the *paribhāṣā* commentators. Cf. *vārt.* 9 on P.6.1.158.

[373]This argument normally occurs with the *paribhāṣā* itself (see footnote 372, p. pagerefloci78). See also *Laghuśabdenduśekhara* IV.458:18–21, Kaiyaṭa's *Pradīpa*, V.149^b, and in general the commentaries on P.6.1.158.

Comments The word *nighāta* (78:2) is a term from the milieu of phonetics or the *prātiśākhyas*, rather than *vyākaraṇa*.

Argument 78.2[374] [78:4

— What is the point of intimating this?

— Here in *cinuté* 'he builds up' and *krīṇīté* 'he buys' the accent on the verbal *sārvadhātuka* inflection is valid, though it is after the accent on the thematic suffix.

Explanation The relevant steps here are:

i)	*ci*			+	*laṭ*	by P.3.2.123
ii)	*ci*			+	*té*	by P.3.4.77–79
iii)	*ci*	+	*śnu*	+	*té*	by P.3.1.73

At stage iii) an acute accent on the thematic affix *śnu* is prevented by the *paribhāṣā* from superseding the acute accent already on the *te* by P.3.1.3.

[374] This example occurs in the *Mahābhāṣya* (see Mbh.III.110:7) and elsewhere.

Paribhāṣā 79

Words employed to mean the whole are also used to mean the parts.[375]

Argument 79.1[376] [79:2

— How is this known?
— From the world. For example in the world one says 'oil has been eaten', 'ghee has been eaten'.

Explanation The point here is that someone has eaten *some* oil, not all the oil in existence.

Argument 79.2[377] [79:2

In the discipline too there is an intimation, because [in P.1.1.58] he teaches the prohibition of items before [the primary nominal suffix] *vara* being like the original [which they replace].
— How come this is an intimation?
— Here in *yāyāvara* 'wanderer' the letter *ā* of the [intensive suffix] *yaṅ*, which is elided by *ato lopaḥ* (P.6.4.48), is prohibited from being like the original. Thus the letter *ā* [at the end of *yāyā*] may not be elided [by P.6.4.64].
— The elision of the letter *ā* is prescribed before an *ārdhadhātuka* [like *yaṅ*], before a vowel, before an item with the marker *k* or *ṅ*. So how could there possibly be elision before a vowel [i.e. *a*] which is only one part of *yaṅ*? It is the whole of *yaṅ* which is an *ārdhadhātuka*; a part of *yaṅ* by itself is not an *ārdhadhātuka*.

---

[375] This saying is cited four times by Patañjali (Mbh.I.12:19, 411:19, 426:28, 427:3). It is not discussed by any other *paribhāṣā* commentators.

[376] This argument is also from the *Mahābhāṣya* (I.12:20, 411:20, 427:1).

[377] The derivation of *yāyāvara* is alluded to by Patañjali (I.152:5; III.216:8). He cites the form as part of a verse, as yet untraced. The *Kāśikā* and subcommentaries on P.1.1.58 (KV.I.205) also discuss *yāyāvara*, but none of these sources link it with the *paribhāṣā*, as the Vyāḍi commentator does.

The elision of *ā* simply cannot take place. There is no point in prohibiting items from being like the original [in this situation]. This being the case, by prohibiting items from being like the original before *vara* [P.1.1.58] he is intimating that 'words employed to mean the whole are also used to mean the parts.'

Explanation The derivation of *yāyāvara* is as follows:

i)	*yā*			+	*yaṅ*			by P.3.1.22 or 23
ii)	*yā*	+	*yā*	+	*yaṅ*			by P.6.1.9, 7.4.56, 7.4.83
iii)	*yāyā*			+	*yaṅ*	+	*varac*	by P.3.2.176
iv)	*yāyā*			+	*yṅ*	+	*varac*	by P.6.4.48
v)	*yāyā*					+	*varac*	by P.6.1.66

The danger now is that we might, by P.1.1.57, posit a virtual *a* for that elided at stage iv):

*v) *yāyā* + [*a*]*ṅ* + *varac*

Then it might be possible to invoke P.6.4.64 and elide the final *ā* of *yāyā*:

*vi) *yāy* + *vara* by P.6.4.64

This is clearly undesirable, so P.1.1.58 prohibits the action of P.1.1.57 in this case where *varac* follows. But since *a* is only a part of the original *ārdhadhātuka yaṅ*, and P.6.4.64 only works if an *ārdhadhātuka* follows we must deduce that when Pāṇini says '*ārdhadhātuka*' he means also 'part of an *ārdhadhātuka*.'

Comments Note the rather drastic conjectures necessary for making sense of lines 79:8–9.

Argument 79.3[378] [79:12

— What is the point of intimating this?
— The prohibition of *guṇa* and *vṛddhi* by *na dhātulopa ārdhadhātuke* (P.1.1.4) is valid when only a part of the root is elided.

[378]This argument, which seem quite sound if the *paribhāṣā* is accepted, is not used in the general exposition of P.1.1.4. It is there merely asserted that *dhātu* equals *dhātvekadeśa* (e.g. *Kāśikā* I.77:3). The Vyāḍi commentator's argument is a good one and, it seems, unique.

A citation form behaves like the original form.[379]

Argument 80.1[380]

[80:2

— How is this know?
— Because he makes mention of *dīrgha* 'long vowel' in *kṣiyo dīrghāt* (P.8.2.46).
— How come this is an intimation?
— The mention of *dīrgha* 'long vowel' here is unnecessary. *Dīrghāt* 'after a long vowel' is understood simply by the specification [in P.8.2.46] of *kṣiyaḥ* 'after *kṣi*'.
— How does the substitute *iyaṅ* get prescribed for the long vowel [at the end of *kṣī*]?
— Because if it were a short vowel he would say *kṣeḥ* 'after *kṣi*' [instead of *kṣiyaḥ* in P.8.2.46].
— This is not so. The substitution of *iyaṅ* would be inapplicable, in just the same way that the appearance of the case inflections is inapplicable here.
— How is the appearance of the case inflections inapplicable?
— It pertains to a meaningful nominal stem, not to a root. But this [*kṣi*] is a root, therefore the case inflections do not appear.
— It is said that this [*kṣi*] is not a root, it is the citation form of a root. The term nominal stem comes after [? belongs to] that *kṣi* which is not a root, because it is not a root.

[379]The *paribhāṣā* is known to Patañjali (Mbh.I.21:7:9, III.408:4:5:9). See also the interesting discussion on citation forms in general, started by Kātyāyana (Mbh.I.20f.).

The *paribhāṣā* is discussed by all the *paribhāṣā* commentators: Puruṣottamadeva (no. 114), Sīradeva (no. 18), Nīlakaṇṭha (no. 23), Haribhāskara (no. 18), Nāgeśa (no. 36) and Śeṣādrisudhī (no. 36).

It is also used in the *Siddhāntakaumudī* (SK.I.286–87 (283)).

[380]In spite of the opacity of the argument, it is the same in essence as that given by Patañjali in discussing P.8.2.46 (Mbh.III.407:20–408:10). See also the other *paribhāṣā* commentators, and Kielhorn 1874.175 f.

[The case inflections] *su* etc., come after a nominal stem. Therefore the appearance of the nominal suffixes is applicable in this case. There is no substitution of *iyaṅ*.

— If there is not [any substitution of *iyaṅ*] then *kṣiya* is validated just because it is specified [as such in the *sūtra*]. There is no point in stating *dīrgha* 'long' [in P.8.2.46]. The teacher observes that 'a citation form behaves like the original form'. Thus, this is the citation form of a root. So as for a root, the appearance of the case inflections does not take place. The substitution of *iyaṅ* is also inapplicable, just as the appearance of the case inflections is certainly applicable. Therefore *dīrgha* 'long vowel' is stated [in P.8.2.46].

Explanation The Vyāḍi commentator's exposition of this argument is very diffuse, and unclear in parts. The core of the argument is the same as that given by Patañjali (see footnote 380, p. pagerefloci801) and is as follows:

In P.8.2.46 Pāṇini teaches a certain operation which occurs after the root *kṣi* when it ends in a long vowel. However he cites the root *kṣi* in an ablative form which is based on the stem *kṣī*, which ends in long *i*. So why is it necessary to add *dīrghāt* 'after a long vowel'?

If we eliminated *dīrghāt* from P.8.2.46 we would be left with a double bind (*ubhayataspāśā rajjuḥ*). If we take *kṣī* in the rule to be a citation form, then it is not a root. Therefore the suffix *iyaṅ* cannot apply, for it is only applied to roots (P.6.4.77).

If we accept the *paribhāṣā* then the citation form *kṣī* must behave like the root *kṣī*. So the problem is solved. But the new difficulty arises that the inflectional endings cannot be applied directly to a root, but only to a *prātipadika* (P.4.1.1).

Patañjali does not seek to establish the *paribhāṣā* from this discussion and it is hard to see how the Vyāḍi commentator intends to do so.

Comments For all its lack of clarity, the Vyāḍi commentator's version of this argument is crucial.

In 80:9 the Vyāḍi commentator says *ucyate*.... He must be quoting. And the words which follow, *naiṣa dhātuḥ | dhātor anukaraṇam etat*, are almost identical with those of Patañjali: *naiṣa dhātur dhātor eṣo 'nukaraṇaḥ*. It would be unreasonable to explain this as anything but a quotation by the Vyāḍi commentator of the text of the *Mahābhāṣya*.

Argument 80.2[381] [80:16

— What is the point of intimating this?

— Here someone says *dviḥ pacatu* 'twice "let him cook" '. So the citation form behaves like the original form. The word-couplet is validated [?] so there is lowering of the accent by *tiṅ atiṅaḥ* (P.8.1.28). The single term *pada* 'word' applies to the whole, noun and verb.

[381]This argument too is found in the *Mahābhāṣya* (I.21:7–8).

The second part of this argument (80:18–20) may bear some relation to Mbh.I.221:1–5, but again see Puruṣottamadeva (no. 114) etc.

So it is not possible to say 'after a word'. Therefore by this means [i.e., the *paribhāṣā*?] it is the whole which counts as a word, so there is this effort.

Explanation

- Someone says *pacatu pacatu* 'let him cook, let him cook'.
- Someone else reports this, saying *dviḥ pacatu ity āha* 'he said, "let him cook" twice'.

By P.8.1.28, a verb preceded by a non-verb is unaccented. In the first case, the first *pacatu* is therefore unaccented, while the second is accented (*pácatu*). In the second case, the difficulty might arise that being a mere citation, *pacatu* is not actually a verb, and so cannot be affected by P.8.1.28. But the *paribhāṣā* tells us to treat it as a verb anyway, so we get the unaccented form *pacatu*.

The remaining points are not clear.

Comments The reading '*padadvayā siddhā bhavati*' (text 80:17) is clearly wrong, but the MSS are unanimous, and it is hard to see what the original reading might have been, given the known mechanisms of scribal error. Reading '*padadvayaṃ siddhaṃ* ...' would at least be correct Sanskrit, but is unjustifiable textually.

When in doubt about the quality of something unmanifested, the neuter gender is employed.[382]

Argument 81.1[383] [81:2

— How is this known?
— Because he mentions *napuṃsaka* 'neuter' in *ardhaṃ napuṃsakam* (P.2.2.2).
— How come this is an intimation?
— Because *ardha* 'half' is valid as neuter only after a neuter. So he is intimating that when in doubt about the quality of something, then out of feminine, masculine or neuter, neutrality or the neuter gender is employed. Thereby [i.e., by P.2.2.2 without *napuṃsakam*], a compound might be formed even if there is a masculine. Therefore 'neuter' is mentioned in P.2.2.2.

Explanation The mention of the word *napuṃsaka* in P.2.2.2 is a genuine puzzle. This rule specifies that under a somewhat complex set of conditions, the word *ardha* may be compounded with a following word as a *tatpuruṣa*, e.g. *ardhaṃ* + *pippalyāḥ* → *ardhapippalī* 'half a pepper'. One of these conditions is that the word *ardha* be neuter, e.g. *ardhaḥ* + *nagaraḥ* → *nagarārdhaḥ*, with *ardha* now as the second member of the compound. But why is it necessary to specify the word *napuṃsaka* explicitly in the *sūtra*? Surely it is enough that the word *ardhaṃ* is expressed in the neuter?

The Vyāḍi commentator suggests that the inclusion of the word *napuṃsaka* is necessary because there exists a *paribhāṣā* such as the present one. If *sūtra* P.2.2.2 were to read only '*ardhaṃ*', then the use of the neuter might arise because of the global effect of the present *paribhāṣā*, and it would not have any true grammatical basis. Thus, if an item were masculine, and *ardha* agreed with it, a compound by

---

[382]This idea is expressed by Patañjali (Mbh.I.250:3–4), but more as a simple sentence than as a formal *paribhāṣā*. Puruṣottamadeva also gives it (no. 60). The maxim instantiates a nice *asamartha-samāsa*.

[383]In spite of the wide discussion from Patañjali onwards about the purpose of *napuṃsaka* in P.2.2.2, this particular answer seems unique to the Vyāḍi commentator. Kaiyaṭa comes close to this idea (*Pradīpa* II.416^a:37) when he says ...: *napuṃsakagrahaṇaṃ jñāpakam nirdeśeṣu liṅgāvivakṣāyāḥ*: ' "neuter" is mentioned to intimate that when items are being specified, there is no intention of stating their gender'.

P.2.2.2 would be feasible. So Pāṇini mentions ***napuṃsaka*** explicitly to rule out this possibility.

Argument 81.2[384] [81:2

— What is the point of intimating this?
— It is valid to say specifically 'what [i.e., neuter] has been born?' [After all,] only two things could be born in general, a girl or a boy. And yet one says 'what has been born?'

[384]Found in the same places as the *paribhāṣā* itself; see footnote 382, p. 259.

Ato lopaḥ (P.6.4.48) does not apply to items part of which has been elided.[385]

Argument 82.1[386] [82:2

— How is this known?
— Because in *nalopaḥ supsvarasaṃjñātugvidhiṣu kṛti* (P.8.2.2) he teaches that the elision of *n* is invalid with respect to a rule about [the augment] *tuk*.
— How come this is an intimation?
— Here in *vṛtrahabhyām* 'with the two slayers of Vṛtra', if the *n* [of *vṛtrahan*] is elided, the elision of the *a* (P.6.4.48) might subsequently apply.
— How come?
— It would not then be possible to say that it [the *tuk*] was [being added] 'to a short vowel' (cf. P.6.1.71). So there is no point in the elision of *n* being invalid. So by teaching that the elision of *n* in invalid with respect to a rule about [the augment] *tuk* he is intimating that this *paribhāṣā* does exist.

Explanation The relevant derivation here is:

i)	*vṛtrahan*	+	*kvip*	+	*bhyām*	by P.3.2.87 etc.
ii)	*vṛtrahan*			+	*bhyām*	by P.6.1.67
iii)	*vṛtraha*			+	*bhyām*	by P.8.2.7

At this point, were it not for the *paribhāṣā*, we might find:

a)	**vṛtrah*	+	*bhyām*	by P.6.4.48
				(N.B. *kvip* is virtual)

[385] This maxim is not known elsewhere in the Pāṇinian tradition.

[386] Similar, but not identical, points with regard to the derivation of *vṛtrahabhyām* (or *bhiḥ*) are raised by Kātyāyana in *vārt.* 5 on P.1.1.39 (Mbh.I.97:19), but in this context Patañjali prefers to refer to *paribhāṣā* no. 7.

The use of the argument to prove the *paribhāṣā* is unique to the Vyāḍi commentator.

This leaves no scope for P.6.1.71, which needs the short vowel of stage iii) to give:

b) **vṛtrahat* + *bhyām*

But it is to stop this happening that P.8.2.2 is given. Thus, by teaching P.8.2.2, Pāṇini is intimating that P.6.4.48 will not apply and stage a) will never arise. The application of P.6.1.71 remains a danger and has to be prevented by P.8.2.2.

And the fact that P.6.4.48 does not apply at stage a) is due to the effect of the *paribhāṣā*. The partial elision of the base is the loss of the final *n* at stage iii).

Argument 82.2 [82:9

— What is the point of intimating this?
— Forms like *rājīyati* 'he wants to be a king himself, *rājāyate* 'he lords it' are valid.

Explanation The derivations relevant here are:

i)	*rājan*	+	*kyac*	by P.3.1.8, 1.4.15
ii)	*rāja*	+	*kyac*	by P.8.2.7

At this point P.6.4.48 might take place, leading to a wrong form. It is barred from doing so by the *paribhāṣā*. Thus:

iii) *rājī* + *ya* by P.7.4.33

and so on.

Likewise:

i)	*rājan*	+	*kyaṅ*	by P.3.1.11
ii)	*rāja*	+	*kyaṅ*	by P.8.2.7
				P.6.4.48 is barred as above.
iii)	*rājā*	+	*ya*	by P.7.4.25 etc.

A rule for an explicitly mentioned word is stronger than an internal rule.[387]

Argument 83.1[388] [83:2

— How is that known?
— Because in *dhinvikṛṇvyor a ca* (P.3.1.80) he mentions the two augments *num*.
— How come this is an intimation?
— One should say *dhivikṛvyor ac ca* here. If it is stated like this, then once *at* [*ă*] has been generated [i.e., *dhivi* → *dhiva*] then subsequently the [augment] *num* will be attached [by P.7.1.58].
— In that case because of the statement *mid aco 'ntyāt paraḥ* (P.1.1.47) the *num* would be heard in the wrong place.
— One must think this over: is it *num* that must be generated, or *at*?
— *Num* is internal. Because it is internal, *num* is generated, and subsequently the *at* will appear.
— How is the *num* internal?
— Because it pertains to the theme.
— How?
— When there is a rule about *num*, the root must be stated as an initial element. Because only at the stage of the root being an initial element does *num* arise for a item with the marker *i*.

So it is internal. So in that case, the *at* is stated for the explicitly mentioned words *dhinvi* and *kṛṇvi*. *Num* is a general prescription. *Num* is prescribed in general for items with the marker *i*

[387] This maxim seems unique to the Vyāḍi commentator, at least in this form. It is not used in the *Mahābhāṣya*, discussed by the *paribhāṣā* commentators or cited by the *Kāśikā* or *Siddhāntakaumudī*.

[388] Although the question of the nasals in P.3.1.80 is discussed by some subcommentators, the question is never related to the *paribhāṣā*.

(cf. P.7.1.58). If the *at* is generated [first] because of being prescribed for the explicitly stated word then *num* may potentially be heard in an undesired location. Therefore he mentions the two augments *num*.

Explanation In the *Dhātupāṭha*, some roots are listed with a final *ĩ*. This *anubandha* is a signal that such a root takes the infix *n* (*num*) when followed by a suffix (P.7.1.58). Thus, *dhivĩ* becomes *dhinv* + suffix. Why, then, does Pāṇini mention the form *dhinvi* in P.3.1.80? Surely he should say either *dhinv* or *dhivĩ*, but not an amalgam of both?

The standard derivation of the 3rd. sg. present of the root *dhiv* is:

	dhivĩ					Dhp.1.624
i)	*dhinv*			+	*tip*	by P.7.1.58
ii)	*dhina*	+	*u*	+	*tip*	by P.1.3.9, 3.1.80, 1.1.52
iii)	*dhin*	+	*u*	+	*ti*	by P.6.4.48
iv)	*dhinoti*					by P.7.3.84, 1.1.56

The Vyāḍi commentator proposes adding the *a* first to just *dhiv*:

a)	*dhivĩ*			+	*tip*	
b)	*dhiva*	+	*u*	+	*tip*	by P.3.1.80 etc.

The next step, adding the nasal augment *num* by P.7.1.58, would give the wrong form **dhivan*, because of the marker *m* which sends the augment to the place after the last vowel.

On further consideration the Vyāḍi commentator decides that the claim of *num* to be applied first is that it is *antaraṅga* 'internal'. The claim of the *a* (*dhinv-* → *dhina-*) to be applied first is that it is prescribed specifically for *dhinv* and *kṛṇv* in P.3.1.80.

Thus, by teaching the roots in P.3.1.80 with their nasals already in place, Pāṇini is intimating that otherwise the latter of the two above choices would prevail: and this is the *paribhāṣā*.

Comments The term *anuṣaṅga* (83:3:5:12) is phoneticians' terminology for *āgama* 'augment'. It is used by Kātyāyana (Mbh.I.115:5), and, following him, by Patañjali (*ibidem* and I.58:21).

Argument 83.2 [83:13

— What is the point of intimating this?

— Where both an internal item or an explicitly mentioned word might apply, the explicitly mentioned word is stronger.

Comments This is, of course, no argument at all.

Paribhāṣā 84

The explicit mention of a marker is stronger than the explicit mention of a root.[389]

Comments Note the non-technical use of the word *prātipadika*.

Once again the Vyāḍi commentator is demonstrating his independence of thought in presenting fresh arguments for this rare *paribhāṣā*.

Argument 84.1[390] [84:2

— How is that known?
— Because he mentions *catur* 'four' in *na vṛdbhyaś caturbhyaḥ* (P.7.2.59). The mention of *catur* here is not necessary.
— If it is not done how does one know [that P.7.2.59 applies] 'after four'?
— After reading the four [roots] beginning with *vṛt* [Dhp.1.795–98] we shall put the marker *vṛt* at the end.
— This is unnecessary. It is done in the text itself. [The fifth root], *kṛpū* 'capability' [Dhp.1.799], will be regarded as the same as the marker *vṛt*.
— The prohibition of the augment *iṭ* would apply to *kṛp* too [by P.7.2.59].
— But it is desired [that it should do so: see, for example,] *tāsi ca klpaḥ* (P.7.2.60). So even without this mention of *catur* 'four', the augment *iṭ* will be prohibited after just the four. There is no point in mentioning *catur* [in P.7.2.59].
— This *vṛt* [marker] is not for the purpose of delimiting the items beginning with *vṛt* [the root].
— What, in that case?
— It is for the purpose of delimiting the items beginning with *dyut* [Dhp.1.777].

[389] This maxim seems to be peculiar to the Vyāḍi commentator.

[390] The problem of *catur* in P.7.2.59 is discussed in the *Kāśikā* (KV.V.739 f.) in terms similar to the Vyāḍi commentator's, but without reference to the *paribhāṣā*.

— How?
— If this *catur* [in P.7.2.59] is not mentioned it is possible to state that the marker *vṛt* is for the purpose of delimiting the items beginning with *vṛt* [the root]. For if the *catur* is mentioned then it would not be fore delimiting the items beginning the *vṛt* alone, because 'a prescription or a prohibition applies to the nearest item' (*paribhāṣā* 13). It would only be for delimiting the items beginning with *dyut*.
— Even so, the mention of *catur* is unnecessary.
— How?
— We shall distinguish the items beginning with *vṛt* from those beginning with *dyut*. 'After the *vṛts*, that is, after those items beginning with *vṛt* which are part of those beginning with *dyut*.'
— This, then, is a purpose [for mentioning *catur* in P.7.2.59]: *syandū* 'to flow out' [Dhp.1.798]. At the stage *syand sya ti* [in forming the future] the augment *iṭ* is prohibited by *na vṛdbhyaś caturbhyaḥ* (P.7.2.59), and it is optional because of the marker *ū* [on *syandū*: see P.7.2.44]. Here, the marker *ū* makes an operation which is due to the explicit mention of that marker; *na vṛdbhya* ... (P.7.2.59) has the explicit mention of a root. Because the explicit mention of a marker is stronger, the augment *iṭ* would be optional. By virtue of mentioning *catur* [in P.7.2.59], the one having the explicit mention of a root takes place. So this *paribhāṣā* is known to exist.

Explanation This argument is very clear. The only slight difficulty is an apparent inversion of the correct sense between 84:9 and 84:13. The *paribhāṣā* no. 13 should, in this context, suggest that the marker *vṛt* would primarily delimit those items closest to it in the *Dhātupāṭha*, i.e., the *vṛtādi* group (Dhp.1.795 f.), and thus be inapplicable to the larger, more distant *dyutādi* group (Dhp.1.777 f.).

Comments The phrase *kriyate nyāsa eva* (84:5) is a particular idiom of Patañjali's, occurring very frequently throughout the *Mahābhāṣya* and meaning 'this desideratum can be satisfied by the text of the rules as it stands'.

Argument 84.2[391] [84:20

— What is the point of intimating this?
— *Kṛtrimā kriyā* 'an artificial action' is validated. The rule *kṛñaḥ śa ca* (P.3.3.100), which is prescribed by the explicit mention of the root, does not block *ktri* which is taught by a marker [in P.3.3.88].

[391]This question is not discussed in the *Mahābhāṣya* or *Kāśikā*.

Explanation The conflict here is between P.3.3.100 which would apply *śa* and *kyap* after the root *kṛ* in the feminine, and P.3.3.88 which leads to the proper formation of *kṛ* + *tri* + *ma* + feminine suffix. The *paribhāṣā* selects the latter option.

Paribhāṣā 85

When there is an extension of generalities there is an extension of particulars.[392]

Explanation Several of Pāṇini's rules teach the extension of a prescription from one context to a larger, or different context (e.g., P.1.2.1 etc.). The present *paribhāṣā* teaches that when this happens it is the general conditions and properties of the first context which are transferred, not those which are in some way special to the initial context.

Argument 85.1[393] [85:2

— How is that known?

— Because he says *gotrād aṅkavat* (P.4.3.80).

— How come this is an intimation?

— One should say [instead] *gotrāntasyedaṃvat* 'what ends in a *gotra* [suffix] has [suffixes] like *idaṃ* [cf. P.6.3.120]. Then whatever is prescribed in the sense 'this is his' will arise [after a word ending in a *gotra* suffix].

And what is prescribed in the sense 'this is his'? It is just the same as [what is prescribed for] *aṅka*.

This being the case, by stating *gotrād aṅkavat* (P.4.3.80) he is intimating that the *paribhāṣā* does exist. Thereby, the word *tasya* 'his' in *tasyedam* 'this is his' (P.4.3.120) is a general reference: any item ending in the sixth [genitive] inflection should may be there. Therefore he states *aṅka* [in P.4.3.80].

---

[392] This *paribhāṣā* is originally Kātyāyana's third *vārttika* on P.1.1.56 (Mbh.I.134:16). It is repeated as *vārt.* 3 on P.6.3.68 (III.166:17). It is not used by Patañjali other than in these contexts. It is discussed by Puruṣottamadeva (no.164), Sīradeva (no. 106), Nīlakaṇṭha (no. 97), Haribhāskara (no. 108), Nāgeśa (no. 101), Śeṣādrisudhī (no. 93), and used in the *Siddhāntakaumudī* (SK.III.634:1–2 (2790)) and *Kāśikā* (on P.3.3.132, KV.III.101).

[393] This argument seems to be unique to the Vyāḍi commentator.

Explanation The thrust of this argument seems to be that if we tried to align P.4.3.80 with the general rule P.6.3.120 rather than with P.4.3.127, we would be able to use the suffix *aṇ* alone, and not *vuñ* too. By referring P.4.3.80 to the more specific *sūtra* (P.4.3.127), Pāṇini intimates that otherwise we would lose the specifics and gain only the generally applicable suffixes.

Comments This is not a sound argument since the changes proposed to P.4.3.80 do not improve the rule in any way. There is no original redundancy (*vaiyarthya*). No *prayojana* is offered.

All other commentators, including Patañjali, take this *paribhāṣā* to be *lokasiddha*, based on mundane experience.

Twice fixed is well fixed.[394]

Comments The Vyāḍi commentator's style changes abruptly here and in the next *paribhāṣā*, no. 87.

Argument 86.1[395]

[86:2

— How, then, is one to know that this *paribhāṣā* exists?
— It is said, 'since in *peṣaṃvāsavāhanadhiṣu ca* (P.6.3.58) he prescribes that *udaka* become *uda* before the word *dhi*.'
— How could one not say this?
— It is said, 'because it is achieved by the previous rule, *udakasyādeḥ saṃjñāyām* (P.6.3.57).' This being the case, by teaching the second rule, *peṣaṃvāsavāhanadhiṣu ca* (P.6.3.58) he is intimating that the *paribhāṣā* 'twice fixed is well fixed' does exist.

Explanation The unstated prerequisite for this argument to work is that *udadhi*, derived by P.6.3.58, is a proper name and can therefore satisfy the condition *saṃjñāyām* of P.6.3.57.

Comments The Vyāḍi commentator's repeated use of *ucyate* (86:2:4) and the slightly untypical use of words like *gamyate* (86:2) strongly suggests that he is quoting this discussion from some unknown source.[396] The style of the remainder of this work too is in a noticeably different idiom from the earlier parts of the book.

Furthermore, the rule under discussion, P.6.3.58, appears not at all in the *Mahābhāṣya*. Candra, however, regards *udadhi* as a *saṃjñā* and derives it by his equivalent of P.6.3.57 (Ca.5.2.65). In his commentary on Ca.5.2.65–68, Candra even uses the phrase *udakasya udabhāva*, which the Vyāḍi commentator also uses (86:3).[397] These terms betray a non-Pāṇinian approach to morphophonemic change. They suggest the transformation of one item into another, as opposed to the metaphor of replacement.

---

[394] This maxim is used once by Patañjali (Mbh.III.119:21) is his discussion of *vārt.* 2 on P.6.1.223. It does not seem to appear elsewhere in the Pāṇinian literature.
[395] This argument seems to be unique to the Vyāḍi commentator.
[396] Cf. the *Kāśikā* on P.6.3.58 (KV.V.257:4–5): ... *udakasya uda ity ayam ādeśo bhavati.*
[397] Ca.5.2.65: *nāmny udakasyodaḥ| udakasya saṃjñāyām uttarapada udabhāvo bhavati.*

The *Kāśikā* in its gloss on these rules replaces this mode of expression with the normal idea of substitution: *uda* replaces *udaka* (KV.V.257).

It is possible, then, that the Vyāḍi commentator is here actually quoting or referring to Candra's grammar, or to a common source, no longer extant.

Argument 86.2[398] [86:8

— What is the point of intimating this?

— Something fixed once occurs nowhere. Thus for example,

aciraprakāśakā vidyut 'the briefly shining lightning',

by *pratyayasthāt kāt pūrvasyāta id āpy asupaḥ* (P.7.3.44).

It is to be used after pondering things such as this and other things too.

Explanation The point here seems to be that by P.7.3.44 we should expect the form *aciraprakāśikā*. But because the rule is not reinforced elsewhere, the (strictly speaking illegal) form *-prakāśakā* occurs.

Comments The reading '*-prakāśakā*' is that of P_1 only, unfortunately. Reading with the majority of the manuscripts would make nonsense of the example.

398 This argument seems to be unique to the Vyāḍi commentator.

Paribhāṣā 87

When a primary nominal suffix is mentioned a preceding *gati* prefix or case-related word is also meant.[399]

— When a word ending in a primary nominal suffix is mentioned, that item with a preceding *gati* prefix or a preceding case-related word (*kāraka*) is meant.

Explanation The *gatis* are a subset of the general group of particles (*nipātas*), and are defined in P.1.4.60–82. The case-related words (*kārakas*) are defined in P.1.4.23–55.

Normally a primary nominal suffix (*kṛt*) is prescribed after an item such as a *dhātu* or *aṅga*. Then, by *tadantavidhi* (P.1.1.72) any reference to the *kṛt* also refers to the whole unit of root + *kṛt* or *aṅga* + *kṛt* etc.

The present *paribhāṣā* extends this principle so that a reference to the *kṛt* also covers any *gati* or *kāraka* which is prefixed to the root or *aṅga*.

[399] This *paribhāṣā* is widely accepted and used. It is originally a *vārttika* of Kātyāyana, no. 9 on P.1.4.13 (Mbh.I.318:8). It is also obliquely referred to in the *ślokavārttika* on P.7.1.37 (III.256:8–11).

Patañjali mentions it seven times (I.318:9:16, 346:11; III.128:12, 255:23, 256:1:3).

It is discussed by Puruṣottamadeva (no. 46), Sīradeva (no. 62), Nīlakaṇṭha (no. 35), Haribhāskara (no. 64), Nāgeśa (no. 28) and Śeṣādrisudhī (no. 28). It is cited in the *Kāśikā* on P.6.2.49 (KV.V.57) and 7.1.37 (KV.V.573), and *Siddhāntakaumudī* on P.2.1.32 (SK.II.39:5 (694)).

Argument 87.1[400] [87:3

— How does one know that this *paribhāṣā* exists?
— Because, concerning *vyākrośī* 'altercation' he says *ṇac* in the sense 'reciprocal action' (P.3.3.43).
— How come this is an intimation?
— This rule is apparently unnecessary.
— † But if this [rule] were not specified, would not *y* and *v* exist [and be affected?] by *na yvābhyāṃ padāntābhyāṃ pūrvau tu tābhyām aic* (P.7.3.3). †
— There is no problem. Since this is under the general heading 'presuffixal base', one understands the words 'that item after which there is a rule about a suffix, up to but not including the suffix' (P.1.4.13).
— Surely only an item beginning with a root is a presuffixal base. The term presuffixal base does not apply to [the prefixes] *vyā*. Therefore *karmavyatihāre* ... (P.3.3.43) is not necessary. By giving it, he is intimating that the *paribhāṣā* 'when a primary nominal suffix is mentioned a preceding *gati* prefix or case-related word is also meant' does exist.

Explanation *Vyākrośī* is formed from the string

vi + *ā* + *kruś* + *ṇac* + *añ* + *ṅīṣ*

Ṇac is prescribed by P.3.3.43, and following it *añ* by P.5.4.14.

Why does Pāṇini say that *ṇac* has the particular sense '*vyatihāra*'? So that P.7.3.6 will prevent P.7.3.3 giving the wrong form **vaiyākrośī*. But this assumes that P.7.3.3 applies to the whole of *vyākrośī* including the *gatis* *vyā*, and not just to the *aṅga*, *kruś*. Therefore Pāṇini must have had the *paribhāṣā* in mind.

Comments This argument is curious for what it is not, as much as for what it is. In his comments on *vārttika* 6 and P.6.2.47, and again on *vārttika* 10 and P.1.4.13, Patañjali unequivocally declares that this *paribhāṣā* is intimated by P.6.2.49 which contains the apparently unnecessary word *anantara*. It is not common for Patañjali to be this clear cut about such issues, and by quietly giving a totally different justification for the *paribhāṣā*, the Vyāḍi commentator is loudly ignoring the *Mahābhāṣya*.

All other commentators use Patañjali's arguments.

[400] This argument is apparently unique to the Vyāḍi commentator.

Argument 87.2[401] [87:12

— What is the point of intimating this?
— In [the examples]

> *prayāyiṇe, prayāyiṇaḥ* 'to or from going forwards',
> *māṣavāpiṇi* 'in sowing the rice'

the retroflexion of the *ṇ* by *prātipadikāntanumvibhaktiṣu ca* (P.8.4.11) is valid.

Explanation The first two words are examples of a *gatipūrva* word, the last two of a *kārakapūrva* (in this *karma*).

The rule P.8.4.11 teaches the optional substitution of *ṇ* for the final *n* of a nominal stem, *num* or an inflexional *n* in the second member of a compound, when the first member contains *r* or *ṣ* and only the items specified in P.8.4.2 intervene.

Mention of a nominal stem includes mention of the first member of the compound too, by this *paribhāṣā*.

Comments This argument is not cogent for the simple reason that not all *prātipadikas* are *kṛts*; there are also *uṇādis*, *taddhitas* etc. The *paribhāṣā* is not really applicable in P.8.4.11.

Thus ends the *Paribhāṣāvṛtti* according to the Vyāḍi commentator.

Comments This colophon is, strictly speaking, ambiguous. It could signal the end of the commentary on the Vyāḍi commentator's *paribhāṣās*, or it could signal the end of the Vyāḍi commentator's discussion of the *paribhāṣās*. As mentioned in the introduction, there is a separate manuscript tradition of a *Vyāḍīyaparibhāṣāpāṭha*, a bare list of *paribhāṣās* attributed to the Vyāḍi commentator, so the former interpretation might have some weight. For our purposes, however, this is not an important matter. We have been interested in the author of the present commentary, whatever his name, and it has been established beyond reasonable doubt that this commentator is not the same person as the Vyāḍi mentioned in the *Mahābhāṣya*.

---

[401] This is again unique tc the Vyāḍi commentator, although the examples *māṣavāpin*, *vrīhivāpin* are found in the *Kāśikā* on P.8.4.11 etc. (KV.VI.618), and in the *Mahābhāṣya* (I.115:22).

Bibliography

Abhyankar, Kashinath Vasudev, 1955. "A Short Note on Paribhāṣā works in Sanskrit Grammar", *ABORI*, **36**. 157–62.

—, 1961. *A Dictionary of Sanskrit Grammar*. Baroda: Oriental Institute.

—, 1967. *Paribhāṣāsaṃgraha (vyāḍiśākaṭāyanādiproktaparibhāṣāpāṭhānāṃ tatpraṇītavṛttīnāṃ ca saṃgrahaḥ)*. Poona: BORI.

—, and Govind Vinayak Devasthali (eds.), 1978. *Vedavikṛtilakṣaṇasaṃgraha (a Collection of Twelve Tracts on Vedavikṛtis and allied topics)*. Poona: BORI.

Aklujkar, Ashok Narhar, 1974. "The Authorship of the Vākyakāṇḍa-ṭīkā", in *Festschrift Charudeva Shastri*, ed. Suniti Kumar Chatterji, et. al. New Delhi: Charu Deva Shastri Felicitation Committee. Pp. 165–88.

Allen, William Sidney, 1953. *Phonetics in Ancient India*. London: Oxford University Press.

Amara, 1969. *Amarakośa saṃkṣiptamāheśvaryā ṭīkayā ṭippaṇyā ca sametaḥ*. 10th edition. Mumbai [Bombay]: Nirṇayasāgara Prakāśana.

Aṣṭavikṛtivivṛti of Madhusūdana Maskarin: references to Abhyankar and Devasthali 1978.75–111.

Ayer, Alfred J. 1972. *Russell*. London: Fontana/Collins.

Bālamanoramā of Vāsudevadīkṣita: references to Caturveda and Bhāskara, 1958–61.

Belvalkar, Shripad Krishna, 1938. *Descriptive Catalogue of the Government Collections of Manuscripts in the Government Mss. Library ...*, vol. 2, *Grammar, part 1: Vedic and Pāṇinīya*. Poona: BORI.

Bhārgavaśāstrī Bhikājīpanta Jośī, 1942–1945. *ŚrīmadbhagavatPatañjalimaharṣipraṇītasya Pāṇinīyavyākaraṇamahābhāṣyasya ... ṛṣikalpopādhyāyaKaiyaṭapraṇītena Mahābhāṣyavyākhyānena pradīpena parivṛtaḥ ... Nāgojībhaṭṭakṛtena Bhāṣyapradīpavyākhyānenoddyotetyanvarthanāmadheyena samullāsitaś ca*. Vols. IV (1942), V (1945). Bombay: Nirṇayasāgara Press. [Covering P.4.1–5.4 and P.6.1–6.4; see *Mahābhāṣya* entry below for details of other parts.]

Bhartṛhari, see *Mahābhāṣyadīpikā* and *Vākyapadīya*.

Bhāṣāvṛtti of Puruṣottamadeva: references to Chakravarti 1918.

Bhattacharya, Dinesh Chandra, 1946. *Paribhāṣāvṛtti, Jñāpaka-samuccaya, Kārakacakra by Puruṣottamadeva. Edited with Introduction, Appendix &c.* Rajshahi: Varendra Research Museum.

Birwé, Robert, 1966. *Studien zu Adhyaya III der Aṣṭādhyāyī Pāṇinis*. Wiesbaden: Harrassowitz.

—, 1967. "Fragments from three losts Kośas: Vyāḍi's Utpalinī II", *Journal of the American Oriental Society*, **87**, pp. 39–52.

Bloomfield, Leonard, 1933. *Language*. New York: H. Holt & Co.

Böhtlingk, Otto, 1887. *Pāṇini's Grammatik: Herausgegeben, Übersetz Erläutert und mit Verschiedenen Indices Versehen*. Leipzig: Haessel.

Bronkhorst, Johannes, 1983. "On the History of Pāṇinian Grammar in the early centuries following Patajñjali," *Journal of Indian Philosophy*, **11**, pp. 357–412.

—, 1987 (ed. and tr.). *Mahābhāṣyadīpikā of Bhartṛhari. Fascicule IV: Āhnika I*. Poona: BORI. [A facsimile reproduction of the complete surviving manuscript was published by BORI, Poona, 1980.]

—, 1986. *Tradition and Argument in Classical Indian Linguistics: The Bahiraṅga-Paribhāṣā in the Paribhāṣenduśekhara*. Dordrecht: Reidel.

Bubenik, Vitus, [1978]. *An Introduction to the Study of Morphology. Manuscript for Internal use of Students of morphology at Memorial University of Newfoundland*. Unpublished: circulated in 1978.

Bühler, Georg, 1877. *Detailed report of a tour in search of Sanskrit MSS, made in Kāshmīr, Rajputana and Central India*. Bombay, London: Bombay branch of the Royal Asiatic Society.

Cāndravyākaraṇa of Candra: references to Chatterji 1953–61. See also Liebich 1902.

Cardona, George, 1970. "Some principles of Pāṇini's Grammar", *Journal of Indian Philosophy*, **1**, pp. 40–74.

—, 1976. *Pāṇini: a Survey of Research*. The Hague: Mouton & Co. (Reprinted, Delhi: Motilal Banarsidass, 1980.)

—, 1978. "Still again on the history of the Mahābhāṣya", *ABORI*, **58–59**, pp. 79–99.

—, 1988. *Pāṇini: His Work and its Traditions*, volume 1: *Background and Introduction*. Delhi: Motilal Banarsidass.

Caturveda, Giridharaśarmā and Parameśvarānandaśarma Bhāskara (eds.), 1958–61. *ŚrīBhaṭṭojīdīkṣitaviracitā Vaiyākaraṇasiddhāntakaumudī, śrīmadVāsudevadīkṣitapraṇītayā Bālamanoramākhyayā vyākhyayā śrīJñānendrasarasvatīviracitayā Tattvabodhinyākhyayā vyākhyayā ca sanāthitā*. 4 vols. Dillī, Vārāṇasī, etc.: Motilal Banarsidass. [Volume IV includes Jayakṛṣṇa's commentary *Subodhinī* and Nāgeśa's subcommentary *Laghuśabdenduśekhrara* on the *svara* sections of the *Siddhāntakaumudī*.]

Chakravarti, Srish Chandra (ed.), 1918. *The Bhāṣāvṛtti, a commentary on Pāṇini's Grammatical Aphorisms Excepting those which Exclusively Pertain to the Veda, by Purushottama deva; Edited with Annotations*. Rajshahi: The Varendra Research Society.

Chatterji, Kshitish Chandra (ed.), 1953–61. *Cāndravyākaraṇa of Candragomin*. 2 vols. Poona: Deccan College.

Chimpa, Lama and Alaka Chattopadhyaya (trs.), 1980. *Tārānātha's History of Buddhism in India*. Calcutta: Bagchi.

Coulson, Michael, 1976. *Sanskrit, an Introduction to the Classical Language*. London: Hodder & Stoughton.

Dadhirāmaśarman, 1988 (reprint). *ŚrīmanmaharṣiPatañjalivinirmitaṃ Vyākaraṇamahābhāṣyam, śrīmadupādhyāyaKaiyaṭapraṇītena Bhāṣyapradīpena śrīmanNāgeśabhaṭṭaviracitaBhāṣyapradīpoddyotodbhāsitena samullasitena*. Vol. VI (1988 reprint). Delhi: Chaukhamba Sanskrit Pratishthan. [Covers P.7.1–8.4. NB: page numbering restarts for *adhyāya* 8.]

Deshpande, Madhav Murlidhar, 1965. *Critical Studies in Indian Grammarians I: The Theory of Homogeneity* [*Sāvarṇya*]. Ann Arbor: University of Michigan.

Devasthali, Govind Vinayak, 1942. "On the probable date of Śabara-Svāmin", *ABORI*, **23**, pp. 84–97.

—, 1949. "Positive data for the date of Śabarasvāmin", *The Journal of the Ganganāth Jhā Research Institute*, **6**, pp. 231–40.

—, 1951. "Śabara and Patañjali", *Journal of the University of Bombay*, **20**, pp. 101–6.
—, 1967. *Anubandhas of Pāṇini*. Poona: University of Poona.
Dvivedī, Vindhyeśvarī Prasāda, 1917. *Śabdakaustubha by Paṇḍit Bhaṭṭoji Dīkshita, vol. III (Śabdakaustubhaḥ sarvatantra svatantraśrīmadBhaṭṭojīdīkṣitaviracitaḥ)*. Benares: Chowkhamba. [Covers P.4.]
Filliozat, Pierre-Sylvain, 1988. *Grammaire Sanskrite Pâninéenne*. Paris: Picard.
Frauwallner, Erich, 1973. *History of Indian Philosophy ... translated from original German into English by V. M. Bedekar*. 2 vols. Delhi etc.: Motilal Banarsidass.
Gadā of Vaidyanātha: references to Gokhale 1913.
Gaṇapāṭha: references to Böhtlingk 1877.
Garuḍpurāṇa, 1978. *The Garuda Purana*, translated by a Board of Scholars. 3 vols. Delhi etc.: Motilal Banarsidass.
Geiger, Bernhard, 1909. "Mahābhāṣya zu P. VI,4,22 und 132 nebst Kaiyaṭa's Kommentar, ubersetzt, erläutert und mit einem Anhang", *Sitzungberichte der kaiserlichen Akademie der Wissenschaften zu Wien*, **160.8**, pp. 1–76 [references to reprint in Staal 1972].
Gokhale, Gaṇeśaśāstri (ed.), 1913. *VaidyanāthakṛtaGadāṭīkā saṃvalitaḥ Paribhāṣenduśekhara*. Poona: Ānandāśrama.
Grierson, George, 1916. "On the Sarada Alphabet", *Journal of the Royal Asiatic Society*, **17**, pp. 677–708.
Grünwedel, Albert, 1914. *Tāranātha's Edelsteinmine, das Buch von den Vermittlern der Sieben Inspirationen, aus dem Tibetischen übersetzt*. Petrograd: L'Académie Impériale des Sciences.
Haracaritacintāmaṇi of Jayadratha, : Chapter 27 of this work is reproduced in *Mahābhāṣya* (q.v. below), part I, pp. 6–10.
Haribhāskara, *Paribhāṣābhāskara*: references to Abhyankar 1967.311–774.
Housman, Alfred Edward (ed.), 1903–30. *M. Manilii, Astronomicon, recensuit et enarravit A. E. Housman*. 5 vols. London: Grant Richards.
Iyer, Subramania K. A. (ed.), 1963. *Vākyapadīya of Bhartṛhari with the commentary of Helārāja; kāṇḍa III, part 1*. Poona: Deccan College.
Jayadratha, *Haracaritacintāmaṇi*: Chapter 27 of this work is reproduced in *Mahābhāṣya* (q.v. below), part I, pp. 6–10.
Jhalkīkar, Bhīmācārya, 1978. *Nyāyakośa or Dictionary of Technical Terms of Indian Philosophy, by Mahāmahopādhyāya Bhīmācārya Jhalkīkar, Revised and re-edited by Mahāmahopādhyāya Vāsudeva Shāstrī Abhyankar*. Poona: BORI.
Joshi, S. D., 1975. *Patañjali's Vyākaraṇa-Mahābhāṣya Kārakāhnika (P.1.4.23–1.4.55). Introduction, Translation and Notes*. Poona: University of Poona.
—, 1980. *Patañjali's Vyākaraṇa-Mahābhāṣya Vibhaktyāhnika (P.2.3.18–2.3.45). Introduction, Text, Translation and Notes*. Poona: University of Poona.
—, and Jouthe A. F. Roodbergen, 1969. *Patañjali's Vyākaraṇa-Mahābhāṣya Avyayībhāvatatpuruṣāhnika (P.2.1.2–2.1.49). Edited with Translation and Explanatory Notes*. Poona: University of Poona.
—, and Jouthe A. F. Roodbergen, 1971. *Patañjali's Vyākaraṇa-Mahābhaṣya Karmadhārayāhnika (P.2.1.51–2.1.72). Edited with translation and explanatory Notes*. Poona: University of Poona.
—, and Paul Kiparski, 1979. "Siddha and Asiddha in Pāṇinian Phonology", chapter 5 in *Current Approaches to Phonological Theory*, ed. D. Dinnsen. Bloomington: Indiana University Press.

—, and Saroja Bhaṭe, 1983. "The Role of the Particle *ca* in the Interpretation of the *Aṣṭādhyāyī*", in *Proceedings of the International Seminar Studies in the Aṣṭādhyāyī of Pāṇini*, edited by S. D. Joshi and S. D. Laddu. Pune: University of Poona. Pp. 167–227.

—, and Saroja Bhaṭe, 1984. *The Fundamentals of Anuvṛtti*. Pune: University of Poona, 1984.

Kaiyaṭa, *Mahābhāṣyapradīpa*: references are to the volumes enumerated under *Mahābhāṣya* below (q.v.).

Kāśikā of Vāmana and Jayāditya: references to Shastri and Shukla 1965–67. Cf. also Śarmā and Deśapāṇḍe 1970.

Kātantradhātupāṭha: references to Palsule 1955.

Keith, A. Berriedale, 1920. *A History of Sanskrit Literature*. Oxford: Oxford University Press.

Kenney, E. J., 1974. *The Classical Text: Aspects of Editing in the Age of the Printed Book*. Berkeley etc.: Univ. of California Press.

Kielhorn, Lorenz Franz, 1887. "Some devices of Indian Grammarians", *Indian Antiquary*, **16**, pp. 248–63. (Reprinted in Staal 1972, pp. 128–64.)

—, (tr.) 1874. *The Paribhāṣenduśekhara of Nāgojibhaṭṭa*, Part II, *Translation and Notes*, Bombay: Government Central Book Depot. Second edition by K. V. Abhyankar, 1960. Poona: BORI.

—, (ed.), 1880–85. *The Vyākaraṇa-Mahābhāṣya of Patañjali*. 3 vols. Bombay: Government Central Press. Third edition by K. V. Abhyankar, 1962–72, Poona: BORI.

Kiparski, Paul, 1971. *Pāṇini as a Variationist*, ed. by S. D. Joshi. Poona and Cambridge, Mass: University of Poona and M.I.T.

Kṣīrataraṅgiṇī of Kṣīrasvāmin: references to Mīmāṃsaka 1957/58.

Laddu, Sureshachandra Dnyaneshwar, 1973. "The Device of Contiguity as a Key to Interpreting Pāṇini's Rules", in *Centre for the Advanced Study of Sanskrit Studies, number I*, edited by R. N. Dandekar. Poona: University of Poona. Pp. 157–171.

Lagefoged, Peter, 1971. *Preliminaries to linguistic phonetics*. Chicago and London: University of Chicago Press.

Laghuśabdenduśekhara of Nāgeśbhaṭṭa: references to Caturveda and Bhāskara, 1958–61.

Lahiri, Prabodh Chandra, 1935. *Concordance Pāṇini–Patañjali (Mahābhāṣya)* Breslau: Marcus. [N.B. corrections from Birwé 1966.204–7].

Liebich, Bruno, 1902. *Cāndra-Vyākaraṇa, Die Grammatik des Candragomin, Sūtra, Uṇādi, Dhātupāṭha*. Leipzig: Brokhaus.

Lyons, John, 1968. *Introduction to Theoretical Linguistics*. Cambridge: Cambridge University Press.

—, 1978. *Chomsky*. 11th Impression. Glasgow: Fontana/Collins.

Mādhava 1977. *Śrīmādhavācāryapraṇītaḥ Sarvadarśanasaṃgrahaḥ. Madhusūdanasarasvatīkṛtaḥ Prasthānabhedaś ca. Etat pustakam ānandāśramasthapaṇḍitaiḥ saṃśodhitaiḥ.* 4th edition. Puṇyapattana [Poona]: Ānandāśrama. [Granthāṅkaḥ 51.]

Mādhavīyadhātuvṛtti of Sāyaṇa: references to Śāstrī 1867 and Shastri 1964.

Mahābhāṣya of Patañjali: for the *mūla* referemces are to Kielhorn 1880–85. For the commentaries *Pradīpa* by Kaiyaṭa and *Uddyota* by Nāgeśa, the editions used are as follow:

I. Raghunātha [Kāśīnātha] Śāstrī and Śivadattaśarmā [D. Kudāla] 1932. (Covers P.1.1)

II. Śivadattaśarman 1988 (reprint): (Covers P.1.2–2.4)

III. Raghunātha [Kāśīnātha] Śāstrī, and Śivadattaśarmā [D. Kudāla], 1937. (Covers P.3)

IV. Bhārgavaśāstrī Bhikājīpanta Jośī, 1942. (Covers P.4.1–5.4)

V. Bhārgavaśāstrī Bhikājīpanta Jośī, 1945. (Covers P.6.1–6.4)

VI. Dadhirāmaśarman, 1988 (reprint). (Covers P.7.1–8.4)

Mahābhāṣyadīpikā of Bhartṛhari: references to Bronkhorst 1987.

Mahābhāṣyapradīpa of Kaiyaṭa: references to the volumes enumerated under *Mahābhāṣya* above (q.v.).

Mahāvṛtti of Abhayanandin: references to Tripāṭhī and Chaturvedi 1956.

Maitreyarakṣita, see *Tantrapradīpa*.

Maten, E. P., 1973. *Budhasvāmin's Bṛhatkathāślokasaṃgraha: A Literary Study of an Ancient Indian Narrative*. Leiden: Brill.

Matilal, Bimal Krishna, 1971. *Epistemology, Grammar and Logic in Indian Philosophical Analysis*. The Hague, Paris: Mouton.

Mīmāṃsaka, Yudhiṣṭhira (ed.), 1957–58. *Kṣīrataraṅgiṇī: Kṣīrasvāmiviracitā Pāṇinīyadhātupāṭhasya paścimôttaraśākhāyā Vyākhyā*. Amritsar: Rāma Lāl Kapūr Trust.

—, 1973. *Saṃskṛta Vyākaraṇa-śāstra kā Itihāsa (tīn bhāgoṃ meṃ pūrṇa)*. 3 vols. Sonipat: Rāma Lāl Kapūr Trust.

Nāgeśa, *Paribhāṣenduśekhara*: references to Gokhale 1913 (but numbering according to Keilhorn 1874).

—, *Mahābhāṣyapradīpoddyota*: references to the volumes enumerated under *Mahābhāṣya* above (q.v.).

Nāmaliṅgānuśāsana of Amara: references to Amara 1969.

Nene, Gopāla Śāstrī (ed.), 1929. *The Śabda Kaustubha by Pandit Bhattoji Dīkshit vol. II ... from the second pāda of the 1st adhyāya to second pāda of 3rd adhyāya ....* Benares: Chowkhamba.

—, and Mukund Śāstrī Puntamkar (eds.), 1933. *The Śabda Kaustubha by Śrī Bhaṭṭoji Dīkshita, vol. I, ... first pāda of the first adhyāya complete*. Benares: Chowkhamba.

Nīlakaṇṭha, *Paribhāṣāvṛtti*: references to Abhyankar 1967.292–416.

Nyāyakośa: see Jhalkīkar 1978.

Nyāsa of Jinendrabuddhipāda: references to Shastri and Shuka 1965–67.

Ojihara, Yutaka and Louis Renou. 1960–67. *La Kāśikā-vṛtti (adhyāya I, pāda 1) traduite et commentée*. Three fascicules, the last by Y. Ojihara alone. Paris: École Français d'Extrême-Orient.

Padamañjarī of Haradatta: references to Shastri and Shukla 1965–67.

Palsule, Gajanan Balakrishna, 1955. *A Concordance of Sanskrit Dhātupāṭhas (with Index of Meanings)*. Poona: Deccan College.

—, 1966. *Saṃjñāyām in Pāṇini*. Volume A.10 of *Publications of the Centre of Advanced Study in Sanskrit*. Poona: University of Poona.

—, 1970, *Some Views of Pāṇini and his Followers on Object Language and Meta-Language*. Volume A.36 of *Publications of the Centre of Advanced Study in Sanskrit*. Poona: University of Poona.

Pathak, S., and S. Chitrao, 1935. *Word Index to Pāṇini-sūtra-pāṭha and Pariśiṣṭas*. Poona: BORI.

Patkar, M. M. 1970. *Descriptive catalogue of manuscripts in the Shri Ranbir Sanskrit Research Institute, Jammu (Kashmir)*. Vol. 1. Jammu: SRSR Institute.

Pinchuk, Isadore. 1977. *Scientific and Technical Translation*. London: A. Deutsch.
Prakriyākaumudī of Rāmacandra: references to Trivedī 1925–30.
[*Mahābhāṣya*]*Pradīpa* of Kaiyaṭa: references to the volumes enumerated under *Mahābhāṣya* above (q.v.).
Puruṣottamadeva, *Laghuparibhāṣāvṛtti*: references to Abhyankar 1967.115–360. See also Bhattacharya 1946.
Raghavan, V., and K. Kunjunni Raja (eds.), 1968²–. *New Catalogus Catalogorum. An Alphabetical Register of Sanskrit and Allied works and Authors*. Vols. 1–. Madras: University of Madras.
Raghunātha [Kāśīnātha] Śāstrī, and Śivadattaśarmā [D. Kudāla], 1932–37. *ŚrīmadbhagavatPatañjalimuninirmitaṃ Pāṇinīyavyākaraṇamahābhāṣyam, etadvyākhyānabhūta upādhyāyaKaiyaṭapraṇīto Bhāṣyapradīpas tadvyākhyānabhūto Nāgeśabhaṭṭaviracito Bhāṣyapradīpoddyotaḥ*. Vols. I (1932), III (1937). Bombay: Nirṇayasāgara Press. [Covering P.1.1 and P.3.1–3.4; see *Mahābhāṣya* entry above for details of other parts.]
Rājataraṅgiṇī of Kalhaṇa: references to Stein 1892.
Rau, Wilhelm. 1977. *Bhartṛharis Vākyapadīya: die Mūlakārikās nach den Handschriften herausgegeben und mit einem Pāda-Index versehen*. Wiesbaden: Franz Steiner.
Rây, P. 1956. *History of Chemistry in Ancient and Medieval India, Incorporating the History of Hindu Chemistry by Acharya Prafulla Chandra Rây*. Calcutta: Indian Chemical Society.
Ráy, Prafulla Chandra. 1907–09. *A History of Hindu Chemistry*, 2 vols. London: Williams and Norgate.
Ṛgvedaprātiśākhya: references to Shastri 1931.
Robins, R. H. 1967. *A Short History of Linguistics*. London: Longmans.
Rocher, Ludo, 1986. *The Purāṇas*, vol. II.3 of *A History of Indian Literature*, ed. Jan Gonda. Wiesbaden: Harrassowitz.
Roodbergen, Jouthe A. F., and Shivaram Dattatray Joshi. 1974. *Patañjali's Vyākaraṇa-Mahābhāṣya Bahuvrīhidvandvāhnika, (P.2.2.23–2.2.38), Text, Translation and Notes*. Poona: University of Poona.
Śabdakaustubha of Bhaṭṭojīdīkṣita: references to Nene and Puṇtamkar 1933 (*adhyāya* 1.1), Nene 1929 (*adhyāyas* 1.2–3.2), and Dvivedī 1917 (*adhyāya* 4).
Saduktikarṇāmṛta of Śrīdharadāsa: references to Sternbach 1978.
Sainsbury, R. M. 1979. *Russell*. London: RKP.
Sammatākāra. Unknown author of *Sammatā*, apparently a commentary on the *Dhātupāṭha*.
Sarasvatī, Dayānanda (ed.), 1969, *Atha vedāṅgaprakāśaḥ, tatratya ekādaśo bhāgaḥ Dhātupāṭhaḥ* .... Ajamerunagara: Vaidika yantrālaye mudritaḥ.
Śarmā, Āryendra, Khanderāva Deśapāṇḍe and Da. Go. Pādhye (eds.), 1969–76. *ŚrīVāmanaJayādityaviracitā Pāṇinīyāṣṭādhyāyīsūtravṛttiḥ Kāśikā*. 3 vols. Hyderabad: Sanskrit Academy, Osmania University.
Sarvadarśanasaṅgraha of Mādhava: references to Mādhava 1977.
Śāstrī, Bhāradvāja Dāmodara (ed.). 1867. *Mādhavīyadhātuvṛtti, Nāmadhātuvṛttiś ca, śrīyuta Mādhavācāryasodareṇa śrīSāyaṇācāryeṇa viracitā*. Kaśī: Medical Hall Press.
Sāyaṇa 1867: *Mādhavīyadhātuvṛtti*. references to Śāstrī 1867.
—, 1964: *Mādhavīyadhātuvṛtti*. references to Shastri 1964.
Scharfe, Hartmut, 1977. *Grammatical Literature*, Vol. V.II.2 of *A History of Indian Literature*, ed. Jan Gonda. Wiesbaden: Harrassowitz.
Śeṣādrisudhī, *Paribhāṣābhāskara*: references to Abhyankar 1967.378–465.

Sharma, Raghunatha (ed.), 1968. *Vākyapadīyam, Part II, with the commentary Ambākartrī*. Varanasi: Vārāṇaseya Saṃskṛta Viśvavidyālaya.

Shastri, Dwarikadas (ed.) 1964. *The Mādhavīyā Dhātuvṛtti (a treatise on Sanskrit Roots Based on the Dhātupāṭha of Pāṇini) by Sāyaṇācārya*. Varanasi: Prāchya Bhāratī Prakāshana.

—, and Kalika Prasad Shukla (eds.), 1965–67. *Nyāsa or Pañcikā commentary of ācārya Jinendrabuddhipāda and Padamañjarī of Haradatta Miśra on the Kāśikāvṛtti ... of Vāmana-Jayāditya*. 6 vols. Varanasi: Prāchya Bhāratī Prakāshana and Tara Publications.

Shastri, Mangal Deva (ed.), 1931. *The Ṛgveda-Prātiśākhya with the commentary of Uvaṭa ... vol. II, Text in Sūtra Form ....* Allahabad: The Indian Press.

Siddhāntakaumudī of Bhaṭṭojīdīkṣita: references to Caturveda and Bhāskara 1958–61.

Sīradeva, *Bṛhatparibhāṣāvṛtti*: references to Abhyankar 1967.161–272.

Śivadattaśarman, 1988 (reprint). *ŚrīmanmaharṣiPatañjalivinirmitaṃ Vyākaraṇamahābhāṣyam, śrīmadupādhyāyaKaiyaṭapraṇītena Bhāṣyapradīpena śrīmanNāgeśabhaṭṭaviracitaBhāṣyapradīpoddyotodbhāsitena samullasitena*. Vol. II (1988 reprint). Delhi: Chaukhamba Sanskrit Pratishthan. [Covers P.1.2–2.4.]

Speijer, J. S. 1886. *Sanskrit Syntax*. Leyden: Brill. (Reprinted 1980, Delhi: Motilal Banarsidass.)

Staal, Johan Frederik (ed.), 1972. *A Reader on the Sanskrit Grammarians*. Cambridge, Mass.: The MIT Press.

Stein, Marc Aurel, 1892. *Kalhaṇa's Rājataraṅgiṇī or the Chronicle of the Kings of Kashmir ....* 2 vols. Bombay: Education Society's Press.

—, 1894. *Catalogue of the Sanskrit Manuscripts in the Raghunatha Temple Library of His Highness the Maharaja of Jammu and Kashmir*. Bombay: Nirnaya-Sagara Press.

Sternbach, Ludwik, 1978. *A Descriptive Catalogue of Poets Quoted in Sanskrit Anthologies and Inscriptions*. 2 vols. Wiesbaden: Harrassowitz.

Subodhinī of Jayakṛṣṇa: references to Caturveda and Bhāskara 1958–61.

Tantrapradīpa of Maitreyarakṣita (also known as *Tantravārttika*): Prof. S. D. Joshi informs me that Kṣitīśacandra Cakravārtī of Calcutta was reported to have a complete MS of this text. See also Abhyankar 1967.30, note 1.

Tārānātha, *History of Buddhism in India*: references to Chimpa and Chattopadhyaya 1980.

Tattvabodhinī of Jñanendrasarasvatī: references to Caturveda and Bhāskara 1958–61.

Trikāṇḍaśeṣa of Puruṣottamadeva: referred to in Mīmāṃsaka 1973.

Tripāṭhī, Shambhu Nath, and Mahadeo Chaturvedi (eds.), 1956. *Jainendra Vyākaraṇaṃ by Pūjyapāda Devanandi with Jainendra Mahāvṛtti of Shri Abhayanandi*. Kāshī: Bhāratīya Jñānapīṭha.

Trivedī, Kamalāśaṅkara Prāṇaśaṅkara, 1925–31. *ŚrīRāmacandrācāryapraṇītā Prakriyākaumudī [pūrv/uttar]ārdhaṃ śrīViṭṭhalācāryakṛtayā Prasādākhyayā ṭīkayā sametaṃ*. 2 vols. Poona: BORI.

[*Mahābhāṣyapradīpa-*] *Uddyota*: references to the volumes enumerated under *Mahābhāṣya* above (q.v.).

Uṇādisūtra: references to Pathak and Chitrao, 1935.728–62.

Upalekhasūtra: see Abhyankar and Devasthali 1978.xiv.

Utpalinī of Vyāḍi: see Birwé 1967.

Vaidyanātha, *Gadā*: references to Gokhale 1913.

Vaiyākaraṇasiddhāntakaumudī of Bhaṭṭojīdīkṣita: references to Caturveda and Bhāskara 1958–61.

Vākyapadīya of Bhartṛhari: references to Rau 1977.

Vasu, Śrisa Chandra (ed. and tr.), 1891. *The Aṣṭādhyāyī of Pāṇini, Edited and Translated into English*. 2 vols. Allahabad: The Pāṇini Office.

Vikṛtivallī of Vyāḍi: references to Abhyankar and Devasthali 1978.1–3.

Verpoorten, Jean-Marie, 1987. *Mīmāṃsā Literature*, vol. VI.5 in *A History of Indian Literature* ed. Jan Gonda. Wiesbaden: Harrassowitz.

Viṭṭhala, *Prasāda*: references to Trivedī 1925–31.

Vogel, Claus, 1979. *Indian Lexicography*. Vol. V.II.4 in *A History of Indian Literature* ed. Jan Gonda. Wiesbaden: Harassowitz.

Weber, Albrecht. 1886. *Die Handschriften-Verzeichnisse der Königlichen Bibliothek zu Berlin, Fünfter Band, Verzeichnisse der Sanskrit- und Prākṛit-Handschriften, Zweiter Band, Erste Abtheilung*. Berlin: Königliche Bibliothek.

West, Martin L., 1973. *Textual Criticism and Editorial Technique*, Stuttgart: Teubner.

Wezler, Albrecht, 1969. *Paribhāṣā IV, V und XV. Untersuchungen zur Geschichte der einheimischen indischen grammatischen Scholastik*. Berlin, Zürich: Gehlen.

—, 1976. "Some Observations on the Grammatical Terminology of Pāṇini", in *German Scholars on India, Contributions to Indian Studies, edited by the Cultural Department of the Embassy of the Federal Republic of Germany*. Bombay: Nachiketa Publications Ltd. Vol. 2, pp. 361–79.

Whitney, William Dwight. 1889. *Sanskrit Grammar, including both the Classical Language and the Older Dialects, of Veda and Brāhmaṇa*. 14th issue of 2nd edition, 1975. Cambridge, Mass: Harvard University Press.

Wujastyk, Dominik, 1981. "Notes on Traditional Sanskrit Teaching", in *South Asia Research*, 1, pp. 30–36.

—, 1983. "Do *Paribhāṣās* Wrongly Immunize Panini's Theory Against Criticism?", in *Proceedings of the International Seminar on Studies in the Aṣṭādhyāyī of Pāṇini*, ed. S. D. Joshi and S. D. Laddu. Pune: University of Poona. Pp. 97–103.

Citation indexes

References are to page numbers in the present volume.

*Sūtra*s of the *Aṣṭādhyāyī*

1.1.1 .... 129, 178
1.1.2 178
1.1.3 100
1.1.4 .... 69, 236, 237, 255
1.1.5 .... 25, 100, 103, 165
1.1.6 .... xxvii, 165
1.1.8 75
1.1.9 188
1.1.10 130
1.1.11 180
1.1.13 10
1.1.15 .... 35, 36, 39, 40
1.1.20 69
1.1.21 200
1.1.22 .... 44, 47, 227
1.1.23 .... 49, 54–57
1.1.24 .... 57, 69, 73, 74
1.1.26 .... 43, 85
1.1.27 .... 58, 62, 63
1.1.28 .... 21, 67, 68
1.1.29 .... 67, 68
1.1.31 .... 67, 68
1.1.37 .... 36, 204
1.1.39 .... 69, 70, 72, 73, 75, 241, 261
1.1.42 101
1.1.43 101
1.1.44 217
1.1.45 .... 117, 118
1.1.46 12
1.1.47 263
1.1.48 125
1.1.49 .... xxx, 86, 87
1.1.50 132
1.1.51 135
1.1.52 .... 86, 155, 178, 264
1.1.53 178
1.1.54 86
1.1.55 .... 85–87, 178
1.1.56 .... 57, 65, 143, 264, 268
1.1.57 .... 147, 255
1.1.58 .... 254, 255
1.1.59 .... 238, 239
1.1.60 xxx
1.1.61 .... xxx, 160
1.1.62 .... xxx, 9, 150, 192, 241
1.1.63 xxx
1.1.66 .... 115, 116, 207
1.1.67 .... 115, 116
1.1.68 .... 3, 5, 8–10
1.1.69 .... 18, 39, 132, 188
1.1.70 .... 39, 87
1.1.71 105
1.1.72 .... 121, 201, 203, 222, 223, 226, 272
1.1.73 137
1.2.1 .... 15, 268
1.2.4 .... 149, 151, 165
1.2.9 .... 190, 191
1.2.14 149–151
1.2.18 .... 103, 104, 191, 232
1.2.22 232
1.2.28 .... xxx, 155
1.2.31 58
1.2.33 .... 214, 215
1.2.42 120
1.2.45 121
1.2.47 .... 212, 213, 241
1.2.49 .... 162, 212

1.2.55 ... 221
1.2.58 ... 221
1.2.59 ... 221
1.2.63 ... 220, 221, 230
1.2.64 ... xiv, xx
1.2.69 ... 122, 123, 207, 218
1.3.1 ... 4, 62
1.3.2–8 ... 84
1.3.2 ... 43, 84
1.3.4 ... 189
1.3.6 ... 28
1.3.8 ... 10
1.3.9 ... 28, 35, 73, 84–86, 90, 264
1.3.10 ... 88
1.3.11 ... 211
1.3.12 ... 134
1.3.13 ... 62
1.3.14 ... 54, 56, 141–143
1.3.15 ... 142
1.3.16 ... 142
1.3.28 ... 150
1.3.60 ... 96, 97
1.3.78 ... 134
1.3.90 ... 134, 135
1.4.1–2.2.38 ... 80
1.4.2 ... 47, 80, 111, 243, 247, 248
1.4.3 ... 79
1.4.4 ... 79
1.4.5 ... 79
1.4.6 ... 79
1.4.7 ... 79, 80, 179
1.4.8 ... 80
1.4.9 ... 80
1.4.13 ... 70, 105, 203, 272, 273
1.4.14 ... 226
1.4.15 ... 262
1.4.23–55 ... 272
1.4.31 ... 56
1.4.42 ... 55, 56
1.4.45 ... 56
1.4.49 ... 56
1.4.60–82 ... 272
1.4.61 ... 36, 40
1.4.94 ... 49, 50
1.4.95 ... 49, 50
1.4.102 ... 73
1.4.109 ... 83
2.1.2 ... 206
2.1.3 ... 120
2.1.4 ... 120, 206
2.1.9 ... 206
2.1.11 ... 120
2.1.32 ... 272
2.1.40 ... xv
2.1.49 ... 119, 120
2.1.57 ... 29
2.1.59 ... 29
2.1.61 ... 29
2.1.67 ... 119–121
2.1.70 ... 119, 120
2.2.2 ... 259, 260
2.2.6 ... 24
2.2.24 ... 21, 58
2.2.26 ... 21, 67, 68
2.2.34 ... 214
2.3.1 ... 56, 73, 181
2.3.13 ... 71, 111
2.3.18 ... 55
2.3.36 ... 56
2.3.46 ... 102, 157
2.3.47 ... 102
2.3.48 ... 102
2.3.50 ... 93
2.3.65 ... 50
2.4.12 ... 220, 221
2.4.13 ... 56
2.4.17 ... 230
2.4.21 ... xviii, xix, xxi
2.4.31 ... 6
2.4.35 ... 92
2.4.42 ... 199
2.4.52 ... 178
2.4.71 ... 35, 213
2.4.74 ... 236, 237
2.4.77 ... 166, 167
2.4.79 ... 184, 246, 247
2.4.81 ... 69, 75
2.4.82 ... 206
2.4.85 ... 252
2.4.134 ... 56
3.1.1 ... 12, 121
3.1.2 ... 12, 121
3.1.3 ... 13, 23, 24, 252, 253
3.1.6 ... 109, 110
3.1.8 ... 262
3.1.11 ... 80, 134, 217, 262
3.1.12 ... 134
3.1.13 ... 134, 135
3.1.16 ... 69
3.1.17 ... 55, 56
3.1.22 ... 237, 255
3.1.23 ... 111, 255

3.1.32 90
3.1.33 .... 65–67, 252
3.1.35 .... 6, 7
3.1.36 75–78
3.1.37 .... 6, 7
3.1.38 7
3.1.39 88
3.1.40 76
3.1.44 149–151
3.1.48 224
3.1.67 .... 65, 66
3.1.68 .... 65, 66, 88
3.1.69 .... 65, 66
3.1.73 253
3.1.77 97
3.1.79 .... 246, 247
3.1.80 .... 263, 264
3.1.91 127
3.1.94 .... 88–90, 127
3.1.97 .... 91–93, 112, 197
3.1.100 230
3.1.106 197
3.1.107 197
3.1.120 89
3.1.124 .... 89, 92, 93, 112
3.1.134 237
3.1.139 90
3.1.143 135
3.2.1 .... 49, 90
3.2.3 90
3.2.4 49
3.2.56 .... 60, 61
3.2.57 20–28
3.2.64 .... 240, 241
3.2.71 169
3.2.76 241
3.2.84 43
3.2.87 261
3.2.107 152
3.2.112 102
3.2.113 102
3.2.114 102
3.2.115 .... 75, 239
3.2.121 136
3.2.123 .... 97, 136, 253
3.2.124 136
3.2.134–177 127
3.2.136 26–28
3.2.138 27
3.2.139 xix
3.2.146 127
3.2.149 .... 127, 128
3.2.150 127
3.2.152 128
3.2.153 .... 127, 128
3.2.167 128
3.2.176 255
3.2.178 244
3.3.13 65
3.3.15 252
3.3.19 228
3.3.32 228
3.3.43 273
3.3.57 .... 44, 48
3.3.88 .... 266, 267
3.3.100 .... 266, 267
3.3.103 .... 77, 78
3.3.108 6
3.3.132 .... 157, 268
3.3.133 65
3.3.173 13
3.4.4 101
3.4.26 196
3.4.59 196
3.4.60 196
3.4.69 65
3.4.70 43
3.4.75 101
3.4.77–79 253
3.4.77 .... 11, 13, 15, 65, 75, 252
3.4.78 .... 11–13, 15, 16, 65, 75, 97, 239
3.4.79 11
3.4.82 .... 75, 239
3.4.99 14
3.4.102 13
3.4.103 14
3.4.106 11–15
3.4.113 65
3.4.116 13
4.1.1 .... 119, 121, 122, 257
4.1.2 .... 73, 79, 179
4.1.4 .... 78–80, 222
4.1.13 101
4.1.14 222
4.1.15 173
4.1.26 116
4.1.27 116
4.1.49 .... 162, 174, 175
4.1.80 xv
4.1.82 61
4.1.83 .... 170, 251
4.1.88 162

4.1.92 122
4.1.95 .... 70, 223, 251
4.1.99 223
4.1.112 .... 70, 107
4.1.128 .... 123, 124
4.1.129 123
4.1.152 .... 222, 223
4.2.1 122
4.2.9 171–173
4.2.11 62
4.2.24 .... 162, 169, 170
4.2.32 .... 33, 34, 40
4.2.35 52
4.2.45 226
4.2.59 202
4.2.60 .... 201, 202
4.2.67–70 102
4.2.67 102
4.2.71 102
4.2.91 160
4.2.114 160
4.2.129 123
4.2.138 xv
4.2.140 178
4.2.142 .... 107, 108
4.3.53 .... 45, 160
4.3.80 .... 268, 269
4.3.97 49–52
4.3.115 .... xviii, xxi
4.3.116–118 170
4.3.116 .... 116, 169, 170
4.3.117 116
4.3.120 268
4.3.127 269
4.3.159 123
5.1.20 222
5.1.22 57
5.1.64 45
5.2.25 115
5.2.56 222
5.2.86 201
5.2.87 .... 200, 201, 222
5.2.100 10
5.2.127 21
5.2.140 61
5.3.1 61
5.3.3 132
5.3.55 .... 44, 215, 216
5.3.56 215
5.3.57 .... 44, 214, 215
5.3.60 216
5.3.61 216
5.3.70 113
5.3.71 .... 105, 113, 114, 219
5.3.72 219
5.4.4 .... 181, 182
5.4.5 .... 181, 182
5.4.11 215
5.4.14 273
5.4.50 .... 35, 61
5.4.57 134
5.4.69 50–52
5.4.85 234
5.4.91 .... 50, 233
5.4.127 56
5.4.154 .... 212, 213
6.1.1 .... 59, 238
6.1.6 62
6.1.8 .... 75, 152, 238, 239, 248
6.1.9 .... 110, 237, 255
6.1.13 183
6.1.15 .... 30, 43, 46, 191
6.1.38 207
6.1.39 207
6.1.61 159
6.1.64 157
6.1.65 8
6.1.66 .... 124, 255
6.1.67 .... 35, 241, 244, 261
6.1.70 .... xxi, 123, 124
6.1.71 .... 241, 242, 244, 261, 262
6.1.77 .... 147, 244
6.1.78 .... 23, 24, 191, 193
6.1.79 92
6.1.81 145
6.1.85 168
6.1.86 .... 243, 244
6.1.87 .... 30, 31, 145, 175, 216, 244
6.1.88 .... 145, 175, 176, 240, 241
6.1.89 .... 163, 241
6.1.93 40
6.1.95 .... 145, 146
6.1.96 .... 30, 31, 145
6.1.97 174–176
6.1.98 175
6.1.100 134
6.1.101 .... 130, 145, 175, 176, 210
6.1.102 .... 130, 131
6.1.103 130
6.1.108 .... 43, 46, 145, 152, 191
6.1.109 35
6.1.122 35

6.1.123 136
6.1.125 .... 10, 35, 39, 40
6.1.131 133
6.1.132 105
6.1.135 .... 105, 137
6.1.158 252
6.1.162 106
6.1.163 .... 23, 233
6.1.168 .... 102, 187
6.1.170 187
6.1.176 .... 93, 137
6.1.177 .... 91, 93
6.1.182 102
6.1.186 252
6.1.193 .... 218, 219
6.1.195 218
6.1.196 .... 218, 219
6.1.197 .... 138, 169
6.1.213 137
6.1.223 .... 9, 137, 270
6.2.2 .... 20, 24, 172
6.2.14 .... xviii, xxi
6.2.36 xv
6.2.38 29
6.2.44 29
6.2.45 29
6.2.46 .... 20, 29
6.2.47 273
6.2.49 .... 272, 273
6.2.56 172
6.2.67 96
6.2.86 xv
6.2.139 215
6.2.156 .... 172, 173
6.2.160 21–28
6.2.193 233
6.2.197 233
6.3.26 .... 33, 34
6.3.27 34
6.3.39 209
6.3.41 209
6.3.43 227
6.3.44 44
6.3.57 270
6.3.58 270
6.3.59 83
6.3.67 .... 23, 24
6.3.68 .... 145, 268
6.3.120 .... 268, 269
6.3.138 211
6.3.139 141
6.4.2 43
6.4.3 .... 87, 93
6.4.8 74
6.4.11 126
6.4.16 .... 155, 156, 208
6.4.19 .... 144, 243, 244
6.4.20 .... 117, 182
6.4.22–175 152
6.4.22 .... 144, 149–152, 160, 161, 238
6.4.24 .... 150, 151
6.4.34 143
6.4.35 143
6.4.36 143
6.4.37 .... 149, 150, 246
6.4.48 .... 150, 151, 236, 237, 254, 255, 261, 262, 264
6.4.62 .... 83, 84
6.4.64 .... 152, 238, 239, 248, 254, 255
6.4.77 .... 237, 257
6.4.78 75
6.4.89 .... 86, 87, 198, 199
6.4.108 .... 70, 152
6.4.111 193
6.4.113 132
6.4.119 141
6.4.120 96
6.4.121 152
6.4.125 5
6.4.127 85
6.4.131 .... 152, 158, 211, 240
6.4.132 .... 144, 145, 240, 241
6.4.134 183
6.4.141 179
6.4.143 .... 124, 171, 173
6.4.146 .... 184, 185
6.4.148 .... 70, 171–173
6.4.153 159–161
6.4.154–163 216
6.1.177 93
7.1.1 .... 60, 235
7.1.2 .... 123, 124, 223
7.1.9 .... 174, 175, 177
7.1.11 .... 105, 204
7.1.12 .... 174, 175, 177
7.1.13 .... 69, 71, 72, 124
7.1.17 85
7.1.20 73
7.1.22 73
7.1.28 131
7.1.30 139
7.1.34 .... 174, 177

7.1.35 143
7.1.36 171
7.1.37 .... 244, 272
7.1.39 .... 123, 124
7.1.52 .... 104, 226
7.1.58 .... 263, 264
7.1.61 231
7.1.62 231
7.1.72 73
7.1.75 178
7.1.77 141
7.1.80 168
7.1.84 173
7.1.87 235
7.1.90 .... 40, 139
7.1.91 129
7.1.101 212
7.1.103 111
7.2.1 .... 98, 99, 178
7.2.3 99
7.2.4 .... 98, 99
7.2.5 98–100
7.2.7 .... xxi, 99
7.2.10 .... 17, 22, 43, 44, 164
7.2.11 .... xix, 43, 44, 46, 47, 164, 190, 191
7.2.12 .... 17, 164, 190, 191
7.2.14 .... 43, 44, 46, 47
7.2.35 .... 13, 14, 17, 22, 24, 27, 43, 46, 103, 152, 158, 164, 191
7.2.38 17
7.2.41 .... 17, 18
7.2.44 .... 164, 166, 167, 266
7.2.49 .... 164, 195
7.2.57 65–67
7.2.59 .... 265, 266
7.2.60 265
7.2.67 .... 95, 96, 117
7.2.74 16–19
7.2.75 16–18
7.2.80 207
7.2.82 .... 207, 235
7.2.101 .... 69, 71, 177
7.2.114 9
7.2.115 .... 169, 212
7.2.116 241
7.2.118 223
7.3.3 .... xv, 273
7.3.6 273
7.3.7 .... xv, xviii, xix
7.3.27 .... 209, 210
7.3.28 .... 209, 210
7.3.44 271
7.3.50 45
7.3.54 154
7.3.56 224
7.3.64 92
7.3.74 155
7.3.78 .... 97, 139
7.3.79 139
7.3.83 165
7.3.84 .... 23, 24, 92, 104, 135, 191, 264
7.3.85 104
7.3.86 .... 75, 76, 154, 212, 240, 241, 252
7.3.94 198
7.3.101 .... 71, 72, 123, 124, 139
7.3.102 .... 72, 111
7.3.103 .... 104, 111
7.3.105 179
7.3.113 .... 78, 79
7.3.116 .... 79, 80
7.3.117 78–80
7.3.118–119 .... 69, 79, 80
7.3.118 79–81
7.3.119 .... 78–81, 206, 217
7.3.120 .... 179, 206
7.4.1 154
7.4.7 212
7.4.13 .... 212, 213
7.4.14 .... 212, 213
7.4.25 .... 71, 72, 140, 262
7.4.27 140
7.4.33 262
7.4.41 136
7.4.56 255
7.4.59 .... 110, 152
7.4.60 .... 75, 110
7.4.66 109
7.4.71 126
7.4.78 139
7.4.79 110
7.4.82 .... 9, 109, 199, 237
7.4.83 .... 109, 110, 112, 255
7.4.85 .... 109, 110
7.4.143 252
7.7.3 165
8.1.4 134
8.1.28 .... 257, 258
8.1.62 40
8.1.67 51–53
8.2.1 .... 28, 179

8.2.2 .... 261, 262
8.2.3 179
8.2.4 137
8.2.7 .... 69, 261, 262
8.2.19 .... 154, 168
8.2.20 135
8.2.21 135
8.2.27 .... 149–151, 246, 247
8.2.30 .... 5, 189, 247
8.2.36 .... 3–5, 189, 247
8.2.39 189
8.2.45 43
8.2.46 .... 256, 257
8.2.56 135
8.2.73 .... 186, 187
8.2.74 .... 186, 187
8.2.78 144
8.2.80 .... 133, 179, 180, 183
8.2.81 180
8.2.88 228
8.2.106 126
8.3.4 63
8.3.15 144
8.3.59 .... 23, 24, 28
8.3.60 30
8.3.65 .... 38, 157, 225
8.3.79 38
8.3.82 .... 32–34, 37, 38
8.3.98 38
8.3.110 30
8.4.1 .... 23, 24, 63, 126
8.4.2 .... 63, 175, 274
8.4.3 63
8.4.11 274
8.4.14 8
8.4.17 250
8.4.18 250
8.4.22 98
8.4.41 157
8.4.46 107
8.4.55 .... 22, 25
8.4.61 157
8.4.66 138

Vārttikas from the *Mahābhāṣya*

Śivasūtra 1.6 90
Śivasūtra 2.4 37
Śivasūtras 3.1–4.6 ... 125
Śivasūtra 4.4 39
Śivasūtra 4.11 126

1.1.1.12 129
1.1.4.7 .... 236, 237
1.1.4.8 69
1.1.6.1 .... xxvii, 165
1.1.8.7 75
1.1.10.4 130
1.1.20.6 69
1.1.22.1–3 44
1.1.23.1–2 54
1.1.23.3–4 57
1.1.23.4 54–56
1.1.24.2 73
1.1.24.3 69
1.1.26.3 85
1.1.27.1 .... 58, 62, 63
1.1.39.3 .... 69, 75, 241
1.1.39.4–9 69
1.1.39.5 261
1.1.39.7 72
1.1.39.9 .... 73, 75
1.1.39.10–16 70
1.1.39.10 70
1.1.44.16 217
1.1.56.3 268
1.1.56.25 143
1.1.62.11 9
1.1.68.2–4 10
1.1.71.7 105
1.1.72.3 223
1.1.72.7 203
1.1.72.15 201
1.1.73.4 137
1.2.28.1 155
1.2.31.3 58
1.2.49.7 212
1.2.64.35 xiv
1.2.64.45 .... xiv, xx
1.3.9.10 90
1.3.9.15 .... 85, 86
1.3.10.6 88
1.3.14.1 141
1.3.14.2 141
1.4.2.21 243
1.4.13.4 .... 105, 203
1.4.13.9 272
1.4.13.10 273
1.4.14.1 226
1.4.109.10 83
2.2.34.1 214
2.3.46.8 157
2.4.12.5 220
2.4.35.3 92
2.4.81.4 69
3.1.3.7 13
3.1.6.2 109
3.1.13.1–2 135
3.1.16.5 69
3.1.32.1 90
3.1.35.1 6
3.1.36.1 .... 75, 76
3.1.36.2 77
3.1.36.3 .... 77, 78
3.1.36.5 .... 75, 76
3.1.44.5 149
3.1.94.4 .... 88, 90
3.1.94.5 88

3.2.56.1 60
3.2.56.3 60
3.3.19.3 228
3.3.108.2 6
3.3.132.2 157
3.4.77.2 11
3.4.79.2 11
4.1.1.4 ..... 119, 121, 122
4.1.14.1 222
4.1.15.2 173
4.1.128.1 124
4.3.116.1–3 170
5.2.52.1 119
5.3.55.3 215
5.3.72.1 113
5.3.72.2 113
5.4.5.1 181
5.4.50.1 61
5.4.69.1 50–52
6.1.1.15 59
6.1.13.5 183
6.1.85.9 119
6.1.108.7 145
6.1.108.9 145
6.1.158.9 252
6.1.177.1 93
6.1.223.2 .... 137, 270
6.1.223.3 137
6.2.2.2 20
6.2.46.3 20
6.2.49.6 273
6.2.139.2 215
6.3.68.3 268
6.3.68.5 145
6.4.22.9–12 151
6.4.22.12 149
6.4.132.1 240
7.1.1.12 119
7.1.82.2 248
7.1.84.3 173
7.2.1.2b 248
7.3.56.2 224
7.3.116.2 79
7.3.118–119.4 80
7.3.118–119.5 ..... 80, 81
7.3.118–119.6 ..... 69, 80
7.3.119.4 217
7.3.119.5 78
7.3.119.6 78
7.4.10.3 248
7.4.82.2 109
7.4.83.4 109
8.1.67.1 53
8.2.7.3 69
8.3.65.3 225
8.3.65.4 225
8.3.82.2 32
8.4.1.1 126
8.4.3.6 63

Prose citations from the *Mahābhāṣya*

Citations are by volume, page, and line of Kielhorn's edition.

I.1:3 .... xxv, 2
I.1:6 xxv
I.1:14 xxv
I.4:13 72
I.5:13 xxv
I.6:8 .... xvi, xxv
I.6:9 xvi
I.6:12–14 xvii
I.6:12 ...... xx, xxiv, xxv
I.6:21 .... xvii, xxiv
I.6:26 194
I.7:5 194
I.8:10 2
I.11:23 194
I.12:19 254
I.12:20 254
I.16:1 210
I.16:26 90
I.19:18 2
I.20:17 2
I.20f. 256
I.21:7–8 257
I.21:7 256
I.21:9 256
I.21:13 37
I.23:24 125
I.24:1 125
I.24:2 125
I.25:19 126
I.26:5–6 125
I.26:14 144
I.28:13–15 107
I.34–35 194
I.35:15–18 194
I.35:16 194
I.40:21 117
I.40:22 117
I.41:11 129
I.41:13 130
I.42:13 194
I.48:4 183
I.51:9 144
I.52–53 236
I.53:4 236
I.53:15 69
I.54:12 144
I.54:17 178
I.55:1 178
I.55:4 144
I.57:21 129
I.57:22 130
I.58:21 264
I.59:13 75
I.60:18 117
I.63:21 125
I.63:23 125
I.66:10 130
I.66:11:26 178
I.66:11 178
I.67:1 178
I.68:2 236
I.68:22 178
I.70:5–8 10
I.70:6 3
I.70:8 20
I.70:9 3
I.70 3
I.71:16 20
I.71:18 .... 32, 35
I.71:19–20 35
I.74:2 20
I.74:21 20
I.74:26 3
I.74:28 3
I.74 3

I.75:22 69
I.76:10 91
I.76:23 200
I.76:111 91
I.79:13 47
I.79:21–22 44
I.79 44
I.80:11 .... 49, 55
I.80:13 49
I.80:16 49
I.80:21 49
I.80–81 57
I.81:2 49
I.81:5 54
I.81:8 54
I.81:10–11 56
I.81:11 55
I.81:12–14 55
I.81:12 54
I.81:14 56
I.81:15–16 56
I.81:15 54
I.81:16–20 57
I.81:25 3
I.81 3
I.83:13 73
I.83:14 .... 73, 74
I.83:18 69
I.84:20 85
I.84 f. 14
I.86:2–8 .... 62, 63
I.86:5 59
I.86:6 58
I.86:7 59
I.86:9 ff. 63
I.86:11 63
I.89:15 105
I.90:9–10 67
I.90:9–26 67
I.90:14–16 67
I.90:14 64
I.90:17 20
I.90:19 20
I.94:23 117
I.95:4 117
I.97:10 69
I.97:11 69
I.97:13 69
I.97:16–18 241
I.97:17 69
I.97:18 144
I.97:19 .... 259, 261
I.97:21 69
I.98:1 69
I.98:4 72
I.98:6 69
I.98:11 69
I.98:16 69
I.98:20 73
I.98:21 69
I.98:22 f. 78
I.98:23 .... 69, 75
I.98:24 69
I.99:1 70
I.99:3 .... 69, 70
I.99:23 69
I.101:11 .... 98, 101
I.105:3 181
I.111:11–12 117
I.111:12 117
I.115:3 113
I.115:5 264
I.115:22 274
I.117:1 144
I.118:14 ff. 87
I.118:16 86
I.119:24 194
I.121:21 86
I.123:26 132
I.128:16 137
I.128:19 137
I.132:4–5 86
I.132:5 85
I.134:16 268
I.139:5 20
I.139:14 91
I.140:10–12 143
I.140:11 248
I.140:12 141
I.140:17 .... 141, 248
I.140:23 248
I.140:24 141
I.144:8 147
I.145:6–8 147
I.145:7 147
I.145:11 147
I.145:14 147
I.145:16 147
I.145:18 .... 144, 147
I.145:20 137
I.145:22 144
I.145:23 ff. 147
I.145:25–28 147
I.151–52 168
I.152:5 254
I.153:22 162
I.157:1 238
I.158:4 117
I.161:5–10 241
I.161:10 144
I.163:15 9
I.164:7 157
I.167:11 98
I.175:20–23 8
I.175:23 .... 3, 9
I.177:24 132
I.178:7 132
I.183:17 223
I.183:20 223
I.184:3 ff. 204
I.184:12 203
I.184:13–15 203
I.184:13 .... 105, 203
I.184:21 .... 105, 203
I.184:24 .... 105, 203
I.185:22–186:1 201
I.185:22 200
I.185:23 200
I.186:5–6 201
I.186:5 200
I.189:20 137
I.194–95 47
I.196:15 208
I.200:17–20 232
I.201:16 232
I.205:5 155
I.206:14–15 137
I.207:24 58
I.207:24 ff. 58
I.210:6–7 215
I.210:6 214
I.210:9 214
I.211–12 214
I.212:17 129
I.216:3 98
I.221:1–5 257
I.223:15 144
I.223:16 144
I.223:21 144
I.224:17 168
I.224:19 200
I.225:4–12 212
I.225:6 98

I.227:3 181
I.232:4–5 230
I.238:11 181
I.240:25 181
I.241:24 181
I.250:3–4 259
I.252:8 181
I.254:8 173
I.257:22 117
I.264:14 205
I.265:23 90
I.266:16 194
I.267:1 .... 88, 90
I.267:2 85
I.267:3–4 86
I.267:3 85
I.271:16 194
I.272:27 194
I.273:4 194
I.274:7 205
I.274:22 178
I.274:24 117
I.274:26 117
I.275:1 117
I.277:12 98
I.277:14–16 141
I.277:23 49
I.278:3–4 54
I.278:4–5 54
I.278:8 141
I.278:10 141
I.278:16 98
I.284:22 98
I.286:5 236
I.300:17 96
I.305:17 141
I.305:18 248
I.305:23 141
I.305:26 248
I.310:5 244
I.310:7 243
I.310:8 243
I.316:7 144
I.316:17 203
I.316:18 .... 105, 203
I.316:19–20 203
I.316:26 .... 105, 203
I.317:3 .... 105, 203
I.318:8 272
I.318:9 272
I.318:16 272
I.318:20–25 226
I.319:1–2 226
I.319: 98
I.330:21 49
I.346:11 272
I.348:19 181
I.354:12 .... 32, 35
I.356:7 83
I.369:16 129
I.370:19 181
I.378:3 129
I.378:4 130
I.382:16 59
I.390:16 181
I.393:24 117
I.402:1–5 120
I.402.4 119
I.402:20 20
I.405:23 58
I.405:24 .... 58, 59
I.411:19 254
I.411:20 254
I.422 219
I.426:22 58
I.426:23 .... 58, 59
I.426:28 254
I.427:1 254
I.427:3 254
I.435:1–2 230
I.435–36 214
I.444:24 20
I.449:10 117
I.457:2 163
I.461:9 130
I.461:12 129
I.462:22 157
I.468:11 xxiv
I.468:12 xxiv
I.476–77 230
I.476–477:2 220
I.483:14–16 92
I.488:14 134
I.495:14 166
I.496:17 3
I.496:19 3
I.496:20 3
I.496:21 3
I.496:23 69
I.500:11 248
I.502:5 236
I.502:8 248
I.502:13 248
II.7:24 236
II.8:6 13
II.9:3 144
II.10:12 236
II.11:8 117
II.11:15 109
II.11:22 109
II.15:15 181
II.16:6 171
II.20:22 217
II.20:23–24 218
II.21:21 217
II.22:13 186
II.22:15 186
II.23:15 181
II.28:7:8 236
II.28:7 236
II.42:10 90
II.42:20 66
II.42–43 65
II.44:13 ff. 6
II.44:16 3
II.44:20 75
II.44:21 75
II.45:1 77
II.45:4 77
II.45:5 77
II.46:7–9 75
II.46:8 .... 69, 76
II.46:9 69
II.51:22 149
II.52:4 149
II.54:22 64
II.59:17 98
II.61:22 20
II.75:7 200
II.79:12 ff. 250
II.79:20 88
II.79:21 90
II.79:25 88
II.80:7 .... 88, 90
II.82:7–9 92
II.85:5 xxvii
II.95:14 64
II.97:3–4 238
II.105:3 60
II.105:22 22
II.106:2 25
II.106:4 194
II.106:8 20

II.106:18 194
II.110:14–15 252
II.113:5 117
II.118:5 157
II.118:11 157
II.126:13 117
II.126:16 117
II.127:12 134
II.133:16 127
II.134:5 127
II.139:8 117
II.139:11 157
II.142:12 129
II.144:13 214
II.145:18 186
II.145:20 186
II.146:5 228
II.146:7 228
II.152:14 64
II.158:22 157
II.165:4 135
II.169:23:24 236
II.169:23 236
II.172:20 214
II.178–79 250
II.181:12 3
II.181:13 .... 3, 11
II.181:14 3
II.181:15 3
II.182:17 11
II.184:22 64
II.185:16 144
II.192:3 .... 119, 122
II.197:18 117
II.199:3 181
II.201:13 222
II.201:21 222
II.202:2 200
II.202:5 222
II.202:8 200
II.202:20 3
II.204:10 101
II.205:12 222
II.208:5 173
II.208:8 171
II.212:24 115
II.215:23 159
II.216:1 159
II.223:5–6 240
II.224:16 64
II.240:10 117
II.245:20 214
II.258:18–22 123
II.258:22 119
II.263:7 236
II.274:2–6 171
II.274:4 .... 171, 173
II.274:7–8 171
II.280–81 226
II.284:4 xxv
II.316–17 170
II.322:9 64
II.322:14 64
II.327:3–6 64
II.327:5 64
II.345:11 222
II.345:16 222
II.346:12 3
II.346:16 3
II.357:18–20 159
II.357:19–20 159
II.370:1 222
II.375:12 115
II.385:1 119
II.385:9 236
II.385:18 222
II.392:22 181
II.401:7 222
II.411:13 3
II.416:3 215
II.418:1 205
II.431:2 181
II.437:10 3
II.439:8 20
III.1:8 200
III.3:20 59
III.3:21 58
III.3:22 58
III.3:23 59
III.4:7 236
III.5:1 130
III.5:8 130
III.5:15 130
III.6:5 111
III.6:22 111
III.6:24 113
III.9:3 205
III.10:6 236
III.10:26 129
III.10:27 130
III.14:24 236
III.21:1 183
III.21:2 183
III.21:7 183
III.21:11 183
III.21:20 183
III.21:23 183
III.21:24 178
III.22:5 183
III.22:10 183
III.22:15 183
III.22:21 183
III.23:19 183
III.26:22 125
III.31:11 183
III.33:7 144
III.33:19 ff. 207
III.34:12 186
III.34:14 186
III.34:22 80
III.44:19 144
III.45:16 3
III.48:18 168
III.50:6 144
III.51:2 186
III.51:4 186
III.60:1 168
III.61:13 119
III.64:18 144
III.68:10 144
III.69:4 163
III.69:5 64
III.70:22 144
III.73:19 20
III.74:8 144
III.74:20 115
III.76:16–19 30
III.76:17 3
III.80:6–9 64
III.80:8 64
III.83:10–84:3 145
III.83:20 20
III.83:25 145
III.85:17 144
III.85:24 144
III.88:23 144
III.89:16 208
III.93:3 144
III.94:16 186
III.94:18 186
III.98:4 111
III.98:21 178
III.100:9–11 252

III.103:19 3
III.104:17 163
III.107:15 163
III.109:8–9 93
III.109:8 91
III.109:9 91
III.109:19 91
III.110:7 253
III.110:16 132
III.110:17 132
III.110:19 133
III.115–16 218
III.117:3 144
III.117:18 xxvii
III.119:18 137
III.119:20 137
III.119:21 137, 270
III.120:6 137
III.120:9 137
III.120:15 137
III.120:23 9
III.121:23 111
III.121:24 113
III.123:8 20
III.123:9 20
III.124:19 144
III.125:11 xv
III.128:12 272
III.136:1–3 215
III.140:6 233
III.145:5 20
III.153:13 186
III.153:15 186
III.157:2 119
III.158:17 248
III.158:18 141
III.160:17 20
III.160:19 20
III.161:2 32, 35
III.163:18 83
III.165:23 91, 178
III.166:17 268
III.167:11 144
III.167:12–14 145
III.169:2 3
III.169:3 173
III.174:6 117
III.176:9 49
III.177:9 248
III.177:10 141
III.178:20 86
III.180:17 3
III.180:18 3
III.181:25 91
III.183:22 173
III.183:23 173
III.183:24 171
III.184:2 91
III.184:9 3
III.190:11 ff. 151
III.190:22 149
III.190:23–25 151
III.190:23 149
III.194:7 20
III.197:22 149
III.200:9 125
III.204:14 20
III.207:1 248
III.207:2 141
III.212:7 149
III.213:2 149
III.214:6 236
III.216:8 254
III.218:6 163
III.221:17 236
III.222–23 240
III.223:12 119
III.223:16 119
III.229:7–14 159
III.229:10–11 161
III.229:13 159
III.230:17 139
III.230:22 132
III.232:16 111
III.232:21 163
III.232:22 111
III.232:23 113
III.233:1 163
III.233:3 64
III.234:7 127
III.234:21 37
III.238:12 3
III.238:17 119
III.246:1 20
III.246:3 194
III.246:19 144
III.248:6 98
III.250:17 141
III.252:11 139
III.254:8 173
III.255:4 144
III.255:17 186
III:255:19 186
III.255:23 272
III.256:1 272
III.256:3 272
III.256:8–11 272
III.258:10 141, 248
III.259:3 173
III.259:8–16 6
III.259:12 105, 168
III.259:21 173
III.260:10 141
III.260:15 134
III.263:18 111
III.264:12 248
III.264:13 111
III.264:15 113
III.266:11 141
III.266:22 3
III.266:24 20
III.270:7 248
III.270:7 ff. 248
III.271:1 173
III.271:2 173
III.271:16 144
III.272:19–22 20
III.272:20 20
III.273:8 117
III.274:3 178
III.274:11 173
III:278:9 248
III.278:15 144
III.279:20 98
III.281:3 154
III.286 43
III.292:10 168
III.294:16 91
III.295:20 163
III.296:1 163
III.300:24 91
III.303:18–23 207
III.308:20 64
III.309:9 69
III.309:12 69
III.312:24 144
III.313:21 9
III.315:6 111
III.315:9 113
III.315:11 163
III.322:4–6 209
III.322 209
III.324:11 154

III.324:16 168
III.328:15 205
III.329:8 20
III.330:10 154
III.331:12 20
III.334:19 139
III.335:4 139
III.335:12 91
III.336:9 98
III.342:2–5 20
III.342:3 20
III.343:1 217
III.343:3 .... 78, 81
III.343:4–7 78
III.343:5 .... 69, 78
III.343:6 69
III.344:18 154
III.345:16 236
III.346:4 69
III.346:15 144
III.347:4 248
III.347:22 144
III.348:3 248
III.349:10 139
III.350:10 135
III.354:8 111
III.354:17 111
III.354:18 113
III.356:4 83
III.357:1 109
III.357:12 109
III.357:17 109
III.357:18 9
III.358:11–18 109
III.359:21 154
III.360:13 236
III.364:17 130
III.375:4 20
III.385:8 178
III.385:10 178
III.385:20 178
III.387:16 69
III.389:4 137
III.389:12 144
III.390:10 236
III.398:9 xxvii
III.399:10 168
III.401:9 144
III.407:6 144
III.407:20–408:10 256
III.408:4 256
III.408:5 256
III.408:9 256
III.414:16 183
III.417:3 181
III.417:20 3
III.417:21 3
III.418:18 178
III.426:7 144
III.426:13 .... 144, 178
III.426:14 144
III.426:16 144
III.426:17 144
III.427:20 20
III.434:9 144
III.438:14 3
III.438:15 3
III.438:16 3
III.439:2 129
III.439:4 130
III.442:22–443:4 225
III.445:20 .... 32, 35
III.447:11 3
III.448:11 38
III.450:6 64
III.452:2 126
III.452:6 126
III.452:11 125
III.452:18 144
III.453:13 129
III.453:14 130
III.455:1 ff. 63
III.458:13 3
III.458:14 3

Citations from the *Kāśikāvṛtti*, and the commentaries *Nyāsa* and *Padamañjarī*

References are to the Shastri and Shukla 1965–67 edition.

I.77:3 255
I.114–15 35
I.125:10 47
I.125 44
I.128:5 74
I.128:18 f. 74
I.129:19 f. 74
I.130:21 58
I.130:29 62
I.130 f. 58
I.134:30 63
I.160 f. 117
I.182:27 f. 85
I.205 254
I.215:2 238
I.236 116
I.237 115
I.253:3 223
I.254:18–20 223
I.297 f. 232
I.372:1–4 220
I.372 230
I.385:23–28 207
II.26:4 206
II.88 f. 119, 120
II.92 120
II.145:10 ff. 214
II.208 102
II.266 xviii
II.266:13 xxi
II.266:15 xxi
II.266:26–27 xix
II.352:2 155
II.417:8–14 78
II.417:9 ff. 75
II.417–18 75
II.418:16 76
II.418:17 ff. 78
II.493–94 88
II.496 91
II.540:8 49
II.578:2 f. 61
II.579:1 f. 61
II.581 20
II.652 27

II.658 127
II.660 f. 127
II.662 f. 127
III.75:21 f. 78
III.101 268
III.192 196
III.193:7–8 196
III.193–94 197
III.211 101
III.215 .... 11–13, 16
III.231 14
III.233 12
III.253 ff. 119
III.255 121
III.256 121
III.276 222
III.434:22–24 251
III.515 171
III.681 f. 52
III.698 .... xviii, xxi
IV.18 xviii
IV.30 222
IV.143 115
IV.176 222
IV.197:21–25 201
IV.197 .... 200, 222
IV.241:1 f. 61
IV.292 f. 113, 114
IV.293:6 219
IV.361 ff. 35
IV.435:27 ff. 59
IV.435:32 59
IV.495:14–16 207
IV.556 163
IV.561 40
IV.569 xxvii
IV.607 105
IV.612 137
IV.659 137
IV.660:7–8:14 ff.:30 91
IV.660 93
IV.663:21 102
IV.676:8 218
IV.676:21 ff. 218
IV.691 137
V.18 xxi
V.57 272
V.153 28
V.184 233
V.257:4–5 270
V.257 271
V.320:6 141
V.340 126
V.358 .... 144, 243
V.364–65 149
V.368–69 151
V.369 144
V.479:22 85
V.484 144
V.494:8 184
V.495:1 185
V.504:1–3 159
V.504 159
V.526 235
V.541 105
V.544:5 72
V.544 69
V.563 139
V.571 171
V.573 272
V.586:2 38
V.586 141
V.624:1 141
V.626 168
V.635 ff. 40
V.635 f. 139
V.659 f. 98
V.679:28 xix
V.688:25 44
V.729 195
V.739 f. 265
V.764 207
VI.11:27 xix
VI.32–33 209
VI.69 154
VI.87 139
VI.123:6 81
VI.123:7 f. 80
VI.123:24–29 81
VI.124:26–27 .... 205, 206
VI.130 154
VI.136:3–4 212
VI.186 109
VI.190 126
VI.198 .... 109, 110
VI.312 52
VI.359 137
VI.370 154
VI.437:4:10 186
VI.441 144
VI.445:2 183
VI.497 144
VI.559:3 225
VI.571:30 38
VI.586 38
VI.602 105
VI.608:8 63
VI.618 274

Citations from the *Siddhāntakaumudī*, and the commentaries *Bālamanoramā* and *Tattvabodhinī*

Citations are by volume, page, and line of the Caturveda and Bhāskara 1958–61 edition.

I.9 (3) 43
I.19:1 (10) 188
I.35:2 (25) 9
I.38:14–16 (26) 223
I.52–53 (47) 144
I.53:1 (46) 211
I.54:8 ff. (46) 211
I.54:18 ff. (46) 211
I.179 f. (182) 121, 122
I.198:2 (204) 72
I.198 (204) 69
I.207:9 ff. (213) 62
I.207:20 (213) 58
I.207:25 (213) 58, 62
I.209:3 (214) 85
I.215:3 (217) 226
I.245:1 (244) 180
I.257:10 (258) 49

I.258:12 (258) 49
I.286–87 (283) 256
I.368:2 (359) 98
I.383:1 (369) 74
I.383:26 (369) 74
I.392 (378) 5
I.424:3 (417) 211
I.444:4 (435) 211
I.507 (461) 101
II.39:5 (694) 272
II.122:17–18 (818) ... 221
II.122:26–27 (817) ... 221
II.159:2 (847) 184
II.210:28–30 (935) ... 207
II.383:8 (1311) 159
II.384:1 (1311) 159
II.654 (2117) 35
III.25–26 (2183) 149
III.25:28 ff. (2183) ... 151
III.26:3–6 (2183) 151
III.29:4 (2186) 66
III.30:2 (2189) 154
III.53:26 (2232) 77
III.195 (2354) 5
III.250 (2414) 207
III.291:8 (2471) 141
III.338:24 (2519) 155
III.374:1 (2547) 184
III.480:1 (2651) 198
III.634:1–2 (2790) ... 268
IV.3:8 (2830) 88
IV.10:2 (2844) 88
IV.46:24 (2916) 49
IV.65:8 (2973) 60
IV.65 (2973) 60
IV.116–117 (3101) ... 207
IV.198:1 (*Uṇādi* 223) . 36
IV.198:25 (*Uṇādi* 223) 36
IV.525:11 (3732) 219
IV.597 (3931) 233

Other commentators' *paribhāṣā*s

References are to Abhyankar's *Paribhāṣāsaṃgraha*, and Gokhale's 1913 edition of the *Paribhāṣenduśekhara* (Kielhorn's numbering). Page references follow rule-number references.

Candra
14 83
37 174
82 91
Haribhāskara
1 194
3 117
6 85
9 .... 3, 5, 10
10 11
11 132
16 .... 220, 230
17 188
18 256
20 .... 141, 143
21 248
27 226
28 119
31 186
36 111
39 .... 91, 92
40 88
41 20
44 .... 58, 60, 62
45 127
46 64
48 196
49 64
50 98
51 211
53 171
55 137
57 .... 222, 223
58 200
62 168
64 272
65 233
66 69
70 198
71 144
72 243
73 184
74 .... 159, 162
77 105
80 129
81 130
84 42
85 190
86 166
87 .... 95, 96
89 113
90 .... 208, 209
93 224
94 139
98 109
100 235
101 157
102 .... 32, 35
103 49
108 268
112 231
113 .... 192, 193
114 183
122 205
123 220
125 134
p. 325:17 3
p. 351:9 72
p. 357:14 47
p. 369:11 193
p. 374 .... xiii, xxii
Kātantra
50 174
55 83
Nāgeśabhaṭṭa
1 194
4 88
6 .... 85, 89
7 89
8 88–90
9 .... 49, 54–57
14 .... 3, 11
15 .... 32, 35
27 226
28 272
30 201
31 222

32 200
34 . . . . 220, 230
36 256
37 37
38 47
39 248
40 141
42 . . . . 47, 237
43 236
45 238
46 47
50 . . . . 21, 144, 145
51 243
56 211
57 163
59 64
60 64
61 . . . . 98, 101
67 127
71 . . . . 119, 121
74 186
76 91
77 . . . . 58, 60, 62
78 196
79 137
82 171
84 233
85 69
86 . . . . 159, 162
89 . . . . 105, 204
90 166
91 224
92 139
93.1 184
93.2 235
93.7 192
93.8 190
93.9 198
95 183
99 134
101 268
104 108
105 20
107 129
108 130
111 208
114 220
120.2 42
p. 11:1–3 89
p. 12:1–2 89
p. 15:1–2 55
p. 32:5 10
p. 59–62 201
p. 93:5 ff. 145
p. 103:6 147
p. 106:2–3 151
p. 149 99
p. 170:5 ff. 59
p. 177:7 70
p. 178:7–10 70
p. 181:2 72
p. 197:2 199
p. 229–30 44
Nāgeśabhaṭṭa (Kielhorn's tr.)
p. 256 f. 151
p. 320 163
p. 446 199
Nīlakaṇṭhadīkṣita
1 194
3 117
6 85
8 88
10 115
11 . . . . 3, 10
12 11
14 32
15 42
16 132
22 . . . . 220, 230
23 256
25 141
26 248
34 226
35 272
38 119
41 186
45 111
47 113
48 163
49 64
50 64
51 98
53 127
55 91
56 58
57 196
58 144
59 243
61 211
64 157
67 137
71 222
72 200
74 233
75 69
76 198
77 159
78 184
81 105
83 166
85 224
86 139
87 235
88 . . . . 49, 54–57
93 134
94 183
97 268
102 20
104 129
105 130
111 208
115 220
120 168
131 . . . . 188, 189
136 190
137 192
138 231
140 . . . . 95, 96
p. 302 99
p. 304:13 197
p. 304:2–5 59
p. 308:10 72
p. 315:18 188
p. 316:5 190
Puruṣottamadeva
1 . . . . 3, 10
2 11
3 20
4 . . . . 42, 47
5 . . . . 32, 35, 38
6 . . . . 58, 60
7 . . . . 49, 54–57
8 64
9 64
10 . . . . 69, 75, 78
11 85
12 . . . . 88, 90
15 . . . . 91, 92
16 . . . . 95, 96, 98
17 . . . . 98, 101
19 105
20 109
21 111

23 ... 113
25 ... 115
26 ... 119
28 ... 127
29 ... 129
30 ... 130
31 ... 132
32 ... 137
37 ... 171
39 ... 141
40 ... 248
41 ... 144
42 ... 243
46 ... 272
50 ... 220, 230
51 ... 168
60 ... 259
62 ... 134
64 ... 268
65 ... 159, 162
67 ... 166
71 ... 139
72 ... 198
73 ... 224, 225
78 ... 222, 223
79 ... 200
81 ... 226
82 ... 233
83 ... 184
84 ... 235
86 ... 208, 209
87 ... 196
88 ... 205–207
89 ... 188
90 ... 190
91 ... 192, 193
94 ... 107, 108
96 ... 117
97 ... 186, 187
98 ... 231
100 ... 220
104 ... 211
107 ... 183
113 ... 157
114 ... 256, 257
120 ... 194
p. 12 ... 99
p. 113:13 ... 21
p. 114:7 ... 45
p. 115:14 ... 59
p. 116:8–13 ... 55
p. 117:25 ... 72
p. 118:10 ff. ... 89
p. 149:6 ... 185

Śākaṭāyana
13 ... 83
18 ... 91

Śeṣādrisudhī
1 ... 194
6 ... 88, 90
7 ... 85
9 ... 49, 54, 56, 57
14 ... 3, 5
15 ... 32, 35
18 ... 115
27 ... 226
28 ... 272
31 ... 222
32 ... 200
34 ... 220, 230
36 ... 256
39 ... 141
40 ... 248
42 ... 144
43 ... 243
48 ... 211
49 ... 163
50 ... 64
51 ... 64
52 ... 98, 101
63 ... 186
65 ... 91
66 ... 58
67 ... 196
72 ... 233
73 ... 69
74 ... 159, 162
77 ... 105, 204
78 ... 166
79 ... 224
80 ... 139
81 ... 184
82 ... 235
86 ... 198
89 ... 183
93 ... 268
97 ... 20
99 ... 129
100 ... 130
103 ... 208
p. 44:16 ... 72
p. 397:21 ... 3
p. 435:17 ... 59

Sīradeva
1 ... 194
3 ... 117
6 ... 85, 87
8 ... 115
9 ... 3, 10
10 ... 11, 13, 15
11 ... 132
16 ... 220, 230
17 ... 188
18 ... 256
20 ... 141
21 ... 248
27 ... 226
28 ... 119
31 ... 186, 187
35 ... 111
37 ... 91, 92
38 ... 88
39 ... 20
40 ... 37
42 ... 58, 60
43 ... 127
44 ... 64
46 ... 196
47 ... 64
48 ... 98
49 ... 211
51 ... 171
53 ... 137
55 ... 222, 223
56 ... 200
60 ... 168
62 ... 272
63 ... 233, 234
64 ... 69, 78
68 ... 198
69 ... 144
70 ... 243
71 ... 184
72 ... 159, 162
75 ... 105
78 ... 129
79 ... 130
81 ... 42
82 ... 190
83 ... 166
84 ... 95, 96
86 ... 113
87 ... 208, 209

90 .... 224, 225
91 139
96 109
98 235
99 157
100 .... 32, 35, 38
101 54
106 268
107 107
110 231
111 .... 192, 193
112 183
120 .... 205, 206
121 220
124 134
p. 30:9–10 72
p. 184:27 248
p. 209:18 21
p. 210:26–31 59
p. 210:6 37
p. 216 99
p. 235:27 185
p. 241:29 47

Other texts cited

See the bibliography for details of the editions used.

Aṣṭavikṛtivivṛti xxiii
Bhāṣāvṛtti
P.5.3.71–72 219
P.6.1.70 xxi
P.6.4.146 185
Bṛhatkathāmañjarī xv
Cāndravyākaraṇa
Dhātupāṭha 7, 8
Ca.1.1.52 .... 75, 76, 78
Ca.1.2.93 27
Ca.2.1.21 74
Ca.2.3.14 101
Ca.3.1.32 52
Ca.3.3.63 52
Ca.4.3.57 219
Ca.5.1.128 40
Ca.5.2.65–68 270
Ca.6.1.18 xviii
Ca.6.2.61 .... 80, 81
Ca.6.3.105 186
Ca.6.3.106 186
Ca.6.4.85 38
Ca.6.4.86 38
Ca.6.4.89 38
Gadā
103:13–14 148
103:25–26 147
106:12 ff. 151
169:28 ff. 92
170:28 f. 60
215:17 21
32 5
Gaṇapāṭha
231.14 xv
231.4 xv
256.6 xv
67.3 xv
74.34 xv
91.4 xv
Garuḍapurāṇa xxiv
Haracaritacintāmaṇi xv
Kātantra
Dhātupāṭha 8
Kathāsaritsāgara xv
Kṣīrasvāmin 5
Kṣīrataraṅgiṇī 5
Laghuśabdenduśekhara
IV.458:18–21 252
IV.525:30–526 218
IV.526:17 219
V.70 72
Mādhavīyadhātuvṛtti
1964.41:22 27
1964.84–89 5
1964.88:26 5
Mahābhāṣyadīpikā
Āhnika I.15:3–4 xvi
Āhnika I.16:17–18 xvi
Āhnika I.17:27 xx
Āhnika I.19:29–20:2 xvii
Mahāvṛtti
on Jainendra 1.2.1 xxi
Maitreya 5
Nāmaliṅgānuśāsana xviii
Pāṇinīyadīpikā of Nīlakaṇṭha 197
Pradīpa
P.1.1 (I.5:6) xx
P.1.1 (I.55^a:3) xx
P.1.1.15 (I.251^b) 35, 36
P.1.1.22 (I.273^a) 47
P.1.1.39 (I.328^b) 74
P.1.1.39 (I.328–29) 73
P.1.1.39 (I.329^a:10 ff.) 78
P.1.1.39 (I.329^a:11) 79

P.1.1.71 (I.525^b:18–19) 203
P.1.2.64 (II.94^b) xx
P.2.2.2 (II.416^a:37) 259
P.3.1.36 (III.83^b:28) 77
P.5.3.72 (IV.395^b) 113
P.6.1.96 (V.107^b) 30
P.6.1.108 (V.120–21) 145
P.6.1.158 (V.149^b) 252
P.6.1.196 (V.174^b) 218
P.6.1.196 (V.174^b:6) 219
P.6.3.46 (V.240:15 ff.) 78
P.6.4.22 (V.290^b:33) 238
P.7.2.44 (VI.134) 166
P.7.3.28 (VI.195) 209
P.7.3.118–119 (VI.231:22) 81
P.8.3.82 (VI.201^2) 32

Prakriyākaumudī
I.134 58
I.134:9 62
I.134:12 63
I.642:13–16 207
I.778:19 52
I.814 xxi
II.173:9 207
II.530 60

Rājataraṅgiṇī
1.176 xxvi
4.488 xxvi

Rāmāyaṇa xxviii
Rasarājalakṣmī xxiv
Rasaratnapradīpa xxiv
Rasaratnasamuccaya xxiv

Ṛgvedaprātiśākhya
3.23 xiv
3.28 xiv
6.43 xiv
13.31 .... xiv, xxiii
13.37 xiv

Śabdakaustubha
on P.1.1.68 .... 3, 5

Saduktikarṇāmṛta xxiv
Sammatākāra 5
Sarvadarśanasaṅgraha xxiv
Trikāṇḍaśeṣa xxii

Uddyota
P.1.1 (I.55^a:4) xxii
P.1.1.15 (I.252^a) 35
P.1.1.22 (I.273^a) 47
P.1.1.39 (I.328–29) 73
P.1.1.71 (I.526^a:20) 203
P.3.1.36 (III.83^b:31) 78
P.5.3.72 (IV.395^b) 113
P.6.1.108 (V.120–21) 145
P.6.1.196 (V.174^b:14) 219
P.7.2.44 (VI.134) 166
P.7.3.28 (VI.195) 209
P.8.3.82 (VI.201) 32

Uṇādi
170 30
222 36
223 36
225 36

Upalekhasūtra xxiii
Utpalamālā xviii
Utpalinī .... xviii, xix

Vākyapadīya
II.481 xxv
II.482 xxv
II.483–84 xxv
II.484 xxvi
II.485 .... xxv, xxvi
II.486 xxv
II.487 xxv

Vikṛtivallī xxiii

Citations from the *Dhātupāṭha*

References are to Böhtlingk 1887.

1.1 22
1.175–197 5
1.194 .... 4, 5
1.380 xxi
1.404 7
1.503–509 8
1.510–511 8
1.624 264
1.625 7
1.654–656 7
1.656 7
1.764 216
1.777 265
1.777 f. 266
1.795–98 265
1.795 f. 266
1.798 266
1.799 265
1.874 5
1.875 .... 4, 5
1.975 157
1.1018 44
2.2 84
2.34 157
6.73–108 15
6.120 17
8.10 60
9.13 13
9.61 84

Index of word forms discussed

*adakaska 114
*agnīsoma 37
*agnīṣoma 37
*ánāḍhyambhaviṣṇuḥ 24
*arrkka 107
*avāmadevyám 172
*bhaviṣṇu xix
*brahhmmā 107
*dhivan 264
*idakaṃka 114
*indranī 175
*jyautiṣam 169
*kusrā 30
*lavasīya 14
*mahārājñaḥ 50
*nadĭtara 44
*pavasīya 14
*pāvyam 93
*sāmikṛtakam 182
*śatan xi, 73
*saumendra 170
*tay asanti 193
*uvoṣāṃ cakāra 75
*vaiyākrośī 273
*vṛkṣat 175
*vṛkṣes 175

abhavat xi
abhipreya 243, 244
abhiṣāvayati 225
abhiṣunoti 225
acakād bhavān 187
aciraprakāśakā 271
aciraprakāśakā vidyut 271
aciraprakāśikā 271
adhijigāṃsate 155
āḍhyaṃ karaṇaṃ 61
āḍhyaṃbhaviṣṇu 23–25
āḍhyaṃbhaviṣṇú 23, 24
adīdhayur 165
adyoḍhaḥ 145, 146
agnau 79
agnisoma 33, 41
agnĭsoma 34
agnīṣoma 33, 34, 40, 41
agnisomau 33
agnĭsomau 38
agnisomau māṇavakau 34
āhata 149–151
akṛta 246
akṣadyūḥ 244
amunā 179
anāḍhyaṃbhaviṣṇu 24
anāḍhyaṃbhaviṣṇúḥ 24, 25
anas 183
anastakṣan 183
anastakṣṇaḥ 183
anvaśād bhavān 187
apāsīt 167
apat 167
ardhapippalī 259
arkka 107
ávāmadevyam 172
avyaḍa xv
babhruśe 10
bahuka 57
bailvaka 161
bailvakīyā 160
bhāsate bhāsvaraḥ 128
bhavati 65
bhinnaḥ 182
bhinnakaḥ 182
bhinátti 106
bhrāj 4
bhrājiṣṇu 27
bhūṣṇu xix
bilvakīya 161
bilvakīyā 160
brahmmā 107
bubhūṣati 208
caṭakā 124
caṭakāyā 123
catvāriṃśat 57
chinátti 106
cicīṣati 208
cinuté 253
citragur ānīyatām 59
dadaridrau 177
daivaraktāḥ kiṃśukāḥ 246
dākṣi 70
daśahuṣkaraṇa xviii
dāśaratha 251
daśendra 162
devatrāta 135
dhāvati iti 135
dhinoti 264
duṣkaraṇa xviii

dviḥ pacatu 257
dviḥ pacatu ity āha 258
eṇī 124
eṇyā 124
galaḥ 135
gamiṣyāmi xi
gaṇaka 57
gantāsmi xi
gara 135
gatau 79
gatyām 79
gauritarā 227
gavakṣa 136
gavākṣa 135
gā́rgyâḥ 138
glauḥ 36
go 35, 36
go 'bhavat 35, 39, 40
graha 84, 135
grāha 135
grāmaṇi kulam 241
gūha 87
gūhati 87
hana 84
hanti 9
hanti iti 135
hāriṣeṇya 222
ikṣūṇām 94
ikṣūṇā́m 93
indrāṇī 162, 174, 175
iṣṇu 27
iyeṣa 75, 77
jaghnur 199
jaṅgamyate 109, 110
jānīte 139
jāyate 139
joguhīti 198
jyāyān 216
jyeṣṭha 216
jyotir 169
jyotiṣam 169
kamana 128
kamrā 128
kāraḥ 123
kāryam 112
kāśe 10
kaṣṭāya 72
kā usrā 30
khalati 120
khaṭvāḍhakam 210
kosrā 30
krīṇīté 253
kriyate 140
kártā 252
kṣīrahrada 108
kumāra 119, 120
kumāraśramaṇā 119
kumārī 120
kumārī gauritarā 227
kuśe 10
laviṣīya 13
lohitoṣṇīṣā ṛtvijaḥ pracaranti 59
loluvaḥ 236, 237
lulavitha 219
mahāhrada 108
mahāpravṛddha 29
mahārāja 50–52
māhārājika 52
mā́hārājikaḥ 52
māṣavāpiṇi 274
mīmāṃsate 110
mṛdvyā 147
nāḍāyana 223
nadītara 44, 47, 48
nadyām 79
nagarārdhaḥ 259
nartiṣyati 66
nartsyati 65, 66
nauḥ 36
nāvyâm 137
nīcais 204
nīcakaiḥ 204
nṛtyati 65
pacamānaḥ 235
pacānaḥ 235
pacatu 258
pacatu pacatu 258
paddhatau 78
paddhati 78, 81
palāyate 168
palāyate iti 135
pañcan 57
pañcendra 162
pañcendrāṇī 162
papatuḥ 239, 248
papau 174
papivān 152
papur 239
papuṣaḥ 152, 158
parādhvani 234
parāyate 168
paṣṭauhaḥ 240, 241

paṣṭauhaḥ paśya 240
pati 80, 81
paṭpaṭāyate 134
paṭpaṭāyati 134
paṭvyā 147, 148
paviṣīya 13
pavyam 92, 93
pácati 106
pácâti 138
pácatu 258
plakaṣāya 71
plakṣebhyaḥ 111
popuvaḥ 237
pradīyatāṃ dāśarathāya maithilī 251
prakāraḥ 123
praśasya 216
pratirājá 233
pravāhaṇeyaḥ 209
prāvāhaṇeyaḥ 209
pravṛddha 29
prayāyiṇe, prayāyiṇaḥ 274
priyagrāmaṇika 213
priyagrāmaṇikaḥ 213
páṭhâti 138
puṭiṣīya 15
rāj 4
rājāyate 262
rājīyati 262
sahasrāṇi 73
śakaṭa 79
śakaṭau 78, 79, 81
śakaṭi 78, 81
sakhi 80, 81
sāmikṛtam 182
saṃkhyā 57
saṃśātavrata 136
saṃśitavrata 135, 136
saṃvyāḍa xv
śāmyati 155
sāṅgrahasūtrikaḥ 201
saptati 57
sarvanāma 63
sarveṣām 104
ṣaṣ 57
śatāni .... xi, 73, 74
sautranāḍi 223
sautra 201
śiṣṭāt 143
śiva 70
śīyate 97
somendra 169
spardhate 108
śramaṇā 119
śreṣṭha 216
śreṣṭhatama 215
stambhī 61
stambhī karoti 61
stauti 157
śuklavāsasam ānaya 59
śūna 43
sunoti 157, 225
svāyaṃbhuva 185
śvayitvā 191
syandū 266
tasthuṣaḥ 158
te santi 193
trāhḥ 135
trāṇaḥ 135
uccais 204
uccaistarām 215
uccakaiḥ 204
usrā 30
uvoṣa 75, 76, 78
vāmadevya 171
vardhrīṇasaḥ 63
vāriṣeṇya 222
varṣati iti 135
vā́tsyâḥ 138
vāyū́nām 93
vāyūnā́m 93
vibhrāj 5
vibhrāṭ 5
viḍ 189
virāṭ 5
vṛkṇa 247
vṛkṣaiḥ 174, 176
vṛkṣais 175
vṛkṣāt 174, 175
vṛkṣāya 71, 72
vṛksāya 71
vṛkṣebhyaḥ 111
vṛtrahabhyām 261
vyāḍa xv
vyā́ḍiśālā xv
vyākrośī 273
vyatigamyante grāmāḥ 142
vyatihanyante dasyavaḥ 142
yayā́thâ 219
yāyāvara 254, 255
yuvapalitā 120
yuvatiḥ palitā 120
yuvati 120